BILL HOBBY

Bill Hobby in the pressroom at the Houston Post, *ca. 1972.* Bill Hobby Papers, Briscoe Center for American History.

BILL HOBBY

A Life in Journalism and Public Service

DON CARLETON & ERIN L. PURDY

BRISCOE CENTER
FOR AMERICAN HISTORY
THE UNIVERSITY OF TEXAS AT AUSTIN

DISTRIBUTED BY TOWER BOOKS, AN IMPRINT
OF THE UNIVERSITY OF TEXAS PRESS

Copyright © 2024 by the Dolph Briscoe Center for American History
All rights reserved
Printed in the United States of America
First edition, 2024
Distributed by arrangement with the University of Texas Press

Requests for permission to reproduce material from this work should be sent to:
Office of the Director
Dolph Briscoe Center for American History
University of Texas at Austin
2300 Red River Stop D1100
Austin, TX 78712-1426

♾ The paper used in this book meets the minimum requirements of ANSI/NISO z39.48-1992 (r1997) (Permanence of Paper).

Library of Congress Control Number: 2024937226

ISBN 978-1-953480-12-5 (hardcover)
ISBN 978-1-953480-13-2 (ePub e-book)
ISBN 978-1-953480-14-9 (PDF e-book)

CONTENTS

PROLOGUE vii

1. Will and Oveta 1
2. St. Albans and the Rice Institute 19
3. The Navy and Diana 42
4. The JFK Assassination 60
5. The *Houston Post* 71
6. The Campaign of 1972 89
7. The First Term 117
8. Artesia Hall and the Constitutional Convention 142
9. Constitutional Reform Redux 158
10. The Hobby-Clayton Commission 169
11. Bill Clements and the Killer Bees 187
12. The Campaign of 1982 204
13. Hobby Takes Control 224
14. "No Pass, No Play" 243
15. Hobby versus Clements 266
16. The Presidential Election of 1988 286
17. The Final Term 296
18. Sine Die 308
19. Requiem for the *Post* 319
20. Rescuing the University of Houston 332
21. A Champion for Higher Education 342

EPILOGUE 359
ACKNOWLEDGMENTS 362
NOTES 365
BIBLIOGRAPHY 395
INDEX 402

PROLOGUE

The bow ties were the first sign that something strange was happening.

The lieutenant governor of Texas, fifty-seven-year-old Bill Hobby, expected May 5, 1989, to be a typical, midsession day in the Texas Senate. As the state's longest-serving lieutenant governor and the president of the Senate, Hobby was completely attuned to the rhythm and nature of the assembly's proceedings. Hobby had announced back in the summer of 1987 that his fifth term as lieutenant governor of Texas would be his last, and he was now presiding over his final regular session of the Senate. He undoubtedly hoped the fifty-eighth day of the seventy-first regular legislative session would be the kind he favored: "predictable, bland, and boring." As he would later note, "If there was a debate, I liked it courteous and brief. Bills came up for consideration and were approved in orderly fashion with regular thuds of the gavel." The bills to be voted upon had developed under his watchful eye and were likely the versions he had approved. The thuds of the gavel? Hobby's own. In other words, an orderly day under Hobby's leadership—as the Senate had been since he had first presided in January 1973.[1]

But as the senators assembled that Friday, Hobby noticed something odd: many of them had donned bow ties. Why were so many senators wearing Hobby's preferred style of neckwear? "That was my first clue that something unusual was going on," Hobby said later that day. What he would soon realize was that the bowties were a tip-off to Bill Hobby Day: a formal Senate celebration in his honor, complete with special guests, multiple resolutions, and countless tributes to Hobby's legacy as lieutenant governor. And that legacy was a considerable one. Longtime staff member and friend Saralee Tiede would later reflect, "He had come to occupy this pinnacle of respect in the Senate, even among senators who perhaps weren't personally close to him. They did not cross him. . . . And so things could go his way. He was the master of the Senate."[2]

Weeks before, guests had been asked to mark the occasion of Hobby's last regular legislative session—and to keep the event a secret from the honoree. The Hobby family, lifelong friends, and countless former elected officials were invited to join the ceremony by a group of six senators who were part of Hobby's inner circle, including John Montford and Kent Caperton. That inner circle was an integral part of Hobby's control of the Senate and an excellent example of how he used legislative rules to his favor—rules he had first learned as Lieutenant Governor Ben Ramsey's parliamentarian in the late 1950s. Hobby's innate brilliance was coupled with deep knowledge of how state government worked—and how he could work senators to his advantage. *Texas Monthly* noted, "He is so far ahead of other leaders that he sets the agenda for the entire state." According to Senator Hector Uribe, "Hobby had his team, [and] he depended on the team to deliver bills in a timely fashion—the bills that he wanted out of committee—and to kill the bills when he wanted [them] killed. It was a top-down structure that was set up through the first order of business in the Senate rules. And in the rules, every state senator relinquishes their power to name committees to the lieutenant governor."[3]

It was under Hobby that the lieutenant governor's role had expanded to become the most powerful political position in the state. As Rodney Ellis, a Hobby family protégé and eventual state senator, noted, "I don't think we ever really knew just how powerful the Texas Senate could be until Bill Hobby became the presiding officer." Much of the acceptance of such a concentration of power was due to the respect Hobby had earned over his years in office. His integrity was unquestioned. And he was known to act in a way that was balanced, not dictatorial. "Senators took note that even when he personally felt strongly about legislation . . . he would not stand in the way of majority rule," according to Tiede.[4]

Still, Hobby was not shy to use the powers of the office in ways he thought best served the people of Texas. From committee and chair appointments and setting the Senate calendar to the drafting of the appropriations bill as head of the Legislative Budget Board, Hobby's influence shaped the efforts of the Senate and spread to the larger machinations of Texas politics. As political consultant and power broker Jack Martin summarized, "He was playing chess in a building full of people who played checkers."[5]

Hobby's brilliance was wrapped in an unconventional package, at least by typical politician standards. He was an intellectual with a deep love of data and statistics. A lifelong athlete, he was a passionate horseman with an affinity for foxhunting. He was introverted and quiet, with a lifelong stammer that made him a notoriously succinct public speaker. As his elder daughter Laura Hobby Beckworth would later explain, "He was known for his brevity of public address, and bluntness to a probably offensive degree. But that was probably because he wanted to get his message out as efficiently as possible without detracting from his own message by starting to stutter. How on earth he ever made it as a politician I don't know. But he did it because it was the right thing to do. And he felt like he had the time and tools to do it."[6]

It was a shock when, at the height of his power, Hobby abruptly announced he would not run for another term as lieutenant governor. Nor was he interested in running for governor, a goal many had presumed would be his next step. The news surprised everyone, even his closest family and friends. And while the timing of his announcement was unexpected, the style was classic Hobby: short, decisive, and with little discussion of his personal motivations. As elder son Paul Hobby remarked of his father, "He is private in the sense that he was raised to not put his business on the street. . . . He was authentic, and authentic for him was thoughtful, quiet. He couldn't imagine, why would anybody else be interested in [his] personal emotions or grief?"[7]

And so, facing the end of Hobby's leadership, the Senate came together to honor him with all the pomp, circumstance, and bow ties it could muster. It is hard to believe that any official Senate proceedings could happen without Hobby's knowledge, let alone a full-fledged tribute like the one on May 5. The proceedings that day were typical business already in progress: the invocation, introductions of honorary guests, a message from the House on elections related to drainage districts in Galveston County, and a proclamation in celebration of Cinco de Mayo from the Texas Senate Hispanic Caucus.

But as the Senate doorkeeper announced that Hobby was at the Senate door, Senator Chet Brooks quickly invited Hobby to join him at the podium for "a little special Cinco de Mayo recognition." Senator Uribe kicked off the tribute with Senate Resolution 586, which compared Hobby to Mexican patriot and hero General Ignacio Zaragoza Seguín, including their ability to face adversity (in Hobby's case, in the form of "low revenue estimates, cries of 'No New Taxes,' Republican governors, Democratic governors," and more), their riding skills, and their efforts to champion help for the poor and needy. The resolution declared that Hobby was "a Generalissimo in the war on injustice and inequality."[8]

After reading the resolution, Uribe continued, bringing up the battle of the Killer Bees. In 1979, during the sixty-sixth session, twelve state senators hid off-site for five days to prevent the Senate from voting on a bill related to the timing of the state's presidential primary. Hobby dubbed the absentees the Killer Bees. He later admitted his attempt to push the legislation and the resulting "fiasco" was the biggest mistake in his presidency of the Senate. The irony that the first senator to speak during the tribute to Bill Hobby was a member of the Killer Bees was not lost on anyone in the chamber. When Senator Brooks admonished Uribe, "You promised you wouldn't bring that up," laughter echoed through the chamber. Uribe eventually yielded the floor as additional guests were announced by the Senate doorkeeper.[9]

As the special guests tucked away by the west gallery entrance filed into the Senate chambers, Hobby must have felt like the guest of honor for an episode of *This Is Your Life*. Hobby's beloved wife and closest confidant, Diana Poteat Hobby, joined the group on the Senate rostrum. Together, they had raised four children—Paul, Laura, Andrew, and Kate—and eventually would have nine grandchildren. Laura Hobby Beckworth and Paul Hobby were present in the Senate gallery, as were Paul's wife, Janet, and Laura's children Will and Carter. Her infant son, John Pettus, was too young to attend. John Davis, Bill's high school teacher and lifelong friend, was in attendance, as was Hobby's executive assistant Delores Chambers and close friends Margaret Behrens, Matthew Kreisle, and Ann Ramsey, to name a few.

The list of current and former public officials in attendance read like a who's who of Texas politics. Governor Bill Clements was there to pay his respects to Hobby, as was Speaker of the House Gib Lewis and Comptroller of Public Accounts Bob Bullock. There was Ben Barnes, the former lieutenant governor who directly preceded Hobby, and former governor Preston Smith. And there was a congregation of former senators, including Jack Hightower, Oscar Mauzy, John Sharp, Babe Schwartz, Kent Hance, Don Kennard, Bill Patman, and some of Hobby's closest friends, Ray Farabee, Max Sherman, and Don Adams.

Back down on the Senate floor, another of Hobby's close friends, Senator Carl Parker, gave a lengthy and humorous tribute to Hobby, listing his many excellent characteristics, including his tact, leadership, and ability to attract broad and varied support: "If you've ever been hunting with Bill Hobby, you can understand how he can garner both the support of the NRA for the use of ammunition and firearms and, at the same time, be honored by the Audubon Society." Parker concluded on a serious note, with the nomination for Hobby to be named the first Senate president emeritus of Texas. "The Hobby family, the Hobby name is synonymous with Texas and history and service. Lt. Gov. Hobby, you have honored your family name," Parker declared.[10]

Throughout his life, Hobby's accomplishments were accompanied by mention of his famous parents. His late father was Houston newspaper publisher William P. "Will" Hobby Sr. Will had served as lieutenant governor for three years before becoming governor of Texas in 1918. Bill's mother, Oveta Culp Hobby, had stopped making public appearances by the mid-1980s and did not attend the ceremony. Like her son, she had served as parliamentarian, but for the Texas House of Representatives. She was best known as the "Little Colonel" who had organized and led the Women's Army Corps during World War II and as the first secretary of the Department of Health, Education, and Welfare under President Eisenhower—only the second woman in US history to serve on a presidential cabinet. Together, Will and Oveta had built a pioneering media empire centered on the *Houston Post* and its related broadcast properties, and they had played a significant role in the transformation of Houston into the fourth-largest city in the United States.[11]

Bill Hobby consistently credited his parents and their forebears with his involvement in politics: "A political, or public service, gene lurks in my family's DNA," he would write in his 2010 memoir, *How Things Really Work*. "Hobbys have infested the Senate chamber off and on for 137 years." On another occasion, he called the family's political involvement a "genetic defect." Five generations and thirty-five members of Bill Hobby's extended family—including in-laws—had been associated with the Texas Legislature, some as members and others as parliamentarians, staffers, and mascots. "His family had that sense of noblesse oblige," close friend and colleague Kent Caperton would later reflect. "They always gave of themselves to public service. I think they were truly one of the great families of Texas. And [Bill] saw what his mother had done, and his dad, and I think that legacy of public service was instilled in him."[12]

Senator Parker was sure to point out that Hobby's greatest talent was his "eye for sartorial splendor." Parker shared comments from Bob Armstrong: "I didn't have a bow tie, but in honor of it being 'Hobby Day' I got my oldest sports coat and my scruffiest shoes and put them on. As I walked by the back hall, Hobby saw me and said, 'Bob, you look really nice today.'" Much was made throughout the tribute of Hobby's fashion sense or, more accurately, his lack thereof. Multiple senators made jokes about his orthopedic shoes, old suits, and terrible taste in neckties.[13]

Hobby was also teased for his close rapport with the business community, his limits as a public speaker, and his tendency to abruptly end conversations. Senator Bob McFarland asked, "[How] did Gov. Hobby terminate a conversation with you before he had his personal computer to turn around and play with? How did he get Senate chairmen to the weekly meeting before he hired Dick Harper as bartender? And how did you know his position on any issue before he met with Jess Hay and Peter O'Donnell?" Hobby was known to walk out of meetings midconversation with little to no warning. As Caperton later said, "I'd be sitting in his office, and we'd be having a discussion and I'd think we were making progress. . . . And he'd just turn around in his chair and start doing something else."[14]

Senator Montford presented a poem (attributed to his cousin "Robert Frost Montford") that read in part:

> I'm smart, I'm cunning, I'm part of the academic clergy.
> I'm so exciting, I pioneered charisma bypass surgery. . . .
> I've presided over countless Senate duels.
> Frankly, I'd rather ride horses than suspend the rules.

But the Hobby Day tributes went much deeper than quips about Hobby's bow ties or quirky behavior. Senator after senator rose to second Parker's nomination of Hobby as lieutenant governor emeritus and to share their genuine respect and admiration for Hobby and all he had accomplished. He was praised for his ability to serve all the people of Texas, notably in his meaningful reform of the state's educational systems and human welfare programs. He was also lauded for his integrity. As Senator Cynthia Krier noted, "You are the Senate's leader, conscience, and spirit."[15]

Hobby's own comments during the proceedings were characteristically brief. "This has truly been a great day," he said, "because the Senate hasn't passed any bad bills." His response to the mention of the Killer Bees was to quote Shakespeare's *Henry V*: "Whiles any speaks that fought with us upon St. Crispin's Day." And he noted how moved he was by the day's comments, concluding, "Diana and I thank you all very much."[16]

Comptroller Bob Bullock said in his Hobby Day remarks, "You know, it's easy to make some wisecracks about Bill Hobby's tenure in office, but it's really not easy to make a wisecrack about Bill Hobby personally. . . . In the years that you've been here, you've defined what the lieutenant governor's office should be and what it will be in the future. . . . You rose to each occasion, Governor Hobby; each problem was solved and turned into an opportunity." There was well-known animosity between Republican governor Bill Clements and Hobby. The two worked closely together but undoubtedly through gritted teeth. Theirs was a clash of substance as well as style; the brash Clements was termed "His Orneriness" by author Stephen Harrigan with good reason. But on Hobby Day, even Clements gave Hobby his due: "I am satisfied that your decisions as a leader of this great body have always been based on what's good for Texas. Those kinds of decisions override party; they override different constituencies; they are in the sense of an overall good for our people and for the betterment of this state."[17]

Even during this most laudatory of occasions, politics could not be ignored. One particular issue cast a long shadow: workers' compensation. The issue had bubbled up in 1987 when the workers' compensation fund for state employees required emergency appropriations. The resulting efforts to fix the system pitted business interests against labor, complicated by the involvement of attorneys, insurance companies, and budgetary complexities. As Senator Bob Glasgow (rhetorically) asked Hobby in his tribute remarks, "If you're so dammed smart, why haven't we got this workers comp thing worked out already?" Senator Brooks quickly fired back, "Because he put it in your charge." And in his own remarks, Hobby himself noted, "I'd point out that I originally gave it to [Ray] Farabee, and he had sense enough to resign." The battle over workers' compensation would continue through multiple special sessions and persist until the end of the year. It became one of the most bitter fights Hobby had to navigate.[18]

Hobby was also leaving as a sea change was taking place in state politics. The Democratic Party's long-standing domination of Texas politics was crumbling. In his Hobby Day comments, Bullock pointed out, "[Clements] did bestow a compliment onto you, Governor Hobby. He said that through the years you must have done something right because today Texas has more Republican Senators than at any other time in our history." By the end of the month, the *New York Times* would report on the rise of the Republican Party: "Signs of a fundamental change in Texas politics could be seen: the power of the traditional conservative Democrat was receding, leaving a political void between an increasingly liberal Democratic Party and an increasingly strong Republican Party." That Republican ascendancy would mean the reversal of many of Hobby's legislative accomplishments. But on May 5, 1989, those future concerns were mere shadows as Hobby Day came to a close. The Senate Ladies' Club presented a special charm to Diana Hobby, and two senators presented her with a bouquet of yellow roses. Senate Resolution 557, which listed Hobby's many accomplishments and virtues, was offered and unanimously adopted. The resolution called for a bronze bust of Hobby to be placed in the Texas Senate. He was presented with a special book of memories. The ceremony ended, and a group of the special guests headed to the Austin Marriott for a celebratory luncheon.[19]

The Senate returned to its regular business. Even for a lieutenant governor emeritus, there was plenty of work yet to be done.

BILL HOBBY

CHAPTER 1

WILL AND OVETA

"Former Gov. Hobby Proud Father of Boy," exclaimed a headline in the *Houston Chronicle* on January 19, 1932, announcing the birth of a son to William Pettus Hobby, the editor of a rival paper, the *Houston Post*. "Mrs. Hobby," the article noted, "the former Oveta Culp," formerly the parliamentarian of the Texas House of Representatives, was resting well. Named for his father, William Pettus Hobby Jr. (soon to be known as Bill) was newsworthy from the moment he was born, due to the prominence of his parents, who were both deeply involved in politics and public service.[1]

Will was twenty-seven years older than Oveta and a figure of considerable importance in Houston and Texas. He was known not only for his tenure as lieutenant governor and governor but also for his success as a newspaper editor and publisher, first at the *Beaumont Enterprise* and later at the *Houston Post*. Born in 1878 in Moscow, a small town in deep East Texas, Will was raised to have respect for the written word, the rule of law, politics, and public service. His father, Edwin Hobby, was an attorney with a distinguished career in public service: he served three terms in the Texas Senate and was a state judge for ten. Known for his legal acumen, Edwin wrote a book on Texas land law that was the definitive source on the topic for several decades. Will's mother, Dora Pettus Hobby, came from a prominent family in Fort Bend County, and she was a graduate of what would later become the University of Mary Hardin–Baylor.

Edwin Hobby and his family moved to Houston in 1893 after Edwin lost a reelection bid. At an early age, Will became fascinated with the newspaper business. When he was seventeen, he dropped out of high school to work at the *Houston Post*, moving up the ladder from circulation clerk to reporter, city editor, and managing editor. In 1907, Hobby's success at the *Post* attracted the attention of Walter Crawford, a prominent attorney in Beaumont, who recruited Will to serve as the managing editor and part owner of the *Beaumont Enterprise*. At that time, urban newspapers and their publishers throughout the United States actively partnered with local business and civic leaders to help promote their city's economic interests. Will played that role with enthusiasm and energy. His main project was an effort to secure federal funds to support dredging the Neches River to make Beaumont a deepwater port, which was a landmark development for the city. That accomplishment also gave Will a statewide reputation as an urban Progressive.

Will's love of politics and his increasing stature as a civic booster and newspaper editor eventually led to his election in 1914 as Texas's lieutenant governor. He was not the prototypical backslapping politician. In his memoir, Bill Hobby said of his father, "He was quiet, modest, unpretentious, and rather short." But Will was adept at building relationships and using his allies to his advantage. In both politics and journalism, he greatly benefited from his early connection to a network of prominent individuals who had been close associates of his father, Edwin, in the tiny village of Peach Tree in Polk County, Texas. That network included the influential US congressman from East Texas Samuel Bronson Cooper (whose daughter would become Will's first wife); lumber industry tycoon John Henry Kirby, one of the wealthiest men in Texas at the turn of the twentieth century; and Ross Sterling, a founder of the Humble Oil Company and a Houston real estate developer who served as governor of Texas during the Depression.[2]

Will went on to serve as governor after the Texas Legislature impeached and removed Governor James "Pa" Ferguson in 1917 for corruption. Will was thirty-nine and the youngest governor in state history. He defeated the scandal-ridden Ferguson in the 1918 Democratic primary and served a full term as governor to 1921. As governor, Will led Texas through World War I and deftly managed the difficult issue of Prohibition. One of his most significant accomplishments was his support of women's suffrage. He signed the Texas law that allowed women to vote in the state's primaries, and he later campaigned for passage of the Nineteenth Amendment. "I cannot say whether I learned my political philosophy from my father or whether it was just in my DNA, but, in fact, his mindset was much like my own," Bill reflected. "He believed in cooperation in government between the three branches created by the Texas Constitution. He also believed that real progress meant progress for everyone, rich and poor alike."[3]

Willie Chapman Cooper, Will's first wife, greatly influenced his outlook on women's right to vote. She and Will had been longtime friends before their marriage in 1915. Willie was well known in Washington, DC, political society during the last years of her father's service in the US Congress. She worked in his office and was his escort to social functions in the capital, including parties at the White House during the presidencies of William McKinley and Teddy Roosevelt. Culturally sophisticated and politically astute, Willie was an active supporter of women's suffrage. As first lady of Texas, she was also deeply involved in the effort on the home front to support the US military during World War I.[4]

Will decided not to run for another term as governor, preferring to return to the *Beaumont Enterprise* and to seek new business opportunities. By 1922, he and Willie moved to

Houston, where Will dabbled in several business ventures, including insurance and real estate investments. Two years after arriving in Houston, family friend Ross Sterling, one of the founders of the Humble Oil Company, persuaded Will to accept his offer to return to the *Houston Post* as managing editor. Sterling had purchased the paper and combined it with the city's other morning paper, the *Houston Dispatch*. In 1925, Will played a key role in Sterling's founding of KPRC-Radio, one of the first broadcast stations in Texas. Will and Willie were also highly politically active, notably in the Democratic Party and its 1928 national convention, held in Houston. But tragedy struck on January 14, 1929, when Willie died in her sleep from an apparent cerebral hemorrhage. His wife's sudden death devastated Will, who was despondent. Eager to fill the void left by Willie's passing, Will began a new endeavor: the romantic pursuit of Miss Oveta Culp.[5]

Will had known Miss Culp since the 1919 legislative session, when the fourteen-year-old Oveta had frequently accompanied her father, Isaac "Ike" Culp, to Austin during his tenure in the Texas House of Representatives. Oveta was born on January 19, 1905, in Killeen, Texas, the second of Ike and Emma Hoover Culp's seven children. A precocious and strong-minded girl, Oveta was raised in a pious Baptist family. Her father, a prominent attorney and politician, favored her over his other children and encouraged her to consider herself the equal of any man. Ike also encouraged his daughter's interest in public affairs, and Emma influenced Oveta's views on women's suffrage. Oveta's maternal grandmother, Cordelia Hoover, also played a major role in shaping her character, insisting on the importance of living up to the high standards and sterling reputation of the Culp and Hoover families in Killeen.[6]

Ike moved his family to Temple in 1918, shortly after his successful run for the Texas House. By the summer of 1919, he helped Oveta secure a position as a legislative clerk at the tender age of fifteen. After that year's summer sessions, she and her father returned to Temple, and she enrolled in what was to be her senior year of high school. Oveta soon withdrew from high school due to a conflict with the school principal over a speech she planned to give. Her education continued at Baylor Academy, the secondary school run by Baylor Female College (later Mary Hardin–Baylor College), but Oveta ended her studies without receiving a diploma. Although she attended some classes at Mary Hardin–Baylor, she felt that school was "a big bore" after the excitement of working in the legislature. Oveta soon relocated to Austin, helping her father during special sessions of the legislature and auditing classes at the University of Texas Law School. She eventually took a full-time job at the state's Banking Commission.[7]

In 1925, Oveta moved to Houston at the urging of her family friend and mentor, former suffragist leader Florence Sterling, the sister of Ross Sterling and secretary of Humble Oil. Florence helped Oveta get jobs with the Houston League of Women Voters and in the *Houston Post-Dispatch*'s circulation department. In subsequent years, one version of the story of how Will and Oveta met was that it was at the *Post* in 1926. But Oveta would later explain that Will had been a friend of the family whom she had met while working for her father in the legislature. In May of 1926, Texas House Speaker

Lee Satterwhite appointed Oveta, then twenty years old, to the position of House parliamentarian. The role suited her, given her familiarity with the legislative process and the procedural rules of the House. Oveta also had a strong attraction to order, efficiency, and control, which was the essence of the job. Her appointment further raised Oveta's profile in the state's political scene. She would return to Houston during the legislative break, continuing her work at the *Post-Dispatch* and her involvement with the Democratic Party and other women's political organizations, which also enhanced her public visibility.[8]

Will began an ardent courtship of Oveta in the summer of 1929, eventually proposing marriage in January 1931. In many ways, the couple had more differences than similarities. Will was fifty-two-years old and often described as rotund and jug-eared. Oveta was a twenty-six-year-old beauty with a budding sartorial elegance. Will's political heyday seemed to be over, whereas Oveta was just beginning her career. And their public personas were markedly dissimilar. Will was quiet, even shy, but personable and warm, with a dry wit. Oveta was outgoing and dynamic. However, theirs was a relationship built on mutual affection, shared values, and respect. The couple shared a passion for civic affairs and journalism (and horseback riding, which would become an important Hobby family pastime). Both were dedicated to their careers and knew how to manage relationships to make things happen. And both were highly intelligent, ethical individuals who cared deeply for Houston and Texas.

Will and Oveta married on February 23, 1931, at the home of Oveta's parents in Temple. Afterward, the newlyweds moved into a new six-bedroom, four-bath house near Rice Institute, at 2115 Glen Haven in Houston's Braeswood Addition, an upper-class housing development in which Will had been one of the first investors. Not quite two months after the Hobbys settled in to their new residence, Oveta had to cancel a trip due to what she thought was a stomach bug. In fact, she was pregnant. The Hobbys were to be parents.[9]

At 8:20 a.m. on January 19, 1932, at Houston's Hermann Hospital, Oveta delivered a baby boy whom she and Will proudly named William P. Hobby Jr. In a striking concurrence, it was her twenty-seventh birthday. The *Houston Chronicle*, not the *Post*, broke the news of the birth of the Hobbys' son. The news of William Jr.'s birth was met with publicity worthy of royalty. Ross Sterling, who had been elected governor of Texas in 1930, immediately appointed the infant Hobby a colonel in the Texas National Guard. Humble Oil Company legal counsel Jacob Wolters, commander of the state guard units and another longtime friend of Will's, declared that he had assigned baby Hobby to the headquarters staff of the guard's Fifty-Sixth Calvary Brigade. The *Dallas Morning News* reported that the new colonel was "on leave of absence from duty for a few years. . . . At present, the Colonel's uniform is basically that of Mahatma Gandhi," comparing the infant's diaper to Gandhi's simple dhoti. Another Texas newspaper pointed out, "Former Governor W. P. Hobby's infant son was born on Robert E. Lee's birthday, on Joan of Arc's birthday, and on Mrs. Hobby's birthday. He ought to be a political personality someday.

Also, the lad might turn out to be a newspaper personage. His father is editor of the *Houston Post* at this time, after having spent a lifetime in the newspaper business."[10]

As news of their son's birth spread, the Hobbys received warm congratulations from their circle of friends. Given his parentage, many of the well-wishers expressed ambitious hopes for the newborn. US Senator Tom Connally sent the newborn a message with a warning: "Young man . . . you will have the responsibility of carrying on a splendid tradition because of the distinction of your parents on both sides of the house." Lumber baron John Henry Kirby, Will's longtime friend, wrote to Oveta, "Knowing the mother who will train him I have no hesitation in predicting that forty years hence he will occupy the White House as its master." Texas attorney general—and one of Oveta's former boyfriends—James V. Allred sent Will a handwritten note: "Congratulations! Just heard about the new 'President of the United States.'" Another one of Oveta's former boyfriends, future US congressman Bob Poage, continued the theme that a future president had been born. In a telegram to Will and Oveta, Poage shared the congratulations of "an old bachelor to the father and mother and future president. Nineteenth of January has always been a great day for the South and especially for the Culp Family."[11]

Other friends predicted that a future governor or senator had been born. Florence Sterling wrote that she was "so happy to know W. P. Hobby Jr. has arrived. May he grow to be . . . the Governor of Texas and United States Senator." Governor Sterling and former governor Dan Moody cosigned a telegram to Will stating that they were "wondering just what size hat it will now take to fit you." On behalf of Governor Sterling's entire staff, his assistant Jessie Ziegler, who was a close friend of Oveta's, sent a message addressed to the newborn: "Dear Bill, we understand you arrived in Houston today to be the permanent guest of Governor and Mrs. Hobby. You certainly have good taste in picking such splendid and able parents, and greeting them on the anniversary of the birth of . . . Robert E. Lee. We hope that you will follow in the footsteps of your illustrious parents and keep the name Hobby in the hearts of as many Texans as they have theirs." Will quipped to Oveta that if he had known "babies were so popular, I would have put them in my [campaign] platform."[12]

One friend wrote to Oveta, "I admit that it distresses me a little to think of the brilliant Parliamentarian putting her mind to bottle formula. . . . The fall of the great is mighty! Thought it would be just like you, Oveta, to be smart enough to do both career and family." In fact, Oveta had no plans to abandon her career or civic activities. A few weeks after the baby was born, Will hired a registered nurse to stay with Bill while Oveta was at her desk at the *Post* during the day. By mid-March, she and Will were spending time in Austin visiting Ross Sterling and other friends in the Capitol. Even with the help of a nurse, Oveta found it hard to balance motherhood with work. In an interview she later gave to the *New York Daily News* in 1953, Oveta admitted that she had believed she could handle being a businesswoman, wife, and mother all at the same time but that "in the early years it was sometimes difficult." After intense days in the office, where she was assuming increasing editorial responsibilities, she still had to do a "great deal of the household work" herself after office hours. Her intense drive and her zeal for work, along with her obsession with order, were interfering with her need to bond with little William.[13]

Early in July 1932, six months after Bill's birth, Oveta was on an early morning ride when her horse suddenly bolted, tossing her to the ground. She suffered a badly broken leg, a shattered left wrist, and deep bruises to her right hand, nerve damage in one arm, and numerous cuts and abrasions from head to toe, which required her to be hospitalized for several days. After she was released from the hospital, Oveta was confined to home and disabled for several weeks. Nearly a month after her release from the hospital, Will brought news about the pace of Oveta's recovery to Governor Sterling and his staff. Jessie Ziegler reported to her mother, "Governor Hobby was in today and said that Oveta, while she had to wear a high-top shoe, was getting along nicely but her arm was still practically useless. Her fingers are still numb and kind of useless." According to Ziegler, Will also candidly admitted that there had been one benefit from Oveta's forced confinement at home: "He said that Oveta had gotten to love the baby and that while she had fought against it, she just had to succumb to the little darling."[14]

Baby William's next newspaper appearance was on Mother's Day, May 14, 1933. He and Oveta posed for a photograph as part of a feature in the Society and Clubs section of the *Post* on "five lovely young mothers." Oveta, fully recovered from her accident, held her "fine young son, William Pettus II," on her lap. This created a perfect picture of a stylish mother and cherubic son and underscored the family's growing stature in Houston society. In 1935, the Hobbys commissioned a portrait of Bill that reflected pride in their firstborn and a sense of his, and by extension their own, importance. The painting was done by Boris B. Gordon, a prominent Swiss-born artist who would later be known as the "painter of presidents." Thirteen of Gordon's portraits of politicians of note hang in the US Capitol.[15]

Early in the summer of 1934, when Bill was two and a half years old, Oveta's younger sister, Lynn Culp, moved in with Will and Oveta while she attended business school in Houston. She had recently graduated from high school in Temple and wound up staying with her sister and brother-in-law for nearly two years. During that time, Lynn helped Oveta by babysitting young William, occasionally with the aid of Lyndon B. Johnson's brother, Sam, who worked at a Houston bank. "I used to go with [Oveta's] sister a little bit down there [in Houston]," the future president's brother later recalled. He claimed that after he brought Lynn home late one night, Oveta wouldn't let them get together again unless it was to help Lynn babysit Bill, which he recalled required changing "that kid's diapers."[16]

After Lynn moved into her own residence in Houston early in 1936, Oveta and Will leased out their house on Glen Haven and moved to apartment 12F in the Lamar Hotel in downtown Houston. The Lamar was built in 1927 by real estate tycoon, banker, and *Houston Chronicle* publisher Jesse H. Jones, who kept a residence on the sixteenth floor even during the years he lived in Washington and served as head of the Reconstruction

Finance Corporation in President Franklin D. Roosevelt's administration. The Lamar was a power base for Houston elites, with suites permanently rented to major figures in oil, politics, and banking. The hotel was also the home of the KPRC-Radio broadcast studios, which had moved there in 1935.

Jesse Jones was now Will Hobby's "silent" boss. As a result of the Depression, Ross Sterling had been forced into bankruptcy while still serving as governor, which cost him ownership of the *Houston Post-Dispatch* and KPRC-Radio, as well as his extensive real estate and bank holdings. Jones maneuvered successfully to take control of a significant portion of Sterling's assets, including the newspaper and the radio station, while Jones also continued his ownership of the *Houston Chronicle* and radio station KTRK. Concerned about potential criticism that he now had a monopoly on the news business in Houston (the Scripps-Howard newspaper chain's tabloid *Houston Press* was a distant third in circulation), Jones exercised indirect and silent control of the *Post-Dispatch* through a holding company managed by a close business associate, oilman Jack Josey, whom Jones installed as the company's chairman. Jones was now not only managing editor Will Hobby's boss but also his landlord, a situation that Oveta much resented, although quietly.

This was a stressful time for the Hobbys. The United States was in the midst of the Great Depression, which Oveta would later refer to as the time when "profits were nil." Will's investments, including the Braeswood Addition, had lost most of their value. Although the Hobbys remained relatively affluent because of their salaries at the *Post-Dispatch*, they were fighting a particularly tough financial battle over the paper's future. The paper was struggling to keep its printing presses rolling. Pressured by Jones to cut costs, Josey ordered Will to make reductions in staff that went beyond what Will believed was necessary to keep the newspaper financially afloat. Will's increasing discomfort with the severe budget cuts was obvious to his friends, which led to rumors that he might leave the newspaper. Despite his disagreement with Josey over his management of the *Post-Dispatch*'s budget, Will remained as editor. All the while, he looked for an opportunity to eventually purchase the newspaper with which he had been associated, off and on, since the late 1890s.

Will and Oveta's worries increased further only a couple of months after they moved into the Lamar Hotel. Four-year-old Bill fell seriously ill, possibly with influenza. Consisting of body aches, high fever, and chills, his condition gave Will and Oveta a real fright, especially with their memories of the great flu epidemic of 1919. Both stayed at the apartment while Bill slowly recovered. Their colleagues at the *Post-Dispatch* monitored the situation closely, sending them flowers, cards, and cookies. When Bill was finally out of danger, Judd Mortimer Lewis, Will's old friend and the newspaper's longtime columnist and poet, published a poem in the *Post-Dispatch* titled "I Am So Glad." Lewis wrote, "I am so glad to know your little feet will tread the ways of life and make them sweet. For those who love you so, who bent above your bed of pain . . . and through each terror-stricken day and night gave of their strength to help you win the fight."[17]

A few weeks after Bill recovered from his illness, in May 1936, Oveta learned she was once again expecting. Her second child was due around the turn of the new year. At the time, in addition to her work at the *Post-Dispatch* and her volunteer activities, Oveta was hard at work writing *Mr. Chairman*, a high school textbook on parliamentary rules, drawing from her extensive experience as parliamentarian of the Texas House of Representatives. Oveta, however, refused to slow down during her pregnancy. She continued her writing and soon became actively involved in the official celebration of the centennial of Texas's independence from Mexico, which included a highly publicized visit to the state by President Roosevelt and First Lady Eleanor Roosevelt. Jesse Jones, who was serving in President Roosevelt's cabinet, invited the presidential couple to make a "noncampaign" visit to five Texas cities, starting in Houston, to celebrate the centennial. That the visit occurred when Roosevelt sought a second term as president in the November elections was undoubtedly no coincidence. After the Roosevelts arrived in Houston on June 11, they traveled on the Houston Ship Channel to the San Jacinto battleground. The Hobbys accompanied the presidential party as guests of Jones—Will joining FDR on a boat and Oveta getting to know the first lady on a yacht. The next day, they traveled with Jones to Dallas to attend FDR's speech at the Cotton Bowl.

On their return from Dallas to Houston, the Hobbys experienced a horrific plane crash. The couple had joined Jones, his secretary, and his two pilots in a private plane. A fuel-line leak caused a fire, which forced an emergency landing about twenty miles south of Dallas. The plane was destroyed, and the passengers banged up, including Will. Both pilots suffered severe injuries. Fortunately, Oveta and the baby she was carrying were largely unscathed. The Hobbys were devastated to learn the following day that one of the pilots, Eugene Schacher, had died from smoke inhalation. The couple, with Bill and their unborn child on their minds, decided they would never again fly together on the same aircraft.[18]

On January 19, 1937, Bill made his fourth appearance in the *Houston Post-Dispatch*. His fifth birthday was commemorated by the poet Judd Mortimer Lewis in his "Tampering with Trifles" column in the *Houston Post*. Titled "Bill," the poem celebrated how the young boy had battled through a serious illness. Its hyperbolic conclusion read:

> And so on your fifth birthday we
>   Are glad beyond compare;
> More than we've ever been before;
>   And all the world is fair;
> And we go forward happily
> Into new ways of song,
> Thankful and glad beyond all words
> Because you are along.

By coincidence, on the same day Lewis's poem was published in celebration of Bill's birthday, Oveta and Will's second child, a girl, was born, thus resulting in the unusual situation of Oveta and her two offspring sharing the same birthday, January 19. Will apparently named his daughter Jesse Oveta Hobby in honor of his friend and boss, Jesse H. Jones. He entered the name on his daughter's official birth certificate without telling Oveta beforehand. "Mother was not happy. She detested Jesse Jones," Bill Hobby later recalled. "Mother issued orders that my sister's name would be Jessica, and that's what she was called her entire life." Oveta recovered from Jessica's birth at the family's apartment at the Lamar Hotel, but as per her usual drive, she soon returned to her office at the *Post-Dispatch*.[19]

On July 11, 1937, Bill made his next appearance in the *Post-Dispatch* just six months after his fifth birthday—a rather precocious start to his career as a journalist. His byline appeared in the book review pages of the paper (edited by Oveta). Published in the section "For the Young and Very Young," his review was of *Long Live the King!*, an illustrated history by Alice Dalgliesh of the coronations of famed kings and queens of England. Young Hobby, who had only recently learned to read, had become such a frequent visitor to the children's room of Houston's main public library—all the time under the watchful eye of his nanny—that he got to know the pioneering longtime head librarian, Julia Ideson, in whose honor the beautiful library building was eventually named. The library was conveniently located a few blocks from the Lamar Hotel. In his review, Bill shared some of the book's takeaways, observing that "Queen Elizabeth was called 'Good Queen Bess,' though she was sometimes not at all good." He concluded that the book was "very interesting. I liked it as much as 'Adventures in Puddle-Muddle' and better than 'Alice in Wonderland.'"[20]

Soon after Jessica's birth, Will and Oveta decided that the Lamar Hotel was not a suitable place to raise a family. For one thing, their hotel suite was too small to accommodate an additional child. When the renters' lease to the Glen Haven house expired late in the summer of 1937, the Hobbys reclaimed possession and remodeled and enlarged the home. They had already moved some of their furniture back when a fire broke out on the first floor. The house was saved, but the damage was extensive enough to delay their return for several weeks while the house was being repaired. The Hobbys were forced to find temporary living quarters in the Rice Hotel (also owned by Jesse Jones), as they had already given up their suite at the Lamar. They finally moved into their newly remodeled home on Glen Haven early in 1938.

The family's return to the house on Glen Haven was a happy development for young William Hobby, who was called Bill by his friends and family, with one exception. Oveta continued to call him William for most of her life. The Braeswood Addition, where Glen Haven was located, was transected by Brays Bayou and adjacent to undeveloped open pastureland. A large city park, named for philanthropist George Hermann, was nearby. The park featured picnic areas, playgrounds, a zoo, and other amenities that appealed to Bill. In addition, the area provided plenty of opportunities for horseback riding, an activity especially attractive to the horse-loving Hobby family. Although Oveta had suffered her traumatic riding accident in this area, it did not seem to discourage the family from continuing that leisure activity, especially Bill, who spent much time on horseback. As he later recalled, "When I was very young, [I rode] at the horse stables on Alameda. Both my parents kept horses there. And, of course, the bridle paths were in Hermann Park. I hung around the stable and mucked out stalls and groomed horses and so forth." Years later, when asked about growing up in Houston, Bill noted, "Where we lived, south of Bellaire just off Main Street, that was out in the country!"[21]

The escape from living in downtown Houston gave Bill the freedom to explore the nearby pastures, where he also enjoyed rabbit hunting with George Hightower, a Black former prison trusty whom his father had pardoned as governor. By this time, Hightower had already worked for the Hobby family for several years as a handyman, gardener, and, along with Vernon Wiley and Cecil McBride, one of their three chauffeurs. Hightower kept greyhounds for rabbit hunts, and Bill often went with him and his dogs to hunt in the open field near the intersection of Main Street and Bellaire Boulevard, where the massive Shamrock Hotel would later be built and eventually torn down to be enveloped by the Texas Medical Center. "George spent the rest of his life working for our family, which amounted to about 50 years," Bill recalled, "and he helped raise me."[22]

Bill's eldest son, Paul, observed that his father "was raised by help a lot of the time," because his parents were either older, in the case of his father, or high-achieving and gone, in the case of his mother. "Vernon would tell stories about driving my father around when my father was eight, nine, ten years old, and he'd have his nose buried in a Shakespeare book. He'd be reading Shakespeare intensely. You could have a car accident; you could park the car and get out. You could go to the ice cream shop. It didn't much matter, because Bill was going to sit there with his nose happily buried in his Shakespeare book."[23]

In March 1938, the *Houston Post-Dispatch*'s management, led by Jesse Jones's proxy, Jack Josey, was so impressed with Oveta's work at the newspaper, they promoted her to executive vice president, effectively giving her chief responsibility for the newspaper's daily operations, although Will continued to make overall policy and editorial decisions. In the fall of 1939, the Hobbys finally negotiated the purchase of the *Post-Dispatch* (they immediately dropped *Dispatch* from the name) and KPRC-Radio from Jones. Will and Oveta had to go into debt to finance the purchase, but the newspaper was now their exclusive property. The Hobbys were already well known in Houston's civic and business power circles, but the purchase of the *Post* greatly enhanced their status and influence as power brokers, and it would also play a key role in making Oveta a national figure.

With the purchase of the *Post* completed and the economy recovering from the Depression while the country began preparations for national defense as war erupted in Europe and Asia, the Hobby family's financial situation rapidly improved. They settled in comfortably at their newly refurbished and remodeled house on Glen Haven. Jessica and Bill were tended to by nannies, longtime Hobby manservants, and their father, while Oveta focused much of her time on the *Post*. This is not to say that Will, who was now in his early sixties, was at home all the time and not busy with his own projects, or that Oveta neglected her children, but of the two parents, Will was more of a presence at home than was his wife. As *Time* magazine would later report, "The old governor was inclined to spoil his children, but Oveta was not. She taught them everything from horsemanship to management of their allowances." She closely monitored their childhood pastimes: performances in school plays and church pageants, birthday parties, and trips to the circus. Bill was a member of Troop 36 of the Boy Scouts, which had exclusive use of Camp Spring, located three miles north of the town of Spring, Texas. At the time, the camp boasted a deep swimming hole created by a double bend in Spring Creek. As one observer described, "The boys have canvas kayaks for canoe practice and recreational use, as well as a diving platform and a rope hung from a tall tree for swing diving. Camp Spring, the boys say, is nature's own laboratory for the study of birds, snakes, fish, land and water plants, the stars, as well as a fine place for water sports."[24]

Oveta also made the decisions about her children's schooling. For example, she decided to remove her son from the Oaks kindergarten school in favor of the exclusive and nonsectarian Kinkaid School, founded in 1906 by Margaret Kinkaid. In her letter to the Oaks, Oveta noted, "After seeing William with a group of children I determined he would do better with a group nearer his own age. For that reason, I am entering him at Kinkaid School. With appreciation for your many kindnesses and expressing the hope that you will have a place for Jesse when she is ready for kindergarten." Bill would later tell a reporter that he and his sister had a governess while growing up, but that his mother "never relegated" them to her care. "Mother never attempted to press her views on either of us," he continued. "We have always followed our bent—within reason, of course. She always had time to listen to our troubles. But we were given to understand that we should work out our own problems, and that running to mother might ease our hurt feelings but wasn't a solution to whatever difficulty we were in."[25]

An amusing example of the impact of Oveta's hands-off approach in shaping her children's own views surfaced early in Bill's life during the presidential campaign in 1940. Oveta and Will had been loyal Democrats until FDR's second term, when he pushed a progressive legislative agenda, which included the Wagner Act guaranteeing the right of private-sector workers to organize into trade unions, engage in collective bargaining, and take collective action such as strikes. Will was a lifelong opponent of labor unions. The final break occurred when FDR attempted to pack the US Supreme Court and then broke historical precedent by running for a third term in 1940. As a result, the Hobbys actively supported the Republican presidential candidate, businessman Wendell Willkie. Oveta even worked in Willkie's national campaign. Bill, who was a precocious eight-year-old student at Kinkaid School in Houston in 1940, wrote a school paper during the presidential campaign that he titled "An Account of National Affairs." In what was perhaps an early indication he would develop some political views that differed from his parents', Bill wrote that because of the war in Europe, America "must have a leader who can build up a defense and offense. Franklin D. Roosevelt is the man for the job! He is eligible for a third term. As many of us say, 'We shouldn't swap horses in the middle of the stream.' *We don't want Wendell Willkie.*"[26]

Despite Oveta's dominance in deciding and monitoring his schooling and leisure activity, if not his political views, Bill later stressed that he was closer to his father than to his mother. The fact that Will was old enough to be Bill's grandfather, treated him in a grandfatherly way, and was readily available to him during this period of his boyhood, surely played a role in Bill's positive memories of his father. "My grandfather was so much older than Dad that [their relationship] was, in most ways, completely free of any of the regular father-son tensions in terms of expectations," Laura Hobby Beckworth later noted. "It was just pure love, in the way that you would love a grandfather. I know my grandfather was much more emotive, emotional, just unguarded in his adoration for his children than my grandmother, who was never unguarded really of anything, except perhaps being a grandmother. But there were no barriers for my grandfather's love for my father and for Jessica."[27]

Bill loved the time he spent with his father. An undated note preserved in the Hobby family archive, written when his father was suffering a brief illness, reflects the warm and affectionate nature of their relationship. Uncharacteristically addressing his father by his first name, Bill wrote, "Dear William, I love you. I am going to school now. What do you want the Easter Bunny to bring you? Hurry up and get well. I love you." Bill particularly enjoyed listening to his father's stories about his experiences in politics and journalism, especially anecdotes about the famous people Will had met when he was a "kid" staff member for the *Houston Post*, including the famous short-story writer William Sydney Porter, whose later pen name was O. Henry. Porter was a columnist for the *Post* during Will's first year at the paper. Will also told Bill stories about meeting Texas governor James Stephen Hogg and boxing legend "Gentleman Jim" Corbett, and seeing the captured Apache warrior Geronimo at the Houston train station as he was being transported to the Indian Territory. Bill was also fascinated by his father's anecdotes about when he was governor and had a conference with President Woodrow Wilson during the First World War, and his acquaintance during his governorship with the president of Mexico, Álvaro Obregón, the famed one-armed general of the Mexican Revolution.[28]

Bill also joined his father at times in visiting Will's friends, who happened to be some of the most powerful and influential people in Houston. "My father had the custom on Sunday mornings [of calling] on his friends and they would do the same thing," Bill later remembered. They would visit wealthy businessman and philanthropist Ben Taub, attorney and banker Judge James A. Elkins, and Mr. and Mrs. George Cohen, "the manager and owner of Foleys," a local department store. "I saw a lot of Houston history," Bill recalled. "And [Mayor] Oscar Holcombe was one of those. All those people, they were a group of friends." One of Bill's favorite excursions with his father was to go to the KPRC studios in the Lamar Hotel. "I remember when my parents bought the radio station. The studios were in the Lamar Hotel. Kern Tipps was the manager and then Jack McGrew. And certainly, I hung around the studio as a kid there all the time." McGrew later recalled that Bill was an "inquisitive and mischievous little kid" who, despite being watched "like a hawk" by the radio staff, "more than once managed to get into the announcer booth and punch a couple of buttons, just to watch the little red lights go on and off."[29]

Will occasionally took his son with him on trips to Austin, where they swam in the Barton Springs Pool and visited Will's old friends, including colorful cotton baron and developer Edgar "Commodore" Perry and T. C. "Buck" Steiner, a former rodeo star, law officer, and movie stuntman who owned the Capitol Saddlery, a famed boot and saddle shop on Guadalupe Street. "Buck was a colorful guy," Bill noted in his own memoir. "He claimed to have been friends with Al Capone and Pancho Villa, and he has his own wing in the Rodeo Hall of Fame. When I was lieutenant governor, I frequented Buck's establishment, which was close to the Capitol, visiting with Buck as he sat in a big armchair by the old-fashioned counter. As long as he lived [he died in 2001 at age 102] he called me 'Young Hobby.'"[30]

During these years, Bill also began spending some of his time in the summer at Camp Rio Vista, a boys' camp in the Texas Hill Country. Laura Hobby Beckworth later shared a story she had heard from Cecil McBride, one of the Hobby family's household staff. "Cecil was a big part of [my father's] life. Cecil told me that he and Neany, which is what we call our grandfather, drove Papa [Bill] to Camp Rio Vista when he was old enough to go. They took him and dropped him off, and then they drove back to Houston. And maybe three or four days later, my grandfather said, 'Cecil, let's go see him.' I think my grandmother was out of town; she wouldn't have permitted this. They got back in the car and drove back to Camp Rio Vista to visit."[31]

The comfortable and secure lifestyle Bill enjoyed as a young boy underwent a major disruption in January 1941 when he was nine years old. He was suffering from chronic sinusitis and severe pollen allergies during that winter. At the urging of Houston physician Ralph Bowen, a nationally recognized allergy and asthma specialist, the decision was made to have Bill attend a school located in a desert climate. Like Oveta, when she had been a child, Bill also had a stutter, which his sinus problems seemed to make worse. "I did take speech lessons when I was a child, but the fact is that I'm a poor public speaker. I do a lot of 'err' and 'ahh,' which is not good for public speaking," he later recalled. Following Dr. Bowen's advice, Oveta investigated suitable schools. On the recommendation of a friend, she requested a catalog from Green Fields Preparatory School for Boys, a boarding school in the desert near Tucson, Arizona. In her letter to the school, Oveta, who mistakenly reported that her son would be ten years old in a month (he would be nine), stated that she had been told that Green Fields would be "the ideal school for my son who . . . is in the high fourth grade. . . . Would you advise me whether you would have an opening in the spring term?" Satisfied with what they had learned about Green Fields, Will and Oveta enrolled Bill in the school for the spring semester of the school year.[32]

Founded on an old alfalfa farm in 1933 by George and Rubie Atchley, Green Fields was a "felicitous blend of the eastern academic tradition and western, outdoor, ranch style living." The school's student population was small—just a few dozen boys at the time of Bill's enrollment—which allowed for individualized instruction and small classes, often held outdoors. Bill and the other students lived in bunkhouses or cabins on the school's grounds. The boys started their days by going horseback riding and performing their daily chores before breakfast. Classes and study hall occupied the time from eight until noon and from one until two-thirty. Bill and his schoolmates cared for their horses and rode again from about three to five every weekday in the afternoon. Dr. Bowen checked on Bill in early February, sharing in a letter to Oveta his confidence in the move to Green Fields. "I truly believe that with the continued inclusion of those pollens and environmental factors which are perennial irritants," Bowen wrote, "William will establish an excellent tolerance. Asthma is a disease which is much like a living death during an attack. Asthmatic patients usually develop an unusual psychology because of frequent upsets, and the majority are handicapped in their work and play." In her reply to the doctor, Oveta reported that "Gov. Hobby is with him and reports that he is full of energy and enthusiasm for the new life. He is eating well and playing thoroughly."[33]

Although Oveta's claim that Bill was doing well may have been accurate, young Bill was nevertheless homesick—not an unusual feeling for any child who has been uprooted and separated far away from his parents, caretakers, and friends. A few weeks after entering Green Fields School, Bill wrote a letter to his parents where he pleaded for them to visit: "I forgot, did you want to learn how to ride a horse or fall off one? I fell off one yesterday. It was quite a mean horse. I think it was because I was not riding right. Please come to see me again soon. Please send a comic book. Please send gum. Tell Jessica and Grandmother [Emma Culp] to come see me soon." Despite his loneliness, Bill made it through the semester and returned to Texas at the end of May.[34]

"I think [my] dad's childhood was very formal," Laura Hobby Beckworth later observed. "I don't think it was that unusual for young boys, particularly, to be sent to camp or military school. My father was asthmatic as a child and there was some thought that it was better for his health. It had to be terribly lonely for him. But I know they wanted the best for him." Bill's elder son, Paul, has noted that his father "was raised by help, he was asthmatic, they sent him off to Arizona and then he was at St. Albans. He wasn't unloved by any measure, but he just wasn't raised in the company of his parents." As to Bill's feelings about being away from home for much of his youth, Paul described them as, "You can't miss what you didn't have. But has he talked about it? Or would he talk about it? Never." That reticence to discuss his inner feelings was a characteristic Bill carried throughout his life.[35]

Bill would soon suffer an even greater disruption in his home life as another world war rapidly approached—a war in which his mother would eventually play a key role as the first woman to officially serve in the US Army. After getting her son settled in at summer camp in early June 1941, Oveta traveled to Washington, DC, to consult with Federal

Communications Commission staff about regulatory issues of concern to KPRC-Radio. While in Washington, the War Department asked her to accept a temporary appointment as a consultant to help plan a women's unit of the army's public relations bureau. The army was overwhelmed by an avalanche of letters from mothers and wives of men recently drafted in the first peacetime draft in American history who were worried about how their loved ones were being treated by the military. The news media was also being bombarded. The army had no clue how to handle what was quickly becoming a significant public relations headache, so the officers in the public relations bureau decided to organize a women's department to develop a public relations strategy to deal with the problem. Oveta's position as one of the only women in the nation working as publisher of a major newspaper attracted the War Department's attention and led to their request for her help.

When Oveta discussed the offer with Will, he encouraged her to take the job for patriotic reasons. He also assured her that the children and the *Post* would be in good hands in her absence. In late July 1941, the army announced her appointment as the "Expert Consultant to the Secretary of War," with a convoluted official title typical of army bureaucracy: "Chief, Women's Interests Section, Planning and Liaison Branch, Bureau of Public Relations." Because Oveta's schedule allowed her to spend only ten days a month back home, her mother moved to Houston to take care of three-year-old Jessica. Bill was sent back to Green Fields School in Tucson in September.[36]

By the beginning of December 1941, Oveta had successfully carried out her job as chief of the Women's Interests Section and was preparing to resign and return home to Houston. When Japan attacked Pearl Harbor on December 7, plunging the United States into World War II, General George C. Marshall, Army Chief of Staff, asked Oveta to remain in Washington to help the army lobby Congress to pass legislation authorizing a Women's Army Corps. After she accepted her new assignment, Oveta flew from Washington to Houston on December 21 to spend nearly two weeks with Will and the children over the holidays. Bill, who was back from Green Fields School in Tucson, would be returning to Kinkaid School in Houston for the spring semester of 1942. A news story about Oveta's visit to Houston included a quote from her nine-year-old son, who was unhappy about his mother's absence while she worked as a consultant for the army. He told a reporter that he would never be a journalist because "Mother is, and she has to work too hard."[37]

In May 1942 after Congress passed the bill to create a Women's Army Corps, initially as an "auxiliary" rather than an official component of the army—the Women's Auxiliary Army Corps, or WAAC—General Marshall and Secretary of War Henry Stimson persuaded Oveta to take an assignment as the WAAC commander. Once again, Will urged her to accept the appointment for patriotic reasons. Will was comfortable with the management team he and Oveta had in place at the *Post* and at their radio station, which operated under his general supervision. He also had the care of their children well in hand. In May, Secretary Stimson announced his appointment of thirty-seven-year-old

Oveta Culp Hobby as director of the newly authorized WAAC. General Marshall soon gave her the rank of colonel. Oveta, who faced the daunting task of organizing the WAAC from the ground up and then commanding it once it was a reality, embarked on a difficult and controversial journey that would keep her in Washington until the summer of 1945.[38]

On June 13, 1942, Will and the children arrived at Oveta's newly leased house near the Sidwell Friends School off Wisconsin Avenue, where they stayed for most of the summer. Will had remained with Oveta for a week after her oath-taking ceremony as commander of the WAAC on May 16, and then he returned to Houston to bring Jessica and Bill back to Washington. Earlier in the year, Will had one of the family chauffeurs deliver Oveta's sporty Lincoln Zephyr to Washington, although she rarely drove it herself and instead used the services of an army driver. Will made use of the car and a private driver to take the children sightseeing while Oveta spent long hours working in her office preparing for the upcoming officer training camp. After the training was completed, Oveta and Will traveled to New York City on August 23, taking Bill with them and leaving Jessica in Washington with a nanny. While in New York, they took time to sit for a long interview with a group of reporters in their room at the Savoy-Plaza Hotel. One reporter asked Bill what he thought about his mother's uniform. "The uniform's all right," the ten-year-old answered. "What I like is aviation. Yes, sir! I really like aviation." He then "rattled off" a description of "every known American fighting plane." Oveta told the journalists that she had been delighted to have her husband and the children with her that summer, but that Will would have to make do alone with Bill and Jessica during the coming winter. When someone suggested that Oveta's absence from her domestic duties must be difficult for Will while he was also managing his newspaper and radio properties, Will stressed that he employed a governess for Bill and Jessica, as well as a cook and other household staff.[39]

When their brief visit to Manhattan ended, Will and the children soon departed for Houston, while Oveta returned to WAAC headquarters. In mid-December, Oveta traveled to Houston to spend the Christmas holidays with her family and, hopefully, to get a few days' rest. While Oveta was home, she and Will took the opportunity to have a christening ceremony for Jessica and Bill, with the family physician, Dr. Ernst William Bertner, and his wife, Julia, and Humble Oil Company executive Harry Weiss and his wife, Olga, serving as the children's godparents. As she departed Houston after Christmas, Oveta had the comfort of knowing that Will was spending much time with Bill and Jessica and that her mother would be making frequent trips from Dallas to stay with the grandchildren. In addition, Oveta had significant help from the dutiful and efficient Helon Johnson, Will's executive secretary who had been a *Houston Post* employee since 1932. Johnson also served as Oveta's right hand back in Houston. Oveta sent instructions to Johnson by telephone and correspondence about what meals to prepare for Will and the kids and what kind of shoes, clothes, and toys to purchase for them. One Christmas, when Johnson reported that most of the shopping had been done, she added, aware that Oveta strongly preferred that her son be called William, "We have gotten William's chemistry set." Johnson also reported that Bill had made a last-minute request. "William told me that he wanted me to go with him to do his Christmas shopping," Johnson wrote, "so we are going Thursday evening after school. Since the stores will be open Thursday night, that will give us more time." Bill would later fondly remember the Captain Midnight decoder badge he received as his favorite toy. On another occasion, Johnson informed Oveta that Bill had received his Boy Scout uniform and was "just thrilled beyond all words." Johnson also reported that Bill had told her that the boys who recently joined his Scout troop had been unable to buy their uniforms. "You can imagine how proud he will be," Johnson wrote, "when he goes to the meeting tomorrow night in his full uniform."[40]

Early in May 1943, after an inspection tour of WAAC training camps, Oveta flew on a military plane to Houston, where she had an opportunity to stay with Will and the children. While in Texas, she and Will, with Bill in tow, traveled to Belton, where Oveta was the guest of honor at a formal banquet at her mother's alma mater, Mary Hardin–Baylor College. The next day, Fort Hood commander General A. D. Bruce guided Oveta, Will, and an excited and bedazzled Bill on a tour of his base, which bristled with heavy armament, including the Sherman tanks that Bill had seen in newsreel features at movie theaters in Houston. Two months later, when Congress finally passed legislation to transform the WAAC into the Women's Army Corps (WAC) as an official unit of the army, with Oveta as its commander, Will traveled to Washington to be with Oveta when she took her oath as head of the new corps. Bill and Jessica were attending summer camps in the Texas Hill Country, so Will decided to remain in Washington with Oveta for the rest of July. When a reporter asked Oveta why Bill and Jessica weren't also in Washington with her, she replied, "Last summer when they were with me in Washington was the only summer they didn't spend on the ranch. And much as I'd like them with me again, Washington is no place for them. There's such a problem with housing and the heat. They're much better off on the ranch."[41]

At the beginning of August, three months after his memorable trip to Fort Hood, Bill had another opportunity to be with his mother when she came home to Glen Haven for several days on sick leave to recover from extreme fatigue caused by a thyroid condition. When Oveta felt well enough to return to her duties in Washington in September, Will, deeply concerned about Oveta's health, decided that he and the children would stay with her in Washington and spend most of the fall in her spacious, antiques-filled apartment. A few days after the family arrived in Washington, Will, now sixty-five years old, suddenly took ill with a painful kidney ailment and was hospitalized. He had surgery five days later. It was the beginning of a very gradual decline in his general health that would continue off and on for another two decades. Soon after Will was released from the hospital, he and Bill returned to Houston. Jessica, who was minded by a nanny during the day, remained with Oveta in Washington until Christmas.

In February 1944, another medical emergency in the family added to Oveta's stress and exhaustion, but this time it wasn't Will who was sick. Soon after Oveta returned from an exhausting tour of WAC stations in the United Kingdom, North Africa, and Italy—the latter at an active battlefront—an attack of appendicitis sent young Bill into surgery. Oveta boarded a hasty flight to Houston in time for his operation and stayed a couple of days while he fully recovered. That summer, Oveta's thyroid problem struck again with a vengeance, sending her to the hospital at Brooke Field in San Antonio, where she stayed for several days. After her release, Oveta relaxed at home for a month.[42]

When Oveta returned to Washington in mid-August, Bill, who had finished his last semester at Kinkaid, went with her to enroll in the highly regarded St. Albans, an Episcopalian all-boys school affiliated with and located near the National Cathedral. The Hobbys selected St. Albans because they were impressed with the school's high academic standards and its boarding facilities, which gave Bill relatively close proximity to Oveta while she spent what they anticipated might be her last year leading the WAC. St. Albans would play a significant role in Bill's education and in shaping his moral and ethical views.[43]

CHAPTER 2

ST. ALBANS AND THE RICE INSTITUTE

St. Albans sits on the highest point in Washington, DC, with a sprawling vista of the nation's capital. It was established in 1909 by the bequest of Harriet Lane Johnston (a niece of President James Buchanan) as a "National Cathedral School for Boys," with one of its purposes being the education and training of choirboys for the National Cathedral. For the Hobbys, the school's religious affiliation, with its promise of ethical and moral teaching, was a plus but not the deciding factor. Although they were Christian, neither Will nor Oveta was devoutly religious. Will was raised as a Methodist, but when asked about his religion when he was an adult, he typically answered that it was the Lord's Prayer and the Sermon on the Mount. Oveta grew up as a Baptist, but in the late 1920s she left behind the evangelism of her father in favor of Unitarianism, although that affiliation was relatively brief. By the 1940s, both Will and Oveta were self-identifying as Episcopalians, but neither attended church regularly, and their beliefs were solidly ecumenical.[1]

While religion may not have been a prime factor in Bill's enrollment, it was of great importance to the school in its early years, notably under the leadership of Reverend Albert Hawley Lucas, headmaster from 1929 to 1952. Lucas saw the spiritual education of his students as central to their St. Albans experience, and while he took an ecumenical stance, some form of religious practice was required. Attendance at daily chapel services was compulsory for all the students, and twice a day for boarders at the school. Philip Stansbury, a classmate of Hobby's, described Lucas as "a firm, indeed total, believer in the Christianity he taught. For those not put off by his faults—his temper and autocratic behavior on matters he believed crucial—his imperfection did not reduce his religious influence but perhaps enhanced it." Lucas elevated the school's academic standing by recruiting highly skilled teachers, almost entirely men.[2]

Hobby later recalled, "St. Albans was an excellent school. A quarter or so of the students were boarders. They were mostly sons of military and diplomatic families. It was an interesting group." John Davis, who joined the faculty in 1942, later described the school of the 1940s era to the *Washington Post*: "St. Albans was a close-knit, autocratic Episcopal school aimed at 'molding Christians of the Anglican tradition.' When New England boarding schools were struggling . . . St. Albans had to turn applicants away. That was because it was in the unique position of being a city school preferred by the old Washington families. There were no black students, Roman Catholics were in small numbers, and . . . only Episcopalians were selected for the student vestry." The *Washington Post* story, published in 1991, noted that the school's educational excellence was reflected in the careers of its students: "an astronaut, a Rhodes scholar, a congressman, a senator [John Warner], two ambassadors and the obligatory assemblage of lawyers, military officers and businessmen that make up official Washington."[3]

Bill thrived at St. Albans. In a letter to his parents, he wrote, "I like everything here, all the teachers and boys." His Lower School experience included his selection as a prefect, considered "one of the highest honors for a St. Albans boy." Chosen by their fellow classmates for their judgment and leadership, prefects helped to maintain order while students queued up to go to and from chapel services. Bill also played on the Baby Blue football, basketball, and baseball teams. His chief academic interest was in mathematics, and he later recalled that as a child, he had wanted to be a mathematician. He performed well academically and was popular with his classmates and the faculty. As his November 2, 1945, report card noted, "We are delighted with Bill in every way. He is very well and is always a fine influence." A similar note on his next report card, in December 1945, read, "Bill is [a] very grand, well-balanced youngster. His instructors all speak of him with respect—finding him courteous, cooperative, thoughtful, and mature. Spiritually, he is advanced beyond his years—reverent and intelligent." As his daughter Laura later said, "My father loved St. Albans. He flourished there. He was very athletic, successful in kind of every field which, given his quiet nature and his socially reticent personality, I'm sort of surprised at. He was a very reserved person and a shy child, I think. But he found his niche at St. Albans."[4]

Athletics were of great importance to St. Albans's headmaster, who believed "tough competitive sports, especially football, are man-builders, builders of character through discipline, effort, pain, cooperation, and hard knocks." Given the small size of the student body, boys were encouraged to play multiple sports, and Bill was no exception. He played soccer and was quite proud of his varsity football career at St. Albans, including earning a spot as the team's starting center. During one game, he was roughed up by a kid on the opposing team. His teammate Michael Collins, who played left guard, helped him stand up and asked him which boy had smashed him harder than necessary. Bill identified number sixty-four as the culprit. "After the next play," Hobby later recalled, "they carried 64 off, and he didn't come back." Collins, Bill's guardian angel and fellow classmate, went on to become the astronaut who piloted the Apollo 11 Command

Module that circled the moon while Neil Armstrong and Buzz Aldrin made the first landing and walked on the surface.[5]

To Will and Oveta's delight, Bill—brought up by journalists and raised in the shadow of the *Houston Post*—also joined the staff of the school newspaper, the *St. Albans News*, which had recently transformed from a thin, sporadically published journal to a full-size newspaper that soon earned awards in scholastic journalism contests. Working on the newspaper was an early opportunity for Bill to get some practical experience for a possible future in the family business. Bill's classmate Philip Stansbury wrote that "the *News* provided, for all who desired, an opportunity to gain substantial writing experience plus the basics of journalism—the style and aesthetics of headlines and layout, the give and take of editing, the skill to produce accurate and clear material against an unbending deadline." Bill served as a reporter and the "Lower School Notes" editor. His byline appeared in the October 11, 1945, edition of the paper, with an article on the largest class to enter St. Albans: eighty-six boys from seven states, the Dominican Republic, and public and private schools in the DC area. By the fall of 1946, Bill was a staff reporter. He became the features editor in 1947 and was the editorial editor during his senior year.[6]

St. Albans was also where Bill made one of the most important friends of his life: John Davis, a graduate of Union College and Princeton University who taught history, religion, and languages at the school from 1942 to 1986. One of Bill's classmates later described Davis as an instructor who taught an "Anglo-Catholicism rooted in history and principle rather than in music or ceremony, a pacifism rooted in Christian pessimism about human nature rather than in utopian idealism, and a conservatism rooted in skepticism directed at all governments, old and new." After his death in 2009, his *Washington Post* obituary credited Davis with expanding the school's traditional curriculum to include international affairs and global history, environmental studies, law, and even a wilderness program. In Davis, Hobby found a caring and attentive mentor. He was not alone. Davis fostered deep relationships with many of the boys at St. Albans. Stansbury noted, "For some of those whose imagination he stimulated, [Davis] was the strongest intellectual and cultural influence in their lives." One of Davis's students later described his teacher as "a friend and confidant who has influenced a number of students to join the Church. . . . He is a sensitive man who stimulates a student's imagination, turns natural instincts and prejudices inside out; yet an impatient one who pounces on a complaint of unfairness with a harangue that the world is neither equitable nor fair." Hobby would later describe Davis as "a kind and patient man, my oldest friend. I took Spanish, American history, European history, and sacred studies from him. I was one of his protégés, as were many others."[7]

For the students at St. Albans, there was no escaping the difficulties of the world outside the school. Among the articles in the school paper about school dances and football scores and the editorials calling for better table manners were obituaries for alumni killed in combat or executed by the Germans. Bill, whose mother was commanding the

Women's Army Corps (WAC), felt an especially close connection to the war. Although Oveta usually worked from the safety of her office in the recently constructed Pentagon, Bill was deeply worried after learning she had traveled to Europe in January 1944 to inspect WAC stations just as the war had reached an especially deadly stage. He later learned that she had been at a field camp very near an active battlefront in Italy. In the spring of 1945, he grew anxious when rumors reached him that she would soon be sent to war zones in the Pacific to visit WACs serving in that theater. Oveta's health issues, however, kept her safely in Washington.

Early in 1945, Bill was an eyewitness to two historically significant and memorable events. The first was a ceremony at the Pentagon on January 8, when Secretary of War Henry Stimson, with General George C. Marshall looking on, presented the Distinguished Service Medal to Bill's mother—the first woman to receive the prestigious award. The second was when Franklin D. Roosevelt was inaugurated for his unprecedented fourth term on Saturday, January 20, 1945, a bitterly cold and rainy day in Washington. Because of the president's failing health and the austerity of wartime, the unusually brief inaugural ceremony was conducted on the South Portico of the White House instead of at the Capitol. Will Hobby, as a guest of his close friend Jesse Jones, who was then serving as FDR's secretary of commerce, joined five thousand people who watched from the South Lawn of the White House as Chief Justice Harlan Stone administered the oath of office to FDR. Prior to the ceremony, Will rented a room in the Hotel Washington, located across the street, to the east of the White House, to make it possible for Oveta and Bill to view the event. The WAC colonel and her son watched the ceremony from a vantage point at the hotel's outdoor rooftop restaurant and bar. "My mother and I were up on the roof using binoculars to see what little we could of the ceremony," Bill later remembered.[8]

After the ceremony, Will had planned to join his family at the hotel for lunch. Instead, he went with Jones to the White House luncheon for cabinet members, congressional leaders, Supreme Court justices, and more than 1,700 other dignitaries and their guests in the State Dining Room. Overwhelmed by the crowd, Jones and Will soon fled to the Shoreham Hotel for a more relaxed lunch, then returned to Jones's office. It was there that a fateful phone call came to Jones from Grace Tully, the president's private secretary. Tully asked Jones to come to a meeting with FDR at noon the next day. A messenger from the White House arrived a few minutes later with a letter from Roosevelt to Jones, informing him that he was being removed as secretary of commerce to allow the outgoing vice president, Henry A. Wallace, to have the job. "When my father came back to the Hotel [Washington]," Bill later recalled, "he told us how extraordinarily cordial the President had been to Mr. Jones" at the inaugural reception, but that the subsequent dismissal letter he received from FDR had "infuriated and humiliated Jones." Three months later, FDR would be dead, the victim of a cerebral hemorrhage.[9]

In June 1945, a month after declaring that she intended to remain at her post until the end of the war, Oveta's thyroid problem flared badly once again. Army physicians told her that she needed to be hospitalized. At the same time, Will learned that he would need another major surgical operation. Faced with this bad news, Oveta decided to resign from the WAC and go home to Houston after performing difficult and stressful but successful service for the army for nearly five years. Oveta had resumed her work at the *Post* by the time the news came on August 15, 1945, that Japan had surrendered. Bill also returned to Houston soon after his mother left Washington that summer, but in the fall he returned to St. Albans to begin his second year as a student.

By the fall of 1945, Bill was comfortably ensconced in the academic and extracurricular activities of St. Albans and in the thick of an active social life. It was the beginning of an important period in his life, lasting nearly four years, when his emotional, spiritual, and intellectual development ascended to a new level of maturity. Bill's letters to his parents and friends, and to his teacher John Davis, during these years provide a partial picture of his social evolution during the St. Albans years. In a letter to Oveta and Will in the fall of 1945, Bill pleaded, *"Is it by any means possible to get me a tux by November 30? It is very urgent that I have it by that date for the Football Prom. I will send you my measurements as soon as possible."* The tux was soon dispatched. An undated photo shows a tuxedo-clad Bill enjoying a dance with a young lady during the prom. Letters that flew back and forth over the summer of 1946 reveal that Bill had asked a girl named Amy Sanders to go on a date, which she apparently declined. Amy wrote to Bill, "My grandmother wouldn't let me go as she said I was too young to single date. Thank you for the invitation tho and let's let bygones be bygones." Another friend, Dianne, noted in her own letter to Bill that Amy liked a different boy named Jim. "I think that's horrible," Dianne told Bill, "Cause you were the ideal boy for her." And another friend, Sam, asked Bill to keep an eye on his love interest, a young woman named Brenda who lived in Houston.[10]

Bill had also become more independent in his excursions away from school. At the end of a fall semester, Bill traveled with schoolmates to New York City, flying up for the weekend and staying at the Biltmore Hotel at Forty-Third and Madison Avenue. In addition to visits to Hayden Planetarium and Radio City Music Hall, he attended an exhibition of Salvador Dalí's artwork and reported in a letter to his parents, "This artist's[?] works are somewhat unusual, to say the least." He enclosed a copy of Dalí's mock newspaper, noting, "It will, no doubt, hold up to you a journalistic standard which the *Post* may one day reach." The letter home concludes, "I am quite proud of myself for writing such a long letter and all I ask is how did the Thanksgiving Game come out?" Bill also spent a couple of weeks in California with friends from El Paso during the summers of 1946 and 1947. In a letter to Davis during the second of those stays on the West Coast, Bill noted, "Here I am again in sunny California. It's a great place. Like any other place outside Texas, it makes one appreciate Texas all the more."[11]

His letters to John Davis give us a view of his social, intellectual, and spiritual development. From his first short notes addressed to "Mr. Davis" to detailed, multipage letters, on occasion entirely in Spanish, Bill's correspondence with his religion teacher covered everything from everyday activities and travels to the young man's deepest concerns and aspirations. One letter regarding Davis's upcoming trip to Texas gave Bill the opportunity to exercise his comedic writing skills. In a note to Davis (written on Los Angeles Ambassador Hotel letterhead) of August 7, 1946, Bill referred to his teacher's upcoming trip to Texas:

> May I give you a little friendly advice pertinent to your forthcoming trip to the Republic? If, as you are landing, a cow wanders across the field don't let that disturb you—the pilot has had years of experience dodging them. Also, don't be alarmed if a few Indian arrows glance off the plane. Whenever a plane lands a company of rangers surrounds the field to hold off the Injuns. They almost never get close enough to kill more than one or two people. Since the police force was organized a year ago the drunk cowboys usually stay in town. If, however, one reels up to you and starts waving his gun around just hit him in the stomach. It will probably sober him up and he will be too drunk to mind anyway. If a stray paisano starts to pull a knife just yodel for the nearest Ranger. . . . If there's none . . . you'd better say a quick rosary.[12]

During another summer at home, Bill wrote to Davis about his work at the *Post*. "Back in God's country . . . Whoopee! I must have a penchant of some sort for features work, because that's what I'm working on at the *Post*, too. It's very interesting work. In addition to learning journalism pretty thoroughly, one learns a good deal about other things, too. I have acquired at least basic knowledge on such varied subjects as sulphur mining, alfalfa raising, hillbilly music, and girl scouting." Bill added that before he went to work at the *Post* every morning, he managed to fit in an hour or so of riding. "Our horse had not been ridden since I was last at home at Christmas, so, as you can imagine, he has been giving me a pretty rough time, but I think I will soon have him so that my sister and mother can ride him too." He also had time in the summer, despite his job, to go swimming at the country club daily. Every Tuesday night he enjoyed the Houston Symphony Orchestra's open-air concerts in Hermann Park, which was within walking distance of his parents' house.[13]

In one of his letters to Davis, Bill assured his mentor that he was continuing to tend to his spiritual needs while working at his summer job in Houston. He informed Davis that he and a friend were teaching a class for altar servers at church one evening a week. Another letter delivered a striking bit of news: "Next summer . . . I will make my application to be admitted a postulant. That is between you, me, my parents and the gatepost." Given not only his close rapport with Davis but also the teacher's own devotion to religious studies, it makes sense that Bill would share his intention to take the first steps to becoming a priest. Davis was pleased, but he cautioned Bill that he was facing quite an important decision, and he expressed hope that Bill would think it over carefully. He added that "the tide is turning on the type of people going into the priesthood. Formerly people were so preoccupied with business and making money . . . that the best types did not always go into it. Now with the war over, it seems that practically everyone embarking on the ministry is a fine type person."[14]

Bill's interest in the priesthood was in keeping with his dedication to religious service while at school, where he was an active member of the St. Albans student vestry. "Its members are boys belonging to the Church and chosen from the School on the basis of Christian character," the school's yearbook, the *Albanian*, noted. "Their broad function is to direct, under the guidance of the Headmaster and the Chaplain, the religious and charitable activities of the School," including the care of the Little Sanctuary. They also participated directly in the services through a weekly Bible reading and directed the two annual charity drives, allocating funds to what they considered the worthiest charitable institutions.

The student vestry also selected Bill to be one of the seven servers at the National Cathedral, one of the highest honors of the school. "Duties include preparing the Chapel before each service, directing the weekly system of offerings, and reading the Scripture Lessons each Tuesday morning during the service," the school paper reported. "Great care is exercised by the Student Vestry in selecting the boys for this duty." The servers were deeply entrenched in the ceremonial rituals of the church services. At seven thirty every morning, a server would assist the priest at the thirty-five-minute Holy Communion service: "Robed in purple gown and white cotta, the Server lights the two Altar candles before the service, and during the service acts with a firm voice as the leader of the congregation in saying the Creed, the General Confession, and the responses. His most important duties, however, are to hand the priest the Elements, to move the Prayer Book from the Epistle side of the Altar to the Gospel side, and to administer the Lavabo, or purifying of hands. After the service, the Server extinguishes the Lights, clears the Altar, and prepares the Chalice and Plate for the next service."[15]

The school paper lauded the efforts made by the servers, noting that most of their classmates rarely saw their efforts. "He is at the Cathedral before they are awake; he is serving while they are eating breakfast; he is eating his breakfast while they are enjoying a period of leisure," the paper reminded its readers. "Truly they are servants without reward except the satisfaction they must derive from their share in making St. Albans a Church School." For Bill, the satisfaction he felt at being a server was coupled with his respect for the sanctity of the church and its services. In an open letter in the April 15, 1949, *St. Albans News*, he shared his desire for the cathedral to have a truly "devotional spirit." Bill decried the constant presence of tourists, which meant that there were few opportunities for quiet prayer without interruption. "I write as one who, in five years attendance at St. Albans, has come to have a real love for the Cathedral," he said. "My plea is for a more prayerful atmosphere."[16]

In addition to his religious and journalistic endeavors, St. Albans gave Bill an outlet for his interest in politics. The Government Club was another student activity that flourished at the school. Bill would later recall that the club meetings were held on Friday nights and featured political discussions by about twenty upperclassmen: "We divided ourselves into liberals and conservatives. I don't remember which I was. The club was presided over by Bertram Hulen of the *New York Times* Washington bureau." According to one of Bill's classmates, the Government Club encouraged the free expression of an "extraordinary range of opinions, from bellicose to pacifist, from Dixiecrat to super-liberal. No one felt any social pressure to think in any conventionally consistent way. The atmosphere of discussion about political or social questions was genuinely open and tolerant." Bill's fellow student added that "Bill Hobby, '49, was then a conservative Southern Democrat and a pacifist, a combination which did not appeal to everybody but which was not found offensive or peculiar." Bill even invited longtime family friend Jesse Jones to speak to the group. In October 1947, Jones, who was no longer in government but was still the active publisher of the *Houston Chronicle*, wrote to journalist Henry J. Taylor, "William P. Hobby, Jr. . . . is attending St. Albans School for Boys in Washington. He is a fine young man about seventeen. He saw the Redskins beat the Giants today with Mrs. Jones and me, and he and I have just been having a visit [at the Hotel Statler in Washington]. He told me that Friday nights they had discussions on public questions, and asked me if I would not come out and discuss the Marshall Plan. I felt that I should not, but told him that I would write you, and suggest that it might be convenient for you to spend a Friday evening with them some time. He will probably write you, and I hope you can."[17]

The final edition of the *St. Albans News* of his senior year documented Bill's successful effort to be a fully rounded student. He was featured in a column titled "Men of Saint Albans" that profiled upperclassmen. He had served as class president, *News* staff member and editor, and Government Club member, and he had lettered in varsity football and soccer. "If there is anyone who has added prestige to a position, it is Bill Hobby," the paper reported. "In his many varied capacities he has not only fulfilled his duties but also has broken away from the beaten path, to take strides in new ground." The paper cited his many contributions, including his high-minded and courageous leadership on the editorial page, which had increased interest and readership; his athletic efforts as center on the varsity football team and center forward on the varsity soccer team; and his leadership in Government Club, including his "calm forcefulness" as a speaker on the conservative side: "From the issues of our foreign policy to our Electoral College, Bill has played a large part in shaping the final outcome." The profile even referenced his forceful stance against socialism, describing its followers as "one who 'loses his saddle.'" The profile concluded, "Probably the work that has been of most importance to Bill has been that which he has done for the Church. . . . He is seriously thinking of studying for the Ministry."[18]

Bill, now seventeen years old, graduated from St. Albans on June 4, 1949, with plans to attend Rice Institute in Houston for college that fall. He had excelled in academics in secondary school, with the fifth-highest GPA in his class in June 1948 and membership in the school's cum laude society. When Bill graduated, Jesse Jones sent him a note of congratulations: "You are a credit to your family, your friends, to St. Albans and to all young people." Jones, who remained bitter about his dismissal from FDR's cabinet and had turned against the Democratic Party, warned Bill that the country being led by Harry Truman and the Democratic Congress was drifting into socialism and that the free enterprise system was in danger. Jones stressed that capitalism had made the United States the "strongest in the world." He expressed hope that "your generation will be able to meet the issues, and am sure you will be in the vanguard of leadership."[19]

Following his graduation from St. Albans, Bill joined John Davis in August for an extensive trip to Mexico, with visits to Oaxaca, Cuernavaca, Mexico City, and Puebla. He wrote his parents, "Living here is ridiculously cheap. Here in Oaxaca it shouldn't be over $20 a week. What do you want in the way of silver, pottery, knick-knacks, perfume, etc? I am allowed $400 worth duty free. My Spanish is coming along pretty well, and in another two weeks I should be speaking it with a fair degree of fluency." He was also sending articles back to the *Post* that were published in the paper's travel section. He assured Will and Oveta that he would file "one or more pieces . . . for each of the next three days."[20]

A few days after his trip to Mexico, Bill enrolled at Rice. Established by a gift from wealthy businessman William Marsh Rice, the university had held its first classes in 1912. At the time Bill became a student, the institute, which changed its name to Rice University in 1960, was a racially segregated private university that had earned a reputation for its tough admission requirements and high academic standards. The institute was located only blocks away from Will and Oveta's newly purchased mansion, a huge, three-story, red-brick structure that had been built decades earlier by Texaco oil company founder Joseph Cullinan. The location of their new residence allowed Bill to live at home while he was taking classes. And although he missed out on the Rice football team's 17–15 upset of the University of Texas Longhorns in Austin that fall, he was able to attend the January 1, 1950, Cotton Bowl game when Rice defeated North Carolina.

Bill was soon disappointed by what he perceived was a lack of interest in the humanities, philosophy, theological issues, and even current political affairs among his fellow students. He wrote John Davis that he now realized the "religious training I got from St. Albans in general and you in particular . . . by a process resembling osmosis was a very wonderful thing." He complained that at Rice, however, "intellectual activity is funneled off into the physical sciences." It seemed to him that "variations in the Taylor Series and log differentials are the subjects for bull sessions rather than the Donatist heresy or the latest encyclical. Discussions are usually just that—rarely arguments." He was dismayed that at Rice even "fire-eating Baptists," who were one of his "carefully nursed favorite prejudices . . . don't eat nearly as much fire as I thought they did. The Baptists [at Rice] don't seem to do much but put-up signs saying 'Go to Church.'"[21]

Bill's spirits soon lifted, however, when he was selected associate editor of Rice's student newspaper, the *Thresher*. The managing editor soon recognized that the freshman was skilled at writing headlines and laying out the newspaper because of Bill's experience with the St. Albans student paper and his occasional summer work at the *Houston Post*. Those were tasks the editor had little interest in doing, so Bill assumed the basic duties of putting out the paper, which he found both challenging and enjoyable. Although he would eventually also serve on the school's honor council, which served as an orientation team for new students on the honor system and adjudicated the trials of students found cheating on exams, the student paper became Bill's main interest. Years later, he recalled that he "really majored in the *Thresher* more than anything else, and took little part in other campus activities." He also soon began to contribute editorials and stories. His first story with his byline was a report about one of Rice president William V. Houston's speeches to the freshmen. The story was featured prominently on the *Thresher*'s front page.[22]

One of Bill's first editorials was a criticism of the effort by the American Federation of Labor (AFL) to picket the campus construction site of Rice's new football stadium. The AFL was protesting the construction company, Brown & Root, because of the firm's refusal to pay union wages and its rejection of establishing union-approved working conditions. Reflecting his parent's anti-union views, Bill took pointed aim at the demands of the union, noting, "An AFL spokesman has said that, so far as he knows, there are no union men working on the stadium. How, then, can the union fairly ask to be recognized as the bargaining agent for the men on the job?" Bill's hostility to the AFL was deeply influenced by his father. Will had a long record of enmity toward labor unions. When he served as governor, he had imposed martial law to break a strike at the Port of Galveston in 1920. Will and Oveta's negative public reaction to a wave of major labor union strikes that spread across the nation in 1946 and 1947 was further confirmation of their break from the national Democratic Party and its pro-union orientation. Centering in the steel, rail, electrical, mining, and auto industries, the strikes had involved more than five million workers. No doubt reflecting the discussions he heard at home, fifteen-year-old Bill Hobby had contributed a column to the *Houston Post* denouncing the union strikes in 1947. "The labor leaders of the country are deliberately, and with malice aforethought doing as much damage to the nation and its economy as they possibly can," young Bill wrote. "We, the people of Houston, also have experienced the effects of the almost unbelievable selfishness and irresponsibility of the union heads in the building strike." Proud of his son's column, Will sent a transcript to Jesse Jones, whose construction projects had been hit hard by the strikes. Bill's anti-union views would eventually become more moderate later in his life.[23]

By February 1950, Bill had a regular column in the *Thresher*, which he titled "Casting Pearls." It generally focused on political issues related to legislative rules and procedures. In one column, Hobby reflected on a tax bill under consideration by the Texas Legislature. He described the issue as "the political question closest to the hearts—and pocketbooks—of most Texans" and pointed out that the issue was a simple one, in language that foreshadowed his future approach as lieutenant governor: "Do we pay more taxes or do we go in the hole? . . . It has been impiously suggested that the line of division is drawn between those whose seats in the legislature are secure and those who are not." Another essay delved into the issues of euthanasia and genocide, topics that were also the subject of his English 100 term paper. Bill wrote passionately against the idea of "mercy killings" in the column and concluded, "Some pseudo-religious justifications of this particular brand of killing on the grounds that it relieves 'needless suffering' are perfect examples of the corruption that Christian doctrine and tradition have undergone at the hands of some 'liberal' sects. It has always been the Christian position that sin, not pain, is the only thing to be avoided at all costs."[24]

Late that same month, Will and Oveta surprised Bill with the news they were purchasing Houston's only television station, which was struggling financially. Bill had unwittingly played a role in convincing his father that buying a television station might be a smart business move. When the opportunity initially came up, the owner, Albert Lee, a local oilman, had offered only half ownership. Will was skeptical about the wisdom of investing in the ownership of a television station, especially one that was losing money, and at a time when commercial television was in its infancy. Will also was not keen on a partnership. Bill's passive role in making the deal occurred when he was ill with hepatitis and confined to bed for several days in his room at home. Will borrowed one of the televisions his staff had purchased to test the broadcast quality of KLEE-TV, the station the Hobbys were thinking about buying. After the set was installed in Bill's room, Will decided to spend time with his son watching some of the programs, which ranged from *The Milton Berle Show* to local wrestling matches. According to one of his staff members, Will was enthralled by the programs and was soon spending more time watching the broadcasts than was his son. So enamored with what he was seeing in these early pioneering telecasts, Will called Jack Harris, the manager of KPRC-Radio who was negotiating the purchase, and asked him to see if Lee would sell 100 percent of the station, instead of half. Lee agreed.

When Bill learned that his family now owned KLEE-TV, he sent a letter to John Davis. "The Hobbys just bought themselves a television station," Bill wrote. "There's only one [in Houston], and applications for licenses are frozen, so it's a pretty good bet. The only trouble is that the thing has been in operation for two years and has yet to make one thin dime. In fact, it's lost quite a few dimes. Another trouble is the price. [Which means] two meals a day for the next year or so. The folks figured it was one of those things that had to be done, because if we didn't somebody else (guess who?) would." The "who" was obviously Jesse Jones. Although Jones was a close friend of Will, his *Houston Chronicle* was locked in a fierce competition with the *Houston Post*. The Federal Communications Commission approved the Hobbys' purchase of KLEE-TV's broadcast license on June 1, 1950. The Hobbys immediately changed the call letters to KPRC-TV. On Monday, July 3, 1950, the station made its first broadcast on Channel 2 under its new ownership. When the station went on the air that day, Will appeared on camera to announce the station's new call letters and that it was now part of the *Houston Post* corporate family, which included KPRC-Radio. Will declared that it was now "possible for the *Post* to provide our readers with a newspaper to read, our listeners with a radio to hear, and our lookers-on with a telecast to see."[25]

Bill, however, was not in Houston to witness that first broadcast. As he wrote to John Davis, "Plans for summer are changed. I'm going to England with the Winant Volunteers—group of college students that have been going over to England every summer since the end of the war and working in various sections of London—the bombed out parts, slums, etc." The Winant Volunteers were the brainchild of Father Phillip Clayton, known affectionately as "Tubby." From 1922 to 1962, Clayton served as the vicar of All Hallows Church, which was located in London's East End. Because German bombing during World War II had badly damaged the church, Clayton traveled to the United States in the fall of 1947 to raise money to rebuild the structure. At a luncheon, Clayton connected with an old friend: John Gilbert Winant, the former US ambassador to Great Britain during World War II. The two discussed the idea of bringing young men and women from the United States to England to help build understanding and cooperation between the two countries. Although Winant asked Clayton to visit him to further discuss the idea, two days later Winant was dead by suicide. Clayton continued with his efforts to create the volunteer program, which would be named the Winant Volunteers as "a living monument to the late statesman."[26]

While the first year of the program was a success, enrollment in the second year dropped significantly, with only eight volunteers enlisted for the 1949 class. It was the energy and effort of Clayton that kept the Winant Volunteers program alive. "Without him the program would not have started, and without his tireless energy, optimism and goodwill it would never have continued," noted Nicholas Robertshaw. The charming and persuasive Clayton undertook an extensive recruiting trip in America in the fall of 1949 to promote the program and enlist young men and women to the cause. One stop on the trip was in Texas, a state for which the rotund clergyman had a great affinity. Clayton was known to wear cowboy boots under his robes, not only during visits to Texas but also while in London. As the organization's history noted, "Tubby would describe himself as an honorary citizen of Texas, and there seems no doubt that the individualistic spirit of the traditional Texan struck a chord in him." Clayton's recruiting efforts paid off, with thirty-four Americans joining the 1950 class of volunteers, including five from Texas—one of those being Bill Hobby.[27]

Bill flew to London from New York City on June 10, 1950. He and many of the other volunteers lived at Wakefield House, next door to Talbot House in Trinity Square, just steps away from the Tower of London. After receiving their ration cards, the volunteers were assigned various duties; they served as counselors in youth church groups and camps, assisted with parish work in the East End, and helped rehabilitate church buildings. Writing to Oveta and Will, Bill shared, "I've been working in a big Jewish Settlement House here, taking the place of one of the other fellows. . . . It has been great fun, really. The work has been mostly calling on homes to see why little Isaac hasn't been at his club lately and taking charge of some of the various boys clubs, teaching baseball, football, dispersing fantastic notions about Texas, etc. The more I see of this bunch of fellows . . . over here, the more I like them. Almost without exception, they are all outstanding in one way or another." That sentiment was repeated to John Davis: "There is absolutely a minimum of 'uninteresting people' among [the Winant Volunteers]. Almost all of them are outstanding in one field or another. Some are better than average athletes, a few are very good musicians, etc. . . . and for that reason make a pretty lively crowd to be around."[28]

Bill's opinion of the driving force behind the program was less effusive. He described Clayton to Davis as a "great man and a great priest, but he's getting a bit old and querulous and generally hard to live with." Bill noted that he was serving Clayton as his "part-time chauffeur and aide-de-camp. Actually it's a lot of fun, and I have enough free time to make it enjoyable." He later speculated that Davis would like Tubby Clayton "very much, I think, although I don't particularly. He's an odd mixture, to say the least. There must be—or have been—something pretty dynamic about the man, but I haven't as yet been able to appreciate it. He has wonderful people around him who see his faults and love him still. When he was in his prime, he must have been great. Toc H [Talbot House], of course, is quite an impressive monument to his efforts."[29]

Bill's volunteer work also included publicity efforts, including public speaking on behalf of the Winant program. As he shared with Will and Oveta in July, "I'm getting in some very good public speaking experiences. In one 24-hour period last week, I addressed three of the most varied types of groups you could possibly imagine. I and two other of the fellows harangued a Tower Hill crowd on the subject of the Winant Volunteers, their aims and objectives." Like the famed Speakers' Corner in Hyde Park, Tower Hill was the site of a public forum that fostered free speech and debate, accompanied by robust heckling. Bill noted, "The Tower Hill crowds have a reputation for being a rough bunch to speak to, with more than their fair share of professional hecklers. It was stormy, but fun. It was the first time I had ever had the experience of handling a crowd of that size or nature, answering what questions I could, parrying those I couldn't, and it was a lot of fun." Oveta responded, "I'm glad you are having 'The Tower Hill' experience. *It will just fit for Texas politics.* KPRC-TV televised the city room election night. Each reporter now is a television star. We all send love. We miss you much and much."[30]

The Winant Volunteers also had time for sightseeing and excursions in London and beyond. For example, Bill reported to Davis that he and a friend had gone to a concert at the Royal Albert Hall, "the most beautiful building from the inside and the ugliest from the outside that I have ever seen." At the end of June, Bill joined a group of about nine of his fellow volunteers on a trip to Oxford as guests of the Rhodes Trust. The three-day visit included the university, Stratford-upon-Avon, Warwick Castle, and stays in the private homes of university professors, including the forty-six-year-old Humphrey Waldock, a law scholar at All Souls College, Oxford. Waldock would later be knighted after earning international recognition as a distinguished jurist, serving as the British judge in the European Court of Human Rights and the president of the International Court of

Justice. Bill described Waldock to Davis as a "fascinating" person with whom he enjoyed a conversation and a glass of sherry in front of the professor's fireplace. "As you can easily imagine, we learned far more that way and imbibed the spirit of Oxford far more than would have been possible in the usual guided tour type of thing," he concluded. Bill and his companions were shown a few of the colleges at Oxford by "a wonderful old chap who was so British he made the 'Britishers' laugh. . . . He knew the place inside out, including all the fascinating little stories and incidents which give each place its own flavor." While at Oxford, Bill also saw his first play by George Bernard Shaw, *Man and Superman*. Bill judged it "quite hilarious, rather pointed in spots, and thoroughly enjoyable." After a "beautifully done" church service at Christ Church Cathedral, the group traveled to Stratford, which Bill found disappointing; Shakespeare's birthplace was "just another building that you had to pay one and six to get into. Warwick castle, though, was beautiful."[31]

Bill took advantage of his time in London to do some shopping. He wrote to Will and Oveta, "May I have my Christmas present early? As you know, Peal and Co. in London is the most famous bootmaker in the world. I need a pair of black boots for show wear, and would like, if possible, to get them made here. The price is . . . only about $10 more than what Lucchese would charge." Will sent Bill a telegram in reply on July 3: "Get boots there. W. P. Hobby." Oveta seconded the purchase in her July 7 letter to Bill: "I take it that you are enjoying the work and learning a lot—to coin a phrase. I am delighted that you discovered Peals. They are indeed the best boot makers in the world." She continued, "The house, I must say, is not quite the same. I miss you more than I can tell. That quiet opening of the door and quiet young man poking his head in and saying, 'Good night, mother.' There are times when I am convinced I am rather fond of you."[32]

For Bill, his time in Europe was also an opportunity to sharpen his skills as a journalist. As a staff correspondent for the *Post*, he penned a series of articles with observations on life in postwar London. He devoted one article to the differences in English and American dialects, quoting (and then demonstrating) Churchill's aphorism that England and the United States are two countries divided by a common language. Another story reflected on the general character of the Brits: while Bill praised their tolerance of the eccentricities of others, he found that they lacked American warmth and courtesy. In an effort to better understand the socialism of the majority of the English electorate, he published an interview with one such voter, a white-collar worker named Bill Cherry. Hobby also documented postwar rationing and privations, noting that tobacco, alcohol, first-run movies, and quality clothes were out of economic reach for the average Londoner. He also detected a subtle jealousy of Americans in the average Brit, "partly due to the persistent belief that all Americans are rich and partly because he knows that the American has taken over the position in the world that was once his—that of a citizen in the world's largest empire."[33]

After his first few articles ran in the *Post*, Oveta sent Bill her feedback, noting that she was "enjoying your pieces very much as well as your letters. I asked Mr. [Arthur] Laro if he had any comments or suggestions to make to you on your Sunday features and he said to tell you he liked them very much and to keep them in the same easy, free style you are doing.... You are building quite a following in Houston and its immediate environs. In fact, there may be a clamor for you to continue your Sunday epistles ad infinitum." She also updated Bill on the impending war in Korea: "America has a fair case of war jitters and I for one am afraid that this is chapter one. And for your information—the draft law was extended." Bill kept up with the United States' involvement in Korea but wrote to his family on the British sentiment regarding the impending war: "The news from Korea is being taken exceedingly calmly here, i.e., they don't give a damn. The feeling definitely is that this is our [America's] war, and there is certainly no great desire to aid, despite anything [British prime minister Clement] Attlee ... says. The interesting angle of the Korea show ... is that we seem to have set a constitutional precedent by declaring war without the consent of Congress." Bill went on to speculate, "Maybe, however, a show of force will be sufficient to make Russia back down, for the time being, at least. It seems though, that even if they do back down, the Pacific will be to World War III what the Balkans were to World War I and Czechoslovakia was to World War II. A series of crises leading to war certainly seems like a good bet at this point."[34]

Bill's most solemn piece ran in the *Post* on July 9, 1950, titled "British Calloused by German Blitz." While in London, he attended a dinner hosted by Coleman Jennings, a prominent leader of charitable work in Washington, DC, and member of the board of the National Cathedral. The dinner speaker, the mayor of Stepney, gave a "very graphic account" of the German Blitz, the Battle of Britain, and the German V-1 and V-2 rocket attacks, which inspired Bill's article. Bill observed that due to their characteristic reserve, most Englishmen did not discuss the scars left by the war. His article provided a detailed look at the years of suffering and terror. He described the waves of German attacks that left London in ruins: first the high-explosive bombs, followed by firebombing that decimated the financial district, and then the V-1s and V-2s that left the English with "a callousness born of continuous danger of sudden death." He reminded the *Post*'s readers, "For four years, Englishmen day and night saw their nation crumble under aerial attacks, lived in fear of an invasion which could easily have overrun the British Isles, and could never forget their existence as a nation hung by a slender thread."[35]

In August, Hobby left the "austerity, grimness, and pessimism" of England and traveled to Ireland to attend the Dublin Horse Show. First held in 1864, the show was one of the largest and most famous equestrian events in the world. Hosted by the Royal Dublin Society, it featured military and civilian jumping competitions, undoubtedly a thrill for Bill to witness, as was the spectacle surrounding the show, which he described as "a national fair, social event, and tourist attraction." He also enjoyed Ireland's "good-time" spirit and relative lack of wartime privations. In an article published by the *Post* on August 20, Hobby delved into the economics behind the pageantry. Like many other European countries, the main hope of the Irish was to attract American tourists to close the "dollar gap" to pay for US imports. "Ireland's problem is typical," Hobby wrote.

"She must buy fertilizer, chemicals, and machinery to keep her economy going.... Irish horsemen believe, rather optimistically, that the Irish horse can pay the bill." (Later in life, Hobby would pump US dollars into the Irish economy when he and his wife, Diana, became devotees of the Irish hunt in the 1970s and 1980s.) Hobby also pointed out the nationalism of the Irish government, concluding, "Ireland is as proud of her independence as Texas is of hers, and with about as much reason."[36]

On the next leg of his European trip, Hobby traveled to Oberammergau, a small town in Bavaria, Germany. His time on the Continent was certainly more sobering than the festive atmosphere he had encountered in Ireland. After taking a channel steamer from Dover to the Belgian coast, Hobby boarded a "midget-sized train" that traveled across Belgium and Germany. In his next *Post* dispatch, Hobby vividly described the country's widespread "ruin, destruction, and defeat.... As we passed through Carlsruhe [Karlsruhe], a small town entirely in ruins, I heard a Frenchman say, 'This is the most beautiful town in Germany.'" When Hobby asked why, the man replied, "Because it is the city the Allies bombed the most." The widespread destruction made a deep impression on Bill, especially in comparison to what he had witnessed in England, where German attacks were limited to London and a few other towns. He wrote, "Almost every city of any size or importance sustained murderous bombardment, and was a hell of a terror and destruction that we who have not been through it can only guess at."[37]

Hobby's ultimate destination was to attend the famed Oberammergau passion play. According to town legend, after losing almost half of their population to plague in 1633, the residents pledged to perform a passion play every decade so that God would spare them any further deaths. The first performance was held in 1634; from 1680, the performances took place in years ending in zero. The play faced some controversy in the years following World War II, with critics such as Leonard Bernstein and Arthur Miller leading a petition to cancel the play's 1950 performance because of its negative portrayal of Jews. As one critic later noted, "It is undeniably true that the play was virulently antisemitic through most of its history, and that it gained an extra dose of notoriety after Hitler endorsed the 1934 production." Nevertheless, the play went on in 1950, unchanged from the prewar version. Hobby's review did not address any of the controversy. Instead, he gave a detailed summary of the play's events, praising the reverence and devotion of the performers. He called the play "deeply moving because of its simplicity. The play is long—eight hours—and tiring, but it's worth it." It was fitting that he ended his trip with a play of such spiritual significance. As he had shared with Davis earlier in the summer, "This trip has meant a lot to me from a spiritual point of view in giving me a boost that I badly needed. The big thing which I've learned over here about personal religion is that, for me at least, the heart of the whole matter is a personal love for Christ, in some measure reciprocating his love for us. I now see more meaning in the passage in Corinthians about faith, hope, and charity."[38]

Hobby returned to Houston in August 1950 to begin his sophomore year at Rice and to serve as the *Thresher*'s managing editor. On October 27, the paper published his editorial about Ku Klux Klan protests at the University of Texas Law School against the enrollment of Heman Sweatt, the school's first Black student. That fall, a cross was burned in front of the law school, and the letters "KKK" were painted on the building. Hobby made the incident the subject of an editorial, noting that it had not received due attention in Houston. Stating the actions were the work of the KKK, Hobby deemed it "the last gasp of the bigoted, hate-blinded cowards who form the organization." Hobby also challenged Rice's policy of barring Black students from enrolling in the school. Referring to an earlier dispute over the admission of Black graduate students, Hobby wrote, "The question of admitting Negroes to Rice was fought out . . . several years ago. The result of that fight was a temporary victory for those who would maintain segregation. That the victory was temporary is a certain fact—made temporary by the trend of judicial and public opinion which has in the past few years so diminished racial hatred and prejudice." Hobby's argument implied that if Rice would not lead, it would have to follow: "It will not be many years, we feel sure, before the Rice Institute will admit qualified Negroes, whether under orders from the courts or voluntarily."[39]

Bill continued to serve as editor of the *Thresher* in the fall of 1951. He wrote a regular editorial, "The Editor's Corner," in which he addressed a range of issues, including the need to reform Rice's student council bylaws and honor system. His last "Editor's Corner" expressed support for academic freedom of the press on college campuses, which he deemed "part of a larger freedom of the individual to know. This 'freedom to know' is a nebulous thing. . . . But it is the most fundamental freedom of them all." By the time the *Thresher*'s February 22 issue went to press, Bill had been replaced by Allyce Tinsley Cole, and his name was no longer on the paper's staff list. "The *Thresher* editor, of course, was one of the biggest things that I did, and I fell into that," Cole later recalled. "I ran against Bill Hobby and lost to him, and then it was my good luck to have him fail to pass a math course. And so I got to edit the *Thresher* for the last part of his term." In the March 31 issue, Bill was back as a writer, with a byline on the front page, but he would not reappear on the paper's staff list until the beginning of his senior year in September 1952, when he served as the paper's political analyst while his mother was working on the Eisenhower presidential campaign in New York City.[40]

Bill's academic misstep in the spring of his junior year may have come from a general neglect of his coursework at Rice. He enjoyed his classes with Bill Masterson, a history professor who joined the faculty in 1951 and would later serve briefly as the university's president. Years later, Bill noted that Masterson was his favorite teacher at Rice and that his favorite course was History 110. However, as he wrote to John Davis in January 1952, "School is very dull, and has ceased to have any real interest, with the exception of one or two courses, and, of course, the paper. It may be a passing feeling, but right now at least, I am tired of school. Not of the people or the place, but . . . of what I am doing. I have the feeling that I am marking time." But that lack of engagement at Rice was not because of the absence of intellectual activity on Bill's part. In his letter to Davis, Bill included a critique of William F. Buckley Jr.'s newest book: "Have just finished reading and laughing at the latest academic cause celebre, viz., Buckley's *God and Man at Yale*. It is a little difficult in spots to disentangle his prejudices, with which I am in thorough and complete agreement, and his thesis, with which I could not agree less. He is simply not an educated man, but neither are a lot of other people." He also shared with Davis his take on John Dos Passos's *U.S.A.*, the controversial book that had played a role in the firing of University of Texas president Homer Rainey in 1944 by ultraconservative members of the university's board of regents. "I don't see why they fired Rainey from the University for not taking it off the shelves," Bill wrote. "In fact, I can't imagine anybody taking it off any shelf except under compulsion. Have also been reading Emerson, for whom I have acquired a good healthy contempt."[41]

The year 1952 brought a presidential election. For almost the entire year, Bill's mother was deeply involved in Dwight Eisenhower's bid for the presidency. She had bonded with the general in London during World War II when she was serving as WAC commander. In the spring and summer, she played a key role in Ike's successful effort to secure the Republican presidential nomination. After spending a busy and intense summer campaigning for Eisenhower, Oveta joined Will on a trip to Paris, soon followed by a family vacation with Bill and Jessica at the Greenbrier resort near White Sulphur Springs in West Virginia. Bill, who had attended summer courses at Columbia University in New York City, wrote John Davis, "By [August] the 25th, I will be lolling in Lucullan luxury in West Virginia, where the folks have taken a cottage and are vacationing as much as possible with the telephone nearby. They plan to stay there a month, but I have no idea that they really will stay away from home that long in an election year."[42]

In September, Bill returned to Rice for his senior year. Three days after Ike's election on November 4, he wrote a letter to Davis: "I'm going to school (making good grades for a change) and working nights down at the paper from 4–12, a most agreeable schedule." He went on to share his reaction to Eisenhower's victory. "The election was quite something, a much more clear-cut victory than I had expected. Down in the city room here we were all quite grateful to [Democratic nominee Adlai] Stevenson for thoughtfully conceding in time for the home edition." Bill hinted at being less than thrilled by Ike's victory, despite his mother's total commitment to the general's cause, including serving as the leader of the Democrats for Eisenhower organization. Referring to Stevenson, Bill complained, "Why in hell didn't the Democrats find him four years earlier? I feel that his stature diminished slightly during the campaign, but he's still the best damn candidate we've seen in a year or so. Mother is slowly recuperating from her exertions of the last few months. She really did a helluva job up there as one of the happy few that fought from the dark pre-convention days. By the time the election came, though, most of us down here were so glad to have it over with that it didn't make much difference who won."[43]

Three weeks after the election, President-Elect Eisenhower announced the appointment of Oveta Culp Hobby as head of the Federal Security Agency (FSA), the massive agency that included the Social Security Administration. He also declared that she would attend his cabinet meetings. On January 18, 1953, Bill accompanied Jessica and

Will on a flight to Washington to attend Eisenhower's January 20 inauguration and related celebrations, as well as the Senate hearing to approve Oveta's appointment to lead the FSA. They met Oveta at her large suite at the Mayflower Hotel that would serve as her home for the next two months. After reuniting at the Mayflower, the Hobbys were driven to the nearby Statler Hotel, where they joined eight thousand other guests at a preinaugural party. The chaotic gathering included Vice President-elect Richard Nixon, Governors Earl Warren and Thomas Dewey, and other prominent Republican officeholders, as well as Hollywood and Broadway personalities Abbott and Costello, Ethel Merman, Hedda Hopper, and Constance Bennett. The *Chicago Tribune* noted that the guests "walked on one another's feet, knocked hats askew, kicked loose the carpeting, and gaped to see who was wearing what." Typical of Oveta's experiences dating back to her WAC days, as one of the only women in a prominent leadership position in the federal government, the *Tribune* photographer had her pose for a photograph with the wives of the cabinet members designate instead of with their husbands.

The next morning, the Hobby family made their way to a room in the Capitol, where the Senate Finance Committee, chaired by Senator Eugene Millikin, held a hearing to confirm Oveta's nomination as head of the FSA. As Will, Bill, and Jessica took seats in the visitors' area in the hearing room, Texas senators Price Daniel and Lyndon B. Johnson escorted Oveta to a chair at the table from where she would answer the committee members' questions. Lady Bird Johnson later recalled that her husband took Oveta "under his wing" and introduced her to all the senators. Sitting in a chair next to Oveta, LBJ asked the committee to confirm her appointment. Assuring his Senate colleagues that she would administer the FSA not only with skill but also in an honest and honorable manner, he added, "Mrs. Hobby is the kind of woman you would want as a trustee of your estate." Recalling the moment years later, Oveta said that LBJ's remark not only "delighted and very much touched me, [it was] a remark that I have never forgotten." After LBJ's introduction, Oveta submitted her impressive résumé to the committee. After only six minutes of discussion, the committee voted to confirm Oveta's appointment.[44]

After the hearing, Will treated Oveta, Bill, and Jessica to a special brunch to celebrate their shared January 19 birthdays: Oveta's forty-eighth, Bill's twenty-first, and Jessica's sixteenth. The family gathering caught the attention of an Associated Press correspondent, who filed a report on the various happenings in Washington on the day before Eisenhower's inauguration. The reporter noted that the luncheon was one of the most "unusual celebrations of the day" because of the triple birthdays. Afterward, the Hobbys opted out of attending the special events scheduled for the rest of the day. Oveta wanted to spend that time reading informational material about the FSA. She told Inez Robb, a reporter she knew from her WAC days, that she was working hard to "come to grips with the new job."[45]

At 9:30 a.m. on Inauguration Day, Tuesday, January 20, the Hobbys joined the president-elect and the cabinet-level designees for a communion service at Washington's

National Presbyterian Church, which was followed by the inaugural ceremony at the East Portico of the Capitol. After the inauguration, the president and invitees were driven to a grandstand on Pennsylvania Avenue to watch the inaugural parade from their reserved seats. The parade lasted several hours longer than scheduled, finally ending at seven o'clock that evening. The Eisenhowers remained until the end, but the exhausted Hobbys left early to rest and dress for a special dinner that preceded the inaugural ball. Jessica had purchased a new strapless evening gown to wear to the ball, but Oveta thought it too daring, especially for a teenage girl, so she brought out a mink stole and instructed her daughter to drape it over her shoulders. With the family now properly attired in formal evening clothes, Oveta herded everyone downstairs to attend a dinner hosted by hotel tycoon Conrad Hilton that included Herbert Hoover, California senators William Knowland and Thomas Kuchel, Attorney General Herbert Brownell, *Los Angeles Times* publisher Norman Chandler, and several Hollywood producers. From there they proceeded to one of the two inaugural balls.

The next morning, the Hobbys went to the White House to attend the swearing-in ceremony for all of Ike's cabinet members except Charles Wilson, whose appointment remained stalled in the Senate. Although Oveta was not yet an official member of the cabinet, the president included her in the ceremony because of his request that she attend cabinet meetings. Ike had Abraham Lincoln's cabinet table moved into the East Room of the White House, and he and the cabinet members and Oveta stood by it as Chief Justice Fred Vinson administered the oaths of office. A *New York Journal-American* correspondent reported that the "small, delicately pretty" Oveta had "shadows under her brown eyes. She looked pale and tired from her efforts to enjoy the Inaugural ceremonies with her husband and their two children." Ike soon asked Congress for authorization to create a new cabinet-level department that would consolidate several independent federal agencies, including the FSA. When Congress passed the legislation creating the Department of Health, Education, and Welfare (HEW), Ike immediately appointed Oveta its head, officially making her the second woman to serve on a presidential cabinet.[46]

Not long after Oveta assumed her job as secretary of HEW, she joined a large number of federal officials who became targets of Republican senator Joseph McCarthy of Wisconsin and his extremist followers. Two years prior to Ike's election, McCarthy had launched his demagogic Red Scare campaign, making unsubstantiated charges that the federal government, particularly the State Department, was riddled with Soviet spies and Communist sympathizers who were part of a vast conspiracy to undermine the United States. Among those McCarthy accused of subversion was General George C. Marshall, one of Oveta's heroes. After Ike's inauguration in January 1953, McCarthy even implied that the new president was somehow aiding the Communist cause. Because HEW oversaw the Public Health Service, the Social Security Administration, the Office of Education, and the Food and Drug Administration, Oveta's new department was directly involved in many aspects of the nation's domestic affairs. That made HEW the most controversial cabinet department in Eisenhower's administration. To many conservatives, it was a symbol of dreaded big government and federal interference in the private lives of Americans, including especially hot issues such as racial integration, federal control of public education, and socialized medicine. As a result, the department soon attracted the attention of Senator McCarthy and Red Scare groups. Oveta abhorred the Republican senator from Wisconsin and his fanatical supporters, who had spread unfounded fear throughout the nation. She had made her feelings clear when she publicly denounced anti-Communist demagoguery while delivering the keynote speech at the annual meeting of the Alabama Press Association in Montgomery in February 1950. Oveta denounced the role local newspapers were playing in encouraging Red Scare extremists. She criticized the press for its "fuzzy-minded habit of labeling all Communists, socialists and liberals together as left wing." Such false assertions, she complained, played "directly into the hands of Russia, which makes capital of it for propaganda purposes."[47]

Bill shared his mother's disdain for Joe McCarthy and irresponsible anti-Communism. In a *Rice Thresher* column in February 1953, Bill reacted to Senator McCarthy's plans to investigate "subversion in education." He pointed out the difficulty in defining what that term would mean, noting, "Is it advocacy of social reform? Then Charles Dickens was a subversive. Is it protesting certain policies pursued by the government? Then all members of the opposition party are at all times subversives." Hobby noted that if McCarthy could find proof of Russian interference in higher education, that would be of service. "Unfortunately, however, the past record of the gentleman from Wisconsin does not lead us to hope for such a nice observation of distinctions which, to a mind like his, probably appear subtle at best, non-existent at worst." In another *Thresher* column, Bill pointed out that the US Constitution prohibits Congress from passing laws prosecuting anyone for breaking a law before it is passed. "Congressional investigating committees have repeatedly violated the spirit of this clause," he wrote. "They have, in more than one case, condemned a man for sympathizing with Russia at a time when sympathizing with Russia was quite 'legitimate' and in no way considered treasonable." He cited the case of a teacher in Virginia who was attacked because she had attended a Communist Party rally in the 1930s as part of a comparative politics course. "It's unbelievable, but it happened. Thus far have the witch-hunters gone."[48]

While Bill continued his summer work at the *Post* after graduating from Rice in May 1953, Houston was experiencing its own version of the Red Scare. That June, the local chapter of the American Legion's Americanism Committee, which was actively engaged in spreading anti-Communist hysteria, demanded that a theater in Houston abandon its plan to screen Charlie Chaplin's motion picture *Limelight*. The Legionnaires accused Chaplin, who was in self-exile in Europe because of his opposition to Joe McCarthy and the Red Scare, of being an agent of the Soviet Union. A spokesman for the Legion declared that "Americans aid and abet Stalin's Communism when they patronize and pay money to see Limelight." The *Houston Post* printed an editorial charging that the

Legion's accusation was a "false concept of Americanism. . . . It is not the office of the Legion to decide for all the people whether or not the film affects the public welfare." The straightforward denunciation of the Legion's censorship efforts reflected Oveta's publicly stated opinion that if a person objected to the contents of a movie, that person should simply not go see the movie. Bolstered by the *Post*'s editorial support, the theater ignored the protest and screened *Limelight*. The Legion immediately denounced the *Post*, charging that the newspaper must be "tolerant of Communist sympathizers" and "intolerant" of "pro-American views." A large number of letters assailing the Hobbys as "left-wingers" soon arrived in the *Post*'s mail room, most of them personal attacks against Oveta. The episode outraged her son. In a letter to John Davis, Bill reported that there had been "a little hassle . . . with the American Legion over the showing of the Charlie Chaplin film 'Limelight.' [A] theatre that had been planning to run the film cancelled it under threat of picketing by the Legion. The next day, we ran a strong editorial condemning the Legion for trying to get the film banned and the theatre for knuckling under to them, and the film was shown. Since then, we have received a very nasty letter from the Legion saying that we are Communists, enemies of home, chastity, the flag, and everything else."[49]

Three months after the *Limelight* incident, along with similar local Red Scare episodes carried out by McCarthyite organizations in Houston—including the Minute Women, the Committee for the Preservation of Methodism, and Doctors for Freedom—Oveta struck back. She directed the news editors at the *Houston Post* to conduct an investigation to expose the damage the groups were inflicting on the city's religious and educational institutions. The exposé, written by *Post* reporter Ralph S. O'Leary, was printed in October in a series of eleven articles prominently featured on the newspaper's front page. O'Leary's exposé, which attracted national attention, including that of *Time* magazine, charged that despite Houston being "remarkably free of Communistic influences," this coalition of organizations had initiated a "reign of terror" against liberals and nonconformists in the city. By this time, although Bill was a cadet in a naval officer school in Rhode Island, he continued to monitor the anti-Communist hysteria in Houston closely. He sent O'Leary a letter thanking him for writing the exposé. He told the reporter that it was "a masterful job of reporting, researching, and writing. I think you have done Houston—and the *Post*—a service that will be much noted and long remembered. It was a job that needed to be done in the worst way."[50]

Bill's hostility to McCarthyism and demagoguery of any type would remain a part of his worldview throughout his career in journalism and politics. As Bill's time at Rice Institute drew to a close, his future plans were in place. The priesthood was no longer mentioned. Instead, his next step would be military service, but there is no record as to why he made that decision. During his freshman year, he had tried to enlist in the Naval Reserve Officers Training Corps (ROTC) but had been turned down because of his color blindness. As he later recalled, "The commander of the Naval ROTC at that time was Leonard Sparks Mewhinney, brother of Hubert Mewhinney, my mentor on the *Houston*

Post. Captain Mewhinney told me to apply to Officer Candidate School (OCS), where they could get a waiver for color blindness. So, when I was a senior at Rice, I tried again." In his memoir, Bill describes how he ended up in Naval Intelligence: "The recruiting officer was a crusty old seadog who told me that even if I were accepted, I could only be a 'limited duty officer'—not eligible for command at sea, fit only for such stuff as communications and intelligence. Certainly no red-blooded American boy would want to do that! I allowed as how I was willing to try. That's how I got into Naval Intelligence."[51]

In an April 29, 1953, letter to Davis, Bill shared his motivation for choosing to serve in the navy: "I decided that three years as an ensign in the Navy would be considerably shorter time than two years as a corporal in the army. So I applied for Navy OCS. . . . I have spent most of the month filling out forms, taking physicals, appearing before examining boards, etc, but haven't heard the word yet." Given that his examination was handled by the Intelligence Screening Board, Bill expected he would be accepted for the intelligence section. "If I am accepted," he continued, "I will be up there [in Washington] about the middle of June and spend a few weeks there before going on to Newport."[52]

CHAPTER 3

THE NAVY AND DIANA

Bill graduated from Rice with a bachelor's degree in American history on June 5, 1953. Oveta took a brief break from the Department of Health, Education, and Welfare (HEW) and flew back to Houston to attend the commencement ceremony. "Your correspondent is now William Hobby, B.A., Rice, 1953," Bill wrote to John Davis that July. "I fear, however, that I noted very little significant change in my life at the moment I received the coveted bit of parchment." Bill was eagerly awaiting the results of the character and security checks that would determine if he had been accepted into the Naval Intelligence service. He jokingly asked Davis, "Incidentally, have any of the gentlemen been around school digging into the more infamous episodes of my past? I hope you didn't tell them the truth, or at least not the whole truth." While he waited to hear from the navy, Bill worked in the family business as a cameraman for KPRC-TV. He confessed to Davis, "It's a fascinating business that I know absolutely nothing about. The only consolation is that nobody else does either. . . . There's only one trouble with it. It isn't the newspaper business. I'm afraid that's where my interest lies, rather than at the TV station, even though it's the television that pays the grocery bills." Bill shared his excitement with Davis over the *Post*'s plans for a new building, with final construction decisions made over the Fourth of July weekend while Oveta was in Houston for the holiday. Bill's patience was rewarded with his acceptance to the navy's Officer Candidate School (OCS) in Newport, Rhode Island. He began his training in September. Although he joined the military as the Korean War was ending, the Cold War continued.[1]

Bill entered a naval reserve OCS training program based on the Holloway Plan, which expanded naval training beyond the US Naval Academy in Annapolis to additional locations on civilian college campuses. As *Time* noted in 1947, "The Navy had realized that it would desperately need officers for the postwar fleet—far more than the Naval Academy could turn out." Bill wrote to John Davis on November 7, 1953, the halfway point of his sixteen-week OCS training program, which he called "this mess." "I suspect that this is one of those experiences that, 30 years from now, I will tell my son that I wouldn't have traded for anything—but wouldn't go through again for anything," he noted. "In two short months, I have formed some quite definite opinions about the Regular Navy. They are opinions that Herman Wouk's Willie Keith shared and expressed quite ably." Willie Keith was the main character of Wouk's Pulitzer Prize–winning novel, *The Caine Mutiny*. The book detailed Keith's experiences serving on a navy minesweeper in the Pacific during World War II. According to *Time*'s review of the book, "Willie Keith is no tragic hero, but he is recognizably like thousands of civilians turned naval officers who took their lumps, helped win the war and shucked their rancors at the end of it, along with their uniforms." Hobby could likely relate to the character, a privileged Princeton graduate who enlists in the navy to avoid being drafted into the army. Over the course of the novel, Keith grows from a young, privileged idealist to a seasoned, and disillusioned, naval officer. Bill continued to Davis: "The work here isn't actually too hard—it's just that there is so much of it. The pressure is high, partially because they have a lot of material to get across in 16 weeks, and partially to separate the wheat from the chaff."[2]

At the conclusion of his OCS training, the navy ordered Hobby to report to the Naval Intelligence School in Washington, DC, on February 1, 1953. Bill relayed to Davis that he found the orders "highly satisfactory." In addition to looking forward to his holiday leave, the intensity of his training had lessened. "For the first time in three months, I actually read a book: *Tender Is the Night*. Good, but [not] nearly as good as *The Great Gatsby*," he wrote. "Am now working on *Connecticut Yankee in King Arthur's Court*. Also some of Ray Bradbury's Orwellish-prose: *Fahrenheit 451*." He also enjoyed some time with friends, spending several weekends in Boston with Bob Shorb, a former St. Albans classmate and a graduate of Harvard Law School who went on to become a partner at the Pogue & Neal law firm, a predecessor of the legal giant Jones Day. Shorb and Bill would remain friends well into the 1970s. Bill also admired Shorb's wife, Katherine, who was known as "Teeny." He told Davis, "What a lucky **** Shorb is to get a girl like that." Bill had certainly dated, but there was no indication of any marriage prospects of his own. Little did he know, that was about to change.[3]

Bill graduated from OCS on January 29, 1954, with Oveta there once again to hand him a diploma. Now an ensign, he entered Naval Intelligence School in Washington, DC, where he lived in the Cleveland Park neighborhood near St. Albans School and the National Cathedral. Hobby's supervisor at the intelligence school was Donald Morris, a New Yorker who had served in the navy since 1942. After World War II, Morris had attended the Naval Academy and earned two combat stars in Korea. He would later join the CIA and served in Soviet counterespionage until he left the agency in 1972. As Bill later described it, "[Morris's] job was giving grief to Soviet [KGB] agents in Paris, Berlin, Kinshasa, and Saigon. He babysat KGB defectors in Washington and thereabouts."

Bill later hired Morris as a foreign affairs columnist for the *Post*, where Morris would work for seventeen years. It was during the spring of 1954 that Bill received a fateful invitation from Morris. According to Bill's memoir, "We were closing up one night in 1954 when [Morris] invited me home for dinner. He told me that his sister-in-law was in town and his wife had told him to 'bring home a tall one.'" The sister-in-law was Diana Poteat Stallings, a teacher at Chatham Hall in Virginia who was visiting her sister, Donald's wife, Sylvia Stallings Morris. At six feet, Bill qualified as "a tall one"—taller, at least, than the five-foot-ten Diana.[4]

Diana Poteat Stallings was born in New York City on April 22, 1931. Her father was Laurence Tucker Stallings, a noted playwright, screenwriter, and book critic. Her mother was Helen Purefoy Poteat. Laurence and Helen met at Wake Forest University, where Helen's father, Dr. William Louis Poteat, was the revered president of the university. "Dr. Billy," as he was fondly called, came from a slaveholding Baptist family and was a professor of natural science and biology before being named president of Wake Forest. A devoted Baptist, he nevertheless strongly believed in the teachings of Charles Darwin on evolution: "His then-liberal ideas concerning education, race relations, and scientific thought frequently brought Dr. Poteat into conflict with conservative North Carolinians." Such views were controversial at a Baptist institution, but Poteat survived as president from 1905 to 1927, and in 1925 he helped defeat a legislative attempt to ban the teaching of evolution. He and his wife, Emma Purefoy, had three children, including Helen, who was born on April 6, 1896.[5]

Diana's father, Laurence Stallings, was born in 1894 in Macon, Georgia. He entered Wake Forest in 1912, where he edited the campus literary magazine. He and Helen dated while he attended Wake Forest, graduating in 1916. He joined the US Marines Reserve the next year and was assigned to active duty on July 25, 1917. Serving in the marines' Second Division in France, Laurence was "horribly wounded" during the Battle of Belleau Wood, when he attacked an enemy machine gun post. His kneecap was blown off, but he pressed on and threw a grenade that destroyed the enemy position. For his bravery, the US Army awarded him a Silver Star, while the French honored him with the Croix de Guerre. Surgeons eventually amputated Laurence's leg years later when he suffered a bad fall after slipping on ice. He and Helen married on March 8, 1919. Three years later, after Laurence received a master's degree in foreign service from Georgetown University, the couple moved to New York City, where Laurence worked as a reporter and entertainment critic for the *New York World*.

While at the *World*, Stallings collaborated with famed playwright and journalist Maxwell Anderson to write *What Price Glory?*, a play that followed two US marines fighting in France during World War I. According to one critic, *What Price Glory?* "shows us war happening and disillusioned men in mortal danger, all to create an intensity and authenticity that have seldom been matched." At roughly the same time, Stallings wrote his semi-autobiographical novel *Plumes*, centered on the postwar experiences of the titular character Richard Plume. *Plumes* received critical praise and commercial success upon publication in 1924, and it was adapted into the film *The Big Parade*. But it was somewhat overshadowed by the success of *What Price Glory?*, which premiered that same year in New York. The play was critically acclaimed and inspired two films. It ran for 433 performances on Broadway, generating enough royalty revenue to enable Laurence and his wife to retire to her family's 620-acre plantation, Forest Home, in Caswell County, North Carolina.[6]

Forest Home is located just outside of the town of Yanceyville, which sits just south of the Virginia border. The plantation house, also known as Poteat House, was the two-story, antebellum Greek Revival home of James Poteat, built from 1855 to 1856 (likely by the enslaved people whom he owned). It was the birthplace of painter and art instructor Ida Isabella Poteat, born in 1858. The family lost most of their wealth as a result of the Civil War, but they never lost title to the plantation, which was largely unoccupied after 1870. In 1928, Helen purchased the plantation from her father and his brother and sister. A 1942 article about Caswell County in the *State*, a weekly magazine of North Carolina, paints an idyllic picture of Forest Home: "It is located in a beautiful grove of ancient trees. Its pillared portico rises through two stories to the roof line: immense boxwoods surround it. The house is unchanged . . . except for the wings, which are a recent addition."[7]

Poteat House became home for Helen and Laurence's two daughters: Sylvia, born in 1926, and Diana, born in 1931. As Diana's daughter Laura recalled, "[My mother] was born in New York, but she really was a creature of North Carolina, and the name Poteat is a North Carolina name." Just a few years after Diana's birth, Laurence Stallings left his family. Helen would eventually go to Reno for a divorce in 1936. According to Laura, "My mother's memory was that her father left the family when she was around two. He was a very accomplished playwright and later screenwriter in Hollywood. He went on to marry one of his colleagues from Movietone Studios and had another family in California. And so, this farm in North Carolina, which we still have, was [Helen Stallings's] principal asset." Diana's son Paul later recalled, "My mother came from a very tragic circumstance, abandonment by her father, and she could have let that rule her life and define her outlook. All of us realize that single fact can often lead to a life rent with anger and therapy and mistrust. And she just refused. She just decided to have a positive view of the world. If happiness is a choice, she made it. She made a decision to go forward to raise a family free of the echoes of that painful history. She faced her demons by denying the vanity that demons need to flourish."[8]

Laurence Stallings went on to a successful career as a cultural critic and screenwriter (his screenplays include the John Ford movies *She Wore a Yellow Ribbon* and *3 Godfathers*). He died in 1968. In a poignant note to John Davis on March 11, 1968, Diana wrote in response to Davis's condolences on her father's death, "I know only what the news stories said, but I am grateful that his death appears to have been a quick one. I regret that he never knew his grandchildren, nor they him." In 1955, Diana's mother married Boston businessman Gordon P. Marshall. In 1971, she placed Forest Home in a revocable trust, with her daughters, Diana Poteat Hobby and Sylvia Stallings Lowe, and attorney James E. Hughes of New York serving as trustees. She died on April 6, 1980, at the age of eighty-four.[9]

Diana attended secondary school at Chatham Hall, an Episcopal girls' school in Chatham, Virginia, located about forty-five minutes from Forest Home. After graduating, she entered Radcliffe College as an English major, attending the school on scholarship. A gifted writer, her love of literature is apparent in her college assignments. Her senior thesis, "The Praise of Life," was a study of the dramatic works of William Butler Yeats. She also tried her hand at fiction, including one short story about an idealistic college student leading a choir in a women's prison (Diana had sung in the Radcliffe chorus). She graduated Phi Beta Kappa from Radcliffe in 1952 and then attended North Carolina State University for a year. As her daughter Laura recalled, Diana "studied farm management and agriculture, and even tried her hand at acting." According to Laura, "Her real pleasure that year was [when] she joined a theater company called the Little Theatre Group. One of her friends in that Little Theatre Group in Raleigh was Andy Griffith, the actor." Diana then returned to Chatham Hall as an English teacher. It was there that she met Ginny Holmegreen, who was in charge of the equestrian program. Originally from San Antonio, Ginny would eventually marry Charlie Zimmerman, another equestrian. The Zimmermans would have a lifelong connection with Diana over their shared love of riding, eventually serving as riding instructors for Diana's children in Houston.[10]

The elegant and intelligent Diana made an immediate impression on Bill. As her son Paul remembered, "She was just so gracious and so kind to everyone she met. She could relate on any level, whether it was a well-digger in North Carolina to the English PhD at the state dinner. She could stand and punch with anybody, but she never pulled mental rank on you. And she could—easily." For Bill Hobby and Diana Stallings, the dinner at the Morris home sparked an instant romance, as their daughter Laura recalled: "It was absolutely love at first sight. They just adored each other." Despite the geographical distance, the two began dating. Their first date was in Middleburg, Virginia, where they stayed at a gatehouse on the Huntland Farm and went foxhunting. Huntland Farm was owned by George Brown and Herman Brown, the Houston brothers behind the politically powerful construction company Brown & Root. The Brown brothers were close family friends of Will and Oveta, who along with the Brown brothers were members of the influential "8F crowd" in Houston, named for the suite in the Lamar Hotel that Herman used as his headquarters. "My parents' love of horses is pretty much what they bonded over, after they met," explained Laura. "All of their dates were horse-related. And that was the defining theme of their marriage, our family's life; it's still the language that we all use to communicate in some ways, even now."[11]

Bill and Diana's courtship was relatively brief. They became engaged after only six dates, shortly after Bill's June 25, 1954, graduation from Naval Intelligence School. Bill's relationship with Diana delighted Will and Oveta, who readily accepted her into the Hobby family. Oveta helped select Diana's engagement ring, a twenty-three-carat peridot mounted in platinum with four baguette diamonds as accents. As Bill and Diana's son Paul noted, the immediacy of their relationship was uncharacteristic of his father, whom he described as "the least impulsive person in the history of the world. He is calculated, thoughtful, and sometimes ponderous. But I think he recognized instantly that [Diana] filled all his voids. He was exactly right about that. She was his intellectual equal by any measure. And then in every other way, in the family arts and the social arts, his superior. And he would know that." On July 4, Diana and Bill's engagement was announced in Margaret Lacey's society column in the *Houston Post*, which noted that "a fall wedding is planned." Because of Oveta's celebrity as a member of President Eisenhower's cabinet, news about the engagement also ran in outlets ranging from the *New York Times* and *New York Daily News* to the *Southern Newspaper Publishers Association Bulletin*.[12]

On September 13, 1954, Bill and Diana were married in a simple and intimate ceremony at Forest Home, followed by a reception in the gardens. Diana's sister, Sylvia, and Bill's sister, Jessica, served as bridesmaids. Will Hobby was his son's best man. Oveta, who took a break from her duties as secretary of HEW, hovered over the affair. Diana was an elegant bride in an off-the-shoulder, tea-length dress. Bill wore his navy dress whites. Albert H. Lucas, Bill's former headmaster at St. Albans, presided over the wedding. The *Houston Post*'s society column noted that the couple would take a wedding trip to Cape Hatteras, North Carolina. Bill and Diana were registered at Sabino of France, an antiques and furniture store with locations in Houston and Paris, and their gifts reflected the Hobby family's prestige. They received a number of pieces of Sheffield sterling silver, from serving platters to a toast rack; English silver flatware; crystal items from Waterford, Lalique, and Sabino (including that 1950s necessity, the ashtray); and place settings for twelve and a tea set in Wedgewood china. Despite the lavish wedding gifts, Bill and Diana lived fairly modestly, residing in a garage apartment in McLean, Virginia. As Diana wrote to Helon Johnson, who had the unenviable task of securing insurance for the couple, "Bill's only exceptional garments are three pairs of riding boots and his evening clothes; I have one pair of boots and one evening dress (and not much else). I have no furs or jewelry except my peridot engagement ring." They would later add one pair of pear-shaped peridot and diamond earrings to the insurance inventory in 1955.[13]

Diana enrolled at Georgetown University that fall, taking courses in English literature, with a focus on Elizabethan- and Stuart-era literature and drama. While still serving in the navy, Bill had taken classes at Georgetown toward his master's degree in history over the summer. In the fall he continued his studies with coursework on Russian history and the rise of the Soviet state (undoubtedly influenced by Cold War geopolitics and his work in the navy). In January 1955, he was granted an extension for his fall semester term paper in Russian history; despite the extra time, Bill did not finish his coursework and drew an incomplete. Diana took a job with the Institute of International Education, where she organized tours and activities for foreign exchange students in the Washington area. She also had a job editing classified economic reports for the CIA. According to Bill, "Her office was in 'Temporary M,' a frame building left over from World War II—the same building where Mother had worked fifteen years earlier." He would later write, "What did Diana, an editor by trade, do for the spooks? She and some other ex–English teachers and newspaper types translated the stuff CIA economists wrote into English so ordinary folks could understand it." Years later, Diana described the work as "unbelievably dull." The Hobbys also continued their weekend hunts, including visits to Middleburg, the site of their first date.[14]

Bill was fully immersed in his work as an investigator for the Office of Naval Intelligence (ONI). Although it was one of the oldest intelligence agencies in the United States, having been formed in 1882, the ONI was also one of the least well known. As a matter of policy, the ONI rigorously avoided publicity. While the size and scope of the office had diminished in the years immediately following World War II, the onset of the Cold War, the fear of Communist espionage, and the outbreak of hostilities in Korea had resulted in a major increase in background investigations of applicants for jobs in the federal government. Hobby's branch of the ONI was described as "a research and evaluation unit, coordinating and disseminating intelligence relating to sabotage, espionage, and counter-subversion. . . . [It] keeps track of the danger spots; its work is primarily a desk job." The sorts of investigations that Bill undertook were central to ONI efforts in the 1950s and 1960s, with about five hundred agents working in criminal investigations, counterintelligence, and background investigations for the navy. "My main job was in counterintelligence," Bill later recalled. "Part of my job was to keep track of the activities of foreign naval personnel who were in the United States. We'd get FBI reports to help us keep track of them." Hobby found the work fascinating. "By far the best part of the job was that [at] 10:30 every morning I'd go over to the reading panel and . . . read the entire take of the U.S. intelligence community," he recalled. "That was absolutely the most interesting part of the job. It was an incredibly instructive three-and-a-half years. It gave me a lot of knowledge about how the world works."[15]

In their leisure time, Bill and Diana also built a thriving social circle in Washington, including the company of Hobby family friends in the area. A month after the wedding, journalists Les and Liz Carpenter, whose news service, the Carpenter News Bureau, covered the nation's capital for the *Houston Post,* hosted a Sunday morning brunch party at their home in Northwest Washington in honor of Bill and Diana's marriage. Oveta was late to the party because of a prior commitment to appear on NBC's news program *Meet the Press*. Bill, Diana, and the other guests gathered around the Carpenters' television set to watch Oveta talk about her initiatives at HEW. At the end of the broadcast, Oveta raced to the party, where the guests gathered under a Lone Star flag flying on the front lawn to sing "Deep in the Heart of Texas" and "The Eyes of Texas."[16] Oveta resigned from her cabinet position on August 1, 1955, and returned to Houston to become the resident editor of the *Houston Post*.

While living in Virginia, Bill and Diana became close with Frank Calvert Oltorf, better known as Posh, whom Bill described as "a distant Pettus cousin and close friend." At the time, Posh was the Washington-based lobbyist for Brown & Root. He was close to Texas senator Lyndon B. Johnson. "Posh, Diana, and I had many good times in Washington," Bill later recalled. On July 2, 1955, LBJ suffered a heart attack that he barely survived. While the senator was recovering at his home in Washington, Bill extended an invitation to him and his wife, Lady Bird, to attend a dinner party at the Hobbys' McLean apartment. "I called Walter Jenkins, Johnson's longtime administrative assistant, to invite the senator to the party," Bill explained. "Walter, of course, told me that the Johnsons were not going out in the evening because of his health. I told Walter that I realized that but asked him to let the Johnsons know we were thinking of them and would miss them." The night of the party, Jenkins called Bill at about 8:00 p.m. to let him know that the Johnsons were on their way to Bill and Diana's home. "Panic! Diana had just put dinner in the oven, but she took it out quickly," Bill recalled. "I looked up the number for the Bethesda hospital and wrote it in big letters inside the telephone book cover. I had visions of the majority leader dying in a lieutenant j.g.'s apartment. But he didn't. All went well!"[17]

Happily settled in Washington and enjoying his work, Bill remained involved in the Hobby family business and philanthropic activities. For example, he was credited as part of the team that covered the 1956 national political conventions for the *Houston Post*—reporting that netted the paper a second-place award at the Gridiron Show in Houston in 1957. Bill and Jessica moved into a more active role in the family's foundation in 1956. Established in 1954, the Hobby Foundation was the mechanism by which the family managed their charitable giving. At a meeting in late November 1956, Oveta and Will added Bill and Jessica to the foundation's board, joining Will, Oveta, and prominent Houston attorney and family friend George Butler. A year after joining the board, Bill made a motion at a foundation meeting to make a $150,000 gift to Rice Institute "for the Advancement of Literature, Science and Art." Oveta also kept Bill abreast of the news in Houston, including a letter to him in which she reported, "I wish you and Diana could have been with us Tuesday night when the Nixons were at the house. Dick seems even to have converted Jessica." In that same letter, Oveta also commented on a news story that was highly critical of her in the Communist *Daily People's World*, which Bill had mischievously sent his mother: "Thanks for the clipping. I hope you don't believe all you read, but if you do, please judge your poor old mother by the enemies she makes."[18]

Ultimately, it was Bill's "poor old mother" who, dealing with a husband whose health had continued to decline, brought Bill and Diana to Houston to help her manage the *Houston Post*. Consequently, Bill officially left active duty in the navy on January 19, 1957. According to Laura, "I think my grandmother no doubt put a lot of pressure on my dad to come back and help run the paper, which I think he always knew he was going do anyway." News that Oveta Culp Hobby's son would return to Houston to help run the *Post* soon spread. In January 1957, United Press International correspondent Patricia Wiggins reported in her society column, "Lt.(jc) W. P. Hobby, Jr. is making plans to head back to the Lone Star state. The son of Oveta Culp Hobby, ending 3 ½ years with the Navy, will head back to Houston to resume his newspaper career on the paper published by his father and edited by his mother." The February 11 syndicated column of celebrity reporter Dorothy Kilgallen seconded the news: "Oveta Culp Hobby's son, Bill, is seeing Gotham after winding up his Navy hitch. After he's celebrated properly, he'll fly to Houston to assume his position in the family newspaper empire." While Bill had given serious consideration to making a career in Naval Intelligence, he later said that he came back to Houston because he felt it was his duty and responsibility to help his mother "run the family business." The plan was for Bill, who had turned twenty-five, to get more experience as a reporter. Paul Hobby confirmed Oveta's part in Bill's return to Houston and to journalism: "I think he would have been perfectly happy being a career military guy, but Oveta summoned him home. I think she probably put the family guilt on him and said, 'The *Houston Post* is your legacy. You have to come run it.' He came back home, and he did all the menial jobs that he was supposed to do to learn how to run the newspaper. She brought him back, and then she wouldn't step aside."[19]

A few days after Bill ended his naval service, he and Diana went on a vacation to the Mediterranean, following a brief stay in Manhattan. When they returned to the United States, they packed up their belongings and moved to Houston, where they settled in a house near Rice University. Bill soon reported for duty at the newspaper. It was not his first job at the *Post*. While studying at Rice and living at home, Bill had held a part-time job at the *Post* during the fall and spring semesters and a full-time position during the summers. In a confidential letter Oveta sent to her editor at the *Post* at the time, she revealed the underlying reason for her giving Bill a job at the *Post* while he was still taking classes at Rice. She told her editors that Bill was not to be given easy jobs just because he was the publishers' son. She made it clear that if he had no knack for the business, she needed to know right away. Now that he was back on a permanent basis, Oveta decided to put her son though a period of additional training to gain journalistic experience before he eventually assumed higher-level responsibilities. Because of his strong interest in politics, Oveta had Bill work as a political reporter. His first assignment was in Austin, where he joined the *Post*'s Capitol news team, led by bureau chief Bill Gardner and chief correspondent Felton West, to help cover the state legislature. It was while Bill Hobby was covering the Texas Senate that he met Bill Moore, the powerful senator from Bryan whom the press corps often referred to as the Bull of the Brazos, which was the river that ran through his district. Moore had been elected to the Senate in 1948, and when Hobby met him, Moore was serving as the upper chamber's president pro tempore. Moore would still be an influential and combative member of the Senate sixteen years later when Bill assumed his duties as lieutenant governor.

Bill also did general reporting and contributed to the *Houston Post*'s editorial page. For example, Bill contributed to the newspaper's stories about Nelson Rockefeller's Special Studies Project, which Rockefeller organized to identify the challenges the United States would face in the coming fifteen years and to propose strategies to meet those challenges. Rockefeller, who had served as Oveta's deputy when she was secretary of HEW, appointed Oveta to the project's board of expert advisors, and she was actively involved in the board's deliberations. Not surprisingly, the *Post*'s coverage of the Rockefeller project was strongly favorable. In addition, Bill wrote an editorial enthusiastically praising the project. Oveta sent clippings of the *Post*'s news stories and Bill's editorial to the project's executive director, Henry Kissinger. Oveta attached a note to the clips assuring Kissinger, in a statement that fudged the truth, that the favorable stories and her son's editorial had "appeared without any influence from me."[20]

In October, Governor Price Daniel called the members of the Texas Legislature back to the Capitol to convene for a special session, which was immediately followed by a second special session that lasted until early December. In a full-page ad published three days after the first special session opened, the *Post* touted the excellence of the newspaper's legislative coverage, emphasizing the benefit of a morning newspaper to give its readers more complete coverage of the legislature's efforts, notably the late-night proceedings of the special session. The ad pointed out that the *Post*'s Austin staff included "Bill Hobby, Jr." In the special session, Governor Daniel, an ardent supporter of segregation, asked the legislature to pass a bill giving him the power to resist federal enforcement of the Supreme Court's 1954 ruling in *Brown v. Board of Education of Topeka*, which declared that racial segregation of public schools was unconstitutional. However, the specific event motivating the governor to call the special session was the Eisenhower administration's action to use federal troops to enforce integration of the public schools in Little Rock, Arkansas. Hobby covered the ebb and flow of the "segregation bloc" of legislators who supported Daniel's bill. With an eye to the rules of the Senate, Hobby's front-page story on November 4 predicted that procedural rules would probably defeat the governor's efforts, given that the segregation bloc did not have sufficient votes to suspend the rules. His prediction turned out to be accurate. Daniel was forced to call a second session, and on November 26, 1957, the legislature voted overwhelmingly to give the governor the power to immediately close any school where federal troops might be sent to enforce integration. Hobby's coverage of the legislative sessions in 1957, which required a knowledge of Senate procedures in order to explain the proceedings to readers of the *Post*, was valuable experience he would later put to good use in his own legislative career.[21]

Bill wasn't the only family member whom Oveta recruited to help with the newspaper. Eight months after Bill and Diana moved to Houston, Oveta installed Diana as the *Post*'s book review editor, a position Oveta had once held. This was a job for which Diana, a voracious reader and intellectual, was well prepared and one in which she excelled. The book section was part of the *Post*'s Sunday magazine entertainment supplement, *Now*, which also covered music, TV, radio, and art. Diana wrote the section's lead column (which often featured interviews she conducted with authors, book industry leaders, and reviewers), assigned books to reviewers, and edited the book reviews. She continued that job until the 1970s. Her columns ranged from reviews of books on record (the precursors of today's audiobooks) to an analysis of Texas academic journals. Like the rest of the *Post*, the book section was a family affair. Bill also contributed a few reviews, including one of Winston Churchill's *Age of Revolution*, which in Bill's opinion revealed the "less attractive characteristics of Sir Winston's historiography." Bill also decried Churchill's oversimplifications and ancestor worship, but he accepted the former British prime minister's "legitimate right to assess the abilities of such statesmen and generals as Pitt, North, Shelbourne, and Fox." Diana also commissioned her sister, Sylvia, and Bill's former St. Albans teacher John Davis to contribute book reviews.[22]

Not long after Diana assumed her job as the *Post*'s book page editor, she had the delicate task of assigning a review of her father-in-law's biography, *The Tactful Texan: A Biography of Governor Will Hobby*, published in March 1958. The book's progress had not been smooth. Will had worked with James A. Clark, who produced a first draft of the book in 1957 and turned it over to Will and Oveta to review and correct. Will also shared the manuscript with Bill and Diana. Both couples were unhappy with the results. Bill later admitted that he and Diana had agreed that Clark's "manuscript was unreadable." Bill called Weldon Hart, a veteran journalist who had served as chief of the *Austin Statesman*'s Capitol news bureau, and asked him to "reorganize and rewrite" Clark's text. Hart did additional research, added some of his own memories, and thoroughly revised Clark's manuscript, sending the draft to Bill, who turned it over to his mother to read. Oveta took the manuscript to *Post* reporter Marguerite Johnston, who helped Oveta make further revisions. When Will's biography was published, Diana assigned the review to W. D. Bedell, a *Post* columnist. His favorable review appeared in Diana's books section on April 27, 1958. "Gov. Hobby's thousands of friends will especially enjoy it," Bedell wrote. "They will recognize its lacks. But they will understand that there is no way to put into words the full quality of this man—friendly, humble, witty, keen, direct, generous, kind." Unfortunately, Will had suffered a sudden illness in January, during which he underwent major surgery on his throat and almost died. He was bedridden for most of that spring and summer.[23]

Bill continued his political reporting in 1958, notably with a series of front-page stories that provided detailed analysis of the demographics behind election results in Harris County. His articles supplemented the *Post*'s overall election coverage with deep dives, often district by district, into how results were shaped by the geographic and racial composition of Houston. In July, the results of the Democratic primary elections led him to conclude, "The liberal faction of the Democratic Party has rolled up immense gains in voting strength since the Daniel-Yarborough gubernatorial runoff in 1956." Hobby went on to note that those gains came in areas that had been strongholds of conservative Democrats. According to his coverage of the August runoff elections, that trend continued, with the takeaway that the liberal faction had performed a complete "mopping up operation . . . defeating every candidate of the conservative faction in a manner that will leave its mark on Harris County politics for many years." His election coverage in November focused on the Houston Independent School Board elections, where Hattie Mae White (identified in the paper as Mrs. Charles White, the wife of a Black optometrist) unseated the incumbent and became the first Black person to be elected to public office in Harris County since Reconstruction. In his front-page analysis of the elections, Hobby provided detailed demographics on 91 of the 181 precincts that had voted in the three races, noting they fell into "13 distinct geographic groups and one racial group." While he pointed out that the election was "a strange affair—one which observers of many political viewpoints will ponder for a long time," he did make one clear conclusion: that White's surprising victory had only been possible because she had drawn votes from areas beyond Black precincts. Bill's coverage earned praise from *Post* readers. In one letter to the editor, his August postelection analysis was called "a thoughtful and effective method of presenting the facts showing the comparison and between this and the first primary election in July." Another reader wrote, "Bill Hobby's scholarly post-mortem on the Democratic run-off deserves high praise. It was written and edited to merit my confidence."[24]

On October 25, 1958, Bill and Diana's first child, Laura Poteat Hobby, was born. Baby Laura was named for Will's favorite sister. For the couple that had longed for a child, the birth of Laura was a joyous occasion. According to Laura, "They were trying to get pregnant earlier in their marriage and apparently not very successfully, because at some point they discussed the process of adopting Korean war babies." That happy event was followed by a troublesome one. On November 29, 1958, after taking one of his auto tours around the city, Will was struck with severe pain in his abdomen. An ambulance rushed him to nearby Hermann Hospital, where he had emergency surgery the next morning to remove a hemorrhaging stomach ulcer. His survival was in doubt the night after his surgery. Oveta, Bill, and Jessica (who drove over from San Antonio) spent the night at the hospital, monitoring his condition. Will once again managed to survive, but this bout of illness robbed him of his mobility and finally ended his active involvement in the Hobby businesses. He would spend the rest of his life as an invalid.[25]

In January 1959, after working as a political reporter and occasional editorial writer for nearly two years, Hobby accepted an offer from Lieutenant Governor Ben Ramsey to join his staff as the Senate parliamentarian, following in his mother's footsteps, albeit on the other side of the Capitol (she had served as the first female parliamentarian for the Texas House of Representatives). Bill would later note that "Ramsey had a weakness for gubernatorial offspring" to serve in the position of parliamentarian. Bill was preceded in the position by Dan Moody Jr., son of Governor Daniel Moody, and he would be succeeded by Nancy Moody, Governor Moody's daughter. Ben Ramsey was a native of San Augustine, a small East Texas town where he had worked in his father's law office and on the family farm. He eventually studied law at the University of Texas. His public service included two terms in the Texas House of Representatives, eight years as a Texas senator, and a brief stint as secretary of state under Governor Beauford Jester before successfully running for lieutenant governor in 1950. Ramsey was starting his fifth consecutive term in that position in January 1959. He would become a political mentor to Bill Hobby. A conservative Democrat, Ramsey nevertheless believed in the ability of government to improve the lives of Texans; he "strongly supported rural electrification, water conservation and development, paving of farms roads, and stricter laws regulating insurance companies." He was known as fiscally prudent, with a deep-seated understanding that the budget was central to the running of the Senate. As Ramsey noted in his inaugural address of 1959, "The hard, cold facts of the balance sheet must be recognized, of course. Money is a problem of this Legislature. It always is. . . . In my opinion, a tax program should accompany each request for new or additional state services. . . . I know the people of Texas will support sound essential projects for the betterment of our state. Our job is to separate the essential from the non-essential. . . . The fundamental question is, not where can we get all the money we want—but rather, how much can we afford to spend?"[26]

Ramsey was adroit at navigating the somewhat fractious party politics of the 1950s. The state's Democratic Party split into factions over the 1952 and 1956 presidential elections, with the conservative wing, led by Governor Allan Shivers, abandoning the national Democratic Party to back Republican candidate Dwight Eisenhower over Democrat Adlai Stevenson. While he was in alignment with Governor Shivers on a number of issues, including "raising revenue necessary for higher teachers' pay, state hospitals, and prisons," Ramsey stayed loyal to party lines and was named chair of the Texas Democratic Party in 1955.[27]

Ramsey was not a typical politician. He had an aversion to the glad-handing of politicking, although he never lost an election. As columnist Bob Bowman recounted, "Ramsey hated to campaign and seldom made a political speech." And he did not look the part, either: "With his slouch hat, rumpled suits and scuffed shoes, Ramsey sometimes resembled an unmade bed." Bowman shares a story of a friend visiting Ramsey in his office as the lieutenant governor sat quietly reading his newspaper while a group of VIPs waited to see him. "Mister Ben, there's a roomful of important people out there, waiting to see you," the friend reportedly said. Bowman noted that "without lowering his newspaper, Ramsey muttered: 'Well, sit down and be quiet. Maybe they'll go away.'"[28]

Hobby's tenure as parliamentarian extended through the Fifty-Sixth Regular Legislative Session, which began on January 13, 1959. He was paid $16.50 per day for his services—the same as the sergeant at arms, but more than the Senate chaplain and assistant secretaries. The job's role is vaguely defined: "The Senate parliamentarian assists the presiding officer in matters of procedure and Senate rules." Each lieutenant governor shaped the role to his requirements. "Governor Ramsey needed a parliamentarian like a boar hog needs tits," Hobby reflected in his memoir. "Senate rules and traditions were engraved in his brain, as they came to be in mine. You can read the rules until you have them virtually memorized and learn the traditions as you go, but it takes a session or two for them to become instinctive." Hobby would later joke about his role as parliamentarian under Ramsey: "Now that is not to say I didn't have important duties! I had to drive the governor's children to school [and] take Madame Ramsey to the beauty parlor." Those "duties" aside, his time under Ramsey was significant. It gave Hobby a ringside seat for the inner workings of the Senate, not to mention a firsthand lesson in how the lieutenant governor could wield power over the operations of the state. "I met with Governor Ramsey before the session each morning to get instructions on what bills to refer to what committee," Hobby recalled. "Occasionally he would refer a bill to the Committee on 'S—t' by tossing it in the lower left-hand drawer. Talk about final disposition!"[29]

Hobby also learned to gauge what was important to Ramsey. As the Senate held afternoon meetings in the later days of the session, Ramsey preferred to play poker with his friends. "He left me the telephone number for where he could be reached, with instructions that if a senator wanted to reach him in a real emergency I should dial the number and hand the phone to the senator," Hobby recounted. "Sure enough, what I thought was an emergency arose, and I followed instructions. The next day Governor Ramsey told me that there had been no real emergency. There were no more emergencies."[30]

Hobby would later call Ramsey "my role model as lieutenant governor." Bill was clearly influenced by many of Ramsey's characteristics, notably his expert ability to use Senate rules to his advantage—and how a bit of subterfuge could be employed to manage the senators. "At that time, there were so few bills on the Senate calendar that the parliamentarian kept them in a file box at the rostrum," Hobby wrote in his memoir, noting,

> Then, as now, senators came to the rostrum during the morning call (the routine business period) to seek recognition on their bills. Ramsey knew everything. Occasionally when he saw a senator on his way, he would tell me to lose Senate Bill XYZ. I put the bill in my coat pocket. When the senator asked Ramsey to recognize him on the bill, somehow I couldn't find the bill in the box. "Senator, are you sure it's out of committee? I can't find Senate Bill XYZ here," I would ask. "OK, Ben," the senator would usually say, "I'll vote for your damned old so-and-so bill." I suddenly found Senate Bill XYZ.

Hobby's tenure as parliamentarian ended on May 12, 1959, the last date of the regular legislative session.[31]

When Hobby returned to Houston, the other family business became his sole focus. Having demonstrated his journalistic abilities over the previous two years, he was promoted to associate editor of the *Post*, which included, among other duties, serving as the newspaper's liaison with its Austin and Washington bureaus. Bill would continue his role as a political analyst—one he hadn't completely abandoned while serving as parliamentarian and commuting back and forth between Houston and Austin during the regular session of the legislature in the late winter and early spring of 1959. In February, the *Post* published a massive special section, "Suburbia," featuring multiple articles investigating every angle of the postwar boom in subdivisions and the accompanying lifestyle that was beginning to have a major impact on Houston. Hobby's contribution to the section was an analysis of the suburban voter, which he pointed out had defied the initial assumption that "suburbanites, in the immemorial manner of the middle class are conservatives in the classic, Burkian sense . . . opposed to 'big government,' taxes, in favor of the sanctity of contract and private property." Hobby noted that as "new acres of prairie were covered with Saint Augustine grass and enclosed with chain link fence," the voters in question defied those expectations. And while the suburban vote had helped secure Eisenhower's victories in the 1952 and 1956 presidential elections, Hobby explained, it was not that the suburbs were more Republican but rather that "so many more people live there." Hobby cited a range of examples from the Houston suburbs that confounded any stereotype, and he concluded, "Suburbia has been the graveyard of many political experts already. They will be joined by others."[32]

On August 10, a front-page story in the *Post* presented another example of the kind of political analysis in which Bill was now specializing. In a data-driven look at political conditions in Texas a year prior to the presidential election of 1960, Bill identified US Senator Lyndon Johnson as the front-runner among Texas political leaders of both parties. Among the Democrats surveyed, a whopping 67 percent favored Johnson, with John F. Kennedy coming in fourth with a puny 7 percent. Republicans greatly favored Vice President Richard Nixon, with 92 percent of respondents choosing him over all challengers. Bill also noted that a majority of those surveyed believed that the Democrats would carry the state, regardless of who ended up as the nominee.[33]

In December 1959 Bill covered Eisenhower's trip to India and the summit meeting between Eisenhower and Western European heads of state in Paris. On his "Flight to Peace" goodwill tour, which took place from December 4 to 23, 1959, the president visited eleven nations, including five in Asia, flying twenty-two thousand miles in nineteen days. In an editorial prior to the trip, the *Post* predicted it would be "a high point" of the president's personal diplomacy efforts, with the opportunity for "man-to-man" discussions with leaders of the countries on the tour. "Above all, the journey will demonstrate as nothing else could this country's interest and concern for the free nations of the world," the editorial concluded. Hobby's coverage of the trip was featured almost daily on the *Post*'s front page, with his detailed on-the-ground dispatches supplementing the dryly factual news service articles about the visits. Hobby went beyond the basic recounting of events to provide colorful and detailed descriptions of the tour: the mood of the crowds, the weather, and the spirits of the president and his entourage. His articles also provided insight into the tone of the president's meetings with foreign leaders, with an eye to the larger foreign-relations goals of the trip. The reporting drew on not only Bill's experience as a journalist but also his service in Naval Intelligence, where he had been privy to the inner workings of international relations.[34]

The trip began in Rome, where Eisenhower met with President Giovanni Gronchi and Pope John XXIII. Bill likely attended the pope's meeting with the one hundred or so journalists accompanying Eisenhower, where the pontiff urged them to "give valiant service to the cause of truth and peace in the world." From there, Eisenhower traveled to Ankara, Turkey; Karachi, Pakistan; and Kabul, Afghanistan, holding informal meetings with the leaders in those states. As Hobby noted in his summary of Ike's visit to Karachi, the president's message was clear: "He posed the hope of improved international relations but made clear the United States stands firmly behind Pakistan in upholding free nations against aggression." The president's comments continued to call for disarmament: "There can be no winners in any future global war," Eisenhower said to a crowd of twenty-five thousand Pakistanis. "The world, the entire world, must insist that the conference table, rather than force, is to be used for settlement of international disputes."[35]

Hobby called the welcome the president received in India the equivalent of "the Fourth of July, New Year's Eve and the Thanksgiving Day game rolled all into one." Throngs of crowds numbering in the hundreds of thousands swarmed the presidential motorcade, turning the thirteen-mile parade route into a two-hour procession. Eisenhower met with Prime Minister Jawaharlal Nehru and President Rajendra Prasad, visited multiple locations in New Delhi, addressed the members of the Indian Parliament, and made a respectful stop at the Gandhi cremation shrine, where he paid homage to the late leader by laying a wreath and planting a sapling. As the trip took a midpoint pause in New Delhi, Hobby provided the *Post*'s readers with a thematic framework for the tour, noting that the predominant theme of the trip's first half was in reaction to the Communist military pressures on South and Southeast Asia. He also provided context for the significance of the trip's second half, pointing out the issues facing the meeting of the "Big Four" in France (the leaders of the United States, France, Germany, and Great Britain) that would be the trip's conclusion. Hobby wrote, "The hammering out of a Western position that all members of the alliance can adhere to strongly will be no easy task. The issues that divide the Big Four are not, of course, fundamental ones of political ideology. They are, however, important. They relate to the North Atlantic Treaty Organization and the political and economic organization of Europe."[36]

After a stop in Tehran, Iran, the tour continued in Athens, Greece. Hobby contrasted the president's welcome there with the ones he had received in the "Asian countries," where the throngs of people saw his visit as an occasion for a public festival. Hobby ascertained that the response in Athens was a reflection of a "real depth of feeling for Eisenhower the man and the symbol of America." Ike then went on to Tunisia before arriving in Paris for his conference with French president Charles de Gaulle, British prime minister Harold Macmillan, and German chancellor Konrad Adenauer. After a stop in Madrid and a meeting with Generalissimo Francisco Franco of Spain, the president's trip concluded with a visit to Morocco.[37]

Hobby wrote a detailed postmortem analysis of the trip for the *Post*'s December 27 edition, in which he noted the tour's most significant results. As the competition between Communist and anti-Communist nations increased, the conflict would focus less on military force and more on political and economic incentives to those nations that were not committed to either side of the Cold War. He predicted the United States was entering a period of "détente diplomacy," with emphasis on reducing tension between the two sides. Eisenhower's administration was encouraging other Western nations to provide economic aid to "underdeveloped" nations. In addition, the emphasis on economic aid for anti-Communist countries—notably the Asian countries visited by Eisenhower—meant that military aid would continue but that those governments should increase their "living standards." Hobby wrote, "Economic growth . . . was stated time and again as a goal of United States policy—growth without appalling sacrifices of human freedoms of values as in Communist China." He also noted that the outpouring of affection that greeted the president at every stop represented a singular benefit that the United States enjoyed—one that would not be possible for Great Britain or France, who were seen as representatives of "old-style" colonialism.[38]

As the 1950s drew to a close, Bill and Diana were comfortably settled in Houston and in their jobs at the *Post*. By the end of 1959, the continuing growth and success of the newspaper and of KPRC-TV were bright spots for the Hobby family at a time when Will's physical decline continued. In a story about the *Post*'s increasing editorial influence, the *Dallas Morning News* characterized the paper as "very much a Hobby enterprise." The Dallas paper pointed out Oveta's role as president and editor and Bill's role as an associate editor, with "his desk in the midst of the busy city room." Diana Hobby, the story added, was editing "one of the better book sections in the Southwest."[39]

Regardless of the fulfillment Bill had found in military service, he was now fully engaged as a journalist at the *Post*, having found his niche in political analysis, with an eye to data and demographics, which were among his intellectual strengths. In December of 1959, Bill's essay "Journalism: Literature's Fourth Dimension" appeared in the *Texas Quarterly*, a journal from the University of Texas Press that featured scholarly articles on the arts and sciences, edited by Harry Ransom. Diana had covered the journal's debut issue in her "Books" column on April 20, 1958, noting the inaugural issue helped make the case that "Texas literature [is] gaining in stature and importance." Bill's contribution explored how journalism differed from other forms of literature, including a discussion of the role of journalism in American letters. Before presenting a survey of how American news had changed over its first two hundred years, the essay tackled the nature of journalism as a literary form (as well as the nature of journalists themselves). Hobby argued that the element of time is the genre's most distinctive characteristic, noting, "Journalism is literature in motion." It was also the nature of a journalist to be a "miscellanist," as "Tutankhamen's tomb makes at least as good copy as Elizabeth Taylor."[40]

Now a seasoned member of the Fourth Estate, Hobby articulated the dissenting nature of the newsman. "Journalism is the literary bridge between thought and action," he wrote. "Because the journalist guards this always troubled frontier, he is usually dealing with the stuff of controversy and is often—or at least often should be—at odds with constituted authority." He went on to note that journalists are "likely to be an ill-tempered, cantankerous, and thoroughly difficult lot where authority is concerned."

Hobby was most convincing when he attempted to correct the common expectation of journalistic neutrality, which he pointed out confuses objectivity with fairness. While some critics expect that journalists be "purely" objective, Hobby pointed out, "In the case of a competent journalist writing on a subject of which he has expert knowledge, it is inconceivable that he should be without a point of view." Hobby continued, "This is not to say that [a journalist] cannot write a fair account of what occurred. Fairness is not only a quality of the mind but a function of judgment." As the next decade began, Hobby would be frequently called to exercise his judgment as his influence at the *Post* continued to grow.[41]

CHAPTER 4

THE JFK ASSASSINATION

On May 14, 1960, the *Houston Post*'s executive editor, Frank H. King, announced that twenty-eight-year-old Bill Hobby had been named the paper's managing editor. Bill replaced Jack Donahue, who took a job at the *Los Angeles Mirror-News*. To counter potential criticism that Bill was too young to lead the newspaper, the *Post* pointed out in a press release about his promotion that Bill's father, Will Hobby, had been twenty-six when he assumed the same job. *Time*, which had long shown an interest in Oveta's career, observed that under his mother's guidance, "Bill Hobby is likely to continue putting out one of the Southwest's better newspapers." After visiting Bill in the *Post*'s newsroom, a *Time* journalist wrote a story that emphasized Bill's youth and hinted that his promotion was the result of the obvious family connections. "Entering the crowded city room," the reporter wrote, "the first desk a visitor runs into is that of a crew-cut young man in shirtsleeves, who looks like a cub reporter fresh from journalism school. The young man is, in fact, William Pettus Hobby Jr., 28, who last week was named managing editor of the powerful *Houston Post*, which is owned and run by his parents."[1]

The *Post*'s daily and Sunday circulation had now surpassed the *Houston Chronicle* to become the largest in Texas. Its financial success made it possible for the Hobbys to move forward with a plan to build a $2.5 million expansion of the printing plant. As Bill was assuming his duties as managing editor in May 1960, contractors began work on a three-story addition to house the *Post*'s new high-speed color presses. That additional space trebled the size of the pressroom, making it possible to handle the paper's rapidly increasing circulation more efficiently. Will's ill health prevented him from attending the ground-breaking ceremony, but with Bill at her side, Oveta presided over the event in a parking lot next to the Post Building on May 11. The new presses became operational in June 1961.²

Now that he was managing editor of the *Post*, Bill became more active in the civic, cultural, business, and charitable life of Houston, as was expected of someone in such a publicly visible position. He took leadership positions with the Houston Symphony Society, the Houston Chamber of Commerce, the United Fund, the local unit of the American Cancer Society, the mayor's advisory committee on aviation, and the Bank of Texas. His professional memberships included the American Society of Newspaper Editors and the state and national associations of the Associated Press Managing Editors. In April 1962, as an active member of the South Texas Press Association, Bill addressed its annual meeting in San Antonio, where he signaled his continuing interest in the Texas Senate after serving as Lieutenant Governor Ben Ramsey's parliamentarian, calling for an end to its "secret" (executive) voting sessions. "That's wrong and newspapers can do something about it. That's what God put newspapers on earth for," Hobby told the editors. "We have the right to know how our senators vote. The public still can't find out how the Senate votes on some of the most important issues in our state government—the appointments to the boards and commissions made by the governor." He also continued to stress the point about journalistic objectivity that he had raised in his article in the *Texas Quarterly*: "We can't be objective. Objectivity is an absence of a point of view, and any good reporter must have a point of view." He argued that by weighing the facts and sticking to the truth, newspapers can be fair yet not be colorless.³

Soon after Bill assumed his new duties as managing editor, he was involved in coverage of two local news stories of national significance: one on racial integration and the other on the issue of presidential candidate John F. Kennedy's Catholicism.

In the spring of 1960, peaceful protests in Greensboro, North Carolina, against racially segregated lunch counters inspired students at Texas Southern University (TSU) to protest Jim Crow practices in the South's largest city. In early March 1960, Eldrewey Stearns, a twenty-eight-year-old army veteran and student at the TSU Law School, led a group of approximately one hundred TSU students in a sit-in demonstration at a grocery-store lunch counter in south Houston. The store's management closed the lunch counter to keep from serving the students. On March 25, 1960, Stearns led a student group to Houston City Hall, where they picketed and sang church songs. Afterward, they entered the city hall cafeteria and asked to be served. To their shock, white Houston city councilman and future mayor Louie Welch joined them at the counter and ordered the manager to serve the students, who were subsequently sold coffee and food. Under Oveta's leadership, the *Post* had been one of the few newspapers in the South to support the Supreme Court's public-school desegregation decision in the *Brown v. Board of Education* case. After the *Post* ran the city hall story on its front page, angry white Houstonians flooded city hall with mail and telephone calls denouncing Welch's action. Houston mayor Lewis Cutrer announced that in the future, any Black customers who tried to be served at the lunch counter would be arrested, but the chief of police, Carl Shuptrine, informed the mayor that because the protesters would be breaking no laws, his officers would not make the arrests. Encouraged by this success, the TSU students targeted other businesses in Houston. The specter of events in Little Rock, Arkansas, where the school integration controversy had damaged the business community in that city, hung over Houston's merchants. With growing anxiety, the city's Retail Merchants' Association advised its members to respond to the protests in a manner that would allow the business community to "continue to grow and prosper free of the disorder and violence which took their toll on business and community life in Little Rock."[4]

In August 1960, fearing violence, Robert Dundas, vice president of Foley's department store in downtown Houston, sought a resolution to the racial tension. Dundas wanted to desegregate Foley's restaurant, but he worried that if his department store was the first to break the color barrier, it would bear the brunt of white racist anger and lose customers. He decided to convince the owners and managers of other downtown lunch counters that if they all desegregated at the same time, white protesters would be unable to single out an individual business for reprisal. After a series of private talks, Dundas persuaded downtown lunch counter operators to join with Foley's to end racial segregation in downtown Houston. Retailers soon quietly removed the "Colored" and "White" signs over water fountains and on restroom doors. The retail executives insisted, however, that they would desegregate only if the news media agreed to not cover the event. They were aware that news coverage in other southern cities had led to violence by white racists. It was hoped that a news blackout would allow Houston to avoid a similar fate.[5]

Dundas explained his strategy to Oveta and Bill Hobby and to Jesse Jones's nephew, John T. Jones, who had succeeded his uncle as publisher of the *Houston Chronicle*. Oveta was determined to prevent another Little Rock situation in Houston. Accordingly, she, Bill, and Jones agreed to impose a news blackout on their newspapers and broadcast properties. Oveta was making the major decisions at the *Post*, but Bill strongly supported the decision. Oveta ordered her photographers, reporters, and editors not to print photographs of or stories about the lunch counter protests. *Post* reporters, including city editor Ralph O'Leary, civil rights specialist Blair Justice, and managing editor Frank King, pleaded with Bill and Oveta not to impose the blackout, arguing that the *Post* was obligated to report news. Oveta ignored their pleas. Other radio and television stations agreed not to cover the event, largely due to Foley's advertising power. Dundas quietly spread news of the desegregation decision throughout Houston's Black community. On August 25, 1960, he welcomed a contingent of TSU students when they arrived at Foley's lunch counter and asked for service. The operators of the other Houston lunch counters followed Dundas's lead on that same date.[6]

When the national press learned about the coordinated news blackout in Houston, several papers printed editorials criticizing the decision. The liberal *Texas Observer*, understanding that news coverage was important to raising public awareness of segregation practices, complained, "We are still blinking our eyes—we can't believe it! The entire Houston press—newspapers, radio, and TV—entering into an overt conspiracy to suppress a major news development they had covered fully up to the time of its climax! Inflammatory reporting is one thing, but truthful reporting is another." The Oveta Hobby–friendly *Time* magazine, however, was less critical. In a story with the headline "Blackout in Houston," *Time* emphasized the public safety and security motivations, as well as the economic reasons behind the decision, quoting an anonymous Houstonian that the retail stores desired "to integrate the lunch counters at the least possible cost. They wanted to lose neither Negro nor white business. They felt that not publicizing the event was their safest course of action."[7]

The month after Houston's downtown lunch counters were desegregated, Bill Hobby became involved in the controversy over presidential candidate John F. Kennedy's Catholicism, which had caused a backlash in many of the anti-Catholic evangelical Protestant congregations in Texas and other Southern states. A traveling fundamentalist preacher held a series of religious revivals in Houston during which he denounced Kennedy as a stooge of the pope who would impose Catholicism on the country if elected. When Bill heard about the revivalist's attacks on Kennedy, he assigned a reporter to attend one of the revivals and write a story about what he heard. The resulting news piece was not flattering to the preacher or to his message. As Bill later told *Time*, he soon caught "all sorts of hell" from a delegation of Houston's fundamentalist preachers who showed up at his office at the *Houston Post* to demand that the newspaper print a statement supporting the evangelist's criticism of Kennedy's religion. They threatened that if Bill rejected their demand, they would stop purchasing notices in the *Post* about church services and would ask members of their congregations to cancel their subscriptions and any ads their businesses were placing in the paper. Bill refused to print the statement and asked them to leave. There was no noticeable loss in advertising.[8]

The year 1960 was notable for Bill and Diana Hobby for reasons other than Bill's promotion at the *Post*. In September Diana gave birth to their second child, Paul William Hobby. Now the parents of two children, the Hobbys moved from their residence on Southgate to a larger house at 1506 South Boulevard, located several blocks north of Rice University and less than one mile from Will and Oveta's mansion on Remington Lane. During the next three years after the move, Diana and Bill would have another son, Andrew, born in 1962, and another daughter, Kate, born in 1964.[9]

Paul recalled growing up in the house on South Boulevard. "That house was comfortable, and it was cozy. My mother is from North Carolina, so you had wood everywhere. My grandmother had stone, but my mother would have wood, which reflected their personalities. It was cozy, livable, approachable. It wasn't grand but it was tasteful. That's just my mother's style." John Davis was an occasional overnight guest at Bill and Diana's house on South Boulevard. The Hobby children referred to Davis as "Uncle

John." "Our guest room awaits," Bill wrote Davis, inviting him for a visit. "Its chief hazard [is] the proclivity of dogs and small children to get in bed with all newcomers, knowing that the regulars (their parents) kick them out faster." One of the memories Paul Hobby had of the house was Oveta being driven up the driveway by a chauffeur for one of her regular after-work visits. "We had a dog named Murphy," Paul recalled. "My grandmother would come over with her driver, and she'd come up the driveway. And Murphy wouldn't let her out of the car. We were all tickled pink, because Murphy was our hero. You know, here was this woman, she was not used to anybody telling her what she could and couldn't do. And here this dog wouldn't let her out of the car." Bill and Diana would raise their four kids in the home and continue to make it their primary residence for nearly fifty-five years, except for the three years they lived in Austin.[10]

As the *Houston Post* continued to generate healthy profits, Bill, with Oveta's support, decided to expand the family's newspaper ownership into nearby Galveston County. In February 1963, the Hobbys purchased the historic *Galveston News*, the oldest continually operating newspaper in Texas, founded in 1842. That acquisition also included the island city's afternoon paper, the *Galveston Tribune*, as well as the *Texas City Sun*, a small circulation journal founded in 1912 in the oil-refining town on the mainland. The combined circulation of the three dailies was about thirty-six thousand. The purchase was not without controversy. The papers were owned by the Moody family company, founded by wealthy financier and entrepreneur William L. Moody Jr. The company sold the newspapers to the Hobbys over the objection of Moody's daughter, philanthropist Mary Moody Northen, who was outvoted by the other stockholders in a contentious two-hour meeting. The purchase attracted the attention of *Time* magazine. In a story published in March 1963, the *Time* reporter who interviewed Bill described him as "the crew-cut Post Managing Editor William P. Hobby Jr., 30, Oveta's boy." When the reporter asked Bill if the purchase of the Galveston newspapers was the start of a much larger news media corporation, he replied, "Much as I like the sound of the phrase, this is not the start of an empire."[11]

Oveta and Bill moved quickly to tamp down worries in Galveston that the venerable *Galveston News* was going to be folded into the *Houston Post* and that Galveston would lose an important part of its identity as a separate city from its rapidly growing and sprawling neighbor and historic urban rival. Accompanied by her son, Oveta addressed a sold-out luncheon sponsored by the Galveston Chamber of Commerce at the Jack Tar Hotel on April 1. Her remarks illustrated Oveta's view of the role a newspaper could play in boosting the business prospects of a city. She and Bill also pointed out the Hobby family's historical connection to Galveston, where Bill's grandfather Edwin and granduncle Marmaduke had fought in the Battle of Galveston during the Civil War and had later lived for a time after the war. The Hobbys later underscored their stake in Galveston by building an expensive new printing plant for the *Galveston News*. Oveta and Bill also merged the Texas City and Galveston newspapers to form the *News-Sun Today* to cover the booming residential and business area surrounding NASA's Manned Space Center. The Hobbys' ownership was short-lived, however. They would sell the papers in 1967.[12]

A month after buying the *Galveston News*, Bill continued to show his strong interest in the affairs of the Texas Senate. He went to Austin and testified at a hearing of the Senate Committee on Constitutional Amendments, where he argued against the practice of holding executive sessions of the Senate, an issue he had raised in his speech to the South Texas Press Association a year earlier. Hobby stressed that it was not "morally right to conduct public business behind a veil of secrecy. Passing upon governors' nominations is one of the most important of the basic constitutional functions assigned to the Senate in our system of government. There is no more reason why the Senate should exercise this function in secret than there is a reason why the Senate should, for example, vote on a tax bill in secret." He declared that "the people's best defense against the unwise or capricious use of power is the right to scrutinize the actions of those who exercise that power."[13]

When John F. Kennedy was sworn in as president on January 20, 1961, the Hobby family had no special ties to the White House for the first time in eight years. The Hobbys, however, did maintain their close relationship with Lyndon and Lady Bird Johnson while LBJ was vice president. Bill and Oveta attended the vice president's lavish outdoor barbecues on his ranch in the Texas Hill Country, including one honoring United Nations officials in spring 1963. Bill also paid visits to LBJ's office when he was in Washington on business. Whenever the vice president was in Houston, he would stop at the Hobby mansion on Remington Lane to visit with Will, whose poor health made him permanently bedridden.[14]

On November 21, 1963, President Kennedy, the first lady, Vice President Johnson, and Lady Bird traveled to Texas to raise money for JFK's 1964 reelection campaign and to unify the state's bitterly divided Democratic Party. A political feud between Senator Ralph Yarborough and Governor John Connally and their respective followers threatened JFK's hopes of carrying Texas. After delivering a speech in San Antonio, JFK and his party flew to Houston, where he spoke at a sold-out testimonial dinner honoring US congressman Albert Thomas. Because Oveta was on a trip out of state, Bill Hobby and *Houston Post* columnist and advertising agency executive Jack Valenti met the presidential party at Houston's municipal airport. Valenti was also a friend and an occasional advisor to Vice President Johnson. After the dinner that night, Valenti went to Fort Worth with JFK and LBJ, and the next morning he rode in the Dallas motorcade.[15]

Bill was in his office at the *Post* at 12:36 p.m. when stunning news came over the Associated Press wire: "Bulletin. President shot. Dallas." Hearing a shout, Bill rushed to the wire-service room and stood by the Teletype printers, watching for additional information. "Then, after what seemed like an interminable time—it probably was a few minutes," Bill recalled, "New York breaks in and says, 'BUREAUS DOWNHOLD. DALLAS ITS YOURS.'" At about twelve forty-five, he was handed the following AP wire copy:

BULLETIN

DALLAS, NOV. 22 (AP)—PRESIDENT KENNEDY WAS SHOT TODAY JUST AS HIS MOTORCADE LEFT DOWNTOWN DALLAS. MRS. KENNEDY JUMPED UP AND GRABBED MR. KENNEDY. SHE CRIED, "OH, NO!" THE MOTORCADE SPED ON.

BULLETIN MATTER

DALLAS-FIRST ADD KENNEDY SHOT X X X SPED ON.

AP PHOTOGRAPHER JAMES W. ALTGENS SAID HE SAW BLOOD ON THE PRESIDENT'S HEAD.

ALTGENS SAID HE HEARD TWO SHOTS BUT THOUGHT SOMEONE WAS SHOOTING FIREWORKS UNTIL HE SAW THE BLOOD ON THE PRESIDENT.

ALTGENS SAID HE SAW NO ONE WITH A GUN.

AP REPORTER JACK BELL ASKED KENNETH O'DONNELL, PRESIDENTIAL ASSISTANT, IF KENNEDY WAS DEAD. O'DONNELL GAVE NO ANSWER.

KENNEDY WAS REPORTED TAKEN TO PARKLAND HOSPITAL, NEAR THE DALLAS TRADE MART, WHERE HE WAS TO HAVE MADE A SPEECH.[16]

The *Post*'s newsroom filled up as word of the shooting spread around the building. "Here I am a kid, 31 years old or something," Bill later recalled, "aware that this was the biggest story I would ever handle, aware that my reputation as a newspaperman would depend on what I did in the next few minutes." In a candid admission, Bill admitted he hadn't had "the foggiest idea of what to do. Managing editors are supposed to know what to do." As Bill stood by the wire-service machines, stunned and nearly paralyzed with shock, J. D. Hancock, the *Post*'s city circulation manager, was standing beside him. "I had known J. D. most of my life," Bill later recalled. "He had been selling the *Houston Post* for fifty years—longer than I had been alive." Hancock turned to Bill and asked, "You're going extra aren't you?" Hancock's comment brought Bill out of his stupor. "Suddenly I knew what to do—put out an extra edition." The problem, however, was that the *Post* hadn't published an extra edition since 1947, when the French freighter *Grandcamp* blew up the Texas City docks, killing hundreds of people. "Television news had pretty well killed off extra editions," Bill noted, and another problem was that it was now early afternoon. "There aren't many folks in the newsroom of a morning paper at 1 p.m."[17]

Bill called Jean Buttrell, the production manager: "Can you get some printers, engravers, and stereo-typers and pressmen here?" Buttrell promptly called everyone in. Bill was astounded by how quickly the printers and pressmen streamed in. "We were on the street in about 2-1/2 hours, which was amazing." Above the headline on the front page of the extra edition, Bill placed a black reverse bar with four crosses on it and the word "EXTRA" inserted in the middle of the crosses. While the extra was being printed, he chartered a plane and sent four *Post* staff members to Dallas, including Owen Johnson, the newspaper's chief photographer. While the *Post* hurried to get its extra edition out on the streets, KPRC-TV and Radio were broadcasting live feeds from the NBC television and radio networks. As was the case with the news media across the United States, the unfolding story of the assassination and the events that followed dominated the pages of the *Houston Post* and the broadcasts of KPRC for several days. Bill kept the original paper copy of the Teletype bulletin, framed it, and hung it on his office wall. When he recalled the episode years afterward, he marveled at his lack of emotional reaction while he was getting the *Post*'s extra produced. "I mean, your job was to get the paper out. But it was after the story was covered and the paper was on the street that the emotional reactions came. That feeling went on for years. I would suddenly tear up just thinking about it."[18]

On November 24, the Sunday after the assassination, Dallas night club owner Jack Ruby shot and killed Lee Harvey Oswald in the basement of the Dallas police station. That morning as Bill and Diana drove to church, Diana suggested that they stop by Jack and Mary Margaret Valenti's home. Mary Margaret, who had been on Lyndon Johnson's staff before she married Valenti, had just had their first child, and she was back from the hospital. Diana had bought a baby present, and she suggested to Bill that they stop by and deliver it to Mary Margaret, whom Diana was concerned about, since her husband was now with LBJ in Washington. When the Hobbys arrived at the Valentis' house, they heard the telephone ringing continuously with calls from reporters, friends, and relatives. Mary Margaret, recovering from her recent hospital stay, was having difficulty managing the situation while she tended to her newborn, so Bill manned the telephone while Diana helped Mary Margaret. At about eleven thirty that morning, the Hobbys were stunned to see on the Valentis' television set the broadcast of Ruby shooting Oswald. They never made it to the church service. "Jack came back that Sunday afternoon, really just to get some clothes before he returned to Washington to help LBJ," Bill remembered. Valenti gave Hobby a detailed account of LBJ taking the oath of office on Air Force One. Hobby's interview with Valenti, published the next morning in the *Post*, was the first eyewitness news account of LBJ's swearing in. Hobby's story also broke the news that LBJ had called Attorney General Robert Kennedy from Air Force One and that Kennedy had urged Johnson to take the oath of office before he left Dallas. LBJ handed the phone to Valenti, who was told the wording of the oath. Valenti wrote the words on a piece of paper and then gave it to federal judge Sarah T. Hughes to use when she administered the oath.[19]

As an old friend of the new president, Oveta was among those who understood that LBJ was well prepared by skill and experience to do whatever was necessary to calm a grieving nation and to keep the ship of state on a safe course moving forward. Two days after the assassination, an editorial in the *Post*, "New Leader of Free World Well Prepared," expressed the solid confidence Oveta had in LBJ's leadership. Bill Hobby immediately dispatched a copy of the editorial to LBJ. In response, LBJ wrote to Bill, "These have been somber hours. I wanted you to know that your letter and editorial comforted me greatly. How I wish I had the wise counsel of your father right now, for he was always a beneficial influence in my life." LBJ's lament about the absence of Will Hobby was a reference to Will's being near death and inaccessible by December 1963. LBJ added, "I am going to lean on you, Bill, for much help in the months ahead."[20]

By the beginning of 1964, it was clear to all who were close to him that Will Hobby was in his last days. He had long ago stopped going to his office at the *Post*. He rarely left his bed at the mansion on Remington Lane, and when he did, it was only with the help of his attendants, and he usually remained in his room. Bill and Diana's oldest children, Laura (now six) and Paul (now four), would occasionally spend the night at their grandparents' Shadyside mansion. Will's room was at the end of the hallway on the second floor of the house. "He was in a fairly narrow bed that was sort of high," Paul recalled, "but it wasn't a hospital bed in today's terms." Despite Will's fragile condition, "he'd encourage Laura and me to climb up on the end of the bed and he would laugh and play with us. We'd hear [Oveta's] heels clicking on the marble floors as she walked down the hallway to check on us. She would shoo us off the bed. 'Oh, gosh, what are you doing? You're going to hurt him.' He would wait until she was comfortably gone and then he would motion us back on the bed."[21]

Early in 1964, receiving word that the end was near, the Harris County Commissioners Court voted to honor the former governor with the naming of a new sixty-five-foot-long automobile ferryboat, to be used at the Lynchburg crossing of the Houston Ship Channel. On February 26, Oveta christened the *William P. Hobby* when the boat was launched at the Todd Shipyards on Greens Bayou. Jack Harris arranged to broadcast the launching ceremony live on KPRC-TV so that Will could watch from his bed.[22]

After lingering for more than three months, the end for the eighty-six-year-old Will Hobby came on the evening of June 6, 1964, when he suffered a stroke. His physician Mavis Kelsey pronounced him dead at 10:30 p.m., with Bill and Oveta at his bedside. Jessica was in San Antonio and unable to get to Houston in time. Bill immediately telephoned the news to the *Post*'s night desk, and the morning edition's front page was redone to announce Will's passing. Bill had his staff gather and publish comments about Will from several of his old friends. He also sent a letter with the news of his father's death to his former teacher John Davis, acknowledging what many who were close to "the Governor" must have felt: that Will's health "had been such for several years that his passing could not have been other than a release for him."[23]

Will Hobby's death was met with an outpouring of condolences to the Hobby family. Governor John Connally, who was still recovering from the gunshot wound he had received while riding in JFK's limousine on that tragic day in Dallas, declared a week of official mourning and ordered the lowering of the flags over state buildings to half-mast. President Johnson issued an official statement from the White House declaring, "Texas and the Nation are diminished by the loss of Governor Hobby. Throughout the last 30 years he was a wise, charitable, and loyal friend to me."[24]

Will's funeral was held on June 8 at 11:00 a.m. in the 1,500-seat, 125-year-old, Episcopalian Christ Church Cathedral in Houston. Pallbearers and executives of the *Houston*

Post and KPRC followed Will's flag-draped casket into the church. Because Will had complained to Oveta that most eulogies were pompous, none were delivered at his service. A silk US flag that had been displayed in his office at the *Post* for more than thirty years draped his casket. Before the casket was lowered into the grave, Jack Harris and funeral director George Lewis Jr. removed the flag and presented it to Oveta, who then handed it to Jessica and Bill. On July 2, less than one month after Will's death, the Houston City Council honored his legacy in an especially noteworthy way. The council voted to change the name of the city's commercial airport to William P. Hobby Airport.[25]

When Lyndon and Lady Bird Johnson, Oveta's friends of many years, moved into the White House after the horrific event of November 22, 1963, the Hobbys once again enjoyed a close connection to the presidency. Two days after LBJ's nomination in August 1964 to run for his own term as president, Johnson telephoned Oveta to invite her and Bill to a luncheon at the LBJ Ranch with his newly nominated vice presidential running mate, Minnesota senator Hubert Humphrey. During the call, Oveta told the president that she and Bill would soon publish an editorial endorsing his election. She also told him her intention to print a news story about Humphrey's visit to the ranch and the ticket's plans for the coming campaign. With Bill's ascension to the role of president of the *Post* after the passing of his father, the paper now had a new managing editor, Bill Woestendiek, whom Oveta and her son wanted to bring to the ranch to interview LBJ and Humphrey. If LBJ had no objection, Oveta would also send a *Post* photographer to the ranch to take photographs for Woestendiek's story. The photos would be featured prominently with the story. Obviously aware that the *Post*'s article would not be negative, LBJ gave his consent. The next morning, he sent a small air force JetStar to Houston to pick up Oveta, Woestendiek, George and Alice Brown, and Houston insurance company tycoon Gus Wortham and his wife, Lyndall. Bill was unable to go to the ranch because Diana, who was pregnant with their fourth child, Kate, was in the hospital recovering from an operation on the small veins in her legs. Shortly after Oveta and her party landed at the ranch, the *Post*'s photographer arrived and took pictures of LBJ and Humphrey as they stood under large oak trees by the Pedernales River and sat on horseback. The photo op was an exclusive for the *Post* for which Oveta told LBJ, "Thank you, dear. I'm very grateful."[26]

On August 30, the day after Oveta's visit to the LBJ Ranch, the *Post* published its editorial along with Woestendiek's news story and the photographs. Oveta asked Bill to write the editorial, whose headline declared, "For a Better USA—Vote for LBJ." Bill pulled a quote from the Democratic Party's 1964 platform as one of the *Post*'s reasons for opposing Goldwater, who had voted against the Civil Rights Act of 1964: "We are firmly pledged to continue the nation's march toward the goals of equal opportunity and equal treatment for all Americans regardless of race, creed, color, or national origin." LBJ, who had received his copy late that same morning, was delighted. He tried to call Oveta, but she was at the cemetery visiting Will's grave. He finally located her at Bill's house. "I just wanted to tell you that I didn't think it could have been better," the president enthused.

Telling Johnson that Bill had written the editorial, Oveta handed the telephone receiver to her son. LBJ complimented him on the editorial and the photographs that ran with it. The president was so happy with the coverage that he asked Bill to send him several copies of the newspaper. Humphrey also spoke with Bill, declaring the photo of him on horseback to be "the finest picture I've ever taken," adding that he wanted Bill to send copies to the newspapers in Minneapolis and Saint Paul. When Oveta got back on the phone, LBJ said that she should be pleased she got the photo scoop on *Time* and *Life* magazines, both of which were now demanding that the White House grant their photographers access to take similar photographs on the ranch, a request the president was ignoring. As expected, LBJ won a landslide victory over Senator Goldwater on November 3.[27]

CHAPTER 5

THE HOUSTON POST

At the time of Will Hobby's death in June of 1964, the *Houston Post* was continuing to prosper, along with the boomtown it covered. The newspaper continued to enjoy the largest circulation in Texas, with more than 220,000 subscribers at a time when the city's population was slightly less than one million. From spring 1964 until early fall 1965, the *Post* gained more new subscribers than in any comparable period in its history. As the *Post* grew in size, its influence in the Texas news media industry increased, making Oveta Culp Hobby and her friend Houston Harte—founder and head of the Harte-Hanks newspaper chain, which included the *San Antonio Express-News*—arguably the most influential individual newspaper publishers in the state, now that the *Houston Chronicle*'s Jesse Jones and the *Fort Worth Star-Telegram*'s Amon Carter Sr. had passed from the scene, and the *Dallas Morning News*'s ailing Ted Dealy wandered in the wilderness of the extreme right wing. The *Post*'s domination would be short-lived, however. The newspaper lost its lead to its chief competitor when the *Houston Chronicle* bought the *Houston Press* from the Scripps-Howard chain and closed it down in March 1964. The *Chronicle* grabbed the *Press*'s subscribers, which increased its circulation to over 250,000, and it added the *Press*'s most popular syndicated features. By late 1965 the *Chronicle* had taken a lead over the *Post* that it never lost. A year after Will's death, Oveta took her late husband's position as chairman of the *Houston Post* board and chief executive officer. She promoted Bill to her former job as president and executive editor and moved Jack Harris up to executive vice president of the Houston Post Company and president of its broadcast division.[1]

In May 1965 the *Post* received a Pulitzer Prize, the first ever won by a Houston newspaper. Native Iowan Gene Goltz, whom the *Post* had hired in 1962 as its suburban reporter, won the prize for a series of articles exposing decades of city hall corruption in Pasadena, a major oil-refining center on the north side of the Houston Ship Channel. Bill Hobby later noted that because the series had "enormous potential for libel," he sent each one of Goltz's stories to the *Post*'s lawyer, Jack Binion of the Butler & Binion law firm, who was Bill's godfather. After a thorough legal review, Binion cleared the series for publication. After the *Post* published the exposé, Pasadena mayor James Brammer and his lawyers demanded a meeting with Oveta, Bill, and *Post* managing editor William Gardner. The Hobbys and Gardner agreed to meet only if their attorney was also present, but Binion was called out of town and was unable to attend. Bill said later that Binion assured him that "there was nothing to worry about and gave me a magic wand to wave if the meeting got unpleasant." Brammer's lawyers had a tape recording of Goltz making highly critical statements about Brammer and claimed that the statements supported their charge that the exposé had libeled Brammer. When the lawyer played the tape, it upset and frightened managing editor Gardner. Bill then used the "magic wand" Binion had given him, informing Brammer's lawyers, "If your client thinks he has been libeled, you know where the courthouse is. Jack Binion will begin discovery Monday morning." Bill recalled, "I never heard from them again." He observed that "the last thing a crooked public official wants is to give subpoena power to a newspaper."[2]

Oveta and Bill's new managing editor, Bill Woestendiek, was a self-assertive and outspoken journalist who encouraged and supported aggressive investigative reporting. One of the first signs that Woestendiek and Oveta and Bill had differing definitions of investigative journalism and editorial freedom came in 1966, when the *Post* fired the politically liberal editorial cartoonist Thomas Darcy, whom Woestendiek had hired the year before. Darcy was an early critic of the Vietnam War, and he had frequently drawn unflattering cartoons of the Hobbys' good friend Lyndon Johnson, which Woestendiek claimed was the reason Oveta had ordered the cartoonist's dismissal. Darcy's firing signified that not all was well in the *Post*'s newsroom in the mid-1960s, despite its newly won Pulitzer. Tension between Woestendiek on one side and Oveta and Bill on the other escalated as Woestendiek claimed that Oveta was killing some op-ed columns he wanted to publish that were critical of LBJ. The brash managing editor also alleged that Bill had censored stories written by his investigative reporters that the Hobbys feared would anger their key advertisers.[3]

Woestendiek's complaints and his criticism of Oveta led to a predictable result: Bill Hobby fired him. The *Post* story about his departure, however, said he resigned. Oveta later charged that Woestendiek was "not a competent managing editor" and that he had been trying to get rid of longtime and highly valued employees of the news staff to replace them with people who would be loyal to him. A few years after Woestendiek's dismissal, an anonymous *Post* "insider" told *Texas Monthly* that Woestendiek was fired because he "popped off" to Oveta one too many times. Woestendiek, however, said he was fired because his philosophy of what a newspaper should be differed radically from Oveta's. With Woestendiek's firing, peace was soon restored in the *Post*'s newsroom, and the paper moved forward successfully, but it remained behind the *Houston Chronicle* in circulation.[4]

On January 19, 1965, Bill Hobby celebrated his thirty-third birthday, while his mother celebrated her sixtieth. In the eight years since he and Diana had moved to Houston to work in the "family business," as he termed it, Bill had worked for brief periods of time in most of the news positions at the newspaper, from reporter to managing editor. He was obviously the heir apparent, the chief in waiting, for the Hobby media companies. Bill's sister, Jessica, still in her twenties and married to Henry Catto, lived in San Antonio, where she was determined to follow an independent path that didn't include the *Houston Post* or the family's television and radio properties.[5]

At sixty, Oveta was as vital and energetic as ever, and she showed no signs of giving up control over the Hobby enterprises. She continued to run the *Post* with an iron grip, and there was no question in anyone's mind about who was in control. Nevertheless, Oveta generally stayed out of the paper's newsroom, unless it strayed into coverage of which she disapproved, but the editorial page was her exclusive domain. Bill was also a member of the editorial board, but he only played a token role there. Journalist Saralee Tiede became friends with some of the staff at the *Post* in the late 1960s. They made it clear to her that "Oveta was very much in charge of the *Post*. My friend told me that at editorial meetings she just dominated [Bill]. And if he brought something up, she could quickly be very dismissive of him." Laura Hobby thought that although her father had been "ready to take the paper probably in some riskier directions, probably in more aggressive editorial and investigative directions," Oveta's "position was we're a profitable, respected news organization, [so] why push the envelope?" Laura noted that at that time, Bill Hobby was still "a young man and smart and he is a true journalist at heart. And, you know, journalists want to get to the bottom of the story and tell the whole story, and that was not always possible while my grandmother was in charge."[6]

Despite Oveta's tight control over the *Post*'s editorial positions, there were occasions when Bill would go around his mother. When Albert Thomas, Houston's long-serving Democratic congressman, died in 1966, state representative and liberal Democrat Bob Eckhardt entered the race to fill the vacant congressional seat. Bill Hobby and Bob Eckhardt had become friends in the late 1950s when Bill was covering the legislature for the *Post*. During the 1966 congressional campaign, the Brown & Root Company worked hard to elect Eckhardt's opponent, conservative Larry McKaskle. Eckhardt was solidly pro-union, but Brown & Root's president, George R. Brown, hated the labor movement. Brown was also one of Oveta's closest friends. She published a strongly worded editorial in the *Post* endorsing McKaskle. When Bill learned, presumably at an editorial board meeting, that the *Post* was supporting McKaskle, he warned Eckhardt. Assuring Hobby that he understood the difficult position he was in, Eckhardt told him that he was going on a campaign boat ride on the Houston Ship Channel with the mayor of Baytown and some labor leaders. He wondered if the *Post* might give the event some positive coverage as a news item. Agreeing to this idea, Bill sent a reporter with a camera to shoot a photograph and write an objective story about Eckhardt's boat trip. The photo and the story were placed in a prominent location in the *Post*.[7]

It appears that Bill Hobby began to think more seriously sometime in 1965, possibly earlier, about establishing his own public identity and finding a place for himself separate from his mother. Paul Hobby believed his father's yearning to run for political office was his way of stepping away from Oveta's world. Bill's eventual run for lieutenant governor, Paul felt, was his father's way of "exerting himself and striking out on an independent path." Because of his family history, especially his beloved father's, Bill decided he would go into politics, not because he wanted to be a politician but because it was a necessary means to an end. As an introvert, Bill didn't savor the idea of campaigning and backslapping. He was a policy wonk who, as a lover of math, enjoyed tinkering with budget details, data, and statistics. He also had a genuine desire to continue his family's tradition of public service. He had grown up hearing his father reminisce favorably about his days as lieutenant governor and governor, and he had greatly enjoyed the short time he had covered the legislature for the *Post* and the months he had worked for Lieutenant Governor Ben Ramsey. As a result, Bill set his sights on playing a key role in state government as an elected official, taking the route his father had followed. He would run for lieutenant governor—possibly followed later by an election to the governorship.[8]

Consequently, early in 1965 Bill decided to quietly gauge possible public interest in his plan to run for office. He apparently leaked the idea to a prominent political journalist who would treat it as coming from an anonymous source. On February 9, Allen Duckworth, the veteran political editor of the *Dallas Morning News*, reported that Hobby was contemplating running for lieutenant governor in 1966. He cited his source as someone "closely associated with the Hobby family." It's not known if that direct source was Bill or if it was someone Bill asked to leak the news on his behalf, but it seems obvious Bill initiated it. He also didn't confirm or deny Duckworth's story.[9]

Duckworth's story didn't launch a "draft Bill Hobby for lieutenant governor" movement, but that wasn't the purpose of the leak. And Bill didn't receive any negative reactions. After the story was published, Bill vastly increased his public activities in 1965. He became a member of the board of the Texas Bill of Rights Foundation, the Texas Election Bureau, and the Texas Social Welfare Association. Governor John Connally appointed him to the board of regents of the University of Houston, an institution Hobby's family had long supported, which had recently become a state-supported school. For the second consecutive year, Columbia University named Bill one of the jurors on a thirty-five-member panel for the Pulitzer Prize for eight journalism categories. Each board membership was publicized by press releases, which newspapers across the state carried.[10]

Although Bill continued to struggle with his stutter, he accepted more speaking invitations than he had in the past. In May, for example, he addressed the Gulf Coast Press Association meeting in Galveston. The speech was an early indication of Hobby's political ambitions. Instead of focusing on news industry issues, his speech was a call for more investment in the state's public schools, an early sign of his interest in issues related to education, which would be one of his causes while he was in elected office. He pointed out that the national ranking of "wonderful, booming, progressive Texas" for investment in education had fallen in the past quarter century from twentieth to thirty-seventh: "In short, we are going backward at an alarming rate." He argued that there were two reasons why. "The first is our failure to keep pace in education. The second is the structure of the economy in Texas." The basis of the state's economy would become another policy theme he would continue in the future. He pointed out that growth had declined in both the agricultural and the oil sectors and that the only economic growth in the future would be in science and technology instead of in traditional manufacturing. "The future will require us, not so much to exploit natural resources, as to develop human resources." He argued that failure to do so would raise the state's social welfare costs because of an increase in the number of citizens who were poorly educated. "Every dollar that we 'save' by not spending it on education in this state, we are going to spend many times over in providing relief payments in the future to people who are unemployable just because they have not been well-enough educated to hold a job." Bill also showed foresight by predicting, years before the Reagan revolution, that state government would become more powerful as the federal government continued to look to the states to take more responsibility in such areas as social welfare and education.[11]

At the annual meeting of the Texas Social Welfare Association at Houston's Shamrock Hotel in November, Bill repeated his warning about the economic transformation Texas would soon face and the crucial importance education would play in meeting the challenges the transformation would produce. Bill also argued that Texas had to expand and better fund its programs to help the poor. In a reference to President Johnson's war on poverty, Bill proclaimed, "A citizen who is underfed, who malnutrition has made susceptible to disease, cannot be a contributor to the great society, but must be a drain on it."[12]

This theme of the crucial importance of education and its relationship to the transformation of Texas's economy from commodities to human resources would be one that Bill would continue to stress in his speeches for many years to come. One of his consistent refrains was that Texas was "going backward" because of the lack of state investment in education. As a result of this flurry of public appearances and his advocacy for improving public education in the state, as well as his active involvement in a wide range of civic and business enterprises, the Houston Junior Chamber of Commerce selected Bill as one of the Outstanding Young Texans for 1965.[13]

In the fall of 1965, President Johnson and Lady Bird drew the Hobbys ever closer to their circle. On September 4, Oveta, Bill, and Diana accepted the president's invitation to fly with George and Alice Brown to the LBJ Ranch to go boating on Lake Lyndon B. Johnson for the Labor Day holiday. The trip to the lake also included Jack Valenti, KTBC-TV general manager J. C. Kellam, federal judge Homer Thornberry, and influential entertainment lawyer Arthur B. Krim. After sunset while still at the lake, Lady Bird heard "a stir of excitement and then squeals of laughter" in the distance. A Secret Service agent told her, "The President has Mrs. Hobby and Diana in the little [amphibious] car." Without telling Oveta and Diana that the blue convertible was also an amphibious vehicle, LBJ drove them down a steep road that led straight to the lake. He yelled, "Oh, oh, our brakes don't work," as the car entered the lake and the water rose to within three or four inches below the windows. He then hit the switch and they motored around in the lake. Oveta and Diana "squealed," Lady Bird wrote in her diary, "and Lyndon enjoyed himself hugely." Afterward, Bill Hobby told his wife and his mother that at LBJ's urging, he and Arthur Krim had tried to follow the amphibious vehicle as it headed down to the lake, but they took the wrong gravel road and missed seeing them go into the water. "Damn it," LBJ responded. "I wanted . . . to see what [Bill Hobby] would do if he saw the President and his mother about to drown." That night after the adventure on the lake, helicopters transported the Johnsons and their guests back to the LBJ Ranch. Bill and Diana Hobby and the Thornberrys flew back to Austin with the Browns, while Oveta remained with the Johnsons.[14]

LBJ wasn't finished with the Hobbys, however. Oveta accepted President Johnson's requests for her to serve on a series of task forces, committees, and commissions in his administration. The president tapped Bill for service in his administration much less often than he did Oveta, but Bill wasn't a stranger in the White House. In March 1966, LBJ appointed him to the newly formed National Citizens Advisory Committee on Vocational Rehabilitation. The sixteen-member committee, chaired by Dr. Howard A. Rusk, director of New York University's Institute of Rehabilitation Medicine, was charged with studying the effectiveness of joint federal-state vocational rehabilitation programs in "restoring the disabled to useful and meaningful lives." Because committee members included several corporate executives, such as ABC television network president Leonard Goldenson, whose business responsibilities precluded active involvement, the committee's staff members conducted the basic work and reported their findings in reports to the committee. As a result, Bill was little involved in the committee's work. However, he did join with his fellow committee members in approving its final report to the secretary of the Department of Health, Education, and Welfare, which to no one's surprise found many programs to be inadequate and underfunded at every level. The committee's work ultimately led to the passage of amendments to the Rehabilitation Act of 1954, which included the expansion of the federal grant program to support special projects to improve rehabilitation services at the state level.[15]

LBJ also included Bill in his campaign to use the news media to raise public support for the war in Vietnam and to counter the antiwar movement. Bill attended a conference at the White House in April 1967, where LBJ tried to persuade newspaper and news magazine editors that all was well in Vietnam. The president brought General William Westmoreland, the commander of US forces in Vietnam, back to Washington to make a presentation at the meeting. Westmoreland claimed that the United States was winning the war militarily, but that "unpatriotic" antiwar criticism on the home front was threatening that effort. Bill Hobby, whose previous service as a naval officer inclined him to give credence to the military's point of view, accepted Westmoreland's argument. When Bill returned to Houston, he briefed Oveta on Westmoreland's statements. She had recently returned from a trip to South Vietnam as a member of a task force to study how a version of LBJ's Great Society could be implemented there to defeat Communism. Oveta's own strong promilitary views also predisposed her to agree with General Westmoreland's accusations. She approved an editorial in the *Post* denouncing the antiwar movement as "giving aid and comfort to the enemy." Bill proudly sent a copy of the editorial to LBJ the day before it was published to show that the president had his and Oveta's solid support.[16]

In February 1967, *Ramparts* magazine, an antiwar New Left publication, printed an exposé revealing a secret program of the Central Intelligence Agency that provided covert funds to the National Student Association. When the *New York Times* followed up on the *Ramparts* exposé, its own investigative reporters discovered that over a period of twenty years, the CIA had funneled approximately $500 million of secretly appropriated congressional funds not only to the National Student Association but also to various foundations that in turn gave the money to nongovernment organizations, including the Crusade for Freedom, which then granted the funds to Radio Free Europe. The purpose for hiding congressional funding for Radio Free Europe in this convoluted manner was to make it appear that the media organization, which broadcast news and information to the Communist nations in Eastern Europe, was independent of US government control. The story in the *Times* revealed that the Hobby Foundation was among several foundations that had served as conduits for CIA funding to the Crusade for Freedom, which falsely claimed that the donations it raised from the public were the main source of funding for Radio Free Europe.[17]

Oveta had been among the original members of the Crusade for Freedom board when it was organized in 1950. In addition to joining the Crusade, she offered the Hobby Foundation, the family's philanthropic foundation, as a secret conduit to channel CIA money to overseas projects. When the *New York Times* asked Oveta for an interview about the Hobby Foundation's connections to the CIA, she asked Bill to respond. Bill had no apologies to make about the foundation's secret work with the CIA. Not only did he have a background in Naval Intelligence, his brother-in-law, Donald Morris, had been a CIA agent for seventeen years. Accordingly, Bill gave the *Times* one of his typically short, but forthright, statements. "The Hobby Foundation had for several years cooperated with the CIA in funding projects in the national interest," Hobby said. "We are proud to have been of service to our government in these matters and remain ready to cooperate in any way we can." Bill's unapologetic response ended the matter.[18]

Continuing his effort to persuade the press to print more positive news about the Vietnam War, LBJ invited Bill Hobby to the White House on September 6, 1967, to participate in a meeting with *Dallas Morning News* publisher Joe Dealy, *Dallas Times*

Herald publisher James Chambers, and prominent Dallas attorney Eugene Locke, who was serving as deputy ambassador to South Vietnam. Joined later by Texas congressman J. J. "Jake" Pickle, LBJ's appointment secretary Jim Jones, and lawyer and lobbyist Jake Jacobsen, the group flew that afternoon on Air Force One from Washington to Randolph Air Force Base near San Antonio, from where they were flown in a small JetStar to the LBJ Ranch. After being greeted by Lady Bird, LBJ gave his guests a tour of the ranch before dinner, when they were joined by the Johnsons' daughter Lynda, who was accompanied by her fiancé, Chuck Robb. The extent of influence this gathering of three urban Texas newspaper publishers had on actual news coverage of the war in Vietnam can only be surmised, but future events indicated that it had little to none. We do know, however, that the first lady enjoyed the group's visit to the ranch. Before going to bed that night, Lady Bird wrote in her diary, "I have never spent a more fascinating day."[19]

A month after the trip to Washington and the Texas Hill Country with LBJ, the Hobbys announced plans to build a two-hundred-thousand-square-foot headquarters for the *Houston Post* at the corner of the Southwest Freeway and I-610. The *Post*'s offices and printing facility on Polk Street had long needed updating. The newsroom was shabby and crowded, the building badly needed repairs, the printing equipment was out of date, and the neighborhood around the building had long been in decline. The Hobbys determined that it would be more cost effective to construct a new building than to renovate the *Post*'s old home. They also decided to build their new facility in a more prestigious and visible location and to hire an architectural firm capable of designing a landmark structure. The *Post* had continued to be highly profitable, which provided the financial resources needed to carry out the plan. Once the decision had been made but not announced publicly, they began to search for a suitable location. Bill noticed the future location by accident. "When we were looking for a new home for the *Post*," Bill later recalled, "I noticed a for-sale sign [on a lot on Southwest Freeway] and realized that the telephone number was that of Rice University's." He learned that the property had been donated to Rice by the late Herman Brown and his brother George R. Brown, a Hobby family friend and Rice University patron. To enhance the property's value, George Brown had built a street connecting it to existing road thruways at no cost to the university. Bill called Rice to find out what the university was asking for the property. The price seemed reasonable, so Bill brought the idea to Oveta. After inspecting the twenty-one-acre site and consulting with her business advisors, she agreed to make the purchase.[20]

It took three years to design and construct the facility. Although Bill was much involved in this project, Oveta remained in charge. After many months of planning, including working out a design by the firm of Wilson, Morris, Crain & Anderson, who were the architects of the Astrodome, the *Post*'s new campus was finally ready for occupancy late in 1970. The complex consisted of seven buildings, most of which were connected, containing a total of more than 440,000 square feet. The four-story main building fronted one of Houston's busiest freeways. With its eight turreted, exposed-concrete modules that some compared to grain elevators, some Houstonians soon began referring to the *Post*'s new home as Fort Hobby.[21]

By the late 1960s, Bill and Diana were beginning to emerge from Oveta's shadow to become publicly recognized figures in their own right, at least in Texas. That emergence was symbolized in April 1968 by a profile on Bill and Diana published as part of *Vogue* magazine's special issue on Texas, which celebrated the opening of HemisFair '68, a world's fair in San Antonio. The issue also featured other prominent Texans, including Bill's sister and brother-in-law, Jessica and Henry Catto; Governor John Connally and his wife, Nellie; Houston heart surgeon Dr. Michael DeBakey; and Houston art patrons John and Dominique de Menil. *Vogue*'s writer observed that Bill and Diana, who posed together for a photograph in their "simple, rambling" home, were "known throughout Texas and beyond, partly because he is the executive editor and president of the impressive *Houston Post*, she partly because she is its book editor. Together, they are good-looking, reticent, laughing, solid, intelligent, with an easy rein on power."[22]

In July 1968 Bill gained additional media attention when he traveled with thirty-two other news executives and columnists on Pan American Airways' inaugural flight from New York City's JFK Airport to Moscow. The invitation from Pan Am was sent to Oveta, who had traveled on Pan Am's first scheduled round-the-world trip in 1947, but she asked Bill to go in her stead. His travel companions included *TV Guide*'s publisher, Walter Annenberg; newspaper columnist Art Buchwald; the *Fort Worth Star-Telegram*'s publisher, Amon Carter Jr.; the *Los Angeles Times*' publisher, Otis Chandler; *Look* magazine's publisher, Gardner Cowles; and *Life* photojournalist Stan Wayman. The trip, which was featured in a cover story in *Life*, marked the opening of direct commercial air service between the Soviet Union and the United States. In Moscow, Bill stayed with some of the American entourage in the Rossiya Hotel, said to be Moscow's finest. He also visited Leningrad, where he attended an opera, despite that not being one of his favored forms of entertainment. He flew back to New York City from Leningrad and then reunited with Diana at Forest Home, their farm in North Carolina.[23]

As the presidential election approached in the fall of 1968, political observers in Texas speculated about whether the *Houston Post* would endorse the ticket of LBJ's vice president, Hubert Humphrey, and his running mate, Maine senator Edmund Muskie, or that of Eisenhower's former vice president, Richard Nixon, and his surprising choice for a running mate, the relatively unknown Maryland governor Spiro Agnew. The question was raised because of the potential clash between the Hobbys' intimate friendship with Lyndon Johnson and Oveta's close affiliation with and service in Dwight Eisenhower's presidential administration and her longtime identification with the Republican Party.

As it turned out, however, it was an easy decision for Oveta to make. Deeply influenced by what she judged to be the disgraceful treatment of LBJ by an ungrateful Democratic Party that seemed fatally wounded and paralyzed by the antiwar movement and the political and social violence that had engulfed the country, Oveta threw her support behind Richard Nixon. Although she had never been enthusiastic about

Nixon as a person, she had much more in common with his political views than those of Hubert Humphrey. Bill Hobby, who continued to identify as a Democrat, supported Humphrey and continued his close connection to the Johnson administration. He and Diana attended receptions in the White House early in 1968. In May, two months after Johnson announced he would not run for another term, they were overnight guests at the White House. Bill's sister, Jessica, also continued to support the Democratic Party, although her husband, Henry Catto, maintained his affiliation with the Republican Party and backed Nixon. Oveta agreed to serve as vice chair of the Eisenhower Team for Nixon-Agnew, but she was little involved in the ebb and flow of the campaign.[24]

As Oveta approached her seventies, she was increasingly the subject of rumors that she had ceded control of the *Post* to Bill and that she spent most of her time engaged in her social and intellectual life. When a magazine writer mentioned the rumors to Oveta shortly after she celebrated her sixty-sixth birthday in 1971, she was quick to dismiss them. "You better believe I run this newspaper," Oveta said. "Regardless of what some people think, I am still the chief executive and I make the decisions around here." An example of Oveta's insistence on making the important decisions at the *Post*, including its editorials, occurred in June 1971 when, over the objections of the White House, the *New York Times* published the Defense Department's classified history of the war in Vietnam, which was known to the public as the Pentagon Papers. Oveta decided to print an editorial in the *Post* criticizing the *Times* for publishing a classified national security document. Veteran *Post* reporter and politically liberal editorial board member George Fuermann strongly disagreed with Oveta's decision. Knowing that Bill shared his view on the matter, Fuermann persuaded Bill to go with him to try to dissuade Oveta from printing the editorial. When they met privately with Oveta, she replied that the *Post* would publish the editorial and she would sign it, which is exactly what she did.[25]

With their daughter Kate's birth in 1964, Bill and Diana Hobby's family was complete. That same year, Laura was six, Paul was four, and Andrew was two. The period from Kate's birth through the 1970s were the years the Hobby children grew up. Of course, with six years' difference between the oldest child, Laura, who was born in 1958, and Kate, the youngest, the four Hobby children would leave the family nest at different times, but their recollections of childhood provide an intimate picture of the private side of Bill's and Diana's personalities and the dynamics of their family life when they lived in Houston, as well as for the relatively brief period later when they resided in Austin.

After Kate's birth, Diana, who'd had four kids in six years and continued to work as the book editor for the *Houston Post*, was often drawn into other concerns at the paper. These included dealing with complaints from influential elites when the paper was perceived to fall short in its coverage of literary events in Houston. In May 1969, for example, wealthy art patron John de Menil wrote Bill to express his displeasure that the *Post* had failed to adequately cover the Black Arts Festival sponsored by him and his wife, Dominique, which had featured the poet LeRoi Jones. "We had a great American poet in town Friday. He made a speech, aggressively black—and so intelligent.

I would like to share with you my regret that the *Post* did not mention the visit of LeRoi Jones, a writer of whom Americans can be proud." Bill passed the letter to Diana for a response. Her reply included a clip of the *Post*'s story about the Black Arts Festival. She explained that the *Post*'s reporter had tried to set up an interview with Jones but was unsuccessful. John de Menil responded that trying to arrange an interview with LeRoi Jones would have been "much too difficult" for the *Post*'s reporter. "The thing was to be in the auditorium and to listen. The speech was more informative than any interview could possibly have been. And the poems he read and pounded and chanted: that was extraordinary. It would have been a revelation for a perceptive reporter, as it was for Dominique and me."[26]

As a working woman with young children, Diana dealt with the perennial issues other working women faced then as well as now: how to maintain a home, shepherd four little kids (one of them an infant), and continue to work at an intellectually satisfying job that brought her much enjoyment. Despite money not being an issue, it seemed "odd," as Laura later noted, that her parents resisted the idea of hiring domestic help to end the "general chaos at our house." Laura noted that Bill and Diana "grew up with nannies and drivers and cooks. Both sets of grandparents had household help and help with the kids, so it seemed that it would be a natural solution for mother to have done the same thing." Diana's parents had divorced when she was young, and her father, Laurence Stallings, had essentially abandoned the family, so any reluctance Diana had about a nanny for the children might have stemmed from her childhood. Bill might also have had mixed feelings about a nanny. As we have seen, he too had nannies while his mother was managing the *Post* with his father in the 1930s and a governess while Oveta was in Washington, DC, commanding the Women's Army Corps during World War II. The result, as he later acknowledged, was that he always felt much closer to his father than his mother.[27]

Diana's household situation was eventually resolved. "It was my grandmother, as usual, who took hold of the situation," Laura recalled. Around the time of Kate's birth, Oveta contacted an agency in London to engage a proper British nanny to help Diana. The woman she employed was Joan Robins. "It was a good move," Laura observed. "She was British old school, no nonsense, in a fun way. But it was a really good thing for all of us." Paul also recalled that his mother "ran the family" but that it became too much. "Joan Robins was around for all of my growing up," Paul said. "She was sort of house manager and nanny." She remained with the Hobbys for thirty years.[28]

Despite Joan's firm hand, life in the Hobby household remained comfortably informal and cozy, if somewhat frenzied, with four small, energetic kids and dogs running around. "We had a pack of dogs that lived with us forever," Laura said. "Horses and dogs were a huge part of Dad's life and a huge part of our lives. And our home was very much his happy place." The house was often filled with neighborhood kids and a diverse group of visitors to Houston whom Diana invited to stay at the Hobbys' home while they were in town. Laura described the situation as "an open-door policy. Anyone and everybody were welcome." Diana's overnight guests included members of the Harvard track team working out at Rice University in Houston's warmer weather late in the winter, patients receiving treatment at the nearby MD Anderson Cancer Center, and campaigning politicians.[29]

Bill's meetings with politicians often took place in the library. That was also where the family's television was located, which meant the kids would often watch their favorite shows while their father was trying to have discussions with his visitors, including Congressman Bob Krueger, who was campaigning for the US Senate. Before entering politics, Krueger had been a professor of English at Duke University. Paul was attending St. John's School, and Krueger would edit his school papers after a long campaign day. "That was very sweet," Paul said. "I'll never forget it."[30]

Joan Robins did her best to moderate the Hobbys' domestic style of laid-back disorder, especially Diana's open-house policy. For example, Robins rarely knew to whom Diana had given keys to the house. Speaking with a tone of frustration, she would tell the Hobby children that if they were ever locked out of the house, they should just wave down anybody on the street, "because your mother has given them a key." Diana and the kids usually spent part of the summer at Forest Home in North Carolina. While they were away, Robins would have all the house door locks changed. When the family returned, Robins would give them a new set of keys. Joan also dealt with a constantly ringing telephone, because Bill insisted on keeping the house telephone number listed in the phone book. "Dad thought that's what you were supposed to do as a newspaper publisher," Paul noted. "As a result, we grew up with a lot of drunken phone calls and death threats and stuff like that." Laura admitted that it was "barely organized chaos. I don't know how we got to school every day. I still marvel at that one. But we did."[31]

The easygoing but simultaneously hectic domestic environment at the Hobby house on South Boulevard was also reflected in the laissez-faire manner in which Bill and Diana guided their children. Laura and Paul characterized their parents as "kind of hippies with nice clothes. They had social obligations, and they had family appearances to keep up. But in their hearts, they were a progressive kind of hippie-style parents and hands-off to a fault sometimes." The Hobby children eventually realized that their friends had much more structured lives than they did. "There was very little supervision," Laura recalled. "But we knew they had very high expectations that we would do well in school, and that we would be kind and polite to others." Paul confirmed his sister's point that light supervision of their activities didn't mean attention was not paid to manners. "My mother wouldn't let us brag," Paul stated, "and my father wouldn't let us whine." But other than that, there was no "micromanaging." Generally, Bill and Diana's parenting style was, as Laura later noted, "benign neglect, in an incredibly loving way, and generous." Kate agreed, noting that "there wasn't a lot of helicopter parenting." Kate also stressed that her parents created an atmosphere at home that discouraged any feelings that she and her siblings were better than others. "I never felt entitled at all," she said. "I felt like we had to go work our butts off and be us. It was more like, go to school and do your work and be a good person." Paul said that one result of Bill and Diana's raising him to be independent was that as a teenager he was never particularly rebellious. "I didn't really have anything to rebel against," he noted. "I was trusted."[32]

Bill and Diana's parenting might not have been like most households in this era, but in other ways their individual roles were more traditional. "Dad was the head of the household," Paul observed. "He could be playful, but in general, he was a pretty stoic, removed figure doing his man thing." Kate said that when her father came home from work, "we'd have dinner, and he would ask me about my day. He was always very supportive about whatever I was doing. And that was about it. I don't really remember getting a lot of advice from him. That was definitely more my mother's role. I would say he was a busy father, but he wasn't neglectful. He was kind and supportive, but you know, he wasn't going to show up at all of my soccer games. But that didn't bother me. It didn't even really occur to me that he was supposed to be there." Kate stated that her mother was "the one who drove us everywhere and there was always at least one friend in the car with us, sometimes more." Laura remembered that when her mother was book editor, she worked in an office at the old Houston Post Building on Dowling Street. "We would go to the office with her, and we would sit at her desk and type, which was very fun for us."[33]

Despite their father spending much of his time on the family business, and later in politics and state government, Bill's children recalled that one of his favorite activities was to take them to breakfast at a drugstore near their home. "We often walked," Laura said, "especially on weekends." Bill also was the family disciplinarian, although he seems to have played that role infrequently, and it was largely symbolic. Laura remembered that she and her siblings would occasionally have typical preadolescent fights in the back seat of the family car while Bill was driving. "My father literally had a horse crop, above the visor on the driver's side. And if we were fighting, he would reach up and take his horse crop and just sort of swing towards the backseat while driving down the road. He couldn't even really make contact, but we got the message."[34]

Diana oversaw the Hobbys' social life, mainly because Bill was shy and quiet by nature and not one for small talk. "My father does not have the art of what you would think a lot of people in the world of politics have to have," Kate noted. "If he doesn't feel like he needs to say something then he won't say anything. And then my mother would fill in the gap. She'd chatter away when he was tired of talking." During the children's youth, Oveta also helped maintain a social life for Bill and Diana. Laura recalled that her family's entire "social life was really because of my mother and my grandmother. My father had people that worked for him that would help organize lunches and dinners, but that was not his strong suit, that was my mother's. She gathered people together, and he loved those gatherings, having dinners with interesting people. But that was really my mother who did that."[35]

The most important recreational interest for the entire Hobby family was horseback riding. It was a family legacy that went back at least as far as Oveta's father, Ike Culp, who had owned a stable of horses and had been an expert trainer. Oveta and Will were both skilled equestrians who passed their love of horses on to Bill and his sister, Jessica, who also became accomplished riders. When Jessica was a teenager, she frequently participated in horse-riding competitions and shows. Bill became a certified horse-show judge and a foxhunter. Diana, who grew up surrounded by horses at Forest Home, became a talented equestrian at a very early age. A mutual love of horses seems to have been one factor, among many, that played a role in the attraction Bill and Diana had felt for each other when they met in Washington, DC. Considering this history, it's no surprise that Bill and Diana's children continued their family's tradition.[36]

As Laura later recalled when talking about the family's recreational activities, "We rode horses, and we attended horse shows. That was our extracurricular activity." Ginny and Charlie Zimmerman, whom Bill and Diana met in Virginia early in their marriage, played a key role in providing professional guidance and supporting the efforts of the Hobby kids as they learned how to ride and handle horses. The Zimmermans later moved to Houston, where they ran the Edge Park Stables near Houston's Memorial Park in an area now occupied by the Houston Polo Club. When the kids were growing up, Bill spent much of his leisure time riding horses on the grounds adjacent to the stables. "It was a wonderful, happy environment for my father," Laura recalled. Laura was particularly close to the Zimmermans. Charlie was her godfather, and she was equally devoted to his wife, Ginny.[37]

Bill and Diana also took their kids on vacation trips in the summer, most often to Forest Home. Laura recalled that the only times she ever flew in an airplane as a little kid were the flights to North Carolina. "We'd get dressed up and fly to Atlanta and then we would board a Piedmont Airlines flight to Raleigh or Greensboro, North Carolina, and then drive to Forest Home." Diana would remain in North Carolina with the children, while Bill would come and go from Houston. When the children were older, the Hobbys took family trips to Pinedale, Wyoming, near the Tetons, where they rode horses into the Bridger Wilderness. They also traveled as a family many times to Colorado to ski in Aspen, where Jessica and Henry Catto had a ranch. At least two memorable trips were made to Manhattan, New York. "My father loved Broadway plays—musicals, really," Laura said. "He was not an opera, symphony, or a ballet fan." They timed their travel to New York to coincide with the National Horse Show at Madison Square Garden, which they also attended. "Those were the only trips my father ever really initiated," Laura recalled. Although Bill enjoyed trips to mountainous regions, beaches held no attraction for him. Diana enjoyed the beach and would take the kids to Galveston, but Bill skipped those trips. However, whenever the family traveled to Corpus Christi to enjoy the beach at Padre Island, Bill would go with them because they stayed with the Ed Harte family. Harte was the publisher of the *Corpus Christi Caller-Times* and the son of newspaper magnate Houston Harte, a longtime friend of Will and Oveta. Bill visited with Ed Harte while Diana and the kids enjoyed the sun and the sand.[38]

The most exciting trips were to Ireland, which the Hobbys tried to take annually.

"My parents had a whole life in Ireland," Laura said. One trip to Ireland was made in January 1968, when they stayed in County Clare while they hunted foxes in the ruins of abandoned abbeys. In a postcard to John Davis, Diana wrote that the abbeys were "fox-factories. You can usually flush three or four out of a good run, with hounds pouring after them through the windows and doorways. We shall have hunted two weeks straight when we head home from Dublin." Diana, a Yeats scholar, was excited to add that they had visited Thoor Ballylee Castle at Gort in County Galway, where William Butler Yeats had once lived.[39]

Oveta continued to be a major presence in the family in these years, especially with her grandchildren. That was particularly the case for Laura because she was the oldest of the children and therefore had the opportunity to be around Oveta longer than her brothers and sister, although Paul was not far behind Laura in that regard. "Our grandmother was ever present in our lives," Laura said. "We saw her if not every day, probably twice a week, sometimes more. I had a very comfortable, happy, relaxed relationship with her." Laura and Paul recalled that when Oveta stopped by their house after work, she would check to see that they were doing their homework. "I don't think you can describe Oveta as the grandmother that made you cookies. She was very formal and always perfectly turned out," Kate said, "but she was always very interested in all her grandchildren. She wanted to know what we were doing and where we were headed."[40]

Throughout the 1960s, Bill saw Oveta almost daily at the *Houston Post* offices, which included the weekly meetings of the *Post*'s editorial board and the KPRC executive management. Diana also visited frequently with her mother-in-law in person or on the telephone. On weekdays after work, when Oveta was being driven from the Post Building back to her mansion on Remington Lane, she often had her driver stop at Bill and Diana's house, where she had drinks with Diana and Joan Robins. Oveta and Diana shared many interests, including gardening, performing arts such as ballet and opera, and literature.[41]

The kids also often spent weekends at Oveta's mansion—Laura more often than the others. The Shadyside mansion was less than a mile from Bill and Diana's house, so the kids were able to ride their bikes to see their grandmother and to enjoy the property's amenities, including a swimming pool, greenhouse, and tennis court, all of which Paul described as "utopian." Kate recalled that she and her siblings would ride their bikes across busy Bissonnet Street and then sneak through the large backyard of a house in Shadyside to visit Oveta's pool. The mansion itself held its own attractions. As a young girl, Laura loved to go upstairs to the third floor to admire and try on Oveta's many fashionable ball gowns.[42]

When the grandkids visited Oveta, they also experienced a much more controlled environment than they had at home. Oveta was the one person in the family who was a micromanager, and she felt an obligation to instruct. Laura recalled that her grandmother planned every minute of the day when Laura and her siblings stayed with her. "My grandmother would correct our diction, our manners, our wardrobe, my skin, our weight," Laura recalled. "There was no area in which she felt like she needed to hold back." Kate had the same memory. "God forbid you would ever say something grammatically incorrect. She would immediately correct you, although in a loving way." Paul later noted that Oveta was "never a warm and fuzzy, grandmotherly type, although she would be playful at times, and she had a dry sense of humor."[43]

An example of Oveta's understated wit appears in a letter she wrote to Paul when he graduated from the University of Virginia. She apparently dictated the letter to one of her assistants at the *Post*, who typed it with a script font. Paul recalled that the letter expressed her "congratulations on the occasion of your graduation from the University of Virginia. I find you thoroughly acceptable as a grandson." Paul showed the letter to his fraternity brothers, "who got cookies and stuff from their grandmother and, they're going, no way, you made that up. And I would say, nope!" One of Paul's friends suggested that Oveta was obviously the ultimate professional woman, businesslike and even militaristic, but in private she must be much different. "And I would answer: 'No, not really.' That was the way she really was." Despite Oveta's occasional aloof manner and frequent instructions to her grandchildren about proper behavior, appearance, and speaking, it appears not to have generated any lasting resentments, especially with Laura, who would work professionally with her grandmother after she earned her law degree.[44]

Oveta also directed the Hobby family's holiday traditions, especially Christmas and Easter. Bill and Diana and the children opened Christmas presents in their house on South Boulevard. Afterward, they dressed and went to church, followed by a luxurious lunch at Oveta's mansion. The Hobbys also observed Easter together at Oveta's place. "She had the best Easter egg hunts in the world," Kate recalled. "She of course would have her helpers dye the Easter eggs and plant them in her incredible yard. My grandmother organized and prepared it all. And we had a ball. My cousins, the Cattos, would come over from San Antonio and we would hunt Easter eggs together."[45]

Attending church services on Christmas and Easter with Oveta was a tradition, but attendance on normal Sundays was hit or miss. "We were members of Christ Church Cathedral growing up," Paul said. "But we didn't actually go to church on Sunday very much, because we were always at a horse show somewhere." Oveta frequently took her grandchildren to services at Christ Church, located in downtown Houston, and Bill and Diana—more often Diana—would sometimes accompany them. The Hobbys all self-identified as "high-church Episcopalians" who were attracted to the rituals and formality of establishment Anglican tradition. Diana, especially later in her life, frequently attended services by herself at nearby Palmer Memorial Episcopal. "My father really would only go when my mom or my grandmother made him," Paul said. "But he would tell you that his Episcopal faith is just one of the parts of who he is. And that was true. It seemed that there always were Episcopalian priests and other church officials in our lives. My father had a great religious education at St. Albans, and he can, to this day, quote more tracts of the Bible than I can. But he dislikes hypocrisy in religion.

The Christian Moral Majority people were always ugly and opposed him in politics. I have tried to get him to distinguish between the church and personal faith, and I'm not sure I've gotten anywhere." Because his father was a graduate of St. Albans School in Washington, DC, and had maintained connections with the institution and some of the faculty, particularly John Davis, there was some pressure on Paul to attend high school there. "My godfather, John Davis, was very close to my family," Paul noted, "so it was always the plan that I would go to St. Albans." Occasionally, Bill and Diana sent Paul to Washington to spend long weekends with Davis with the thought that the experience might entice him to transfer from St. John's School to St. Albans. "When I'd come back from my trip, they would ask me if I had a good time," Paul recalled. "I would answer, 'Sure, I had a great time.' And they'd ask, 'Well don't you want to apply to St. Albans?' I'd say, 'Thanks, but no. I'm doing great at St. John's, and I like my life in Houston.'"[46]

As Oveta spent more of her time on the various Hobby media properties, Bill and Diana became more involved in the daily operation of the *Post*. Bill enjoyed a good relationship with the *Post*'s news staff, and he was loyal to those who were loyal to the paper. For example, Bill deeply respected Felton West, a top-notch political reporter who held several positions at the *Post* as an employee for more than fifty years, including city editor, Austin bureau chief, columnist, and Washington bureau chief. When Bill sent him to Washington to be the *Post*'s bureau chief, West tried to buy a house but lacked the money for a down payment. When he decided to leave the *Post*'s retirement plan so he could tap the money for a down payment, Bill found out about it from the manager of the fund. Bill persuaded West to leave his retirement money in the newspaper's retirement system. He gave West an interest-free loan to make it possible for him to buy the house. After West retired, he wrote a letter to Bill, recalling, "Except for your action, I might never have saved my money for retirement and had nothing to supplement Social Security." West wrote the letter a month before he died in 2005. Felton ended the letter with, "I love you and Diana and I loved your mother, who was always very nice to me."[47]

After Bill was elected president of the Texas Daily Newspaper Association in 1971, he was profiled in the association's *Round-Up* newsletter. The story described Bill as an unassuming and informal thirty-nine-year-old who drove "a Ford, smokes Roi-Tan cigars, trods across the carpeted city room in ancient Naval issue black shoes and is called 'Bill' by everyone from copy boy to corporate vice president." The reporter followed Bill as he attended the afternoon news conference and "afterwards lingers awhile with Ed Hunter, the *Post*'s managing editor, mulling aloud over the morning's paper and the afternoon's competition. Then, clipboard in hand, he wanders through the city room, antenna attuned, as the newsroom staff of 155 reporters, deskmen, photographers, critics, librarians put out another edition of the *Houston Post*." The story noted that Bill "worries about the state's poor, its dirty water, and polluted air, and its restless students." Bill told the newsletter writer that an "aggressive newspaper can obviously exert some influence over the way a community grows. It can exert some leadership in environment and public ethics." When the writer told Bill that it was obvious he enjoyed his work, his answer was revealing in its reference to the military job he had been reluctant to give up. "I really never wanted to do anything else, except when I was in Naval Intelligence."[48]

As it turned out, Bill Hobby did want to do something else.

CHAPTER 6

THE CAMPAIGN OF 1972

There are conflicting versions of exactly when Bill Hobby decided to run for lieutenant governor of Texas. Over the years, Hobby made contradictory statements about when he made the decision. In some interviews he gave late in life, he inexplicably stated that he hadn't thought about being a candidate until he decided to run for lieutenant governor in 1971. For example, when Hobby gave an interview for an oral history project in 2007, the interlocuter asked if he had considered running for lieutenant governor before 1972. Hobby replied, "No, I had not run for anything before and had not really considered it."[1]

In his memoir published in 2011, however, Hobby stated that he had "always wanted to run for office" and that from the time he had been the twenty-seven-year-old Senate parliamentarian for Lieutenant Governor Ben Ramsey in 1959, he had known that "lieutenant governor was the office to which I was best suited." As previously discussed, in February 1965, the *Dallas Morning News* published a report from an anonymous source that Hobby was thinking about running for lieutenant governor. Soon after that report, Hobby worked to raise his public visibility, but he apparently decided the time wasn't ripe in 1966 for him to make a bid. A year later, a wire-service story reported speculation in Austin that Hobby would run for lieutenant governor in 1968 if the incumbent in that office, Preston Smith, ran for governor. As it developed, Smith did successfully run for governor, but the dynamic young House Speaker Ben Barnes, the fastest-rising political star in the Texas Democratic Party, decided to run for lieutenant governor. Hobby decided that Barnes was too formidable to challenge, so he postponed his plans to be a candidate once again.[2]

It's clear that as early as 1959, probably earlier, Hobby intended to enter the political arena, and his specific target was the lieutenant governor's office. Just as clearly, he believed it was his calling. "My life has centered around public affairs, first as a journalist and then as a public official," he noted in his memoir. "I have spent most of my life in and around Texas government. A political, or public service, gene lurks in my family's DNA. All this is by way of saying that the workings of government were a part of household conversation—and of life—from childhood." As Hobby's longtime confidant Saralee Tiede has observed, "I believe Bill went into politics because it was expected of him. From the very beginning, he was raised in a highly political environment."[3]

Bill Hobby had another motive for pursuing elective office: a need to establish his own identity separate from his famous mother. Ron Kessler, one of Hobby's campaign coordinators in 1972 who became well acquainted with him, also believed Hobby "was seeking an identity separate from the newspaper and from his mom, but also even from his dad. I mean, think about the noble purposes that other leaders have pursued to rise to find their own identity." Hobby's astute friend, San Antonio attorney Maury Maverick Jr., a political liberal who had served in the state legislature in the 1950s, shared his perception with Ann Richards, at the time a campaign worker in Austin and not yet an elected official, about one of the private forces driving Bill Hobby's political ambitions in the early 1970s. "He has a private hell of his own: Mother," Maverick said. "That mother makes my mother, yours, and David's [Ann's then husband], rolled into one, look like a simpering worm. He desperately wants to escape."[4]

Saralee Tiede has observed that Hobby had "tremendous respect for his mother, he knew her legacy, but I think Bill spent his whole life trying to live up to whatever image that his mother had created that he was supposed to be. I had the impression from people I knew at the *Houston Post*, that his mother was completely in control of the paper, and he was basically a nonentity, even despite his titles. It wasn't a pleasant place for him. He was in her shadow." Tiede believed that one of the reasons Bill often told the story about his handling of the *Post*'s coverage of President Kennedy's assassination was that it was entirely his story and not his mother's. "Nobody second guessed him. He was in charge because she was out of the country, which allowed him to make those decisions."[5]

Despite Hobby's yearning for more than ten years to run for lieutenant governor, Ben Barnes's election in November 1968 convinced him he would have to place his ambitions on hold for another four years. Hobby assumed, correctly as it turned out, that Barnes would run again in 1970 as the overwhelming favorite for reelection. As Hobby told an oral history interviewer years later, he knew he would have to wait for a more "propitious time."[6]

It soon became apparent that the "propitious time" was going to be 1972. In the summer of 1969, only six months after starting his first term as lieutenant governor, Ben Barnes confirmed to his friends, including Bill Hobby, that he intended to be a candidate for governor in 1972. Barnes assumed he would easily win reelection to a second term as lieutenant governor in 1970, which would place him in a prime position to move into the governor's office two years later. Barnes's decision, if carried out, meant there would be no incumbent in the 1972 Democratic primary election. In addition, there appeared to be no clear favorite to replace him waiting in the wings. "After Ben was reelected in 1970," Hobby recalled, "it was well understood by everyone who knew him that the next stop was the Governor's Mansion." Barnes's decision was the most significant factor affecting Hobby's plans. "I wasn't going to run against Ben," Hobby said.[7]

His decision now made, if not publicly announced, Hobby accepted a temporary assignment from Ben Barnes in June 1969 to serve as chair of the Texas Senate's Interim Committee on Welfare Reform. Barnes later claimed that political strategy played a role in his decision to appoint Hobby to the committee. In the midst of a meteoric rise in his political career, Barnes fully expected to be elected governor in 1972. Looking ahead, he was aware that some of the members of the state Senate who were less than friendly to him could make it difficult for him to get his legislation passed. As a result, he claims that he encouraged Bill Hobby to make his bid for lieutenant governor in 1972. Barnes felt that if Hobby was presiding over the Senate, Bill would play a key role in getting Barnes's legislative agenda passed. Barnes claims that he appointed Hobby to the welfare reform committee to give Bill more public visibility as well as experience in dealing with a difficult policy issue.[8]

The members of Hobby's welfare reform committee included East Texas senator Charles Wilson, who served as vice chair; powerful senator Bill Moore; and Houston senator Barbara Jordan. The Senate resolution authorizing the committee asked for a report to be submitted to the legislative session to convene in January 1971. Although the resolution was passed in June 1969, it took several months to recruit and appoint staff support. Hobby persuaded Dr. June Hyer, an administrator at the University of Houston–Clear Lake, to take a leave of absence to direct the committee's support staff. Hobby hired consultants to analyze parts of the complex Medicaid system. He also engaged Electronic Data Systems in Dallas, which was multimillionaire Ross Perot's company, to make a thorough study of the Texas Department of Public Welfare's operational systems. Hobby finally held the first meeting on February 13, 1970, in Austin. Committee meetings continued periodically through November.[9]

Hobby later noted that chairing the committee "wasn't exactly a high honor" because of the negative image in Texas of welfare recipients. "Welfare has pretty much always been associated in the public mind with lazy, shiftless folks who won't work—'welfare queens' who supposedly live high on the hog on welfare payments." As Hobby has explained, however, living like a queen on welfare "would be difficult considering that Texas's welfare payments have always been among the lowest in the nation." He noted that the Texas Senate's sudden interest in the state's welfare system had little to do with "concern for the least among us," but was driven more by worries about how much it was costing the state budget.[10]

Hobby's committee submitted its report, "Breaking the Poverty Cycle," to the Senate in January 1971. The report declared that the state's welfare system had a sad history of treating the blind, the disabled, and the poor "as persons to be maintained only on a level at or below that of decency." The report made wide-ranging recommendations. The Senate ignored some, including the call for a statewide system of free day-care centers, but others were adopted. The latter included the removal of the constitutional ceiling on state appropriations for welfare, the replacement of food commodities with food stamps, and the garnishment of wages for child support. Some of the reforms, however, had to wait until future legislatures put them in place. Overall, Hobby was satisfied with the committee's report. "It was a good piece of work," he later said, "and my participation left me with a better understanding of the arcane and impossibly complex laws surrounding the provision of health and human services."[11]

In October 1969, while he continued to guide the work of the Interim Committee on Welfare Reform, Hobby added another job in state government to his résumé when he accepted Governor Preston Smith's invitation to join the nine-member Texas Air Control Board. The board's mission was to protect the state's air resources by monitoring and reducing levels of air pollution. That appointment, as well as his service as chair of the welfare reform committee, burnished Hobby's credentials as a person well informed about the workings of state government. Both assignments provided him with in-depth information related to two areas of state government that were rapidly growing in significance: social welfare and the environment. Hobby's knowledge of the workings of state government had also been built by his work for the *Houston Post* as a reporter covering the legislature, and later as an editor directing the coverage of his Capitol correspondents; his service as Ben Ramsey's Senate parliamentarian in 1959; and his four years (1965–1969) as a member of the University of Houston Board of Regents, dealing with the legislature's public education policies. And, of course, he had grown up in a family that had been part of state government for a couple of generations.[12]

Hobby's work on the Interim Committee on Welfare Reform and the Texas Air Control Board also gave him the opportunity to work closely with some of the leaders in the Texas Senate. Among them was Max Sherman, who first met Bill Hobby when Hobby was chairing the welfare reform committee. Sherman was in attendance when Hobby made a presentation to his State Affairs Committee about the findings and recommendations of Hobby's committee on welfare reform. "I was very impressed with the thoroughness of the report and how well it was done," Sherman later said. "But my real introduction to Bill was when I read the entire report afterward. I thought it was one of the finest analyses of our welfare problems that I'd ever read. It was a fitting introduction to Bill Hobby."[13]

Another senator Hobby got to know during this period was the liberal state senator from Galveston, A. R. "Babe" Schwartz. "Hobby was on the Texas Air Control Board in 1969 when I was going crazy about air and water pollution," Schwartz recalled. "I asked him if he was going to vote for the special interests or for the people and try to give us clean air. He convinced me that his heart and mind and thoughts were in the right place and sure enough I found out that indeed he was a good environmentalist.[14]

With Barnes out of the lieutenant governor's race, Hobby knew that the 1972 election was the time for him to seek the public office to which he had long aspired. Not only would there be no incumbent in the job, but there were also other factors that helped him make his decision. One was that the terms for all thirty-one members of the state Senate would be up in 1972, which meant that any one of them who ran for lieutenant governor would be giving up their Senate seat, unlike in other years, when they might be in the middle of their term. "I hoped, wrongly," Hobby later noted, "that the absence of mid-term 'free rides' would reduce the number of senators running for lieutenant governor." That hope didn't pan out, however. Three senators eventually declared their candidacies: Wayne Connally from South Texas, who had statewide name recognition because he was former governor John Connally's brother; El Paso's Joe Christie, who had strong support from labor, the *Texas Observer*, and the liberal faction of the Democratic Party; and North Texas conservative Ralph Hall.[15]

An important factor that eventually had a profound impact on Hobby's candidacy stemmed from a totally unexpected development that eventually became known as the Sharpstown bank scandal. The scandal was the result of the reckless financial wheeling and dealing of Houston land developer and banker Frank Sharp and his efforts to skirt federal banking and insurance regulations and laws. The Sharpstown affair first came to the public's attention on January 18, 1971, when US Securities and Exchange Commission (SEC) attorneys filed a civil lawsuit in federal court in Dallas charging Frank Sharp, former Democratic state attorney general Waggoner Carr, former state insurance commissioner John Osorio, and several other defendants with stock fraud. Sharp's corporations, including the Sharpstown State Bank and National Bankers Life Insurance Corporation, were also named in the suit. Each of the accused denied the charges. The accusations against a former attorney general, an insurance commissioner, and a prominent businessman were surprising by themselves, but the greater shock was the SEC's allegation that to carry out the fraud, Frank Sharp had bribed current Texas governor Preston Smith, House Speaker Gus Mutscher, Representative Tommy Shannon of Fort Worth, state Democratic chairman and state banking board member Elmer Baum, and some of their aides to use their power and influence to pass new state bank deposit insurance legislation in 1969 that was favorable to Sharp's business interests.[16]

The SEC claimed that Sharp had granted more than $600,000 in unsecured loans from his Sharpstown State Bank to the state officials named in the suit as a scheme to have bills passed by the legislature that would exempt state-chartered banks, which would include the Sharpstown Bank, from FDIC regulations. The FDIC had been threatening to withdraw insurance coverage of the bank's deposits because of its highly questionable loan practices. The officials had been given loans to buy stock in Sharp's National Bankers Life insurance company. Sharp promised his accomplices that he would soon artificially increase the value of their stock with a scheme to manipulate the price, which they could then resell at huge profits. However, Sharp would not make the loans until the legislature passed the legislation he wanted.[17]

Back in September 1969, Governor Smith had called a special session of the legislature, during which Speaker Mutscher and Representative Shannon, with the help of some of their staff members and others, were able to rush Sharp's bills to passage. After the law was passed, but prior to it going to Governor Smith for signing, Sharp's bank went forward with the loans he had promised. Sharp—whom Pope Paul VI had earlier officially recognized for his contributions to the Catholic Church (although Sharp was a Methodist)—conned the administrators of the Jesuit Fathers of Houston Incorporated, which owned and operated Strake Jesuit High School in Houston, into investing enough of the school's money to raise the value of his insurance company's stock. The public officials who had received his loans suddenly sold their stock in Sharp's company, generating a total of $250,000 in profits. Prosecutors said that the day after the bills passed, the defendants sold the stock to a priest friend of Sharp's for twice the market price that day. The insurance company later collapsed. Interestingly, Smith later vetoed the bills on the advice of the state's top bank law experts, but not until he had made $62,500 in profit on the bank loan/stock purchase deal.[18]

The federal lawsuit against Sharp, Carr, and others was filed as the Texas Legislature began its regular biennial session in January 1971. Soon after the news broke, liberal Democrats in the Texas House, with Corpus Christi representative Frances "Sissy" Farenthold among the leaders, joined with their few Republican colleagues (their coalition would later be known as the Dirty Thirty) to demand a legislative investigation into the affair. Speaker Mutscher, however, thwarted their effort by appointing a committee controlled by his political cronies, and it went nowhere. Despite Mutscher's self-defensive maneuvering, the Dirty Thirty continued their protests, with Sissy Farenthold eventually entering the race for governor as a progressive anti-corruption candidate in the 1972 Democratic primary.

Every official to whom Sharp had made loans and who had taken a profit from the sale of stock denied any knowledge of a scheme, claiming that the stock purchases were normal business transactions with no connection to any legislation. Unfortunately, as the stock value collapsed when the news of the Sharpstown scandal broke, the Jesuit Fathers of Houston would eventually end up with forty thousand almost-worthless shares of National Bankers Life stock and a $6 million cash loss. The legal case proceeded slowly through the courts, and by the summer of 1971 any person in state government who had even a slight connection to Frank Sharp was under intense scrutiny from the news media, public interest groups, and political rivals. As a result, political pressure greatly increased not only on Smith, Baum, Mutscher, and Shannon but also on Ben Barnes, who had once received a loan from Sharpstown Bank and had been connected in tangential ways to Frank Sharp and the bank bills.[19]

Bill Hobby was foxhunting in Ireland with Diana in January 1971 when the news broke about the SEC lawsuit against Sharp and the other defendants. When he returned to Texas later in the month and was told about the case, he was slow, like many of his fellow Texans, to grasp the potential political ramifications of the lawsuit. But as more details about corruption leaked out in the coming weeks from the US Justice

Department's separate investigation of Frank Sharp, Hobby grew increasingly appalled. He believed, however, that the evidence against Ben Barnes, but not the others, was tissue thin and circumstantial—as indeed it continued to be.[20]

In June 1971, Frank Sharp pleaded guilty to two counts of violating federal banking and security laws. The judge fined him $5,000 and sentenced him to three years of probation. Sharpstown was now a confirmed episode of criminal behavior, even if the other participants had not yet had their day in court. It was now fair game as a campaign issue—one that would eventually help Hobby's chances for victory. As one of his campaign staff later recalled, "By the summer of 1971, one couldn't read a newspaper in Texas without reading about Sharpstown."[21]

By the late spring 1971, Hobby was ready to enter the primary as a candidate for lieutenant governor. Before he made his official announcement, however, he decided to make the trek to the LBJ Ranch, near Stonewall, Texas, to get former president Lyndon Johnson's endorsement. The former president gave Bill a warm welcome. Johnson told Hobby that he would gladly endorse his candidacy in the Democratic primary, but not if one of his opponents turned out to be George Christian, LBJ's former press secretary. Christian was also a good friend of Hobby's. "George was a prince of a man," Hobby later observed. "George lent his astute advice, boundless wisdom, and political good sense to me as long as he lived." Hobby assumed, correctly, that Christian would not be a candidate in 1972. On the bookcase shelves in LBJ's ranch office were several gavels Johnson had used when he presided over the US Senate as vice president. He gave Hobby a gavel that had belonged to President Andrew Jackson. "[It was] made from wood that had come from Old Hickory's office," Hobby recalled. "Of course, I used that gavel the first day I presided over the Texas Senate." Afterward, Oveta wrote LBJ, "William appreciated your seeing him and all the wonderful advice you gave him. I appreciated it, too." Johnson replied, "You and the Governor [Will Hobby] did a wonderful job on Bill. I want to help any way in the world I can, and will again the next time he passes this way."[22]

Having secured LBJ's blessing, Hobby decided to drop a hint to the public and to his potential opponents that he would be a candidate. While on a visit to Dallas on June 4, 1971, he gave an interview to KDFW-TV's popular news director Eddie Barker, who noted how active Hobby had become in government service in Austin recently. Barker asked him if that might be a sign that he had political plans in the near future. Hobby smiled and replied that he was "thinking very strongly" of running for lieutenant governor. As he obviously intended, Hobby's remark was duly reported in several Texas newspapers.[23]

A month later, on Tuesday, July 6, 1971, Bill Hobby, now thirty-nine years old, announced his candidacy for lieutenant governor at an 11:00 a.m. press conference in the Texas Senate Chamber. The event was a low-key affair and short on excitement, as Hobby quietly delivered a dry speech focused on the significant but unexciting subjects of federal-state relations, the necessity for writing a new constitution to replace the current "archaic" one, the importance of "modernizing" state government, the need to make legislative procedures more efficient and rational, and the prescribed duties of the lieutenant governor. In his announcement speech, Hobby made no reference to the widening Sharpstown scandal and the charges of bribery and stock fraud. His only mention of law and order was a vague statement calling for "promptness and equity in law enforcement." Years later, many of Hobby's friends and associates remembered Hobby's entrance into the lieutenant governor's race as a crusade against the corruption in state government revealed by Frank Sharp's admission of guilt and the indictment of his collaborators. Those memories have been misremembered as the years have passed, however.[24]

Hobby's failure to mention Sharpstown in his announcement speech did not mean he had no concerns about the scandal. Even if it developed that some or all of the accused were able to escape criminal convictions—which some did—Hobby felt that at the very least, their greedy behavior had been inappropriate and their judgment catastrophically bad. Worst of all to Hobby, their sleazy, money-grubbing deals, legal or not, had cast legitimate doubts about the financial mores of the state's public servants and the basic integrity of the legislative process. Although his own reputation for steadfast integrity and fairness meant much to him, Bill Hobby was no puritanical, holier-than-thou judgmental moralist. But to him, holding elected office was an act of public service in which selfless and ethical behavior was a requirement, not a luxury. Bill Hobby accepted and understood that the governor, lieutenant governor, and individual members of the legislature would have their own positions on policy and ideas about the role of government, no matter how right or wrong or even crazy they might be, but he looked at dishonesty with disdain.[25]

Hobby has never explained why he failed to mention Sharpstown in his announcement speech or in the press conference that followed, but the evidence is clear that it had nothing to do with any personal link to the scandal or sympathy for those who had admitted their guilt. Although this is speculative, the likely reason was his friendship with Ben Barnes, whose enemies were actively seeking to link him to the scandal, despite the lack of hard evidence that Barnes had been involved in the affair. At this point, Barnes's name was being mentioned in news stories about the Sharpstown scandal because of the loan he had once received from Sharp's bank and because he had presided over the Texas Senate when Sharp's bills were passed. Most of the members were eventually forced to admit the embarrassing fact that they had never read the Sharpstown bills. Except for the small number of members who were actively pushing the bills forward on Sharp's behalf, Barnes and many senators viewed the legislation as normal and inconsequential special "local" bills of no interest to them. Barnes always vigorously denied any involvement in the efforts to get Sharp's bills out of the Senate, and no hard evidence has ever been discovered to counter his claim.[26]

It is possible that in June 1971, Hobby was reluctant to be perceived as a Sharpstown crusader, not only because of his belief in Barnes's innocence but also because the judicial process was ongoing for most of the accused, including Speaker Mutscher and two other members of the state legislature. Another factor was the rumor circulating that the Nixon administration had launched the Sharpstown investigation to destroy Ben Barnes, who was being touted as a potential Democratic candidate for the presidency. Hobby later stated he believed there was substance to those rumors, and he suspected that Nixon or one of his cronies had ordered the IRS to conduct an extensive audit of his own taxes.[27]

After Hobby gave his announcement speech, which was as short on specifics as it was brief in length, he held a press conference during which members of the Capitol press corps were able to get details about his views on policy. In answering a question about the high level of poverty in many areas of Texas, Hobby stressed that his experience as chair of the welfare reform committee had convinced him of the need to overhaul the state welfare system. He also declared his opposition to state income and corporate taxes. A corporate income tax, Hobby argued, "just gets passed onto the consumer in the form of higher prices." He admitted, however, that the state was "at or near a practical ceiling" on how high the sales tax could go. "One area that we ought to look at," he suggested, "is to levy the ad valorem tax on all property, not just real estate, but also stocks and bonds and bank accounts and other forms of wealth."[28]

Pointing out that Texas was "now overwhelmingly an urban state," Hobby argued that he was more knowledgeable about and sensitive to the issues related to the state's rapidly growing cities than any other candidate in the race. One of those issues was air and water pollution, which was primarily an urban problem. Citing his work as a member of the Texas Air Control Board, from which he was now resigning because of his candidacy, he declared his strong support for improved pollution controls, including a class-action bill that would permit private citizens to directly sue companies or government agencies for pollution violations. He repeated his call for overhauling Senate procedures, which gave him the opportunity to remind reporters of his previous experience as Ben Ramsey's parliamentarian.[29]

Years later, an oral history interviewer asked Hobby if he had thought he was going "to make great changes" when he decided to run for public office in 1971. "Well, I wanted to save the world and reform the state," he answered. "But the world and the state somehow do not seem to want to be reformed very much." By then he had retired from public office, and he told the interviewer that one of the key things he had learned since 1971 was "you don't solve problems in government, you manage issues, which are mostly financial."[30]

At the press conference following his announcement, reporters asked Hobby if he was running as a Democrat or a Republican, citing his newspaper's past editorial endorsements of Republicans Dwight Eisenhower and Richard Nixon for president, as well as of Republican George H. W. Bush over Democrat Lloyd Bentsen for the US Senate in 1970. "I am a Democrat," Hobby answered without hesitation. "I have never been anything but a Democrat." He did admit, however, that he had occasionally voted for Republicans in the November general elections. "If the people want a Lt. Governor who makes all judgments on a party label," Hobby said, "they better vote for someone else." As the campaign continued, however, Hobby stressed that if he succeeded in winning his primary, he would be an official representative of the Democratic Party and he would vote for the party's candidates at all levels. On another occasion, when he made a campaign stop in Austin, he was asked, if he had always been a Democrat, then why had the *Houston Post* endorsed Nixon in 1960 and 1968? He answered that the *Post*'s editorials weren't under his control, without identifying who had made the endorsements—his mother. Hobby explained that although the *Post* had supported Nixon, he had voted for Kennedy in 1960 and Humphrey in 1968. "I have never voted for Nixon." He added that the only imaginable way he could support Nixon in the general election in 1972 was if the Democrats nominated George Wallace for president.[31]

Bored with the interest in the degree of his party loyalty and the issue of the *Houston Post* editorials supporting Nixon, Hobby feigned ignorance when he was reminded that Oveta had endorsed Nixon in a signed editorial. "Did she really?" he asked. "Yes," the questioner responded. "Well, everybody makes mistakes," Hobby replied. A few years later, when he was asked why he was a Democrat, he answered, "Well, the short answer is, I'm not a wacko! You know when I grew up in politics in Houston, you kind of knew vaguely [that] Republicans and homosexuals ... existed but you didn't know anyone who admitted to being one! No, I was born and bred a Democrat."[32]

Laura Hobby Beckworth noted that "back then there was a strong conservative George Bush Republican bias in our family. My uncle Henry Catto was a George Bush Republican. And my grandmother [Oveta] had been a Republican. But I don't think my father's positions on issues were really that different from those a Rockefeller Republican or a George H. W. Bush Republican took. I know my father's view on social issues was 'live and let live' but quite conservative fiscally. That's who he is. I mean he is not a big spender. To put it mildly."[33]

Soon after Hobby declared his candidacy, speculation began that he would tie his campaign directly to Ben Barnes's gubernatorial campaign. The news media knew that Hobby and Barnes were friends and political allies. Barnes was a popular figure in Texas, and political pundits assumed he would easily win the Democratic primary. According to Hobby, he and Barnes did discuss the possibility of the two running their campaigns as one ticket. But Hobby ultimately decided against it. Nearly every key position in Texas state government was occupied by an independently elected person. Political tickets were not the tradition in Texas. The only thing uniting state officeholders during this era of one-party domination was their identification as Democrats. Hobby told Barnes he believed it would be better for them to run entirely independent campaigns. He was afraid that running as a ticket would only unite their enemies. Criticism of Hobby could spill over on Barnes, and vice versa. When an interviewer for the *Dallas Times Herald* asked Hobby if the rumor was true that he and Barnes would run as a team, Hobby replied, "Ben is running his race and I'm running mine."[34]

After the election Hobby admitted he'd had "a guardian angel looking over" his shoulder at that time, because rumors that Barnes had been implicated in the Sharpstown scandal soon escalated. "Ben was not involved in Sharpstown," Hobby has argued, "but he was in the wrong place at the wrong time." But Hobby believed that didn't matter to the voters. "The Sharpstown scandal had tarnished incumbents (rightly or not)," Hobby wrote, "and voters were angry with just about everyone in office that year." The rumors were effectively used against Barnes by his primary opponents in the governor's race, especially Sissy Farenthold. As a result, Barnes, who had once been heavily favored, finished in third place behind rancher Dolph Briscoe and Representative Farenthold. The loss ended Barnes's once-promising career in elective office. If Hobby and Barnes had campaigned as a team, Bill might have gone down with Barnes.[35]

Bill's announcement that he would run for lieutenant governor surprised many Democratic Party leaders and officeholders outside the *Houston Post*'s circulation area, where he was not well known, although his family name had widespread recognition because of his parents' public careers. After Hobby made his candidacy formal, he was invited to speak at various places around the state, even though he had yet to put his campaign organization together. On August 20, he traveled to Amarillo to preside as president over a meeting of the Texas Daily Newspaper Association, where he was besieged with questions about his decision to run for lieutenant governor. Three weeks later, Hobby gave a Labor Day speech to a printers' union convention at the Baker Hotel in Dallas. The union named him "fair employer of the year" because of the good working conditions over the years for union printing tradesmen at the *Houston Post*. With one wary eye on potential opponent Joe Christie, a favorite of the state's labor unions, Hobby addressed bread-and-butter issues of special interest to his audience, including the need for increased funding for education and vocational training and reform of the auto insurance industry, charging that the cost of premiums was too high.[36]

The Sharpstown scandal entered a new phase on September 23, 1971, when a grand jury indicted Speaker Gus Mutscher and legislators Tommy Shannon and W. S. Heatley on the charge of accepting a bribe from Frank Sharp. Governor Preston Smith was named as an unindicted coconspirator. The indictment greatly escalated news coverage, and it turned up the heat on every incumbent running for reelection to an office in state government. Pretrial publicity continued to interact with news about the ongoing Democratic primary campaign until March 15, 1972, when a jury in Abilene needed only two and a half hours to find Mutscher and his associates guilty. Judge J. Neil Daniel assessed punishment at five years' probation.[37]

The more Bill Hobby learned about the Sharpstown controversy as the weeks went by, especially after Speaker Mutscher's indictment, the more he understood its potential effects on the coming year's Democratic primary election and the impact it would have on current state officeholders. As Hobby later noted in his memoir, "The Sharpstown scandal made [1972] a good year for new faces." As he thought about the scandal and how it might affect his campaign, Hobby's mind became fixed on the word "honesty." During his father's election campaign for governor in 1918, Will Hobby's opponent, James Ferguson, had called him a short, fat, and ugly man who had been "slighted by the Creator." One of the charges against Ferguson that led to his impeachment as governor in 1917 was that he had used public money for his personal needs. Will Hobby's response had been, "My friends, when the good Lord created me, He at least gave me the ability to tell the difference between my own money and the money of the people of Texas." Bill Hobby understood that honesty was also the issue at the heart of the Sharpstown scandal, and that it would be much easier for the voters to understand that simple concept than the complexities of financial fraud and stock manipulation. The simple word "honestly" would soon result in a catchy slogan for the Hobby campaign.[38]

Accordingly, Hobby's campaign speeches began to refer more often to the Sharpstown scandal. In October, when he appeared on Austin's influential political issues television show *Capital Eye*, Hobby referred to Ralph Hall's vote in favor of the Sharpstown State Bank legislation in 1969. Hall had been chairman of the Senate committee that sent Sharp's bills to the floor of the Senate without holding a hearing. Hobby argued that "any conscientious and responsible committee chairman would have wanted to hear what the banking commission and the banking industry had to say about these bills." He would continue that strategy against Hall throughout the campaign. At one point, Hall charged that Hobby was unprepared for the office he was seeking because he lacked legislative experience. Hobby responded that he "would like to debate our respective degrees of experience. I would also like to ask him how his committee reported the Frank Sharp bills to the Senate without debate."[39]

Hobby spent most of the fall and winter of 1971 organizing his campaign while also appearing at public forums such as *Capital Eye*. For his campaign manager, Hobby hired Steve Oaks, a young lawyer who was a partner in the prominent Houston firm Butler & Binion, which had long represented Hobby family business interests. Oaks recruited campaign coordinators across Texas, mainly from his law school buddies. Among them were West Texas coordinator Kent Hance, who later became a state senator and a congressman. Helen Farabee, who had worked for Hobby's welfare reform committee, served as a coordinator in Wichita Falls. Helen later became Hobby's trusted advisor on health and human services. She and her husband, Ray, who would later be elected to the state Senate, would be among Hobby's closest friends. Other key field lieutenants were attorneys David Chappell in Fort Worth, Ron Kessler in Dallas, Lee Godfrey in Austin, Don Rives in northeast Texas, and John Watson and Joe Bill Watkins in Houston. Each was a young, successful, and influential lawyer in their local area.[40]

Reflecting on the campaign years later, Hobby's Dallas coordinator, Ron Kessler, observed that he was deeply impressed with the team Hobby and Oaks assembled. "You have to give Hobby the credit for being so purposeful, so intent on winning that election. It was a brilliant campaign. I don't think there'd ever been a campaign put together that was as structured on the ground. We also made very effective use of radio and television ads. It targeted markets that Hobby really wanted to win, and he did win." Kessler's recruitment as the campaign's Dallas coordinator was typical of Hobby's and Oaks's overall organizational methods. Kessler's political mentor, liberal state senator Oscar Mauzy, asked Kessler and his wife, Vicki, to join him for lunch with Hobby and Oaks, neither of whom the Kesslers had ever met. Hobby had learned that white conservatives in Dallas who tended to vote Republican didn't vote in the Democratic primary. The primaries attracted more minority and progressive white voters, so Hobby wanted a coordinator who had strong connections with leaders of those groups. "It was a very wise strategy that they carried out across the state, and it proved effective," Kessler noted. "Hobby devised the strategy and Oaks implemented it." Influenced by Mauzy and impressed with Hobby, Kessler agreed to manage the Dallas campaign.[41]

Kessler was pleasantly surprised when Hobby also invited Vicki to join the campaign organization. Vicki, who was a political activist with experience as a campaign worker, later noted that Hobby was aware that she and her husband always worked as a team. Ron observed that it wasn't common in those days to have women in campaign leadership, but they quickly learned that Hobby had "grown up with a strong-willed mother, and he married one of the strongest women I've ever met in Diana Stallings Hobby, and I think he had a high comfort level with such women." The Kesslers cited Helen Farabee as another example of Hobby's admiration for strong-willed and talented women.[42]

With the organization largely in place statewide, the campaign had its official opening on Hobby's fortieth birthday at his headquarters near the Houston Post Building. Diana and Oveta joined more than one thousand supporters who crowded into the headquarters to watch him blow out the candles on his birthday cake and to celebrate the opening of the campaign. It was a raucous event. Attendees mingled and talked about the campaign while a band and singers performed in the background. Many attendees were also helping to drain the large number of beer kegs, surrounded by multicolored balloons bearing Hobby's campaign slogans. At one point, Hobby went to a microphone and thanked his guests for coming and explained the issues he would stress in the campaign. The list included those he had been talking about for several months, especially constitutional reform. But he also placed more emphasis on the Sharpstown scandal and his goal to restore confidence in state government.[43]

The Hobby campaign focused on his three major opponents, Senators Hall, Christie, and Connally. Each was an incumbent member of the legislature running in an anti-incumbent political environment, and each had been in the Senate when Frank Sharp's corrupt legislation had been passed with little opposition. "My father was running against people that had a lot better political names and political experience," Paul Hobby noted, "but there was a strong anti-incumbency mood in the air and the campaign was able to take advantage of it." Famed San Antonio architect O'Neil Ford, who was designing a new home for Oveta, was a friend of brothers Wayne and John Connally. He sent Oveta a confidential note, however, to tell her that he had talked to "many persons and all of them wish Wayne would not run at all. (e.g. Houston and Ed Harte and Mr. LBJ). I wouldn't want Wayne and John to know how I feel as I like them both—BUT. I honestly feel Bill has the right position and the right attitudes to win and serve—effectively. All of us ecologists and environmental alarmists are for him."[44]

Ron Kessler thought Christie was the biggest threat to Hobby. "Joe Christie was a good looking, smart, and a very effective guy," Kessler recalled. "He had solid support from the liberal, Ralph Yarborough wing of the Democratic Party, which had some clout at the time, and that was a bloc vote." One of those liberals was future Texas governor Ann Richards, who was working full time in the primary campaign for liberal Corpus Christi representative Sissy Farenthold, the reform candidate for governor. Richards supported Joe Christie for lieutenant governor, especially because of his strong position on protecting the environment.[45]

Hobby, however, did manage to attract some liberal support, and in his campaign statements, except for his occasional criticism that Christie had voted for Sharp's bills without understanding what was in them, he was much easier on Christie than he was on Ralph Hall and Wayne Connally. At a campaign appearance in Austin in early February, he declared that he didn't know if Hall and Connally were dishonest or simply incompetent because of the role they played in allowing the Sharp banking bills to go to the floor without a hearing. But he didn't include Christie in those charges.[46]

In April, when Richards, who supported Joe Christie, learned that a fellow progressive, Maury Maverick Jr., was supporting Hobby, she wrote a letter to Maverick scolding him for his decision. Based on the conservative editorial policy of the *Houston Post* and Oveta Culp Hobby's record as a Republican, Richards considered Bill Hobby to be the business-establishment candidate. Maverick was unimpressed. "I never heard of your candidate in my life," he responded. "I doubt if he is as good as you say he is or if Bill is as bad as you think he is. Hobby gave me more space [in the *Houston Post*] than any other newspaperman in Texas when I ran for the Senate 15 years ago, [when] I said things like Red China ought to be in the UN." Not one to mince words, Maverick pointed out that Hobby "helped me more than you did." Maverick discounted any influence Oveta might have on her son's politics, explaining that Bill was trying to establish a political identity separate from his mother, whom Maverick characterized as domineering. Maverick believed Hobby had the potential to do the right thing if he won. "Bill has a high sense of duty to country. He may not do any good with it, but I think . . . he will please you more than anyone you have known in your life in the same job."[47]

With a new focus on corruption in the statehouse, Hobby did his best to position himself as the antidote to the average Texas voter's "crisis of confidence" in state government. He expressed in print his view that his most significant asset was honesty, which clearly referred to the Sharpstown scandal. Hobby's campaign soon bought highway billboards and newspaper ads around the state proclaiming, "Bill Hobby will make a good lieutenant governor. Honestly." As Ron Kessler observed, "That tagline, 'honestly'—was what really caught the eyes and the hearts of the Texas voter." Hobby and his campaign team were embarrassed, however, when some of their billboards mistakenly declared, "Elect a good man, not a good politician," instead of the intended phrase,

"Elect a good man, not *just* a good politician." Hobby learned about the error when he received complaints from local officeholders, including El Paso county commissioner Sam Blackham. Hobby quickly had the offending billboard ads removed. "I sincerely regret that I have unintentionally insulted some good men who are experienced politicians," Hobby wrote the county commissioner. "This state desperately needs honest men with political savvy who are willing to work for the best interests of the state."[48]

Unlike his strongest opponents, Hobby worked hard to attract minority voters, especially urban Black voters. That was one of the reasons he and Oaks recruited Ron Kessler, who had strong connections to Black leaders in Dallas. The Hobby campaign also recruited young Black people to work for the campaign at the community level. Saralee Tiede has observed that "Bill and his family had good Black friends, and they were very respectful of achievements in the Black community. They rejected racism. They just thought discrimination was wrong."[49]

Rodney Ellis recalled that early in 1972, when he was a senior and student body president at Evan Worthing High School in the Sunnyside section of Houston, the principal, Allen Norton, asked him to come to his office to meet Steve Oaks. "My principal told me there are some people here who want to get some young folks involved in Bill Hobby's campaign for lieutenant governor." Impressed with Ellis, Oaks invited him to lunch at a downtown hotel to meet other members of the Hobby campaign team. "That was a big deal for me, to go downtown and meet with people like that," Ellis noted later. "They asked me to help Governor Hobby in his campaign by hanging up signs and kind of like being an intern at the campaign headquarters. At some point, they took me to meet Bill Hobby. I also remember meeting his mother. That's when I found out that his father was the person Hobby Airport was named after." Ellis not only performed ground-level work but also accompanied Hobby to campaign appearances in Houston. "I was around him quite a bit," Ellis remembered. "It was an exciting experience. I was very impressed by how mild-mannered, soft-spoken, and bashful he was."[50]

Hobby's quiet modesty and shy behavior in public impressed Rodney Ellis, but it was a problem for Hobby's campaign team. Ron Kessler later recalled that early in the campaign, he and other coordinators had serious concerns about Hobby's speaking ability, his obvious dislike for mixing and mingling, and his lack of charisma. As political commentator and writer Larry L. King, who was famed as the playwright of *The Best Little Whorehouse in Texas*, noted, "Bill Hobby could take the excitement out of an earthquake." Hobby's campaign team understood that he had never been a candidate for public office, and they had anticipated that at the start of the campaign he would have the problems all novices did. But it was worse than they had expected.[51]

Looking back on the 1972 campaign a few years later, veteran *Dallas Morning News* political reporter Sam Kinch Jr. agreed that Hobby had been an awkward candidate. He observed that in politics, "you have to be a glad-hander and a ball-buster, and he's not either one. It took him a long time to get used to the idea of going through the process of being a candidate. He was a horrible speaker. Hell, he still is. But he is excellent at putting words together." A profile of Hobby in the *Dallas Morning News* noted that he was "not your traditional kind of candidate—the ego tripping, back-slapping politician who basks in the adoration of his supporters. Rather Hobby seems to prefer an informality that permits him to stroll around a group of his backers and chat individually with them." Referring to his natural informality, a reporter for the *Houston Chronicle* observed that he encouraged people to call him Bill, adding that "he whistles a lot, the tune rarely discernable. He is left-handed. He'll take a drink. And you might see him smoking a Kool cigarette (usually bummed from someone), a cigar, or a pipe. He is quiet, reserved, calm and cool, even under pressure." A reporter from Hobby's own newspaper, the *Houston Post*, wrote that Hobby "dislikes hand-shaking tours of shopping centers . . . because of his private nature and his belief that such contrived, strained confrontations with voters are of little value." Hobby told a reporter that "one television appearance is worth a thousand handshaking expeditions in shopping centers." Years later, when an interviewer asked Hobby if he ever enjoyed campaigning, he uttered one of the typically brief answers he nearly always gave when asked such questions: "Uh, no."[52]

In addition to his lack of charisma and his discomfort in public settings, Hobby also had to deal with his stutter. Laura and Paul Hobby recalled that when their father decided to run for lieutenant governor, he took speech lessons to improve his stutter. As Laura noted, "It was a real source of concern to him, and he worked really hard to overcome it. He was known for the brevity of his public addresses and his bluntness to a probably offensive degree, but in part that was probably because he wanted to get his message out as efficiently as possible without detracting from his message by stuttering." Ron Kessler had a good friend who, after he met Hobby, warned, "'Ron, you've made a big mistake. This guy stutters when he talks. He doesn't make a good impression. I'm not sure that you're aligned with a guy who's going to win this race.'" Democratic state senator Hector Uribe observed that campaigning "was painful for Bill because of his stuttering. To me, it was painful, not just for Bill, but for the person listening as well, if they had any empathy whatsoever for the man." Uribe discovered how shy and reluctant Bill was to speak when he met him for the first time during the campaign in 1972. "I was doing civil rights litigation in El Paso, and I was invited to a fundraiser for him. Having grown up outside of the State of Texas, I didn't know anything about Bill Hobby or his family. I went up to him and I asked, 'What do you do?' He just said, 'I run a newspaper.' And that was it. End of discussion." As he got to know Bill better, Uribe understood that running for public office "was such a courageous thing that he did, something that wasn't natural for him. To overcome that, to me, is a wonderful accomplishment."[53]

As the campaign progressed, Hobby employed a strategy that helped him control, but not eliminate, his stammer. He learned that when he was giving a speech, if he felt a stutter coming on, he could usually alleviate it by pausing briefly to clear his throat. As a result of that effort, Hobby's campaign coordinators noted that his speaking improved, as did his confidence, and that he even became adept at dropping in humorous one-liners.[54]

Hobby knew his stutter was more likely to be a problem early in the morning or as he became fatigued late in the day. Saralee Tiede recalled an incident when Hobby agreed to record a series of five-minute radio spots about why a quality public-education program was important to the state's economy. "I think he was tired and some of the recordings were really not very good. He was stuttering and stammering. But they were on tape and were edited. I think when he talks about himself, he's more inclined to stutter and stammer than if he's telling some story about or, just recounting some event that he liked. But you start asking him questions that require him to say something personal, and he just shuts down." Tiede felt that Hobby worked "to formulate the words that he might stutter over. I could see him sometimes making that effort." After Hobby had served as lieutenant governor for a few years, Tiede noted that he "had pretty much mastered it. He wasn't embarrassed about it. He never turned down an interview because he was worried about it. But I never heard him stammer or stutter when he was presiding over the Senate and I can't explain that."[55]

Another concern for some of Hobby's staff, but one that was far less serious than his stammer, was their candidate's inattention to his personal appearance and lack of regard for current fashion. "Just look at the way he dressed," his friend Kent Caperton said. "He had the worst taste in clothes of anybody I have ever known. His shoes always needed to be shined, his suits were rumpled. It looked like he bought them in some basement store somewhere." Ron Kessler recalled a campaign event for Hobby at the Kessler home in Dallas. "When he arrived before the other guests, he had on a tie that probably came from the 1920s and may have been one of his dad's." Vicki immediately went to the kitchen, grabbed a pair of scissors, and cut off the befuddled Hobby's tie. She then went upstairs and got one of Ron's ties and had Hobby put it on.[56]

In the early weeks of the campaign, except for the Houston-Galveston area, Hobby's campaign suffered from his lack of widespread name recognition, especially in the Dallas–Fort Worth metroplex and in West Texas. This was especially worrisome to his coordinators, because his strongest opponent was Wayne Connally, whose last name was well known throughout Texas because of his older brother, former governor John Connally, who had continued to be a newsmaker in 1971 and 1972 as Nixon's treasury secretary.

Ron Kessler recalled that the name recognition problem was at its worst in the campaign's early stage, when "nobody knew him. I remember having a cocktail party in Dallas at the start of the campaign and literally, nobody showed up. It was just Bill and me." But as the campaign trudged on, it began to gain noticeable momentum statewide. Hobby attracted much more attention in Dallas when prominent businessman and conservative Democratic activist Jess Hay decided to support him. "Jess Hay was a kind of a godfather of Dallas democratic politics," recalled Kessler. "That was back when there was a good number of conservative Democrats who had not yet left the party. But Bill and Jess hit it off and that really helped. Jess could draw a crowd to our events that I couldn't." As a result of their working together in 1972, Bill Hobby and Jess Hay forged a warm friendship and a close political relationship that would continue until Hay's death in 2015.⁵⁷

Almost as soon as Hobby announced his candidacy in the summer of 1971, a reporter asked if his mother would be campaigning for him. Bill replied that he hadn't asked her to campaign. What went unsaid was that he was trying to establish his own identity separate from Oveta and that he intended the campaign to be about him, not his more famous mother. As the time for intense campaigning drew closer in early 1972, however, Hobby and his campaign team became concerned about San Antonio and the conservative Democratic vote in West Texas. John Connally's influence remained strong in those areas, and most of the former governor's campaign organization was working for his brother Wayne. Hobby planned to make his own campaign stops in specific areas in West Texas, where his effort had the potential to garner votes, but he eventually realized he needed additional help. Accordingly, Hobby decided to have Oveta take a visible role in the campaign, as well as Diana and his sister, Jessica Catto, with the latter having solid connections in San Antonio.⁵⁸

The Connally home base was Floresville—Wayne and John Connally's hometown—where the former governor still owned a ranch. Because Floresville, which was also in Wayne Connally's Senate district, is only thirty miles southeast of San Antonio, the Hobby campaign staff realized they would have to pay special attention to the Alamo City. San Antonio was also the home base for Jessica and her husband, Henry Catto. Although Henry was a moderate Republican who was serving as Nixon's ambassador to El Salvador, he was quietly supporting Bill Hobby's bid for lieutenant governor. Jessica, however, was a Democrat who openly worked for her brother's candidacy. With the Hobby campaign's blessing, Jessica, who spoke fluent Spanish, returned temporarily to San Antonio to campaign for her brother in the city's Mexican American neighborhoods.⁵⁹

Initially, Oveta was somewhat troubled by Bill's decision to run for public office. Laura Hobby Beckworth later remembered her grandmother worrying about the impact that Bill's campaign and, if successful, his removal to Austin would have on the *Houston Post*. Oveta continued to hold tight control over the paper, but she depended on Bill's assistance with important administrative matters. "I know she worried about trying to manage the newspaper," Laura recalled, "which was very much a going concern and the source of income. She also probably had all the same reservations that a mother would have that politics was a rough game. It's one thing being an observer and chronicler of the political world, another thing to be the candidate." Oveta had had her own unpleasant experiences as a young woman when she ran a losing campaign for the state legislature. "So, I think her reservations were on both fronts," Laura added. "But once my father decided to run, she was all in."⁶⁰

Oveta also had to decide how the *Post* would cover the campaign. She made the not-surprising decision to promote her son's candidacy in editorials, while maintaining neutrality in news coverage. Accordingly, during the campaign the *Post* published four highly laudatory front-page editorials in support of Bill's bid for lieutenant governor.

The goal of neutrality in news coverage, however, proved to be somewhat elusive. *Time* magazine observed that there were two "curious things about the *Post*'s quadruple blessing of Hobby: the paper declined to take a stand on any of the other statewide contests, and it neglected to mention Hobby's position as president and executive editor of the newspaper."[61]

Although Oveta would not go out on the campaign trail until the spring because of her direct involvement in overseeing the construction and furnishing of the Hobbys' new radio and television studios, her decision to take a more visible public role was shown at the opening of the campaign headquarters in Houston, where she was on prominent display. In March, Oveta generated more indirect publicity for her son's campaign when she hosted the formal opening ceremonies for the new KPRC-Radio and TV studios on Southwest Freeway. By coincidence, the studio's location in southeast Houston was close to Sharpstown, the subdivision built by land developer Frank Sharp. Although it was not a campaign event, Bill Hobby was a visible presence at the widely publicized ceremony. In addition, Oveta persuaded Lyndon Johnson to make a rare trip away from his ranch in the Texas Hill Country to be the guest of honor and speaker at the luncheon held at the building. The news of his participation appeared in newspapers across Texas. The celebration was officially nonpartisan, but LBJ's presence sent a message to the public about his friendship with Bill and his mother.[62]

Oveta went on the road for the campaign on April 11. Accompanied by Diana Hobby, Oveta first stopped in Fort Worth, where she attended a brunch at the River Crest Country Club, followed by a coffee and press conference at Bill's Fort Worth campaign headquarters. Afterward Vicki Kessler drove her to Dallas, where Oveta held a press conference that afternoon in her suite in the Stoneleigh Hotel, proudly sporting her Distinguished Service Medal on her coat lapel. Her friends, Neiman Marcus department store board chairman Stanley Marcus and his wife, Billie, hosted a formal cocktail reception and dinner at their house on Nonesuch Road, near White Rock Lake.[63]

A reporter for the *Dallas Times Herald* who attended the press conference at the Stoneleigh noted that "Mrs. Hobby . . . does not feel her association with a Republican administration will hurt her son's campaign." Oveta explained to the small group of reporters gathered in her hotel suite that the Hobbys were "a close-knit family but will do our own thing. Bill is his own man. He will have his own thoughts." Referring to the Sharpstown scandal, she declared, "Dishonesty anywhere is indefensible. Corruption in the highest levels of state government is offensive to every Texan who believes in government by and for the people. He will go to Austin not to seek career and fortune, but to discharge a public trust."[64]

On April 12, Oveta and Diana flew from Dallas to San Angelo on a leased two-engine, six-seat Cessna 310 piloted by Bob Cargill, a young *Houston Post* reporter who was on an official leave of absence to work in the campaign. Shortly after landing, Oveta was rushed to a local television studio to appear on a morning television program. Later in the afternoon, Diana took a commercial flight back to Houston, and Cargill flew Oveta to Midland, where she attended a reception in her honor at the Midland Country Club. She hoped to win over some of the area's conservative, well-heeled oil company executives and independent oil operators, whose loyalty to the Democratic Party was fading rapidly. Oveta told the audience that her son had "always wanted to serve the people of Texas since he was a little boy and sat around listening to his father and me discussing the problems and challenges of government." She stated that Bill favored constitutional revision and that he wanted more legislative support of public schools. In a reference to Bill's work on the welfare reform committee, Oveta told the country club audience that Bill wanted to help Texans escape poverty, and one important way to accomplish that goal was through increased funding for vocational schools and community colleges. As Laura Hobby Beckworth later observed, "My grandmother was tireless, you know. She was on the stump, the whole campaign. I traveled with her actually quite a bit during that time."[65]

Bill Hobby's opponents took sharp notice of Oveta's campaign efforts. At a press conference in Dallas the day after Oveta visited the city, Wayne Connally was asked what he thought about her involvement in the campaign. Connally answered that he was "a little bit surprised she has come out and decided to actually campaign for him. I'll have to assume they have a strong and serious concern about the way Bill Hobby is doing the job campaigning alone." He added, "This is not totally unexpected," and implied that Oveta wouldn't turn over control of the *Post* to Bill because he wasn't up to the job. Another opponent, Joe Christie, recalling the 1972 campaign several years later, admitted, "You know, I had a stupid notion I could beat Bill Hobby. And I think I could, but I couldn't beat his mother [*laughs*]."[66]

The campaign team also sent the candidate's wife on the road, deeply confident that the sociable and highly intelligent Diana Hobby would make a good impression in personal visits with voters, especially talking to local community organizations in small towns. "I loved campaigning," Diana later recalled. "I got to go into rural areas. I would visit with a few people in the town's only dress shop or only hardware store or only drug store. It was my chance to . . . know my state." Vicki Kessler often traveled with Diana on her campaign trips, and they became good friends. Max Sherman, who was serving his first term in the Texas Senate in 1972, representing a district centered in Amarillo, was also strongly impressed with Diana, whom he met when she came to Amarillo on a campaign trip. "Diana, of course, was very passionate about reproduction issues. I first met her when I was on the board of Planned Parenthood in Amarillo. She spoke to our local chapter and made it clear that her husband shared her views about the good work Planned Parenthood was doing. She spoke well and made a very good impression."[67]

Of course, the actual candidate, Bill Hobby, was on the road on an almost constant basis, explaining his views on various issues, including positions that were controversial. The election of 1972 was the first to be held when registered voters eighteen years and older were allowed to vote. With that in mind, Hobby gave speeches on several college campuses, hoping to attract those new voters by addressing issues of concern to students. At an appearance at the University of Texas at El Paso, for example, he declared that he was in favor of reducing the penalty for private use of marijuana from a felony to a misdemeanor, with mandatory probation for first convictions. Months before the US Supreme Court ruled in *Roe v. Wade* that laws prohibiting abortion were unconstitutional, Hobby made it clear that he supported liberalizing Texas's abortion laws to make it "a personal matter for the woman involved, with medical consultation." On some hot-button issues over which the Texas Senate had little or no authority, he was happy to point that fact out to his questioners. When asked about his position on busing, for example, he answered that the lieutenant governor's authority over that matter was "roughly the same as his authority over the Vietnam war." That matter, he stated, was going to be resolved "at the federal courthouse, not the State Capitol."[68]

For most of his travels during the campaign, Hobby's only company was his pilot, Bob Cargill, who was also his traveling staff man. Together they flew about ninety thousand miles around the state. On one flight when the ceiling was low, Cargill wasn't certain where they were, so he flew down out of the clouds to determine their location. They found themselves flying parallel with a highway but unable to read any road signs. This problem inspired Hobby to explain to Cargill that his first legislative act as lieutenant governor would be to get a bill passed to make highway directional signs much larger and facing up to the sky so that pilots like Cargill would always know where they were. "Of course," Hobby added with his characteristic dry humor, "that presupposes that the pilot can read." Cargill's successful handling of flying in a low cloud ceiling was not the only example of the pilot's ability to remain cool and handle a problem. On August 22 Cargill was flying Hobby from Fort Worth to a speaking engagement in Lubbock when part of the Cessna's propeller broke loose from the engine, narrowly missing the cabin. Cargill safely navigated the airplane to a forced landing on ranchland in King County, ninety miles east of Lubbock. A representative of the Federal Aviation Agency later reported that Cargill and Hobby had barely escaped disaster.[69]

Cargill and Hobby began campaign days at 6:00 a.m. and worked until late, typically making more than a dozen stops a day. When they arrived at an airport, which sometimes was no more than a landing strip with a hanger and/or a small office for the manager and a pay telephone, they would be met by a couple of local supporters who drove Hobby to wherever he was scheduled to speak. Most of Hobby's stops were brief. He usually depended on local volunteers for logistical support, but those appearances were coordinated through the campaign's headquarters in Houston.[70]

By the last month of the campaign, Hobby, who was predicting that he and Wayne Connally would face each other in a runoff, was aiming his harshest attacks at Connally. He repeatedly charged that any senator such as Connally "who voted for the bread tax, against the 18-year-old vote, and signed the floor report recommending the Sharp bills forfeits his right to consideration for higher office." A week before the election, as Bill campaigned in Corpus Christi, President Nixon was making a highly publicized visit to John Connally's hometown, Floresville, which is a ninety-minute drive from

Corpus Christi. Wayne Connally issued a news release announcing his attendance at the invitation-only dinner being held in the president's honor, implying that Hobby hadn't been invited and that Connally had Nixon's endorsement. When a reporter asked Hobby if he thought Nixon's visit would help Connally's campaign, he laughed and said, "President Nixon will be as helpful to Wayne as he was to George Bush [in his failed 1970 US Senate race]."[71]

A few days before election day, Hobby filled the state's newspapers with an ad that asked in large print,

> Had enough of the same old gang that brought you the Frank Sharp banking bills and ignored needed reforms in the interest of all Texans? Several members of the now infamous 62nd Legislature want to be promoted. There's Senator Wayne Connally. He's running to restore confidence in state government. Yet, he, along with Senator Ralph Hall, were the very legislators responsible for signing the Frank Sharp bill out of committee. Even after the scandal was exposed, Connally refused to see the need for an ethics bill. His vote against the 18 year-old-right-to-vote is matched by Senator Hall's count against utility regulation and welfare reform. Then, there's Senator Joe Christie. When the chips were down during the food tax filibuster, Senator Christie took an untimely walk. Where did he walk? According to the *Texas Observer*, he was in Preston Smith's office when the vote was taken to cut off debate and thus pass the bread tax through the Senate. If you're tired of this kind of leadership, do something about it at the voting booth. Elect a man on May 6th who will make a good Lt. Governor. Honestly.

When primary election day finally arrived on May 6, it was clear the vote was going to be close in both the lieutenant governor's and the governor's races. Most of the election prognosticators were unsure about how the Sharpstown scandal was going to affect the outcome, but the consensus was that Ben Barnes would still prevail in the governor's race and avoid a runoff because he had not been indicted or directly tied to Sharp's fraudulent activities. The lieutenant governor's race was considered a toss-up, but some news commentators were predicting Wayne Connally would receive the most votes.[72]

When the ballots were tallied, however, Bill Hobby was in first place, four percentage points ahead of Connally, but he failed to attract enough votes to avoid a runoff. Hobby carried all the major cities except for Austin and El Paso, which were won by Joe Christie, who wound up in third place, with Ralph Hall in fourth place behind Christie. The day after his loss, Christie endorsed Hobby over Connally. Hobby won more support from liberals than had been predicted, which hurt Christie, and Hobby's focus on the Black vote had paid off handsomely, as he ran well in Black precincts. The *Houston Chronicle*'s political reporter Bo Byers noted that Hobby had done well with the college vote. Byers also observed that despite Oveta's record of supporting Republican presidential nominees, Bill was "hard to tag with a political ideology label but comes off . . . as a moderate, middle of the road type." In the governor's race, Ben Barnes was unable to escape the wave of anti-incumbent sentiment resulting from the Sharpstown scandal. He ran a poor third, but still far ahead of the incumbent governor, Preston Smith, who had barely escaped indictment. Uvalde rancher Dolph Briscoe won the most votes in the governor's race, falling slightly short of a majority, forcing him into a runoff with reform candidate Sissy Farenthold.[73]

As had been the case with Will Hobby's elections decades earlier, the Hobby connections with other Texas newspaper publishers paid off for the campaign, as did Bill's easy manner with fellow journalists. Nearly two dozen of the state's newspapers endorsed Hobby. As Sam Kinch Jr., the veteran political reporter for the *Dallas Morning News*, observed, "Unlike most politicians, Hobby was especially comfortable with local newsmen, either at press conferences or on a one-to-one basis." Kinch noted that Hobby was candid with reporters, which also put him in good stead with the press. "He does not hesitate to discuss his more controversial positions when someone raises a subject," Kinch said.[74]

Preparing for a month-long runoff campaign, Hobby turned his attention to the problem all candidates face in runoffs: low voter turnout. Hobby issued statements imploring his supporters not to let him be buried "in that gigantic graveyard of Texas politics in which lie candidates who led in the primary but got zapped in the runoff because their voters didn't come back to the polls." He told the *Dallas Morning News* that he was working to bring his voters back to the polls on election day. Although he expected to win, "when you're running against someone named Connally, you'd better run scared." He and his campaign team were optimistic, however, that the primary runoff between Dolph Briscoe and Sissy Farenthold for governor would attract a larger voter turnout than usual. Their optimism proved to be justified. The *Dallas Morning News* observed, "This year's lieutenant governor race has attracted more attention than any since 1962 when Preston Smith beat [former Texas House Speaker] Jimmy Turman."[75]

From May 4 until election day on June 3, Bill Hobby and Wayne Connally engaged in a heated runoff campaign—one that the *Houston Chronicle* described as "bitter." At one point, Hobby declared to the press that he had considered taking legal action to remove Connally's name from the ballot. He claimed that Connally had accepted campaign contributions from corporations "in clear violation of state law," which would legally disqualify his candidacy. Hobby told reporters he had decided against filing a lawsuit, however, because of the example his father had set when he was running against James Ferguson in 1918. Will Hobby and his allies had believed that the legislature's impeachment of Ferguson as governor in 1917 banned Ferguson from holding public office in Texas, a view that would later be confirmed by state courts, but not until after the election. Nevertheless, Will Hobby had thought it best to let "the people decide." "My father ran against a corrupt opponent," Bill declared, "and I'm running the same kind of campaign he did." When a reporter asked if he was comparing Connally to Ferguson, Hobby replied, "There is a strong similarity." When he was asked how he felt about charges that the race was "dirty," Hobby replied, "It's not me who's making it dirty."[76]

Hobby's campaign received a boost on May 9, when the Texas AFL-CIO's Committee on Political Education endorsed his candidacy. The *Texas Observer* noted that with the committee's endorsement, Hobby "geared up to meet labor half-way: he said he thinks public employees should have the right to unionize, but not to strike." Several environmental leaders in Texas also announced their support for Hobby.[77]

Armed with support from labor leaders, liberals, and environmentalists, Hobby also continued to pay attention to Black Texans and the newly enfranchised youth voters, especially those on the state's college campuses. Speaking at a Black church in Houston, Hobby hit Connally hard, describing him as "the brother of the man [John Connally] who called Martin Luther King a rabble-rouser who brought the [assassination] on himself." He appeared at several universities, focusing on those with the largest number of students, such as the University of Texas at Austin and the University of Houston. Reporters noted that Hobby seemed to relish campaigning at universities, "where the students can be blunt, grueling questioners." Wayne Connally also had college student committees working for him, but they struggled a bit with the fact that their candidate had vocally opposed and voted against lowering the voting age to eighteen. Wayne Connally's student committee at the University of Texas at Austin tried to solve that problem by running an ad in the student newspaper, the *Daily Texan*, with the surprising claim that Connally had actually voted for enfranchising eighteen-year-olds. The *Daily Texan*, however, ran an editorial pointing out that the ad was a "drastic misrepresentation" of Connally's position, citing the official record of his vote.[78]

Molly Ivins, who at the time was coeditor of the *Texas Observer*, noted that Connally's strategy for the runoff campaign was "to brand Bill Hobby a L-I-B-E-R-A-L." Hobby told a news conference in Dallas that Connally calling him a liberal showed "how desperate he is. Tell me what the word means. I'm a businessman. I'm president of a medium sized corporation with over 1,000 employees. My whole approach to government or business is solving the problem." Hobby's statement was an honest description of his political philosophy. Although he usually shunned labels, he sometimes referred to himself when speaking to reporters as a "progressive on social issues and a conservative on fiscal issues." He strongly preferred, however, to be identified as a "pragmatic problem solver."[79]

During a debate on Dallas's WFAA-TV near the end of the campaign, Connally continued to paint Hobby as a liberal who was out of touch with "true" Texas values. He accused Hobby of wanting to decriminalize marijuana, although Hobby's actual stance was in support of reducing punishment for private possession from a felony to a misdemeanor for first offenders, but not for drug dealers. Connally also charged that Hobby supported busing as a means to racially desegregate public schools. Hobby responded that he opposed busing because it "simply doesn't do the job of achieving equal educational opportunity." When Connally claimed that Hobby's support for lowering the voting age from twenty-one to eighteen was simply a political tactic to win over eighteen-year-old voters, Hobby responded that he believed that "the young people who have to fight our wars should have the opportunity to vote on the people who decide to wage those wars." In the opinion of one journalist, Hobby knocked Connally off balance at least three times. "Connally, red-faced and fuming with anger, never regained the initiative," the journalist observed. "In the heat of confrontation, Bill Hobby is double tough. Under pressure, he can be quietly deadly." A reporter at the *Houston Chronicle* was surprised that Hobby had shown "not a shred of nervousness" and had maintained "an almost incredible calm" despite Connally's attacks. Soon after the debate, Hobby's campaign aides were amazed to see him back at his motel in his swimming trunks, quietly reading a novel and getting some sun while lounging beside the pool.[80]

Hobby made good use of call-in radio shows broadcast from stations in the state's larger cities, especially Houston, Dallas, Austin, and San Antonio. Radio offered him a relaxed forum in which to answer questions about issues. His fast thinking and dry wit served him well when exchanging comments with listeners. For example, when a caller asked if he thought public officials indicted in the Sharpstown scandal were simply victims "of the times," Hobby quickly replied that he didn't know if they were "victims of the times," but they were "quite likely to serve some time."[81]

The campaign got dirtier a week prior to the election. "Thus far during the runoff campaigns," Molly Ivins reported, "the lieutenant governor's race is attracting the lion's share of the attention, mostly because that's where the mud's being slung. Great, gooey gobs of it." Hobby submitted photocopies of checks totaling $3,072 that Connally had received from the president of Frank Sharp's insurance company, National Bankers Life, for a hunting lease on Connally's ranch. Connally explained that the charge was based on the going rate for leases and had nothing to do with his support of the banking bills. On the checks themselves, however, the reason for payment was listed as "promotional expenses" for National Bankers Life. Hobby also accused Connally of accepting seventeen other illegal contributions from corporations. Molly Ivins noted that "Hobby was having a good day. But Connally . . . roared back gamely the very next day and announced that Bill Hobby is a child molester. If he'd thought of it, he probably would have added that Hobby is an egg sucker too."[82]

Connally's "child molester" accusation stemmed from an incident on September 10, 1967, when Hobby was accused of assaulting a minor. One of Hobby's neighbors in Houston alleged that when Hobby witnessed her eleven-year-old boy painfully wrenching the arm of his three-year-old son, Andrew, he went out in the yard and grabbed the older boy by the arm and loudly chastised him. The boy's mother called the police and filed an assault charge, but the Harris County district attorney concluded that the case was "not meritorious" and refused to refile it, which was equivalent to dismissal. During a speech in Lufkin, Connally said that in 1967 Hobby was "not attacking problems, he was attacking children." Hobby did not deny the charge, but he did say that he couldn't "imagine a self-respecting parent [who] wouldn't have" done the same thing. Connally declared, "I think Mr. Hobby owes an explanation to the people of Texas on why he attacked this minor and then managed to get the matter dropped or hushed up." After she investigated the matter, however, Molly Ivins learned from *Houston Post* staff members that Hobby had insisted that the *Post* report on the incident, which it did. "The *Post*, like any other major daily," Ivins explained, "would ordinarily have no more bothered with charges stemming from a neighborhood incident than they would front-page the DAR's dahlia contest." As Hobby would later recall, "The campaign was long and nasty."[83]

Hobby spent $523,000 (or $3.4 million in 2021) of his own money on the campaign. Hobby's friend, Senator Max Sherman, recalled that Hobby "enjoyed getting elected without having to have a super PAC or having to go chase after people to raise money, because he had the money. My own guess is that Bill probably had very few outside contributions. Which meant he wasn't beholden. And I think that's a real asset." Much of Hobby's campaign expense was for media ads during the runoff. In his no-frills, thirty-second television spots, Hobby stood in front of a plain background, speaking directly to the voters as the camera slowly zoomed in. Each ad had a theme based on typical voter concerns, such as education, drug problems, the economy, and welfare reform. In one ad, Hobby reassured prospective voters, "Only one machine can get me in office, and the person behind that machine . . . is you." The camera came to a stop on a tight shot of his face as the campaign's slogan ran across the screen in simple white type. A reporter for the *Houston Post* noted that Hobby had been considered "a poor public speaker" but that he had become "rather skilled at it, especially in the forceful image he projects on TV." The reporter also observed that Hobby had no more charisma on television than he had in other forums, but he made no attempt to be charismatic. His personal appearance remained unimportant to him as well. "His reasonably close-cropped hair is anything but mod," the reporter added, "and he still prefers narrow ties and white shirts with his stylish double-knit suits."[84]

By the time of the primary runoff, Hobby had accumulated much practical knowledge about the workings of Texas political campaigns at the local level. In his memoir, he recalled learning in 1972 that "there were maybe a dozen counties in Texas that were one-stop shopping. If The Man was for you, you got 70 per cent of the vote. If The Man was against you, you got 30 per cent. Either way, your business in that county was done." He noted that the Man might be a mayor, a judge, or a sheriff. In Fayette County, which is located between Austin and Houston, the Man was the politically powerful sheriff Jim Flournoy. "Jim and I got along fine, and he supported me," Hobby recalled. "Jim publicly anointed his candidates by having them join him in his convertible in the July 4th parade. I rode with Jim for several years." The brothel known as the Chicken Ranch was located near La Grange, the Fayette County seat. The Chicken Ranch would soon inspire a popular Broadway musical and movie, *The Best Little Whorehouse in Texas*, which featured a character based on Sheriff Flournoy who protected the brothel. Hobby's runoff campaign mailed at least one postcard to as many registered voters in Texas as possible. For distribution in Fayette County, Sheriff Flournoy took Hobby's postcards to the Chicken Ranch, "where the girls addressed them on slow afternoons," Hobby remembered. "We got 100% coverage in Fayette County, and I carried it handily."[85]

Hobby had a similar experience in another rural county. Late in the afternoon on election day, Hobby's campaign manager, who was an attorney in one of the large counties in West Texas where Connally was considered the favorite, called Hobby and told him he was going to win the county by a few votes. "That's wonderful!" Hobby replied. "But how do you know? The polls won't close for hours yet." The campaign manager answered, "Bill, my friend Marilyn is the county clerk here. I got her divorce for her years ago, and we have maintained a close personal relationship." Hobby carried the county by a few votes.[86]

Hobby's campaign also benefitted from his relationship with another influential and popular local political figure, state senator Max Sherman. Hobby has said that it was during a visit to Amarillo a few days before the runoff election that he realized he would defeat Connally. Bob Cargill flew Hobby to a private airport in Amarillo—an area in the Panhandle he expected Connally to carry. He was pleasantly surprised when Senator Sherman met him at the airport. Sherman drove Hobby to a campaign event, where he gave Hobby an enthusiastic introduction and announced that he was endorsing him for lieutenant governor—the first senator to do so. "I knew that was a good sign," Hobby recalled. Sherman, who had been deeply impressed by Hobby's work on the welfare reform committee the year before, later remembered that when he met Hobby at the airport, "I told him that I would help him and I hoped that he would win that runoff. We shared the fact that we were on the same platform and that we really had the same goals about good government."[87]

In late May, as the date for the runoff election drew near, Oveta was informed by Ed Harte that Bill seemed to be competitive against Connally in Corpus Christi. Harte suggested that it would be a big help if Oveta made an appearance there and that the *Caller-Times* would give her visit extensive coverage. She accepted Harte's invitation and held a press conference in Corpus Christi, during which she was able to discuss a wide range of issues. When a reporter told her that Connally had accused Bill of being "inconsistent, contradictory, and dishonest," Oveta replied, "Well, it's that season of the year for making political statements. What Mr. Connally says is his business. I believe in freedom of speech. I know of no dishonest statement made by Bill."[88]

On Election Day, June 3, 1972, Hobby defeated Connally in the Democratic primary runoff by 240,000 votes. Dolph Briscoe defeated Sissy Farenthold for the gubernatorial nomination. The large voter turnout was unprecedented for a runoff election in Texas. After Bill's victory, the publisher of the *Bryan Eagle* wrote Oveta: "Of great personal satisfaction was the fact that Brazos County . . . gave Bill sixty-five percent . . . of the votes. There is no question in my mind but that Bill has a unique opportunity . . . in the massive rejection of established politics. It is not very often that the populace rises en masse to register such wide sweeping disapproval as was manifest during the primaries."[89]

Texas was still a one-party state, which meant winning the Democratic primary practically guaranteed a victory for Democratic nominees for statewide office. Facing a token Republican opponent, Hobby soon made preparations for assuming office three months before the general election in November. Accordingly, the Hobbys moved to Austin a few weeks after Bill's victory. Because they had four kids, Bill and Diana decided to move into a house rather than live in the lieutenant governor's apartment in the Capitol. Diana Hobby told reporters that she and Bill would use the apartment for entertaining and as an interesting place for overnight guests to stay. "But to try to shoehorn our brood into it would be a disaster." Paul Hobby, who was eleven at the time, later noted that "Ben Barnes's family had actually lived in that apartment in the Capitol, but my mother disliked the whole idea of living there. That wasn't going to happen even for five seconds. But as a kid, it was fun to go up there and scrabble around." Laura, who was thirteen when her family moved to Austin, recalled that she also enjoyed her visits to the apartment and to her father's office. "The people that were on Papa's staff were just extended family to us." But Laura noted that whenever she and her brother, Paul, went to the Capitol, "We were always cautioned to be quieter than normal and respectful when we were there and to dress appropriately." The Hobbys bought a house in the Northwest Hills section of the city. Laura, who entered the eighth grade that fall, recalled, "As a family, we were sort of sad to leave our friends, so we kept our house in Houston, and we returned there for lots of things. It was a big adjustment for us to go from private school in Houston to public school in Austin. But I don't recall anybody being heartbroken about it."[90]

CHAPTER 7

THE FIRST TERM

With no Republican opponent in the general election in November, Bill Hobby's quest to be lieutenant governor was complete. With the 1972 election in effect decided, the *Houston Journalism Review*, an upstart, new, but short-lived newsletter local journalists produced independent of their employers, published an article analyzing the *Houston Post*'s coverage of Bill Hobby's campaign. The article alleged that in the first primary campaign, the *Post* had printed more stories about Hobby than all the other candidates combined. "Nobody in the state could whisper a good word about him, or he about himself, that didn't end up as three inches in the *Post*," the writers complained. "Four months after his announcement, the *Post* was still printing news about Bill Hobby [while] neglecting to mention his political aspirations."[1]

In an editorial, the *Review* also raised a larger question about the propriety of journalists and newspaper publishers being directly involved in political campaigns. "As journalists and as citizens we are inclined to believe that Hobby could better serve the public by devoting his energies to improving the *Post* instead of the state." Although Hobby declared that he would take a leave of absence from the *Post*, which would remove him from editorial and news coverage decisions, the editorial argued it was "almost beyond the realm of possibility that the *Post* will be able to do critical, fair, investigative reporting of the lieutenant governor's performance. The fact that his mother is chairman of the board and editor and that he very well may return to the paper in the future will not be lost on the *Post* management and news staff. Pressures or not, reporters inevitably will fear reprisals for writing stories critical of Hobby and his political allies."[2]

Curiously, the *Dallas Morning News* was less concerned about the *Houston Post*'s objectivity or a journalist taking an elected office than it was about the possibility of Bill Hobby withholding information from the news media because he was a journalist. The newspaper's veteran Capitol correspondent Richard Morehead observed that Hobby had joined a long list of journalists and newspaper publishers who had become state officials, including Governor James S. Hogg, editor of the newspapers in Quitman and Longview, as well as Hobby's own father. "More often than not," Morehead noted, "it is harder to get information from an ex-newsman in government than it is from the other types. Perhaps it takes one to know one."[3]

Because Hobby would not take office until January 1973, he turned his attention during the last six months of 1972 to the mundane but necessary tasks of securing office space and assembling a staff. But he also had other, more significant goals. The first was the writing and approval of Senate rules for the upcoming legislative session. After that, his most important goal was to help pass an amendment to hold a constitutional convention to rewrite Texas's "antiquated" 1876 constitution. The amendment was on the ballot of the general election in November. Free of concerns about his own election, Hobby's political efforts prior to November focused almost exclusively on behalf of the constitutional convention amendment. Accordingly, Hobby traveled around the state in support of the amendment, stressing the need for annual sessions of the legislature and an expansion of the governor's powers. The amendment passed.[4]

In September, during the last special session of the Sixty-Second Legislature and four months prior to his inauguration as lieutenant governor, Hobby fought an effort to strip his office of its power to control the Senate by revising the Senate's procedural rules. Galveston's liberal senator Babe Schwartz had drafted the revised rules, which reduced the number of standing committees and the number of members on each committee. Hobby approved of those changes and most of the other rules Schwartz revised, but he opposed a rule that would restrict his ability to appoint committee members. Another liberal, Arlington senator Oscar Mauzy, offered a different set of rules that would essentially strip the lieutenant governor of even more power than Schwartz's proposed rules. Although he would not become lieutenant governor until January 1973, Hobby worked with Schwartz and Ben Barnes, who was still lieutenant governor, to persuade enough senators to reject Mauzy's proposal. Hobby remained opposed to Schwartz's rule stripping him of the power to assign members to committees, but he decided to wait until January, when he had taken office, to fight to get that rule rewritten.[5]

Hobby's preparations for his new job included several meetings with his legislative mentor, Ben Ramsey, who was now a member of the Texas Railroad Commission. Ramsey advised Hobby to act as soon as the Senate convened for its new term in January to fight to restore the powers that had been taken away from his office during the last special session. Hobby was an eager student who would adopt Ramsey's legislative style when he presided over the Senate. "I never realized just how much I learned or absorbed from Ben Ramsey until I first started presiding. I would answer a question from a senator and the words that came out of my mouth were Ramsey's words!" Hobby later stated that he "learned at the knee of an awfully good teacher. Ben Ramsey was the master of the art." Ramsey would be a frequent visitor to Hobby's office throughout his first regular session. Hobby told his staff that whenever Ramsey came to his office for a visit, he didn't "care how many reporters or lobbyists or whatever" were waiting to meet with him, they would "have to wait until Governor Ramsey says what he has to say." Hobby would rely on Ramsey's advice until Ramsey's death in March 1985.[6]

On August 25, with the primaries over and a slate of fresh new reform candidates on the ballot after most of the incumbent state officeholders had been wiped out, the Texas Democratic Party honored one of those fresh new faces, Bill Hobby, with a one-hundred-dollar-per-plate fundraising dinner in Austin, featuring US Senator Lloyd Bentsen, Texas Land Commissioner Bob Armstrong, and Texas Agriculture Commissioner John White. The new guard present at the dinner included gubernatorial nominee Dolph Briscoe and his wife, Janey, and attorney general nominee John Hill. Newly nominated Houston congressional candidate Barbara Jordan drew as much attention at the dinner as the honoree, Bill Hobby. Jordan would soon be the first Black woman from the South to be elected to the US House of Representatives. Houstonians Jordan and Hobby had forged a friendship when they both served on the welfare reform committee. During the event, Jordan went to the podium and declared her pride that "Bill Hobby is joining the leadership of Texas. Texas is better for it." As usual for such gatherings of public officeholders, lobbyists were the main source of financial support for the event, as they purchased all 102 eight-person tables at $1,000 each. Hobby aides later reported that the dinner had raised more than the original goal of $150,000.[7]

As the Democratic Party's nominee for lieutenant governor, Hobby was also involved in the 1972 presidential campaign. Democratic Party presidential nominee George McGovern, the liberal antiwar senator from South Dakota, was deeply unpopular in Texas. Nearly every Democratic officeholder in the state avoided an association with the McGovern campaign, but not Hobby. McGovern was too liberal for Hobby's more conservative economic views, and he refrained from traveling around the state making speeches for the South Dakota senator. However, Hobby, whose past loyalty to the Democratic Party had been questioned during the primary campaign, could ill afford to be perceived as not supporting the Democratic nominee for president. Accordingly, unlike most of the Democratic leadership in Texas, Hobby not only publicly endorsed McGovern for president but also appeared with McGovern when the US senator addressed a joint session of the Texas Legislature. Hobby accompanied the presidential nominee into the House Chamber and sat with the McGovern entourage on the Speaker's dais. Having no Republican opponent in the general election, Hobby had no practical concerns about his endorsement of McGovern threatening his election chances in November. In addition, Hobby strongly disliked President Nixon, who was running for a second term. Despite news media suspicions about Bill's party loyalty, Oveta nevertheless published an editorial in the *Post* endorsing Nixon's reelection.[8]

On November 7, 1972, Bill Hobby was elected lieutenant governor of Texas, winning 93 percent of the vote. Dolph Briscoe was elected governor, although by a surprisingly narrow margin. Richard Nixon was elected to a second term as president. Now lieutenant governor elect, Hobby decided in early December to host a retreat to include every member of the Senate—the sixteen incumbents as well as the fifteen newly elected rookies. With almost half of the Senate filled with newly elected members, Hobby hoped a three-day, two-night legislative retreat would help the freshmen and the incumbents to become acquainted not only with each other but also with him. He asked Bill Jenkins, one of his aides, to find a remote place away from the news media where they could spend a weekend to mix and mingle and plan for the upcoming legislative session. Hobby also hoped to round up enough vote pledges to support his revision of the recently amended Senate rules. Jenkins knew the perfect place for the getaway: the Provident Hotel, a private establishment in Provident City, a ghost town in Colorado County, between Houston and Victoria.[9]

Before he attended the retreat, Hobby met with Ben Barnes on December 2 in Brownwood to get his advice and a pledge of support for his fight to restore the rules. Barnes agreed to do whatever Hobby asked of him. Although Barnes was a lame duck, his term would not end until January 16, when Hobby was sworn into office. His last duty as lieutenant governor would be to preside over the Senate from January 9 until Hobby took over. Barnes agreed to attempt to restore the old Senate rules during his last week in office. If successful, this strategy would allow Hobby to avoid a difficult confrontation with the senators at the very beginning of his term. His chances looked slim, however, because as a lame duck Barnes lacked the influence he'd once had, and the same senators who had changed the rules in the last called session would still be in place until January 16.[10]

Hobby soon gathered with thirty-one senators for a weekend of male bonding, having lost Barbara Jordan, their only female senator, to the US Congress. As it developed, however, being locked up in a legislative retreat with a bunch of lively, heavy-drinking politicians turned out not to be Bill Hobby's idea of a good time. One of the incumbents, Oscar Mauzy, later described the retreat as "primarily a deer-shooting contest, hunting, drinking whiskey, and playing poker." East Texan Don Adams, who was one of the newly elected senators, recalled, "Governor Hobby was sort of reticent around all these guys. I mean, you get that whole Senate together and they are boisterous. And Bill Hobby is not boisterous."[11]

After dinner on the first day, it became clear that Lubbock senator H. J. "Doc" Blanchard, who had supported Wayne Connally, was going to lead an effort to take power away from the new lieutenant governor. At an after-dinner meeting, Blanchard tried to persuade a majority of the senators to agree to lock in the recently passed Senate rules when the new session convened. By this time, everyone was "good and drunk," Oscar Mauzy recalled. With inhibitions and guards lowered, Hobby was able to identify which members intended to vote to strip his powers come January. Mauzy soon realized that Hobby's real purpose in calling the retreat had been to persuade the newly elected members to vote to restore his power. Hobby's effort paid off. "He picked up a bunch of freshmen," Mauzy noted. "A bunch of them didn't know anything about the rules, didn't understand them at all." Nevertheless, Mauzy was determined to join with Blanchard to force the vote for their version of the rules as soon as the Senate convened in January.[12]

As a result of the Provident City weekend retreat, Hobby knew that his plan to revise the Senate rules faced tough resistance, and it would be his first real challenge as lieutenant governor, but he felt confident that he had rounded up enough freshman support to prevail. As Don Adams, the newly elected senator from East Texas, later noted, "Senate rules are the province of the lieutenant governor. For a senator to attempt to bypass the lieutenant governor's traditional sphere in adopting the rules is pretty bad." The Provident City gathering also gave Hobby a hint about which senators he might have problems with and which he could depend on—including Adams, who had turned down Hobby's request for an endorsement during the election campaign because Adams had been running his own campaign and hadn't wanted to alienate any of his potential voters. However, as Adams was leaving the retreat in Provident City, he told Hobby, "I want you to know I'll support whatever you want the Senate rules to be." As Adams later explained, "It became very apparent to me early on that Bill Hobby had a vision and he was trying to implement his vision." That was the beginning of a political alliance and a long friendship between Hobby and Adams.[13]

On January 9, 1973, the Sixty-Second Texas Legislature convened for the traditional official last meeting before the newly elected and reelected members of the Sixty-Third Legislature were sworn into office a week later. That traditional meeting was the last over which the outgoing lieutenant governor, Ben Barnes, would preside. Bill Hobby was in the Capitol for this session, even though it would be another seven days before he took his oath of office. After his victory in the primary, Hobby had spent much time in Austin getting ready for his new job, which included conferring with Ben Barnes. After Hobby taped an appearance on a political interview program at Austin's KTBC television station, he returned to the Capitol, where he saw Barnes walking down a hallway. "He invited me to come with him to [Senator Tom] Creighton's office for a drink," Hobby wrote. "Barnes, Sen. A. R. 'Babe' Schwartz of Galveston, Creighton, and I were there. It was a very fruitful meeting, not in terms of anything decided, but because of the beginning of a fine personal relationship."[14]

That meeting connected Hobby to valuable legislative allies, particularly for his upcoming battle to restore the powers of the lieutenant governor under the Senate rules. Referring to his chance visit with Barnes and Creighton, Hobby noted that "the first good thing that happened in my relationship with [Tom] Creighton was one of those things that I could never have planned, it just happened." Schwartz, a combative liberal who had supported Joe Christie for lieutenant governor, recalled that he "kind of suspected that [Hobby's] coming from the Houston establishment didn't bode well for my future in the Senate. I was not for him as lieutenant governor. I was not one of his troops." Schwartz, however, soon became a key member of the Hobby team.[15]

During this interim period between his victory in November and his inauguration on January 16, Hobby organized his staff, including the Senate parliamentarian, a post critical to the lieutenant governor's ability to preside. Hobby selected Dr. June Hyer, an academician who had served ably as the chief of staff for Hobby's welfare reform committee. Hyer took on additional duties as one of Hobby's executive assistants. Margaret Behrens, Barnes's office manager, continued in that same role for Hobby and worked for him until she retired in 1987. Hobby's campaign manager, Steve Oaks, stayed on as his chief executive assistant. Hobby's staff also included administrative assistants Tom Hagan, formerly with the Houston Chamber of Commerce; Bill Jenkins, who had been on Hobby's campaign staff; and Jason Perlman, formerly on Barnes's staff. Bob Cargill agreed to serve as Hobby's press spokesperson, while also continuing in his role as Hobby's pilot. Hobby appointed North Carolina native Delores Hunter, who had earned a doctorate at the University of Houston, as one of his major policy advisors; she thus became the first African American to serve in a professional position in the lieutenant governor's office.[16]

While Hobby appointed his staff, he devoted a week to meeting privately with individual senators to win support for a compromise proposal to restore most of the lieutenant governor's powers that had been taken away during the fourth special session in 1972. The amended rules had left only two appointments available to Hobby during his first term, which would greatly weaken his power as president of the Senate. Hobby's meetings with each senator were critical to his effort to restore power to the office. His strategy was to promise specific committee assignments and chairmanships to members who would agree to vote in favor of his compromise proposal for the new rules. June Hyer and Steve Oaks helped him determine committee assignments. Hobby's plan would also allow some of the senators to retain their old committee assignments. These meetings also gave him another opportunity, in addition to his discussions at the weekend retreat in Provident City, to make his case to the newly elected senators, who now made up almost half of the Senate—this time in private, one-on-one conversations. Hobby later noted that as a result of these private meetings he was "able to gain substantial support for a compromise proposal." The new rules, which Babe Schwartz drafted in conference with Hobby and Barnes, would give Hobby the power to fill the remaining open seats on each committee without regard to seniority, as well as to appoint the chair. It was this proposal that Hobby would submit to a vote of the Senate on the first day of the new session.[17]

One way Hobby was able to restore the rules was by agreeing to keep four influential veteran members as chairmen of their committees: A. M. Aiken Jr. on Finance, Bill Moore on State Affairs, Charles Herring on Jurisprudence, and Jack Hightower on Administration. Hobby offered the chairmanship of the Natural Resources Committee to Max Sherman, who had helped his campaign in Amarillo. And he punished one of his opponents, Lubbock senator Doc Blanchard, by removing him from his chairmanship of the Economic Development Committee. "Blanchard, of course, had strongly supported Wayne Connally," Hobby said later, "and had been one of the sponsors of the effort to strip the [lieutenant governor's] office of its powers." He replaced Blanchard with another new ally, incumbent senator Tom Creighton, a conservative Democrat from Mineral Wells. Creighton's new committee included responsibility for savings and loan, insurance, and banking legislation. "I was absolutely floored," Creighton later recalled. "I looked at him, and said, 'I don't know a thing about insurance.' He said, 'Maybe that's good. I don't want any more Sharpstown legislation passed. From what I know about you, you have the beady eyes and the guts to kill it.' Of course, that flattered me." Hobby allowed Creighton to pick his own committee members.[18]

While making committee selections, Hobby singled out Don Adams, the new senator from Jasper, in East Texas, as an ally. Hobby invited Adams to meet with him in Houston. "I didn't know what to expect," Adams recalled. "I went down there to his office in the *Post*. He was very coolly cordial to me. Hobby wanted to know what committee I was interested in and I told him I was interested in the Rules Committee and in the Jurisprudence Committee. And he gave me them to me." Babe Schwartz later noted that Adams "became Hobby's best man for everything."[19]

Late in the afternoon on Monday, January 15, 1973, Hobby was preparing for his inauguration as lieutenant governor of Texas the following day. Bill Jenkins informed him that Lyndon Johnson had failed to respond to Hobby's mailed invitation for him and his wife, Lady Bird, to attend the event. That news disappointed Hobby. His family's connections to the Johnson family went back more than five decades. The presence of the Johnsons at such a landmark occasion for the Hobby family would please and honor both Bill and his mother.[20]

Before the inaugural dinner that night at Austin's Municipal Auditorium, Hobby made a special effort to lure the Johnsons to the inauguration as his guests, where he hoped they would sit in prominent places on the inaugural platform. When Hobby dialed LBJ's private telephone number at his ranch near Stonewall, Texas, the former president answered the phone with a gruff, "Yes?" "Mr. President, this is Bill Hobby. I didn't want the day to pass without telling you how much it would mean to me and Diana and my mother if you would come to the inauguration." LBJ asked when the inauguration would occur. Hobby replied, "Tomorrow." Showing impatience, LBJ said he knew it was the next day, "But what time?" Hobby said it would be at noon. "Noon!" LBJ exclaimed. "That's when I take my nap. You're just trying to kill a sick old man!" With no further comment, Johnson slammed the phone down.[21]

Very soon after that abrupt conclusion to the telephone call, Mary Rather, LBJ's secretary, called Bill Jenkins and said that the Johnsons would attend the inaugural ceremony after all. When Jenkins asked Governor-elect Dolph Briscoe if he approved of making space for the Johnsons on the crowded inaugural platform, Briscoe insisted there was no room for them. There were two reasons for Briscoe's negative reaction. The primary one was that the governor-elect's wife, Janey, had long disliked LBJ. The other was that Dolph Briscoe feared that the news media would focus most of its attention on the former president, who had rarely appeared in public since leaving the White House, rather than on the inaugural ceremony. Knowing Hobby would not take Briscoe's decision well, Jenkins decided to take an indirect path to get the news to him. Aware that Hobby had been told that every seat on the platform was taken, he asked Hobby where on the platform the Johnsons were supposed to sit.

"Next to Diana and me on the platform. Where else?" Hobby answered. "There isn't room for them on the platform," Jenkins replied. "Okay," Hobby responded. "Diana and I will give our seats to the Johnsons. I'll just stand out in the crowd and raise my right hand and swear to 'preserve, protect and defend the Constitution of the United States and this state.'" Jenkins replied, "I knew that's what you would say. I'll go back to the inaugural planning committee and give them your decision." As Hobby wryly noted later, "It turned out there was room for the Johnsons on the platform after all."[22]

Inaugural day began early on January 16, 1973, with a prayer breakfast at the Villa Capri, a large motel adjacent to the University of Texas. It had one of the few dining rooms in Austin in the early 1970s that could accommodate the five hundred ticketed guests attending the breakfast. Bill and Diana Hobby sat with Dolph and Janey Briscoe as preachers prayed from the podium asking for divine support for the newly elected leaders of the Lone Star State. Tom Landry, the celebrated head football coach of the Dallas Cowboys, served as the featured speaker. Briscoe later recalled that Landry gave "an inspirational talk that set the moral tone for the remainder of the inauguration."[23]

After breakfast, the Hobbys, the Briscoes, and the other elected officials of Texas state government made their way to the Capitol, where an audience of approximately five thousand had gathered on the South Lawn. Austin had endured freezing temperatures for several days prior to the event, but the weather had improved, with the morning's temperature in the low fifties, although the breezy and cloudy conditions made it seem colder. Shortly before noon, VIPs took their seats on the inaugural platform alongside three former Texas governors, Allan Shivers, Price Daniel Sr., and Preston Smith. The crowd reacted with surprised cheers and applause as the thirty-sixth president and the former first lady walked onto the platform. After the Johnsons took their seats, Bill and Diana Hobby, followed by Dolph and Janey Briscoe, walked out of the Capitol to the inaugural platform under an archway of drawn swords formed by the white-uniformed Ross Volunteers honor guard of cadets from Texas A&M University. A nineteen-gun salute echoed across the Capitol grounds. The entire event was broadcast live over a statewide television network.[24]

At noon, Bill Hobby, with his wife, Diana, at his side, swore before Texas Supreme Court chief justice Robert Calvert that he would faithfully execute the duties of lieutenant governor. He was now officially the thirty-eighth lieutenant governor of Texas. Immediately after taking the oath of office, Bill delivered his inaugural speech, in which he declared that his efforts as lieutenant governor would concentrate on giving every child in Texas an opportunity for a good education, reforming the state's antiquated criminal justice system, and writing and passing a new state constitution. He ended his brief speech with gracious comments about the new governor, the wealthy rancher, banker, and former state legislator from the southwest Texas town of Uvalde. Hobby pledged that in performing the duties of lieutenant governor, he would remain "at the right hand of Dolph Briscoe, whom we principally honor here today."[25]

After Briscoe took his oath of office as governor and delivered his inaugural speech, the ceremony ended. As the VIPs stepped off the inaugural platform and entered the Capitol rotunda, well-wishers mobbed LBJ. Despite his initial negative reaction to the Johnsons' being seated on the platform, Governor Briscoe invited the couple to be his guests at the official luncheon in the Governor's Mansion. LBJ declined, saying that he didn't want to impose on Briscoe's special event, but with Briscoe's insistence, he eventually accepted the invitation. Lyndon and Lady Bird arrived at the mansion ahead of the Briscoes and the Hobbys. The Briscoes were surprised when they entered the dining room to see that LBJ had grabbed the governor's seat at the head of the table and was enthusiastically holding court. Oveta sat next to LBJ, and they exchanged memories of their long relationship. The Briscoes took chairs reserved for other guests as LBJ, clearly energized by the warm reception he had received at the inauguration, told war stories and ate food off of his neighbors' plates while Janey Briscoe silently fumed.[26]

After the luncheon, the Briscoes and the Hobbys took their seats on a raised platform on Congress Avenue to view the inaugural parade. Two hours later, Dolph Briscoe and Bill Hobby hosted a public reception in the great rotunda of the Capitol. There were no special or invited guests for this event. Briscoe later recalled that he and Hobby "felt strongly that we should be available to greet and shake the hand of any member of the general public who wanted to attend." They were both acutely aware that public trust in state officials had been badly damaged by the recent Sharpstown corruption scandal, which had ended the political careers of several state officeholders and played a key role in Briscoe's and Hobby's own election victories. "Bill and I decided," Briscoe later said, "to throw open the doors of the Capitol for an event to symbolize our determination to conduct a state government that would be open to the scrutiny of the people." The reception lasted two hours. "We had invited to the reception those who had elected us, the Texas public," Hobby recalled, "and we shook hands until there were no more to shake." At eight o'clock that night, Bill and Diana attended the governor's black-tie inaugural ball at the Municipal Auditorium on the shore of Austin's Town Lake. Public galas were held at Gregory Gym (a rock concert), City Coliseum (a square dance), and the Terrace Square Ballroom ("candlelight dancing").[27]

On Wednesday, January 17, the day after the exhausting round of inaugural celebrations that had lasted from breakfast until midnight, a tired but proud Bill Hobby stood at the dais of the ornate Texas Senate Chamber and gaveled the thirty-one-member legislative body to order. The gavel he used was the one LBJ had given him during the primary campaign. Sixty years earlier, Will Hobby had gaveled open his first session of the Texas Senate. Following in his father's footsteps, Bill had finally found a prominent place of his own. And it was of his own making—one to which he had long aspired. Diana, the Hobbys' four children, and Bill's mother, Oveta, stood with him on the dais. Bill's sister, Jessica Hobby Catto, and her husband, Henry Catto, also attended the ceremony.

After the opening gavel, the dean of the Senate, A. M. Aiken, a Democrat who had served in that legislative body since 1937, presented Will Hobby's official portrait as lieutenant governor to Bill, who showed it to his mother. Oveta smiled warmly and waved to the members of the Senate. Bill later hung the portrait, on loan from the Texas State Library, in a prominent location in his formal office in the Capitol, where it remained for the remainder of his service as lieutenant governor.[28]

After the Senate's ceremonial gathering adjourned, the senators moved to the House Chamber to attend the joint session for Governor Briscoe to deliver his first official speech to the legislature. However, before House Speaker Price Daniel Jr. introduced the new governor, Daniel announced that the legislature was deeply honored by the presence of Bill Hobby's mother, Oveta Culp Hobby. He noted that she had won national fame as the wartime leader of the Women's Army Corps; as the first secretary of the US Department of Health, Education, and Welfare; and as the publisher of the *Houston Post* and the owner of a radio and television station. Daniel added that Oveta's legacy also included her pathbreaking service in the Texas Legislature as parliamentarian of the House from 1926 until 1931 while only in her twenties. As Oveta rose from her chair to be recognized, she received a standing ovation and scattered cheers. When his mother stood up on the House floor, it reminded Bill that because he was born in January 1932, his mother had been carrying him while she was still working as House parliamentarian in the spring of 1931. It was something he often joked about when he emphasized to friends how long he had been involved with the legislature. "Therefore," he loved to say, "I attended my first session of the legislature *in utero*!"[29]

Depending on who holds the office, how active the officeholder chooses to be, and the goodwill of the Senate, the lieutenant governor of Texas has typically exercised more legislative power than the governor. The 1876 state constitution established a "weak governor" form of state leadership in which the governor's powers are mainly restricted to vetoing legislation, the exclusive authority to call special sessions of the legislature, and authority to set the agenda for those sessions. The lieutenant governor's constitutional role is to assume the office of the state's chief executive in the event of the governor's resignation, death, or impeachment. All three of those situations have occurred in Texas history. The only duty the Texas Constitution assigns to the lieutenant governor is to serve as the Senate's chief presiding officer. The constitution also allows the lieutenant governor to cast a vote whenever a Senate vote is tied. The lieutenant governor also chairs the Legislative Budget Board, which writes the first draft of the state budget, giving the lieutenant governor the ability to influence the financial direction of state government. Hobby especially enjoyed the role he played on the budget board because it allowed him to dig deeply into the financial math that made government operations possible. He would later state that presiding over the Senate was important, but it was more important to serve as a chairman of the Legislative Budget Board. "That's really my greatest interest in state government. The budgetary and appropriations process is the principal work product of any legislative session."[30]

But what makes the lieutenant governor a more powerful position than the governor are the rules the senators pass at the start of each session to impose order on their operational procedures. As the Senate has evolved over several decades, its members have used the rules to enable the lieutenant governor to serve as their legislative guide and manager in addition to carrying out constitutionally mandated duties as the Senate's presiding officer who issues parliamentary rulings. In recent history, Senate rules have given the lieutenant governor authority to select members of committees, designate the chairs, assign bills to specific committees, and establish the Senate agenda, which includes deciding which bills can come up for debate and which cannot. Those Senate-delegated responsibilities give the lieutenant governor solid control over the flow of legislation.[31]

Another key to the lieutenant governor's power, especially during Hobby's time in office, was the Senate rule that required a favorable vote of two-thirds of the Senate for consideration of legislation. Eleven senators could shut down bills that had passed the House. Hobby soon found that the two-thirds rule was "a very good one." He learned to depend on it, "to prevent things from being considered by the Senate until they are ripe for consideration."[32]

Before the new lieutenant governor could exercise his powers, the Senate had to decide what those powers were going to be. Which meant that the first item on the agenda had to be a debate about and a vote on the Senate rules for this new session. Not only was passage of the Senate rules the first item on the agenda, but it was also Hobby's first challenge as the Senate's presiding officer. As Ben Ramsey's parliamentarian, he had seen firsthand how important the Senate rules were in making the lieutenant governor a significant player in the shaping of legislation. As Hobby later stressed, he had no intention of allowing the lieutenant governor of Texas to become "the kind of glorified clerkship that it is in many other states." That was the reason he had worked carefully in the previous weeks to lay the groundwork for the Senate to restore most of the lieutenant governor's powers that had been lost during the second special session in the summer of 1972. That strategy had included an attempt by Ben Barnes to persuade the outgoing Senate to restore the old rules, but that effort failed.[33]

Nevertheless, Hobby did persuade all fifteen of the new senators (nearly half of the members) and some of the incumbents to support his plan. But first, Hobby had to stave off Oscar Mauzy's floor fight against the compromise proposal that Hobby and Babe Schwartz had worked out before the session. The debate lasted four hours, but the outcome was twenty-four to six in favor of Hobby's proposal. During the rules fight, Tom Creighton offered an amendment to tighten requirements for bringing bills to the Senate floor. Because the vote was fifteen to fifteen, Hobby exercised his constitutional power to break ties, casting the deciding vote in favor of Creighton's amendment. Hobby later recalled that after the vote, Creighton "came up to the rostrum to confer his highest compliment: "Man, you've got brass balls." The venerable dean of the Senate, A. M. Aiken Jr., also came up to the rostrum that first day of the session and pointed out to the new lieutenant governor—who, as usual, was unaware of how he had dressed for the occasion—"Bill, you're not wearing a suit." Hobby later admitted, "That was the first and last time I ever presided over the senate without wearing a suit."[34]

After Mauzy lost his battle to strip the lieutenant governor of most of his power, the senator argued that his fight wasn't personal. "[Hobby] knew before he ever ran for lieutenant governor how I felt about the rules because I told him," Mauzy recalled. "He got out and hustled some votes and beat me." Hobby patched up his relationship with Mauzy after he prevailed in the rules fight by reappointing him chairman of the Education Committee. Hobby considered Mauzy "the most knowledgeable member of the Senate in the area of educational finance."[35]

The reason Hobby wanted an expert on school finance to lead the education committee was because of a class-action lawsuit, *Rodriguez v. San Antonio Independent School District*, which claimed that the Texas system of school finance was unconstitutional because of unequal funding between poor and wealthy school districts. In December 1971, a federal court had ruled in favor of the plaintiffs, but the state appealed. When the Senate convened in January 1973, the US Supreme Court was reviewing the case. Because of *Rodriguez*, Hobby knew public-school financing would be a major area of legislative concern for the next several years, no matter what the Supreme Court decided. The court ruled in March 1973 that the Texas system did not violate the federal constitution, but that it was a problem that should be resolved by the state legislature. After that decision, other lawsuits were soon filed on behalf of plaintiffs seeking more equality in public-school financing.[36]

The public-school financing controversy inspired Hobby to dig out an old letter his father had received in 1918 when he was governor that complained about the same problem. "That the constitutional provision for equal and uniform taxation has never been enforced in any county in Texas is indisputable," the writer observed. "That glaring inequalities exist in every county in Texas is well known to all." More than half a century later, the problem remained. At the beginning of the session, Hobby placed the letter on his desk in the lieutenant governor's office as a reminder that comparable issues had plagued the state for decades. He kept the letter in place throughout his service as lieutenant governor, not as an excuse for inaction but as a reminder to not let his frustrations get out of hand when solutions were hard to find. In an interview with a reporter, Hobby admitted that it was vexing to see how many similar issues were still being confronted more than half a century later. Those issues included women's rights, prohibition, and political ethics. When his father was governor, the main issue for women's rights had been suffrage, "but now it's abortion." Will Hobby had also confronted the controversy "over a widely used but prohibited drug, alcohol. Now it's marijuana." In addition, Bill Hobby pointed out that "there was the issue of ethics of state officials, with my father becoming governor when Jim Ferguson was impeached. There would appear to be a rhythm to our concerns that seems to reoccur."[37]

After Hobby's victory in the Senate rules fight, Governor Briscoe asked him to represent Texas at the inauguration of Richard Nixon to his second term. Accordingly, Bill and Diana flew to Washington, DC, on January 18, 1973, where they attended two events soon after arrival. One was a reception for Vice President Spiro Agnew at the old Smithsonian Castle on the National Mall, which Hobby later complained was "a mob scene." He and Diana quickly fled the reception and went to the Kennedy Center, where Frank Sinatra was staging an event in honor of all the state governors. Bored by the program, which the Hobbys thought was "incredibly" bad, they fled during the intermission, which didn't occur until 11:15 p.m. Bill later observed that "the people I saw the next day who did not have the foresight did not get out of there until 1:30 a.m."[38]

Bill Hobby and Steve Oaks, who had flown to Washington the day before the Hobbys, devoted the next morning to meetings with members of the Texas congressional delegation, including Senator Lloyd Bentsen and Representatives Bob Eckhardt and Barbara Jordan. While Bill was visiting with Bentsen, the senator hinted that at some point in the future, perhaps in 1976, he might be a candidate for vice president or even president. Bentsen would also be up for reelection to the US Senate in 1976, and he planned to run for a second term. In the event he was nominated for a national office, Bentsen wanted to take advantage of the Texas law allowing the state's US senators to run simultaneously for reelection and for vice president or president. The bill had been passed when Hobby was Ben Ramsey's parliamentarian in 1959. It had been for LBJ's benefit, as he prepared for his run for the presidency in 1960. Hobby assured Bentsen that, "wisely, there is no thought of changing this law, although we doubtlessly will change the dates of the primaries."[39]

That evening Bill and Diana hosted a dinner party for a few of their old friends living in the Washington area, including John Davis and Bill's St. Albans classmate Bob Shorb and his wife, Teeny. At noon on the following day, the Hobbys attended Nixon's inauguration, which was held at the East Portico of the Capitol. Bill later said that Nixon's sixteen-minute-long acceptance speech, as well as the entire ceremony, was "depressing." As soon as the ceremony ended, he and Diana raced to National Airport to return to Austin.[40]

On the afternoon of January 22, two days after the Hobbys arrived home, Lyndon Johnson suffered a fatal heart attack at his ranch in the Texas Hill Country. Bill was attending a reception at Austin's Commodore Perry Hotel when he heard the news. He immediately went to his office at the Capitol to confer on the phone with Briscoe about state arrangements and procedures for honoring Johnson. The news of LBJ's death was a surprise but not a shock to Hobby or to Briscoe. The last time they had seen the former president had been at the state Capitol on inauguration day. "President and Mrs. Johnson were just mobbed by everybody wanting to shake their hands," Hobby recalled. "I remember standing there with Diana and saying, 'You know, if this is that old man's last hurrah, it is a good one.' He was sick, and obviously so." It was LBJ's last public appearance.[41]

A few days after LBJ was buried on his ranch near Stonewall, Texas, on January 25, the members of the Sixty-Third Legislature reconvened in Austin to carry out its most important job: governing. The members had a constitutionally prescribed time frame during which they could get the job done. The Texas Constitution restricts the number of days that a regular biennial session of the legislature can meet to a maximum of 140, which are usually spread over five months, starting on the second Tuesday in January of odd-numbered years.

Hobby normally convened each meeting of the legislature at noon. He would then ask the secretary of the Senate to call the roll of the thirty-one members in alphabetical order. The roll call was followed by a prayer given by a guest chaplain. Hobby would then give the Senate secretary a list of all bills that had been filed. As he handed the bills off, he designated the committees to which they would be submitted. After the bills had been assigned, Hobby introduced special guests in attendance. Then individual senators could make remarks on any subject. Deeper into the legislative session, as committees completed their meetings and public hearings, the committee members voted on the bills. If a bill passed the committee, it was eligible for the intent calendar, which brought it to the full Senate for debate. Every morning each member received a list of all the bills eligible for debate and a vote on that day. No member was allowed more than five bills on the intent calendar at one time. When a senator thought there were enough votes to carry his or her bill, the senator would call for debate and a vote, which required a two-thirds majority.[42]

Although Hobby was the new lieutenant governor, he knew the procedures well because of his previous experience as Ben Ramsey's parliamentarian in 1959. "[Hobby] really knew how the process worked," Max Sherman noted. "He learned things that he would do and not do when he worked for Ramsey." For example, Hobby preferred to leave it entirely up to the Senate to kill or not kill a bill. Sherman recalled Hobby telling him that Ramsey "tossed bills he didn't like into a little drawer to be forgotten. Well, Bill Hobby, I think, determined he would not do that." Every Monday or Tuesday morning, Hobby hosted breakfast in his apartment in the Capitol for the committee chairs to talk about bills that were moving through the Senate. Sherman recalled that the breakfasts were important because they made the chairmen "aware of various things that were going on," as well as gave the senators a sense of how Hobby felt about pending legislation.[43]

The main question among Senate members and the Capitol press was whether the Senate would lead Hobby or Hobby would lead the Senate. As he began his first session as the presiding officer of the Senate, Hobby was keenly aware that a majority of senators could decide at any time to take his powers away from him. From the very beginning of his first term, Hobby's operative strategy was always to strike a delicate balance that would placate senators and preserve his powers, while also getting needed legislation passed. This was in sharp contrast to the style of his immediate predecessor, Ben Barnes. Hobby was "very low key, low profile, slow, easygoing," Tom Creighton observed. "Barnes was more aggressive, more dynamic, more impulsive." At the beginning of the session,

Hobby was asked by a reporter if he would be the same kind of lieutenant governor Ben Barnes had been. "The only answer I know is that I'm going to be the kind of lieutenant governor Bill Hobby is."[44]

Hobby's view of his role was that he should help guide legislation, not try to impose it on the Senate. The lieutenant governor "doesn't run the senate, he is merely the presiding officer," he said. For Hobby, passing bills was the process of compromise. "Until you reach some sort of consensus, something isn't really ripe for legislative consideration. Those great victories that you win by one vote will turn around and bite you in the back, sooner or later. Until you've been able to build a consensus for a program, it's probably not a good program anyway." Hobby's experience as he worked his way through his first session as lieutenant governor confirmed his belief in the necessity of a compromise approach. "You take positions or don't take others that you really would like to, because of the vital necessities of compromise, which is what the system is all about. And you are not going to have your way on everything." That was the basis for how Hobby tried to work over the next eighteen years.[45]

Hobby's go-slow approach for the sake of compromise drew criticism from some of the liberals who had supported him in the primary runoff. They charged that Hobby had abandoned his campaign promise to be a "moderate progressive" and was instead acting increasingly conservative. However, Hobby defended his strategy as the "method for accomplishing constitutionally sound legislation." He didn't see the point of passing laws that the Texas attorney general and the courts were clearly going to declare unconstitutional. He explained that it would do no good if the Senate looked "silly by enacting poorly thought-out" unconstitutional legislation. "There is a careful and meticulous way of doing things and I want to see that they get done right." A close Hobby ally, Pasadena senator Chet Brooks, who was a former *Houston Post* reporter, argued that under Hobby the Senate would pass bills that were "going to be clear and easy to enforce," unlike the versions passed by the fast-moving, passion-driven Texas House. When criticized for moving too slowly on legislation, Hobby responded that he favored "quality over quantity."[46]

Although Hobby would take a stronger lead as he gained experience, during his first term he depended on a small group of veteran senators—including Charles Herring, Bill Moore, A. M. Aiken, Tom Creighton, and Babe Schwartz—for leadership. Except for Schwartz, each was a conservative and felt no need to make concessions to the reformers, because they could depend on the uncritical support of their conservative constituencies. For example, the gruff and iconoclastic Moore, the so-called Bull of the Brazos, was quite happy to be the only member to cast a vote against a bill. "Moore was a notoriously difficult kind of cantankerous fellow," one senator recalled. "He was used to doing things his way and he was Chairman of the State Affairs Committee and kind of ran it by his own rules. He had an ongoing battle with Babe Schwartz and frankly, he was a constant source of difficulty for Bill Hobby."[47]

As a result of the Sharpstown corruption scandal, the voters of Texas had filled the

Sixty-Third Legislature, especially the House, with new members who were determined to pass strong ethics and lobby reform bills and so-called sunshine laws aimed at making all operations of state government more transparent. "The voters had spoken out about corruption and bad government," Hobby noted, "and those of us elected that year got the message." The new Speaker of the House, thirty-one-year-old Price Daniel Jr., who was elected Speaker after serving only two terms in the legislature, led the effort to pass the reform bills. The Senate, however, had conservative incumbent holdovers such as Bill Moore who were less than enthralled with some of the laws Daniel and his reform-minded House colleagues were sending to the Senate with what they thought was unseemly haste. The Senate's new presiding officer was among those who sought a more measured approach. "I had some reservations and took some hits in the media for slowing down Daniel's legislative freight train," Hobby said. "The bills that passed were better for having more scrutiny."[48]

The first of the legislative freight trains Hobby slowed down was a package of ethics, lobby control, campaign finance, and other reforms, including the establishment of an ethics commission with enforcement power. Hobby was not in favor of some parts of the package because of a basic dislike of laws that were intended to, as he put it, "force people to be ethical." He also argued that the Texas courts and the election system made an ethics commission unnecessary. Keenly aware that some of the Senate's conservative stalwarts would oppose the House's ethics and lobbying reforms, Hobby decided he would select 150 citizens representing every House district to participate in a conference to study the reforms. Hobby explained that he intended to "help pass meaningful ethics reform but only after careful deliberation maximizing citizen participation." He noted that during his primary campaign he had promised to have a citizens' conference for such a purpose and that he was simply carrying out his campaign pledge.[49]

As Hobby expected, Speaker Daniel and several other members of the House accused him of deliberately stalling their reform legislation. In a speech on the floor of the House, Lufkin representative Arthur "Buddy" Temple Jr., son of a wealthy East Texas lumber tycoon, complained it was presumptuous of Hobby to assume his 150-member committee could do a better job on the reform package than the 150 members of the House. Twenty of the twenty-four members of the Harris County delegation in the House signed a petition asking Hobby to reconsider his decision. The acerbic, liberal *Texas Observer* coeditor Molly Ivins accused the lieutenant governor of hoping to kill the reform bills by stalling consideration until the end of the regular session. "Everybody's mad at Bill Hobby, with cause.... You just wouldn't believe how many ways there are to stall legislation at the end of a session."[50]

Hobby enjoyed more support and understanding in the Senate, however. Even a progressive such as Senator Oscar Mauzy, who favored most of the reform package, defended the lieutenant governor. Mauzy told reporters he had little hope that a strong ethics or lobby bill or other reform measures would come out of the Senate, but he blamed the conservative makeup of the Senate rather than Hobby reneging on any campaign promises. Hobby's other defenders argued that the lieutenant governor simply felt it was wrong to enforce ethical standards. Hobby had always disclosed more than the ethics law required, including his net worth. Bo Byers, the *Houston Chronicle*'s longtime Capitol correspondent, noted, "It's not that [Hobby] doesn't care about ethics. His thinking is: 'I'm ethical, but I'm not going to tell other people how to be ethical.'" As the *Dallas Times Herald* observed, there was no question about Hobby's ethical standards. The paper noted that "probably because of his own personal wealth" he did not "appear to be a child of big business or the lobby. He refuses gratis plane trips offered by lobbyists and sends back courtesy football tickets to University of Texas games." A member of the Capitol press corps observed that "whether Hobby can whip veteran Senate conservatives in line on the reform issue without sparking an all-out revolt will be a major test of his leadership skills this session."[51]

At a meeting of the state Democratic executive committee in Fort Worth, Hobby defended his plan for a citizens' conference. Referring to the Sharpstown scandal, he claimed that the House was "legislating in a climate that's almost guaranteed to produce bad legislation. We really don't need to enact any new legislation that is universally ignored, that is obviously unconstitutional and does very little to improve respect for law and order and the legislative process." Hobby's 150-member Citizens Conference on Ethics in Government finally met for two days in late March at the Lyndon B. Johnson School of Public Affairs on the University of Texas at Austin campus. The conference released a final report that was tougher than Hobby had expected. Its recommendations included calls for extensive public financial disclosure by state officials, registration of all paid lobbyists and their employers, stronger campaign contribution and spending laws, a term limit for the Speaker of the House, and creation of a state ethics commission to enforce ethics laws, among other measures. The report was a minor embarrassment for Hobby, who announced he generally agreed with the recommendations, but he did not support the creation of an ethics commission. He believed that the enforcement of any ethics laws the legislature might pass should be left to the state's district attorneys. He now found himself in the awkward position of refusing to accept the recommendations of his own ethics advisors.[52]

The chairpersons of the conference's subcommittees soon filed reports that were distributed to members of the Senate. Senators Charles Herring and Don Adams joined Hobby at a press conference where they declared that the House's ethics bills either had unconstitutional provisions or were unclear and contradictory and needed to be rewritten in "plain English." Offering an example, they argued that the House Speaker term limit bill was "unconstitutional on its face." Led by Price Daniel, the House quickly voted to endorse most of the conference's recommendations. Ultimately, however, Hobby ignored the conference's proposals. The bill to create the ethics commission would eventually die in the Senate.[53]

After Hobby made it clear he would ignore most of his conference's recommendations, the Senate busily made changes in several of the House versions of the reform laws, especially the ethics code and the lobby statute, which were largely rewritten. Hobby also sought advice from his friend and mentor Railroad Commissioner Ben Ramsey, who also opposed most of the liberal-inspired reforms. Some felt that Charles Herring in particular, chairman of the powerful Senate Jurisprudence Committee, was a major influence over Hobby during the reform fight. His committee weakened several ethics bills, but ultimately, the measures were restrengthened in conference and passed by the legislature.[54]

Despite complaints that Hobby was being influenced too much by Commissioner Ramsey and the conservative old guard, the reality was more complex. Hobby quietly worked with liberals behind the scenes to reach compromise solutions for various provisions of the ethics bill. For example, the House version required appointed (i.e., unelected) officials such as university regents and agency board members to submit financial disclosure statements. A majority of the Senate opposed financial statements for appointees to boards or agencies. Hobby called Oscar Mauzy, who was on the conference committee, to come to the lieutenant governor's office to work out a compromise. They carefully went through the appropriations bill and identified every agency that made financial decisions that could privately benefit the appointees in some way. They placed in the bill a requirement for appointees to those specific agencies to file financial reports. Appointees who were serving on boards or agencies that provided little to no opportunity for self-benefit were not required to report. The compromise was accepted by the Senate. "Hobby's entitled to a lot of credit for it," Mauzy later admitted. "It was his idea, not mine."[55]

During the conference committee, lobbyists also made a strong effort to kill the provision to adopt strict requirements for lobby registration. Mauzy later credited Hobby for defeating that effort. Tom Creighton didn't share Mauzy's view of Hobby's efforts with the conference committee, but he admitted, "For the lack of experience that Hobby had, he did a good job." Mauzy also believed that the "glare of public opinion" persuaded Hobby to change his mind about some of the conservative revisions of the ethics and lobbying bills. "He was willing to change his mind. It's an interesting exercise in a fellow having to learn the ropes and learning who he can rely on and who he can't."[56]

Speaker Daniel didn't share Mauzy's, Creighton's, and other senators' positive view of Hobby's performance. Daniel and Hobby clashed almost from the first day of the legislative session in January. That clash developed into what one Capitol correspondent called a "running feud" that lasted until the session ended. Daniel complained to reporters that the Senate had greatly weakened the House version of the lobby control act. Irritated that Daniel went public with his criticism instead of quietly working out a compromise that might satisfy both houses of the legislature, Hobby issued a press release angrily accusing Daniel of "childish bickering, hasty and immature reaction, and public posturing. The Speaker's record of ineffectual efforts at intelligent legislation speaks for itself." Hobby noted that Attorney General John Hill had ruled five sections of the House version of the lobby control bill as unconstitutional. Daniel responded that Hobby's comments had "startled and dumbfounded" him. Daniel's fans in the press criticized Hobby's attack. In his column in the *Dallas Morning News*, Stewart Davis accused Hobby of hampering the reform effort and of trying to tear down Daniel as a potential opponent in the upcoming election in 1974.[57]

Daniel called a press conference, during which he denounced the entire Texas Senate, claiming its members had "raped, pillaged, and ridiculed" the House's reform bills. Alarmed by the escalating feud and the threat of a stalemate that might force a special legislative session, Governor Briscoe decided to intervene despite his deep reluctance to interfere with the legislative process. Briscoe had served four terms in the Texas House in the 1950s, and he understood that legislators generally resented direct gubernatorial involvement in their work. Briscoe knew from personal experience that near the end of a long session, "legislators can become quite stubborn."[58]

The governor arranged a meeting in his office with Daniel, Hobby, and the members of the conference committee. He warned them he would not, under any circumstances, call a special session to finish business that should be settled in the regular session. "I asked them to find a middle ground and get their work finished on time," Briscoe later recalled. He asked Mark White, his young secretary of state who was the governor's liaison with Hobby and the Senate, to work with the leadership of both houses to work out their differences in a way that would also satisfy Briscoe.[59]

White served as the go-between for Briscoe and Hobby in this matter, as well as others, during the nearly five years he served as secretary of state. He was liked and respected by both officeholders. When a problem occurred in the Senate over a vote on a bill that Briscoe and Hobby both supported, they would often meet to discuss the role White would play to help resolve the problem. When necessary, Briscoe, Hobby, and White would split the senators up between them. White hadn't known Hobby before he became secretary of state, but he soon became an admirer of the lieutenant governor. "It came as an interesting phenomenon for me to see that Bill Hobby was not the wild-eyed liberal that his opponents had said about him when he was running for office," White later recalled. "He was very moderate, and he and Dolph Briscoe, who everybody knew was a conservative, got along famously. They were both gentlemen, they were both mature in their understanding in their roles in the government, and they worked very closely together."[60]

Briscoe was eager to resolve the problem between Daniel and Hobby before the legislature was forced to adjourn after meeting for the prescribed 140 days. He had pledged during the election campaign that he would not call special sessions of the legislature. Briscoe would be under tremendous pressure to break that pledge if the much-anticipated reforms weren't passed during the regular session.

But Briscoe was not an objective broker in the Hobby-Daniel dispute. Within weeks of Inauguration Day, Briscoe and Hobby had forged a close relationship of mutual respect. In his memoir, Briscoe noted that his father and Bill Hobby's father had both worked for Texas governor Ross Sterling—Briscoe's father had been Sterling's ranch manager—but he hadn't known Bill before the election. "We quickly developed an excellent working relationship. Bill was extremely easy to work with. He and I had very similar goals." Accordingly, the governor stayed away from the Senate, but as he later noted, he was happy to work directly "with some of the senators when Bill Hobby asked me to do that. We made a good team."[61]

During the two terms Briscoe served as governor, he and Hobby didn't agree on everything. Dolph was more conservative than Bill, while Bill had reservations about some of Briscoe's proposals to vastly increase spending on road and highway funding and to grant rural property tax relief. Briscoe opposed adoption of a new Texas Constitution, which was Hobby's pet cause, and they disagreed about tax policy. Dolph was against new taxes; Bill thought they were necessary. Regardless of those differences, they got along well on a personal level. Briscoe appreciated that it was Hobby's responsibility to lead the Senate, and he never interfered with the lieutenant governor's leadership. Hobby had deep respect for the governor's office and was deferential to Briscoe. And their families' close links to Ross Sterling didn't hurt the relationship. Sterling was one of Dolph's heroes, and Bill was aware of how important Sterling had been to his father Will's career. That link was the subject of many of their conversations. Several years after they both left public office, Briscoe stressed in his self-titled memoir that he and Hobby had been "steadfast friends" while he was governor, and "we remain so."[62]

Briscoe's relationship with Daniel, however, had become problematic by the time the regular session was approaching its end. "I often thought that [Daniel] was more interested in getting his name in the media than he was with doing the best job possible for the people of Texas," Briscoe complained. "I never had to watch my back with Bill Hobby. But that was not the case with Price Daniel Jr." The Senate finally passed the ethics bill on May 22, after Oscar Mauzy's attempts to amend it were defeated, but to Daniel's displeasure it was significantly different from the one that came out of the House. With the Speaker leading the way, the House defeated the Senate's version, which sent the bill to a conference committee. After a bitter battle, the conference committee passed a compromise bill. A bill on financial reporting went through a similar process, which resulted in another compromise hammered out by a conference committee. Daniel called the final bills "weak" and "watered down." Hobby responded that "cooler heads" in the Senate had prevailed to counter the House's "emotion-laden," "hasty," and "haphazard" actions.[63]

Ethics and lobby reforms weren't the only contentious issues with which the Sixty-Third Legislature struggled. Another was the issue of consumer fraud and deception. In late March, Mauzy sponsored a bill in the Senate and Bob Gammage submitted a matching bill in the House filled with strong protections against a wide range of deceptive and misleading business practices. Attorney General John Hill, who was a consumer protection advocate, helped Mauzy and Gammage write their bills. As the sponsors expected, the business lobby quickly expressed its opposition to many of the provisions. The most vocal opponent was the insurance industry, which demanded that the bill be stripped of all regulations that applied to its business practices. The conservative members of the Senate who were closely allied with the business lobby made it clear to Hobby that they could not support the bills without significant revision. Hobby wanted to strengthen consumer protection, but he had problems with the bill. He wanted to add a provision against frivolous lawsuits, and he wanted to give authority to the attorney general to make additions to the list of deceptive trade practices as needed. Hobby also agreed with the insurance lobby that the Texas Department of Insurance should continue to regulate the industry.[64]

To preserve the basic provisions of the bill while also making it palatable to the senators with close ties to the business lobby, Hobby brought Attorney General Hill and Senators Mauzy and Herring to his office to work on a compromise version. Hobby stressed that there weren't enough votes in the Senate to pass the bill without revisions. He proposed to send it to Herring's Jurisprudence Committee for rewriting. Hill angrily expressed his opposition to Hobby's proposal, because he claimed that Herring was "carrying water for the insurance industry." Hobby adjourned the meeting with the issue unresolved.[65]

After consultation with some of his colleagues in the Senate, Mauzy persuaded Hill that Hobby's fears were well grounded. To get a consumer bill out of the Senate, provisions related to the insurance industry had to be removed and a ban against frivolous lawsuits added. Mauzy also withdrew his opposition to Herring's revisions because of his realization that Governor Briscoe would veto the bill unless they were made. With Hill's and Mauzy's reluctant support, Herring's committee revised the bill, and the Senate passed it. Speaker Daniel was furious about the revisions. Ignoring Daniel's protest, Briscoe signed the Deceptive Trade Practices Act at a public ceremony in his office.[66]

Despite his original complaints about Hobby's compromise bill, Hill later admitted that it "was probably the most far-reaching law ever enacted by the Texas Legislature that did not originate in a major law firm representing business interests. The law worked exactly as intended." After its passage, the attorney general's office used the law to prosecute nursing home owners who were negligent, swindlers who sold phony oil and gas investments, and retailers who used scams to sell their products. In the 1990s, however, those gains in consumer protection would be significantly weakened by new tort reform laws.[67]

Battles were also waged over bills regulating pollution (fought by the energy industry), requiring oil and gas field unitization (supported by Hobby and the major oil companies), revising rules to limit the authority of conference committees to insert new items into a bill that had already been passed by both houses of the legislature (favored by Daniel), and seeking the equal funding of public schools (a contentious battle between poor and wealthy school districts). Each of those bills was defeated. Hobby was particularly frustrated by the defeat of the compromise stopgap school-financing plan.[68]

The Sixty-Third Legislature also passed a breathtaking amount of legislation that didn't face nearly as much opposition or generate as much controversy as the compromise ethics and lobbying reform acts or the bills that were defeated. It included new open-records and open-meetings laws inspired by the Sharpstown scandal, a path-breaking bill mandating bilingual instruction in elementary schools, an act to make automobile insurance rates more competitive, a bill outlawing credit discrimination on the basis of gender or marital status, a law lowering the penalty for possession of less than four ounces of marijuana to a misdemeanor, and an act overhauling workers' compensation that included unlimited death benefits for widows and orphans and freedom of choice in picking a doctor. Hobby was particularly involved in the passage of bills that reformed and streamlined the state's budget-making process (a special interest of the math-loving lieutenant governor), increased the power of the Texas College and University System Coordinating Board to veto expansion of state university facilities, and lowered the legal age of adulthood to eighteen.

The debate over lowering the legal age of adulthood to eighteen brought out Hobby's strong feelings against Senate filibustering. "Filibusters make the Senate look silly," Hobby has said. He opposed them because they "consume precious time when numerous bills await attention." Senator Don Adams opposed the bill lowering the legal age of adulthood to eighteen, largely because it would drop the alcohol drinking age from the age of twenty-one. On the day the Senate was scheduled to consider the bill, Adams decided to delay the vote by using an old ploy to warn that he was considering a filibuster, although he never intended to do it. He had the sergeant at arms get stacks of books from the Legislative Reference Library and put them in plain view on top of his desk and Bill Moore's desk. By tradition the stacked books were a visual signal that the senators were going to filibuster. Adams hoped delaying the vote would give him time to lobby support for his position. Not long before the vote, Robert Fulton Battise, the principal chief of the Alabama-Coushatta Tribe of Texas, which had its reservation in Polk County in Adams's Senate district, visited the lobby outside of the Senate Chamber. He called for Adams and Moore to come out to the lobby to pose for a photograph with him. When they left the Senate floor to have their pictures taken with Battise, Hobby suddenly called a vote on the eighteen-year-old-adulthood bill. The bill quickly passed while Adams and Moore were absent. Adams had no hard feelings about the trickery. He later reported that "Hobby thought that was funny, you know, and we laughed about it."[69]

Hobby also acted quickly on another occasion to avoid a filibuster that would have stopped the passage of Houston senator Jack Ogg's bill to loosen regulations capping interest rates on mortgage loans. The bill, which had already passed the Senate, had passed the House with some minor amendments and was returned to the Senate for concurrence. Bill Patman, who was one of Hobby's least favorite senators, feared the bill would allow lenders to charge excessive interest rates, and he planned to filibuster. Drawing from his deep knowledge of the Senate's rules of procedure, which he had learned when he served as Ben Ramsey's parliamentarian in 1959, Hobby used a complicated parliamentary maneuver to head off Patman's filibuster.

Hobby and Ogg knew that Patman was going to block the bill because of its main provisions—even though the Senate had already passed them—and not because of the House's amendments. Hobby persuaded Bill Moore and Babe Schwartz to conspire with him and Ogg in a procedural maneuver to thwart Patman's plan. When Ogg took the floor and asked the Senate for a vote to accept the House's amendments, Hobby quickly recognized Schwartz, who proceeded to make a few comments about the bill. While Schwartz was speaking, Hobby interrupted him to recognize Moore, who made a motion for the Senate to vote on Ogg's previous request to vote, which meant that Schwartz would be the only senator who would make remarks about the issue. According to Senate rules, Moore's motion had to be voted on before the Senate could conduct other business, including allowing any additional speeches. Schwartz, who shared Hobby's negative view of Patman, promptly stopped speaking, and the Senate immediately voted nineteen to twelve in favor of Ogg's motion to concur in the House amendments. An observer who watched Hobby's maneuver later recalled that "Patman was left fuming and furious because Hobby had faked him out of a chance to filibuster." Even though Ogg's bill made it to Briscoe's desk, the governor vetoed it.[70]

The Sixty-Third Legislature adjourned at midnight on May 28, 1973. Veteran observers of state government praised the lawmakers for producing more substantive legislation than any in recent memory. Even Oscar Mauzy, who was prone to skepticism, shared that positive view. "We passed a damn good consumer protection act and a damn good bilingual act," Mauzy noted. "We revised the penal code. We totally revised the family code that deals with domestic relations and parent-child relationships. The eighteen-year-old [adulthood] bill is a major piece of legislation. Competitive automobile insurance rates have now become law."[71]

Bill Hobby and Dolph Briscoe were equally satisfied with the legislative results. Briscoe was especially pleased because it was the first legislature since 1947 that had not passed new taxes, thanks to a boom in the state's oil economy. Hobby, however, warned it would be difficult to meet the state's needs during the next biennium without a tax increase, possibly even an income tax. That was a prediction with which Briscoe, who had pledged "no new taxes" during his election campaign, publicly disagreed. Despite his pride in the legislature's achievements, Hobby lamented the defeat of a compromise stopgap school-financing plan, which Briscoe also called a disappointment.[72]

Hobby received generally good reviews for his first-term performance as lieutenant governor. He had his critics, however—chiefly the *Texas Observer*'s coeditors Molly Ivins and Kaye Northcott. After the Sixty-Third Legislature adjourned, they complained that Hobby had relied too much on Senate Jurisprudence Committee chairman Charles Herring, who had stalled many of Speaker Daniel's reform bills for months. "[Herring's] committee," Ivins and Northcott argued, "can be blamed for the fact that three of the bills were not passed until the last day of the session." As a result, they claimed, Hobby ended the session "with significantly fewer friends than he had in January."[73]

The lost friends to which the *Observer* referred were members of three key Democratic Party constituencies: environmentalists, consumer advocates, and legislative reformers. Hobby did lament to the press that very little of significance was done for the environment, but he noted that the Senate seemed to have little interest in the issue during the session. Hobby also upset consumer advocates when he prevented Bill Patman's filibuster against the bill to allow higher profits on mortgage loans. Briscoe vetoed the bill, but that didn't spare Hobby from criticism. At the time, Hobby explained that he had taken the action because he opposed filibusters. However, at the end of the session, Senator H. J. Blanchard, using the filibuster, killed Mauzy's bill to give tenure to public-school teachers, despite it having enough votes to pass. Hobby, who opposed the bill, sat silently while Blanchard filibustered. That inaction was noted by public-school teachers, who accused him of a double standard. Despite the criticism from progressives and reformers, Hobby did strengthen his support among minorities, particularly Black constituents. Hobby also improved his standing with conservatives by maintaining a good working relationship with Briscoe. And in supporting less restrictive ethics and lobbyist registration laws, he solidified his support with business interests who had previously supported Wayne Connally.[74]

After the legislative session was over, the *Dallas Times Herald*'s Austin bureau chief, Dave Montgomery, published a critique of Hobby's performance. Montgomery claimed Hobby was regarded by some members of the Senate "as a lightweight, easily influenced by the Senate's longtime power brokers," such as Tom Creighton, Bill Moore, and Charles Herring. The Dallas reporter admitted that Hobby's "even tempered and sedate" personal style, "to the point of being colorless," probably contributed to his appearing "weak." He noted that Hobby was not an "outgoing glad-hander," that he appeared "shy and uncomfortable amid crowds," and that his speeches were delivered in "a dull monotone punctuated by a frequent cough." Montgomery credited Hobby for his "bold" candor and for his constructive work in "non-sexy" areas that the public paid little attention to, such as budget-process reform, and his efforts to "weed out unnecessary state expenditures." Oscar Mauzy, however, rejected the image that Montgomery, Ivins, Northcott, and other journalists drew of Hobby. He agreed that the lieutenant governor was his own worst enemy because of his colorless personal style, but Mauzy told an interviewer that Hobby was not nearly the weak leader the press claimed him to be. He charged that too many reporters were making judgments about Hobby that were based on form instead of content.[75]

Because of the constitutional requirement that regular sessions of the legislature could be held only once every two years, and Governor Briscoe's decision not to call a special session for the remainder of the life of the Sixty-Third Legislature, it appeared that the Texas Senate would not reconvene until January 1975. However, US support of Israel in the Yom Kippur War in October 1973 led to an Arab embargo of oil shipments to the United States, which resulted in a major fuel shortage. When President Nixon urged states to lower speed limits to fifty-five to conserve oil and gas, Briscoe called a special session in December, during which the legislature passed a law lowering speed limits on the state's roads and highways. But that special session was a brief interlude. Although his duties as presiding officer of the Senate seemed to be over for the rest of his first term in office, Hobby wasn't idle. He continued to engage in state affairs throughout the summer and fall of 1973. He also looked forward to playing a leading role in the constitutional convention, which would convene in the Capitol in January 1974. And, of course, he had a decision to make about running in the Democratic primary in the spring of 1974 for nomination as the party's candidate for a second term as lieutenant governor.

But before any of that, in the summer of 1973, Bill Hobby suddenly found himself in the middle of a highly contentious public controversy caused by inadequate state regulation of residential centers for children with behavioral problems.

CHAPTER 8

ARTESIA HALL AND THE CONSTITUTIONAL CONVENTION

In early June 1973, soon after the Sixty-Third Legislature adjourned, Bill Hobby flew to Atlanta, Georgia, to meet with Governor Jimmy Carter and other state officials to learn about that state's zero-based method of budgeting, which required justifying the cost of every continuing or new item in the budget each time a new budget was prepared. Hobby became interested in the method after hearing Governor Carter give a speech on the topic during the summer of 1972. Carter had borrowed the concept from the Texas Instruments company in Dallas. Carter convinced Hobby the method could be applied to the Texas state budget with positive results, including the elimination of waste and redundancies. After he returned to Austin, Hobby met with his fellow members of the Legislative Budget Board and urged them to adopt the budgeting method during the interim between sessions. With Governor Briscoe's enthusiastic support, the board adopted Hobby's proposal in September 1973, and scheduled it to begin with the 1976–1977 biennium. Although the method was frequently revised and adjusted over time, the Texas Legislature eventually abandoned zero-based budgeting in the early 1990s.[1]

On June 15, while Hobby was still in Georgia, law enforcement officers in Liberty County, Texas, arrested fifty-eight-year-old Joseph Davis Farrar, who owned and operated Artesia Hall, a private residential school for "emotionally disturbed" teenagers, and charged him with murder. The Houston news media's extensive coverage of Farrar's arrest grabbed the attention of Hobby's chief of staff, Steve Oaks. Farrar had been dean of men at the College of William and Mary in Virginia when Oaks was an undergraduate student leader in the mid-1950s. Oaks and some of his classmates discovered that Farrar had recruited students to spy on other students at the college. They also knew he was obsessed with rigid enforcement of the school's rules and regulations and applied harsh and inflexible punishment for the slightest infraction. When these issues came to light, the college's administration removed Farrar as dean.[2]

Back in August 1972, nearly a year prior to Farrar's arrest, Oaks had been shocked to read in a front-page *Houston Chronicle* story that Farrar was in Texas operating a residential center for troubled teens. Oaks knew that after Farrar had left William and Mary, his work record had included dismissal as headmaster of a private school for embezzling money from the school's funds. At that time, Oaks warned Harris County judges about Farrar's past. As a result, the judges stopped sending youngsters to Artesia Hall. Oaks was frustrated that the residential center had remained in operation despite his warnings about Farrar. Most of the kids in Artesia Hall were placed there voluntarily by their parents, who paid a monthly fee of $400 with a contract of twelve months. Juvenile courts in counties outside of Harris County had continued to send teenagers to the school.[3]

Established in 1970, Artesia Hall was located on twenty-two heavily wooded acres in an isolated rural area in northern Liberty County, forty-five miles from Houston. Its prisonlike facilities, surrounded by tall cyclone fences topped with barbed wire, consisted of a collection of mobile homes and temporary buildings. Living conditions were primitive and unsanitary. For most of the time that it was in operation, the school operated without a license or supervision by the Texas Department of Public Welfare, despite a law requiring a state license. Apparently, Farrar's success at keeping the Department of Public Welfare from closing the school was aided by the work of his attorney, Price Daniel Jr., who had been a state representative before becoming House Speaker. Farrar falsely claimed that he was an accredited psychologist, even though he lacked a doctorate in the field, as required by state law.[4]

It was eventually revealed that the children in residence at Artesia Hall had suffered under Farrar's sadistic theories about the therapeutic benefits of severe physical discipline. Children were punished with ice-cold baths, forced to squat in a large pail used to feed the livestock as other students scrubbed them with wire brushes until they bled. Other punishments included being forced to dig ditches for no practical purpose, and being stripped, bound in chains, and repeatedly dipped into a septic tank. Farrar gave parents very limited access to their children and censored their mail.[5]

Residents of Liberty County who lived near Farrar's "school" had long suspected that he was physically abusing his students. Many referred to the facility as a "concentration camp," but their complaints to the Texas Department of Public Safety were largely ignored or downplayed. Farrar's practices finally made news in June 1973 when a grand jury indicted him on a charge of murder for willfully failing to provide proper medical treatment and timely hospitalization for Danna Annette Hvalboll, a seventeen-year-old resident who had died in early November 1972 after swallowing rat poison. Eyewitnesses later testified that after she drank the pesticide, Hvalboll was slapped, forced to sing and vomit, and marched around the school grounds. According to testimony, Farrar and/or his staff kept her strapped to a bed while she suffered convulsions. As her condition worsened, Farrar finally drove Hvalboll to Ben Taub Hospital in Houston, where she soon died.[6]

After Bill Hobby returned to Texas from Georgia on June 18, Oaks told him about Farrar's arrest and the bad conditions at Artesia Hall. Deeply concerned, Hobby told Oaks to contact Raymond Vowell, the commissioner of the Texas Department of Public Welfare (DPW), to demand that he take action to protect the students at Artesia Hall. Attorney General John Hill later recalled that "Oaks' take-charge response, despite the fact the Lt. Governor's office lacked any legal or historical control over the DPW, enjoyed the full support of his boss." Indeed, Hobby was well informed about the department's problems. In 1970 his special Senate Interim Committee on Welfare Reform had examined the agency and determined that its management was "shockingly bad" and incapable of adequately carrying out its responsibilities.[7]

On June 19, Vowell dispatched DPW staffer George Campbell to Liberty County to investigate conditions at Farrar's school. The next morning Hobby summoned Vowell to his office in the Capitol and demanded to know what his agency was doing to protect the students at the school. Hobby's knowledge about serious administrative problems in the DPW put Vowell on the defensive. During the meeting, they took a call from Campbell, who reported over speakerphone that the environment at Artesia Hall was "repressive" and that he had uncovered plenty of evidence not only that students had been abused but that the abuse was likely to continue. After Campbell ended the call, Hobby told Vowell to contact the attorney general's office and the Texas Department of Public Safety and ask them to do whatever was necessary to stop the abuse. He then helped his staff draft a press release that accused the DPW of a "dereliction of duty" and stated he was "appalled and deeply distressed that [Artesia Hall] ever operated with the approval of the Department of Public Welfare in view of the serious charges that have been made about this operation over the last several years." He added that the problem was "part of a larger failure of DPW to establish effective regulations governing licensing of childcare and foster care facilities." Hobby stressed he would do whatever was necessary "to achieve and maintain the integrity and accountability of the institutional program licensing by this state."[8]

Hobby sent a letter to Vowell on June 20 demanding that the DPW immediately contact the parents of children at Artesia Hall to advise them of the situation there. He also dispatched his staff assistant Harry Ledbetter to fly to Liberty County in a state plane with two assistant attorneys general, DPW staff members, and freshman state representative John Whitmire of Houston to investigate the school. The next day, Hobby delivered a long-scheduled speech at a Trinity River Authority awards dinner in Anahuac, which is only twenty-five miles south of Liberty County. After the dinner, Jim Sterling, a funeral director and former mayor of Dayton, a town in Liberty County, went to Hobby and explained that he was foreman of the grand jury that had indicted Farrar. Sterling was related to former Texas governor Ross Sterling, who had been a close associate of both Bill Hobby's father and Governor Briscoe's father. Jim Sterling had managed Briscoe's campaign in Liberty County, and he and the governor were good friends. Sterling asked Hobby to tell Briscoe about Farrar and the abuses at Artesia Hall. He also gave Hobby details he had learned while a member of the grand jury about the horrific punishments Farrar had administered to his students. "I was listening to a funeral home operator who was accustomed to scraping bodies off the pavement," Hobby recalled, "and he was horrified by what was happening at Artesia Hall."[9]

The next morning, Hobby met in the governor's office with Briscoe and his wife, Janey, who were appalled by what Hobby told them. The Briscoes were the parents of three teenagers, and the Hobbys' two oldest kids were also teenagers, which made both families especially sensitive to what was happening to the residents at Artesia Hall. "Bill's description of Farrar's abuses really upset Janey," Briscoe recalled. The governor was outraged. "Dolph was usually a mild-mannered fellow," Hobby recalled, "but this made him angry." The Hobbys and the Briscoes decided to fly to Artesia Hall to get a personal view of the situation, but first Briscoe and Hobby held a meeting with Steve Oaks, Attorney General Hill's first assistant Larry York, officials from the Department of Public Safety, Representative John Whitmire, and Raymond Vowell. Governor Briscoe asked Vowell to explain why Artesia Hall was still open. As Vowell struggled to give an answer, Briscoe interrupted and ordered him to take immediate action to rescue the children still housed at the school. Briscoe also called upon the commissioner of the Texas Department of Mental Health and Mental Retardation to move the children at Artesia Hall who had been placed there by juvenile courts to Rusk State Hospital, where they would receive better care. The parents who had voluntarily sent their children to Artesia Hall would be given the choice of bringing them home or letting them be moved to Rusk.[10]

Hobby and the Briscoes flew to Liberty County immediately after their meeting. They went directly to the courthouse, where Attorney General Hill was already seeking a temporary injunction to close Farrar's school and evict Farrar's staff from the property. State district court judge Clarence Cain granted the injunction, which allowed staff from Rusk State Hospital to take temporary control of Artesia Hall. A week later, Cain made the injunction permanent. After the hearing, Hobby and the Briscoes were driven to Artesia Hall. They were appalled by what they saw. Dolph Briscoe later recalled that his wife had been deeply distressed by "the stark fear" on the teenagers' faces and had expressed that conditions at Artesia Hall were worse than she had expected.[11]

Artesia Hall's closure was permanent. Joseph Farrar's son Dale, who also worked at the school, was indicted in Liberty County on the charge of beating students, but Liberty County's district attorney dropped the charge after the school was closed. Bill Hobby's involvement with the Farrars was far from over, however. In 1975 Joseph Farrar filed a civil rights and malicious prosecution lawsuit in federal court against Hobby, Judge Cain, the Liberty County sheriff, and two state welfare workers involved in the closure of the facilities. He asked for $17 million in damages. One year later, a judge dismissed the murder charge against Farrar because the crime of "murder by omission" with which he had been charged had been dropped from the state penal code prior to the death of Danna Hvalboll. The lawsuit against Hobby and the other defendants was finally tried in federal district court in Houston on August 15, 1983. Because Joseph Farrar had died six months earlier, his son Dale and the executors of Joseph's estate replaced him as plaintiffs. Hobby testified at the trial. He later observed that the attorney for the plaintiffs, former attorney general Waggoner Carr, "worked hard to convince the jury that my actions were political grandstanding by a powerful politician." The judge, Robert O'Conor Jr., repeatedly sustained objections against Carr's argumentative and repetitive questions.[12]

When the jury decided against the plaintiffs, Judge O'Conor ruled that they would not be awarded damages and that all parties would have to pay their own legal costs. However, the jury concluded that Bill Hobby's actions had deprived Farrar of due process because the school had been closed without a proper hearing. Nevertheless, the jury also decided that Hobby's role was not "a proximate cause of any damages." As a result, Judge O'Conor ruled that Hobby would have to pay a nominal penalty of one dollar in damages. Farrar's son appealed, and federal judge Lynn Hughes ordered Hobby to pay $317,662 in attorney fees and other costs. Hobby, who told the press that "this case isn't over," filed an appeal, which eventually went to the US Supreme Court. In *Farrar v. Hobby*, the court voted five to four to reverse the lower court's decision that Hobby was liable for the plaintiff's legal fees. In her comment about the ruling, Justice Sandra Day O'Connor noted, "If ever there was a plaintiff who deserved no attorney's fees, that plaintiff is Joseph Farrar." The Supreme Court's ruling ended nearly twenty years of Bill Hobby's involvement with the Farrars and the horrors of Artesia Hall. As Hobby later noted, it had ended "long after many people had forgotten Artesia Hall. It was expensive, time-consuming, and worrisome, but I'm quite sure I would do the same thing over."[13]

The Artesia Hall episode led Governor Briscoe to appoint a task force on youth care and rehabilitation to investigate conditions in the state's private schools for "troubled" children. The legislature and the news media also conducted investigations. Eventually thirty-nine unlicensed childcare institutions were discovered, with revelations that many had their own horror stories. Private schools in Centerville, Wimberley, Boerne, rural Travis County, and other locations were discovered to have administered severe physical and emotional punishments such as beatings and solitary confinement in cages and small closets. Mark White, who was secretary of state at the time, later observed that staff at many of the schools had committed "terrible abuse," which was able to occur largely because of a lack of state supervision. He declared that "Bill Hobby had the courage to do something about it. He took the lead on it and he made the biggest strides in improving mental health in Texas of any person prior to his days in office."[14]

After decades of neglecting the problem of unlicensed private schools and the abuses committed against children at many of those institutions, the legislature eventually overhauled childcare institutional licensing in the state. Dolph Briscoe later noted that the state's action had been "better late than never, but we'll never know how many of our children were battered, abused, and scarred for life."[15]

On January 13, 2004, Bill Hobby learned the name of one of those victims. On that day a woman who identified herself as Beth Warren left a message on his voicemail. "I have been doing some research on the Internet and found that . . . Joseph Farrar sued you as lieutenant governor back in the 1970s . . . over an academy . . . that [was] closed down in Liberty, Texas. . . . I was sent to Dr. Farrar when I was sixteen years old, and was beaten, thrown around, threatened and given a gun and told to kill myself." She explained that after all that had happened to her at Farrar's school, her life had drifted by. "I nearly lost my life," Beth said—but she survived. "God bless whoever closed down those schools," she proclaimed. Hobby later noted that the voicemail was "a heartwarming reminder that some had not forgotten and a fairly dramatic reminder of my attempt thirty-one years earlier to prevent harm to children incarcerated in an East Texas institution named Artesia Hall."[16]

As he had promised during the 1972 campaign, Hobby announced on the day of his inauguration that he was immediately taking an official leave of absence as president of the *Houston Post* and that he would not be involved in the *Post*'s editorial decisions as long as he was in office. Members of the press who had doubted Hobby's assertions that he was a loyal member of the Democratic Party and that he had never agreed with his own newspaper's editorial support of Richard Nixon received his latest statement with skepticism. Hobby meant what he said, however, and he made an effort in public to separate himself from his mother's editorial decisions. Despite her continuing to express support for Nixon in her *Post* editorials, Hobby persisted in his criticism of the president. Soon after one of Oveta's pro-Nixon editorials, Hobby addressed a group of students at the University of Texas at Austin, where he charged that Nixon was trying to destroy freedom of the press and that his administration was "the most corrupt the country has seen in years."[17]

In a speech at the University of Texas at Arlington, Hobby charged the Nixon administration with using the Sharpstown scandal in a partisan attempt to destroy the state's Democratic Party and help Republican candidates running for office. He argued that the Nixon administration's efforts had failed, but because of its actions "individuals have suffered great injustices." Hobby believed that Ben Barnes had been one of Nixon's targets.[18]

Many of Hobby's speeches in the fall of 1973 focused on oil and gas policy because of his role as chairman of the governor's Energy Advisory Council, which Dolph Briscoe established to study the state's future energy needs. The council sponsored studies about ways to conserve existing oil and gas supplies as well as the options for providing alternative sources of energy, including nuclear and wind power. Hobby's work on the energy council appealed to his interest in mining data in support of policy development. As chairman, Hobby brought together thirty-four experts on energy use and resources to serve as the council's consultants. He asked them to produce detailed statistical information documenting a wide variety of subjects ranging from how much of the nation's refining capacity was located in Texas to the size of the state's natural gas reserves. He barraged the consultants with questions: "What do we have? What do we need? How do we bridge the gap? What will the effect be on tax revenue, the environment, and regulatory issues?" As Hobby later recalled, "It soon became obvious no one really knew the answers to my questions, and for a very good reason. There had been no particular reason to find out before." Hobby was able to secure funding from the energy industry as well as from state and federal government sources for the council's research to find answers to his questions.[19]

Briscoe's decision to establish his Energy Advisory Council soon proved to be timelier than anyone could have predicted when it was created. On October 6, 1973, Egypt and Syria attacked Israel in an effort to regain the Sinai Peninsula and the Golan Heights, which they had lost in 1967 in the Six-Day War. When the Soviet Union sent military equipment to the invaders, the United States responded by resupplying Israel. After the war ended in late October with an Israeli victory, the Arab members of the Organization of Petroleum Exporting Countries (OPEC) retaliated by reducing oil production and embargoing oil shipments to the United States, which led to fuel shortages and major spikes in the price of gasoline. The embargo would last until March 1974.[20]

Armed with data from his energy council consultants, Hobby gave a speech in Austin on the status of the energy supply. Hobby argued that the reliance on gas and oil to produce electricity was "sheer madness" because 93 percent of America's energy reserves were in coal and lignite, while only 7 percent were in oil and gas. He predicted that because of OPEC's cutback on oil production and its embargo of heating oil shipments to the United States, Americans could face a "pretty grim" energy situation in the coming winter. At this time, approximately 17 percent of oil consumed in the United States was imported.[21]

Although there was increasing awareness among climate scientists in the early 1970s that the use of fossil fuels was harming the environment and raising temperatures worldwide, the governor's Energy Advisory Council seems to have either ignored or been unaware of those findings. Hobby called for more oil and gas drilling in coastal waters and in Alaska, an increase in imports of oil, heavier reliance on coal, and more nuclear energy plants. In support of the latter option, he argued the country could no longer afford the "luxury" of waiting to solve nuclear waste disposal problems before building new plants. Although most of Hobby's recommendations were the standard ones advocated by the energy industry, he also understood the need for conservation measures. Declaring that "we are going to have to cut down on our demand," Hobby argued that Americans had to change their consumption habits and adopt practices such as raising their air-conditioning to seventy-six instead of seventy degrees, using smaller horsepower cars, and scheduling fewer airline flights. He claimed that taking those measures could reduce consumption by as much as 10 percent. Warning that oil and gas rationing might have to be imposed for the first time since World War II, Hobby urged Americans to begin carpooling and to improve mass transit services.[22]

As the energy crisis worsened in November, President Nixon requested Americans to voluntarily drive slower than the posted speed limits to reduce gas consumption. Late that same month, when it became clear that the US Congress would soon pass a law to deny federal highway funding to any state that failed to lower its maximum speed limit to fifty-five miles per hour, Governor Briscoe asked the Texas Highway Commission to impose that limit statewide. In a unanimous vote on December 3, the commission voted to lower the speed limit. On December 6, after members of the Texas Legislature challenged the legality of the commission's decision, Attorney General Hill ruled that the highway commission's order was "in excess" of its legal authority and that only the legislature could set the statewide speed limit. Hill's ruling forced Briscoe to call a special legislative session to meet on December 18 to pass a law capping the speed limit at fifty-five. Hobby convened the Senate, and it quickly passed the speed limit law. At the time, the press reported that Hobby was teaching gasoline conservation by example, noting that he showed up at the Capitol driving a Volkswagen Bug. Some of his acquaintances thought that the Volkswagen was more likely a sign of Hobby's basic disinterest in materialism than a conscious symbol of his support for gasoline conservation. His family and friends described Hobby as an "extremely frugal" person who drove either a Volkswagen or a four-year-old Ford to work, despite being a millionaire.[23]

When Hobby attended the National Lieutenant Governors' Conference in February 1974 in Washington, he met with members of the Texas congressional delegation to register his unhappiness about the federal energy bill that Congress had passed that same day. He criticized the bill for giving the secretary of the interior rather than state regulatory agencies the right to set maximum efficiency ratings, and for authorizing the Federal Energy Office to take control over interstate oil and gas. When Hobby returned to Texas, he told the news media that he disagreed with Nixon's assessment that the energy crisis was over, saying the shortages might last another five to seven years.[24]

During the summer and fall of 1973, there had been much speculation among the state's politicians and in the press about Hobby's political plans. In the coming year, would he run for a second term as lieutenant governor? Would he challenge Dolph Briscoe in the gubernatorial election? Or would he leave elected office altogether and reassume his duties at the *Houston Post*? In addition, Hobby's trip to Georgia after the end of the session to gather information about zero-based budgeting seemed to many to be a strong indication that he would run for reelection or for governor. In an appearance on a public affairs television program in Austin in August 1973, Hobby confirmed that he might run for governor in 1974. He indicated, however, that he had a strong preference for running for reelection to his current position, stating, "I like the job I'm in." Privately, Hobby had already decided not to run for governor if Briscoe sought a second term.[25]

A few days after Hobby's television appearance, Briscoe told him in private that he would seek reelection, although he would not make a public announcement until

October. The decision not to challenge Briscoe was an easy one for Hobby to make, primarily because of his respect for and friendship with the governor. They had worked closely together during the legislative session, and they shared moderate political philosophies. In addition, Hobby found his work as lieutenant governor to be deeply satisfying. After Briscoe confirmed his intention to run again, Hobby soon leaked the information that he too would be a candidate for a second term.[26]

Hobby would not make his official announcement that he would run for reelection until early in 1974, but in the meantime, he busily raised money for the upcoming campaign, as well as to pay off the $302,000 he had borrowed for his first run. His main donors included close family friend George Brown, chairman of the board of Brown & Root; Charles Butt, president of the H-E-B grocery store chain; newspaper publisher Houston Harte; Austin attorney and lobbyist Ed Clark; South Texas land developer Lloyd Bentsen Sr., who was Senator Lloyd Bentsen Jr.'s father; Amarillo attorney and power broker Wales Madden; and Dallas land developer John Stemmons.[27]

In a press conference on January 19, 1974, Hobby made his long-anticipated official announcement that he was a candidate for reelection. An amendment to the Texas Constitution passed in 1972 had lengthened terms for all statewide officials to four years. The term lengths of members of both houses of the legislature remained the same. As the *Dallas Times Herald* observed, Hobby's announcement surprised "virtually no one." Reporters were surprised, however, by his attack on constitutional provisions restricting specific state monies, called "permanent funds," which could only be used for highways, public schools, and Texas A&M University and the University of Texas. He described the permanent funds as "bad, evil, and any other word you want to make up." Hobby called on the recently convened constitutional convention to eliminate the permanent funds and make them available for the regular appropriations process. "I don't want a bunch of people who do not have elective office spending money that is not approved by the legislature." Referring to the University of Texas Board of Regents' recent allocation of $53 million for several construction projects, Hobby complained that the board's action was "intolerable." He was against "special dedicated funds that enable people to spend tax dollars without having to explain why they should spend them." Several members of the press pointed out that it was highly unusual for a politician who was seeking reelection to set himself up for strong opposition from the influential regents of the University of Texas and Texas A&M University and the powerful alums of both institutions.[28]

As Hobby prepared for the primary election in May, he had little worry that his attack on the permanent funds would cause him trouble at the polls, despite angering some powerful special interests. No viable candidate had announced or was expected to announce that he or she would oppose Hobby in the primary, and the Republican Party was too weak to threaten his victory in the November general election. Political reporters and other observers who assessed his chances stressed that two factors made Hobby virtually invincible: incumbency and money. In the twentieth century, only one incumbent lieutenant governor had been denied reelection in Texas. House Speaker Price Daniel Jr. did think seriously about challenging Hobby, but he soon determined he would have little financial support for the campaign.

Hobby did have critics other than the defenders of the state's Permanent School Fund. Liberal Democrats who believed he had weakened ethics legislation and reneged on his pledge to support pollution-control bills felt they had sufficient reason to oppose his bid for renomination in the primary. But organized labor's decision to support Hobby blunted their opposition. That decision had been made somewhat reluctantly, because Hobby was not seen as an especially strong advocate of unionism. The state's labor leadership, however, felt that Hobby listened to their concerns and that he would be fair when considering their issues. In addition, Hobby had strengthened his support among minorities, particularly Black voters. Especially important to Hobby's reelection effort, however, was the support he had gained from the state's big business interests. Hobby's failure to back the most progressive provisions in the ethics and lobby reform bills had won over many of Wayne Connally's former supporters. Conservatives also appreciated Hobby's excellent working relationship with Governor Briscoe, who also had solid support from the conservative wing of the party.[29]

From January until May 1973, unconcerned about his prospects for reelection, Hobby concentrated on the effort to write a new state constitution, which the *Dallas Times Herald* called "his pet cause." Ever since his election as lieutenant governor, Hobby had made it clear that he wanted to play a leading role at the constitutional convention. "One of the good government initiatives I embraced wholeheartedly," Hobby later recalled, "was constitutional revision. At the same time that voters elected me in 1972, they overwhelmingly approved convening a constitutional convention to revise the unwieldy, outdated, and highly restrictive state constitution." One month after Hobby's inauguration in January 1973, a reporter asked him what he was willing to fight for. Hobby replied that he would fight to "play a significant role in being able to write the first new constitution in almost a century. That's something to tell your grandkids about."[30]

Work on a new constitution began nearly a year before the January 1974 convention. The Sixty-Third Legislature authorized the creation of a commission to lay the basic groundwork for the convention's work. In February 1973, a panel composed of Briscoe, Hobby, Attorney General Hill, Speaker Daniel, Texas Supreme Court chief justice Joe Greenhill, and Texas Court of Criminal Appeals judge John Onion selected the thirty-seven members of the commission. Speaker Daniel served as president, and Senator A. M. Aiken was vice president. The members were divided into thirteen committees. Committee chairs included Hobby's Senate allies Craig Washington (Local Government), Babe Schwartz (Rights and Suffrage), Jack Hightower (Administration), and Max Sherman (Style and Drafting). When Hobby met with a subcommittee of the commission, he urged its members to propose stronger powers for the governor, especially the power to dismiss members of state boards. He argued that the governor should have no limits on his appointment powers except for Senate confirmation. The commission submitted its official recommendations to the constitutional convention in the fall of 1973. "I hoped the convention would build on the work of the Commission," Hobby noted. "It was a highly representative panel of capable, high-minded citizens. The Commission had tackled tough issues, from taxation to metro government, and produced a thoughtful, middle-of-the-road document."[31]

Despite Hobby's publicly expressed desire to serve as chairman of the constitutional convention, several members of the House, led by Speaker Daniel, soon expressed their opposition. Daniel aspired to higher political office, and it was clear he had hopes that a successful constitutional convention would eventually catapult him into the governor's office. Attorney General Hill ruled that the wording of the referendum authorizing the constitutional convention required its membership to consist entirely of Texas legislators. Therefore, only a member of the legislature could serve as chairman. As lieutenant governor, Hobby was presiding officer of the Senate, but he was not a member of the legislature. "That pretty much left the job to Speaker Daniel," Hobby noted, "for whom I did not have the greatest respect." In an interview with United Press International, Hobby expressed his regret that he had no official role in the convention. He also admitted that from a political perspective, there would have been more of a "downside than upside" to serving. "But from an historical point of view it would be a source of great personal satisfaction to take part."[32]

On January 7, 1974, eleven days before he announced his bid for reelection, Hobby, serving as temporary chairman, called Texas's first constitutional convention since 1875 to order. The convention was composed of the members of the Sixty-Third Legislature, who met in the House Chamber as a unicameral body. Nearly one hundred years earlier, Bill's grandfather Senator Edwin Hobby had been one of the leaders in the Texas Senate who called for a convention to write a new constitution to replace the one adopted in 1869 during Reconstruction. That convention met in Austin from September until November 1875. It produced a new constitution written in large part by former Confederates in outraged reaction to the previous constitution, which had enforced the citizenship rights of formerly enslaved Texans. That constitution severely restricted the powers of the legislature and the governor, returned control of public schools to local authorities, and basically established a commission form of executive administration. The governor was given no authority over other elected state officials or over local officials. The 1876 constitution was a product of white supremacy that had provisions that are unacceptable today, such as the requirement of racial segregation in the public schools and the levy of a poll tax, which are no longer operative. It also established the University of Texas and enacted homestead protection. The constitution of 1876 was created to serve a Texas dominated by an agricultural economy with a vast majority of its citizens living in rural areas. Although Edwin Hobby supported the drafting of a new constitution, he had not been a delegate to the convention. The new constitution was approved by the voters in February 1876 and was still in effect in 1974, although heavily amended.[33]

In his address opening the 1974 constitutional convention, Hobby argued that the 1876 constitution limited the state government's ability to deal with "constantly changing conditions." To correct that problem, it was essential that the constitution be rewritten to provide the legislature "with the power and authority" necessary for timely decision-making, which meant discarding biennial in favor of annual sessions. He also warned about pressure from special interests. "The people want a constitution for everyone, not just special interests," he said. "They want a constitution for tomorrow as well as today." Hobby later admitted that his warning to the delegates about pandering to special interests had been futile. "Rewriting the constitution, since it . . . covered every aspect of government, was a fat target for special interests. All the lobbyists in town wanted their interests protected." Prevented from taking a formal role in writing a new constitution, Hobby nevertheless remained at the Capitol during most of the seven months the convention was in session to lobby delegates for the revisions he favored and to monitor developments.[34]

In a speech in Fort Worth, Hobby argued that the new constitution would bring Texas government "kicking and screaming at least into the early 20th century." The 1876 constitution, he said, guaranteed that we "were going to have an underpaid, amateur, part-time legislature. Really, the wonder is not that state government sometimes fails to perform or respond as quickly and intelligently as you'd like. The miracle is that under the circumstances it functions as well as it does. We have a $5B a year operation with nobody really in charge." Hobby declared that one of the most important constitutional changes needed was a provision giving the governor the authority to appoint the chairs of each state board or commission and the power to remove them with Senate consent. In another speech, Hobby argued that the new constitution should not be burdened with provisions that were best addressed by legislation. Because popular views on issues often evolve over time and require changes in the law, he felt it would be wise to keep most of those issues out of the constitution. "It's much easier to pass or repeal a law," he stated, "than it is to amend the constitution."[35]

Hobby didn't support every proposed change to the constitution, however. He especially opposed a right-to-work provision prohibiting union shops, arguing that it was unnecessary because Texas already had a state law banning union shops. The issue had become a major dispute at the constitutional convention. Hobby was standing on the floor of the House Chamber lobbying and monitoring the deliberations as legislators argued. "Tempers were hot," he remembered. "Dallas Representative Jim Mattox, a strong union supporter who later would serve as attorney general, called Speaker Daniel a liar from the floor. Senator H. J. 'Doc' Blanchard collapsed near the podium and needed medical attention." Hobby sent a note to Craig Washington, who represented Hobby's district in Houston, asking him to vote "yes" on the motion to delete the right-to-work provision from the constitution. Washington was standing on the floor of the chamber. "The son-of-a-bitch doesn't have a vote," Washington told the messenger who delivered the note. As he spoke, Washington didn't notice Hobby standing close behind him. "When I tapped him on the shoulder," Hobby recalled, "we both started laughing."[36]

The convention delegates had their share of disputes over a number of issues, some significant, many trivial. Every special interest in Texas had lobbyists pressuring the convention to write provisions securing their agendas in the constitution. One day the convention members would fight over provisions to overhaul the judiciary, while the next day they would battle over a provision to legalize bingo gambling for the purpose of charitable fundraising. However, Hobby had been generally pleased with the constitutional convention's progress.

Adjournment was originally scheduled for May 31, 1974, but the delegates voted to extend the convention until July 30. Despite criticism that the legislators were taking too long, Hobby defended the time-consuming process as being cautionary and deliberate. But he made that observation in April, which was the month when the going got rougher, as the original adjournment date neared. By then, legislators were drawing lines in the sand that they refused to cross when votes were called. Senator Tom Creighton was among them. As the end approached, he concluded, along with some of the other conservatives in the Senate, that the new constitution would give state government too much power. He also felt it was a mistake for the convention to consist entirely of members of the legislature, because it ensured political divisiveness. The legislature "was not the proper forum to rewrite a new constitution," Creighton observed, "because of all the politics involved."[37]

The delegates who supported a new constitution also had to contend with Governor Briscoe's conflicted views about their work. Briscoe took the position that because the legislature and the voters had decided prior to his election as governor that the constitution would be rewritten, he would make no attempt to influence the process. Prior to the convention, he stated that the Texas Constitution had problems and corrections were needed, although he had serious doubts about the need for an entirely new document. Many delegates interpreted Briscoe's statement as an endorsement of their work. While the convention carried out its work, the news media frequently asked Briscoe for his opinion about various proposals, but he refused to comment.[38]

The fight over the right-to-work provision eventually caused the new constitution to fail on the last day of the convention. When the final votes were cast on July 30, 1974, the new constitution lost by only three votes. "Sadly, the anti-union effort was the specific special interest of the Republican Party that derailed the convention," Hobby later observed. The convention then adjourned. In his published memoir, Briscoe admitted that he had been relieved when the convention eventually adjourned without approving the new constitution. But that outcome deeply disappointed Bill Hobby. He recalled, "I thought the proposed new constitution was an improvement over the 1876 constitution, but there wasn't much I could do." Max Sherman thought the decision to make Price Daniel the convention chairman had been a serious mistake. Daniel alienated his liberal supporters in the convention by joining with conservatives to kill a carefully worked out compromise on the right-to-work provision in the new constitution. Many of Daniel's colleagues blamed the defeat of the constitution on his decision to switch sides on the issue. Daniel further angered the liberals and union leaders by holding a press conference immediately after the convention adjourned, during which he blamed the unions and their "manipulation of Black and Mexican American delegates" for the defeat. Briscoe later observed that while Daniel "had tried to appease every faction at the convention, he ended up alienating just about everyone. His political career actually suffered as a result of his performance during the convention." Sherman believed that if Hobby had been chairman, "it would have ended up much differently."[39]

Despite his disappointment, Hobby resolved to salvage whatever he could of the final product. Concluding that a convention composed of legislators would never get the job done, he decided to gather support for the creation of a citizens' convention to carry out the job the legislature had failed to finish. "That idea proved to be not very popular," Hobby lamented. Those who opposed the idea included Republican representative Ray Hutchison of Dallas, who headed the House Constitution Revision Committee. Hutchison rejected the idea of a citizens' convention as a waste of money. The legislators' constitutional convention had cost the state budget $3 million. Hutchison and Hobby did agree, however, that the failed version of the constitution should be revised and reconsidered during the upcoming Sixty-Fourth Legislature. Implementing that plan would have to wait until the legislative session convened in January 1975. "Those of us who were unwilling to give up on getting a new constitution were optimistic about our chances for success in the next legislature," Hobby stated. "We were especially encouraged by the fact that Price Daniel Jr. would no longer be Speaker because he had decided against running for reelection."[40]

While Hobby monitored and lobbied the constitutional convention, he also took time to raise money and to campaign for the Democratic primary on May 4, although he faced token opposition. In early March, he traveled to Dallas, where he hosted a fundraiser at the Fairmont Hotel attended by three hundred people, including several executives from major Dallas banks as well as key supporters from the city's Black and liberal Democratic ranks. In April, Hobby gave a few speeches that kept his name in the newspapers as voters prepared to cast their votes in the primary. In Austin, he spoke on the University of Texas campus, where he advocated "complete equality for women in all areas of employment and job opportunities in Texas." With a nonbinding referendum on horse-race betting on the statewide primary ballot, Hobby told a meeting of the Houston Chamber of Commerce that he favored pari-mutuel horse-race betting in Texas, calling the law against it "foolish" and saying it bred "disrespect" for the law. "I think it's foolish to have laws against something people are going to do anyway."[41]

As expected, on May 4 Hobby won an overwhelming victory in his bid for renomination as the Democratic nominee for lieutenant governor. An especially weak candidate won the Republican nomination, which practically guaranteed that Hobby would easily win election to a second term. With his political future looking brighter than ever, Hobby turned his full attention to the constitutional convention.

Hobby's political future suddenly appeared to be in danger, however, when Austin police officers arrested him at two forty-five on Thursday morning, June 20, as he waited at a red light. Reporting that he was in "a very drunken condition," the police charged him with driving while intoxicated. He declined to take a breath test. Anne Chisolm, a thirty-three-year-old British journalist and biographer, was in the car with him. Chisolm was in Austin researching a biography of Nancy Cunard, whose papers are archived at UT Austin's Harry Ransom Center, and Hobby had taken her for a driving tour of the Hill Country. Following his arrest, Hobby was released from jail on his own recognizance and thus escaped having to sit in a cell until he posted bail, although it was standard procedure to put anyone arrested on a DWI charge in jail for at least a brief period, typically overnight. "There was no procedure at night for securing the release of someone by posting a bond," recalled Dave Richards, a noted attorney and liberal political activist. "Often we lawyers had to tell some poor soul that he or she must stay the night in the tank and we would see him or her in the morning."[42]

Because Hobby held one of the most powerful positions in state government and he had just been renominated for a second term, the state's news media jumped on the story. That same Thursday morning, despite the bad news from Austin, Oveta insisted on keeping her set schedule at the *Houston Post*, which included her regular weekly news and editorial board meeting. As she entered the boardroom, she calmly told her editors, "I know what's on all of your minds. I want you to run a story [about the DWI] and I want you to put it on page one." She then asked for the first item on the agenda and spoke no more of the incident, continuing the meeting as though Bill's arrest had never happened.[43]

Babe Schwartz remembered hearing the news about Hobby's arrest on the radio when he woke up that morning. A few minutes later, a member of Hobby's staff called Schwartz and asked him to join Bill, Diana, Tom Creighton, and others for a meeting in Hobby's office in the Capitol. "When I walked into the office," Schwartz recalled, "Diana was cold as the last iceberg, just nothing, not a sound. But she opened the meeting and said, 'All right, we're all assembled to find out what Bill should do.'" Schwartz told her that Bill "should find the first judge available at the City Hall, plead guilty, pay a fine and immediately leave." Creighton disagreed and argued that Hobby had to plead not guilty. Creighton and Schwartz had both been prosecutors before their elections to the Senate. "This is not something that you deny," Schwartz argued. "We're all guilty of doing this. We all drink." Bill sat silently while the discussion continued. Finally, Diana told Bill to go to the city hall and plead guilty and pay the fine. "And sure enough," Schwartz remembered, "the next day it was over."[44]

Before Hobby made his court appearance, however, he sought advice from political consultant George Christian, who agreed with Schwartz's recommendation. Diana Hobby and Lee Godfrey, a young trial lawyer, appeared in court with Bill, who pleaded no contest to the charge. Travis County judge Mary Pearl Williams assessed a $100 fine and placed Bill on probation for thirty days. Judge Williams explained that it was standard procedure for the court to assess probation on a first offense. She also ordered

Hobby to attend meetings at an alcohol rehabilitation program. At his hearing, Bill told Judge Williams, "Needless to say, I'm extremely sorry, extremely regretful. We have a fine system of justice for citizens and public officials alike. I hope the citizens of Texas judge me on all my actions, not just one." Paul Hobby later noted that it couldn't have been too difficult for his father to make his plea. "He was not one to lie or equivocate or spin or hide. He's a very straight-up guy."[45]

Hobby's release became known in Travis County as the Hobby Rule, which meant everybody had a right to be released on their own recognizance. "In one of life's ironies," Dave Richards noted in his memoir, "Bill Hobby's name is tied to a major breakthrough in Austin law enforcement. The press and criminal lawyers learned of the incident, and a hue and cry were raised about favoritism. In response, the law enforcement officials changed their policy and instituted what became known in Austin as the 'Hobby Rule.' The new rule enabled a DUI suspect to be released to their attorney in the evening hours and thereby avoid a night in the pokey. I have actually shown up in the city jail to secure release of some inebriated acquaintance and been asked by the jailer if I wanted to 'Hobby' out my friend."[46]

Hobby made few public appearances for five months after his arrest. Because he faced only token opposition in the general election, he was free of the necessity to campaign. His arrest had no discernable impact on his election prospects. Hobby's Republican opponent was a politically unknown commodities broker and former airline executive named Gaylord Marshall. As expected, on November 5, 1974, Hobby easily won his bid for a second term as lieutenant governor with 74 percent of the vote. Briscoe also won a second term, with 61 percent of the vote, against Republican Jim Granberry, an orthodontist from Lubbock, and Ramsey Muniz, a candidate for the La Raza Unida Party.[47]

Hobby held a press conference in Dallas a week after his election. A reporter asked if he thought the DWI charge and guilty plea would eliminate him as a candidate for governor in 1978. "That's a hypothetical question," he replied. "I'm not going to play that game." He also declined to say if he would run for governor, declaring, "That's four years off." The day after the press conference, the *Dallas Times Herald* headline declared, "Hobby dodges questions on DWI case." Nevertheless, the issue soon faded away. Although Hobby continued to drink, he never had another DWI. He never drove at night after he had a drink. If he went to a restaurant, if Diana wasn't available, he would arrange for someone to pick him up at home, drop him off at the restaurant, and take him back home. "Oh, I think [Hobby] probably drank too much when he was lieutenant governor," former senator Kent Caperton observed. "But I never felt like Bill's drinking affected his job." Oveta later told *Texas Monthly*'s Harry Hurt that she never castigated Bill about his DWI arrest. "I never dressed him down," she said. "He is a grown man."[48]

CHAPTER 9

CONSTITUTIONAL REFORM REDUX

Unlike the previous legislature, the sixty-fourth had fewer new members, and with the reelection of Dolph Briscoe and Bill Hobby, there was a strong sense of continuity and a determination to pick up where the Sixty-Third Legislature had left off. But a new Speaker now presided over the Texas House. Price Daniel Jr. had taken the position that no one should serve more than one term as Speaker, and he refused to run for reelection to the legislature in 1974, instead planning to run for attorney general in 1978. Hailing from the South Texas plains, the forty-six-year-old incoming Speaker, Bill W. Clayton—better known as Billy—was a much more conservative Democrat than his predecessor. He was also more conservative than Hobby. The *Dallas Times Herald*'s Capitol correspondent noted that Clayton made Hobby "look almost left-wing by comparison." More conservative or not, Clayton was more helpful to Hobby and Briscoe in carrying out their legislative objectives than Daniel. "It was much easier for us to work with Billy Clayton than Price Daniel, Jr.," Briscoe later noted. "Clayton and I shared a rural, agricultural background and we agreed on practically every issue. He was never unfair in his dealings with me, and he always kept his promises."[1]

There were also three new members of the Texas Senate, all Democrats and attorneys: thirty-three-year-old Kent Hance from Lubbock, twenty-eight-year-old Lloyd Doggett from Austin, and, most important to Hobby, forty-two-year-old Ray Farabee from Wichita Falls. Farabee's wife, Helen, had worked for Hobby's welfare reform committee and served as his campaign coordinator in Wichita Falls. Ray Farabee soon became one of Hobby's key allies in the Senate.[2]

When Hobby convened the Senate in January 1975, he and his colleagues enjoyed an estimated $1.5 billion surplus in the state treasury, largely due to revenue generated by rising energy prices. As the session continued, however, inflation increased the cost of state operations, which eroded the budget surplus. Despite Hobby's warning a year earlier that a tax increase would be necessary to pay the state's bills in the next biennium, the booming economy appeared to eliminate that need. Governor Briscoe, who had campaigned in 1974 on a platform of no new taxes, was especially pleased by the sight of large amounts of money flowing into the treasury. He joined Hobby and many members of the legislature in viewing the strong economic outlook as an opportunity to increase state expenditures in a few limited areas, but he also wanted to eliminate the tax on consumer utility bills and reduce other taxes. Briscoe warned the legislature against "going hog wild" or he would use his veto power to trim excessive spending.[3]

Despite Briscoe's warning, the legislature's agenda for increased appropriations was a long one. Hobby's wish list included resurrection of the constitutional revision effort, creation of a state utilities regulatory commission, tough new laws strengthening Texans' right to privacy (with a special concern about wiretapping), and property tax reform, all of which he stressed in his inaugural address. In addition, several legislators proposed a badly needed 10 percent salary raise for state employees and public-school teachers and substantial increases in the budget for public-health programs, medical and vocational education, and highway construction and maintenance. The legislative agenda also included tightening licensing and regulation of childcare facilities—a critical need exposed by the Artesia Hall controversy—and addressing the daunting problem of public-school finance reform. The state was under intense legal pressure from the courts to make the quality of education in every independent school district as equal as possible.[4]

Hobby and Briscoe were also eager to increase the Texas College and University System Coordinating Board's authority to control all new state college construction projects. They were alarmed at what they considered to be "ill-considered and extravagant building projects" launched primarily by the University of Texas System, the University of Houston, and Texas A&M University. Most of their ire was aimed directly at Frank Erwin, the former chairman of the University of Texas Board of Regents, who had taken advantage of the university's fast-growing revenues from oil production on university land in West Texas to launch major construction projects on the Austin campus, including a performing arts facility and swimming and basketball arenas. The effort to give more power to the Coordinating Board would eventually fail because of Erwin's success at rallying the university's powerful alumni, who included most of the members of the legislature.[5]

As Hobby began his second term, he retained the committee structure from the previous legislature. He was generally comfortable with the senators who had chaired committees during the Sixty-Third Legislature, leaving in place those who had stayed in office. However, his comfort level wasn't his only consideration. One senator noted that Hobby kept troublesome Bill Moore as chair of the State Affairs Committee, because he was one of the members "who had served for a long time and the seniority gave them certain privileges that Hobby wasn't going to upend because it would cause more problems than it could solve." In 1972 Moore had also been the first member of the Senate to declare his support for Hobby's election as lieutenant governor.[6]

Hobby initiated a weekly breakfast with all the chairmen. Senator Tom Creighton later recalled that those breakfasts were "the most worthwhile weekly experiences that we had." Hobby sat at the head of the conference table and led an informal discussion about legislative issues. "I thought that it was a very healthy thing," Creighton said. "We would talk about the issues and what the leadership wanted, and [Hobby] would ask for open and free expression and exchange. And there was a lot of disagreement. We were split many, many times." Hobby usually stayed out of the arguments. As Ron Kessler observed, "One of the reasons Hobby was so darn effective is that he was just able to listen and hear. That's one of the reasons he was such a good policy guy."[7]

Of the large number of special items on the agenda of the sixty-fourth legislative session, the most controversial turned out to be the regulation of homes for so-called troubled youth. Although the effort to improve regulation of youth-care facilities had widespread popular support, the bill met fierce opposition from Lester Roloff, a fundamentalist Baptist minister who in 1968 had opened Rebekah Home, a residential facility for "troubled" teenage girls in Corpus Christi. In 1973, after receiving allegations of physical abuse at the home, child-welfare officials tried to inspect it, but Roloff refused to allow them entrance to the grounds, claiming it would infringe on the principle of separation of church and state. When Attorney General John Hill launched his own investigation of Roloff's operation, his investigators gathered affidavits from several of the girls at Rebekah Home documenting numerous incidents of abuse.

Hill closed Rebekah Home for several months, but it reopened in 1974 when the Texas Supreme Court ruled that the closing had been unconstitutional. When the legislature convened in January 1975, Hobby and several members were determined to pass a bill requiring such youth homes to be licensed and regulated by the state. Roloff rallied evangelical Christians to fight the bill, but the Texas House managed to pass it. The bill ran into trouble in the Senate, however. Despite his otherwise liberal record, Senator Ron Clower from Garland, a Dallas suburb with a large number of evangelicals, insisted on an amendment to exempt church-related institutions from state regulation.[8]

Hobby had persuaded Senator Bill Moore to carry the bill in the Senate. As Hobby later noted, Moore "was a lukewarm sponsor at best, and once again lived up to his reputation as one of the more outrageous members of the legislature." Upon the failure of a vote to suspend the rules and allow the debate to move forward, Hobby saw Moore toss his copy of the bill in a wastebasket. "I don't want to hear about it anymore," Moore declared. "I'm through with it." He complained that he was tired of being harassed by "Brother Lester Roloff and Ron Clower." With the help of Senators Chet Brooks and Carlos Truan, Hobby eventually managed to get a vote on the bill, but it resulted in a fourteen-to-fourteen tie. Exercising his constitutional power to break tie votes in the Senate, Hobby voted in favor of the bill, and Governor Briscoe signed it into law. As Hobby later noted, the legislation made "all residential childcare facilities subject to licensing by the state Department of Public Welfare, including even those run by preachers who claimed the Bible made them do it." Hobby's fight for legislation to regulate childcare facilities surprised a few of the more liberal members of the Senate, who had pegged him as a devoted probusiness conservative who was less than enthusiastic about progressive reforms. As the session continued in the coming months, the liberal perception of Hobby's political views gradually changed. Dave Montgomery, the *Dallas Times Herald*'s Austin bureau chief, noted that although he was "far from a wild-eyed radical . . . Hobby is displaying an uncharacteristic liberal tint in launching his second term in office. During the first term Hobby was often influenced by ranking conservative senators. But now the tables may be shifting."[9]

Hobby's efforts to solve the deeply complex public-school finance problem not only brought additional attention to his nascent liberalism but also indicated his growing self-assurance as presiding officer of the Senate. The Sixty-Third Legislature had struggled but failed to produce an equitable formula for financing schools. That failure as well as the continuation of pressure from the courts created a sense of urgency for the Sixty-Fourth Legislature to resolve the issue. The state's system of formula-based public-school financing was so complicated that some members of the House and Senate had great difficulty understanding the various plans that school-financing experts had submitted for their consideration. Hobby, however, was not among them. He relished the challenge because of his fondness for solving complex mathematical puzzles. But his deep involvement in the issue went beyond a simple interest in math. He also believed in the cause to provide a quality education to every student no matter what school district they happened to live in, whether it was in the barrios of South San Antonio, the ghettos of Houston, or the ultra-affluent Highland Park in Dallas County.[10]

Oscar Mauzy, chairman of the Senate Education Committee, worked closely with Hobby to try to solve the school finance problem. Hobby was "very helpful in this school finance fight," Mauzy later observed. "He's much more enlightened and progressive and knowledgeable on the subject than the governor is, and he wants to make the kind of changes that I want to make in our system." When the House sent its version of the bill to the Senate, Mauzy and Hobby met in private in the lieutenant governor's office to revise it. They increased the size of the enabling appropriation and added a provision for bilingual education, as well as grants to districts based on the taxable wealth of that district. The House version raised the minimum salary for teachers from $6,000 to $10,000, and it also included unemployment insurance for all school employees. Hobby knew a majority of the Senate wouldn't agree to a salary increase of that size. He and Mauzy proposed a compromise that lowered the minimum to $8,000 but retained the unemployment insurance. When the compromise version was made public, the leaders of the Texas State Teachers Association (TSTA) announced they would fight it. Hobby then faced a major battle over teacher salaries and insurance benefits that threatened to kill the overall effort to equalize school funding.[11]

Mauzy persuaded Hobby to convene the Senate as a committee of the whole to conduct hearings on their revised version of the bill, which would not only provide a public forum for the TSTA representatives to argue their case but also allow Hobby and Mauzy to counter those arguments. When the Senate meets as a committee of the whole, a senator serves as chair and the lieutenant governor is allowed to participate in the debate and vote. Hobby appointed Mauzy to serve as the chair with the understanding that during the debate Mauzy would only recognize senators who supported the compromise. "[The lobbyists] for the TSTA made some irresponsible remarks to start with," Mauzy remembered. "We just took them on and made them eat their own damn words. Hobby and I just ate their lunch. It was the best cross-examination I have ever done. Hobby is not even a lawyer, and he did better than I did." Mauzy stated he had never seen Hobby "so outraged and so damn good in making his point."[12]

After the hearings, the Senate accepted Hobby and Mauzy's compromise version of the school finance bill. When it went to the House and Senate conference committee, however, teacher unemployment insurance was deleted. After the failed efforts of 1973, the legislature finally passed a public-school finance bill, although it was clear to all that it was insufficient and that the problem would need to be readdressed in the next legislature in 1977. The *Texas Observer* judged that the effort had made "definite improvements in the state's system of paying for public education," but it had failed to equalize educational quality in all school districts. Other critics also pointed out that the new act continued to rely too heavily on property taxes to support the public schools, which was at the heart of the unequal funding problem. Dolph Briscoe later observed that "few of us had any confidence" in the legislation. "Someone called it a 'Band-Aid' plan and that is what it turned out to be." Nevertheless, some progress had been made.[13]

Another major issue was constitutional revision. For Bill Hobby, writing a new state constitution was the most important item on the legislative agenda. Hobby told reporters that he hoped all the research done in the failed effort to write a new constitution "would not be wasted but somehow salvaged." Soon after the Senate convened in January, Hobby carried out a carefully planned strategy to get constitutional revision done as quickly as possible. He persuaded Speaker Clayton to agree to the creation of a joint special House and Senate committee to draw up a new constitution, largely to be based on the version that the constitutional convention had failed to pass. If approved by the legislature, the new version would be submitted to voters for approval in a statewide election in November 1975. However, Senator Walter Mengden, a Houston Republican known to his colleagues as Mad Dog because of his extreme right-wing rhetoric, threatened to kill the special committee with a filibuster. Hobby ended the threat when he told Mengden that he didn't care if he made an ass out of himself but that "making an ass of the Senate" was a different matter, and it would not be forgotten. Mengden backed off.[14]

The legislature voted to approve the special committee, and Hobby and Clayton filled it with House and Senate members who were strong supporters of revision. Using many of the items from the failed version, except for the troublesome right-to-work provision and other controversial items, the joint committee produced eight amendments.

The voters could pick and choose which, if any, of the amendments would replace their corresponding provisions in the current constitution. "We thought we had a better chance of approval by writing eight separate amendments to the current constitution rather than attempt to submit an entirely new document," Hobby later observed. "That way voters would not have to reject the entire document if they only objected to one or two amendments." The amendments included having annual sessions of the legislature that would last no longer than ninety days, authorizing the governor to name commission chairs and remove appointees, allowing counties to pass ordinances, and merging the Texas Supreme Court with the Court of Criminal Appeals. "The finished product didn't include everything I wanted," Hobby admitted, "but it was still a substantial improvement over the present constitution."[15]

When the joint committee submitted its work to the legislature, Clayton and Hobby used parliamentary procedures to cut off debate. With Hobby working the floor to get the four-fifths vote necessary to suspend the rules, the Senate passed the bill in one day. The House followed suit, and Hobby and Speaker Clayton signed a resolution sending the amendments to the people for a vote. Tom Creighton, an opponent of the bill, observed that "the process was rigged and loaded, and [Hobby] had the votes. [He] very effectively utilized the power that goes with leadership and got it out."[16]

Speaker Clayton, Attorney General Hill, and several legislators joined Hobby in praising the final product. A few members of the legislature, including Senators Tom Creighton and Peyton McKnight, immediately came out against the amendments, but Bob Bullock, who had been elected state comptroller in 1974, was the only statewide elected official to announce his opposition. Bullock published a study titled "Fiscal Implications of the Property Tax Constitution," claiming that if adopted, the proposed amendments would cost the state treasury an additional $1 billion to $11 billion a year in new expenses. Dismissing Bullock's report as "nothing but smoke and mirrors," Hobby based his cost estimates on the Legislative Budget Board's study indicating the additional costs would be $36 million a year, with each annual session adding another $711,000 to $817, 000. More ominous, however, was Dolph Briscoe's silence on the issue. Privately he told his family and his closest friends that he was not pleased with the proposed amendments, especially the one for annual sessions of the legislature. He kept those doubts to himself, however, and he would not take a public position until a month before the election in November.[17]

Utility regulation was another controversial issue. Since the early years of the twentieth century, members of the legislature had tried but failed to pass laws regulating electric, telephone, and water utility companies. By the 1970s, Texas was the only state without a general agency to regulate utilities. Regulation was left to local towns and cities, most of which lacked staff expertise capable of making informed decisions about reasonable electric and telephone rates, which not coincidentally were among the highest in the nation. A survey revealed that half of the city councils in Texas routinely granted rate hikes without analyzing the requests. Many utility companies also engaged in questionable practices such as passing on to ratepayers such expenses as country club memberships and lobbying fees, with Southwestern Bell and the power utilities being the worst abusers. In the early 1970s soaring utility bills stoked public outrage and demands for reform, which the Sixty-Third Legislature largely ignored in 1973, mainly because of the stiff opposition of Speaker Daniel and Governor Briscoe. By the time the Sixty-Fourth Legislature convened in January 1975, consumer groups such as Common Cause and the Texas Public Interest Research Group were attracting so much popular support for the creation of a state public utility commission that the legislature found it difficult to avoid the issue.[18]

Texas's largest telephone monopoly, Southwestern Bell, with state headquarters in San Antonio but controlling management in St. Louis, Missouri, brought the issue to a head on January 20 by declaring its intention to significantly raise the rate for intrastate long-distance phone calls, which were a major source of profit for the company. Because interstate rates were regulated by the federal government, it cost more to make a long-distance call from one city in Texas to another than to make calls from Texas to out-of-state locations. Attorney General Hill, who was especially angered by Southwestern Bell's arrogance in the matter, got a court injunction that temporarily stopped the company from implementing the rate hike. In his opposition to the Bell company, Hill soon found an ally in Bill Hobby.[19]

Hobby supported Senators Ron Clower, Lloyd Doggett, and Bob Gammage in their efforts to write a bill to create a Public Utility Commission (PUC) consisting of three elected members that would regulate telephone, electricity, natural gas, and private water and sewer companies. Although Speaker Clayton was not in favor of a utilities commission, he took a neutral, hands-off approach to the issue because of strong support for it in the House, led by La Grange's John Wilson and Waco's Lyndon Olson. Governor Briscoe continued to oppose the commission, arguing instead for the creation of an advisory board consisting of experts whom local authorities could call on for help in evaluating rate increases. The two PUC bills, with the House version calling for stronger regulation than the Senate version, slowly wound their way through both chambers. In May it looked like the legislature would be unable to pass the bills before the session ended, but the legislation was unintentionally saved when Southwestern Bell lawyers persuaded the Third Court of Appeals to overturn the lower court's injunction to halt the company's rate hike. Bell's announcement that its increase would be implemented immediately outraged Hobby and enough legislators to suddenly put the PUC bills on the fast track. Hobby told the Capitol press corps that the appeals court ruling, and Bell's resulting action, provided the "strongest evidence yet of the need for a public utilities commission.[20]

The legislature passed the Public Utility Regulatory Act, a compromise version of the House and Senate bills, in the waning hours of the session. The vote in the Senate was twenty-two to nine in favor. Despite some misgivings on his part, but urged on by

Hobby's quiet lobbying, Governor Briscoe signed the bill into law. The act empowered the new commission to regulate intrastate telephone rates and services as well as all utilities in unincorporated areas, except natural gas utilities. Liberals complained the bill was too weak, while conservatives complained it was too strong.[21]

By the end of the 140-day legislative session, Hobby was "drawing both praise and brickbats" for his performance as lieutenant governor. *Texas Monthly* complained that in his first term, "Bill Hobby arrived as an enigma and in two sessions has done little to shed light on his political beliefs or for that matter his abilities." Much of the praise Hobby received, however, contradicted *Texas Monthly*'s evaluation. Several newspapers commended Hobby for the strong role he had played in tightening state control over private youth-home facilities, for keeping the prospect for constitutional reform alive, and for working to get the public-school finance and public utilities regulation bills passed. Compliments for those latter two accomplishments were countered, however, by the complaints of some observers that the school bill fell far short of solving the problem of unequal schools and that the utilities act was too weak. Hobby's response was that passing legislation was the art of the possible. He admitted that although the utilities and educational reform bills weren't as strong as many had wanted, they were the best versions a majority in the Senate would accept.[22]

Some members of the Senate disagreed with *Texas Monthly*'s claim that Hobby had done little to demonstrate his abilities as lieutenant governor. Babe Schwartz gave Hobby the most credit for getting the new constitutional amendments bill passed and sent to the voters for approval. "I don't think that damn constitution [bill] was passed by anybody but Bill Hobby," Schwartz said. When Oscar Mauzy was asked if there had been any difference in Hobby's second-term performance as lieutenant governor, he answered, "He was much more confident in his job. He provided a great deal more leadership and direction." Conservative senator Tom Creighton noted that Hobby had been evenhanded in his treatment of conservatives as well as liberals in the Senate. "He has learned how to get along with the members of the Senate." Creighton also agreed with others who believed that Hobby had become more comfortable and self-confident in his role as lieutenant governor. "Hobby has learned his lessons well," Creighton said. "I think that he made a good presiding officer. He really impressed me with his knowledge of the budget. He comes to the meetings well prepared. I think that would be an indication of how he's grown in his office and has prepared himself to lead."[23]

In June, after the legislative session was over, Bill and Diana moved their family back to their home in Houston, which was mainly Diana's decision. According to her friends, Diana was never comfortable with her life in Austin. After residing nearly three years in the capital city, she missed her job as the *Houston Post*'s book editor as well as the intellectual life she enjoyed with her literary friends in the Rice University community. Diana also wanted her children to reenroll in their former schools and reconnect with their friends. Paul Hobby noted that his mother's decision "also was influenced by the fact that she didn't like politics or public life. Austin was basically a small town then and she thought the whole scene was phony. She thought politics was a petty and shallow little business that chews up families like a Cuisinart. And that's true, but she nonetheless supported Dad's political activities and she was a great campaigner, and she knew how to play the game in public."[24]

In a personality profile in the *Austin American-Statesman*, Diana was careful to not express her real feelings about her life as the wife of the most powerful official in Texas state government. She said she was "fascinated" with Bill's work as lieutenant governor. "I follow it with great pleasure. It's a rewarding job for him." She claimed she had no lack of privacy. "The wife of the Lieutenant Governor is not big news. I'm a private person, and state politics are very considerate and humane to people's families. I don't feel that I've been intruded upon as a result of my husband's activities." She noted that she and Bill discussed issues all the time, but legislation less so, "because the process is so enormously technical that you have to be a real student of it, which he is."[25]

After the move back to Houston, Hobby commuted to Austin, where a few days every month he stayed in a duplex he purchased and worked in his office in the Capitol. Back in Houston, he turned more of his attention to his family's media business. Oveta was still very much in control, but Bill remained on the *Houston Post*'s editorial board (except whenever the legislature was in session), which met twice weekly. He also participated in meetings of the executive management teams for KPRC-TV and KPRC-Radio, both of which usually met once a week. The *Post*'s circulation growth had flattened, but advertising had slightly increased. The paper's efforts to automate its operations were going well. All of its want ads and more than half of all editorial copy were now going through the computer. The *Post* was among the most advanced papers in the country in computerized editing and typesetting. As a result, the paper's operating expenses were down $104,000 from 1974, with more than half of those savings in production.[26]

In 1975 Houston was continuing to enjoy an economic boom that began soon after the end of the Second World War. The city's population had nearly doubled since the late 1950s, and its fast-growing suburbs were sprawling in every direction on the compass. Although the *Post*'s growth had stagnated, the family's television and radio stations were flourishing. KPRC-Radio was enjoying high earnings, but KPRC-TV was even more profitable, with the station's programs dominating viewer ratings. Bill informed his sister and brother-in-law that earnings were forecast to be "the largest in [its] history." With the television station generating the largest share of the company's profits, Oveta began to think quietly about adding another TV station to the Hobby business holdings.[27]

In September 1975, Hobby turned his attention to the upcoming election in November, when Texas voters would decide the fate of his "pet project," the eight amendments to the constitution that would fundamentally change the state's basic charter. Hobby,

Attorney General Hill, and Speaker Clayton traveled separately across Texas urging voters to approve all of the amendments. Governor Briscoe, however, remained silent. Bob Bullock maintained his opposition and repeated his warning that the amendments would lead to higher taxes. Several of the state's judges opposed the amendment to reorganize the judiciary. Members of the legislature who had voted against passage of the amendments during the previous spring also urged voters to reject them. The provision for annual sessions of the legislature was the main reason for their objections. Conservative senator Peyton McKnight explained that "the more times the Legislature meets the more laws it has time to pass, and that means more taxes." In addition to those opponents, several influential members of the business elite in Houston spoke out against the amendments, including Hobby family friends George R. Brown, Gus Wortham, and James A. Elkins. Bill Hobby nevertheless continued to campaign for the amendments despite opposition from these powerful old friends.[28]

Despite opposition to the amendments, Hobby and his allies remained hopeful that a majority of voters would favor their passage. On October 14 those hopes suffered a major blow when Governor Briscoe called a surprise press conference during which he declared his strong opposition to all eight amendments. Citing Bob Bullock's claims, the governor charged that passage of the amendments could result in vastly increased state expenditures, perhaps even triggering an income tax. He admitted the amendments included a few good provisions, but in his view the bad ones, particularly the provision for annual legislative sessions, far outweighed the good. Briscoe remained popular with his deeply conservative base of supporters in rural Texas, who were suspicious not only of the federal government but also of state government. That base of voters was not inclined to favor annual sessions of the legislature, and the possibility of higher taxes was even more unpopular. Hobby later noted that Briscoe's opposition "pretty much doomed our effort."[29]

On November 4, the voters overwhelmingly defeated all eight of the amendments. "The vote wasn't even close," Hobby noted. When reporters asked him for an explanation, he replied, "There's not enough of the body left for an autopsy." John Hill and others vehemently criticized Briscoe not only for his opposition but also for his refusal to express his opinion when the legislature was considering the amendments. However, Hobby's disappointment with the governor's stance was expressed more softly, which Briscoe appreciated. As the governor later observed, "Even when we disagreed on specific issues, Bill was always a steadfast friend. In those few cases when we couldn't [come to an agreement], our disagreements never became angry or disrespectful." Hobby eventually realized that he and his allies had basically misjudged the voters. Looking back years later, Hobby wrote that "it was incredible that such substantive change got as far as it did. I attributed the defeat to 'fear of change and innovation.' Texas voters will accept change in small increments when they are convinced of the need for it. But multiple changes with strong and credible opposition is going nowhere in a deeply conservative state." In his memoir, Hobby admitted he had believed "we could create a document more appropriate to governing a populous state in the twentieth century. I was wrong." As Lynn Ashby, the popular columnist for the *Houston Post* humorously observed,

> *Dolph and Bill went up the hill*
> *To fetch a constitution*
> *Dolph backed down*
> *The plan was drowned*
> *So much for our solution.*[30]

CHAPTER 10

THE HOBBY-CLAYTON COMMISSION

After a skiing vacation in Colorado with Diana and the kids during the Christmas holidays, Bill returned to Austin early in January 1976 to preside over an unusual session of the Senate. Hobby and the thirty-one members of the Senate were gathering at the Capitol to conduct the trial of state district judge O. P. Carrillo of Duval County, who had been impeached by the House. They would conduct the first trial of a public official in Texas since Governor James Ferguson's removal in 1917.

After being postponed four times, the trial finally began on Monday, January 5, but not until Hobby was able to rally enough members to defeat two separate resolutions to postpone the proceedings yet again and adjourn. The attempts to postpone deeply annoyed Hobby, who stood at the Speaker's rostrum and sarcastically asked, "Is there anybody else that wants to waste the court's time and shirk their constitutional duty?" His comment offended Senator Peyton McKnight, who had previously butted heads with Hobby over several issues. From the microphone on the floor of the Senate Chamber, McKnight told Hobby that he hoped the lieutenant governor had made his remark in jest. "If not," Peyton continued, "I think you owe this body an apology. I think everybody has the right to speak their own mind. I think you cast aspersions and try to damage the reputation of those who made the motions." Hobby replied, "Senator, everyone has that right to speak and so does the lieutenant governor."[1]

For a period of twenty-two days in January, Hobby, acting in his role as the judge in O. P. Carrillo's trial, pushed the proceedings forward, diligently presiding over witness testimonies, issuing rulings, and performing other duties judges typically carry out in a civil trial, including giving instructions at the end to the full Senate, which was acting as the jury. Carrillo took the witness stand in his own behalf, spending nearly seventeen hours over four days, during which he denied all allegations. The trial featured two

Houston attorneys: Leon Jaworski, the special prosecutor in the Watergate case two years earlier, who served as special counsel to the Texas Senate, and famed trial attorney Richard "Racehorse" Haynes, who was on Carrillo's defense team.[2]

The trial ended on Friday, January 23. After deliberating in a closed session for half an hour, the Senate voted twenty-three to five to convict Carrillo on one charge of financial corruption, followed by a vote of twenty-two to five to bar him permanently from serving in public office. Eager to finish the trial and go home, the Senate voted to dismiss the remaining charges against Carrillo "without a decision as to their merits." Carrillo eventually spent three years in prison after his conviction in a criminal trial. It was the first time in nearly sixty years that the Texas Senate had removed a public official. Coincidentally, that previous official had been Governor Ferguson, whose removal in 1917 had made Bill's father, Will Hobby, governor.[3]

After the Carrillo trial, Hobby turned his attention to the work of the Joint Advisory Commission on Government Operations, better known as the Hobby-Clayton Commission. Inspired by a similar study launched by Governor Jimmy Carter in Georgia, the Sixty-Fourth Legislature created the commission in the spring of 1975 to study the structure, purposes, and practices of 250 state agencies to determine how state government could operate more economically and efficiently. Hobby later referred to the commission's work as "the Carterization of Texas." When Governor Briscoe named Hobby chairman and House Speaker Billy Clayton vice chair, he told them he hoped the commission would result in stopping "the unbridled growth of state government."[4]

The eighteen-member commission was a mix of legislators and laypersons. The bill, which was sponsored by Senator Bill Patman, called for the Hobby-Clayton Commission to submit its findings and recommendations by the beginning of the regular session in January 1977. For most of the summer and early fall of 1975, Hobby and Clayton had focused on hiring staff and making plans for hearings and carrying out research necessary for making recommendations. Once the staff was in place, Hobby directed them to keep their "eyes on the big dollars and chase as few rabbits as you can." He stressed that it was the commission's job to target duplicative agencies and unnecessary regulation.[5]

The Hobby-Clayton Commission held its first public hearings in November 1975, soon after Texas voters rejected the constitutional amendments. In an interview with reporters during the hearings, Hobby predicted the commission's work would "tighten up" state operations, but he cautioned against "overselling" the eventual results of the commission's study. Hobby said he didn't think Texas had a "monstrously wasteful state government" because the legislature generally had been reluctant "to launch all kinds of programs . . . as have some Northeastern industrial states" that were experiencing serious fiscal woes. After the commission held its first full meeting late in 1975, Hobby spent one or two days a week in Austin for most of 1976, monitoring staff work, participating in hearings, and chairing commission meetings.[6]

In between Hobby-Clayton Commission meetings in Austin that summer, Hobby was in Houston working at the *Post*. A reporter who interviewed Bill in his office on the third floor of the Houston Post Building described him as dressed in a wrinkled suit, sporting a bow tie, and wearing his US Navy shoes from the 1950s. Frederic Remington wildlife sketches and paintings hung on the wall along with autographed pictures of LBJ. His bookshelves were filled with spy novels, various histories, accounting and business manuals, journalism texts, media law books, and government publications. As Hobby ate his peach yogurt lunch, he assured his interviewer that the *Post* had "pointedly" avoided anything other than factual reporting of his activities as lieutenant governor. He also noted that the paper routinely printed letters to the editor that were critical of him.[7]

Bill also became involved in Oveta's effort to expand the family's media holdings. Back in the spring of 1975, she had been surprised to learn that her friends at Harte-Hanks Newspapers had purchased a television station in Jacksonville, Florida. At one of her weekly meetings with KPRC-TV chief Jack Harris, Oveta observed that the Hartes had apparently made a "good buy" and wondered if she might have missed a promising investment opportunity—maybe it was time to expand the family's media holdings. Harris felt it was a propitious time. He told Oveta there were indications that Houston's American General Corporation might be interested in selling its WLAC-TV station, the CBS affiliate in Harris's hometown, Nashville, Tennessee. Gus Wortham, Oveta and Will's longtime friend, was the founder of American General. When Wortham's company had bought the Life and Casualty Insurance Company of Tennessee in 1968, WLAC-TV and WLAC-Radio were among the assets of the Nashville-based company. Because the television and radio stations were unrelated to its core business, American General was open to selling them.[8]

Soon after Bill returned to his job at the *Post* following the end of the legislative session in May 1975, Oveta sent him and Harris to make "a clandestine visit to Nashville" to tour WLAC and analyze the Nashville media market. Liking what they saw, Bill and Harris recommended to Oveta that the family make an offer to American General to buy the television station but not its radio property. This recommendation persuaded Oveta to initiate negotiations with American General, whose board agreed to spin the radio station out of the deal. An agreement was eventually reached in October 1975 to sell WLAC-TV to the Hobbys' broadcast entity, Channel Two Television Company, for a reported $17 million. Negotiating with American General proved to be much easier than getting the Federal Communications Commission to approve the purchase. The commission held up the sale for more than one year. Among the issues was the FCC rule prohibiting television and radio stations in the same city from sharing the same call letters but having different owners. Jack Harris received FCC approval to change the television station's WLAC call letters to WTLV, which removed one obstacle to approval.[9]

Other obstacles remained, however—chiefly the FCC's "for the good of the community" public interest standard. That was a vital element in FCC decisions to grant licenses to new stations and to approve the purchase of existing ones. As a result, it was essential for an out-of-town purchaser of a television station to cultivate the goodwill of the civic and business leadership in the city in which the station was broadcasting.

The FCC's interest in keeping ownership local meant that many, if not most, television stations were still locally owned in the 1970s. Increasingly, however, national media corporations were buying locally owned broadcast properties and integrating them into larger companies with corporate headquarters in cities far away from the local station. The same process of consolidation was happening in the newspaper and radio industries.

Jack Harris was aware that local audiences did not always welcome "outside" entities acquiring broadcast stations that were considered to be community institutions. Any local protests voiced to the FCC had the potential to hamper the purchase. With that potential problem in mind, Harris persuaded Oveta to make a public goodwill visit to Nashville with Bill and Jessica in June 1976. Their mission was to assure local viewers that the family would be thoughtful owners considerate of local interests and concerns. Harris's publicity team sent advance notice to the city's two daily newspapers, the *Banner* and the *Tennessean*, that the prospective new owners of WLAC-TV would arrive at the Nashville Airport on June 24 accompanied by native son Jack Harris. Both newspapers took the bait, although Bill managed to evade the reporters, who instead focused on his mother.[10]

After the airport news conference, Oveta, Bill, Jessica, and Jack Harris attended a luncheon in their honor at Commerce Union Bank, one of the city's largest financial institutions. They took the opportunity to visit with the leaders of community organizations, including the local chapters of the League of Women Voters, the Council of Jewish Women, and the National Council of Negro Women. That evening Bill and Jessica accompanied their mother to an early dinner with Tennessee governor Ray Blanton at the Belle Meade Country Club, followed by a charity show at the Municipal Auditorium starring Jerry Lewis and Roy Clark. By all accounts, the expedition to Nashville was a major success.[11]

When the FCC finally approved the purchase, the Hobby family quickly assumed ownership and management of the station. The value of television station properties escalated sharply soon after the purchase, essentially doubling the value of the Nashville station. With the purchase of the new television station, the Hobbys' rapidly growing, privately held communications empire, which had three thousand employees, was estimated in 1978 to have a value of at least $200 million and earnings of about $18 million a year in pretax profits.[12]

In the early 1980s the FCC relaxed its criteria for approving broadcast mergers, making it easier for the Hobby media empire to expand. The company eventually acquired television stations in Meridian, Mississippi; Tucson, Arizona; Des Moines, Iowa; and Daytona Beach and Orlando, Florida. They would make their last media acquisition in 1986 with the purchase of KSAT-TV in San Antonio.[13]

The Democratic Party nominated Georgia governor Jimmy Carter for president at its convention in July 1976, with Minnesota senator Walter Mondale as his vice presidential running mate. Bill Hobby supported the nomination. Carter had impressed Hobby when they met in Atlanta three years earlier to discuss the method of zero-based budgeting. Although Hobby agreed to serve on the Texas Democratic Party's statewide committee for Carter's election campaign, he chose not to campaign actively that fall. Instead, he turned his attention to the upcoming regular legislative session that would convene in January of the new year. Because Hobby, Briscoe, and the state's other top officials had been elected in 1974 to four-year terms, they enjoyed a welcome respite from the chore of campaigning for reelection. That break from politics also allowed the leaders of state government more time to plan the legislative agenda for the Sixty-Fifth Legislature. Governor Briscoe observed to a reporter that "since none of us in statewide offices will be making a race, we should have everything ready to go in 1977. We will be better prepared."[14]

The next statewide election was two years away, but Briscoe and Hobby were already plotting their political futures. Hobby gave thought to running for governor, but he soon decided against it for two main reasons. For one thing, his interest in the job wasn't that strong. For another, Briscoe had privately informed Hobby in late October 1976 that he would run for a third term in 1978. Hobby had no intention of opposing Briscoe. Hobby expected to have no serious opposition in the primary or in the general election if he ran for reelection as lieutenant governor, which meant little campaigning would be required. Additionally, Hobby loved being lieutenant governor, and he venerated the Texas Senate as an institution. The combination of those reasons made his decision an easy one. He announced the news at a fundraising event in Houston on November 29. Briscoe attended the event, undoubtedly grateful for Hobby's decision not to run against him, but also because the two had become friends. The governor spoke at the fundraiser, declaring, "Bill Hobby is the most effective [lieutenant governor] Texas has ever had."[15]

Briscoe was enthusiastic about the upcoming legislative session, especially with anticipated help from his friend, the newly elected president, Jimmy Carter. During the campaign, the president-elect had promised Briscoe, who traveled throughout Texas advocating Carter's election, that he would end federal price controls on natural gas. "The economy seems stronger," Briscoe told the press, adding that "if the federal government will get out of the energy business drilling activity will pick up." The governor predicted that the state's economy would be even more robust in 1976. Budget experts were predicting a state budget surplus of as much as $3 million, which meant no need for a tax increase. Hobby agreed with Briscoe that the legislature would "see a healthy balance in the treasury." But Hobby also warned "there is not enough money to do all the good things people want to do," including his hope of setting aside funds for emergencies. He pointed out that total spending demands for such items as highways, higher education, state employee pay raises, public-school funding, and utility tax relief exceeded the available surplus by at least $2 billion.[16]

Hobby's tasks in the weeks prior to the start of the Sixty-Fifth Legislature included chairing meetings of the Legislative Budget Board and overseeing the completion of the official report of the Hobby-Clayton Commission. Because the state budget was in great shape, the latter responsibility was the most important of the two. After nearly eighteen months of intensive research into the operations of more than two hundred state agencies, boards, and commissions, the blue-ribbon panel of lawmakers and business experts submitted a draft report with more than one hundred recommendations, which the staff worked to revise and edit in time for the start of the Sixty-Fifth Legislature. Hobby traveled to Austin to work with the staff to produce the final report, which was submitted to the legislature and Governor Briscoe on January 11, 1977. Hobby had been an active participant in the commission's deliberations, and he played a key role in shaping the 250-page report.

The Hobby-Clayton Commission's recommendations included abolishment of certain state agencies while forcing the rest to undergo a periodic review to determine the need for their continuing existence, which would later be known as a "sunset" process. Other recommendations included reorganizing health and welfare services to eliminate overlapping responsibilities, consolidating the state's three water resource agencies under a single administration, and reducing the number of state employees by 5 percent. The commission also called on the legislature to pay closer attention to balancing higher education needs against available resources. The legislature could take an important step in that effort, the report stressed, by stopping the proliferation of new state universities and colleges duplicating the mission of the state's ninety-seven existing campuses.[17]

At high noon on Tuesday, January 11, 1977, Bill Hobby gaveled open his third regular session of the Texas Senate. A projected $3 billion budget surplus resulting from the booming oil, gas, and sales tax revenue put the members of the Sixty-Fifth Legislature in a more optimistic mood than usual. An editorial in the *Fort Worth Star-Telegram* observed, "If the 65th Legislature is to have a central theme then it surely will be one tied to dollars for never before has there been so much money available and never before has the demand for spending it been so great." Hobby agreed, telling reporters that "appropriations in general will be at the top of the upcoming legislature's list of priorities. All the rest is poetry. The last time the Texas legislature had to look for new or additional taxes was 1971 and I can assure that it will be at least 1979 before this possibility is faced again." That proved to be an accurate prediction.[18]

A few days before the Senate convened, Hobby announced that school finance and the related problem of the state's antiquated property tax system were the major matters facing legislators. This would be his third attempt to solve those complex problems. "It is apparent there is a pretty widespread desire that the state take over more funding of public education," Hobby observed, "largely due to the inequity and disparity of property taxes." Still stung by the defeat of his pet-project constitutional amendments in November 1975, Hobby thought it might be possible to give it another shot, declaring that passing the amendments was the "great accomplishment of the last session," but he also admitted the voters had disagreed. Nevertheless, he felt it worth the legislature's effort to get portions of the defeated constitutional propositions split off into individual bills and enacted by the legislature. That hope failed to materialize.[19]

Before the Senate could proceed with its normal business on its first day in session, Hobby had to oversee the removal of Charles Schnabel, the Senate's secretary, whose prolonged legal tribulations had created troublesome public-image problems for the upper chamber. Schnabel's troubles began at the end of October 1975, as Hobby and his colleagues in the Senate prepared for the trial of Judge O. P. Carrillo. Hobby had been alarmed by the news that Travis County district attorney Bob Smith was investigating an allegation that Schnabel had abused his position by using state equipment for private purposes. Schnabel denied the allegation, claiming that it had been cooked up by a resentful former employee whom Schnabel had discharged from his job in the Senate. Two months later, headlines in newspapers across Texas announced that a Travis County grand jury had issued three indictments against Schnabel, two for theft and one for official misconduct, based on a charge that Schnabel had ordered a Senate employee to do chores on his personal property.[20]

Schnabel's legal difficulties hovered over the Senate during the impeachment trial of Judge Carrillo in January 1976. On January 4, the night before the Carrillo trial began, Hobby held a three-hour meeting with twenty-five senators to discuss the Schnabel case and whether the Senate should fire him or at least suspend him pending his trial in state court. Senator Walter Mengden urged his colleagues to fire Schnabel, while Senator Lloyd Doggett argued that Schnabel should be allowed to keep his job until a decision was rendered at his trial, which would not be held for at least six months. Hobby, who favored suspension over termination, agreed to hold a vote on the matter the next morning, prior to the opening of the Carrillo trial. The next day the Senate passed a resolution by a vote of eighteen to thirteen to allow Schnabel to remain on the job, but it also took away his authority to hire or dismiss staff and reduced his power to spend state funds. Hobby was not pleased with the decision. He told reporters that if he were a member of the Senate, he would have voted to suspend Schnabel from office "until his exoneration," because the charges involved Schnabel's handling of public funds. Afterward, Hobby asked the Senate Administration Committee, chaired by his close ally Don Adams, to investigate the charges to determine if changes in Senate policy and procedures related to the operations of the office of secretary should be made.[21]

One month later, a grand jury in Austin issued additional indictments against Schnabel, raising the total to eight: two counts of felony theft, one count of forgery, and five counts of official misconduct. The charges included stealing two Senate payroll checks, forging an endorsement on a check, and misapplying Senate funds by paying four Senate employees and one former employee for work at a University of Texas track-and-field event in 1975.[22]

The *Texas Observer* noted that none of the charges against Schnabel were "earth-shattering, but together they add up." Whether or not Schnabel's activities had been illegal, at the very least they raised ethical issues and questions about Senate operations. Austin journalist Winston Bode, a widely read syndicated newspaper columnist, wrote that in the Schnabel case the Senate system was also on trial. Hobby was deeply concerned that the affair, which was spread over the front pages of the state's newspapers, would erase the improvements made in the legislature's public image since the Sharpstown scandal. In addition, as chief administrator of the Senate staff, the secretary worked closely with Hobby, the presiding officer of the Senate. Hobby, who had run for lieutenant governor in 1972 on an honesty platform, decided that Schnabel had to go. He issued a statement to the press asserting that Schnabel's role as Senate secretary was "untenable" and that he "should step aside." Schnabel refused to resign, however. He admitted that he might have bent a few rules for the sake of Senate business, but he had not broken any laws. He remained friends with most members of the Senate, many of whom had gone on fishing and hunting expeditions with him in South Texas. He also was popular with the Capitol press corps. Some felt that the wire service reporters who focused on the affair were too aggressively sensationalist in spreading the Schnabel story, with the hope they would win fame with a scoop similar to the Sharpstown scandal.[23]

The Senate Administration Committee finally submitted a report to Hobby in September 1976 recommending new operational procedures for the office of the secretary of the Senate that included tightening up money handling and stronger accounting rules. Hobby implemented those changes immediately. A few days after the committee sent its report to Hobby, Schnabel pleaded guilty to two misdemeanor charges of official misconduct. In return, Travis County district attorney Bob Smith had the court dismiss five of the felony indictments. The judge gave Schnabel a one-year probated sentence and ordered him to pay a $1,000 fine. The DA told the press, "I don't think anybody seriously wanted to see Mr. Schnabel go to the penitentiary anyway." Schnabel continued to maintain he never profited from any of his actions as secretary, a claim the DA seemed to substantiate by saying he "had never had any proof that [Schnabel] profited personally." Schnabel immediately issued a statement saying that as far as he was concerned, the case "was closed" and he would not resign.[24]

On September 16, 1976, one week after Schnabel's plea bargain was announced, Attorney General John Hill issued a thirteen-page report on the case based on the findings of his task force investigation. Hill's report agreed that some of the original charges against Schnabel had been accurate, but that most were relatively minor, borderline infractions of state rules. Calling Hill's report "a very good one," Hobby noted that many of the problems had been addressed and a new Senate policy was in effect to prevent their recurrence.[25]

Despite Schnabel's insistence on keeping his job, Hobby still wanted him out. On the first day of the new legislative session, Schnabel was forced to resign as secretary of the Senate. Betty King, a fifty-two-year-old former Texas House Appropriations Committee staff member who had held positions in state government for thirty years, replaced Schnabel as Senate secretary. The hardworking Port Arthur native would soon become Hobby's close advisor and loyal guide for the remainder of his tenure as lieutenant governor. As one Senate observer would later note, King was "smart, refined, knowing and discreet, capable of getting things done invisibly in a legislative body full of sometimes difficult personalities." Many years later, when an oral history interviewer asked him what was the best thing he ever did when he was lieutenant governor, Hobby quickly replied, "Make Betty King secretary of the Senate."[26]

With the Schnabel affair finally out of the way, Hobby quickly made committee assignments, and the Senate turned to the normal business of legislation, which included more than one hundred prefiled bills that were ready for Hobby to assign to committees. For the first time in several years, the Senate passed its procedural rules with a minimum of controversy.

The Senate adjourned early in the second week of the session to allow Bill and Diana Hobby, Dolph and Janey Briscoe, and Bill Clayton to lead a delegation of approximately 1,500 Texans to Washington to attend the inauguration of Jimmy Carter as president. After they arrived in Washington, the Hobbys attended the Texas State Society's pre-inaugural party with one thousand other Texans who jammed into the US House Ways and Means Committee room that was designed to accommodate a much smaller group. One journalist described the party as a "melee," with the guests barely able to move, hear each other speak, or hold on to their drinks without splashing the contents on the floor or on the people around them. Although the temperature outdoors was twenty degrees, the room was so crowded the air conditioner had to be turned on. The next morning before Carter's noon inauguration, US Senator Lloyd Bentsen provided the Hobbys, the Briscoes, and his other guests a more comfortable venue for brunch.[27]

On January 25, after Hobby gaveled the Senate back into session, the members began the scramble to grab as much of the $3 billion surplus as possible for pork barrel projects back in their districts. Dolph Briscoe, and to some extent Hobby, worked hard to restrain expenditures, although the governor, in league with Speaker Clayton, also had his own costly tax reduction project: a constitutional amendment to require tax rates on agricultural property to be based on productivity rather than market value, to allow certain exemptions for homesteads, and to prohibit taxes on personal property. With the legislature dominated by rural interests, those efforts eventually proved successful. The state's voters later approved the amendment by an overwhelming majority.

A large boost in highway funding satisfied some of the demand for pork barrel projects because those funds were spread through nearly every Texas Senate district. Combined with the tax reductions and additional funding for schools, with the latter not allocated until a special session that summer, those increases exhausted most of the budget surplus. "I wish we could spend more money on welfare, more on education, more on highways," Hobby told reporters. "It would all be money well spent. But the fact is there are just so many dollars available and it's just a process of cutting the cost to fit the pattern."[28]

The legislature also spent much time studying and evaluating the Hobby-Clayton Commission's recommendations for streamlining state government. Hobby's guess that the legislature would not adopt most of the commission's recommendations proved correct. The House and the Senate eventually adopted thirteen of the forty-seven new laws the commission recommended. The general appropriations bill included twelve other recommendations. The adopted proposals included three that served as the basis of significant new laws in the field of criminal justice: establishment of a statewide adult probation system; authorization for "shock probation," in which first-time offenders would serve sixty days in state prison before going on probation; and a requirement that convicted individuals released early from prison remain under state supervision for the remainder of their sentences. The commission's recommendation for consolidating the three state water agencies into one agency won approval over strong opposition. Among the rejected proposals was a constitutional amendment that would have given access to the Permanent School Fund to all the state's public universities rather than only the University of Texas and Texas A&M. As Hobby had anticipated, that recommendation was defeated by the fierce opposition of the powerful alumni groups of both universities. Of the Hobby-Clayton Commission recommendations enacted by the Sixty-Fifth Legislature, the Texas Sunset Act had the most significant long-term impact on state government. The act created the Sunset Advisory Commission to examine each of the 175 state agencies to determine if they should be continued or abolished. The agencies were required to justify their existence to the commission every twelve years. As of 2022, the commission has abolished or consolidated ninety-two state agencies and claims to have saved $1 billion in state funds.[29]

Although it had no impact on public policy or law, Hobby had the unhappy experience in 1977 of presiding over the longest filibuster in Texas Senate history. Senator Bill Meier of Fort Worth opposed a bill because of a privacy clause that would deny access to the names of people who received workers' compensation benefits. Meier talked for forty-three and a half hours, making his objection the longest in Texas history. Meier's performance deeply annoyed Hobby, who opposed using the filibuster as a legislative maneuver. "Like most filibusters," Hobby later complained, "this one didn't accomplish anything except to delay other bills." In contrast, Senator Oscar Mauzy's filibuster on the last day of the session did accomplish something, although it also peeved Hobby. Mauzy prevented the passage of a school finance bill by speaking until the clock ran out at midnight.[30]

When the regular session of the Sixty-Fifth Legislature ended on May 30, Hobby was generally pleased with the results, especially with the attention paid to the Hobby-Clayton Commission and the adoption of some of its recommendations. His personal victories included his quiet behind-the-scenes work to kill two bills. One was an effort to exempt church-operated childcare facilities from state regulation, which was pushed by Lester Roloff and his supporters. The other was a right-to-life bill setting harsh new limits on abortions. Hobby also succeeded in passing, over intense opposition, a modest increase in payments to welfare families with children—an accomplishment that one observer of the Senate judged to be "one of the few statesmanlike acts of a dismal legislative session." Less pleasing to Hobby was the disappearance of the budget surplus, which ended his attempt to set aside a reserve for emergencies. More significant was the legislature's failure to address public-school financing due to Mauzy's last-minute filibuster. As expected, the Band-Aid plan passed in 1975 had proven unworkable, and local school districts were facing financial disaster. As Hobby later noted, "Texas had become so diverse that it was impossible to create a system that could serve a huge metropolitan district like Houston and a small rural district like Spring Lake [Speaker Clayton's hometown] equally well."[31]

It was clear to Hobby that Governor Briscoe needed to call a special session of the legislature to address the school finance issue to avoid a crisis and judicial intervention. Hobby and Clayton assured Briscoe they had the votes in the House and Senate to pass a bill and that by using the original bill as the starting point for the new one, the session could be completed within a few days. Briscoe disliked special sessions, but he agreed and called for it to convene in July. "I knew that we had an emergency situation," Briscoe said. As he later recalled, equalization of public-school funding was "the most vexing issue I faced during my six years as governor." After the governor announced his decision, Hobby and Clayton asked their education committees to prepare a new school finance bill largely based on the former one.[32]

Hobby returned to Austin to convene the Senate on July 8. Briscoe placed additional items on the agenda other than school finance, including nursing-home regulation reform and legislation to allow the state to issue bonds to build an offshore facility, popularly known as a superport, to handle supertankers carrying oil. It took the legislature nearly two weeks to pass the three bills on its agenda. Starting with the version of the school finance bill Mauzy had killed with a filibuster at the end of the regular session, the legislature's final version allocated $945 million for public-school support, including $341 million to be distributed directly to public-school districts, $345 million for teacher pay raises, and $142 million for equalization payments to property-poor school districts. To reduce costs, the legally required length of the school year was reduced by five days. Mauzy voted against the bill. He predicted the courts would rule the bill unconstitutional, which would force the legislature to reconvene to write another one. That prediction proved to be accurate. A judge ruled the bill unconstitutional only a few days after the special session adjourned, but the judge allowed the legislature to wait until the next regular session in January 1979 to write a new bill. Its business completed, the called session was adjourned on July 21. The 1977 special session would be the last time the legislature would meet before the May 1978 primary election.[33]

The news media's editorial assessments of the regular and special session were mixed, but the overall feeling was disappointment. Paul Burka, *Texas Monthly*'s legislative correspondent, felt that a $3 billion surplus was "more than enough to fund state agencies adequately, make real headway in achieving school district equalization, provide some taxpayer relief . . . or possibly to purchase some park land." Nevertheless, Burka judged that Bill Hobby was "unquestionably the best presiding officer since the mind of man runneth not to the contrary. He is totally free of lobby influence." As one senator observed at the time, Hobby didn't pay attention to lobbyists because "he doesn't have to—after all, they already work for folks like the Hobbys."[34]

Hobby returned to Houston after the end of the special called session and once more turned his attention to the family's business. His activities included attending meetings about the newly acquired television station in Nashville, resuming his normal duties on the *Houston Post* editorial board, and participating in management sessions for KPRC-TV and Radio. In September and October 1977, eager to raise public awareness about how legislation passed during the Sixty-Fifth Legislature would affect local communities, Hobby and Clayton traveled across Texas to make presentations at twenty-five local-impact seminars sponsored by a number of statewide organizations, including chambers of commerce. Hobby, who was troubled by low voter turnout and what he perceived as a decline in citizen interest in state government, hoped the tour would help remedy the problem. The "nonpartisan" tour had an additional attraction for Hobby. He faced reelection in the May 1978 Democratic primary, although he hadn't formally announced his intention to run. The seminars generated local newspaper stories, and local business and civic leaders important to his reelection effort would be in attendance. The seminars gave Hobby an opportunity to impress voters with his accomplishments as the presiding officer of the Senate and his expertise in public policy issues such as taxation, public education, transportation, health care, and law enforcement. Hobby attended nearly twenty of the seminars. Clayton made the presentations at those Hobby was unable to attend, while Hobby covered those Clayton had to miss. At the other meetings Hobby and Clayton made joint appearances. Hobby's tour began on September 8 in Waco, and during the rest of the month he proceeded to Victoria, Corpus Christi, Harlingen, Del Rio, Amarillo, and El Paso. He took time off on September 27 to accompany his mother to Fort Worth for the funeral of her older sister, Juanita, who died on Saturday, September 24. Resuming the tour in October, Hobby appeared in ten additional cities.[35]

During the fall of 1977 Hobby also tended to his responsibilities as chair of the Texas Energy Advisory Council, which Governor Briscoe had established by an executive order in 1973. The legislature made the council a formal state agency in 1975 to work on issues related to the still-lingering energy crisis that began in the early 1970s. Hobby chaired a session of the energy council in Austin on September 9, during which he had to referee an argument Bob Bullock and Peyton McKnight had with John Hill, who complained that the council had not done enough during the energy crisis and demanded that the members pass a strongly worded resolution condemning President Carter's energy policies, which were unpopular in Texas. Bullock and McKnight accused Hill of trying to grab headlines for his political benefit. Hobby interrupted the argument and said, "We all recognize this discussion is getting into the political scene." He ruled the "discussion" was over. He then pointed out to Hill that the council had passed resolutions in previous meetings stating its position on how to manage the crisis. Hobby had already issued a press release on September 3 criticizing Carter's energy policies. At another meeting in early December, Hobby named a seven-member committee to coordinate the state's response to future natural gas shortages in the coming winter in the northern states.[36]

After spending Christmas at home with their family, Bill and Diana traveled to Ireland on December 26 for a vacation. Ireland was a favorite destination for the Hobbys, who took annual trips to the Irish countryside, where they spent much time on horseback, including foxhunting and Diana's show jumping. "My parents had a whole separate life in Ireland," Paul Hobby noted. Diana's scholarly studies of Irish poet and playwright William Butler Yeats inspired some of their interest in Ireland. She had written her senior thesis at Radcliffe in 1952 on four of Yeats's plays, and she would continue her scholarly study of Yeats off and on for nearly forty years. Diana eventually wrote a doctoral dissertation on the correspondence between Yeats and book and magazine illustrator Edmund Dulac, which earned her a PhD at Rice University in 1981.[37]

Bill and Diana returned to Houston on January 7, 1978, where Bill rejoined Oveta to attend *Houston Post* and KPRC-TV and Radio management sessions. At the end of January, he traveled to Washington, DC, to attend a $1,000-per-person Democratic congressional fundraising event at the Madison Hotel. While in Washington, Hobby also met with James Schlesinger, President Carter's secretary of energy, to convey the Texas Energy Advisory Council's concerns about the president's national energy plan and to urge removal of federal price controls on natural gas. Schlesinger accepted Hobby's invitation to attend a luncheon meeting of the council in Houston in early April to explain federal policy.[38]

In February, Hobby turned his attention to the May 6 Democratic Party primary. He had no serious concerns about winning the primary or the general election in November. Two of his three primary opponents were token candidates with no money, name identification, or serious campaign plans. Political pundits also viewed the third opponent, thirty-year-old, 275-pound John Westbrook, as a nonserious candidate. Like Hobby's other opponents, Westbrook had no money, but he enjoyed benefits they lacked: he was a Black preacher with a church in Tyler, he had name identification as the Baylor football player who had broken the color barrier in the Southwest Conference, and he attracted newspaper attention on the campaign trail. Westbrook had no campaign platform other than that he was "the people's candidate." He did, however, bring up Hobby's 1974 DWI arrest during the campaign, calling it "a moral blemish" on the office of the lieutenant governor. Westbrook readily admitted he had decided to run for lieutenant governor because it wasn't a full-time job, which would allow him to continue to preach at his church after he was elected.[39]

Hobby ignored Westbrook as well as the other two opponents, and he had no active campaign. He made only one reference to Westbrook, and that was when he shared a stage with him during an appearance at the Texas AFL-CIO's political education conference in Houston in March. "I have never met the man," Hobby told the audience. "I know he is a man of great accomplishment," referring to Westbrook's breaking the color barrier at Baylor. "I just wish he had run against someone else." Hobby continued to refrain from any obvious campaigning. He and Diana even took a ten-day skiing vacation in Aspen in mid-March when all the other candidates were on the campaign trail. When Hobby returned to Texas, his pilot Bob Cargill flew him around the state to make "nonpolitical" speeches, give interviews about current public policy issues, and attend and be seen at events—just to make certain he remained in the public eye. At each stop, Hobby's speeches were about politically safe issues such as zero-based budgeting, tax policy, constitutional amendments, and recent legislation such as the Sunset Act. After an appearance in Wichita Falls, the local newspaper observed that Hobby "didn't sound much like he was running for re-election. He didn't mention his opponents, didn't talk about his record, and didn't mention his plans if re-elected." Westbrook made the primary campaign slightly more interesting than most expected, however, and he shocked nearly everyone when he received 242,000 votes on election day. It was a larger number than expected but far short of Hobby's more than 900,000, which was approximately 70 percent of the vote.[40]

Hobby's easy primary victory was no surprise, but another election outcome was. Dolph Briscoe lost his bid for a third term as governor to Attorney General John Hill by nearly two hundred thousand votes. Mark White defeated the preelection favorite Price Daniel Jr. for nomination as the party's candidate for attorney general, an outcome that deeply pleased Hobby. In the Republican primary race for governor, Dallas oilman Bill Clements defeated Dallas legislator Ray Hutchison, who was a political moderate and Hobby's friend. Clements, the owner and founder of the Southeastern Drilling Company (Sedco), the world's largest offshore oil-drilling company at the time, had served as deputy secretary of defense in the Nixon and Ford administrations.[41]

When California voters grabbed national attention on June 6 by approving Proposition 13, a referendum that would freeze the state's property taxes, political leaders throughout the country decided to join the rapidly expanding voter tax revolt. Bill Clayton and the Republican gubernatorial nominee, Bill Clements, were among them. Anti-tax groups, many business leaders, and several newspapers in Texas urged the state's political leadership to take advantage of the anti-tax environment and call a special session to reduce taxes, cap the rates, and shrink state government.[42]

Bill Hobby opposed the demands to call a special session. He was well aware of the popular pressure on legislators, and he supported some tax reduction, but he was against hasty action. He argued that the next legislature should address the issue, which would give his and Clayton's offices more time to conduct studies to determine the possible impact the tax cuts would have on essential state services. When Oscar Mauzy talked to Hobby about the demand for a special session, Hobby complained, "The whole thing's crazy. There shouldn't be any such thing." Hobby argued that there was not enough time to prepare for a special session and that Speaker Clayton, who was pressuring Briscoe, had not paid enough attention to the potential fiscal impact. In addition, Hobby had heard from most of the members of the Senate, and a majority were opposed to the special session. Briscoe, of course, had always been an anti-tax crusader and he strongly favored new reductions, but he was reluctant to call the legislature back to Austin because of his longtime opposition to special sessions and his uneasiness about spending an estimated $1 million to pay for the session.[43]

Hobby held a press conference in Austin on June 21 to discuss the prospects for a special session. He noted that Briscoe hadn't made "a firm decision," but he thought it likely the governor would call a session. In a reference to California's Proposition 13, Hobby admitted tax reform had become a popular issue nationwide. If Briscoe decided to call lawmakers back to the Capitol, Hobby could support a special session, but only if the agenda was restricted to repealing the sales taxes on utility bills, lowering the state property tax, and raising the amount of inheritance that would be tax free. Hobby added that it would be "much more practical" to reduce taxes than to cut government spending across the board. Privately, Hobby thought Proposition 13 might be appropriate for heavily taxed California, but not for Texas, which had one of the lowest tax rates of any state. He told friends that Texas needed more public services, not lower taxes.[44]

Despite his lukewarm endorsement of a special session at the press conference, Hobby went back to Briscoe and Clayton and argued against calling one. Caught between the lieutenant governor and the Speaker, Briscoe was unable to make up his mind. On June 23, Hobby broke off his discussions with Briscoe and Clayton to go to Houston to greet President Carter, who was visiting the city to speak at a fundraising dinner for the Democratic National Committee at the Hyatt Regency Hotel. Hobby joined Houston mayor Jim McConn to officially greet President Carter when he arrived that afternoon at Ellington Field. Despite his problems with Carter's energy policies, Governor Briscoe also attended the dinner and gave the president a warm introduction. Afterward, Briscoe told reporters he had not yet decided about a special session, but he believed California's approval of Proposition 13 demonstrated that the political environment was highly favorable for legislative action on property tax reduction.[45]

On July 8, after nearly three weeks of indecision, Briscoe finally gave in to Clayton's demands and agreed to call the second special session, instructing the legislature to convene only two days later, on July 10. That got the entire proceeding off to a bad start because many members openly complained about the short notice. Briscoe asked the legislature to pass five specific constitutional amendments and two acts, each dealing with cuts on current taxes and restrictions on new ones. The session, which lasted the full thirty days allotted, was tumultuous, with the Clayton-led House pushing large tax cuts and the Hobby-led Senate resisting them. Furthermore, as a lame duck, Briscoe had little influence over the proceedings. When the session ended its first week, liberal Democrats Senator Lloyd Doggett of Austin and Representative John Bryant of Dallas complained to reporters that most of Briscoe's proposals were "ill-conceived" and should never have been submitted to the legislature. However, both legislators noted that Bill Hobby had been "the voice of reason in the midst of a lot of hysteria the last two weeks," and that as a result, his stature had "substantially increased."[46]

Hobby didn't hide his lack of enthusiasm for the special session. When Briscoe called the session, the governor declared, "The people of Texas are demanding that a significant portion of existing tax revenue surplus be returned to them." Hobby openly disagreed. In a televised interview, he said he doubted most Texans were clamoring for radical tax relief. He felt there had been no sweeping public sentiment for Briscoe to call the special session, noting that he had received no more than fifty letters on the subject, and "certainly half of those have been against the special session." He also disagreed with Briscoe's request for the state legislature to limit local property tax increases. "I think that if the citizens of Austin or the citizens of Houston think their city governments are spending too much money, there is an available means for them to deal with it. We have elections every year." The *Fort Worth Star-Telegram* observed that "Bill Hobby . . . has found himself cast in the role of a spoiler" in the effort to lower taxes. "At critical junctures during the session Hobby has helped erect roadblocks and assisted in applying the brakes to portions of the Briscoe program." Less than a week before the session was scheduled to adjourn, Hobby told reporters, "This session has been a real tribute to the legislative process. Not much needed to be done and therefore not much will be done and that speaks well for the legislative process. We've gone through six turbulent economic years without the need for changes in our tax structure. If it ain't broke why fix it?"[47]

After all was said and done, the results of the session included the repeal of the sales tax on residential gas and electricity bills and a reduction in state inheritance taxes. Although the impact of the legislation was relatively modest, Hobby's skilled actions in tamping down the more extreme anti-tax efforts significantly enhanced his stature as a leader in the Senate. Most of the members were beginning to defer to Hobby on complex issues such as taxation, welfare, and budgeting. Those areas interested the math-loving lieutenant governor far more than the hot social issues, as he tinkered with and crunched the numbers, walking into budget meetings carrying a pocket calculator. "The style that I saw Hobby use most effectively was what I would call quiet persuasion," said one senator. "He examined issues with a very reasoned, logical, thoughtful kind of analysis." *Texas Monthly*'s Paul Burka noted that Hobby had been aided by a staff that was the best since John Connally was governor. As a result of Hobby's quiet maneuvering, the legislative outcome fell far short of what Republicans and other antitaxers had demanded. And they correctly blamed Hobby for it. Senator Walter Mengden was among those Republicans who complained to reporters that Hobby was the person most responsible for the Senate's failure to enact limits on local property taxes.[48]

Relieved to finish a special session that he thought was a waste of time and money, Bill immediately took Diana to Dublin, Ireland, to attend a horse show and to vacation until they returned later that month. Back in Houston, only their youngest child, Kate, an eighth grader at a private school in the city, was still living at home. Laura, now twenty, was a junior at the University of North Carolina. Her eighteen-year-old brother, Paul, had graduated from Houston's St. John's School the previous May. That fall he was entering his freshman year at the University of Virginia. Laura and Paul's brother, sixteen-year-old Andrew, was in high school, but it was a private boarding school located in Boca Raton, Florida. Their mother, Diana, was also still in school, continuing her work on a doctorate in English at Rice University. A reporter who wrote a profile on the family during this period noted that Bill was the only Hobby who wasn't in school.[49]

In September Hobby began to focus on the upcoming general election on November 7. Hobby had easily vanquished his current Republican opponent, Gaylord Marshall, back in 1974, and he had no worries about defeating him again. Hobby continued the "noncampaign" strategy he had followed for the primary. He made one openly partisan public appearance on September 18, after attending the Democratic State Convention in Fort Worth. He joined John Hill, Mark White, US Senate candidate Bob Krueger, and other Democratic candidates for a campaign rally in Galveston hosted by Babe Schwartz. Each of those candidates except for Hobby faced strong opponents. The *Austin American-Statesman*'s political reporter noted that "[Hobby] is making what only could be charitably called a minimal effort at re-election." Noting that Hobby had faced only token opposition in the May 6 primary election, the reporter observed that Hobby had "yawned his way to an easy victory and has counted on doing the same thing to [Gaylord] Marshall."[50]

Hobby purchased no newspaper, radio, or television ads, but he did go on the road. He spoke mostly at small rallies, breakfasts, luncheons, and dinners across the state during the two months prior to Election Day. He restricted interviews to meetings with the members of the editorial boards of large urban newspapers or with individual reporters in his office at the *Houston Post*. When questioned about campaign issues, he replied that the only issue was competence. A local reporter in Abilene asked him if he was confident he would be reelected. Hobby replied, "Oh, yeah. I don't have any qualms about it." Whenever he was asked about Gaylord Marshall, Hobby would answer, "I don't know very much about him." Another reporter inquired why he wasn't out shaking hands and kissing babies. Hobby simply replied, "I don't believe I've ever kissed a baby." Paul Hobby later explained his father's unusual campaign style. "[Dad's] shy and he's private in the sense that he was raised to not put his business on the street. But he was not a man of the people or a populist, or backslapper. He wasn't good at retail politics, even if he had tried."[51]

On October 18, Hobby took time away from the "noncampaign" to go to Washington, DC, with Diana to attend a black-tie dinner at the Sheraton Park Hotel, where the Association of the United States Army was honoring Oveta with its George Catlett Marshall Medal for public service. While he was in Washington, Bill learned that a *Texas Monthly* statewide poll conducted only three weeks before the election indicated he had a massive lead over his Republican opponent. His solid performance as lieutenant governor had made him politically unassailable, which was largely the reason Republicans had offered only a token opponent to contest his reelection. In a profile in

Texas Monthly published the month before the general election, Paul Burka observed that Hobby had won respect by not exploiting his news media connections and by not grandstanding. "Hobby avoids the limelight, seldom holds press conferences or tours the banquet circuit, and discloses no hint of ambition for higher offices others have ascribed to him. Characteristically, Hobby has never taken credit for any accomplishments." Burka cited an anecdote illustrating how much Bill's performance as lieutenant governor had transformed his image since his election in 1972. According to Burka, the *Houston Chronicle*'s curmudgeonly conservative editor Everett Collier had fiercely opposed Hobby's candidacy in 1972. When Bill was attending a crowded reception in Houston sometime after the end of the regular session of the legislature in 1977, Collier made his way over to him and blurted out, "Bill, you're the best Lieutenant Governor since Ben Ramsey."[52]

As expected, on November 7 Hobby won a third term with 65 percent of the vote, winning by more than 640,00 votes and carrying 250 of Texas's 254 counties. The 1978 election, however, had one stunning political outcome. Bill Clements won an upset victory over John Hill to become the first Republican governor in Texas since Reconstruction. In addition, the Republicans had gained additional seats in the legislature, although still far from a majority in either house. It was also the first time in Texas history the governor and lieutenant governor were from different political parties. It was clear that Clements would be a much more vocal and activist governor than Briscoe had been, which led some political observers to predict that the result would be a lessening of Hobby's influence. Two weeks after the election, however, Ben Barnes, who was speaking at a luncheon in Brownwood, predicted that "Clements is going to have to get along with Hobby, rather than the reverse, because there's really not anything Clements has got that Hobby wants—maybe other than his job someday."[53]

CHAPTER 11

BILL CLEMENTS AND THE KILLER BEES

At high noon on January 16, 1979, on the south steps of the Capitol, Texas Supreme Court chief justice Joe Greenhill swore in Bill Hobby—with Diana at his side—for his third term as lieutenant governor. Bill was three days away from his forty-seventh birthday. Immediately after, sixty-one-year-old Dallas oilman William P. "Bill" Clements was sworn in as Texas's first Republican governor since Reconstruction. A few days earlier, the members of the Texas House of Representatives had elected Billy Clayton to his third term as Speaker. Two hopefuls for the 1980 Republican presidential nomination, John Connally and George H. W. Bush, were among those seated on the inaugural platform. Oveta Culp Hobby was also in attendance, but it would be her last inauguration. Like her son, Oveta was three days away from her birthday—her seventy-fourth. Health issues would prevent her from attending Bill's future ceremonies. At one point in his inaugural address, Clements looked over at Bill Hobby, who was seated to his immediate left, and declared, "You will hear voices during my administration expressing doubts about some of my proposals. But I will persist, I will prevail." When Hobby later recalled the moment, he said, "I smiled. He didn't prevail."[1]

Thus began a four-year struggle between the two multimillionaire state leaders of opposing political parties. The issues over which they would battle included Clements's effort to pass a constitutional ban on a state income tax, tough anti-crime laws that included expanded wiretapping authority for police, increased authority over the state budget for the governor, and a law allowing citizens to use the initiative and the referendum to pass special laws and to accept or reject legislation. Clements's immediate primary goal, however, was to cut tax revenue by $1 billion and reduce teacher pay, state support for higher education, and many state services.[2]

Hobby not only lacked any enthusiasm for most of Clements's legislative priorities but also was strongly opposed to some of them, especially the proposals to reduce state services and support for higher education. Hobby argued that $1 billion simply wasn't available for Clements's reductions and there was no reason for them. He believed Texans wanted better government, not less, and he couldn't see much public support for reducing or eliminating services. "I don't think anyone is more for cutting taxes than I am," he stated, "but when you talk about cutting taxes responsibly you've got to talk about where you can reduce expenditures. Education, welfare, transportation, and criminal justice constitute 85 percent of the budget so if you're talking about a $1 billion tax cut, you're talking about major program reductions, and I haven't heard anybody say where those major program reductions ought to be." In 1979 Texas ranked forty-fifth among the states in state and local tax collections, and the lowest among the top industrial states. It was and remains one of only seven states with no income tax. As Hobby stressed in his memoir, "The state of Texas is as big a tax break as there is."[3]

Hobby argued that instead of a reduction in state services, there was a critical need to increase support for mental health services, education, prisons, and state police. He vigorously opposed Clements's plan to reduce funding for the state's public universities. Years later, Hobby recalled that Clements "hadn't been in office long when he said that higher education had greater waste than any state agency and appointed a committee to look into imposing more financial control." Hobby had strong opinions about the issue. "There exists in the Legislature a virulent strain of anti-intellectualism that does not reflect well on this state," he claimed. He argued that it was Clements's duty "to counteract that sort of thinking rather than to give it redneck reinforcement."[4]

As chairman of the Legislative Budget Board, Hobby was an expert on the state budget. He was appalled by Clements's lack of knowledge about how the state budget was formulated. Hobby later said that Clements apparently never realized that no one, "especially anyone in the legislature," ever wasted their time by reading a governor's budget plan. Clements appointed financial consultant Paul Wrotenbery as director of his Budget and Planning Office. "Before he had been there long," Hobby recalled, "Wrotenbery invited me over to his office and lectured me about budgeting. I never went to any other meetings with Wrotenbery."[5]

Soon after his inauguration, Clements called Hobby and Speaker Clayton to his office to discuss his idea for raising the gasoline tax, which was a consumer tax that Clements favored to reduce taxes on businesses. "Clayton and I just never had any enthusiasm for any of these projects at all," Hobby remembered. Clayton, who had no intention of taking political blame for raising gasoline taxes, explained to Clements that tax bills had to originate in the House and then they had to be passed out of Representative Bob Davis's Ways and Means Committee. Davis was a conservative anti-tax Republican and Clements's campaign chairman. "Davis is a good friend of yours," Clayton said. He suggested that it might be a good idea if the governor called Davis and pushed him to get the gasoline tax out of his committee. Hobby recalled that a few days later Clements's office issued a press release declaring that "after long study of the matter with the lieutenant governor and the Speaker," Clements had independently decided there would be no tax increases. "I thought that was interesting. He was the only one who ever had any interest in the idea."[6]

On February 2 and 3, Hobby returned to Houston to participate in the official visit of Deng Xiaoping, the de facto leader of the People's Republic of China. The historic visit, the first by a leader of Communist China, came after the United States established official diplomatic relations with the country on January 1. When Deng was planning his trip to the United States, he informed President Carter that after meetings at the White House, he and his delegation wanted to visit Atlanta, Houston, and Seattle to gather information on economic and technological development. His reason for including Houston in his itinerary was to tour the Manned Spacecraft Center. President Carter asked longtime Texas Democratic Party activist and public relations expert George Bristol to arrange Deng's visit to Houston. Bristol discovered that the conservative business leaders in the city were hesitant to participate in a program with the head of a Communist country that the United States had long considered to be a deadly enemy. In frustration, Bristol called Oveta Culp Hobby and explained the problems he was having. He asked if the *Houston Post* would host a private press conference and breakfast for Deng on Saturday morning, February 3, before he departed Houston. NASA would be giving Deng a tour of the Johnson Space Center the day before. Oveta, who had long been an internationalist, understood the diplomatic significance of Deng's visit. She immediately told Bristol, "Of course we will do this." Bristol later recalled, "From that point on, if it was good and proper for Oveta Culp Hobby, it was so for the Houston establishment."[7]

Oveta persuaded *Houston Chronicle* publisher Richard "Dick" J. V. Johnson to join with the *Post* as official cohosts of the event, which would be held in a private banquet room on the second floor of the downtown Hyatt Regency Hotel, where Deng and his entourage were staying. Oveta and Johnson gathered eighty news media executives from Texas, Oklahoma, and Louisiana to attend the breakfast. The news executives agreed to keep Deng's remarks off the record. Oveta persuaded her son to come to Houston on Friday, the day before the event, to introduce Deng to the audience the next day and to make a brief presentation. On Saturday, February 3, the audience of news executives gave Deng a standing ovation as he entered the dining room for breakfast. In her welcoming remarks, Oveta told Deng, "We live in changing times, and it is our devout hope that there be an easing of tensions and rapprochement with the People's Republic of China." Seated at the speaker's table with Bill and Oveta were the *Chronicle*'s Dick Johnson, special trade representative and Texan Robert Strauss, and US ambassador to China Leonard Woodcock. Despite the noise from a large group of pro-Taiwan protesters on the street outside the hotel, the breakfast was a major success. Bill Hobby presented the seventy-four-year-old Deng with a painting done in 1932 in Beijing by Texan artist John W. Thomason. After breakfast, Deng flew to Seattle before his return to China. Bill Hobby's involvement in the event resulted a few months later in his leading a delegation of Texas energy industry executives to China.[8]

Soon after Deng's departure, Bill Hobby returned to Austin to reassume his duties presiding over the Senate. The legislative process continued in February and March at its typically slow and deliberative pace, which would accelerate quickly as the 140th day of the session grew closer. The rhythms and routines were ones Hobby was well used to, now that he was presiding over his third regular session as lieutenant governor. The Sixty-Sixth Legislature was also marked by one of those incidents that occurred nearly every session, when members got crosswise with each other, particularly when those senators openly disliked each other, and alcohol was involved.

One morning in March when the Senate was tending to routine business, Hobby arranged for another senator to preside in his place so he could take care of a few matters outside the Capitol. When Hobby returned to his office in the Capitol sometime in the afternoon, Betty King, the secretary of the Senate, told him that the running feud between Senators Bill Moore and Babe Schwartz had led to a major disruption on the floor of the chamber that had stopped proceedings. Both men were Democrats, but Moore was a staunch rural conservative and Schwartz was a pro-union urban liberal. More important, they had a serious personality clash. As Hobby later noted, "Moore couldn't stand Schwartz, and Schwartz couldn't stop taunting Moore, who was known as the 'Bull of the Brazos' for good reason. He was a big man who didn't have much truck with those who disagreed with him. Babe Schwartz was as quick as a featherweight boxer, razor-tongued, and prone to keep punching long after the battle was won or lost."[9]

Betty King explained to Hobby that during the morning session, Moore and Schwartz had engaged in a heated argument over a bill Moore was sponsoring that lessened some of the liability for building contractors who were undertaking projects paid with public funds. Schwartz declared that the bill was too friendly to contractors and accused Moore of letting the Association of General Contractors write its provisions. Schwartz and Austin senator Lloyd Doggett then teamed up to use a procedural rule to table the bill. Harsh words were exchanged between Schwartz and Moore, and then the Senate adjourned for lunch.[10]

When the Senate reconvened after lunch, it became apparent to his colleagues that Moore had enjoyed a few too many alcoholic beverages during the break. Saralee Tiede, who was covering the session as a reporter for the *Dallas Times Herald*, recalled that "Moore wasn't the only member prone to drinking too much during lunch. That's why Hobby didn't like to have any meetings after lunch." Moore found Schwartz interrogating a witness at a meeting of a committee that Moore chaired and Schwartz didn't belong to. Ike Harris had been presiding as the committee's vice chairman in Moore's absence. When Schwartz saw Moore enter the room, he loudly announced that Moore was "obnoxious." Moore replied, "Senator, you're repulsive to me." Schwartz told Moore that if he didn't like the characterization, Moore could try to eject him from the floor. By this time, the loud ruckus had drawn a crowd. Senator Ed Howard was able to pull Moore away while other senators grabbed Schwartz.[11]

"Hobby just hated the fact that everything had gone to hell when he was gone," Tiede noted. According to Paul Burka, *Texas Monthly*'s veteran legislative reporter, "To get ahead in Hobby's Senate, you had to be willing to address the state's major problems without partisanship or demagoguery, and you had to obey his number one rule: Never embarrass the Senate. Hobby set the standard and rewarded those who met it with his respect. Those who didn't meet it were not left in doubt about where they stood."[12]

After hearing Betty King's account of the altercation, which she described as "pandemonium," Hobby called Moore and Schwartz separately into his office. He expressed his displeasure at their conduct and demanded that it not be repeated. Afterward, Hobby sent pairs of boxing gloves to Schwartz and Moore as souvenirs of the incident and as a humorous but serious reminder that he expected it not to happen again. Schwartz displayed his boxing gloves on the wall of his office, but the Bull of the Brazos sent his pair back to Hobby. Nevertheless, the feud between the two strong-willed senators "never got quite that out of hand again," Hobby recalled.[13]

Early in May, as the Sixty-Sixth Legislature reached its final weeks, Hobby found himself in the middle of another major fight, although not a physical one. And the battle wasn't with Governor Clements but with a group of his fellow Democrats.

By early 1979 Jimmy Carter had become an unpopular figure in Texas, casting his prospects for winning the state in the next presidential election into serious doubt. Two well-known Texas Republicans, John Connally and George H. W. Bush, as well as former California governor Ronald Reagan, who had a strong following in Texas, were planning to run for the Republican nomination for president. Texas had held a special presidential primary in 1976 to help support Lloyd Bentsen's candidacy, but the law expired with that election. In the fall of 1978, John Connally's campaign advisors decided to lobby the upcoming Sixty-Sixth Legislature to pass a new law to hold another presidential primary to help his campaign. It was generally accepted that whoever won Texas's Republican primary would have a significant advantage in the contest for the party's presidential nomination. As a result, party activists anticipated that many conservative Democrats who were opposed to Carter would be eager to vote in the 1980 Republican primary. But that would also disqualify them from voting in the Democratic primary for conservative Democrats at the state and local levels. Texas law prohibited voters from casting a ballot in more than one party's primary.

John Connally's campaign team believed that if given an opportunity, conservative Democratic voters would vote for Connally, a former Democratic governor who remained popular with that faction of the Democratic Party. With that prospect in mind, the Connally team, which included Connally's close associate Ben Barnes, decided in October 1978 to lobby Bill Hobby and Speaker Clayton to push a bill through the legislature for a split-primary election structure that would make it possible for Democrats (or any voter) to vote in the Republican presidential primary as well as in the regular Democratic primary. The presidential primaries would be held separate from the regular primaries for nominating congressional, state, and local candidates. Voters would be able to vote in one party's presidential primary and then switch to another party's regular primary, which would be held a few months after the presidential primary. The presidential primary would be held in March 1980, which would also help Connally. A big win in a critical state like Texas that early in the primary season could possibly give Connally enough momentum to edge out Reagan and Bush for the Republican nomination.[14]

Barnes persuaded Hobby to support the dual-primary plan with the idea that it would give Texas more influence in the presidential nomination process. Hobby later cited that argument as the basis for his support. That reasoning seems thin, however, because in October 1978, President Carter was not expected to have a viable opponent for his renomination, which meant Texas would have little influence over Carter's nomination, no matter when the state held its primary. Massachusetts senator Edward Kennedy eventually ran against Carter for the Democratic nomination for president in 1980, but he would not announce his candidacy for more than a year. Liberal Democrats suspected that Hobby's real reason for pushing the primary plan was to help Connally and that it was a favor to his friend Ben Barnes. But Hobby denied that accusation. Years later, when he was asked in an oral history interview if helping Connally had been his motivation, Hobby answered, "Hardly. When I ran for lieutenant governor [in 1972], I ran against John Connally's brother. John Connally was secretary of the treasury and the IRS started investigating me. Pure coincidence, I am sure! So, that's how much regard I had for John Connally." Hobby's longtime associate and advisor Saralee Tiede, when asked the question about Hobby's motives, retorted, "Help John Connally? He didn't even like John Connally."[15]

Hobby has always insisted that he favored an earlier primary date because he believed it would give Texas more influence over Carter in his bid for renomination, not because he wanted to help Connally. "As it is now," Hobby argued at the time, "the agenda for presidential campaigns gets set by people slogging around in the snow of New Hampshire. Of the six primaries before the end of March four are in the New England states and that's where the issues get set." Hobby said those issues tended to be liberal concerns and eastern consumer interests, not Texas interests, especially in federal regulation of the energy industry. "An early primary in Texas would focus attention on concerns of energy and agricultural producers such as those that maintain lobbies in Austin."[16]

On January 31, Dave McNeely, chief political correspondent for the *Austin American-Statesman*, broke the news that Hobby and possibly Speaker Clayton would soon submit a bill to have presidential primaries on the second Tuesday in March in 1980. The bill would also move the regular party primaries from May to July, with runoffs in August. Clayton was believed to favor the plan, but he was letting Hobby take the lead. At that time, primary elections in Texas were held on the first Saturday in May, with runoffs the first Saturday in June. Hobby explained that the second Tuesday in March was chosen for the separate presidential primary because of Democratic Party rules, which designated the date as the earliest that presidential delegate selection could be made.

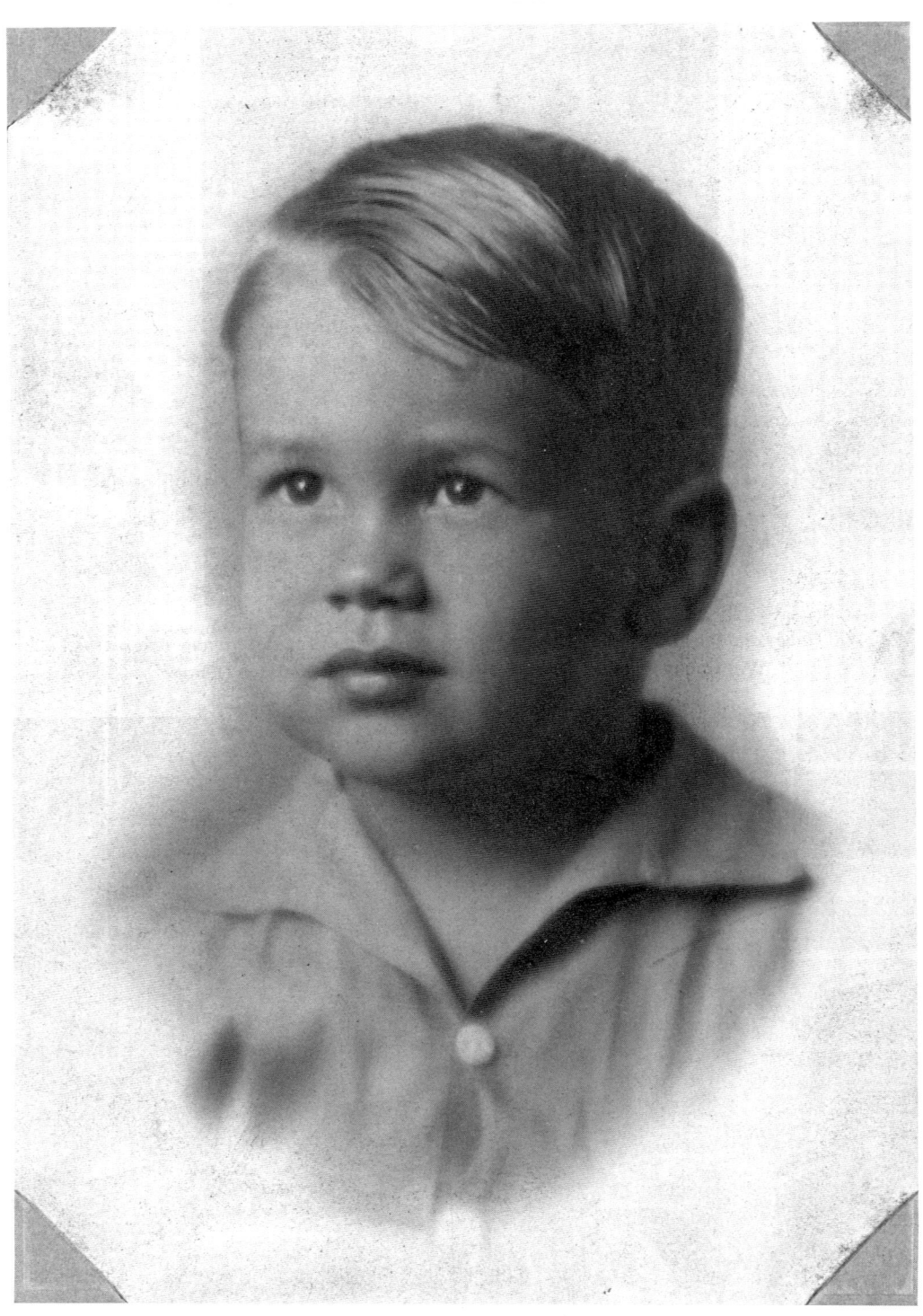

Portrait of Bill Hobby as a toddler. Photo by Elva Cockrell Studio, Houston. Bill Hobby Papers, Briscoe Center for American History.

Bill Hobby and former president Lyndon B. Johnson, January 16, 1973. The 1973 inauguration in Austin was Johnson's final public appearance. Bill Hobby Papers, Briscoe Center for American History.

From left, *Governor Dolph Briscoe, Janey Briscoe, Lieutenant Governor Bill Hobby, and Diana Hobby attend inaugural festivities, January 16, 1973.* Photo by Roger Powers. Bill Hobby Papers, Briscoe Center for American History.

At the time, three states—New Hampshire, Iowa, and Florida—held presidential primaries earlier than March, but the party had given those states special permission to continue their traditional timing. Hobby admitted that his proposal would generate "considerable disagreement. I'm sure it will be the subject of considerable debate." Nevertheless, he made it clear that having a separate presidential primary in March would be one of his main legislative priorities for the session.[17]

A few of the conservative Democratic senators welcomed Hobby's plan. They wanted their conservative supporters, Democrats and Republicans, to be able to vote in the Republican presidential primary and not be barred from voting later in the Democratic primary, which would continue to give the conservatives an advantage over liberals in the regular primary. Liberals, of course, were not happy. They wanted to prevent Republicans from voting in the regular Democratic primary, which they had been doing regularly for decades, since the Republican primary rarely had competitive races for Congress and state offices. The fight between Bill Clements and Ray Hutchison for the Republican nomination for governor had been an exception. When Hobby shared his plan with liberal Babe Schwartz, the senator expressed his outrage. "Bill, do you know what Republicans do who vote in the Democratic Primary? They vote against me and Mauzy and Chet Brooks," Schwartz said. "You're about to give the Republican Party the privilege of having every Republican in Texas vote for Connally in March and then vote against us in July. If that happens you can kiss us goodbye and we ain't gonna sit still for it." Hobby replied that his primary plan was "what is best for Texas." Schwartz responded, "Well if you don't mind, we're going to do what's best for us." Despite liberal opposition, Hobby knew that with the support of the Senate's conservative majority, he had more than enough votes to pass his split-primary bill. However, he underestimated the determination of the liberal opposition.[18]

The effort to conduct a separate presidential primary and move it from May to March also ran into strong opposition from the Republican Party's state executive committee, which issued a statement demanding that the present system be left unchanged. George H. W. Bush denounced it as a scheme to put him and other Republican candidates at a disadvantage in favor of Connally, which was accurate. Governor Clements claimed that Reagan also opposed the plan, but the Texas governor was in a difficult position in the matter because Connally had campaigned for him during his race for governor, as had Bush and Reagan. Nevertheless, he did hint that he might veto any bill that split the primaries. Having nothing to gain from a skirmish over the presidential primary, Clements tried to remain aloof from the controversy.[19]

Despite the opposition, Hobby made passage of the split-primary bill a personal mission, helping to draft the bill and lobbying hard for its passage. He assigned the bill to the Senate State Affairs Committee, optimistic the committee would easily pass it. On March 6, however, Hobby was alarmed when it won committee approval by only one vote, which reflected the deep divisions in the legislature over the issue. Late in the afternoon on the day after the committee vote, Hobby had Gene Fondren, a lobbyist for Texas automobile dealers, gather the state's most influential lobbyists for a meeting with him and Speaker Clayton in Austin in a downtown private club. Hobby asked the lobbyists to help him marshal the votes he needed to pass the split-primary bill. When some of the lobbyists asked him why they should exert themselves for that cause, Hobby answered that the presidential race by itself was not as important as the need to protect conservative Democratic officeholders in the legislature, especially those in the Senate. He also claimed the early primary would give Texas "a greater voice" in the presidential race, especially in the critical areas of energy and agricultural policy. When one lobbyist asked what he wanted them to do, Hobby, as usual, was concise: "What you do best, lobby." He added, "I am just using every device I know of in the Legislature to accomplish this goal."[20]

At the same meeting, Hobby also asked lobbyists to work against Governor Clements's initiative and referendum law, which, if passed, the governor would use to get his massive tax cuts accomplished without legislative involvement. Hobby declared that Clements's bill ranked high on his list of "worst" bills to be considered during the session. Several lobbyists told reporters this was the first time Hobby had engaged in an openly hostile act of defiance against Clements. When Hobby asked for a show of hands from the lobbyists who supported Clements's bills, no hands were raised. Afterward, some of the lobbyists admitted they felt Hobby had put them "on the spot" when he asked them to show their hands, because he was one of the most powerful elected officials in the state. They also pointed out that many Republicans and Democrats they contacted later said they preferred to keep the presidential primary in May, although they agreed with Hobby's opposition to the initiative and referendum bill, which ultimately failed to pass.[21]

Speaker Clayton finally decided to support Hobby's primary bill, but he was faced with competing versions in the House and serious opposition from Republicans as well as liberal Democrats. On April 19 opponents of the split primary, led by Dallas representative John Bryant, added a rider to the general appropriation bill that would force the presidential primary to be held on the same day as the regular primary by forbidding the use of state funds for a presidential primary held on any other day. Representatives who favored a split primary assumed the rider would be removed during the conference committee with members of the Senate.[22]

In the Senate, Hobby convinced Jack Ogg, with whom Hobby had shared his plan back in October, to sponsor the split-primary bill. On May 1, with the State Affairs Committee having approved the bill in March, Ogg announced he would call a vote to bring it to the floor for debate, which required twenty-one of the thirty-one senators to vote yes. But an opponent of the bill, Senator Ron Clower, claimed he had twenty votes against it. Ogg's bill stalled on the Senate calendar for weeks because it lacked the necessary two-thirds vote to suspend the regular order of business and bring the bill up for debate. With the session nearing its end and the bill facing certain defeat, Hobby pulled a parliamentary trick by getting the Senate rules suspended to allow him to bring a bill to the floor with a notice of twenty-four hours, which would require only sixteen rather than twenty-one votes for passage. With that change in the rules Hobby placed a note on the intent calendar that he was submitting an unidentified bill in twenty-four hours. "I gave notice that I would lay out the Regular Order of Business on Friday, May 18," Hobby recalled in his memoir. "That meant the primary bill would be at the top of the calendar." Years later, as he remembered the events that followed, Hobby admitted, "Bad idea."[23]

In the meantime, Hobby set aside Ogg's bill and persuaded Senator Bill Meier to sponsor a "seemingly innocuous" bill dealing with primary filing fees that in reality would create the split primary. Hobby would bring Meier's bill to a vote instead of Ogg's.[24]

On May 17, with the Senate in executive session, Oscar Mauzy walked up from the floor to the rostrum and asked Hobby, "Governor, would you mind telling me what your little note on the intent calendar means?" Mauzy recalled that the lieutenant governor "was as haughty and as arrogant as I've ever seen Bill Hobby. Hobby's usually very open and obvious with everybody. He said, 'Senator, it means just what it says.' I said, 'Well, fuck you, Governor!' I turned around and walked back to my desk and put my feet up on the desk." Hobby also refused to tell Doggett and Schwartz what the bill was about. "We knew what he was going to do," Mauzy later recalled. "We just wanted him to tell everybody." Hobby later admitted that "messing with the Senate calendar was the biggest mistake I made as lieutenant governor."[25]

After the executive session adjourned, the core group of liberal senators, including Babe Schwartz, Carl Parker, Glenn Kothmann, Ron Clower, Lloyd Doggett, Bill Patman, Bob Vale, Carlos Truan, and Gene Jones, gathered in Mauzy's office to assess the situation. They were aware the Meier bill was a Trojan horse that would easily pass in the Senate, and then the House would attach a split-primary amendment to it. That bill would go back to the Senate, where it would only need a simple majority to pass. In that event, the liberals would lack the votes to kill it. Afterward, when the liberals confronted Hobby about his scheme, he admitted that had indeed been his plan.

The liberal conspirators concocted a strategy to thwart Hobby's efforts. Convinced Hobby would be able to break a filibuster, they created a unique plan of action. Schwartz, who was an expert on the Senate rules, proposed they should just break the quorum and prevent a vote from being taken. "We had broken the quorum before and it worked," Schwartz later remembered. "I promised that the Senate would adjourn. I said you don't think any little silly bastard's gonna hang around all weekend just because Hobby wants to do what he wants to do, do you? It's ridiculous." It turned out that Schwartz was wrong. "Little did I know that Hobby had put a lock on the door and that was going to be the end of anybody leaving town."[26]

Schwartz's colleagues agreed to follow his plan. They would disappear early the next morning, May 18, and deny Hobby a quorum. They would hide out for a few days until forty-eight hours prior to the end of the session, when it would be too late to pass the bill. Their maneuver would not be a criminal offense, but they knew Senate rules empowered Texas Highway Patrol officers and Rangers to arrest them and return them to the Capitol. Nevertheless, all but two of the senators agreed to hide in a garage apartment behind a house on Bridle Path in West Austin owned by Senator Carl Parker's assistant Dora McDonald. The other two, Chet Brooks and Raul Longoria, decided to leave town. Longoria, who was in court in Edinburg trying a case, fled across the border to Mexico. Chet Brooks went to Ardmore, Oklahoma, where the Texas Department of Public Safety (DPS) had no jurisdiction.[27]

When Hobby convened the Senate on the morning of May 18, he looked out over the floor and realized most of the liberals weren't there, which meant there would not be enough senators present for a quorum. Hobby stalked the Senate Chamber, angry and confused, even though Mauzy had warned him the day before that the liberals were thinking about "busting" the quorum. Hobby had believed Mauzy was bluffing. After waiting for forty-five minutes, Senator Peyton McKnight, joined by five conservative Democrats and two Republicans, made a motion to call on the DPS and the Texas Rangers to conduct a statewide search for the missing members and arrest them if necessary to bring them back to the Senate. By a vote of fourteen to two, the call was ordered. It was the first such call issued for members of the Texas Senate in ten years. The Capitol press corps ran to the telephones and called their newspapers and radio and television stations, generating intense news coverage statewide as well as nationally, including stories in the *Washington Post*, the *New York Times*, and *Time* magazine. Thirty DPS officers fanned out across Austin and traveled to the missing senators' hometowns in search of the absent legislators. The state troopers eventually staked out a convention, a golf tournament, a religious retreat, and some farms and ranches, but they found nothing. They also openly tailed the senators' wives.[28]

Hobby innocently boosted news coverage when he gave the liberal fugitives a catchy name: the Killer Bees. Africanized honey bees, popularly known as killer bees because of their aggressive nature, had been a media sensation in the late 1970s as they made their way from Brazil, through Central America, and headed straight for Texas, although the bees wouldn't appear in the state until the mid-1980s. Hobby had initially used the term earlier in the session during a battle over a consumer rights bill before the split-primary bill surfaced. During a debate, Hobby called Senator Gene Jones to the dais and, in a reference to the liberals, complained, "You know, I never know where you guys are coming from. You're like a bunch of goddamned killer bees! You're coming from all directions and you're stinging me. You're going to kill me!" When the liberals did their disappearing act, Hobby referred to them publicly as killer bees, a name the news media instantly adopted.[29]

The ten senators who remained in Austin were secretly having breakfast at Dora McDonald's house the morning they disappeared. "Nobody knew where we were or what we had decided to do," Mauzy remembered. Agreeing to stick it out, they moved into McDonald's garage apartment, which had one bedroom with a double bed and one bathroom with a tub, a shower, and a toilet. McDonald brought in a double mattress and put it on the floor, along with three sleeping bags, giving ten men only seven places to sleep. The apartment also had a radio and a television. The property was surrounded by a high wooden fence that hid the backyard from the street, which allowed the senators a place to walk around and sit outside.[30]

The Killer Bees decided to use Hobby's former chief of staff Steve Oaks as their go-between with the lieutenant governor. They were aware that Oaks was sympathetic to their cause. Mauzy sent word through one of their allies who was not in hiding to set up a phone call between Gene Jones and Oaks, who was still in Austin providing legal counsel to Hobby. Oaks agreed to receive Jones's call on a pay phone on the third floor of the Capitol. Jones told Oaks which members were in hiding, but not their locations, and that they would remain in hiding until it was too late to pass the split-primary bill. Oaks said he would give the message to Hobby. They set up a time for Jones to call him on the pay phone. When Jones called back at the arranged time, Oaks told him, "Hobby just says for all you guys to forget it. This is war—no negotiations, no compromise. He thinks he can find you. He's going to get you back here, and, by God, he's going to pass that bill if you've got to stay here all weekend!"[31]

The renegade senators suddenly realized they were going to be stuck in the one-bedroom apartment for nearly five days. They remained anyway. No one left the property during that period except for Gene Jones, who suffered from claustrophobia. Jones fled to his home in Houston, where he remained hidden and safe from arrest. Under Senate rules the DPS officers were not allowed to enter a private residence when responding to a call to bring legislators back to the Capitol. "We just hunkered down," Schwartz recalled. "Our staff sent in food and whiskey and more food and more whiskey than we should have had, and we just set up the bar and set up the food."[32]

Meanwhile, the senators who had remained in the Capitol were forced to bide their time, doing little work and worrying about the fate of their pet bills that were languishing on the calendar as time for the session ran out. Senator Peyton McKnight was among those who were growing impatient with the holdouts. "If the idea of the absent senators is to carve a niche in history," McKnight told reporters, "I would remind them that those remembered in Texas history books are those who stood and fought, not those who cut and run." As payback, the remaining senators began killing the Killer Bees' pet legislation in committee. At a staff meeting that weekend, Hobby expressed his anger and disappointment that the liberal senators had gone into hiding. However, Rodney Ellis, who was now on Hobby's staff, later remembered that "most of the people on the staff, at least the younger ones, thought that he had made a mistake by moving the Texas primary date, essentially to help John Connally." Hobby also complained about the "ineffectiveness" of the DPS search. In an interview with the *New York Times*, he stated that "the effort has not been very impressive. It's 12 prominent senators of the state they've failed to find. It has really been a pretty ludicrous performance on the part of the DPS." Hobby's complaints inspired Kelly Arnold, the Senate's sergeant at arms, to walk around the Senate Chamber wearing a T-shirt that read, "Where the Hell Are the

Killer Bees?" Hobby later admitted, "The whole thing was such a fiasco. The 'Worker Bees,' who stayed behind, spent each session haranguing the absentees, since we didn't have the quorum necessary to transact any business. And we were in the very last weeks of the session with lots of legislation in the pipeline."[33]

At this point, DPS officers in Houston sent a message to Hobby that they had finally apprehended one of the Killer Bees, Gene Jones. They nabbed him as he went out to pick up a newspaper in front of his house. The troopers asked him if his name was Jones and he said yes. They rushed the culprit back to Austin in a DPS helicopter. When Kelly Arnold, the sergeant at arms, met them at the Capitol, Arnold turned to the DPS officers and said, "That's not Senator Jones." The man looked like Jones but turned out to be his brother, Clayton, who told Arnold, "I didn't tell them I was Senator Jones, they just arrested me." As it turned out, Gene Jones had been in his house, but when he saw the DPS officers arresting his brother, he fled though the rear door to his backyard, climbed over an eight-foot fence, and fled to a local radio station, where he gave an on-air interview to prove that the DPS had grabbed his brother. "They brought in the wrong guy," Hobby noted. "A bigger screw-up you just could not imagine."[34]

On the other side of the Capitol, twenty-five members of the House issued a statement of support for the missing senators. Eager to avoid direct involvement in the affair, Governor Clements performed his own disappearing act. He traveled to Hartford, Connecticut, to spend the weekend at the Marine Club. His office told the news media he was unavailable for comment. Most Republicans were opposed to the split primary, but they were divided over approving the drastic tactics of the Killer Bees. Privately, Clements didn't advocate a split primary, but he agreed with Hobby to the effect that the "truants" were neglecting their duty.[35]

On Monday, May 21, the Killer Bees voted to return to the Senate the next afternoon if Hobby would agree to conditions. Schwartz, who had remained in touch with Hobby by prearranged calls to the pay telephone, reluctantly agreed to contact Hobby and ask him if Chet Brooks could come to his office and present their terms. "Bill, I'm calling because they've elected me," Schwartz said, "but I voted against calling you. I want you to know that I'm ready to stick it out. I don't give a damn whether the session ends favorably or not but we have to win this battle." Schwartz told Hobby that Brooks wanted to meet with him in private to negotiate the terms. Hobby agreed to meet with Brooks, who had worked as a reporter at the *Houston Post*. "You've already won the battle, Babe," Hobby responded. "I'm not going to screw around with the primary bill anymore if you all come back and if we can finish the business of the session before midnight tomorrow." Unknown to the news media, Brooks met privately with Hobby that evening and presented the Killer Bees' conditions. One was that they be allowed to come back as a group. Another was that they be given time to shave and shower and get dressed appropriately. And finally, they asked Hobby to agree not only to call off the DPS search but also to give them a DPS escort from their hiding place to the floor of the Senate. Hobby agreed to the terms.[36]

The next morning, the Killer Bees ended their hideout. As the renegade senators entered the Senate Chamber, visitors in the packed gallery cheered and buzzed like bees. Many of the spectators were wearing yellow-and-black Killer Bees T-shirts, and a few wore fake insect antennae on their heads. The group held a press conference and reported that Hobby had agreed not to attempt any parliamentary maneuvers to bring the bill up for a final simple-majority vote.[37]

Mauzy later recalled that when Hobby greeted them, he was "a perfect gentleman as he always is. He had gotten over his bad feelings and his hurt feelings. It finally dawned on Hobby that he was the guy that was looking bad in this whole thing—we weren't. Obviously, he had gotten his feelings hurt by it all, but it didn't carry over very much. I don't think Hobby is a vindictive or a vengeful man." Saralee Tiede noted that "Hobby was a no-drama guy. What Hobby wanted was to have everything orchestrated and worked out. Of course, that didn't happen with the Killer Bee episode." At first, however, Hobby refused to acknowledge that he had made a mistake. On the day the liberal senators returned, he told reporters that he still supported the concept of the early primary. He admitted that he had been hurt politically with liberals but that he had strengthened his support with conservatives. He predicted that the affair would be forgotten when the election was held in 1982. Hobby's attitude quickly changed, however. "After a few days I repented my ways (and still do)," Hobby recalled years later. "The Bees returned to the hive. The bill never passed. It wasn't a very good idea anyway. Neither was putting a call on the Senate. That came about because I made a bad error in judgment. I can't imagine what I was thinking. It was foolishness on my part."[38]

After the Killer Bees returned to the Senate, the editorial columns of Texas newspapers were filled with speculation about the damage the affair had inflicted on Hobby's political reputation. The *Dallas Times Herald* observed that the Killer Bees episode had seriously hurt Hobby's "good-guy image," noting that "liberals and moderates" were furious with Hobby, whom they helped elect in 1972. "Hobby has always been considered progressive in his philosophical outlook, but he aligned himself in this session solidly behind conservative Democratic senators on the presidential primary."[39]

The observation by one newspaper that the Killer Bees episode was "the low point" of Hobby's career as lieutenant governor turned out to be correct, but only in the sense that his reputation only went up from that point on. The political damage to Hobby would be short-lived. As it turned out, John Connally was a stunningly unsuccessful Republican presidential candidate who ultimately netted only one delegate. The experience marked a watershed in Hobby's tenure in office, as it lessened the influence conservative Democrats had over him. Although he blamed himself for the Killer Bees affair, he also realized that he had been led astray by Connally's conservative allies in the business world. Hobby would never leave the political middle ground, but his views shifted more to the liberal side on many issues, if not all. And he refused to allow the episode to harm his effectiveness as the Senate's presiding officer. Not long after the episode of the split primary, Gib Lewis, a conservative Democratic representative from

Fort Worth who would eventually succeed Bill Clayton as Speaker, observed that "as lieutenant governor, Hobby probably has as good a control on members of the Senate as any lieutenant governor we've ever had. He runs the Senate. Despite the 'Killer Bees,' he runs the Senate. Don't ever think he doesn't. A bill does not get passed in the Senate that does not have his blessing."[40]

In 1989, the Killer Bees celebrated the tenth anniversary of the affair at the legendary Scholz Garten in Austin. Hobby had DPS officers "arrest" them and bring them to a reception in the Senate Chamber. Hobby greeted them from the rostrum clad in full beekeeper regalia, including gloves, hat, and face net. The boisterous celebration was a perfect symbolic end to the story, memorialized in the following lines:

> *In the thick of the 66th Session,*
> *Amid all the dirt and the sleaze,*
> *Came a parliamentary maneuver*
> *Called the Flight of the Killer Bees.*[41]

The Sixty-Sixth Legislature's regular session ended on Memorial Day, May 28, 1979. The Killer Bees episode in the Senate would be its historical legacy, but otherwise the legislative results reflected the continuing retreat away from the post-Sharpstown reform days of the 1973 session. It was also shaped by having a Republican living in the Governor's Mansion and the growing realization that the Republican Party was no longer a political force Democrats could ignore. At the end of the session, *Texas Monthly*'s Paul Burka observed that "as Texas' best practitioner of political theatrics since John Connally, Clements managed to come out looking good despite getting virtually nothing he wanted."[42]

The Sixty-Sixth Legislature was notable not for what it accomplished but for what it didn't, in areas such as improving the rights of farmworkers and protecting consumers. After it was over, few observers considered the session to be a great success by most measurements. In an editorial, *Texas Observer* editor Jim Hightower argued, "Before the session started, conventional wisdom among Austin's legislative watchers was that . . . Hobby would come forward to play the 'Man of Reason' role, holding the line against the excesses sought by business lobbyists. Instead, Hobby threw in with the lobbyists, and he attempted to ride roughshod over anyone opposed to their agenda."[43]

It was no secret that Jim Hightower was far to the left of Bill Hobby on almost every issue. His claim that Hobby had let progressives down ignored the obvious fact that Hobby was moderately conservative on most issues affecting business, and his actions were in line with that political viewpoint. The ceiling on interest charges for home buyers' mortgages was raised to 12 percent, an increase of 2 percent, when the national *average* was 11.2 percent. The Federal National Mortgage Association, Fannie Mae, was threatening to stop buying mortgages in Texas because of the low ceiling. The bill "gutting" the Consumer Protection Act removed the previously legislated mandatory amounts for damages caused by fraud and deception but left intact most of the key protections, including allowing class-action suits. That bill had plenty of votes in the Senate to pass without Hobby's involvement. Hobby supported consumer protection legislation in general, but he disliked mandatory damage amounts as much as he opposed mandatory sentences for crimes.[44]

On May 30, two days after the end of the legislative session, Hobby traveled to Washington, DC, where he spent nearly two weeks visiting old friends and taking care of some Hobby family business matters. On June 11, his last day in Washington, Hobby joined Bill Clements in a meeting with the Texas congressional delegation to discuss the governor's "Texas Energy Plan" and to lobby the members to push the plan in Congress. Hobby knew the meeting was an unnecessary exercise since the delegation was already taking the actions Clements was advocating, but for diplomatic reasons he agreed to go with the governor and make low-key and noncontroversial remarks about the need for the United States to be energy self-sufficient. Many of the congressmen were critical of the meeting, including Jack Brooks, who complained that there was nothing new in the plan because most of its proposals had long been advocated by members of the delegation. Afterward, Brooks told one of his colleagues in the delegation that Clements was "just up here to demagogue." Hobby, however, seems to have escaped the delegation's ire over the incident.[45]

After Hobby returned to Texas in mid-June, he put aside his state duties that summer to recuperate from the legislative session and the drama of the Killer Bees and to take care of his business affairs, which included two trips to Nashville for meetings with the management of the Hobbys' television station in that city. In early August, however, Hobby had to temporarily step away from his business activities and vacation time to address a catastrophic oil-well blowout that had occurred in June at an offshore Pemex (Petróleos Mexicanos) well in the Bay of Campeche in the Gulf of Mexico. Prevailing currents carried oil from the well toward Texas. By August the oil poised an immediate threat to the beaches, estuaries, and bays in South Texas. Sedco of Dallas, a company founded by Governor Clements, operated the Pemex drilling site. Clements had left the company several months prior to his run for the governorship and was not involved in its operations, although his son was its chief executive. Nevertheless, the governor suffered political damage in South Texas as a result of the disaster. The damage was made worse by his comment to the press that the accident was "much to-do about nothing."[46]

On August 7, 1979, the day a wave of oil was expected to hit the beaches, the US Coast Guard flew Hobby, Land Commissioner Bob Armstrong, and Railroad Commission chairman Mack Wallace over the area to see the extent of the leak. The Coast Guard also took them in a cutter to see the boom barriers stretched across the entrance to the Port of Brownsville and other areas. On an inspection tour of South Padre Island, Hobby praised the work of the Coast Guard and told reporters that everything that could be done to protect the beaches and estuaries was being done. "Chances are very good that long-term ecological damage can be avoided. But we are going to see some very dirty beaches.

It will look terrible, but they can be cleaned up without lasting damage, but it will take a lot of effort and a lot of money. It will go down in history as one of the most difficult [spills] to control." Governor Clements soon returned from a trip to Europe to inspect the beaches on August 10. The leak would eventually release 3.3 million barrels of oil before the well was finally capped in March 1980, after polluting 170 miles of the state's shoreline. It is impossible to measure how much political damage Clements suffered because of the spill, but it would become an issue when he ran for reelection in 1982.[47]

A week after his visit to the beaches of South Texas, Hobby made another trip to Washington to attend a seven-hour, closed-door meeting in the East Room of the White House. Hobby joined a group of 150 other Texas Democrats at the meeting called by President Carter to hear presentations by senior presidential advisors, including Texan Sarah Weddington, who was one of Carter's assistants; National Security Advisor Zbigniew Brezinski; and Treasury Secretary William Miller. The speakers addressed efforts to get inflation under control and to have the US Senate ratify the Strategic Arms Limitation Talks (SALT). Carter also spoke, urging the Texans to help generate support for his policies when they returned home. It was one of a series of meetings the White House was hosting with various state delegations. As Hobby was leaving the White House, a reporter asked him if he had any new impressions of Carter and his administration because of the meeting. Hobby gave one of his typically brief answers: "No."[48]

After Bill and Diana took a two-week vacation in Jackson Hole, Wyoming, in late August, Bill took advantage of contacts he had made with Chinese officials during Deng Xiaoping's visit to Houston. He led an official delegation of twelve Texas oil drillers, contractors, and equipment manufacturers to China to explore business possibilities. As they toured China, the group concluded that the Chinese oil industry was at least forty years behind the US in drilling technology. In interviews with reporters after his return to Houston, Hobby stressed the potential economic benefits of the new relationship with China, stating, "Obviously, there are billions of dollars of business to be had." Hobby remained in China for a week after his delegation returned to Texas. He visited the printing plant for the *People's Times*, which was still being printed with type set by hand. Hobby was surprised by the air pollution in Beijing, which was caused by coal fires. "If you're unhappy about our environmental standards," Hobby later told the news media, "you should spend a few days in [Beijing]."[49]

In the fall of 1979 Hobby agreed to lead a major fundraising effort for Jimmy Carter's upcoming reelection campaign in 1980. Hobby had his problems with Carter, especially with his energy policies, but he had zero interest in seeing any of the three men who were vying for the Republican nomination—Connally, Bush, and Reagan—living in the White House. Hobby flew around Texas with a goal of raising $2 million for Carter. His stops included San Antonio, where he held a news conference at the St. Anthony Hotel with Austin businessman and civic leader Lowell Lebermann. He declared his agreement with Carter's political philosophy, which he described as "lessening of the federal presence."[50]

As Bill and Diana prepared for the 1980s, they did so with some relief that the legislature would not have another session until January 1981, and if he decided to run for another term, Bill would not have to face a reelection bid until 1982. It all meant that Bill would be spending more time in Houston in the coming year working in the family business, while also paying attention to his political obligations.

CHAPTER 12

THE CAMPAIGN OF 1982

Bill and Diana began the new decade by spending nearly two weeks in the Irish countryside, far away from politics and the family business. After the Hobbys returned to Houston on January 20, 1980, Bill remained relatively free of legislative and political activities for much of the year. The next regular session of the legislature would not convene until January 1981, and he would not face reelection until 1982. As a result, Bill devoted a major portion of his time to family business matters. The day after returning from Ireland, Bill attended a *Houston Post* editorial board meeting, which was followed by conferences later in the week with Oveta and the Hobbys' general counsel, Jim Crowther, and other editors. These consultations with his mother and the executives of the Hobby newspaper and media entities, including KPRC-TV's Jack Harris, usually occurred three times a week. In addition, Bill made several trips to Tennessee during the year to meet with the management of the Hobbys' television station in Nashville.[1]

In between these business activities, Bill stayed busy during the spring and summer, meeting in his office at the *Post* with visitors from the political and civic realms, giving interviews to journalists and magazine writers, and attending a variety of luncheons, dinners, and special events, including a Houston Rotary Club luncheon where he was introduced to Bill Clinton, who at that time was in his first term as the governor of Arkansas. Hobby attended a Carter administration briefing in Washington at the White House and a bridge dedication ceremony in Laredo, both in February. In late May Hobby returned to Washington for meetings with members of the Texas congressional delegation, including Houston congressmen Mickey Leland and Bob Eckhardt and Senator Lloyd Bentsen. Among the topics in those meetings was the upcoming general election campaign in which President Carter faced a difficult bid for reelection against Ronald Reagan, the presumptive Republican presidential nominee. Hobby also made frequent trips to Austin to keep his hand in out-of-session legislative matters. On May 11, the Hobbys attended Laura's graduation ceremony at the University of North Carolina at Chapel Hill. Laura would enter the University of Texas Law School in September. Bill's freedom from facing reelection or having to preside over the Senate gave him and Diana free time to enjoy some leisure travel, including a trip to ski in Taos, New Mexico, in March; a beach vacation in Jamaica in April; and a two-week stay in Jackson Hole, Wyoming, in August.

In the fall of 1980 Hobby altered his routine to help with the Democratic Party's effort to defend itself against a Republican political onslaught that threatened Carter's reelection as well as that of Democrats in Congress and the Texas Legislature. Hobby attended the Democratic National Convention in August, where he threw his support behind Carter against Ted Kennedy's challenge for the nomination despite his earlier unhappiness with the Carter administration's energy policies. A few days before the election he spent a day traveling around Texas with Carter and appearing at his campaign rallies.[2]

Hobby also hosted and attended receptions and other money-raising events to support the reelection bids of several members of the Texas Senate and the US Congress, including former Killer Bees Ron Clower, Gene Jones, and Babe Schwartz and veteran Houston congressman Bob Eckhardt, a liberal who was perceived to be especially vulnerable to the rapidly shifting political ground. Paul Hobby recounted an anecdote that illustrated Eckhardt's long friendship with Bill and Diana. Eckhardt and his wife, Celia, had a cabin in Humble, Texas, about twenty miles northeast of Houston, where they stayed when Congress was out of session (they also had an apartment in Washington near the US Capitol). The cabin had no air-conditioning or heating. Paul Hobby recalled that "occasionally when it got too cold at the cabin, the Eckhardts would just sort of show up in the middle of the night at our house." Oveta had never allowed the *Post* to endorse Eckhardt for any of his reelection campaigns because of the hostility her close friend George Brown had for Eckhardt and his advocacy for regulation of the oil and gas industry, as well as his longtime support for labor unions. Despite his mother's stance, Bill hosted two fundraisers for his old friend in the fall of 1980. Nevertheless, Eckhardt, Clower, Jones, and Schwartz were among the many Democrats who were swept out of office by the Reagan landslide on November 4.[3]

In late November, with the election of 1980 over—with disastrous results, from his point of view—Hobby, who would soon be forty-nine years old, began to focus on his own political future. He intended to run for a fourth term in 1982, despite his continuing discomfort with the necessary campaign rituals. He welcomed the chance to confront the challenges state government faced in the 1980s, and he felt he had learned everything one could know about how to manage the Senate. The Killer Bees affair had been a fiasco, but it taught him a hard lesson he would never forget. "Because of the Killer Bees experience," Saralee Tiede noted, "Bill learned to pick his own battles and be strategic and to decide what's really important."[4]

Hobby had found a professional home in the Texas Senate, which had an honored place in his family's history. "What distinguishes Hobby most of all," *Texas Monthly*'s Paul Burka wrote around this time, "is the contrast between his indifferent attitude toward politics and a feeling toward state government that approaches reverence." Burka quoted one of Hobby's colleagues as saying the lieutenant governor regarded state government "the same way a priest regards the Church." The fact is that Hobby loved the job and the opportunity it gave him to be involved in meaningful public service. He also enjoyed the very thing that others found boring, the nuts-and-bolts duty of tending to the budget and the appropriations process—work for which he had developed a special expertise. The more comfortable he became in the job and the more knowledge about the sausage making of legislation he acquired, the more his interest in being governor diminished. Hobby later said he believed his father had enjoyed being lieutenant governor more than governor, and that it had been one of the factors in Will's decision not to run for reelection in 1920.[5]

With the Capitol press corps speculating that Hobby would challenge Bill Clements for governor, he killed those rumors with an early announcement of his plans to remain as lieutenant governor. He wanted to avoid the inevitable problems he would face with Clements in the upcoming regular session if the governor thought Hobby would be running against him in the next election. Hobby feared that the news media, as well as his colleagues in the Senate, would suspect that his political ambitions were behind every move he made in guiding legislation. He wasted no time in sharing his intentions with a reporter from his own newspaper, which published the news on November 21. He didn't make an official announcement until three days later, when he called a press conference in the Senate Chamber and read a statement announcing his reelection bid. Referring to Reagan's election and the current political environment, Hobby noted that "voters all across the country said clearly that they want a government that understands what financial responsibility is. They want a government that taxes less and spends its tax money better. They want a government that intrudes less on everyday life. . . . In short, they want a government like Texas government." Accordingly, Hobby pointed to his past role in holding down state spending despite the demands of a growing population. Somewhat contradictorily, however, Hobby also promised he would pay more attention to increased funding for higher education, especially faculty salaries.[6]

After making his intentions clear to the public nearly two years before the general election in 1982, Hobby took time off from business and politics to spend several days in December hunting deer in South Texas. He and Diana spent Christmas and New Year's Day at home in Houston before heading back to Ireland for another extended stay prior to Bill's convening the Senate on January 13 for the new regular session.[7]

The morning before Hobby gaveled the new Senate to order at noon on January 13, 1981, for its sixty-seventh regular session, he announced his Senate committee assignments, which signaled that no hard feelings remained from the Killer Bees episode. He appointed Lloyd Doggett to his first subcommittee chairmanship (Consumer Affairs) after serving in the Senate since 1973. He also named Oscar Mauzy chairman of the powerful Jurisprudence Committee, and he retained Chet Brooks as chairman of the Human Resources Committee. All three had been Killer Bees, with Mauzy being a leader. Over on the other side of the Capitol, House members reelected Billy Clayton to another term as Speaker despite a challenge from liberal representative John Bryant of Dallas. Clayton had spent most of the previous year fighting a federal indictment for accepting a bribe from a donor. After a six-week trial, the jury found Clayton not guilty, which allowed him to retain his speakership as well as stay out of prison.[8]

When Hobby convened the Senate on that first day of the session, he viewed a chamber that no longer included liberals Babe Schwartz, Gene Jones, or Ron Clower—all victims of the growing popularity of the Republican Party. Also among the missing were Tom Creighton, who had not run for reelection, and the long-serving Bull of the Brazos, Bill Moore, who had been upset by Democrat Kent Caperton in the primary. New faces included Panhandle senator Bill Sarpalius, who had flipped a Republican seat. It was a younger and much more conservative body than those over which Hobby had presided in the past.[9]

West Texan Bill Sarpalius soon became one of Hobby's legislative allies in the Senate. Sarpalius later recalled that at his first meeting in the lieutenant governor's office, Hobby addressed him as "Senator." Sarpalius asked Hobby to please call him by his first name, explaining that he still felt uncomfortable when anyone called him by his title. "You've earned that title," Hobby replied. "Respect the position and the title that comes with it. It's a title you can use for as long as you live, the same as a person who earns a doctorate degree. Respect those many people who earned the title before you and do everything possible to bring honor to the title." Hobby's lecture impressed on Sarpalius the deep respect Hobby had for the Senate.[10]

Later, Sarpalius had a heated dispute with Senator Walter "Mad Dog" Mengden that illustrated Hobby's management style as he tried to work with the thirty-one strong-willed and often-contentious individuals who served in the Texas Senate. At one point in the session, Sarpalius submitted a bill to raise the legal drinking age in Texas from eighteen to nineteen. Mengden had submitted essentially the same bill in the Sixty-Sixth Legislature, but he couldn't get enough votes to pass it. When he submitted the same bill in the new legislature, he discovered that Sarpalius had already submitted his own version. Mengden told Sarpalius to withdraw his bill and join him as a cosponsor of his own bill. Sarpalius declined and instead asked Mengden to cosponsor his bill. "Mengden pointed out that I was a freshman and didn't even know how to present a bill," Sarpalius remembered. "He was right. But I told him that each member has to have a first time and a first bill."[11]

The next day both bills appeared on the intent calendar, which was highly irregular. The responsibility typically fell to the committee to make a decision about which identical bill should be recognized as the official version. Instead, the committee asked Hobby to choose which senator he would recognize to present the bill. Hobby called

Mengden and Sarpalius to his office, which was near the Senate floor. "No freshman is going to come in here and steal legislation that I have been working on for several years," Mengden informed Hobby. "I've gotten a lot of press coverage from this bill and I want to keep it going as long as I can." Sarpalius interrupted Mengden and said, "Are you crazy? Hundreds of kids are out there getting killed by other kids who don't know how to drink responsibly. You want to keep this bill afloat so you can get good press? You had your chance. You couldn't get it passed, so step aside and let a freshman do it for you." Mengden stood up and walked toward Sarpalius. Fearing a fight, Hobby bolted out of his chair, rushed over, and got between the two angry senators. Hobby told Mengden, who was not one of his favorite members of the Senate, "Look, this has been your issue for a long time. We all know you have worked hard on it, but at the same time, Bill [Sarpalius] has worked hard on it, too, and it means a lot to him personally. The committee left it up to me to decide. To be fair, I'm going to flip a coin. The winner is the one I'll recognize when we go back onto the senate floor."[12]

Hobby reached into his pocket and pulled out a quarter. He asked Mengden to call it. "Heads," Mengden replied. "If heads wins," Hobby declared, "I will recognize Senator Mengden. If tails wins, I will recognize Senator Sarpalius." He flipped the coin over his shoulder, and it landed behind a chair where neither senator could see it. "You two stay where you are," Hobby instructed as he reached around the chair with his back to the senators. He looked at the coin and declared, "It's tails." Unable to view the coin, Mengden demanded he flip it again. "That wouldn't be fair to Senator Sarpalius," Hobby responded. "You'll just have to trust me. Now let's go back into the chamber, and I am going to recognize Bill."[13]

An angry Mengden and a pleased Sarpalius returned to their seats. Hobby rapped his gavel, looked around the room, cleared his throat, and said, "The senator from Deaf Smith County will be recognized," naming Sarpalius's home county. Mengden then stood up and declared, "I object, because you all know this has been my issue, and Lieutenant Governor Hobby gave it to this freshman." Ignoring Mendgen's objection, Hobby asked for a roll-call vote. It was thirty to one in favor of letting Sarpalius present his version of the bill. When the bill later passed on the final vote, Mengden threatened to have it killed in the House. Sarpalius, however, had a good friend on his side, Speaker Clayton, who made sure the bill passed the House, although the liquor lobby managed to water it down. Governor Clements signed it.[14]

Texas Business magazine noted the way Hobby handled the squabble over the bill to raise the drinking age as an example of why he was effective. "Hobby has been willing to leave the grandstanding to others," the magazine's reporter observed, "while quietly working in his chambers behind the Senate floor to sooth bruised egos and seek compromise solutions." Looking back years later, freshman senator Kent Caperton pointed out how Hobby always understood that his authority came from having the trust of the members. "Bill Hobby was a master at handling the dynamics of personalities, "Caperton said. "He was respectful. He wouldn't bad-mouth a member to another member.

He just didn't work that way. Bill Hobby understood that as individual senators we had made promises to our constituents and that his job was to blend all of those various commitments and promises of thirty-one senators into some cohesive policy that could keep Texas moving forward."[15]

The Sixty-Seventh Legislature took care of its most pressing business, passage of the state budget, but it was unable to pass a redistricting bill or resolve continuing problems with public-school finance and an impending insolvency of the state's unemployment fund. Both issues would require special sessions. With the help of the business lobby, Hobby succeeded in killing Clements's initiative and referendum proposal. Hobby was also able to increase state spending despite Clements's demand to reduce appropriations. In the battle with Hobby over state appropriations, Clements found himself at a disadvantage. One lobbyist observed that "no one knows the appropriations process better than Bill, and as chairman of the [Legislative Budget Board], he had the clout to piece together a budget pretty much as he wanted."[16]

However, Clements won his battle with Hobby over the former's wiretapping bill, which allowed the Texas Department of Public Safety, if approved by a judge, to wiretap telephones and to enter homes covertly to plant listening devices as a tool to catch drug dealers. The bill was number one on Clements's legislative agenda. Soon after he was inaugurated in 1979, Governor Clements created a seventeen-member Texans' War on Drugs task force and appointed multimillionaire Dallas businessman Ross Perot as its chairman. Perot made the antidrug war a personal crusade as he spent millions of dollars of his own money to wage a battle against drugs. Critics who believed Perot was going overboard in his work to eradicate "dope," as he called it, from Texas often referred to his task force as the "Reefer Madness" commission because so much of its focus was on cannabis. Perot's task force produced a legislative package to toughen Texas's drug laws that included a mandatory fifteen-year prison term for dealing and a forfeiture law to seize financial assets from dealers. Clements added the wiretapping bill to the task force package.[17]

After the bill passed the House, Clements persuaded Senator Ed Howard to sponsor it in the Senate. Hobby made his opposition clear by sending the bill to Oscar Mauzy's Criminal Jurisprudence Committee. It was well known that Mauzy also opposed the bill, and it was assumed it would die in his committee. Perot, however, hired lobbyists and conducted an aggressive campaign to get public support for the antidrug legislation, including the wiretapping bill, which several polls indicated approximately 70 percent of the people supported.[18]

Hobby hated wiretapping, whether by government or nongovernment entities. He had long suspected that the FBI had wiretapped him in the recent past. In December 1974, Hobby had the Texas Department of Public Safety sweep his Capitol office telephones twice for possible wiretaps. "I have no specific evidence that the phones were tapped," he said afterward, "but I think it's a pretty good assumption in this day and age, with all this stuff coming out of Washington"—meaning Watergate and the BriLab investigation. "I felt it was necessary." There also had been allegations that Southwestern Bell had engaged in illegal wiretapping for its own purposes. The Department of Public Safety failed to find any wiretaps. At that time, Hobby had told the press he was aware that law enforcement officers wanted greater wiretap authority, but "I don't agree with that point of view."[19]

When Clements proposed his wiretapping legislation, supporters of the bill insisted it had enough safeguards to ensure wiretaps and bugs would be used against only drug dealers, not innocent people. "[Clements] wants to wiretap the dope dealers, but that's ok—he's only going to tap the guilty ones," Hobby noted with sarcasm. The bill went against Hobby's libertarian instincts. He inherited from his father a contempt for the many attempts to modify human behavior by passing laws. "It's foolish to have laws against things people are going to do anyway," Hobby told the *Houston Post* in 1974. In that category, Hobby included laws against serving mixed drinks, pari-mutuel horserace betting, and marijuana possession, as well as harsh penalties for drug crimes.[20]

Despite Hobby's disdain for Clements's wiretapping bill, this was a battle he eventually abandoned. At a practical level, he realized he was far short of the votes he needed to defeat the bill. Hobby also assumed that, with Clements's election and the Reagan-driven Republican surge, the days of his enjoying a token Republican opponent in the general election were over, although he didn't yet know for certain who that opponent would be. He was concerned that if he killed what appeared to be a very popular bill, it would become an issue that his Republican opponent in 1982 could easily exploit. He could see his opponent's accusation in his mind: "Hobby protects drug dealers!" He was assured that the final version of the bill would be amended in the House with a provision that it would be automatically repealed on September 1, 1985. At that point, the legislature would have to pass another bill to continue the wiretapping program. Hobby also made certain the wiretapping law couldn't be used to investigate anyone suspected of simply possessing marijuana.[21]

Consequently, Clements was able to persuade Hobby to get the bill out of Mauzy's committee and onto the Senate floor. Clements's aide James Kaster claimed Hobby was "key to that whole thing. We would never have gotten it out without him. Mauzy was chairman of that committee because Hobby put him there, so Hobby called his chit in. Mauzy had a few pet bills that he wanted the governor to sign, so it's a two-way street." Hobby knew the small group of liberal opponents of the bill would criticize him, but that was a chance he would take. "Had I been a member of the legislature," Hobby later explained, "I would have voted against wiretaps because it makes it easier for government to spy on citizens. As it was, I was in the minority, so I did the best I could to make the bill less invasive." When Saralee Tiede recalled Hobby's handling of the wiretapping bill, she argued that a major reason for his decision to abandon the fight was because he wanted "to build a reputation for being fair and evenhanded and letting the Senate work its will. Senators took note that even when he personally felt strongly about legislation, as he did about Clements's wiretap bill, he would not stand in the way of majority rule."[22]

Hobby's retreat on the wiretapping bill and his deference to the governor in their personal relationship discomfited several Senate Democrats, with one complaining to the press that Clements and Hobby had become too "chummy." Senator Peyton McKnight grumbled that he "didn't know [Hobby] was dedicated to passing the governor's legislative program but I guess he is." McKnight's criticism focused entirely on Hobby's withdrawal from the battle against the wiretapping bill, for which Hobby had few allies, while ignoring the lieutenant governor's success at leading the opposition against Clements's referendum and initiative bill as well as others. Hobby also fended off Clements's efforts to lower taxes and reduce the size of state government.[23]

It was true, however, that Hobby and Clements had a mutually respectful relationship during the 1981 session, unlike in 1979, when they hadn't known each other well. During the second regular session, Hobby and Clements met more frequently than in 1979. "[Clements] would go to Hobby's office," James Kaster recalled, "and he'd sit down and have a drink, or Hobby would come over here—[Speaker] Clayton, too. Or [Clements] would walk down and walk up to the podium while they were in session, and they'd sit up there and talk." Senators observed that those chats between the two were often punctuated with laughter. In those discussions at the rostrum or in their respective offices, Hobby would tell Clements if a specific bill had a problem and then suggest to Clements how it could work out. "It was kind of like horse trading," Kaster said. "But Hobby is very correct in his dealings with the governor. He's not trying to step on his turf. He's very conscious of protocol, and it's always been that way. He's a gentleman." That cordial relationship, however, would not last.[24]

The regular session of the Sixty-Seventh Legislature adjourned at midnight on June 1, with a joint House-Senate conference committee on redistricting failing to agree on a plan. The conference had bogged down over Republican attempts to redraw congressional districts in Dallas and in South Texas that would all but assure the election of at least two new Republican members of US Congress while eliminating one incumbent Democrat. Another conference committee also failed to draft bills to fund the state's public colleges and universities and to raise tuition. Because of the time spent on redistricting, little legislation of substance was passed during the regular session, except for Clements's war-on-drugs bills. The failure to finish redistricting forced Clements to call a special session to convene on July 13.[25]

Immediately after the legislature adjourned, Hobby returned to his home in Houston, where he worked in his office at the *Houston Post* on his family's business affairs, including a continuation of his thrice weekly editorial and management meetings with Oveta. He also attended his daughter Kate's horse shows at Houston's Pin Oak Stables and took two separate vacation trips to beaches in Mexico, which were apparently for Diana's enjoyment since Bill was not a fan of the beach. On Monday, July 13, Hobby returned to Austin to convene the Senate for the called session to deal with congressional and legislative redistricting and other issues.[26]

The special session featured a continuation of the fierce battle that had marked the regular session over redistricting, with Republicans and some conservative Democrats on one side and moderate and liberal Democrats on the other, with Hobby holding a middle position. Hobby found himself caught between the intense pressures of party loyalty—supporting the Democrats' goal of preserving all their state Senate and US congressional seats—and sensitivity to the need to create a new Black-majority congressional district in Dallas County. After six days of highly contentious debate and intense maneuvering, the Senate approved Clements's plan by a vote of nineteen to twelve and sent it to the House, where an even more conservative version was passed. When the revised bill arrived back in the Senate, it was passed on August 10 by an eighteen to thirteen margin and sent to Clements for signing. Hobby played an essentially passive role in the Senate battle over congressional redistricting. He played an active role, however, in the effort to draw state senatorial districts. As one observer noted, "[Speaker] Clayton took care of the House Republicans, but in Hobby's Senate, the GOP would take a battering" in the drawing of senatorial districts. Clements stayed out of the fight in the Senate, but after the special session ended on August 11, 1981, he vetoed the final bill, which would have pitted two incumbent Republican senators in Dallas against each other.[27]

The Texas Constitution requires that whenever the legislature fails to produce a redistricting plan or its work is nullified by a veto or court decision, the Texas Legislative Redistricting Board is empowered to draw the districts. Attorney General Mark White, Comptroller Bob Bullock, Land Commissioner Bob Armstrong, and House Speaker Billy Clayton were members of the board, with Hobby serving as chairman. The board convened on August 30. After several rounds of meetings and hearings over a period of several weeks, the board, consisting entirely of Democrats and quietly guided by Hobby, eventually reinstalled the Democrats' redistricting plan in late October. Hobby succeeded in creating a new district in Houston that was all but certain to elect a Black state senator, but it also had the potential for the Republicans to lose two Senate seats, which would preserve the Democratic majority. After Hobby revealed the plan at a press conference at the Capitol on October 21, the *Fort Worth Star-Telegram*'s news headline screamed, "GOP Gutted by Hobby Redistricting." Clements was powerless to do anything about the plan, which was largely the product of Hobby's work, because the state constitution makes the board the final arbitrator, denying the governor veto power over the board's decision. The Republican Party challenged the "Hobby Redistricting Plan," as it came to be known in the news media, in the courts and at the US Department of Justice, but apart from some judicial tweaks slightly altering a couple of legislative districts, the plan remained in force for the 1982 general election.[28]

By the time of the special session in July 1981, Bill Hobby knew that in 1982 he would face his first serious Republican challenger in the general election. In the late summer of 1981, forty-six-year-old Houston oilman George W. Strake Jr., the Republican secretary of state and Clements's former campaign chairman, began to raise funds to support his campaign for lieutenant governor. Like Hobby, Strake was a wealthy man, and he was willing to spend as much money as it would take to win the election. Unlike Hobby's previous Republican opponents, Strake also had name recognition because of his close association with Clements and the fact that he was an official with statewide duties. He was also well known in the circle of conservative donors from the West Texas oil patch, Dallas–Fort Worth, and Houston. After the election of 1972, Hobby had basically enjoyed a free ride in his reelection bids because of the weakness of the Texas Republican Party, but with Clements's shocking upset victory in 1978, Republican gains in the Texas Legislature, and Reagan's election as president in 1980, in which he easily carried Texas, it was obvious that the partisan balance of power was changing rapidly. On October 6, Strake resigned as Texas secretary of state and officially announced he would run against Hobby in the 1982 general election. He declared that ten years of Hobby was enough for the state, while four more years "would be too much." Strake also questioned Hobby's leadership and charged that his political philosophy was much too liberal for Texans.[29]

Hobby had known Strake casually before he became secretary of state because his father, George Strake Sr., had been for many years a prominent civic leader and donor to Catholic charities and schools in Houston. But it wasn't until Strake worked for Clements that Hobby knew him well enough to conclude that he was an intellectual lightweight. Because of that perception, Hobby initially discounted Strake as a threat, which worried some of Hobby's close allies in the Senate. Oscar Mauzy was among them. "I have been telling people for some time, including Hobby, that he is a damn fool for taking this guy Strake for granted," Mauzy said at the time. "First of all, anybody that has been in office for as long as Hobby has, the mood is to 'throw the bastards out,' regardless of their records or anything else. Being an incumbent is not necessarily a political advantage anymore in this state."[30]

Mauzy, Ray Farabee, Kent Caperton, and former senator Don Adams, among others, urged Hobby not to ignore Strake as he had ignored Gaylord Marshall, his Republican opponent in his two previous reelection bids. Don Adams went to Hobby's office on August 3 to warn him that he needed to mount a strong campaign against Strake. Adams said he would pull together a campaign in his old senatorial district in East Texas, where he had deep political ties. Hobby asked Adams to join him for breakfast the next morning to discuss it. At breakfast, Adams told Hobby, "The offer stands, I'll take fifteen counties." Hobby replied, "No, I want you to take all 254 counties in Texas. I want you to run this campaign." Adams begged off. "Bill, I've successfully run several campaigns but nothing like this and I don't feel qualified to do that." Hobby disagreed, telling Adams that he was more than capable of doing a good job and that he really needed his help. Adams finally agreed to take the task on.[31]

With the legislative sessions over by the end of summer and Adams in place as his campaign chairman, Hobby returned to Houston and his normal duties at the family business. He also made trips to Austin to finish the work of the redistricting board, and Bob Cargill flew him to various towns around the state to attend receptions in honor of members of the Senate. One of the highlights of the fall schedule was a private visit to

Houston by King Hussein of Jordan and his wife, Queen Noor, in early November for medical checkups at Methodist Hospital under Dr. Michael DeBakey's direction. Hobby greeted the king's entourage at Houston's William P. Hobby Airport on November 9, and he and Diana attended a chamber of commerce luncheon in the royal couple's honor on November 12.[32]

With Don Adams coordinating, Hobby began his fundraising on December 1 in Brownsville, months earlier than usual, but not because of any worries he had about prevailing in the coming year's May 1 Democratic primary. His opponent, Troy Skates, was a former service station owner who had no money, name recognition, or campaign organization. Hobby's early fundraising effort arose from his awareness that Strake's campaign would have formidable financial resources behind it. By the end of 1981, Hobby had collected $532,000 in donations.

On January 9, 1982, Hobby filed for election to his fourth term. Ten days later, he took a prominent place standing at the podium next to Lloyd Bentsen and his wife, Beryl Ann ("B. A."), as the US senator announced his bid for reelection in Austin. A photograph of Hobby and the Bentsens standing together smiling was published in newspapers throughout the state, which was exactly what Hobby had intended. That press conference foreshadowed political events to come.[33]

Although Hobby was assured of defeating his token opponent in the Democratic primary, he actively campaigned during the late winter and early spring of 1982, never mentioning his primary challenger by name but instead focusing on his Republican opponent in the November election. When a reporter asked him if he was worried about his chances in the party primary, he replied, "No. I do have an opponent, a fellow that's run, I think, three times before. But I'm pretty confident about this race."[34]

In February Bob Cargill flew Hobby on a whirlwind speaking tour of nearly twenty Texas towns and cities, including Victoria, Corpus Christi, Laredo, and San Antonio. At most of his campaign stops, Hobby attacked Reagan's "New Federalism" plan, which, in exchange for federal responsibility for Medicaid, would turn full responsibility for Aid to Families with Dependent Children (AFDC) and the Food Stamp Program over to the states. Calling the social impact of Reagan's proposal "inhumane," Hobby claimed the program would result in Texans paying about four times their fair share of the cost. The plan would reduce AFDC assistance, removing 215,000 Texans from the current rolls. "Humanity must be put back into the program," Hobby asserted. In Waco, he declared that the basic issues in his race against Strake were experience, expert management of the state budget, and a professional and productive government. He then stressed that "the experienced candidate is Bill Hobby. The candidate who understands the budget is Bill Hobby. The candidate who knows how to promote a more professional, more productive government is Bill Hobby. I'm not a bit bashful about describing myself that way." He also attacked Governor Clements for slashing the Texas Employment Commission's budget in half when unemployment was at a record high. "It was an incredible act of inhumanity to cut back on a service more needed than ever before."[35]

That late February tour was immediately followed by a major speech to a Dallas convention of the Texas Classroom Teachers Association. After that speech, Hobby rushed back to Houston to ride a horse in the Go Texan Day parade that traditionally precedes the opening of the Houston Livestock Show and Rodeo. The only breaks Hobby had from his campaign activities were to attend a meeting of the Pulitzer Prize jury from March 1 to 3 in New York, where he served on the editorial cartoon committee, and a skiing vacation with Diana in Taos in late March.[36]

On Hobby's return to Texas in April, he embarked on another fast-paced tour, making brief stops in seventeen mid- and small-sized towns and focusing his efforts on independent voters. At each stop he gave speeches in which he called Texas the "economic flagship of the 50 states" and explained how much his budget reforms had improved the legislature's ability to manage the state's fiscal affairs during the ten years he had served as lieutenant governor. He also stressed that his primary interest was in education and the need to raise the salaries of public-school teachers and college faculty members. At one stop he told his audience it was early in the campaign for him. "My real campaign is in the fall."[37]

As expected, Hobby easily won renomination in the May 1 Democratic primary. The results of the Democratic primary signaled a shift in the balance of power within the party away from the establishment conservatives, who had been led by John Connally and who, like Connally, were moving over to the Republican side. This partisan transformation made it possible for liberals to dominate the Democratic primary. As civil liberties and voting rights attorney Dave Richards later noted, "The primary and general elections of 1982 produced a watershed year in Texas politics."[38]

A group of promising upcoming stars, most of them liberal followers of former US senator Ralph Yarborough, won their primary elections. Jim Mattox, a liberal congressman from Dallas, defeated moderate conservatives Max Sherman and John Hannah for the attorney general nomination, but only after a runoff election, while liberal party activist Garry Mauro defeated conservatives Dan Kubiak and Pete Snelson for nomination as land commissioner. Former *Texas Observer* editor Jim Hightower, another liberal, was the victor in his primary challenge to unseat conservative incumbent agriculture commissioner Reagan Brown. Liberals were disappointed, however, when moderate conservative Mark White defeated their political ally Bob Armstrong for the gubernatorial nomination, while another moderate conservative, Bob Bullock, was renominated as state comptroller. Ann Richards, a liberal member of the Travis County Commissioners Court, defeated incumbent state treasurer Warren Harding. As Dave Richards noted, "The reason these people had the temerity to run in conservative Texas was because, at long last, the Democratic primary had begun to resemble somewhat the Democratic electorate and no longer drew in the entire political spectrum of the state."[39]

In the GOP primary, sixty-six-year-old Dallas congressman and insurance tycoon James Collins defeated Walter Mengden in the race for nomination as the party's candidate for the US Senate. Collins was an ultraconservative Republican from North Dallas who had served in Congress for fourteen years. Clements had a token opponent for the governor's nomination, and Strake ran unopposed for lieutenant governor. The Republican Party had not yet grown large enough in Texas to attract its own candidates for other statewide offices. As a result, the party threw all its fundraising support behind its three major candidates—Bill Clements, George Strake Jr., and James Collins—with each man also able to draw upon his own considerable wealth. Republicans were confident that Clements and their other nominees would easily defeat the Democratic candidates with support from the rapidly growing pro-Reagan conservative base in Texas.[40]

Faced with this formidable threat, Lloyd Bentsen and Bill Hobby realized their reelection prospects were in danger, while Mark White faced what many political pundits considered to be an almost impossible race against the incumbent governor. Bentsen, however, was determined to avoid the same fate suffered by his two longtime Democratic colleagues, Senators Frank Church of Idaho and Birch Bayh of Indiana, who were swept out of the US Senate in 1980 by the Reagan election wave.

Accordingly, Bentsen and his advisors devised a "coordinated campaign" strategy. Late in the fall of 1981, Bentsen suggested to Hobby that rather than take the traditional route in Texas of running independent political campaigns, they should team up and coordinate the races of all statewide candidates. Hobby agreed. In January, when Bentsen announced his candidacy for reelection, he and Hobby met to plan their coordinated campaign. They decided to pool campaign funds and staffs and develop a common strategy for their cause, including an aggressive get-out-the-vote effort targeted at rank-and-file Democrats as well as swing voters. Both skilled fundraisers, Bentsen and Hobby agreed to contribute half of what they raised to the coordinated effort. After the May 1 primary, they would invite the nominees for statewide office to join their combined campaign organization, with the understanding that they would be expected as a group to raise the other half of the campaign funds.[41]

Once the Democratic Party's nominees for statewide office were known, the Bentsen-Hobby campaign leaders invited them to join the coordinated campaign, which would not only make available more money for their campaigns but also tie them in to Bentsen's and Hobby's extensive networks of skilled county leaders. Except for Bob Bullock, the candidates eagerly accepted the invitation. According to biographers Dave McNeely and Jim Henderson, the irascible Bullock was not enthusiastic about the Bentsen-Hobby plan because he saw the upcoming Democratic candidates as future competitors. "The other nominees embraced the 'Coordinated Campaign' idea," McNeely and Henderson noted, "so like it or not, Bullock was compelled to go along."[42]

Bill Hobby happily teamed up with Mark White, with whom he had forged a friendship when White was Dolph Briscoe's secretary of state—a good relationship that continued after White was elected attorney general in 1978. Hobby was also comfortable teaming up with the liberals, although he had little enthusiasm for Jim Hightower, who had often attacked him when Hightower was editor of the *Texas Observer*. Of the liberal nominees, Hobby was closest to Ann Richards, whom he had appointed to his Special

Committee on Delivery of Human Services in 1980. "One of my greatest friends—and worst critics—when I was in office was Ann Richards," Hobby wrote in his memoir. "Her lightning wit transformed the good ol' boy world of politics." Richards's biographer Jan Reid observed that Hobby "would do as much as any politician to tutor and help Ann Richards. But at first, she had a poor opinion of him." Richards, who was an especially fierce liberal in the 1960s and 1970s, was a strong supporter of Joe Christie when he was one of Hobby's opponents in the lieutenant governor's race in 1972. Hobby got to know Richards in 1977 when she was chief of staff for state representative Sarah Weddington, who was famed for her role as legal counsel to the plaintiff in the Supreme Court's *Roe v. Wade* abortion rights case. When Richards worked in the state Capitol, she finally had an opportunity to meet Bill Hobby, quickly realizing he was nothing like the person she had imagined he was in 1972 when she opposed his nomination. "He was the first man outside of my immediate circle of friends who ever talked to me as if we were on equal footing," Richards recalled. "I was really taken with his easy manner and extraordinary kindness."[43]

After Richards was elected to the Travis County Commissioners Court in 1976, one of her causes was expanding public services available for women experiencing intimate partner violence. Hobby later recalled that in 1979 Richards lobbied him relentlessly to put in the state budget funding for a shelter for abused women in Travis County. As usual the state budget was tight, especially for appropriating money to address social causes. "It wasn't an easy sell," Hobby later noted, "but I told her I would do all I could." After the appropriations bill reached the conference committee stage without funding for the shelter, a giant wreath of roses displayed on a metal tripod was delivered to Hobby's office. A gold banner was stretched across the wreath with the inscription, "A promise is a promise." The card attached to the wreath was signed, "Ann Richards."[44]

When he received the wreath, Hobby quickly went back to work to find money for the center for abused women. After he made some trades and called in a few favors, he succeeded in getting the women's shelter put back in the conference committee's appropriations bill, which was accepted by both houses of the legislature. But Clements vetoed the shelter's appropriation. "I still had the roses in my office," Hobby said, "but they had died and turned black. I scratched out the inscription and wrote in 'A veto is a veto' and sent it back to Ann." In the following session in 1981, Hobby succeeded in getting state funds for the women's center by tying the appropriation to one of Governor Clements's favorite items, a sewage treatment plant in Laredo, which made the women's center funding veto proof.[45]

Saralee Tiede noted that Ann Richards "was one of the few people with whom Hobby could really get going and have a lot of fun with. They just went back and forth all the time." Paul Hobby observed that his father and Richards had a special bond. "You know, Austin was a small town then," Paul said in an interview. "There was sort of an intelligentsia around my father that included Ann Richards. They were very much part of our group when I lived in Austin." In an interview in 1985, Richards confirmed that she considered Bill Hobby a mentor. "He taught me you don't have to have an opinion about everything. That if you do, you don't have to express it." Paul Hobby observed that his father was "very, very proud" that Richards had credited him with being her mentor. "I'm sure he was helpful to her, but she helped him as well. She had a gut feeling about people that he hadn't even dreamed about and that was useful to him. So, was Bill Hobby her mentor? On some level, yes. But on another level, she was just playing to his fragile male ego, which is good, you know. We all need that."[46]

Once all the Democratic Party's nominees were on board, the Bentsen-Hobby machine went into action with its unified operation. In contrast, each of the Republican candidates for statewide office conducted campaigns independent of one another. In addition, candidates James Collins and George Strake had their own individual problems. Collins made the mistake of basing his campaign on the accusation that Lloyd Bentsen, a moderate conservative who was one of the darlings of the business establishment, was essentially a leftist. As a result, Collins got no help from Clements, who, when asked by reporters for his reaction to Collins's tactics against Bentsen, answered, "I have never viewed Lloyd Bentsen as what my definition of a liberal is. I've always viewed Lloyd Bentsen as a moderate." Many Republican operatives felt that Collins's ridiculous accusations that Bentsen was a "flaming liberal" were hurting Clements and the other GOP candidates.[47]

Surprisingly, Bill Hobby's well-heeled opponent, George Strake Jr., had his own problems with Bill Clements. According to Clements's legislative liaison James Kaster, Clements "was never going to say anything bad about Lieutenant Governor Hobby. In fact, when George Strake announced he was going to run for lieutenant governor, the governor was not enthusiastic and told George, 'Look, Bill Hobby has helped me a lot . . . and we would not have passed a lot of that legislation [without him].' He reminded Strake that in Texas 'governors and lieutenant governors don't run in tandem. I'm not going to say anything bad about Governor Hobby.'" Some liberal members of the Texas Senate as well as a few Republicans suspected that Hobby had made a deal with Clements. In exchange for Hobby's not interfering with the wiretapping bill, Clements would not help Strake. Kaster denied those rumors. "[Hobby] never asked for anything [in return]," Kaster claimed. "It would be something, quite frankly, that Hobby would not ask. This is not the way Bill Hobby is. He's a gentleman, and he believes in protocol." Kaster stated that Clements took it on his own initiative to tell Strake he wasn't going to campaign against Hobby. "Hobby didn't ask him to do it."[48]

Karl Rove, who would later gain national fame as the mastermind of George W. Bush's quest for the presidency, managed Strake's campaign. Initially, Rove's strategy took the same path as the Jim Collins campaign. Strake labeled Hobby a liberal, but unlike Collins, Strake and Rove soon understood that the tactic was a mistake and dropped it. Instead, Strake declared that Hobby was a poor fiscal manager and that as chairman of the Legislative Budget Board, he had unleashed a frenzy of overspending. Strake also criticized Hobby for supporting the plan to allow undocumented Mexican workers to attend the state's public schools. Years later, when he recalled the 1982 campaign, Hobby said, "Little did I know what dark forces confronted me! Karl Rove came after me with the usual Rove stuff. 'The state budget had grown!' It certainly had, but not by enough. Texas, then as now, was one of the fastest growing states and trailed the nation in public education and public services. Strake didn't want undocumented workers to go to public schools. I guess he wanted them to go on welfare or to prison."[49]

Writing in his column in the *Austin American-Statesman*, political reporter Dave McNeely noted the irony in Strake's claim that Hobby had poor budgeting skills, given widespread understanding that Hobby's skillful fiscal management was his strength. McNeely also pointed out that Strake's charge early in his campaign that Hobby was a liberal "probably came as a shock to liberal Democrats, some of whom had tried but failed to recruit someone to challenge Hobby in the primary because of their view he was too friendly with the business lobby."[50]

Don Adams had organized Hobby's campaign months before the Democratic primary on May 1. Early in the campaign, Oveta telephoned Adams and asked him to come to Houston for a meeting at her office at the *Post*. She had campaigned for Bill in 1972, but she hadn't been involved in his reelection campaigns, mainly because he hadn't needed the help. But Oveta was aware of the threat her fellow Houstonian George Strake Jr. posed to Bill's reelection, especially with Strake's financial resources and his family's name recognition in the Houston-Galveston area.

"Mrs. Hobby called," Adams remembered, "and she asked, 'Senator, would you have time to come to Houston and see me?' Well, you know what the answer to that was. I said, 'Yes, ma'am.'" Oveta asked Adams how much Bill's campaign would cost. Adams told her $4 million. "She replied that the worst thing that could happen to William, which is what she called him," Adams recalled, "is to lose the race because of money." She took Adams to the office of legal counsel Jim Crowther, majordomo of the Hobby business enterprises, and told him, "When Senator Adams calls and asks for money, send it." Adams said that after that meeting, he would occasionally call up Crowther to tell him the campaign needed another million dollars. "He would send it and never asked me for an accounting," Adams said. "For my own protection I hired an accountant. I had a budget, and we had a line for advertisements. Every time I would buy television it would come out of this line. But Crowther never asked me why. He just sent the money. It was the best campaign manager's job that you could have."[51]

Early in the campaign, *Texas Monthly* declared, "The most surprising development has been the high degree of anxiety emanating from the Bill Hobby camp. The ten-year Democratic lieutenant governor is running scared over the challenge by Republican George Strake. . . . This is all the more surprising since Hobby has lots of money, an honored Texas name, a clean if unexciting record in office, a power base (the family-owned *Houston Post*), and no real enemies." The popular monthly magazine stressed that "Governor Clements has coattails and . . . Texans get bored with their lieutenant governors. Strake . . . has money and will use it to buy name recognition, just as Clements did in the 1978 governor's race; he will also be more effective as a campaigner than Hobby, but then who wouldn't? Hobby's greatest speech in office was, 'The Senate will stand adjourned until ten a.m.'"[52]

Strake, however, was having difficulty finding an issue that had much appeal to undecided voters. But his good looks and outgoing personality attracted a sizeable group of supporters, including an endorsement from former Democratic governor Preston Smith. Strake also used his abundant financial resources to purchase extensive television advertising at a cost of $190,000 a week, some of which featured former Democratic state senator Bill Moore, who charged that Hobby had served "too long for any one man in such a powerful position, particularly one who has accomplished so little." Early in the race, political commentators predicted a close election. Pressure from the campaign and Hobby's worries about Strake occasionally caused him to lose his temper. For example, Adams recalled an incident at the Houston airport when he was in Hobby's airplane waiting for him to arrive to go on a campaign trip. "When Hobby finally arrived, he started chewing my ass out about something and I got right back in his face and it just went away. That's the only cross words we ever had."[53]

Cargill flew Adams and Hobby all over Texas. For example, in late June they went on a two-day blitz with Senator Ray Farabee to towns throughout North Texas and the Panhandle. At each stop, Hobby declared that Strake's campaign was "a combination of pathetic and expensive." He countered Strake's criticism of his position in favor of allowing undocumented Mexican immigrants to attend Texas's public schools by pointing out that the US Supreme Court had recently ruled that states must educate those children and that the policy was "just." "An uneducated child is a burden on society," Hobby said. "No other judgment would have been proper."[54]

To counter Strake's television blitz, Adams worked with political and legal consultant George Shipley and campaign advisor George Christian to write scripts for a round of Hobby's own television ads. Adams believed a Shipley script for an ad taped at the Capitol might have been the most effective. "The setting was at night. We'd turned the lights off on the outside of the Capitol. The camera was outside on a big cherry picker, and it swung down and focused through the window of Hobby's office. He was sitting at his desk working and the camera panned in on him. He looked up at the camera and he made a wonderful statement about the importance of education. I mean it was a dynamite ad." Adams also served as Hobby's personal groomer. Hobby was notorious for paying no attention to how he dressed. His eldest daughter, Laura, observed, "I've never met anyone who cared less about his appearance in general and his clothing in particular." At one point when Adams had scheduled Hobby for an important television appearance, he was so concerned about how Hobby would dress for the occasion that he went to Hobby's duplex, while Hobby was out of state on family business, to select appropriate clothes for him to wear. "I picked out a halfway decent looking suit, but he didn't have a shirt. I went to a men's clothing store and bought him a nice dress shirt and a decent looking tie." Adams pinned a note on the suit that said, "Dear Bill, please wear these clothes for the taping tomorrow, and wash your hair." When Hobby arrived at the Capitol for the taping, he had Adams's note in his hand. "He never said a word to me about it, but when he was sitting at his desk, he laid it down in front of him and that note was in every TV commercial we cut. Of course, you couldn't read it."[55]

The campaign dominated Hobby's September and October schedule, but he had to take a brief break on September 7 to gavel open a special session of the Senate. Clements had been forced to call a special session of the legislature because the state's Unemployment Compensation Fund was threatened with insolvency. If the fund went bankrupt, it would trigger a huge increase in unemployment compensation taxes for employers. With the state conventions for both parties scheduled to begin in two days and the candidates eager to return to the campaign trail, it took only two days for legislators to pass a bill authorizing the state to borrow $350 million from the federal government to temporarily replenish the fund.[56]

Hobby hated demagoguery and never engaged in it knowingly. He also generally avoided any behavior that could be perceived as mudslinging. However, he wasn't above playing an occasional dirty political trick. George Strake Jr. was a devout Roman Catholic, and his father was well known for his generous donations to the church. The Strake campaign taped a television ad to be broadcast on stations in San Antonio and South Texas, which has a large population of Catholics. The ad touted Strake's close ties to the Vatican and that the Pope had recognized his father for his charitable activities. Hobby decided it would be interesting if those television ads stressing Strake's devout Catholicism were somehow broadcast in heavily evangelical Protestant East Texas, an area of the state where JFK's Catholicism had been controversial. "Okay, so a few dirty tricks were pulled in that campaign, and I pulled them," Hobby readily admitted years later. "Can you believe it? Somehow, those ads showing the Pope blessing [Strake] and stuff like that also were broadcast in East Texas where all those Baptists could see them. His campaign probably wasn't helped, but stuff happens."[57]

For several weeks, Strake demanded that Hobby debate him, but the only forum Hobby accepted was a seventeen-minute statewide public-television appearance broadcast from the studio of a PBS station in Dallas on October 16. The program also included a separate debate between Ann Richards and her opponent, Vietnam veteran Allen Clark, who had lost both legs in the war. On the day of the debate, before Hobby flew to Dallas, he met in Houston with George Christian, Don Adams, and members of his campaign staff to discuss strategy for the debate later that night. The staff had prepared a briefing book "with answers to every conceivable question and accusation," Hobby recalled, "but I left the briefing book on the plane."[58]

In his opening statement at the debate, Strake revived his accusation that Hobby was a liberal, citing Hobby's support for George McGovern's campaign for president in 1972, his endorsement by Texas AFL-CIO president Harry Hubbard, and his fundraising efforts for the American Civil Liberties Union. Reacting to Strake's criticism of his support for the ACLU, Hobby pointed out that the organization "defends the constitutional rights of the citizens of this state. If he doesn't agree with the constitution, [Strake] would have real trouble taking the oath of office he won." Strake called for a longer time to discuss the issues than the fifteen minutes they were allocated for that night, offering to finance an hour on commercial stations throughout Texas. "What a shame, that we have only fifteen minutes to debate," Strake told the television audience. "It would be impossible to fully air all the great issues of state in that brief time!" With a sober expression, Hobby replied, "George, keep your money. Fifteen minutes is more than enough for you to tell us all you know about state government." News reports observed that the effect was so devastating that in his closing statement, Hobby simply ignored Strake and instead urged the audience to vote in November for a constitutional amendment to increase the welfare payment ceiling "as a matter of humanity and good conscience." Saralee Tiede, who was covering the campaign for the *Dallas Times Herald*, recalled that Hobby's quip was lethal. "I was the moderator of that event. Hobby managed to just destroy Strake in that debate."[59]

Feeling good about his performance the night before, Hobby spent Sunday morning on a tour of Black churches in Dallas before he returned to Houston for a couple of days prior to embarking on the final campaign stops in West Texas and the Rio Grande Valley. In the Valley, Hobby spoke to an audience of about two dozen in a small café in downtown Mission, calling on them to go to the polls and vote with their "hearts," "consciences," and "pocket-books" to send a message to the Reagan administration that "we don't like Reaganomics." His comments were translated into Spanish. With Election Day fast approaching, Hobby was so confident of victory—polls indicated he had built a sixty-point lead over Strake—that he essentially quit campaigning for himself and instead attacked President Reagan and boosted others on the Democratic ticket. Ann Richards campaigned with him in South Texas, and he promoted her race more than he did his own.[60]

Back in Houston the last weekend before the election, Hobby focused on increasing minority voter turnout. He was a guest on a live call-in program with a predominately Black audience in Houston, made appearances at a few Black churches accompanied by Ann Richards, visited with a Black businessmen's group over lunch, and then met with a predominantly Black senior citizens' group. In every campaign appearance, Hobby depicted Strake and the Republican Party as "insensitive, uncaring, and cold" when it came to meeting the needs of Texas's elderly, poor, and unemployed residents. He also continued his attacks on Reagan. "You all know what the Reagan administration is trying to do—balance the federal budget on your backs. If you don't think that's right, vote a straight Democratic lever next Tuesday." He accused the Republicans of running an "anti-government campaign" that did not believe in public schools, welfare, highways, or other public programs. His campaign distributed handbills declaring in large print, "Say no to Reagan, to Reaganomics, and to his supporters!"[61]

The day before Election Day, Lady Bird Johnson sent Bill a donation with a cover note. "You are in my thoughts as Election Day approaches," Lady Bird wrote. "I wanted to send along this small additional bit of help. Just know that I am a staunch supporter and admirer and I'll be cheering you on tomorrow!" The next day, Bill Hobby won reelection to a fourth term, receiving 58 percent of the vote. Mark White stunned Bill Clements by attracting over 232,000 more votes than the incumbent governor. Bentsen demolished Collins, beating the Dallas congressman by 561,000 votes. The forty-nine-year-old Ann Richards received 61 percent of the vote in her bid to be state treasurer, becoming the first woman to win election to a statewide office in Texas in more than fifty years. Bob Bullock, Jim Mattox, Jim Hightower, and Garry Mauro also easily won election.[62]

The joint Bentsen-Hobby get-out-the-vote effort attracted a half million more voters to the polls than expected, blindsiding the Republicans. The results of the coordinated campaign exceeded all Democratic expectations. Bentsen's and Hobby's long coattails carried every statewide Democrat to victory with them. "Bentsen and Hobby financed and put together the real grassroots organization that resulted in the large turnout," Oscar Mauzy observed, "and I give them credit. [They] carried the major financial load." Ann Richards's ex-husband, Dave Richards, later made the additional point that the Bentsen-Hobby team's "money and their organization encouraged straight party voting" that paid huge dividends to down-ballot candidates like his former wife, Mauro, and Hightower.[63]

Texas Democrats had other advantages that year. The national economy was in a recession that had rubbed a bit of the shine off President Reagan's presidency. Voter polling after the election indicated that despite Texas not experiencing the worst of the recession, there was still enough economic pain in the state to help the Democrats. Polling also suggested that Clements had been hurt badly in South Texas by his association with the oil-well blowout in the Gulf and his downplaying of the largest oil-leak disaster in history up to that time, including comments such as "It's no big deal" and "Why cry over spilt milk?" Residents along the Texas Gulf Coast were outraged by his attitude as they watched crude petroleum wash over their beaches and foul their bays and estuaries, killing untold numbers of wildlife and fish.

It was a deeply satisfying victory for Hobby. Soon after the election, he and Diana sought rest and relaxation in North Carolina, where they enjoyed Thanksgiving, followed by a trip to Washington for an additional vacation, returning to Houston at the end of November. For Hobby, his thoughts turned toward the upcoming inauguration and the opening of the sixty-eighth regular session of the legislature, which would convene in January 1983, a little over a month away. As he entered his fourth term and prepared to work with a new Democratic governor, Hobby was more confident than ever about his power and influence as lieutenant governor and his ability to lead the Senate.[64]

CHAPTER 13

HOBBY TAKES CONTROL

On Monday night, January 17, 1983, Bill and Diana Hobby joined Mark White, Lloyd Bentsen, Texas congressman and US House majority leader Jim Wright, and other Democratic officeholders at Austin's Palmer Auditorium to celebrate the party's stunning victory in November's general election. One of the victors, Ann Richards, whom Bill Hobby had sworn into office as state treasurer on January 2, attracted much attention at the event as the first woman to be elected to a statewide office since Governor Ma Ferguson in 1932. An estimated eight thousand people, many decked out in formal dress, paid fifty dollars each for the privilege of participating in the festivities, with the cash going to the Texas Democratic Party's Victory Fund. Country singer Charley Pride provided the background entertainment as the party faithful danced and drank, reveling in their joy at turning back the Republican effort not only to expand its power over state government but also to take Lloyd Bentsen's US Senate seat.[1]

The morning after the Democrats' gala, more than two thousand people slowly assembled under umbrellas and sheets of plastic in a cold, drenching rain in front of a wooden, flag-draped platform on the south steps of the Texas Capitol. They were there to witness the inauguration of forty-two-year-old Mark White as governor and Bill Hobby, whose fifty-first birthday would occur the next day, to his fourth term as lieutenant governor. In the coming months, Hobby would surpass Ben Ramsey's record of ten years and eight months for length of time served as lieutenant governor.

Texas Supreme Court justice Jack Pope, whose recent appointment by Bill Clements to be the court's chief justice was being challenged by Democrats in the Texas Senate, swore Hobby into office at noon. Diana stood at her husband's side, with their four children standing nearby. Missing, however, was Oveta, who was ill. Former governors

John Connally, Preston Smith, and White's mentor Dolph Briscoe Jr. were also seated on the platform. The vanquished former governor, Bill Clements, decided to skip the ceremony, flying to Dallas the night before.[2]

Mark White took his oath of office immediately after Hobby. As the rain continued to fall, Bill's eldest son, Paul, held an umbrella over his father as he delivered an inaugural speech (brief, as was usual for him) that focused on what had become his signature cause: the state's critical need to increase support for education as it prepared for the transformation of the Texas economy from oil and gas to science and technology. "We are being put to the test to prove that we are not an accident of geology," Hobby declared. Journalist Saralee Tiede, who was covering the inauguration for the *Fort Worth Star-Telegram*, was not surprised by Hobby's emphasis on education. She recalled that "education was always at the top of Hobby's list, especially higher education funding. He believed Texas had to make the transition from being dependent on things that come out of the ground to things that come out of people's heads. But it couldn't be done without a good educational system."[3]

Although he didn't read it at the inaugural ceremony, Hobby wrote and presented to Mark White a poem celebrating White's victory in the gubernatorial election:

> *Twas the Spring of '82 when Marco Blanco*
> > *Rode out of the West on a White steed.*
> *Saving Texas for Democracy was his chivalric deed.*
> > *First, he cleansed the Temple.*
> *Then vanquished champions with every stride.*
> > *Clayton, Armstrong, then McKnight fell aside.*
> *Came the Fall, and Marco had a date with Fate,*
> > *So he hinged his fate on a utility rate.*
> *Kind and forgiving as a Baptist should be,*
> > *This time Marco showed no Clemency.*[4]

Immediately after Mark White's inaugural speech, in which he announced the arrival of a "new generation of Texans" to the state's elected leadership, Bill and Diana joined Mark and his wife, Linda Gale, at a buffet luncheon held beneath tents on the north side of the Capitol. "Hobby and White got along really well and largely agreed on the direction of things," Tiede observed. "That was partly because this was after Clements had been defeated, and the contrast was good." Hobby, grateful for Clements's defeat, was in a mischievous mood when he addressed the luncheon crowd. He expressed his sincere thanks to Texas voters for electing White, which he stressed not only gave him a new and more compatible governor with whom he could work but also had relieved him of his status as the state's top Democratic officeholder. "I'm the only politician you'll ever hear stand up in front of a crowd to thank you for demoting me," Hobby announced cheerfully. After lunch, the raincoat-clad White and Hobby waved and laughed as they watched the inaugural parade from a grandstand on Congress Avenue in downtown Austin.[5]

The day after the inauguration, Hobby gaveled the Senate into session as many of its members struggled to recover from the three inaugural balls held the night before. As one of the Capitol reporters noted, the members of the Sixty-Eighth Legislature had a long list of bills they hoped to pass, but with the country in a deep economic recession, they faced the possibility of a budget shortfall of $1.5 billion, with Hobby calling for tax increases to cover the deficit. The Texas House, however, was now led by a new Speaker, former B-52 gunner and Fort Worth businessman Gib Lewis. As a first-term Speaker, the forty-seven-year-old Lewis, who had served as a representative since 1973, was not interested in leading an effort to raise taxes. The mood was not much better in the Senate. In previous sessions going back several years, the legislature had plenty of money to spend, low turnover in members, and little pressure from the public. But things had changed. As writers for *Texas Monthly* pointed out, "The good old days of multibillion-dollar surpluses were replaced by a budget crunch" that was going to make writing a budget difficult.[6]

Before its members could face that complex issue, however, the Senate was forced to resolve a controversy stemming from actions Governor Clements had taken shortly before he left office. As had happened occasionally in the past with previous governors, after Clements lost his reelection bid and became a lame duck, he made so-called farewell or midnight nominations of individuals to fill vacant positions on government commissions and university boards of regents. Those appointments are constitutionally required to be confirmed by the Senate. Although the list was long and it included the appointment of Jack Pope as chief justice of the Texas Supreme Court, most of the nominations weren't controversial. As it turned out, Pope's nomination would be the least controversial.

The foremost sources of controversy were Clements's nominations for the University of Texas and Texas A&M University Boards of Regents, especially those of former governor John Connally to the UT board and the appointment of the most recent former House Speaker, Billy Clayton, to the A&M board. Both of those appointments as well as others grabbed Mark White's attention, which led to his demand that the Senate return the nominations to his office for reevaluation. John Connally was targeted largely because of his much-publicized leadership of the Democrats for Nixon during the presidential campaign of 1972 and his switch from the Democratic Party to the Republican Party in 1973, both of which had earned him the enmity of loyal Democrats. Former Speaker Clayton, who was still a Democrat in 1983 but who would soon switch to the Republican Party, had supported Bill Clements's reelection, which obviously displeased Governor White. When White announced his plan to review the nominations, it was clear he intended to reverse those of Connally and Clayton, as well as the four other regental nominees.[7]

Despite his friendship with White, Bill Hobby considered his decision to kill the nominations an unnecessary controversy that would be a major distraction from the important issues the Senate faced in 1983. He also disliked the attack on Clayton, with whom he'd had a good relationship when Clayton was Speaker. Bill enlisted Ray Farabee to help him work out a compromise for White to consider. Senators Oscar Mauzy and Lloyd Doggett, who supported White's request, led the effort in the Senate to reject the nominations.[8]

On the second day of the Senate's session, Hobby tried to head off a battle over the nominations. He adjourned the Senate until the next day, when the appointments question would be considered. In the meantime, he had arranged a private meeting with White for himself and twenty senators, led by Senator Kent Caperton. Caperton asked White to head off "a blood-letting this early in the session" by supporting a plan to recall only Clements's appointees to university boards of regents and the state College Coordinating Board. During the meeting, when Doggett quietly guessed how many would vote against White, he determined that there were enough votes in favor of preserving Clements's appointments. Faced with the reality that there were enough votes to deny him his request, White offered a compromise proposal. He promised that if the Senate would return all of Clements's nominations, he would support legislation to prevent outgoing governors from filling vacancies on the state's boards and commissions. The senators accepted the compromise.[9]

When the Senate reconvened on January 20, White submitted a request that it return 104 of Clements's 105 lame-duck political nominations. The one nomination White left alone was that of Jack Pope, a lifelong Democrat who had served as an associate justice on the Texas Supreme Court since 1964. Voting separately on each nominee, the Senate finally approved the return of 59 of the appointees. On that list was John Connally, whose appointment was returned to the governor by a vote of nineteen to twelve. The vote to return Billy Clayton's nomination passed by only one vote. Although Hobby, who had no vote in the matter, made it clear to the Senate that he opposed returning the nominations to White, his quiet maneuvering succeeded in reducing the number of returns by more than half. Five conservative Democratic members who agreed with Hobby voted against any returns.

When the lengthy Senate session finally ended, White told reporters that Texas would "benefit throughout the years by this today. This sets policy." In April, White appointed Dallas businessman and Democratic Party fundraiser Jess Hay to the University of Texas Board of Regents in place of Connally. After the nominations dispute was over, the *Dallas Times Herald* praised Hobby for the role he had played in "providing the steady leadership necessary to avert a Senate crisis over whether to confirm" Clements's appointees. "I don't remember how many of the appointees were voted on and not confirmed," Hobby later recalled, "but merit was not considered, only political party. It was a mistake and was done over my objections."[10]

After the battle over Clements's lame-duck appointments, Hobby spent a few days meeting with new members of the Senate; tending to ceremonial duties such as swearing in the new secretary of state, John Fainter; and presiding over US senator from Ohio and former astronaut John Glenn's address to a joint session of the Texas Legislature on January 26. Glenn was in the early stages of his bid for the 1984 Democratic Party presidential nomination. At a press conference before the joint session, Hobby announced he would support Glenn for president "as strong as I can."[11]

During the week following Senator Glenn's speech, Hobby had several private meetings with Governor White and one meeting with the chairs of all the Senate committees to discuss forthcoming bills. The Senate adjourned on Thursday, February 3, and Hobby returned to Houston, where he met on Friday morning with his mother to discuss their mutual concerns about the future of the family's ownership of the *Houston Post*. There were potential estate tax issues and troubling early signs on the horizon about the viability of the newspaper business. Those issues and concerns would require their close attention throughout the spring and early summer. Bill returned to Austin on Saturday to attend a banquet at the Driskill Hotel that concluded the annual meeting of the Texas Hunter Jumper Association. Bill and Diana's eighteen-year-old daughter, Kate, a senior at St. John's School in Houston, was given two riding awards. The Hobbys' dinner guests were Joan and Jimmy Waterman, who owned a farm in New Caney, a village north of Houston, where the Hobbys now kept their horses. Another guest was Kate's friend, twenty-three-year-old horse trainer Matt Hansen. An easygoing native of Arizona, Hansen loved jumping horses and was training for a slot on the US equestrian team. Kate had met Hansen, who worked for the Watermans as an assistant trainer, during the previous summer.[12]

After the banquet, Bill and Diana went to the duplex in West Austin where Bill lived during legislative sessions. Kate and her three guests retired to the lieutenant governor's apartment on the second floor of the Capitol, where they would spend the night. Bill had never lived in the apartment, but he used it as overnight guest quarters for friends and dignitaries. Kate and the Watermans apparently went to bed around 2:00 a.m., while Hansen stayed up to watch television in the library/den of the apartment. At 5:25 a.m. a newly installed heat sensor alerted Capitol police to a fire in the lieutenant governor's apartment. The police notified the fire department at 5:27 a.m., and the first responders arrived approximately ten minutes later. Meanwhile, a police officer went to the Senate Chamber, saw smoke, and summoned help. Another officer, fifty-six-year-old Joel Quintanilla, raced to the lieutenant governor's apartment to awaken Kate and her guests and escort them to safety. As he approached the apartment, he heard Hansen yell for help. Quintanilla kicked open a door to reach him, but he was knocked to the floor by a blast of flames. Other officers pulled Quintanilla to safety while Officers Arthur Patterson and Wilfred Spinks crawled on their knees into the room as Hansen cried out, but they were unable to reach him.[13]

Officer James Mitchell pounded on the apartment door near Kate's room and awakened her. She heard popping noises from lightbulbs and glass breaking from the intense heat. She later said the smoke was "so thick, it was like breathing soup or something and it was such a rancid smell." She immediately unlocked the door to the outside hallway. "The officer was going wild," she recalled. "I guess that's when I realized it was an emergency because he was so upset." She tried to go to Hansen's room, but the smoke was too heavy. She and Officer Mitchell went to another entrance to the den. When they opened a door near the room where Hansen was located, the flames kept them from entering. "It got so hot, I found parts of my hair melted," Kate said. "I knew I couldn't do anything. I knew instantly that Hansen had died." Firefighters found Hansen's body, but it was not in the den. He was later discovered between twin beds in a small bedroom near the master bedroom. The room was undamaged by flames, and Hansen had not been burned. He died from smoke inhalation.[14]

Two Capitol police officers led Kate down the elevator to the first floor, aware that the Watermans had escaped through a side door. Now safely outside, they stood on the grounds and watched the smoke streaming out the windows, illuminated by the floodlights directed at the Capitol dome. Soon, a female custodian who was leaving the Capitol gave Kate and the Watermans a ride to Bill and Diana's duplex. When they opened their front door, the Hobbys found Kate and the Watermans standing on the porch in their nightclothes. Kate immediately gave them the shocking news: "The Capitol's on fire and Matt's dead." Still traumatized nearly forty years later, when Kate was interviewed about the fire all she could say was, "It was just a really horrible, sad day."[15]

While Diana looked after her daughter, Bill dressed and hurried to the Capitol, where he linked up with Mark White, who had been awakened by the police and fire truck sirens as he slept in the Governor's Mansion, only two hundred yards from the Capitol. White's initial thought was the mansion was on fire, but he quickly realized it was the Capitol. The governor dressed and rushed to the scene. By daylight, fifteen fire trucks were on the grounds, circling the 309-foot-tall granite structure. Completed in 1889, it is the largest state capitol in the United States, taller than the US Capitol. "Mark and I watched the Capitol burn from the sidewalk outside the east wing," Hobby recalled. "The fire turned the back corridor into an inferno and was barely contained before it got into the Senate Chamber." When acting Austin fire chief Brady Pool spotted White and Hobby, he gave them a frightening observation: "If I can't control this fire in the next five minutes, we'll lose the whole building."[16]

With more than one hundred firefighters battling the flames, the fire was under control by around 8:00 a.m. Six firefighters were injured, with three having to be hospitalized. "Austin firefighters were heroes that morning," Hobby noted later. "They saved the Capitol." He told reporters at the time that he had "never witnessed a more professional performance. To them goes the credit for saving a historic and irreplaceable building." Chief Pool told the news media the fire had started in the apartment's den, possibly caused by defective electrical wiring in the television set Hansen had been watching that night. Pool added that the second-floor apartment area was a total loss.[17]

The walls of the apartment's dining room were badly charred, and a crystal chandelier Ben Ramsey had purchased in New Orleans thirty years earlier had fallen twenty feet from the ceiling onto the dining room table. A silver tea service given to Bill Hobby's father, Will, when he left office in 1921 was covered in soot and ash. Bill told reporters, "All it needs is some polishing." A hand-carved wooden door and window casements in the second-floor hallway were destroyed beyond repair. Plaster had fallen or been pulled from the walls by firemen as they'd struggled to extinguish flames that had gone up the granite walls to the third floor. As a result, the third-floor hallway on the east side of the Capitol was heavily damaged. The Senate Chamber and some offices also suffered smoke damage. Luckily, few of the Capitol's historically valuable artifacts were lost. Those damaged beyond repair included a portrait of Governor Coke Stevenson's wife and fifteen large framed collections of photographs of former Texas senators. Many other items were scarred to varying degrees, but most could be salvaged.[18]

"The fire was a gigantic wake-up call," Hobby later recalled. After the postmortem, it was now clear to Hobby and the 1,300 people who worked in the Capitol that the structure was a firetrap. That was not news to Hobby or to many of the state workers based in the building. "The dangerous condition of the Capitol could no longer be ignored," Hobby said. "It had cost one life and very nearly others."[19]

After an investigation, it was confirmed that the Capitol had been subdivided and partitioned on every floor. Over the years, workers had converted the open basement, passageways, and even restrooms into offices and put false ceilings in place for wiring and air-conditioning ducts. Fire walls, which originally had been well designed to prevent the spread of fire and smoke, had been removed, or holes had been punched through. The haphazard renovations had compromised safe passage out of the building. Fire inspectors were stunned to discover that the main valve to the sprinkler system had been shut off at some point in the past, rendering it useless.[20]

Amazingly, the Senate didn't miss a day of work. Despite the strong smell of smoke and the lack of heat, lights, or sound system because of extensive damage to the electrical wiring, the Senate still managed to convene in its chamber on Monday, February 7. Senate secretary Betty King called the roll wearing a suede coat, while most of the senators wore heavy overcoats. Hobby moved his office to the third floor, and the Senate staff whose offices had been on the second floor were assigned offices throughout the building.[21]

Nearly three weeks after the fire, the legislature appropriated $7 million to repair the damage. Governor White, however, asked the legislature to pay for a total restoration of the Capitol, to be completed by 1986 in time for Texas's celebration of the sesquicentennial of its independence from Mexico. Hobby supported the plan, but a majority of the legislature objected because of the enormous cost and the members' fear that most of them would be permanently moved to offices in other state buildings away from the Capitol. Much of the partitioning of the building had been done to create offices for legislators. A restoration would eliminate those offices. As a result, the legislature stripped White's total restoration plan from the bill, but it did approve restoration of the damaged East Wing areas. The legislators also created a State Preservation Board and gave it the authority to hire an architect and a curator with responsibility for the care and preservation of the building and grounds. The legislation made the governor the chair of the board, with the lieutenant governor and Speaker of the House also serving as members. The preservation board soon hired an architect to direct the restoration of the East Wing.[22]

Determined to ensure that the work plan would respect the history of the space, Bill, with Diana's aid, played an active role in overseeing the East Wing restoration. "My mother told my father that there was no need for living quarters, and suggested the space should be turned into a great room for meetings and a new kitchen," Paul Hobby later noted. Agreeing with his wife, Bill decided to convert the space entirely into a reception room, a committee room, and the lieutenant governor's staff offices. Hobby had the new committee room named in honor of his mentor, Lieutenant Governor Ben Ramsey. Bill and Diana found authentic American Renaissance antiques to furnish the new rooms, and Diana acquired oriental rugs in New York that were placed in the new reception room. Throughout the process, it was clear that the Hobbys were in charge. As chairman of the Senate Committee on Administration, East Texas senator Roy Blake was responsible for overseeing the restoration. During a tour of the burned-out area, Blake presented a plan to Hobby for converting the apartment into additional offices for members of the Senate. Hobby nodded quietly and then told Blake he had another plan. He wanted the space for his staff. "I guess that rules that out," Blake replied. "Yeah, I guess it does," Hobby answered. The restoration project, with most of the work done while the Senate was in recess, was completed in 1985.[23]

In 1988, the State Preservation Board hired architect Allen McCree to draw up a restoration plan for the entire building, even though funds had yet to be appropriated. "McCree turned out to be a good P.R. man," Hobby recalled. "He took legislators on weekly tours to show them the dangers lurking behind the pink granite façade: faulty wiring, toxic asbestos insulation, and leaky plumbing, to name a few. During one tour, an obliging rainstorm demonstrated just how badly the roof leaked." These facts eventually persuaded legislators to fund the project. Ford, Powell & Carson and other architectural firms produced the master plan that included an inspired solution to the office and meeting-room problem. The plan called for the construction of a 667,000-square-foot underground annex, which was named the Capitol Extension, to contain committee rooms, offices, and a cafeteria. The annex was constructed before the Capitol restoration project began, which allowed legislators to move out of the old building while it was being restored inside and out. The completed Capitol Extension features wide, skylighted corridors and a two-story rotunda that provides a stunning view of the Capitol dome overhead.[24]

Restoration of the Capitol included stabilizing and retrofitting the structure: replacing deteriorated metal and old mortar; installing new wiring, plumbing, security systems, and a fire alarm network; and repairing the metal dome and roof—all at a cost of approximately $200 million. The legislature funded construction of the Capitol Extension and restoration of the Capitol in 1989, and work began in 1990 while Hobby was still lieutenant governor. When the work was finished in early 1995, Hobby observed that it "was worth every penny of the cost. The restoration was a magnificent accomplishment, a national model, and a great lesson in how a horrible catastrophe can be a catalyst for good."[25]

Despite the major disruption caused by the tragic fire, Hobby quickly guided the Senate back to its main job, which was legislating. He anticipated the filing of around five thousand bills during the five-month regular session, which was the typical amount. Only one-fifth could be expected to become law. Almost a third of the House and Senate membership was new. It was the most radical turnover since Sharpstown. Hobby had ten newly elected senators with whom he would have to work, five of them Republicans. The five new Democratic members included the only Black senator, Houston attorney and former state representative Craig Washington. The other four were Lubbock attorney John Montford, who would become one of Hobby's allies and friends, John Sharp from Victoria, Chet Edwards from Duncanville, and John Whitmire from Houston.

Other than fixing the projected shortfall in the state budget, which was a major problem, the main issues on the Senate agenda included toughening DWI penalties, which was being pushed by the pressure group Mothers against Drunk Driving; raising the legal drinking age from nineteen to twenty-one; addressing prison overcrowding, which was the object of a federal lawsuit; funding new highway construction and repairs; replenishing the bankrupted state unemployment fund; deregulating the trucking industry; and overturning the state's blue law prohibiting most businesses from operating on Sundays. At the top of Governor White's list of priorities was a bill to elect rather than appoint public utility commissioners, and another to provide public-school teachers with a substantial pay raise. White wanted a two-year, 24 percent increase, but no new taxes. Before the start of the legislative session, Hobby warned the governor that a teacher pay raise couldn't be supported without new taxes. As Hobby recalled, the Senate "was willing to support a pay raise and the tax increase it would take to pay for it, but the House, which has to originate tax bills, was opposed, and White was not at all excited about endorsing a tax bill."[26]

As he prepared for legislative battles, Hobby retained his leadership group from the previous session, with Ray Farabee serving as chair of the key State Affairs Committee. Farabee, a Democrat from Wichita Falls who was first elected in 1974, had by this time become one of Hobby's closest allies. Ray's wife, Helen, who had worked on task forces for Hobby before he was elected lieutenant governor, had introduced the two men three years before Ray was elected to the Senate. Hobby counted on Farabee and Mauzy to lead the less experienced senators through committee politics. Port Arthur Democrat Carl Parker, whom Hobby appointed to lead the Education Committee, was the only new chairman. Hobby also appointed Republican Senator Ike Harris of Dallas, a Senate veteran, as chairman of the Economic Development Committee. "I always named Republicans to leadership roles," Hobby later observed. "These appointments were based on talent and not political party." According to Saralee Tiede, "From the beginning, Hobby would identify the people that he thought he could really count on and that he really respected for committee chairmen and his leadership team. He had a very good eye for selecting the people who could do what he wanted. And he knew exactly how strong he was all the time."[27]

Hobby continued his Wednesday meetings with all committee chairs as a group, but he moved the gatherings from breakfast time to a cocktail hour in the evenings, and he included a couple of senators who weren't chairs but were part of his legislative team. Tiede recalled that although there was an agenda, "it wasn't a very formal meeting; it was kind of everybody talking. There were recognized experts in the group." For example, Farabee's specialty was prison reform, John Montford's expertise was on finance, and Mauzy was knowledgeable about education. Each committee chair would be expected to explain issues in their area of interest and knowledge, which would help the group hash out bills behind the scenes and reach a consensus, if possible.[28]

Texas Monthly noted that by 1983, Hobby had "reshaped the Senate in his image, changing it from a brawling House of Commons to a restrained House of Lords. The best senators are Hobby's alter egos on the floor: never provincial, always pragmatic, only interested in sound public policy." Senator Kent Caperton agreed. "There was no question he set the agenda. He recognized serious problems and assumed the leadership role in solving them. He was fair to everybody. He stated his case, he let it be known what his feelings were, and he let it rise and fall on its merits. He had no false sense of self-importance. With all the egos floating around the Senate, that was damned refreshing."[29]

"Certainly, by the early 1980s," Saralee Tiede observed, "Hobby had learned to pull all the levers, to work all the gears, and how to forge important relationships." On almost every issue of critical importance, compromises were hammered out in Hobby's office. "If there was a major disagreement among the senators," Tiede noted, "Hobby would get the Senate leaders in his office in the afternoon. And he would say, 'I am going to leave and when I come back, I want this settled.' By the time he returned, he usually found the problem sorted out and then they poured drinks and had fun." However, Hobby could bare his teeth when angry. Nearly always quiet, concise, and abrupt, Hobby could unleash an attack whose ferocity was always unexpected. Mark White noted that Hobby "didn't take kindly to someone putting him in a corner. He'd pull a sword, and your head would be in your hand. But you wouldn't realize your throat had been cut or who had done it. There's wisdom in that method. It instills discipline in the ranks."[30]

Rodney Ellis also recalled these come-to-Jesus meetings. Ellis said that Hobby would call senators who were on opposite sides of an issue into his office. "Hobby understood there are times when that's the only way you can get around a log jam. Get both sides in a room and then bring other people in who could influence them. Hobby mastered the art of how to squeeze somebody, how to bend their arm, break it, if necessary, but with a very masterful touch. He also had the art of knowing how, when all else fails, to just stop and let it percolate for a while and see what happens." For example, during the 1983 regular session, a bill was filed to require oil companies to give service station operators a reduction on the wholesale price of gasoline if the operators assessed surcharges for retail credit card purchases. The fight between oil company lobbyists and service station lobbyists over the bill threatened to stall other legislation, so Hobby called the senators representing both sides of the issue into his office and urged them to find a solution. In only two days, the compromise was forged. "He was the catalyst," Chet Edwards observed at the time. "He brought the parties in and said he wanted us to work together. He's so powerful because he does not abuse his power. He's not doctrinaire." On another occasion, when a feud between House and Senate cosponsors threatened to derail a solution to a battle over college funding, Hobby met with the lawmakers and arranged a truce. Carl Parker described the meeting as similar to "being called to the principal's office." As another senator stressed, Hobby "never bullied. He'd use reason and logic."[31]

In the months before the Sixty-Eighth Legislature convened, it had been obvious to Hobby that the members would face difficult budget issues. One of those issues was the impact on Texas of the Reagan administration's implementation of its New Federalism plan, which had roots in the Nixon administration's domestic policy. The main goal of New Federalism was to make major reductions in the federal budget by transferring certain federal programs, such as education, to the states and providing block grants to implement them. The grant program would give the states and local governments greater control over these programs, but the amount of federal allocations would be reduced, which meant additional funding would be needed to maintain the programs at current levels.[32]

Oscar Mauzy later observed that "when Reagan announced his so-called New Federalism in 1981, Hobby was the only person in state government who fully appreciated what that meant in terms of the cutbacks in federal funds to all state agencies." Accordingly, Hobby organized an interim task force that consisted largely of Senate committee chairmen to determine how the Reagan administration's grant program would impact Texas. The task force eventually released a report warning local governments that they would have to prove they were spending their appropriations effectively or the legislature would cut their appropriations. Two weeks after the November elections in 1982, Hobby used the report to produce substantive proposals for the legislature to consider in managing the transferred federal programs and dealing with their impact on the state budget.[33]

In December 1982, Hobby announced that for the state to meet its needs, the legislature would have to raise taxes by a record $1.25 to $1.5 billion. New taxes had not been levied since 1971. He pointed out that "the heart of the problem" was Texas's rapidly growing population, plus the need to improve highways, raise teacher pay and equalize funding for public schools, build new prisons, and fund payments for families with dependent children. Hobby told reporters that he "was not recommending a specific taxing source," although he did suggest a five-cent increase in the gasoline tax to raise an additional $1 billion.[34]

When the Sixty-Eighth Legislature convened, Hobby's early prediction that new taxes would be necessary proved to be accurate. His skillful lobbying of the Senate before Inauguration Day garnered enough vote pledges to pass a new tax bill. However, the Texas Constitution requires that tax bills must originate in the House, where there was little enthusiasm for the plan. Work on the bill bogged down there in March, while Speaker Gib Lewis tried to undo the damage caused by his failure to disclose some business relationships and investments in his 1981 financial statement. Lewis's problems and lack of enthusiasm for the tax bill, combined with Governor White's indecision about whether to support it, resulted in the session ending without action on the matter.[35]

Hobby and his staff also cobbled together an education package that included teacher pay raises, a formula to aid poor school districts, and an excellence fund controlled by local school administrators. The Senate passed the package, but conservatives in the House led by Speaker Lewis killed it because it would require a tax increase. After these legislative defeats, several members of the Austin press corps opined that the defeats were largely due to Governor White's lack of preparation and the absence of a clear agenda, while Speaker Lewis was distracted by the controversy over his incomplete financial disclosures. After the session ended, Senator John Leedom, a Republican from Dallas, praised Hobby for "the way he's handled this last session, particularly where we had . . . a new governor that didn't know what he was doing, a speaker of the House who was new and was being tested and then immediately had his set of personal problems and indiscretions." Among the more conservative members of the Capitol press corps, it was generally agreed that despite those setbacks, Hobby was ably filling the leadership vacuum. They gave him good grades for using the budget crisis to identify and eliminate fat that had accumulated in the state bureaucracy after several years of riding the oil boom. Senator Leedom agreed with that assessment. "The leadership really fell on [Hobby] to a heavy degree to keep the whole legislature moving forward. I think the record would show that for the first time the Senate passed more legislation than the House. [Hobby] moved it out of the Senate while the House was still trying to figure out which way the doors were."[36]

Ironically, the poor economic situation made it possible to achieve some degree of prison reform and to slow down the almost mindless building of maximum-security prisons. Some legislative observers called the package of prison reform bills the most revolutionary in Texas history, although the characterization was a bit over the top. The reforms included new parole and probation options, community corrections centers for certain nonviolent offenders, and twenty additional district courts. Despite supporting these reforms, Hobby was disappointed that more steps weren't taken to address the problem of prison overcrowding, which had placed the Texas prison system under the supervision of the US Department of Justice and the federal courts. He pointed out to reporters that Texas still had about four thousand inmates living in tents. Hobby nevertheless observed in an interview during the legislative session that the present Texas Senate was the best in the ten years he had served as its presiding officer. "Some [senators] have complained that it's been a dull session. They can't make them too dull for me."[37]

The regular session in 1983 was not without its contentious moments, however. Perhaps the most bitter arose during a fight over a bill to provide workers' compensation insurance coverage to farmworkers. Oscar Mauzy had sponsored the bill in a previous Senate session, but he had been unable to suspend the two-thirds rule to get it to the floor for a vote. At the beginning of the sixty-eighth legislative session, Senator Hector Uribe, a progressive Democrat from Brownsville serving his second term, offered to help Mauzy make another attempt. Knowing that the bill's chief beneficiaries would be the state's Latino agricultural workers and aware that Hobby had appointed Uribe to the Senate Finance Committee as a freshman, which was a strong sign that the lieutenant governor considered Uribe part of his team, Mauzy told Uribe to "take it over." He believed it would be a better strategy for Uribe to sponsor the legislation, with Mauzy and other liberals supporting his efforts.[38]

Uribe went to work "wheeling and dealing," and a few weeks before the end of the session, he had secured the twenty-one votes required to suspend the rules to move the bill to the floor for a vote. "I'd managed to get four Republicans and even some rural Democrats to vote to suspend the two-thirds rule. When Bill Sarpalius realized I had the votes, he decided to filibuster the bill. He never told me why, but it was obvious that he was representing the Texas Farm Bureau, which was controlled by the big agricultural interests." Before Sarpalius could begin his filibuster, Hobby called a brief recess and walked down from the rostrum to Uribe. He said, "Senator, we need to conduct some business," explaining that it was important to vote on some other bills before Sarpalius tied up the Senate with a filibuster. Uribe later claimed that Hobby promised he would call on Uribe to bring up his farmworkers bill soon after the vote on the other bills, and Hobby would cut short Sarpalius's filibuster at that time. "Well, Bill, didn't call on me until there were only a few hours left in the Session," Uribe recalled. Sarpalius, whose district was overwhelmingly rural and agricultural, was able to conduct his filibuster for nine hours, unimpeded by Hobby, until time ran out on the session.[39]

Soon after Sarpalius killed the farmworkers bill, Uribe, joined by Mauzy and Doggett, held a press conference. "We blasted Bill Hobby, which I felt was the right thing to do from my perspective," Uribe said, "but not from Hobby's perspective." After Uribe and other Latino legislators accused Hobby of betraying the Mexican American community, Hobby explained he had upheld Senate tradition in refusing to cooperate with a parliamentary maneuver to cut off a filibuster. Uribe, however, noted that Hobby had stopped filibusters in previous sessions. Supporters of the farmworkers' compensation bill suspected that Hobby, despite his dislike of filibustering, was helping Sarpalius, who was one of Hobby's loyal Senate allies. "I paid a very dear price for blasting Hobby and basically calling him a liar," Uribe recalled. "I lost my position on the Finance Committee in the next session."[40]

Nevertheless, Uribe felt that Hobby soon realized he had mishandled the episode.

"I think Bill learned from that event. After we blasted him," Uribe observed, "I think Hobby recognized that the times were changing in Texas, and he had made a mistake." Uribe believed that although Hobby was inclined to be progressive, El Paso's Tati Santiesteban and Edinburg's Raul Longoria, who represented conservative business interests, had persuaded him to oppose the bill. "But the demographics indicated that there were going to be more poor Hispanics and middle-class Hispanics participating in the democratic process," Uribe said. "Hobby made every effort thereafter to make sure that he gave me the opportunity to get my votes again."[41]

That opportunity came a month later when Governor White called a special session to extend the life of the Texas Employment Commission. At Hobby's urging, White added the farmworkers' compensation insurance bill to the special session agenda. This time Hobby worked with Uribe in support of the bill, but their efforts failed. Nevertheless, Senator Uribe praised Hobby's effort, declaring, "Hobby has rehabilitated himself." The issue would be revisited in 1985 during the Sixty-Ninth Legislature.[42]

After Hobby gaveled the sixty-eighth regular session of the legislature to adjournment on May 30, the *Fort Worth Star-Telegram*'s Capitol correspondent noted that except for Senator Sarpalius's relatively short filibuster, the Senate's final hours had lacked the "drama and frenzied activity when lawmakers race the clock." The reporter also observed that the 1983 legislative session was widely hailed as Hobby's session. "[Hobby] ended the 1983 legislative session in a position of strength unequalled among the state's Big Three. After more than a decade as lieutenant governor, Hobby is as aloof and powerful as ever." A journalist at the *Dallas Times Herald* agreed. After the regular session ended, he noted, "With his old fashioned suits, with an occasional bow tie, Hobby is the antithesis of this generation's blow dried politicians," but Hobby had emerged from the legislative session "as the most influential leader in state government."[43]

Senator Grant Jones, who noted that more than five hundred bills were passed, stated that if Hobby had "not been here with his intimate knowledge of state government, this session could have been chaotic." Hobby's other Senate allies told reporters the session was tailor-made for him "because it centered on his strong point, state finance." Ray Farabee agreed. "[Hobby] has always had a better grip of the fiscal operation of the state than any state leader I know, but it was particularly critical this year." In their nationally syndicated column, Rowland Evans and Robert Novak described Hobby as "perhaps the most popular Democrat in Texas." The politically progressive *Texas Observer*, which criticized some of Hobby's actions during the session, including his failure to cut off Sarpalius's filibuster, nevertheless bestowed on Hobby its Manager of the Year award. The *Observer* stated that Hobby was a "crafty, pugnacious operator" whose strategy had taken advantage of the turnover in the Senate that brought ten "rookies" into the chamber.[44]

Although Hobby was widely praised for his ability to manage thirty-one large egos in the Senate, the biggest budget shortfall in a decade prevented the legislature from dealing with the main issues, including the long-standing, complex problem of equalizing public-school funding and the reauthorization of the Texas Employment Commission, which had been zeroed out by a ruling of the Sunset Commission. The latter issue, however, was remedied during the special called session held from June 22 to 24. Among the other legislative failures were White's and Hobby's attempts to raise taxes on alcohol, tobacco, computer software, and amusement games. Another was White's futile attempt to persuade the legislature to pass a bill to overhaul the Public Utility Commission. Hobby supported White's bill and arranged for Kent Caperton to sponsor it in the Senate, but it was overwhelmingly rejected in both houses of the legislature. Other defeats included not only Uribe's bill to provide workers' compensation insurance to farm laborers but also efforts to provide pay raises to public-school teachers, deregulate the trucking industry, repeal the state's blue laws, raise the legal drinking age from nineteen to twenty-one, legalize pari-mutuel horse-race betting, and replenish the bankrupt state unemployment fund.[45]

With the Sixty-Eighth Legislature and its first called special session over by the end of June, Hobby returned to Houston, where in July he would be involved in one of the landmark developments in the history of the extended Hobby family. That same month, Bill and Diana also saw the marriage of their oldest daughter, Laura. She was engaged to her former University of Texas Law School classmate John Beckworth, whose father, Lindley Beckworth, had served several terms in the US Congress. Bill and Diana's other offspring were also moving forward with their lives. Eighteen-year-old Kate, who had experienced the severe trauma of the tragic fire at the Capitol in February, had graduated in May from St. John's School and would enter the University of Virginia in September. Andrew, who was twenty years old, was an undergraduate at Southwest Texas State University in San Marcos.[46]

Bill and Diana's oldest son, Paul, now twenty-two, had graduated from the University of Virginia in May 1982. He had worked in his father's reelection campaign the previous fall and planned to attend law school. His decision to go to law school had been an easy one for him, but he was unsure whether to attend Stanford or the University of Texas, so he asked his father for advice. Bill's response provides an insight into his personality as well as his indirect approach to parenting. "I was driving my father to the airport in his old, battered Ford Torino," Paul recalled. "I said, 'Gee, I've got to decide between the waiting list for Stanford and the University of Texas. What do you think?' He would never assert himself unless I asked him. He said, 'Gosh, seems to me, if you're going to live in Texas, you ought to go to the UT Law School. Business you can learn when you get there. But law, you can't pick that up on the street. It's a trade.' I was enormously relieved that he had an opinion about it. So, I thought, okay. I'll go to Texas Law School."[47]

By the early 1980s, the Hobbys were becoming aware of the increasingly difficult economics of the newspaper business. Labor and printing costs were rising rapidly. The cost of newsprint, which had gone up precipitously in recent years, was now 40 percent of total expenses. Yet the cost to readers for single copies as well as for subscriptions was almost free. These problems might have been overcome except for the fact that the *Houston Post*'s competition, the *Houston Chronicle*, was winning the subscription and advertising income war with its rival. The *Post* had continued to fall behind the *Chronicle* in circulation. By 1983 the *Chronicle* led the *Post* in daily subscriptions by more than forty thousand. The circulation figures for the *Post*'s Sunday edition, which was its most lucrative edition in terms of advertising space, indicated that it was nearly forty-three thousand subscriptions behind the *Chronicle*. The *Post* had nearly 42 percent of the market, compared to 58 percent for the *Chronicle*. Experts in the economics of the newspaper industry at the time viewed a 60 percent share of the market, which the *Chronicle* was very close to achieving, as constituting dominance in that market. Because the *Post* had a smaller circulation than the *Chronicle*, it could not charge as much for advertising as its competitor, which was a major factor in the decline of the paper's revenue. In addition, the *Chronicle*'s owner was the late Jesse H. Jones's philanthropic foundation, the Houston Endowment, which gave the *Chronicle* significant tax advantages over the *Post*, tilting the field even more in the *Chronicle*'s favor.[48]

In their attempt to contain costs, the Hobbys had also employed a smaller staff than the *Chronicle*, which some critics felt had a negative impact on the quality of the *Post*'s news coverage, which in turn hampered its efforts to increase circulation. In 1983, the *Post* had only 167 editorial employees, compared with 238 at the *Chronicle*. In the opinion of John Morton, a financial analyst specializing in the newspaper industry, the *Post*'s management had not marketed or managed the paper well. Saralee Tiede, who, as the Capitol bureau chief for the *Fort Worth Star-Telegram*, covered the situation at the *Houston Post* because the lieutenant governor of Texas was involved, agreed with Morton's assessment. "The *Chronicle* was winning the circulation battle, [and] therefore the advertising battle." Joel Barna, a writer for *Houston City Magazine*, speculated that the Hobby family "will obviously need cash to cover inheritance taxes. So, the time to sell the *Post* is now." An unspoken factor in the Hobby's deliberations about what to do with the newspaper was Oveta's age. She was now seventy-eight and beginning to have bouts of ill health. Although not especially serious, they were becoming more frequent.[49]

Bill remained an enthusiast for the *Post* and its legacy, but he was deeply focused on his position as lieutenant governor, in which his power and influence had increased with each passing session. He was serving a fourth term and he had one eye on the governor's office. He was also a realist and could see that the *Post*, which was a closely held, private family company, was likely to continue to be a losing proposition. Tiede later noted, "When you're in a publishing family you just come to that point when you're looking down the road at what will happen when you get to the next generation." She added that there are often different opinions and ideas within a family about what should happen next. "Hobby wanted to avoid that. And that was important to him. He also knew that two-newspaper towns were not doing too well. Of course, ultimately, newspapers were on a downhill slope. And this was even before the internet. Hobby was more interested in the TV stations. Jim Crowther and Jack Harris were running the stations, which were just blowing and going. They were doing well."[50]

Paul later noted that his aunt Jessica, who "got paid by the business, [but] didn't work in the business," was the family member who "had the most sense to see that the business was changing." Jessica was aware that as Oveta aged, no one in the family was focused on the day-to-day operations. "[Oveta] wasn't and my father wasn't," Paul said. "The guy that was running it was Jim Crowther, a valued family lawyer. He was diligent and he was honest, but he was not any sort of revolutionary business builder. [Jessica] recognized that if nobody was going to manage the business aggressively in a time of transition then we should sell it, and she was exactly right. But that doesn't mean it wasn't painful for me anyway, and I assume for my father."[51]

Laura also recognized that the *Post* was becoming a financial problem. During her summer breaks from law school, she had worked at the *Post* for Oveta, Jim Crowther, and her father. From the vantage point of the executive suites, Laura could see that the *Post* had a challenging future as a business. "It was clear to me, as it was very clear to them, that newspapers were not a growth industry. Our television stations at that time were just doing great. They were very profitable, but the newspaper was not so much anymore. And so, the idea was that this is not going to get better. We should sell the paper and get what value we can get out of it. My grandmother agreed, but it was really hard for her."[52]

Despite nostalgia and respect for Will and Oveta's legacy, the Hobby family saw no point in trying to sustain a business that would continue to drain their financial resources long into the future. As Barna argued, it was time to get out while they could sell it for a significant price. At 2:30 p.m. on Tuesday, July 23, Oveta summoned the top executives of the paper to meet with her and Bill in the Post Building's Oak Room. After everyone had arrived, Oveta told them, "William has an announcement." Bill then informed the executives that the *Houston Post* was for sale. The staff, including higher management, later admitted that they had expected changes at the newspaper but not an announcement that the Hobby family would sell. The hope had been that the Hobbys would initiate a reorganization and commit more resources to compete with the *Chronicle*. Bill Hobby admitted to the outside news media covering the announcement, "Any time you end an association that long there are many regrets." But he stressed that he and his family were going "to continue to live in Houston and certainly we would not sell to an irresponsible purchaser or to one who did not have the best interests of the community at heart."[53]

The announcement that the *Houston Post* was for sale generated speculation about Bill's future, because many had thought he would become the *Post*'s full-time publisher after he left elected office. With that option eliminated, many political observers and commentators believed the Governor's Mansion would be his next stop, possibly in 1987, if White decided not to try for a second term, which was unlikely. Some guessed that Hobby would run for governor in 1990, while others predicted he would take a shot at a

Texas seat in the US Senate then held by Republican John Tower. A few even speculated that if Senator John Glenn won the Democratic presidential nomination in 1984, Hobby would be the senator's pick to be his vice presidential running mate. The truth was that Hobby was getting too much satisfaction out of being lieutenant governor to think that far into the future. When a reporter asked him about all the speculation, Hobby laconically responded in his dry-witted style, "Oh, I'll probably run for secretary-general of the United Nations." In the same humorous spirit, Hobby also told reporters he wanted to kill the rumors that he was selling the *Post* to pay for his daughter Laura's wedding on July 31. That marriage ceremony was at the top of the list of Houston's social events that summer, with seven hundred guests expected to attend.[54]

After the *Houston Post* went on the market, the Hobbys assumed it would take twelve to eighteen months to sell, but a buyer soon surfaced, and a deal was made much more quickly than the family had anticipated. Sun Media, a Canadian company that published the conservative Canadian tabloid the *Toronto Sun*, made an offer on October 12. After a couple of days of negotiation, Oveta accepted Sun Media's offer of $130 million, with $100 million of it to be paid in cash. The selling price was considerably less than the estimated market value of between $175 and $225 million. The sale excluded the *Post*'s downtown printing plant, which Sun Media agreed to lease, and a portion of the site occupied by the *Post*'s headquarters on the Southwest Freeway. The Hobbys agreed to turn control over to Sun Media.[55]

On Monday, October 17, five days after accepting the offer, Oveta asked the *Post*'s news and editorial staff to assemble in the newsroom. Wearing one of her famous hats and elbow-length gloves, Oveta entered the newsroom with Bill, as well as Jessica Catto, who had traveled to Houston for the event. They introduced *Toronto Sun* publisher Douglas Creighton and announced that the paper had been sold to Creighton's company, Sun Media, which would begin publishing the *Post* in early November.[56]

Paul Hobby recalled that "the first day the *Toronto Sun* owned the newspaper they changed everything. They turned it into a kind of a full-color, *USA Today* newspaper. It was a very radical redesign. I was taking first-year law school exams in Austin. I was careful not to see any newspapers or walk by any newspaper machines, because I knew it would upset me on my exam. It wasn't a happy thing for me."[57]

Selling the *Post* was also painful for Bill. He and Diana skipped the final act of the Hobby family's relationship with the *Houston Post* and traveled to Ireland, taking refuge in a house in County Tipperary, where they spent most of the month of November. John Davis, Bill's mentor from St. Albans, joined them. After his stay with the Hobbys, Davis wrote Diana a letter that provides a peek into how the Hobbys spent their time in Ireland and why it was such a haven of rest and escape for them, especially at this time: "My warm sweater makes me think of Ireland, with the pleasures of early tea, the merry sound of Mrs. Glasheen in the kitchen, the fires, the black raspberries along the mid-November roads, the mud encased megaliths, and the impression of poetry that the landscape gives to those who don't have to live in it. I am also aware of the pleasures of sitting before the fire while you both are leaping over ten-foot ditches, calling it sport, but which has for me all the attraction of a nightmare."[58]

The ten-foot ditches that were the stuff of nightmares for Davis were part of the appeal for avid foxhunters like the Hobbys. Bill and Diana were regular participants in the Scarteen Hunt, considered one of the most prestigious hunts in Ireland. As journalist and equestrian Ray Brady noted, "There are those who swear—and not all of them are Irish—that Irish fox hunting is the finest in the world. The country has vast, open fields, good for galloping, and a fox population that never seems to diminish." Located in County Limerick, the Scarteen boasted a challenging landscape full of drainage ditches that were "the supreme test of a rider's skill."[59]

The Scarteen Hunt had been running for more than three hundred years under the oversight of the Ryan family. During the time the Hobbys were participants, the hunt was run by Thaddeus "Thady" Ryan, a highly esteemed horseman who expanded the hunt to a broader clientele, including British and Americans. The Scarteen's distinctive pack of Kerry hounds, called the "black and tans" for their coloring, were the oldest private pack of hunting hounds in Ireland, dating to the early eighteenth century.[60] The hunt was characterized not only by the thrill of the chase but also by the social gatherings at Scarteen House or other homes that followed the day's hunt (or local pubs that served as stops along the way). The Hobbys were joined not only by English and Irish aristocrats but also by a "democratic" gathering of local professionals, farmers, and international guests. As members, the Hobbys adopted all the hunt's conventions: they regularly "took a house" in the area, ordered their traditional hunting garb from Irish tailors (including scarlet coats for the men, known as pinks, and black coats for the women), and bought an Irish bay named Cody for the hunt in 1987.[61]

In 1982, Hobby was named one of four joint masters of the Scarteen Hunt. Brady described the position in the *New York Times*: "If you notice an authoritative, commanding figure, with the hounds clustered around him, that is the Master of Foxhounds. He runs the hunt and may well donate thousands of punts a year to keep it financially viable. He is addressed, respectfully, as Master." An American being named master was, in Brady's estimation, "no small honor. His word in the field is unquestioned, and a withering look from a master has sent many an erring rider slinking back to the barn."[62]

The days spent on horseback in Ireland were the fulfillment of a lifelong passion for Hobby, from horse rides as a child in Houston's parks to the stables of Ginny and Charlie Zimmerman to the countless horse shows Bill, Diana, and the children had attended. Foxhunting was in line with Hobby's style: patrician without being ostentatious. In 2002, Hobby resigned as hunt master and wrote to Thady Ryan's son Chris that he would be "hanging up the spurs." Hobby noted, "The privilege of being a joint master of Scarteen for the last twenty years has been one of the greatest honors and pleasures of my life." As master, Hobby wielded authority and commanded respect, much like his position as lieutenant governor. But unlike the unruly senators, the horses and hounds never talked back.[63]

CHAPTER 14

"NO PASS, NO PLAY"

The Sixty-Eighth Legislature adjourned in May 1983 without providing public-school teachers the pay raise Governor Mark White had promised them during the 1982 campaign. The pay raise bill and a hike in taxes to pay for the raise had passed in the Senate with Hobby's support, but both failed in the House because of the opposition to a tax increase and White's refusal to endorse that increase. The state's outraged teachers' organizations blamed the governor for the defeat of the pay raise bill and threatened to oppose his reelection. When White sought a way to escape the wrath of the state's public-school teachers, Bob Bullock and Gib Lewis suggested he create a governor's task force to study school finance, which might find the money to support a pay raise. Accordingly, in June 1983 White created the Select Committee on Public Education to "study issues and continuing concerns relating to public education in Texas, particularly school finance . . . and personnel support . . . as well as the source of funding and structure of the system."[1]

To give the committee credibility with the Texas corporate establishment, whose support was essential to the passage of legislation to raise taxes, White persuaded Dallas multimillionaire H. Ross Perot to serve as the committee's chair. White also selected five other committee members, while Hobby and House Speaker Gib Lewis, who were also on the committee, named five members each. Because the committee's eventual recommendations were likely to have an impact on the state budget, State Comptroller Bob Bullock also served on the committee. The energetic and feisty Ross Perot immediately took command of the enterprise, setting its agenda from the beginning and becoming its public face to such an extent that the news media soon named the group the Perot Committee.

A native of Texarkana, Texas, and a graduate of the US Naval Academy, Perot founded the immensely successful software and technical logistics firm Electronic Data Systems (EDS), which had its headquarters in Dallas. By the age of thirty-eight, Perot had become one the wealthiest individuals in the United States. He sold EDS to General Motors in 1984 for $2.5 billion and became one of the state's leading philanthropists. Before accepting White's appointment to serve as chair of the education task force, Perot, who was a Republican, had served in a leadership position in Governor Bill Clements's war on drugs. Perot was fifty-three when he agreed to chair White's public education commission, and he was no stranger to Hobby, who first got to know him in 1969 when he hired Perot's EDS to work for the Texas Senate's Interim Committee on Welfare Reform.[2]

Chairman Perot broadened the committee's mission and led it into a nine-month in-depth study of the state's public schools that included not only the basic issues of teacher salaries, school finance, dropout rates, the needs of the children of migrant workers, and the effectiveness of the State Board of Education but also issues many teachers felt were none of Perot's business, especially teacher competency, curriculum content, and classroom discipline. Hobby later noted that when Perot studied the state's public education system, he "did not like what he found, and he told Texans so in blunt, uncompromising terms."[3]

Perot discovered that Texas was spending a smaller percentage of total state wealth on primary and secondary public education than any other state except Nevada, and he claimed some Texas school districts were so underfunded that their high schools couldn't afford classes in algebra or geometry, only four years of basic arithmetic. As Perot crisscrossed the state making speeches to civic, business, and educational groups, he complained that Texas had world-class education in only three areas: drill teams, bands, and football teams. He accused Texans of not caring enough about education, arguing that Texas children would need quality educations to compete in a high-technology world.[4]

What particularly angered many Texans was Perot's criticism of the state religion—high school football. Not only did he want football programs greatly reduced in size but he also called for banning any student from extracurricular activities, including sports, if he or she failed an academic course. That proposal, which quickly became known as "No Pass, No Play," unleashed a torrent of complaints, which failed to faze Perot. Organizations representing classroom teachers, such as the Texas State Teachers Association (TSTA), were another source of opposition. TSTA leaders argued that the public schools were basically okay. What teachers needed was a pay raise, not radical reforms. Perot also attracted the fierce opposition of the public-school administrative establishment when he demanded a reduction of the size of their bureaucracies. Referring to Perot, political strategist and lobbyist George Christian observed, "It was very difficult to tell during the heat of that battle whether he was a hero or Public Enemy No. 1."[5]

Perot submitted the committee's final report to Governor White at the end of May 1984. It was stuffed with a wide range of recommendations: not only "No Pass, No Play" but also such granular items as restricting most high school sports events to Fridays and

Saturdays, making junior high sports intramural instead of intermural, strengthening discipline management, improving textbooks, scheduling fewer day trips, increasing the school day to nine hours, reducing class sizes, and implementing basic skills testing. He was especially critical of vocational education, calling it a waste of time and money because he deemed the training to be inadequate and out of date. Perot declared that vocational education was "a dumping ground for minorities." The report called for a 40 percent increase in teacher pay and the establishment of a career ladder to reward excellent performance over time.[6]

Perot attached strings to the pay raise and the career ladder recommendations. Those depended on the establishment of a universal teacher competency test as well as the documentable elimination of waste at the administrative level of school districts. The teacher organizations opposed both. Funding the reforms was another potential problem. When Perot launched his study in June 1983, White, Hobby, and Lewis told him that after he completed the work, they wanted to know how much his recommendations would cost to implement and "how they were supposed to find the money to pay for everything." Perot informed them that the entire reform package would require $4.9 billion, which he suggested should be paid with income from increasing the sales tax and levying new "sin" taxes on cigarettes and liquor. If passed, it would be the largest tax increase in Texas history. Hobby was impressed by Perot's recommendations and his effort. He admired Perot's candor, persistence, and dedication, and he enjoyed Perot's sense of humor. He believed Perot was "exactly the right man to head [the select committee]. Select committees have huge advantages in paving the way for controversial bills," Hobby added. "They study issues, build support coalitions, ferret out the opposition, and work out some of the rough spots." Hobby believed Texas had to upgrade its schools to make a smooth transition from an economy dependent on oil and gas production to one based on brainpower. "Perot understood," Hobby said, "that an education designed to prepare students to work as ranch hands and roughnecks wasn't going to be adequate in a world increasingly dependent on knowledge. He knew that Texas's oil and gas prosperity was fading fast. The state needed to spend more on the minds of its people."[7]

Mark White called a second special session to convene on June 4, 1984, to consider Perot's education reforms and the tax bill to fund them. White also included new highway construction and prison reform bills on the agenda. He gave the legislature thirty days to do its business. Perot's recommendations were bundled into two bills: one for the reforms, the other to pay for them. Because it required new taxation, that bill went to the House. It soon became apparent that Perot's bills were in serious trouble, and not only because of the financial cost. A newspaper poll of legislators when the session began revealed that only a few were willing to vote for the bill. Perot had managed to anger some of the most powerful interest groups in Texas, not only because of his criticisms and caustic off-the-cuff remarks, many of which belittled the work of underpaid teachers and members of the state's educational bureaucracy, but also because of his demand for teachers to take competency tests. Hobby and White had to work hard to gain Speaker Lewis's support for the tax increase. "Bill and Mark had weekly breakfast meetings with Gib to persuade him this was the right thing to do," Saralee Tiede recalled. "He finally came around because they convinced him these reforms would make Texas better prepared for the future."[8]

Attacks on the bill began as soon as the legislature convened. To counter the fierce opposition, Perot enlisted five of his own lobbyists and lawyers from his computer services company, as well as three additional lobbyists who were among the most influential in the state. Perot's lawyer and advisor Tom Luce led the effort. Hobby recalled that the Capitol was "crawling with Perot's team." Perot even sent employees from his company to talk to legislators and help host parties. The arrival of a group of attractive female employees to lobby on Perot's behalf greatly amused Hobby, who penned a poem in reaction:

> *What with taxes and all,*
> *Lobbyists were thick as roaches.*
> *So, it took all the Luce women*
> *To win the war against coaches.*[9]

As he tried to move the reform and tax bills through the legislature, Perot stubbornly refused to accept any compromises. He insisted that lawmakers pass all his recommendations or none of them. The executive director of the Equity Center, an association of poor school districts that supported Perot's recommendations, observed that he didn't allow the legislature to chop the bill into "little pieces" that "shortcut all the usual nonsense. Leadership is bringing things to closure and getting on with it. That's what Ross Perot does better than anyone I've ever seen." Hobby, who accepted Perot's no-compromise approach, skillfully managed the bill through the Senate, with effective help from Senator Kent Caperton. The legislature had thirty days to pass a tax bill. "Hardly anyone thought we could do it," Hobby remembered. "It was a miracle of sorts that all of us from the governor on down could pull together so effectively. I had the easy job." After a decade of experience presiding over thirty-one senators, the lieutenant governor had no shortage of knowledge about how to guide legislation. "I referred the Perot reform bill to the Committee of the Whole Senate, a strategy well suited to complicated issues in short, single-issue special sessions when things have to move fast." Hobby also had the advantage of presiding over a Senate that was united, with a large Democratic majority and skilled leaders such as Carl Parker, Ray Farabee, and Kent Caperton working with him.[10]

Hobby teamed up with Perot to forge a new alliance between traditional business groups and the state's growing high-technology industries, which were already demanding an improved education system. An important part of that strategy was to call for an increase in gasoline taxes, a portion of which would support implementation of the educational reforms. That proposal won support from the powerful highway construction lobby because most of the revenue from the tax would be used for new highway construction. The bill passed easily in the Senate, although the "No Pass, No Play" provision had to be revised to make it acceptable not only to hostile senators but also to Ross Perot. The main opposition to "No Pass, No Play" was resolved by requiring students to get a passing grade on all their courses in each six-week period to be eligible to play sports or to participate in other extracurricular activities. That gave students who had failed their courses an opportunity to redeem themselves in the next six-week period rather than being banned for the entire semester. Despite Perot's insistence on no compromise, he accepted that change.

The educational reform and tax bills (officially House Bill 72) remained in trouble in the House until near the end of the session. "Gib Lewis had a harder job than I," Hobby recalled. "He had 150 members, not 31, who disliked voting against their school districts, and they didn't like voting for tax bills." White's and Hobby's successful efforts to persuade Speaker Lewis to support the legislation paid off. When the House Education Committee gutted the reform bill in a daylong session, the Speaker reportedly informed the committee head that he would not retain his chairmanship unless he reinserted Perot's recommendations in the bill. The threat worked, and the House passed the reform bill, but only after a fourteen-hour session. "Speaker Lewis demonstrated firm leadership with every blow of his gavel," Hobby later observed.[11]

Despite Lewis's efforts, the House unanimously rejected the tax bill the Senate had passed. The bill that failed in the House proposed to levy a new tax on businesses, radio and television advertising, repairs, amusements, and other services. The House not only rejected the bill but also declined to join a conference committee to resolve its differences with the Senate over taxation. In reaction, Hobby and Lewis came up with an unusual strategy. They decided to create a "nonconference committee" that would hold "nonmeetings" to work out a solution. White also participated in these irregular conferences, which were held in his office. "We worked nearly all night to find something acceptable to both sides," Hobby recalled. "In the end we substituted a broader-based solution." The final bill spread new tax and fee increases across a broad spectrum, including higher taxes on gasoline, hotel occupancy, tobacco, and alcoholic beverages. The state general sales tax was also slightly increased. The gasoline tax increase was targeted for new highway construction and repairs, but the bulk of the new revenue was intended to pay for the new reforms.[12]

After the House passed the tax bill, it went to the Senate, where John Leedom threatened to kill it with a filibuster because of the tax on automobile and truck repairs. Hobby quickly huddled with Bob Bullock and Legislative Budget Board director Jim Oliver, who were able to find a $32 million surplus in the Texas Department of Corrections budget to transfer to the funding for the Perot reforms. That amount was large enough to eliminate the proposed tax on car and truck repairs, which satisfied Leedom. However, Leedom's threat to conduct a filibuster, as well as his vote against the tax bill, did not sit well with Hobby. When the next legislature convened in January 1985, Hobby removed Leedom from the powerful Senate Finance Committee. "If you don't vote to raise the money," Hobby explained, "you don't get to decide how to spend it."[13]

The tumultuous and historic special session ended on July 3, with the legislature passing a $4.8 billion tax bill, most of it to finance the Perot reforms. It was the first major tax increase in Texas in thirteen years. Applause erupted in both houses when the tax bill passed. Despite ferocious opposition, the final version of the bill changed membership on the State Board of Education from elective to appointed. Perot's criticism of the Board of Education's performance and his effort to eliminate the system of electing its members had led to a bitter dispute between Perot and board chairman Joe Kelly Butler. Perot advocated reducing the size of the board and appointing its members. Hobby was also the target of criticism when he announced his support for Perot's recommendation.[14]

The legislation included the "No Pass, No Play" rule and a requirement that students pass an exit exam before they could graduate from high school. The bill also provided a pay raise to public-school teachers (although not as large as they had demanded), a higher minimum salary, and a career ladder that would reward long-term excellence in teaching. Those gains were made possible only by the legislature's insistence on mandating teacher competency tests, which angered many if not most teachers, who would not forget it when they voted in the 1986 state election. Hobby later noted one of the ironies related to the Perot educational reforms. He observed that "the most extensive education reform bill in Texas became law because Mark White had promised a teacher pay raise and didn't have the money to pay for it." Another irony was the fact that Perot got much of the credit for the new law, but it was Governor White who would later pay a political price because of the anger of the powerful teachers' unions and the coaches' associations.[15]

While Perot and White were most responsible for the educational reforms, it was Hobby who pushed the reforms—and the taxes to support them—through the legislature. It was also Hobby's wizardry with the state budget and his collaboration with Bob Bullock that saved the tax bill from Senator Leedom's filibuster threat. As Hobby liked to say, "The state budget is 90 percent of the Legislature's work, and the rest is poetry."[16]

Years after the Perot reforms were passed and implemented, Hobby wrote in his memoir that although he was proud of the reforms, in retrospect, they "didn't move the ball very far." He lamented that in the end, Texas continued to have the shortest school year of all the states, and that its public-school pupils still spent less time in class than students in other states. But he felt the bill produced several positive results, including the fact that it set statewide standards, for example, in testing in the third, sixth, and twelfth grades; in limits on class size, with only twenty-two children permitted in kindergarten through fourth-grade classes; and in improved teacher education. "The extraordinary thing is that 'No Pass, No Play,' one of the most contentious provisions of House Bill 72, continues to exist in Texas law and practice," Hobby later observed.

"There were early attempts to unravel it in the legislative sessions after 1984, but, by and large, school districts learned to live with it. The world did not end, and Friday night football did not perish from the earth."[17]

As he occasionally did whenever he was inspired by some event in which he was involved, Hobby penned a short poem about the Perot reforms:

> *When all was said and done,*
>   *Who was it that won?*
> *Who was it that finally got their due?*
>   *The school children of Texas, that's who.*[18]

On Friday, July 13, 1984, after attending Governor White's signing ceremony for Perot's educational reform act, Hobby traveled to San Francisco to spend the weekend before the Democratic National Convention convened in that city's Moscone Center on Monday, July 16. Hobby had originally thrown his full and enthusiastic support behind Senator John Glenn of Ohio and served as his Texas campaign chairman. In their nationally syndicated column, Rowland Evans and Robert Novak claimed that "as perhaps the most popular Democrat in Texas, Bill Hobby's decision to back Glenn has galvanized the senator's Texas campaign." Unfortunately for Hobby and Glenn, no one galvanized the senator's campaign in Iowa or New Hampshire, where he lost the caucus in the former and the primary in the latter. After those defeats Glenn withdrew from the race. Despite his concern that former vice president Walter Mondale was too liberal, Hobby decided to support Mondale's successful bid for the nomination over competitors Senator Gary Hart and the Reverend Jesse Jackson. New York congresswoman Geraldine Ferraro, who was nominated to be the party's vice presidential candidate, became the first woman to be on the presidential ticket of a major American political party. On August 1, a couple of weeks after the convention, Hobby hosted Mondale and Ferraro's campaign visits to Austin and Houston.[19]

At the Mondale-Ferraro rally in Austin, held on the south steps of the Capitol, State Treasurer Ann Richards introduced Ferraro. She told the crowd, the majority of whom were women, "People ask me all the time, will Texans vote for a woman? Well, my Mama didn't call me Bubba!" In her memoir she recalled being "very pleased" with the introduction speech. So was Bill Hobby. Later, Richards, Hobby, and other Democratic leaders flew with Mondale and Ferraro to Houston for another rally. During the flight, Hobby, who sat next to Richards, asked if she still had a copy of her speech. Richards answered that she did and asked, "What do you want to do with it?" Hobby replied, "Well, I have to introduce her in Houston." Richards gave Hobby her copy of the speech. When they got on the platform at the rally, Hobby read the same speech verbatim that Richards had just given a couple of hours earlier in Austin. While Hobby was speaking, Mondale leaned over to Richards and said, "He's giving your speech." Richards replied, "Oh, hush, it's the best speech he's ever given in his life." Richards later wrote, "I think that tells you a great deal about the strength of Bill Hobby. There are not many politicians who will get up in front of the national press and repeat a speech he knows they just heard someone else give. It takes a person who is truly secure in himself to do that. But he didn't say that his Mama never called him Bubba."[20]

By the middle of October, Hobby knew the Mondale campaign was a losing effort. Reagan won reelection in a landslide in November, and the Republicans made major gains in Texas, increasing their number of seats in the legislature to fifty-two. Although Democrats retained a majority in both the Texas House and the Texas Senate, the Republicans suddenly had leverage over legislation that they had not enjoyed previously, because many conservative Democratic members were expected to vote with them.[21]

With the 1984 general election campaign over and the legislative road ahead looking even rougher than ever because of the continuing decline of oil prices and precipitous drop in state revenues, Bill and Diana looked forward to taking extended time off to relax. But first, Hobby held a $1,000-per-person fundraiser in Austin on November 8 to help pay his debt from the 1982 campaign and to bank funds for the upcoming race in 1986, in which he expected to draw another strong Republican candidate. Hobby had not announced his intention to run for reelection, but there was little doubt he would make a bid for another term. The fundraiser in Austin, plus a separate solicitation of donors from around the state that had begun a few weeks earlier, netted his campaign fund $13 million. The morning after the fundraiser, on November 9, Bill and Diana flew to Ireland. They remained there for a month of isolation from politics and state government, not returning to Houston until December 9. The day after Christmas, they were off again, but this time to Aspen, where they stayed until January 2.[22]

Bill Hobby returned to Austin the first week of January after his family's ski vacation in the Colorado Rockies. The price of oil had continued to fall, and with it, the specter of a major deficit in state financing hovered over the soon-to-convene Sixty-Ninth Legislature. The Senate and House again faced the dilemma of how to pay the bills. Comptroller Bob Bullock estimated that the state's budget deficit would continue to climb unless oil prices rose, which seemed unlikely. Hobby, White, and Lewis each announced their opposition to an increase in taxes, but their declarations weren't absolute. Hobby didn't call for new taxes or an increase in current ones, but he preferred that solution over any plan to cut services and educational programs.[23]

A federal court ordered Texas to improve conditions in its prisons and mental health treatment facilities, which added to the budget concerns. The business community and Republican members of the legislature criticized the court order and complained that improving conditions in the prisons and mental health facilities would cost so much that it would force an increase in taxes. Hobby's response to those complaints was that those who were arguing against improving conditions in state prisons and mental institutions "haven't visited them lately." The state also faced a water supply crisis because of its fast-growing cities. The legislature understood that the state badly needed a plan to increase water storage capacity and to better protect water quality, as well as to conserve underground water and improve flood control. At a public hearing held a month prior to the new legislative session, White, Hobby, and Lewis announced their proposal for a water plan for 1985, but it attracted strong opposition from the Gulf Coast's multi-billion-dollar fishing industry. Conservationists who feared that a plan for new dams and reservoirs would reduce the flow of river water and harm coastal bays and estuaries joined the fishing industry in opposition. Texas voters had repeatedly rejected bonds to finance water projects, even though the need for a water plan had grown more acute each year.[24]

To pay for the water plan as well as other pressing needs, some members of the Senate voiced a strong preference for increasing taxes or finding other sources of revenue rather than reducing or terminating critically needed state services. There were several ideas for additional revenue sources other than taxes, including a hike in tuition and fees at state universities, legalization of horse-race betting, and a state lottery. White's implied threat that he would veto a lottery bill eliminated that option. Hobby proposed a combination of higher user fees and modest cuts in state agency funding. "We can come in with a budget that nobody will be pleased with," Hobby said, "but we won't have to have a tax bill to pay for it." Hobby announced he was also open to other options for increasing revenue, including elimination of the blue law restrictions on business. The state's blue law banned the sale of forty-two items on the weekend. Stores that had most of the banned items in their inventory typically chose to close on Sundays. The law had survived previous repeal attempts, despite demands from individual retailers that it be ended. Major department stores such as Sears and Montgomery Ward had recently organized the Texans for Blue Law Repeal Incorporated and hired lobbyists to support the effort. But the Texas Automobile Dealers Association supported the law because it forced the closing of all car dealerships, which saved their overhead costs for one day a week. The liquor store industry opposed repeal for the same reason.[25]

Bullock favored repeal of the blue law because he had estimated the state could earn an additional $13.5 million a year in taxes from Sunday sales. Hobby admitted that amount would not come close to covering the deficit, but he supported repeal for a philosophical reason. "Basically, I'm against regulation and restriction," Hobby told the news media. "If it's efficient to stay open seven days a week, I'm for it." He supported legalized horse-race betting for the same philosophical reason. "Why in the world should Texas prohibit an enjoyable diversion that our adjoining states allow?" he argued. "As a past time it should be allowed."[26]

Hobby was also aware that an effort to repeal "No Pass, No Play" would be made in the new legislative session. Prior to the session, Senator Bill Sims, a Democrat from San Angelo, announced he would lead the effort. Forewarned, Hobby took preventative action by removing Sims and two of his anti-reform allies, John Leedom and John Montford, from the Senate Education Committee. That committee would have to pass the amendments before they could go to the full Senate. Sims told his hometown newspaper that Hobby's action wouldn't cause him to be "any less active in trying to amend the education reform measure than if I were on the committee." Countering news reports that Hobby's removal of Sims from the Education Committee was "punitive," the lieutenant governor's office issued a statement explaining that he was simply placing the senators where he thought they could best serve their districts. Of course, Hobby just happened to replace the three recalcitrant senators with pro-reform senators: Hector Uribe, Kent Caperton, and Gonzalo Barrientos, a freshman from Austin. Many observers believed Hobby's moving of Uribe from the prestigious Finance Committee to the Education Committee was punishment for Uribe's angry public criticism of the lieutenant governor in 1983. Hobby and Uribe both denied that accusation, although Uribe later admitted it was true. Uribe, however, was eager to return to Hobby's good graces, especially because of his hopes for reviving the farmworkers' compensation insurance bill. Hobby's support for that legislation was essential to its chances for passage.[27]

Uribe's decision not to complain about his new committee assignment ultimately paid dividends. On April 18, 1985, after some quiet work behind the scenes, Hobby succeeded in having the Senate approve Uribe's cosponsored bill to phase in unemployment compensation benefits for farmworkers. Jim Harrington, legal director of the Texas Civil Liberties Union, declared that the vote was a "historic vindication of the farmworker struggle for justice in Texas. The workers have overcome one more vestige of plantation life, which has subjected them to years of discrimination." The bill extended jobless benefit coverage to 145,900 workers, including migrant and seasonal workers.[28]

During the session Hobby also made considerable progress in his effort to diversify the Texas economy and move the state budget away from its dependence on oil and gas revenue and toward an economy based more on science and technology. He secured a $35 million legislative appropriation to pay for research in "emerging technologies" in telecommunications, microelectronics, energy, and biotechnology. This appropriation was the result of a landmark economic development that had occurred two years earlier, in July 1983, when Hobby had teamed with Mark White, Gib Lewis, UT Austin president Peter Flawn, and others to attract the Microelectronics and Computer Technology Consortium, better known by its acronym, MCC, to Austin. Despite strong bids from San Diego, North Carolina, and Atlanta, MCC selected Austin to serve as the location for its research labs. Headed by retired admiral and former deputy director of the CIA Bobby Ray Inman, a native Texan, MCC was a pioneering research consortium of high-tech companies organized to put the United States in a more competitive position in the race against Japan's efforts to develop semiconductors and dominate the computer industry. It was a prime example of the type of new economic development Hobby had advocated for several years. The appropriation for computer research and development that Hobby persuaded the legislature to pass in 1985 fulfilled a pledge he had made to Admiral Inman two years earlier.[29]

In 1983 Hobby had also promised Inman that the legislature would maintain its level of support for the University of Texas at Austin or even increase it, because MCC's decision to locate its labs in Austin was largely due to the research partnership the consortium had forged with the university. That partnership included land at the university's Balcones Research Campus (later named the J. J. Pickle Research Campus) for MCC to construct a building to house its labs. However, protecting the budget for UT Austin and the state's other institutions of higher education in 1985 turned out to be a more difficult problem for Hobby than he or anyone else could have predicted in 1983, when crude oil prices were high. Early in the new session, legislative budget cutters in the House faced a huge budget deficit and focused on the state's system of colleges and universities as a primary target for budget savings, mainly because the Legislative Budget Board, which Hobby chaired, had recommended a reduction in the higher education budget. Although the board's recommendations are advisory only and often suggest larger budget reductions than what the legislature ultimately adopts, the recommendation nonetheless shocked the leaders of the state's public universities and colleges.[30]

In response to the Legislative Budget Board's call for a cut in the higher education budget, legislators proposed to double the cost of tuition as a means of covering some of the reduction. Understanding that improving Texas's public universities was essential to the effort to diversify the state's economy, Hobby supported a hike in tuition, but he thought the legislature's increase should be higher than proposed. Aware that the state's tuition rates were among the lowest in the nation, he submitted an alternative plan to triple the cost of tuition for Texas residents and quadruple the cost for out-of-state students. Hobby took his proposal to Gib Lewis, who immediately endorsed it. However, Mark White didn't like the idea, preferring instead to raise various user fees to cover the projected deficit in the state budget. Hobby eventually persuaded White to not veto the tuition increase if Hobby was able to get the legislature to include provisions for loans and scholarships for low-income students. Hobby later recalled that a group of UT Austin students "didn't like the idea [of a tuition increase] either. They marched on the Capitol, demanding a meeting. They got it. I spoke to them for nearly an hour in the Senate Chamber." Hobby held his ground despite the student protest. The legislature passed the bill increasing the cost of tuition and setting aside scholarship money. White kept his promise and signed the legislation on June 16, 1985.[31]

"Bill Hobby was a great visionary," Mark White later remarked, "because he understood the basic changes that needed to be made to broaden the economy in Texas and the need for money to get the job done; he did both. We tried to diversify our economy. Because of Bill Hobby we made big investments in research. High-tech was kind of the new oil field for Texas. Bill moved forcefully to get the financing we needed to successfully attract MCC to Texas. We did it and we were the envy of the nation, and now they call it 'Silicon Gulch' in Austin."[32]

As the Sixty-Ninth Legislature entered its final days, one of the major issues that remained unaddressed was funding for County Indigent Health Care, a program the legislature had established in the late nineteenth century requiring counties to "provide for the support of paupers [and] residents of their county who are unable to support themselves." The program, which had been neglected by the legislature for years, needed new management and increased funding at the county level. In 1983 Governor White established a task force to make recommendations for legislation to resolve those problems. At Hobby's suggestion, the governor appointed the highly regarded health and human services public policy expert Helen Farabee, Hobby's friend and Senator Ray Farabee's wife, to head the task force. Farabee submitted the report early in the session and a bill was written, but it hadn't been passed by the time the legislature neared its constitutionally mandated date for adjournment in May.[33]

The legislators who prepared the indigent healthcare bill planned to pay for it with a state cigarette tax, but as the legislature prepared to vote on the bill at the end of the session, White announced his intention to veto it, complaining that the bill broke his pledge to voters not to allow any new taxes. That last-minute threat immediately set off a rushed and ultimately futile search for a way to pay for the bill before adjournment. The bill died in the House as the Sixty-Ninth Legislature adjourned at midnight on May 28. Latino and Black members of the legislature harshly criticized White for the failure to pass the bill, accusing him of insensitivity toward the poor and of "tax paranoia." White quickly realized his mistake. Less than an hour after the regular session adjourned, he called a special session to consider the indigent healthcare bill and required it to convene that same day.[34]

Led by US Senator Phil Gramm, conservative Republicans immediately launched a campaign to kill the bill. Gramm telephoned Texas legislators from Washington, denouncing the program as a "welfare giveaway." Outraged by the efforts of some of his Republican colleagues to destroy the program, state senator and moderate Republican John Leedom urged them to ignore Gramm. In a reference to Gramm's recent switch in party affiliation, Leedom declared he had "been a Republican a little bit longer than Phil Gramm has. To me the difference between welfare and indigent health care is really the difference between night and day. With the indigent health situation, I think you're reaching into an area where government should do for people what they can't do for themselves." The Texas Senate took only two minutes to approve the $70 million bill, with all six Republican senators voting in favor of it. Speaker Gib Lewis saved it in the Texas House when he broke a key 71–71 tie vote, ending the three-day session. After the vote, Governor White stood in the Senate Chamber and declared to the senators, "I'll look forward to seeing you in January of 1987."[35]

Hobby was delighted by the passage of the indigent healthcare act. As soon as Gib Lewis broke the tie in the House, Hobby walked through the Capitol shaking hands with his allies who had helped him get the historic plan passed. The *Austin American-Statesman* gave Hobby credit, noting how hard he had pushed for passage during the regular session and observing that his work on the issue had burnished his reputation for being liberal on welfare matters while also being fiscally conservative. Hobby told reporters the indigent healthcare bill was "recognition of basic equity. I'm sorry there was a need for a special session, but with the bill having failed in the House at the last minute, there wasn't really much choice." Pleased with the accomplishments of the Sixty-Ninth Legislature and the passage of the healthcare bill, Hobby declared, "This is a famous day, and a famous victory. But you look at what has happened in this state in the last year." He proudly noted the passage of other bills, including those to provide worker compensation and unemployment benefits for farmworkers, to equalize funding among rich and poor school districts while overhauling public education, to raise payments for Aid to Families with Dependent Children, to finance full-day kindergartens, and to establish programs to screen schoolchildren for learning disabilities. A major cut in higher education funding was also avoided.[36]

Hobby's list of legislative accomplishments also included the state's new $35 million advanced-technology research program, one of his principal goals for the session. Hobby called the technology appropriation the equivalent of a "Texas national science foundation that will allow Texas colleges and universities to remain in the forefront of high-technology development." Hobby told the *New York Times* that despite the serious budget issues the regular session "was certainly the most productive and personally satisfying session I've seen." The *Times* noted that Hobby "emerged as a hero to many for forging compromises on key financial issues." Federal judge Woodrow Seals joined those praising Hobby's performance in the Sixty-Ninth Legislature. Seals told Hobby he had come "to the conclusion that you are the most effective public officer holder in Texas today. I am personally very grateful that you were able to lead the Legislature through the adoption of the bill for the indigent hungry. That was a remarkable piece of work. You are a really good man." At the bottom of Oveta's copy of the letter, Judge Seals wrote, "Oveta, I know you are proud of William."[37]

As Hobby pointed out, the Sixty-Ninth Legislature was productive. It repealed the blue law, although automobile dealers and liquor stores were exempted. It also mandated seat belt use in the front seats of cars, and it raised the drinking age from nineteen to twenty-one. Lawmakers appropriated $170 million for poor school districts, although they failed to give teachers a pay raise. A "comprehensive" statewide water plan was placed on the November ballot as a constitutional amendment for voters to consider. It won approval. Under federal court orders, the legislature appropriated millions of dollars to improve the state's prisons and mental health system. One victory was a result of doing nothing, and that was the legislature's refusal to amend the Perot educational reforms. The projected $1 billon revenue shortfall was mostly covered by new fees and tuition increases, which allowed Governor White to say that he had not allowed any new taxes. Not buying this smoke and mirrors claim, the *Austin American-Statesman* opined that in reality, "fees are taxes in disguise."[38]

When reporters asked Hobby if there had been any failures during the session, he answered, "I really can't think of anything of significance." As usual, however, there were legislative losers as well as winners. On the losing end were teachers, who failed to get a pay raise; several state agencies that suffered budget reductions; promoters of the bill legalizing horse-race gambling; and advocates for banning open containers of alcohol in cars. Others included conservationists who wanted better protection of the Edwards Aquifer and government reformers who demanded action to close loopholes in the Open Meetings Act.[39]

A few weeks after the special session adjourned, Bill and Diana traveled to Hawaii, Taiwan, and Hong Kong. After they returned home, Hobby embarked on a two-day tour of five Texas cities to urge voters to cast their ballots in November in favor of the comprehensive water plan. At his last stop, Hobby held a press conference at an airport in Sherman, Texas, where he was accompanied by Ray Farabee. With no fanfare, Hobby casually dropped the news that he would run for reelection in 1986. His press secretary and pilot, Bob Cargill, commented that Hobby hadn't made a formal announcement yet. "The only reason I know he's running is we've opened a campaign office, and we're going to have a reception—make that fund raiser." Afterward, a reporter telephoned George Strake, the man whom Hobby had defeated by more than five hundred thousand votes in 1982, for his reaction to Hobby's statement. Strake responded that "nothing short of death or debacle" could stop Hobby from winning reelection.[40]

In October, the University of Texas System Board of Regents conferred the system's prestigious Santa Rita Award to Hobby in recognition of his role in fending off the legislature's attempt to make drastic reductions in the state budget for higher education. The Santa Rita Award is given to "individuals who have made valuable contributions over an extended period of time in the development of the UT System and who have demonstrated generous support to preserve and enhance opportunities in higher education." Jess Hay, the chairman of the UT System Board of Regents, made the presentation. He pointed out that during the last legislative session, Hobby's leadership, dedication, and singular courage had "averted what could have been a financial disaster for Texas higher education."[41]

Bill and Diana spent the month of November in Ireland. When they returned to Texas early in December, Bill divided his attention between planning for his upcoming reelection campaign, improving implementation of the Perot reforms, and dealing with the bleak economic prospects for the current state budget because of the continuing drop in oil prices. The budget shortfall was by far the most serious and difficult situation on that list. Hobby and his two fellow members of the "Big Three" of state government leadership, Governor Mark White and Speaker Gib Lewis, had hoped that oil prices would go back up in the months prior to the next regular legislative session in January 1987. Unfortunately, in December 1985 the Arab oil states announced a significant increase in their oil production. Oil prices fell from $32 a barrel in November to $15 a barrel in February. Texas newspapers announced this development with headlines such as one in the *San Angelo Standard-Times* that described the reaction of the energy sector and those dependent on it, including the banks, whose outstanding loans to oil operators now threatened their very existence: "Oil Price Downturn Fosters Hysteria."[42]

Low energy prices benefitted consumers whose incomes weren't tied to the energy industry, but if the price of oil remained low or fell lower in 1986, the current state budget would no longer be balanced. Because the Texas Constitution prohibited budget deficits, Governor White would have to call a special legislative session to cover the deficit. The only way to do that was to drastically reduce state services and support for higher education and public schools and/or legislate a substantial increase in taxes. Ever since the beginning of the 1970s, escalating oil prices had driven up state income from severance taxes on oil and gas and property taxes on oil refineries and other energy industry facilities. That windfall in revenue gave Texas state government a fiscal free ride. As Hobby and others had warned for several years, the free ride ended as oil and natural gas prices plunged.

At the same time Hobby was watching oil prices fall, he also campaigned to speed up implementation of the Perot educational reforms. He criticized the Texas Education Agency (TEA) and the newly appointed members of the State Board of Education for what he felt was their overly cautious oversight of school districts. The Perot public-school reforms, and Hobby's perception that some school districts weren't carrying them out quickly enough or properly, were among the few issues that brought Hobby's anger out in public. He was proud of the Perot reforms and their potential to improve the quality of public-school education in Texas. The state's increasingly dire economic condition, however, caused Hobby much concern about the future of the reforms. The legislature had increased its appropriation for public schools by $2.7 billion in 1984. As the price of oil fell, Hobby knew not only that the legislature would oppose further increases but that it might also try to reduce the projected state budget deficit by passing drastic cuts in the appropriation for public education, especially if there was a perception, accurate or not, that school districts were wasting money.[43]

Hobby, who was a member of the special Legislative Education Committee, expressed his unhappiness in public at a meeting in Austin on December 17, 1985. Among his concerns was the TEA's administration of the exit test that high school juniors had to pass before they could graduate from high school. Hobby claimed that because the test was only a sixth-grade-level exam, school administrators were "perpetrating a fraud" on students and their parents. The TEA had announced that 91 percent of Texas high school juniors passed the English language arts section, and 88 percent passed the math portion. Hobby, however, was unimpressed. He complained the TEA should have focused not on the percentage of students who passed the test but instead on the validity of the exam.[44]

Early in January 1986, a month after the Legislative Education Committee meeting, Hobby spoke to a Texas Federation of Teachers conference, where he continued to criticize the lack of progress in carrying out the educational reforms. Hobby argued that school districts should be held more accountable for their performance because of the additional money the legislature had provided public schools in 1984. "State aid has increased massively to those districts," Hobby stressed. "I think taxpayers are entitled to see performance for their dollars." He added that the state should reduce the funds provided to school districts where a significant portion of students failed the state-mandated standardized tests, but he would leave it to local school boards to hold superintendents, principals, and teachers accountable. "It's my experience that increased incentive leads to better efforts," Hobby stated. "That's the way our society works. I don't see the logic of putting good money after bad. When you have somebody who's doing a poor job, you don't give them a raise."[45]

Hobby's criticism of the leaders of the state's public schools unleashed a firestorm of negative reactions—an unwelcome development during a reelection year. In January, Hobby enjoyed some respite from his battle with the state's public-school administrators when Sarah Weddington gave him a surprise birthday luncheon at Austin's Westwood Country Club. The party was held five days before Hobby's fifty-fourth birthday because he was scheduled to represent his mother at a ceremony on January 19 to place a historic marker at her childhood home in Killeen. When Bill walked into the Westwood Country Club, he thought he was having lunch with Weddington only. He was shocked to find her with several other women, who promptly began to sing "Happy Birthday." He was also surprised when he realized that he was the only male present. Weddington, the lead plaintiff's attorney in the *Roe v. Wade* abortion case and a former state representative, was practicing law in Austin after having served as a special assistant to President Jimmy Carter. She gathered several women, including Ann Richards and Liz Carpenter, to celebrate Hobby's birthday and to thank him for his support of the Equal Rights Amendment and abortion rights. Weddington was also paying Hobby back for a surprise he had sprung on her back in February 1973 on her twenty-sixth birthday, when she was a freshman legislator. She had spent the day at her desk on the House floor pouting because no one had wished her a happy birthday. When that day's session adjourned, one of her legislative colleagues walked over to her desk and said, "You look sad. Let me buy you a drink. But first I have to stop by the lieutenant governor's office for a minute." When they entered the office, Hobby and several of Weddington's friends in the legislature surprised her with a birthday party.[46]

As Hobby sat in the middle of a circle of guests at Westwood Country Club and sipped wine with them, Liz Carpenter, a former Washington correspondent for the *Houston Post* who had served as Lady Bird Johnson's press secretary during LBJ's presidency, made a toast to Hobby. "To the most powerful person in the state," Carpenter declared. "The one who retrieves the lost clauses and appropriations for human causes. He has made [the Equal Rights Amendment] stick in Texas and that fact alone is one reason we know we will ultimately prevail. What would Texas have been without Bill, [or] without the Hobbys?" When the reporter who attended the party asked Hobby what he thought was his most important accomplishment, he said, "Survived, I guess!" Noting that Bill faced a reelection campaign in the coming months, Ann Richards reminded him they had made a bet that she was going to outpoll him like she had in 1982 when she was elected state treasurer. Richards told the group, "Whoever wins [the most votes] has to take the other to dinner in New York!" Declaring, "Wait a minute," Hobby protested that dinner at a restaurant of Richards's choosing in New York would be more than he could afford.[47]

Hobby soon began to edge away from his criticisms of the TEA and the State Board of Education as he turned more of his attention to the increasingly difficult state budget situation as well as to the upcoming Democratic primary. He also had to make a significant change in his staffing. Bob Cargill decided he liked flying Hobby from place to place more than speaking for him, so he gave up his job as Hobby's press spokesman to be a full-time pilot, including continuing in that role for Hobby. At the receiving end of heat from Texas public-school administrators, while trying to respond to the oil price crisis and entering a reelection year, Hobby lost no time in finding Cargill's replacement. He offered the job to a veteran journalist he deeply respected, Saralee Tiede, a New York native who was the Capitol bureau chief for the *Fort Worth Star-Telegram*.[48]

Tiede and her husband, John, had moved in 1965 to Houston, where she worked as a reporter at the *Houston Chronicle* for five years. Like Bill and Diana Hobby, Tiede enjoyed horseback riding, which brought her to Edgepark Stables, where the Hobbys also rode. They soon became friends because of their love of the sport. After Hobby was elected to his first term as lieutenant governor in 1972, Tiede, by then a reporter for the *Fort Worth Star-Telegram*, renewed her friendship with him. Tiede quickly noticed that Hobby was "media adverse" despite his career in newspapers. "We reporters used to joke that the most dangerous place to be was between Governor Mark White and a TV camera and between Bill Hobby and the door." He also had a disconcerting habit of walking away in the middle of an interview. This behavior was just part of the enigma that was Bill Hobby, and it was why all observers considered him to be the polar opposite of the usual successful politician.[49]

During one of their lunches in January 1986, Hobby asked Tiede if she would take the job as his press secretary. During Hobby's first years in office, Tiede, a political liberal, had thought he was too conservative in his legislative outlook and listened too much to the old guard. "His mentor was Ben Ramsey, who was super conservative. But Bill's views had moderated, especially after the Killer Bees episode. I had a good relationship with him and I thought he was doing really good things, so I said yes. I just thought it would be interesting to be part of government as opposed to reporting on it." Tiede soon became an essential member of Hobby's staff, not only as a skilled liaison with the press but also as an advisor and a confidant. Her work with Hobby would continue long after he left political office.[50]

At the beginning of 1986, Hobby still hoped the current state budget could avoid a deficit for the remainder of the fiscal year. In a speech to the Texas Good Roads/Transportation Association, Hobby said he doubted there would be a need to call a special session, "because I assume Bob [Bullock] has a $200 million to $400 million cushion." Hobby's hope that there would be no deficit in the state's current budget soon proved to be a false one. With the price of oil dropping $10 a barrel from January to February and the unemployment rate rising to over 10 percent, the state was suddenly presented with a $1.3 billion deficit. Faced with a financial emergency, White was forced on February 18 to issue an executive order to all state agencies and universities to cut current spending by 13 percent. Even with White's mandated cuts, the deficit was still $700 million short. A called special session that summer was unavoidable. Closely monitoring the fall in price and the precipitous decline in the state's revenue, Hobby declared, "It's going to be tough with the oil situation. We thought we had an economic crisis last session, but we look upon that as the good ol' times now."[51]

In the meantime, Hobby made campaign plans for May's Democratic Party primary, with Don Adams once again serving as his campaign chairman. With only token opposition, Hobby was confident of winning an unprecedented fifth term. However, Mark White, who faced another campaign against Bill Clements, had to worry about the public-school teachers' vote. Teachers, administrators, and school board members were blaming the governor for the portion of the Perot reforms they disliked, especially the mandated teacher competency exams. For the first time in eight years, the Texas State Teachers Association (TSTA) refused to endorse a candidate for governor, including Bill Clements. The TSTA also refused to endorse Hobby for reelection, but unlike White, he had weak candidates running against him. Nevertheless, Hobby wisely ceased his public criticisms of the TSTA and other public-school employee organizations.[52]

Hobby's main challenger in the Democratic primary was perfume salesman David Young, who had neither money nor name recognition. Nevertheless, all campaigns need some level of funding, and this one was no different. A month prior to the primary, Hobby sent a fundraising letter to his list of financial donors. Asking for their help, Hobby explained why they should continue to provide support by stressing the accomplishments achieved during the last legislative sessions. The list is a key to understanding what legislation mattered most to Hobby. It included a revitalization of the state highway system, a comprehensive water program, reforming public-school financing, an improved indigent healthcare plan, and the creation of the $35 million fund for research in technology. Hobby also repeated his mantra about the necessity for the state to end its dependence on "industries in distress [including] oil and agriculture" and to focus instead on building "a broader-based economy of the future."[53]

Hobby also made efforts to repair his damaged relationship with the State Board of Education. In mid-April he appeared before the board—which he had severely taken to task only three months earlier—and congratulated the members for their performance "in the face of almost constant criticism" due to the "No Pass, No Play" reforms. "The chorus of complaints is sometimes deafening," he said. "Many coaches are still loudly lamenting the simple fact that students have to pass their courses before they can play their games. Some teachers are still furious that they were required to take a simple literacy test. No one hears the chorus louder than you do here on the firing line. No one catches more flak." He cautioned that improvement in public education would take time. "We are aiming at a renaissance, and renaissances do not come quickly."[54]

As expected, Hobby coasted to an easy primary victory on May 3, winning 75 percent of the vote. His reelection in November was almost certain. The Republican nominee for lieutenant governor, David Davidson, a former minister of a nondenominational church in Gonzales, Texas, was ignored by the Republican Party's establishment. The party's state executive committee refused to endorse his candidacy, and some Republican senators announced their support for Hobby.[55]

On June 4, with the primary season over, Hobby and White conducted an inspection tour of two of the impoverished settlements known as colonias, located in unincorporated areas outside Brownsville. Colonias exist along various stretches of the Rio Grande as it flows through Texas. In 1986, an estimated one hundred thousand people lived in the colonias, the vast majority of whom were Latinos. The substandard housing developments lack basic services such as drinking water, sewage treatment, and paved roads. Many of the houses in the colonias are informally constructed of scrap wood, cardboard, plastic tarps, and other materials. These areas also lack access to adequate medical facilities.

Hobby told a crowd of about 150 that gathered outside a home in one colonia that the state had a responsibility "to get the sewage out of the streets and get the water into your homes." The cost to improve about twenty-nine of the colonias was estimated to be $40 to $45 million. White and Hobby pledged to work for $100 million in state money to help improve living conditions. Despite these promises, little would be done, especially as the oil price crisis worsened that summer. A majority of the members of the Texas Legislature, claiming the colonias were the fault of the federal government's inability to curb illegal immigration, opposed state appropriations for improving living conditions in the settlements.[56]

In June it became clear that despite all hopes, the state budget faced a huge deficit. It was obvious that Governor White would have to call a special session of the legislature to address the problem. On June 12, Hobby spoke to a conference of the Texas Science and Technology Council in Dallas, where he summarized the economic realities facing Texans. Noting that members of the legislature were demanding major cuts in the higher education budget, Hobby warned that such an action would make Texas's economic problems even worse. Instead, he called for an increased investment in higher education, which would help make it possible for the state to escape its dependence on oil and gas. Hobby emphasized the importance of advanced university research, through which "we will develop the ideas that will permit us to sustain the prosperity we have enjoyed in the past."[57]

In late July, Hobby embarked on a seven-city tour seeking popular support for his deficit reduction proposals. One of his stops was in Austin, where he spoke to a group of business leaders. Hobby proposed $650 million in spending reductions, including "selective" cuts in state aid to school districts and a rollback of scheduled pay raises for state employees. "Large and significant and painful cuts will have to be made," Hobby said. "But I can get to $650 million without having to cut any bone and muscle." In 1984 the voters had approved bonds to support highways. It would be a "breach of trust," to cut that budget, Hobby argued. He dismissed the idea, however, that budget cuts alone would do the job, calling that approach "clearly not acceptable." It would also be necessary to raise taxes, specifically the sales tax, which he wanted to broaden to cover more types of transactions, with exemptions for food and medicine. Hobby was asked if he was concerned that raising taxes might harm his chances for reelection or hinder any hope he might harbor to serve as governor like his father. He responded that his father had told him that during the first six months he was governor he constantly worried about public opinion. "He woke up one day and decided there wasn't anything he could find in the constitution or law that said Will Hobby had to be governor. After that, he just went on down the road and did what he thought was right and everything went fine."[58]

As expected, Governor White called a special session of the legislature to convene in early August. He asked the legislature to identify spending cuts to eliminate the projected $3.5 billion budget shortage for the coming biennium. He also indicated he might accept a slight increase in taxes. The most controversial question was how much higher education funding should be reduced, with the University of Texas at Austin and the UT System being the special focus of Gib Lewis and members of the House. No other budget reduction proposal raised more powerful opposition. White proposed $25 million in additional budget cuts for the UT System, including those mandated by his executive order issued in February. Hobby's plan required no cuts in the UT System beyond those covered by White's executive order. Speaker Lewis called not only for a reduction of up to $30 million across the UT System but also for the transfer of nearly $300 million from the Permanent School Fund to be applied directly to the state budget deficit. The constitutionally created fund contains the money generated by oil and gas leases, sales, and other sources of revenue from UT System lands in West Texas. A percentage of the annual revenue from the fund is distributed to the UT System (two-thirds) and the Texas A&M System (one-third) to pay for construction bonds at their various schools, although some of UT Austin's share can be used to support operations.[59]

Influential supporters of the UT System quickly organized and launched a major lobbying campaign to defeat the Speaker's proposal. Two days before the start of the special session, UT System Board of Regents chair Jess Hay, a Dallas businessman and Democrat who was close to Mark White and Bill Hobby, organized a rally at the LBJ Auditorium on the UT Austin campus attended by about four hundred supporters of higher education. Hay called for the legislature to combine relatively small cuts in spending with a package of tax increases, which was similar to Hobby's proposal. The rally was bipartisan in makeup, with wealthy businessman and Republican financial donor Peter O'Donnell Jr. also giving a speech and serving as one of the leaders of the lobbying effort. O'Donnell was a major backer of Bill Clements. The president of UT Austin, Dr. William H. Cunningham, who was a major source of information for the group lobbying against the cuts, also spoke.[60]

After the special session convened, Hobby and White both urged the legislature to combine tax increases with spending cuts, but Lewis held firm on his opposition to any tax hike, insisting the deficit would have to be covered solely by a drastic budget reduction. The Senate, however, sided with Hobby. The result was a deadlock between the two legislative chambers. By the end of the second week of the session, Hobby was so frustrated with the House that he considered adjourning the Senate and sending its members home if no tax bill was forthcoming, but he decided against it because of an obscure law stating that if one side of the legislature adjourns and its members leave, they have to return if the other house fails to adjourn within three days. Instead, the Senate Finance Committee continued to mark up the appropriations bill and waited to see what the governor would do. Signs from the governor's office indicated White was prepared to call a second special session if the current one ended in a stalemate.

At this point, the *Austin American-Statesman* reported that "Hobby and his friends are doing everything they can to encourage local business leaders and public officials to tell legislators they favor a tax increase over spending cuts." Years later, when he recalled the 1986 budget crisis, Senate Finance Committee member Kent Caperton remembered that Hobby held a meeting in his Capitol office "with some titans of the business community, including [banker] Ben Love and [developer] Walter Mischer from Houston and Jess Hay and Ross Perot from Dallas. We worked closely with Jess to protect higher education." Hobby invited Caperton, Farabee, and other senators to participate in the meeting. "We talked about how to solve this particular budget crisis and protect higher education," Caperton said. "Hobby appealed to the business community's sense of duty and obligation, and responsibility to not fight us every time we talked about having to raise taxes. His wealth probably enhanced his ability to speak to those other business leaders, rather than just being another elected official." Lady Bird Johnson was among those business leaders who understood Hobby's selfless motives in the matter. During the stalemated session, she sent Bill and Diana an invitation to attend an event at the LBJ Ranch. She handwrote a note at the bottom of the invitation: "Bill, you are our hero for education in this state. This citizen sends a heart-felt thanks and a big salute. And I firmly believe you're expressing the deep wishes of most Texans, even if it means taxes."[61]

At the end of the thirty-day period allotted to the special session, the House and Senate remained more than $300 million apart in their struggle to resolve the budget crisis. Political analysts claimed that Lewis was playing tough because he had a Republican opponent in a district that President Reagan had won by a large majority in 1984. Lewis's opponent was accusing the Speaker of being a "tax and spend" Democrat. On September 4, the special session adjourned with its business unfinished. White promptly called another session, to begin on September 8. When the session convened, the general election was two months away. Speaker Lewis implied that he might consider a tax increase, but only if it was temporary and had a built-in expiration date. In the race for governor, the polls indicated that Bill Clements, who was campaigning on a no-new-taxes platform, was far ahead of White. Midway through the September session, Lewis and his allies in the House concluded that to get past the fast-approaching Election Day, some kind of temporary tax increase would have to be passed that would push the budget problem to the new legislature (and possibly a new governor), which would meet in regular session in January. To help Lewis reach this point, Hobby agreed to support a bill repealing a pay raise for state employees and mandating a reduction in the number of state employees by almost two thousand. "We robbed every reserve fund we could find," Hobby recalled, "[and we] delayed payments to the state retirement fund." A bookkeeping trick delayed the state payroll by a day, which moved that expense to the next fiscal year. State colleges and universities were cut by 10 percent, but public education was left largely unscathed.[62]

The House finally agreed to raise sales and fuel taxes, as well as to provide for additional local-option sales taxes. The taxes were scheduled to expire on September 1, 1987. To Hobby's deep annoyance, Republican senator Buster Brown of Lake Jackson conducted a five-hour filibuster against the tax increases, but Hobby was able to end the delay, and the Senate passed the bill. Hobby admitted the bill was a "small Band-Aid, but it was the best available under the circumstances." The special session ended on September 30, and White signed the bill.[63]

Now that a resolution of the budget crisis had been postponed until January 1987, Hobby sent out a fundraising letter asking for contributions to pay for ads for the general election campaign and to liquidate remaining primary expenses. Even though the polls indicated that his Republican opponent would be easily defeated, Hobby was taking no chances. "As you know, I have an opponent in the November election," Hobby explained to his supporters. "Many people have urged me not to be concerned, but in politics the quickest way to become history rather than helping to make history is to take an opponent for granted."[64]

As expected, on November 4, 1986, Hobby won a fifth term with over 61 percent of the vote. Token Republican candidate David Davidson managed to attract more than a third of the total vote. Election analysts pointed out that Davidson benefitted from Republican straight-ticket voters who cast ballots for Clements. Hobby's victory was generally credited to his long-standing support from minority groups and the Texas business community, which included many Republicans. He even enjoyed the open support of some Republican members of the legislature, including Senator Ike Harris of Dallas. Unfortunately for Mark White, the education reforms he helped pass were popular but the tax increase was not, and White received the unfair blame for that. Adding to White's problems when he faced reelection was the Texas economy, which was in a serious recession caused by the plunge in oil and gas prices. Also, the Texas State Teachers Association continued to accuse him of breaking his promise to provide a substantial pay raise for teachers, and it also attacked him for supporting teacher testing. "Governor White's education reforms have had a lasting impact on Texas public education," Hobby argued years later, "but teachers, who were among the major beneficiaries of those reforms, made it their mission to defeat the man responsible. They succeeded.

Bill Clements, who got a drubbing from White in 1982, resurfaced with deep pockets and a yen for revenge." However, despite a rapidly growing Republican vote, Democratic incumbents Jim Hightower, Garry Mauro, Bob Bullock, Jim Mattox, and Ann Richards were reelected.[65]

A couple of weeks after the election, John Davis, Bill Hobby's mentor at St. Albans, wrote Hobby to congratulate him on his victory. Davis added that his win ought to give hope to "people who have ideas such as making football players pass courses."[66]

CHAPTER 15

HOBBY VERSUS CLEMENTS

On January 2, 1987, Dave McNeely announced in his *Austin American-Statesman* column that Bill Hobby "is finally ready to run for governor in 1990." Hobby had made the much-anticipated decision during the Christmas holidays. At the beginning of the new year, he leaked the news in interviews with *Dallas Morning News* columnist Sam Kinch and the *Statesman*'s McNeely—two of the members of the Capitol press corps whom he trusted and respected. Hobby admitted to McNeely that he had never run for governor because, "since I've been around there has not been the opportunity to run for governor without running against an incumbent." Hobby told McNeely he would have had to oppose Dolph Briscoe, Mark White, or Bill Clements, each of whom he had worked closely with. "And I just couldn't hardly ever see myself doing that," Hobby said. "To run against an incumbent, you've got to run around the state saying that so-and-so is sorry and no good which they're not." Clements had announced after he had taken back the governor's office from Mark White that he would not be a candidate for reelection. With Clements out of the race, the incumbency issue was no longer an obstacle.[1]

McNeely speculated that Hobby made his plans public three years early to ensure that his potential supporters would not give their pledges to other candidates. An early announcement would also help him raise money in the coming three years because he would still have influence as the lieutenant governor. A Hobby gubernatorial candidacy worried Republicans, McNeely noted, because of the impressive support he enjoyed in the Texas business community. McNeely, who knew Hobby well, believed that ever since his election as lieutenant governor in 1972, Hobby had "bided his time, awaiting the opportunity to follow in his father's footsteps. No one with a political nose doubted that the son wanted the governorship." Nevertheless, McNeely discerned a bit of indecision in Hobby's thinking. Hobby had frequently told his friends that he had kept running for reelection as lieutenant governor because he considered the position to be more powerful than governor. If he chose to seek a different office, it would be because he was more interested in a seat in the US Senate. When McNeely asked Hobby if his decision to run for governor now indicated a loss of interest in the US Senate, Hobby replied, "No."[2]

A few days after the *Statesman* published McNeely's column, Hobby consulted with Don Adams, George Christian, and a few other trusted political allies about how he should prepare for his candidacy. At their recommendation, Hobby hired George Shipley, an Austin political pollster and consultant, to provide his candid "thoughts and recommendations" about Hobby running for governor. Shipley gave Hobby and his advisors the candid and tough assessment they requested. His report, based on confidential polling, made several points. One was if Hobby did decide to enter the race, it wasn't too early to start planning. Politically liberal attorney general Jim Mattox, whom Shipley identified as Hobby's main threat, had already begun his campaign and was raising money. Shipley argued that with the rise of the Republican Party in Texas and the move of conservative Democrats to the GOP, the Democratic primary vote was more favorable to liberal candidates, which gave Mattox an advantage. The "sober realization" was that Hobby's current constituency, which was anchored in the business community and among moderate and conservative Democrats, was "not ideally suited to a Democratic primary contest" for governor, because that office attracted far more attention from ordinary voters than lieutenant governor. Despite Hobby's successes, Shipley's polling indicated widespread ignorance about the duties and powers of the lieutenant governor. "We shouldn't assume that people are that well informed about Hobby's accomplishments."[3]

Shipley advised Hobby to drop the "Rose Garden strategy" of his past campaigns, which referred to Hobby's habit of restricting his campaign appearances largely to speeches at receptions, luncheons, and dinners to audiences of local civic and business leaders. That strategy threatened to make Hobby look like an elitist who was "not being interested in pressing the flesh with local officials and activists. The message that sends will cripple his chances." Shipley also believed Hobby's existing campaign organization was in "bad shape" and that he needed to recruit new coordinators and create more alliances in the cities and in South Texas among minorities. He urged Hobby to activate Black political leaders in Houston on his behalf, especially Mickey Leland, Rodney Ellis, and Anthony Hall. In South Texas he should enlist the help of Bexar County judge Tom Vickers and newly elected Laredo state senator Judith Zaffirini.[4]

Shipley also felt that Hobby's fundraising base was too narrow and "special interest oriented." The pollster urged Hobby to expand his funding efforts substantially, especially in Dallas, which was a weak area for him. He added that "something must also be done to slow or cripple Mattox's fund raising efforts this year." Hobby needed a more focused campaign message than he'd had in previous campaigns. "Hobby has been running for reelection on a theme which emphasizes the status quo," Shipley advised. "He needs something more dynamic that gives voters a reason to vote [for] him for governor." Finally, Shipley warned that a gubernatorial race that featured Jim Mattox would inevitably be rough and dirty. Accordingly, "a quiet file should be kept on Mattox and other possible entrants to the race" to counter their mudslinging. This information was a sobering wake-up call. The Shipley report would eventually play a key role in Hobby's campaign planning as the Seventieth Legislature conducted its business during the spring and summer of 1987.[5]

On January 19, 1987, the day before Bill Hobby was to be inaugurated to his fifth term as lieutenant governor of Texas, his staff celebrated his fifty-fifth birthday with a party in the lieutenant governor's quarters in the Capitol. Among those crammed into the crowded room was a gleeful Bill Clements. As is usual in such situations, the guests were in a boisterous and celebratory mood, temporarily setting aside partisanship as well as policy differences as they extended their birthday wishes to Hobby. Many of the guests, however, were aware that state government was experiencing an ever-increasing loss in revenue that was almost certain to cause a contentious battle in the legislature over how to balance the budget as required by the Texas Constitution.[6]

The state was still suffering from the economic bust of the mid-1980s, mainly driven by the drastic drop in the price of oil and the subsequent loss of state revenue. In addition, agriculture, which was also a major component of Texas's economy, was in a slump, as was the real estate industry. State Comptroller Bob Bullock had announced that because of the state's stagnant economy, more than $5 billion in new revenues would be needed to sustain state government for the next three years at its present level. It was well known that Bill Clements and his legislative allies wanted deep cuts in state programs and services—especially higher education—to balance the budget. As a member of the Legislative Budget Board, Hobby was acutely aware that in December 1986, the board had suggested a 26 percent reduction in the budget for publicly supported colleges and universities. Because the Sixty-Ninth Legislature had reduced the higher education budget by 17 percent, the proposed additional cut would mean those institutions would have to operate at a significantly lower level of funding they'd had in 1985, which had been the high point of state support for colleges and universities. Hobby continued his opposition to deep cuts in higher education. Instead, he favored an increase in taxes, including on personal income, as the way to balance the budget—an approach Clements opposed. Accordingly, it was obvious that looming in the immediate future was a major fight pitting Clements against Hobby.[7]

The newly reelected state treasurer, Ann Richards, was also at Hobby's birthday party. Aware that a major legislative fight between the governor and lieutenant governor was imminent, Richards, who was famed for her wit, presented Hobby with a birthday gift that humorously symbolized what was in store in the coming days. When Hobby opened the gift box, Richards declared that she'd wanted to give him something practical to wear for the coming fight: "a beautiful pair of satin boxing trunks."[8]

On January 20, former attorney general John Hill, who had been elected chief justice of the Texas Supreme Court in 1984, administered the oath of office to Hobby, and then to Clements—the man who had defeated Hill in the 1978 gubernatorial election. Immediately after taking their oaths of office, Hobby and Clements delivered their inaugural addresses. Those speeches revealed stark differences in their positions on how to solve the state's financial crisis. Hobby's speech pointedly declared that higher education funding should be increased instead of reduced. Arguing that Texas was far from having a literate workforce, Hobby stated that "more than one-third of our adults don't finish high school. Nearly one-fifth don't finish the eighth grade. Those figures have ominous implications when you consider that 85 percent of the inmates in the Texas prisons are dropouts." Citing the number of faculty members who had recently left their positions at the state's colleges and universities to teach in other states that offered higher salaries and benefits, Hobby also warned that Texas was dealing with a "brain drain." He stated, "It doesn't make sense to balance our budget at the expense of higher education." He also directly blamed Clements's demand for no new taxes during his first gubernatorial term as the reason the state had failed to correct overcrowding in its prisons, which had resulted in federal judge William Wayne Justice's ruling that the state was in contempt of court and would have to pay several million dollars in fines if it failed to pass prison reform in the coming months. It was unusual for a lieutenant governor to make a speech criticizing the governor on Inauguration Day, and it blindsided Clements, who was sitting uncomfortably on the inaugural platform with Hobby.[9]

Afterward, Carolyn Barta, a columnist for the *Dallas Morning News* who was a friend of Clements, commented that Hobby's confrontational manner had shocked the governor because it wasn't Hobby's "normal, laid-back statesmanlike, let's-work-it-out style." Because Barta was aware of Hobby's statements that he would run for governor in 1990, she and her contacts in the Republican Party speculated that Hobby's adversarial speech had been intended to scare off potential rivals in the Democratic primary. This public airing of the differences between the governor and lieutenant governor over policy and the belief that Hobby was positioning himself for the governor's race in 1990 set the tone for the entire legislative session.[10]

On January 26, Clements met with Hobby and the Senate committee chairs in the Ben Ramsey Room next to the lieutenant governor's office to discuss the upcoming session. "Clements arrived in a jovial mood," Hobby later recalled, "eager to talk about his great programs. Clements usually spent weekends in Dallas, and on Mondays he was full of ideas from his friends at the country club." Clements announced that one of his chief legislative goals was to build more prisons and get the state out from under the federal court. Clements stressed that deep cuts in state appropriations, especially public education, would have to be made to help pay for those new prisons. He would oppose any new taxes for that or any other purpose. Clements's good mood quickly soured, however, when Hobby angrily repeated his accusation that Clements was responsible for the state being in federal court in the first place because of his opposition during his first term to raising taxes to address prison overcrowding. Hobby was outraged by the thought that Clements was willing to spend $30,000 a year for each person sent to prison, paid for with money taken from the education of the state's youth. Several of the Senate committee chairs, including Ray Farabee, Carl Parker, and Kent Caperton, also criticized Clements. Harsh words were exchanged, and Clements left the meeting in anger—"sliced and diced by a buzzsaw of powerful senators with strong opinions," Hobby later noted. When Clements returned to the governor's office, he told his staff that Hobby had insulted him. Recalling the incident years later, Hobby said that from his viewpoint, the meeting accomplished "one worthwhile purpose: Clements never came back to the Senate side of the Capitol."[11]

The battle lines between Clements and Hobby were now drawn. At the heart of the dispute was the stark philosophical difference between the two men over the role of government, especially in taxation. To Hobby, a reasonable level of taxation was a necessary evil for support of public schools, higher education, and other programs and services basic to a decent and humane society. He also believed that appropriating funds for education was an investment that would ultimately be paid back to the state with interest in the form of a better-educated and more-skilled citizenry. In addition, Texas needed to build its technology sector, and that couldn't be done without investing in higher education. Clements, on the other hand, was a product of the oil industry and was a Reagan Republican whose philosophy was the less government the better, especially when it came to taxes. A difference over public policy was not the only issue separating Hobby and Clements, however. According to Saralee Tiede, "Hobby basically did not respect Clements as a person." Another of Hobby's staff members, Glenn Smith, observed that Hobby and Clements "were such different personalities, I mean, they were never going to click. They couldn't be more different. Hobby's a very thoughtful guy, Clements was not. Clements had a high opinion of himself. Clements was happy to tell you about all of his many accomplishments in life. And he was crude."[12]

Early in the session, under intense pressure from federal judge William Wayne Justice and a sobering budget analysis from Bob Bullock, Clements reluctantly agreed to a $2.9 billion tax increase to address prison overcrowding, despite intense grumbling by some of the ultraconservative Republicans in the House, including Houston's Mike Toomey and Fort Worth's Bob Davis. Toomey earned the nickname Mike the Knife because of his zealous, single-minded mission to reduce state agency budgets to a bare minimum no matter the human costs. *Texas Monthly* described Toomey as a rigid ideologue whose view of government "had room for no-new-taxes, law-and-order, and little else." Toomey was one of Clements's main advisors on the state budget. Although the governor and Republican colleagues in the legislature considered Toomey to be an expert on budget matters, his analysis of state revenue and expenditures was so misleading and skewed by his ideology that he was giving Clements incorrect budget numbers, particularly for higher education, to push his ideological agenda. Clements's budget staff, who depended on Representative Toomey's math, convinced the governor that most of the remaining deficit could be made up by cutting government fat, most of which could be covered by deep cuts to education and social services, as well as various new user fees. Despite Clements's concession to allow nearly $3 billion in taxes for prison reform, Comptroller Bullock's revenue projections indicated that the state still faced a deficit of approximately $3 billion simply to maintain the status quo. Citing Bullock's highly accurate estimates, Hobby tried to persuade Clements that Toomey's numbers were incorrect. Nevertheless, Clements refused to change his position on the budget, and he repeated his threat to veto any tax bill that exceeded $2.9 billion.[13]

The fierce battle over the budget continued unabated for the entire five months of the regular session of the Seventieth Legislature. Although House Speaker Gib Lewis presided over a branch of the legislature more in tune with Clements's anti-tax stand and was no fan of tax increases himself, he fully understood that more revenue had to be found to prevent reductions that would harm the gains the legislature had made in supporting public education. He was proud of that progress, and he labored to preserve it, but he rejected Hobby's proposal to increase the appropriation for education. Instead, the Speaker advocated a blended package of new taxes and budget cuts in areas other than education. Lewis had a fight on his hands in the House, however. House Republicans opposed tax increases on ideological grounds, while many of the Democrats in the House were frightened of a potential voter rebellion against any increase in taxes. Hobby's Senate took a different stance. Like their colleagues in the House, members of the Senate also worried about political damage, but the Democratic majority supported Hobby's position.

With the Senate holding fast against deep cuts in education, Clements accused Hobby and the Democratic senators of behaving like prairie chickens. He explained that prairie chickens have "a genetic compulsion to thump the ground. And so, I think the Democrats have been going through a thumping period that they felt compelled to do. Now hopefully we will get down to serious business." Recalling the Killer Bees episode, the Democrats immediately ordered T-shirts declaring, "Proud to be a prairie chicken," which they wore under their suit coats while on the floor of the Senate Chamber. Hobby carried the joke further by organizing a softball team named the Lieutenant Governor's Prairie Chickens, which near the end of the session played games against members of the Capitol press corps and members of the Texas Senate.[14]

Meanwhile, as the budget battle increasingly focused on cuts in the education appropriation, Jess Hay and other University of Texas officials organized a coalition to oppose the cuts. The coalition included not just the university but all institutions of higher education, including community and junior colleges. Hay understood that Hobby was the key to their effort to protect the higher education budget. The Dallas businessman had long been a major player in the Democratic Party in Texas as a fundraiser, and he had helped raise money for several of Hobby's campaigns. Over lunch with Hobby, Hay explained the education coalition's strategy, which included hosting public rallies around Texas as well as having seminars with business leaders to explain why it was critical to the state's economy to support higher education. He handed a written plan to Hobby and asked for his active involvement in their effort. Hobby agreed to help, telling Hay he would not only carry the cause in the Senate but also participate in meetings around the state with Hay and his team, which included UT chancellor Hans Mark and UT Austin president Bill Cunningham. The latter had forged a friendship with Hobby, and they frequently played racquetball together at the university's Bellmont Hall athletic facility late in the afternoons after Senate sessions. Cunningham later remembered that when the coalition leaders traveled around the state, Hobby not only went with them but also provided the airplane. "We had rallies in different cities at hotels that the [UT Austin] ex-student association put together for us," Cunningham said. "Hobby certainly was central to our effort. When we went into senatorial districts, he was able to stand up and say we need to avoid cutting higher education, and we must raise taxes. And boy, that was hard to say. Everything went through Bill Hobby in the end, because if he was not behind us, it wouldn't have gone anywhere."[15]

Once Hay had Hobby involved in the campaign, he and his associates—including retired admiral Bobby Ray Inman, head of the Austin-based Microelectronics and Computer Technology Consortium—won the formal support of a majority of the business community leadership in Texas, as well as the support of labor and the various minority interests in the state. Bill Cunningham persuaded the Texas Exes organization to get its members to call their legislators to urge them to support the cause. As a result, a massive number of phone calls were made to members of the Texas House who supported Clements's budget reduction plan. According to Hay, the phones were so overwhelmed in the Speaker's office that Gib Lewis was unable to make outgoing calls. Lewis finally called Hay and asked, "Would you please call off the dogs? I can't make phone calls from my own office."[16]

Wealthy Dallas investor Peter O'Donnell Jr. was the most important ally the coalition recruited from the business community. O'Donnell was one of Bill Clements's key donors and advisors. Although O'Donnell had a deeply conservative political worldview, he was a bit of a maverick among his fellow Republicans in that he was a strong supporter of publicly supported higher education. According to Jess Hay, O'Donnell "had the vision and spent the money necessary to establish clearly the linkage between the state's commitment to higher education and to research and to economic progress in the future." O'Donnell worked with Hay to enlist the sixty top business leaders in Texas to sign a letter urging Clements, Lewis, and members of the legislature to embrace the notion that Texas's future was worth the money invested in education. O'Donnell also eventually played a crucial role in convincing Clements that the budget numbers Toomey was feeding the governor's staff to justify deep cuts in the educational budget were incorrect. "Bill Clements suffered from bad staff advice," Hay later noted. "His staff advice was fundamentally flawed because it simply was based on inaccurate numbers." During the second special session, O'Donnell spent half a day in the governor's office going over the numbers with Clements and his staff, an effort that would eventually pay off.[17]

Former lieutenant governor Ben Ramsey, former lieutenant governor Ben Barnes, Lieutenant Governor Bill Hobby, and former governor Allan Shivers, ca. 1973. Bill Hobby Papers, Briscoe Center for American History.

Helen Farabee and Bill Hobby, undated. In addition to being Hobby's trusted advisor on health and human services, Helen, along with her husband, Ray, was among his closest friends. Bill Hobby Papers, Briscoe Center for American History.

Texas state senator Bob Gammage, state representative Kay Bailey, and Bill Hobby confer on pending legislation in the Senate chambers, February 1975. Hobby and Bailey (later known by her married name Hutchison) became close friends despite belonging to different political parties. AP Images. Bill Hobby Papers, Briscoe Center for American History.

Bill Hobby delivers one of his inaugural addresses. Seated behind him, left to right: *John Connally, Nellie Connally, Diana Hobby, Dolph Briscoe, Janey Briscoe, and Bill Clayton.* Bill Hobby Papers, Briscoe Center for American History.

Vicki Kessler, Jimmy Carter, and Bill Hobby, ca. 1976. Hobby was impressed with Carter's performance as governor of Georgia but was disappointed in his efforts as president. Courtesy of Ron and Vicki Kessler.

Bill Hobby and Betty King. King became secretary of the Texas Senate in 1976 and served as Hobby's close advisor for the remainder of his tenure as lieutenant governor. Bill Hobby Papers, Briscoe Center for American History.

House Speaker Gib Lewis, Lieutenant Governor Bill Hobby, and Governor Mark White meet at the Capitol, ca. 1985. Photo by Bob Daemmrich. Bob Daemmrich Collection, Briscoe Center for American History.

Bill Hobby, Governor Bill Clements, and House Speaker Gib Lewis, ca. 1988. They held regular breakfast meetings during legislative sessions. Photo by Bill Malone. Bill Hobby Papers, Briscoe Center for American History.

Bill Hobby at his desk in the lieutenant governor's office, 1980s. Photo by Bob Daemmrich. Bob Daemmrich Collection, Briscoe Center for American History.

Bob Bullock, the intense and expert comptroller of public accounts, succeeded Bill Hobby as lieutenant governor in 1991. University of Texas Office of Public Affairs records, Briscoe Center for American History.

Bill Hobby listens to the Hobby Day proceedings with his grandsons Will and Carter Beckworth on his lap. Bill Hobby Papers, Briscoe Center for American History.

Bill Cunningham and Bill Hobby, undated. Cunningham, the former chancellor of the University of Texas System, and Hobby served together on the board of Southwest Airlines and enjoyed a close friendship. Courtesy of Bill Cunningham.

Bill Hobby and the McDonald Observatory's Otto Struve Telescope, ca. 1997.
Bill Hobby Papers, Briscoe Center for American History.

Jim Granato, Bill Hobby, University of Houston Chancellor Renu Khator, and University of Houston System Chairman Emeritus Welcome Wilson Sr. unveil the Hobby Center for Public Policy logo. Courtesy of the University of Houston.

Left to right, *Chet Brooks, Grant Jones, Ray Farabee, Bill Hobby, and Max Sherman, November 2000.* Bill Hobby Papers, Briscoe Center for American History.

Diana and Bill Hobby (seated, center) *with their children and grandchildren, ca. 2004.* Bill Hobby Papers, Briscoe Center for American History.

Bill Hobby, Joe Jamail, Herb Kelleher, and Rodney Ellis attend Hobby's eighty-third birthday celebration, River Oaks Country Club, Houston, January 2015. Photo by Michelle Watson.

Although the struggle over the budget dominated the session, other issues also led to legislative fights. One of those issues was abortion. A bill placing new limits on abortions in Texas was submitted on April 13 by Senator Ted Lyon and Representative Mike Millsap, both Democrats. It prohibited late-term abortions and required parental consent for girls younger than eighteen to terminate their pregnancies. Lyon dropped the age-of-consent requirement when he ran into strong opposition from his Senate colleagues. The House revised its version of the bill by allowing abortions at any time in the case of rape or incest. The measure passed on May 18. The bill was supported by Clements, but not Hobby, who abhorred culture warriors and any attempt by government to regulate private personal behavior. "It's a terrible bill," Hobby told reporters. "It obviously is not going to be passed and should not be." Diana Hobby also opposed the bill. When the original version was submitted to a Senate committee in April, she took the highly unusual step, for her, of lobbying three senators to oppose it. She later told reporters she considered the senators—Eddie Bernice Johnson of Dallas, Chet Edwards of Duncanville, and John Whitmire of Houston—"personal friends." She explained that her calls were made as an Episcopalian and that she'd wanted to tell the legislators the church opposed the legislation. All three told the press that Diana's call had no effect on their decisions, but they also worked successfully to weaken the bill before it was passed on May 30. The final version included a provision prohibiting an abortion in the last three months of pregnancy unless a doctor determined the fetus was not capable of living outside the womb, the mother's physical or mental health was in danger, or the fetus was diagnosed as having an irreversible congenital anomaly. Despite the revisions, pro-choice supporters criticized the bill as a first step toward eroding a woman's right to abortion. Hobby kept the final version off the floor until the next to last day of the session, with the hope that time would run out before it could be passed.[18]

Reform of tort law was another contentious issue. Tort law provides a legal pathway in a civil court to redress a wrong done to a person caused by the wrongful acts of others, usually involving the award of monetary damages as compensation. Although tort law is complex and multifaceted, the demand for reform in Texas was basically driven by high insurance rates that corporations and small businesses blamed on excessive jury awards for punitive damages in personal injury cases and high legal fees. The battle pitted plaintiff's lawyers and consumer protection groups against attorneys who represented the business community. John Montford led the effort to pass tort reform in the Senate, while Kent Caperton, Carl Parker, and Craig Washington, all of whom were plaintiff's attorneys, led the battle against what they interpreted as extreme reform. According to Caperton, Hobby's natural inclination was to favor the business lobby's position. But Caperton also noted that Hobby's approach was "very measured and balanced." To find common ground, Hobby brought Montford and Caperton to his office and said, "Well guys, I hear y'all are stuck. Well, I can't have that, we've got to have a solution. I want you two guys to go somewhere and work it out." Caperton explained that it was "a classic example of the Hobby leadership style." Montford and Caperton immediately went to a private location to produce a compromise. The final bill was a true compromise in that it failed to please either side. It failed to limit attorney fees, which was what the House version had proposed, but it did cap punitive damages, although at a higher figure than the House had wanted.[19]

In his effort to wean state government off its dependence on oil and gas revenue and frustrated by the budget stalemate, Hobby decided early in the session to develop a legislative package of constitutional amendments that, if accepted by the voters in a statewide election in November, would authorize the state to issue bonds to pay for programs and projects to encourage business and entrepreneurial expansion outside of the energy economy. Inspired by the example of FDR's New Deal public works program of the 1930s, Hobby also wanted to draft amendments that would fund infrastructure construction and repairs the state badly needed, which in turn would address unemployment and help attract new businesses to the state. He was aware that there would be opposition, especially from Republicans, against the bonded debt the state would be obligated to pay off in the coming years. Nevertheless, he believed it was an especially good time for the state to take on new debt to support projects that would ultimately pay for themselves by boosting the economy and increasing tax revenues. Interest rates were at a fifteen-year low and land prices were falling rapidly. Because of the economic downturn, which had reduced construction demand, building contractors were offering heavily discounted deals to be competitive.[20]

In February, Hobby held a series of lunch meetings in the lieutenant governor's reception room with bond lawyers, economists, mortgage bankers, labor leaders, election consultants, and close political allies to develop the individual amendment proposals, which he unveiled to the public in April. The final package of eight constitutional amendments, which Hobby called the Build Texas plan, included provisions for a state economic development program that would grant and loan money to private businesses such as agricultural enterprises and a loan program for entrepreneurs who were developing new products and businesses. It also included approval to issue bonds to pay for infrastructure projects such as new toll roads, bridges, airports, convention centers, prisons, and mental healthcare facilities. Another amendment would provide bond funding for projects to clean up and prevent water pollution, control flooding, and increase the water supply for drinking and irrigation. The package had additional amendments, including one to establish a state rainy day fund for emergencies, one to continue the system of an appointed rather than elected State Board of Education, and one to provide funding to help Texas be competitive in a bid to be the site of the federally funded Superconducting Super Collider project. Hobby persuaded Lewis to support the package. He also managed to get Clements's endorsement because no new taxes would be required and the package included funding for prison expansion and economic development but not any social welfare programs. The legislature passed Hobby's Build Texas amendment package on the last day of the regular session, when it was added to a list of seventeen other proposed constitutional amendments.[21]

In mid-May, as the constitutionally mandated end of the regular session loomed ever closer and the prospect of the legislature failing to pass a state budget seemed a likely outcome, the tension between Clements and Hobby deepened. To get the state's two most powerful political leaders to reach a middle ground on the tax issue, Speaker Lewis persuaded Hobby to host Clements and the Speaker for a friendly social outing at a trapshooting course thirty miles west of Austin. They were accompanied by top aides as well as lobbyist and former senator Don Adams. After spending more than two hours shooting clay pigeons, Lewis told reporters that although no agreement had been reached on how to balance the budget, Clements and Hobby had agreed to look closely at his latest compromise proposal, which was a blend of spending cuts and additional revenue sources. They also agreed to have at least one more meeting. Otherwise, Lewis stated, "it was strictly just a very casual social type outing." Hobby didn't talk to reporters. Clements's only statement was that they had "all agreed that we wouldn't talk about our scores." As Clements was leaving the club, a reporter asked him if the state budget was discussed. "Oh, of course not," Clements responded. "We avoided that. We had a good time."[22]

Ten days before the clock ran out on the regular session, Clements and Hobby had one last private meeting in Hobby's office to reach a budget agreement. This time the participants in the meeting did not have a good time. It was a disaster. Observers later claimed the discussion degenerated into a shouting match. Clements stormed out of Hobby's office, gathered his staff members, and rushed out of the lieutenant governor's quarters in a huff. Afterward Clements complained to reporters that Hobby was "obstinate" and "unreasonable" and stated he wouldn't meet with him again. Hobby, who claimed his dispute with Clements wasn't personal, told reporters, "I would welcome a conversation with the Governor at any time." He argued that their only differences were over what the future of Texas would look like in the coming decade. Clements, however, stuck to his refusal to meet with Hobby, stressing that he would not change his mind about vetoing any budget bill that exceeded $2.9 billion. "[Hobby] apparently doesn't understand English," Clements added. "I'm not going to change [my mind]."[23]

The regular session ended at midnight on June 1 after the legislature passed bills banning late-term abortions, campus hazing, and drinking alcohol while driving. While lawmakers raised the minimum salary for beginning teachers and partially deregulated the trucking industry, they failed to pass a budget for the coming biennium. Hobby later complained they had failed to do the one thing that the constitution required them to do. The legislature also adjourned without passing several other bills, including the tort reform bill, which Senator Craig Washington filibustered to death the evening the legislature was forced to adjourn. A couple of hours after the end of the session, however, Hobby and Lewis persuaded Clements to immediately call a special session to complete work on the tort reform bill. As Hobby had guessed, the Senate easily addressed Craig Washington's concerns and then passed the bill. The legislature passed the tort reform package a day after convening in the special session. The budget was a more difficult problem, however. Clements called a special session to begin on June 22 to address that critical issue.²⁴

When the Seventieth Legislature convened in its second special session, Gib Lewis and Bill Hobby invited Comptroller Bullock to open it with a report on the status of the state's current revenue. In his typical style, Bullock told the legislators, "The last time you invited me to speak, you asked me to talk about money. I said at the time that I could make the shortest talk in legislative history: You simply didn't have any. Today, I would say you have even less." Bullock stressed that the state still faced a $6 billion shortfall. Because of Bullock's dire news, it took the legislature nearly a month to produce a new budget. Although Hobby continued to advocate passage of a state income tax, that proposal went nowhere. With an income tax not politically possible, the legislature ultimately fell back on the sales and franchise taxes. It was decided to expand coverage of the sales tax to include new areas such as garbage collection, lawn care, pest extermination, private club dues, and telephone calls, as well as to increase the franchise tax rate. The new budget bill increased support for public schools and provided money for college and university faculty merit raises. The final proposed budget totaled $38 billion, which was supported by $5.7 billion in tax increases. That was double the amount of tax Clements said he would accept. Faced with the real possibility of a veto with only six weeks left before the state ran out of money, the legislature postponed a final vote until Hobby and Lewis had a final meeting with Clements.²⁵

On July 15, Clements met with the lieutenant governor and the Speaker in the Governor's Mansion. The meeting lasted into the evening. "We were tired and grouchy," Hobby recalled. "Gib Lewis wanted to wrap things up and 'get out of Dodge.' So did I, but I wasn't willing to squander our children's heritage—and Texas's future." With help from George Bayoud, a key member of Clements's staff who was also present, they finally wore Clements down. The governor agreed to step outside with Hobby and Lewis to announce to reporters that he would not veto the new budget and its tax package. On July 21, the legislature passed the budget bill. The vote in the Senate was twenty-five to six in favor. Clements kept his promise and signed the bill a few hours after the legislature passed it. Two days later, when Hobby spoke at a reception in Houston, he admitted, "We have just finished the toughest legislative session I have endured in 14 years of public service. We did what we had to do. We got the best result possible under very adverse circumstances."²⁶

The tax increase was the largest in Texas history. According to Hobby, when Clements was asked why he changed his mind about the bill after vigorously opposing it for seven months, he replied that Hobby and Lewis wore him down during the meeting and he "was sleepy and I wanted to get to bed." The governor's unexpected decision stunned his friends and foes alike. When several Republican legislators criticized Clements publicly for signing the budget bill, he dismissed their complaints and explained that he was forced to do it because of Mark White's mismanagement during his term as governor. He also blamed Hobby. In a letter to his supporters, Clements wrote, "No one, including me, was totally happy with the outcome. I'm convinced more spending reductions were possible, but Lt. Governor Hobby would not agree. The budget stalemate that he and the other big spenders created threatened to close down services vital to Texas."[27]

Hobby and several members of the Capitol press corps believed that one reason Clements changed his mind was because of his personal involvement in an ongoing scandal in the football program at Southern Methodist University in Dallas. Clements had been a member of SMU's board of trustees until he resigned after winning election in November 1986. A year earlier, the National Collegiate Athletic Association had placed SMU's football program on probation for breaking NCAA rules against paying athletes money or providing them in-kind gifts. It was the sixth time in recent years that the NCAA had punished SMU for breaking its rules. In late February 1987 the NCAA announced it had learned SMU's board members, including Clements, had continued to make cash payments to football players even after the school had been placed on probation. As a result, the NCAA applied the so-called death penalty to SMU's football program by banning it from playing intercollegiate football games in the 1987 football season. At a press conference held a week after the NCAA decision, Clements admitted for the first time that he and other members of the SMU board had indeed been paying the university's football players—as the NCAA had charged and Clements had denied—and that they had continued those payments for several months after the school had been sanctioned. Clements confessed that he had lied to the NCAA when its investigators interviewed him in 1986, but he explained that there had been "no Bible in the room." After Clements made his confession, some members of the legislature urged their colleagues to join them to impeach Clements once the special session passed a budget. Dave McNeely later observed that Clements finally signed the budget bill because with threats of impeachment hanging in the air, he was eager "to get the legislature out of town as soon as possible."[28]

Although Clements backed off from his threat to veto the tax bill, he still extracted a relatively small amount of revenge on his opponents in the higher education coalition by exercising his power to veto line items in the budget. He went after the administrators of the state's college and university systems by vetoing a total of $167.4 million from their operational budgets. Clements also tried to veto other allocations for higher education, but he was foiled by a legislative maneuver that had lumped money for colleges and universities into "protective riders" he couldn't veto on a line-item basis. While he had his veto pen out, Clements also wacked $16.2 million from the state's program to protect children from abuse and neglect. In addition, Clements was able to force Jess Hay to step aside as chairman of the University of Texas System Board of Regents, although Hay remained on the board. In an interview with a reporter after Clements exercised his line-item veto power, Hobby attacked the governor, pointing out that the vetoes "were very heavily directed at education." Hobby declared that Clements's actions were evidence of his anti-education mentality. "[Clements] damaged SMU a lot [and] when he was [deputy secretary] in the Defense Department, he damaged higher education there."

Hobby claimed Clements had opposed the policy of supporting postgraduate education for midcareer naval officers. Hobby characterized Clements's attitude as "kind of a 'I've got mine, Jack, let's pull the ladder up.'" After all was said and done, *Texas Monthly*'s Paul Burka reported that by the end of the special session in 1987, "the two men viewed each other with the total disdain that only Old Money and New Money can have for each other, but in the end, Old Money won and Hobby had his way."[29]

Despite Clements's vetoes, passing the budget was an overall victory for Hobby and the educational coalition that had worked so hard to protect funding for higher education. The legislature also financed a prison building and renovation program with bonds instead of tax revenues. "There's no question in my mind that the hero of the total effort was Bill Hobby," Jess Hay later observed. "He was constant, and in his gentle way, he carefully led the Senate to take the lead in providing support, which was absolutely vital and necessary to the achievement of our objectives."[30]

Although Hobby hadn't officially announced his candidacy for governor, it was assumed throughout the great battle over the budget during the Seventieth Legislature that he would run and that he would be the front-runner. Accordingly, members of the legislature, the Capitol press corps, the leaders of the state Republican Party, and Governor Clements's administrative team suspected that every move Hobby made as lieutenant governor during the session was influenced by his supposed intention to run for governor. Potential rivals in the Democratic primary, such as San Antonio's mayor Henry Cisneros, sent assurances to Hobby they wouldn't run against him.[31]

As expected, incumbent attorney general Jim Mattox, a forty-four-year-old native of Dallas who was eager to run for governor, was not among those who decided to get out of Hobby's way. By late 1986, Mattox had already launched a fundraising drive for his campaign for the Democratic gubernatorial nomination. Mattox's eyes were firmly set on Bill Hobby, whom he perceived to be the one person standing between him and his residency in the Governor's Mansion. Mattox invited a group of state labor leaders to a lunch meeting in Irving on June 3 to discuss his interest in running for governor in 1990. "I believe the trend bodes well for a successful Democratic primary race in 1990 against Hobby," he told one labor leader. "Current public opinion polls indicate my name ID exceeds Hobby's."[32]

Mattox promised in his speeches that the 1990 primary would be a "classic race" between a representative of the "country club set" and a candidate for the common people—the former being Bill Hobby and the latter Jim Mattox. The attorney general relished his reputation for "junk-yard dog" political rhetoric. A joke about Mattox that circulated among the members of the Capitol press corps at the time was if someone was passing out ice cream on one corner and there was a fistfight on the other corner, Jim Mattox would head straight to the fistfight.[33]

Almost from the start of the regular legislative session, Mattox gave speeches mocking Hobby for his wealth and ridiculing him "as a prissy, horsey-set blueblood disconnected from common folk of Texas." One of Mattox's political consultants discovered that Hobby owned a stable full of thoroughbred horses in Houston, and that Bill and Diana vacationed every year in Ireland, where they hunted foxes. After his staff did some research, they learned that a traditional ritual of equestrian foxhunters was to wear expensive red ensembles when they rode after the foxes. Dressing in those red suits was known as "putting on the pinks." Mattox quickly realized that he had the perfect tool for making fun of the Hobbys in a way that stressed their status as members of the elite upper class supposedly out of touch with the everyday problems of average Texans. In a speech to the annual convention of the League of United Latin American Citizens (LULAC) in Corpus Christi, Mattox asked, "Do you know what putting on the pinks is? It's probably not part of your heritage, nor mine either. Putting on the pinks is when you go out there and put on your little red riding coat, and your little pants, your high-top shoes, and chase the foxes through the woods." Mattox then charged that Texas had "too many people that are worried about putting on the pinks, and not worried about whether the average man and woman can feed his or her family and pay his taxes." Saralee Tiede recalled that Mattox "started taking potshots at Hobby. Just nasty stuff. Mattox would get on the phone with reporters and talk trash." According to one source, Mattox even leaked to the press that he had compiled a file on Hobby's alleged past misadventures, but it turned out no such folder existed.[34]

Hobby refused to react publicly to Mattox's gutter-type speeches. One reason was his full-time involvement in the budget battle with Clements, which left him no time to engage in a fight with Mattox. However, on one occasion in July when a reporter for the *Houston Chronicle* asked him how he felt about the possibility of running against Mattox in the 1990 primary, Hobby replied that "a weaker candidate than Mattox one could not imagine." That was essentially all that Hobby cared to say about Mattox in public. In private, he made it clear that he thought Mattox was "a son-of-bitch."[35]

With the 1987 budget war over, Hobby had a major decision to make about the 1990 election and his political future. Saralee Tiede recalled that if Hobby "was going to run, he had to make up his mind to do it. Fundraising was to start in September and a decision had to be made." On Monday, July 27, six days after the legislature passed the biennial state budget and after spending the weekend in Tampa, Florida, attending a political conference about the upcoming presidential election in 1988, Hobby released a statement through his Capitol office announcing that he would not run for reelection as lieutenant governor or be a candidate for governor or for any other elected office in 1990. "I have been asked frequently in recent weeks about whether I am a candidate for governor in 1990," Hobby declared. "The answer is no." Saralee Tiede later stated that she "kind of assumed that was probably going to happen. But he had not been saying anything. He had just let people speculate. I don't remember any particular conversation with Hobby to the extent that 'Oh I'm tired of it, I don't want to do it anymore. I've done all I can.' But I think there was some sense that he was done with it. And, of course, there was Jim Mattox."[36]

Two days later, at the urging of his staff, who were being deluged with requests for interviews with the lieutenant governor, Hobby agreed to hold a press conference in the Capitol to answer questions about his decision and his future plans. Dressed in a white, short-sleeved dress shirt but with no jacket, he stood behind a podium, surrounded by a large contingent of journalists and television crews. Hobby flashed a broad smile and declared, "Contrary to what apparently is popular opinion, I have not died. I will be lieutenant governor of Texas for 3½ years." He admitted that there was some truth in speculation that he had seriously considered running for governor, but he'd concluded he could "better serve the state of Texas by devoting all my time to the office I now occupy." He worried the belief held by members of the Senate that he might run for governor had hampered his effectiveness as lieutenant governor during the past legislative session. He wanted to eliminate political considerations during his last years in office. When asked if he might run against Republican US senator Phil Gramm in 1990, Hobby declined to rule it out but stressed that it was unlikely.[37]

Addressing speculation in the news media that his aversion to campaigning was one reason for his decision, Hobby said he disliked "putting myself forward, projecting myself. I don't like to read stories in the paper or see myself on television. I'm just not basically that kind of person. In 14 years, how many races have I done, counting primaries and general elections? I don't like doing it, but I've done it successfully for a number of years." He also denied the rumor that he was not running in 1990 because he wanted to lobby the legislature in the next session in 1989 to pass a state income tax, which might make him unelectable. He noted that Texas had taken the sales tax as high as it could go and that "clearly the tax system needs to be restructured," but he had "no preconceptions or predispositions one or the other" about an income tax. Finally, when a reporter asked if Jim Mattox was electable, Hobby smiled and said, "If he gets reelected, yes." Otherwise, Hobby refrained from mentioning Mattox.[38]

Although Hobby said nothing about how much Mattox's personal attacks had influenced his decision not to be a candidate for governor, there's little doubt that they did play a significant role. Three days after Hobby released his statement, *Austin American-Statesman* editorial columnist Arnold Rosenfeld, who had been a reporter for the *Houston Post* in the 1960s, wrote that "Jim Mattox recently roughed Hobby up, unfairly and gratuitously as a creature of privilege who could not care about the poor and underdog. Hobby's character and record belie the charge, but Mattox had delivered a credible hint at what was to come." Rosenfeld added, "Unfortunately, impressions can be falsely transformed in the minds of voters as realities. If Bill Hobby has decided who needs it, who can blame him?" Dave McNeely agreed with Rosenfeld. He wrote that Hobby didn't look forward to enduring a mean and nasty campaign with Mattox, who was certain to bring attention to and make misleading innuendoes about the incident when Hobby was accused of spanking a neighbor's child, his DWI arrest in 1974, and the night when his daughter and her friends were spending the night in the lieutenant governor's apartment when a fire broke out that killed one of the guests. No matter how unfair and inaccurate Mattox's remarks might be, Hobby simply didn't want his family involved. "There's no question Hobby was not only troubled by the shift in partisan politics," Saralee Tiede observed, "but also by the shift in the style of campaigning. In the past, with the exception of the campaign against Wayne Connally in 1972, most of his campaigns had been unofficially governed by gentlemen's agreements. With Mattox, the gloves would be taken off. Everything was fair game, every kind of innuendo would be made."[39]

Dave McNeely and Jim Henderson believed that Hobby's dislike of campaigning was a factor in his decision. They pointed out that if Hobby became a candidate for the gubernatorial nomination, he would have to spend the next three years flying to small towns across Texas, where he would have to ride in parades down main streets, eat rubber chicken at endless lunch meetings, and generally do nothing else but run for governor. "To Mattox, who has spent his whole life running for office, that's fun," McNeely and Henderson wrote. "To Hobby, it's work." Saralee Tiede also pointed out that the battle with Clements had tired him. "He had dealt with Clements, which was taxing. And the number of Republican legislators was growing. He was having to deal with the more ideologically doctrinaire Republicans who were taking their talking points from [President] Reagan." Years later, Hobby admitted in an oral history interview, "I just didn't have the same level of fire in my belly in 1987. Eighteen years is a long time. That was enough, you know? I strongly disliked campaigning and the backslapping that went with it. And the thought of having to get into the campaign gutter with someone like Mattox was not very appealing."[40]

Austin political journalist and broadcaster Winston Bode wrote in his political and legislative newsletter, *On the Avenue*, that Mattox and his ability to attract media headlines and throw mud was a significant factor in Hobby's decision. Bode guessed, correctly, that Hobby's "brain trust" members George Christian and Don Adams had played a major role in shaping Hobby's announcement, especially the message that he would be no lame duck during the legislative session in 1989. Bode added, "The truth of the matter is that while Hobby's savvy will be available to state government" and his skill in presiding over the Senate sessions would be helpful during the next regular session, "his announcement has caused him to become a steadily diminishing figure." Hobby's tenure in office, Bode offered, "has been marked by decency and statesmanlike planning for the future, and by a certain self-effacing humor and sense of humanity and appreciation of the ludicrous." But Bode's newsletter article also had a mocking tone. It featured a headline that played on the lieutenant governor's love of horseback riding: "Hobby *Gallops* Down the High Road." Referring to Hobby's "playboy-tinged lifestyle" and his elitist sense of noblesse oblige, Bode wrote that by accomplishing some of his legislative goals in the Seventy-First Legislature, Hobby could go back to Houston where he could "use his wealth and position to pursue the horsey, socializing life he has always so enjoyed."[41]

Whatever the reasons for Hobby's decision, the announcement stunned the state's political activists and news media. Mattox was delighted. He immediately issued a statement that he "was not looking forward to a race against Bill Hobby. He enjoys wide and strong support. I am relieved he will not be making that race." On hearing the news, Bill Clements declared, "While we may have different political philosophies, I have a great deal of respect for Bill Hobby." Bob Bullock, who was eager to seek the lieutenant governor's job, told reporters, "Bill Hobby knows more about state government than any person alive. His record will be unequaled for decades to come and I suspect his talents will be sorely missed." Interestingly, in their own way, Mattox's, Clements's, and Bullock's statements about Hobby clearly reflected their actual feelings about his decision and his record.[42]

Immediately after he made his surprise decision, Hobby turned his attention to the campaign to persuade Texas voters to approve his pet project, the Build Texas plan, in November. Before launching the campaign in September, however, Hobby decided to take a break from his work. After a difficult seven months fighting the budget war and the stress of making his decision about his political future, he and Diana needed to escape Austin and take most of August off for rest and relaxation.

On July 31, accompanied by Ray and Kay Bailey Hutchison, Bill and Diana flew in the Hobbys' airplane to Eagle, Colorado, from where they were driven to the Hutchisons' roomy condominium in Beaver Creek Resort. The Hutchisons, who resided in Dallas, had become close friends with the Hobbys, and they occasionally traveled together on vacation. They also frequently socialized in Austin and in Dallas when Bill and Diana were visiting the latter city. "We were good friends," Kay Bailey Hutchison later recalled. "We had a group which included Ray and me, Bill and Diana, Jess and Betty Jo Hay, and Ron and Vicki Kessler. It was all very informal. We could laugh, and we could debate and have fun doing it." Hutchison noted that she and Ray were stalwart Republicans, and the other members of the group were Democrats, but their party affiliations had no effect on their friendship. "We weren't political at all when we got together."[43]

Once he was back in Texas from his vacation, Hobby turned his attention to the campaign for his $1.9 billion Build Texas plan. Because 1987 was an off-year election with no statewide candidates on the ballot to attract voter attention, he anticipated a low voter turnout, which typically meant an election dominated by "the crazy antispending crowd." Hobby also feared that the long length of the ballot—which was filled with twenty-five amendments printed in single-spaced text—would intimidate and confuse voters. Because of these concerns, Hobby approached the campaign as if he were a candidate. He hired George Christian and George Shipley to provide overall management. Christian and his team produced and distributed a variety of fact sheets and brochures explaining the wording of the amendments and how each would help the state, with an emphasis on economic benefits and infrastructure improvements. They also bought radio spot ads, set up telephone banks, and initiated a direct mail program. Hobby enlisted help from some of his Senate colleagues, including Ray Farabee, Carl Parker, John Montford, and Kent Caperton. Dallas senator Eddie Bernice Johnson helped Hobby in Dallas. She organized a meeting in the Capitol that gave Hobby an opportunity to promote the amendments to minority business leaders. Hobby also made personal appearances at meetings in various locations around Texas where he could discuss the issues thoroughly. It was a grueling schedule that spanned the state from the far northeast (an appearance with Senator A. M. Aiken Jr. in Paris, Texas), to the far west (a speech to religious leaders in El Paso), to far South Texas (a meeting with Valley interfaith leaders in Brownsville), and included speeches in nine other Texas towns and cities as well as multiple appearances in Austin and Houston.

Hobby felt explanations were needed because some of the amendments had potential ramifications that weren't obvious in their wording. One example was the amendment to appoint rather than elect the members of the State Board of Education. Hobby and Ross Perot worried that its defeat would lead to a weakening of the Perot educational reforms, but that possibility was not readily apparent in the language of the amendment. In addition, Hobby scheduled meetings with the editorial boards of the major daily newspapers in Dallas–Fort Worth, Houston, Austin, and San Antonio.[44]

Ann Richards joined Hobby in Austin at what was billed as the official launch of the Build Texas campaign on October 1, although Hobby had been promoting the amendments since the beginning of September. At that joint appearance with Richards, Hobby predicted the passage of the economic enhancement amendments would result in fifty thousand new jobs. "For three or four decades," Hobby said, "Texas' economy has been booming, which made financing with bonds unnecessary. But in a depressed economy it makes sense to go into debt to make the state a better competitor in the struggle to stimulate business." Richards also appeared with Hobby to promote the amendments at other events away from Austin. And she traveled with him to New York City to meet with executives at the brokerage and investment firm Bear Stearns to discuss how the state's bonds would be managed and sold if any or all of the bond amendments passed. While in Manhattan Hobby and Richards attended a performance of the hit Broadway show *Les Misérables*. Hobby was not a fan of operas or symphonies, but he relished musicals.

After Hobby returned to Houston from New York, he and Diana attended the September 28 dedication in Houston's Hermann Park of an outdoor bronze sculpture of explorer Álvar Núñez Cabeza de Vaca that the government of Spain donated to the city. The ceremony included a luncheon at the Warwick Hotel in honor of Spain's monarchs, King Juan Carlos I and Queen Sofía, with Bill and Diana seated at the head table with the royal couple. Following that brief break, Hobby soon went back on the campaign trail. On one Sunday in mid-October, he addressed the congregations at four separate Black churches. Hobby finished the campaign with an op-ed column for the Harte-Hanks newspaper chain and for the *Houston Chronicle*, speeches to the Texas Association of Taxpayers in Austin and to the Greater Houston Association Political Action Committee, and a meeting with the editorial board of the *Fort Worth Star-Telegram*.[45]

On October 24, Hobby ended his Build Texas campaign, voted early, and then embarked on an extended trip overseas, going first to Israel with Ray and Helen Farabee, followed by an overnight stay in London, where his youngest daughter, Kate, was working as an intern. Kate had graduated from the University of Virginia the previous May. Bill and the entire Hobby family—including Joan Robins, who served as nanny to the Hobby kids when they were young—had attended the graduation ceremony. Kate later recalled that when her father visited her in London, he wasn't interested in touring the city's museums but instead indulged his love of musicals by taking her to see *The Phantom of the Opera*. The next day, Hobby flew to Ireland's Shannon Airport and then linked up with Diana in a tiny village in rural County Tipperary. The Hobbys leased for the entire month of November the historic two-story Beechwood House, a former Church of Ireland rectory built in the early nineteenth century. The house served as the base from which they participated in their annual fox hunts in nearby Scarteen, County Limerick.[46]

On November 4, three days after the Hobbys had settled into Beechwood House, Hobby's office in Austin sent him the news that voters had accepted four of the amendments in the Build Texas plan, while voting down the other four. Among the losing amendments was one to provide loans to entrepreneurs to develop new products or to start new businesses. Although Hobby was unhappy about that loss, he was even more chagrined by the defeat of the amendment to maintain the system of appointing members of the State Board of Education. He was also disappointed to learn that the specific amendment to allow the sale of bonds to provide water to most of the colonias had been rejected, along with other local infrastructure projects. Polling later indicated voters were fearful that those local projects would ultimately be paid for with higher taxes levied locally. Nevertheless, Hobby was pleased that the supercollider and the infrastructure amendments, particularly those supporting statewide water projects and the expansion of mental health facilities, had passed. He believed those amendments were among the most important in the package. In a statement he sent to his staff to give to reporters, Hobby, who was identified as "vacationing in Ireland," admitted disappointment in the "mixed decision from the voters." *Austin American-Statesman* columnist Dave McNeely noted that the defeat of some of the amendments "could be seen as a negative for Hobby, who traveled the state selling the idea," but that "some of the amendments may have gone down simply because voters didn't understand them." That had been one of Hobby's fears before the election.[47]

Never one to fret much about an election disappointment, especially one with mixed results, Bill moved on quickly to other interests. Free of the need to run a race for elected office during at least the next three years, Hobby's political plans for the new year included his active involvement in the upcoming presidential campaign, the reelection bids of key members of his legislative team in the state Senate, and the effort to elect candidates for membership on the State Board of Education who would preserve the educational reforms of 1984. The "No Pass, No Play" reforms were among the legislative accomplishments that Hobby was most proud of helping to achieve.

Hobby's friend and close political advisor George Christian told the *Austin American-Statesman* that although his friend was free of any personal political campaigns, Hobby still had "a tough three years ahead of him. The fiscal issues in the 1989 session are probably going to be worse than the last session. I agree with his notion that he doesn't want politics and partisanship interfering with what he has to do."[48]

CHAPTER 16

THE PRESIDENTIAL ELECTION OF 1988

A couple of weeks after Bill and Diana Hobby returned to Houston on December 1, 1987, after a month-long stay in Ireland, they left once more for a three-week tour of India and Nepal with Max and Gene Sherman. Before their departure, Bill's chief of staff, Saralee Tiede, gave him a memorandum in which she expressed in detail her concerns about the state of Hobby's staff. Soon after Hobby had announced back in July that he would not be a candidate for elected office in 1990, some of his staff naturally began to drift away to other jobs, leaving several unfilled vacancies, including the important position of press spokesperson. Tiede reminded her boss that there was "much unfinished business" to address before he left office and that he needed a full staff to accomplish his remaining goals. A few of those goals, including a resolution of the seemingly intractable problem of school financing, were going to be extremely difficult to achieve. Hobby respected Tiede's judgment and heeded her advice. He quickly approved the appointment of Glenn Smith, a former *Houston Post* reporter, to serve as his new press spokesman, while also urging Tiede to fill all remaining job vacancies.[1]

After Hobby returned to his Capitol office a month later, he focused on the challenges ahead. Although the next legislative session was still a year away, he wanted to work in the coming months on building a coalition in the Senate to help him achieve his goals for his last session as lieutenant governor. Some of the senators on whom Hobby depended for support of his legislative agenda, including Grant Jones and Richard Anderson, were facing tough challenges in the Democratic primary and in the general election in November. Hobby planned to help their reelection efforts and to be a far more active player in Democratic Party politics than ever before.

Because of the defeat of the amendment to continue to appoint rather than elect members of the State Board of Education, Hobby also worked with Ross Perot in 1988 to support candidates for membership on the board who would preserve the educational reforms of 1984. Accordingly, he and Perot formed a political action committee and recruited sixty business, civic, and education leaders to join with them to help elect candidates who supported the Perot public-school reforms to the State Board of Education. In addition, Hobby planned to be actively involved in the upcoming US presidential campaign. Hobby was eager to see a moderate Democrat in the White House who could reverse the Reagan administration's social and economic policies, which Hobby felt were harmful to public education, social welfare, and other critical components of civil society.[2]

As Hobby initiated his campaign efforts in the new year, he was delighted to hear positive economic news after three long years of fiscal difficulties. In a speech in Edinburg, Texas, on January 21, Bob Bullock predicted the Texas economy was on its way to recovery in 1988. "Areas least tied to the oil industry will recover fastest. We feel like the worst is over." Three months later, Bullock had even better news. He estimated that by the time the Texas Legislature convened in January 1989, the state would have a $300 to $400 million budget surplus. Hobby received the news with pleasure, noting it indicated actions taken in the Seventieth Legislature were having an effect. And he was pleased that manufacturing, including high tech, was the fastest-growing sector of the economy. "This is not just good news for the immediate future," Hobby told a business organization at a luncheon in San Antonio, "it is an indication that leaders of both the private and public sectors have moved to diversify the once oil-dependent Texas economy into other healthier areas." Hobby cited the recent news that Sematech, a consortium of electronic firms that made semiconductors, had decided to locate operations in Austin. He also observed that Texas had promising prospects for winning its bid for the supercollider. Both operations were expected to bring high-paying jobs to the state and create new businesses related to those projects.[3]

Heartened by the promising economic news, Hobby went on the road during most of January and February to help the members of his Senate team who faced challengers in the March 8 Democratic Party primary. A few of his Senate allies who were running for reelection, including John Montford and Carl Parker, were heavily favored over their opponents, but Hobby still showed his support by speaking at a reception or a dinner held in their honor in their home bases. Grant Jones and freshman senator Richard Anderson, however, faced more serious challenges, so Hobby concentrated his efforts on their campaigns. Both men were strong allies of Hobby, but of the two, Jones's reelection was the most crucial to the success of Hobby's legislative plans. Jones, whose district included Abilene and surrounding counties in west central Texas, had worked closely with Hobby as chair of the powerful Senate Finance Committee during the Seventieth Legislature. Hobby intended to reappoint Jones to head the committee and counted on his playing a key role in the effort to pass tax reform during the upcoming legislative session in 1989.[4]

Near the end of January, Hobby accompanied Jones on a tour of several towns in

Jones's senatorial district, including Brady, where they toured an assembly plant with fifteen reporters in tow, and Gatesville, where Hobby and Jones spoke at a rally at the airport. In the latter town, Hobby told the crowd that Jones was responsible for the constitutional amendment, passed the year before, that provided funding for new prisons, including a $60 million unit for men that would soon be under construction near Gatesville and would create new jobs for the community. Hobby also worked for Anderson's reelection, including hosting a fundraising reception in Houston and speaking at a fundraising barbecue in the senator's hometown of Marshall. Hobby made an extra effort on behalf of Anderson, who was facing a fierce challenge from the conservative mayor of Kilgore, having voted in 1987 for the tax increase despite knowing it would be used against him by his opponent.[5]

On March 8, primary election day, Bill and Diana joined Lloyd Bentsen and his wife, B. A., in the lieutenant governor's reception room for an election watch party. It was an easy night for Bentsen, who defeated a token opponent to become the Democratic nominee for the US Senate for the fourth time. With one significant exception, Hobby's team, including Montford, Parker, and Anderson, were renominated. Hobby was especially gratified by Richard Anderson's victory. However, former Texas House member Temple Dickson, a lawyer and rancher from Sweetwater, defeated Grant Jones, which stunned and disappointed Hobby. When a reporter asked Hobby why he thought Jones lost, he answered in his usual cryptic style: "He didn't get enough votes." Jones's loss was a double whammy for Hobby because another close ally, Ray Farabee, was leaving the Senate to assume the position of general counsel of the University of Texas System. Some legislative observers predicted that Hobby would have much more difficulty passing tax reform and overhauling the workers' compensation system because of losing Jones and Farabee. "You can't take two key leaders out of that Senate and expect it to be the same," George Christian argued. "It's a critical loss. This morning Bill Hobby probably feels like he lost both arms."[6]

While Hobby was campaigning for his Senate team, he was also involved in the state's Democratic presidential primary, which was held the same day as the regular primary. His deep interest in the 1988 presidential election became apparent back in March 1987, when presidential hopeful Gary Hart, the former US senator from Colorado, visited Austin while on an early campaign tour. Hobby hosted a reception and press conference in the Capitol for Hart, whom Hobby introduced as "the next president of the United States." Those words surprised the Capitol press corps as well as Hobby's own political advisors, who had urged him to remain publicly neutral until at least early 1988. The surprise was not so much that Hobby was supporting Hart but that his support was announced so early. But Hobby was enthusiastic about Hart and saw no reason to wait to endorse him. He agreed with Hart's policy positions, particularly his support of an oil import fee, and he believed Hart was going to win the nomination and that he would be the Democrats' strongest candidate against George H. W. Bush. A month later, Hobby and Ray Farabee hosted a reception and fundraising dinner in Houston for Hart. Hobby told his guests, "All of us in Houston know about debt these days. The State of Texas is in the red and so is Gary Hart. Let's help him retire that debt and proceed to the primaries."[7]

At the end of May 1987, a scandal resulting from his extramarital affair forced Hart to withdraw from the presidential race. Hobby then switched his endorsement to Tennessee's Al Gore, pledging his support to the senator during a private dinner at Austin's historic Driskill Hotel in mid-August 1987. Hobby knew much about Gore because of the Hobby family's ownership of a television station in Nashville. "I have always admired your leadership and valued your friendship," Hobby told Gore. "Of course, I must warn you as a friend that my endorsement carries with it certain hazards. For further guidance in this respect, you might consult former Senator Hart and Senator Glenn." Hobby attended a fundraising dinner for Gore in Dallas on February 10, 1988. The event, hosted by Jess Hay, added more than $700,000 to Gore's campaign treasure chest. Prior to the dinner, Hobby and Gore held a joint press conference at which Hobby urged Texas Democrats to vote for Gore in the March primary. He cited Gore's support for education, social justice, and "economic restraint." Hobby argued that Gore "best represents [the] Texas point of view," adding that as a southerner and a military hawk, Gore had the best chance of all the candidates to carry Texas in November's general election.[8]

Two weeks prior to the March 8, 1988, Democratic primary, Hobby recorded a message for Gore that his campaign played on radio stations: "This is Lieutenant Governor Bill Hobby. Al Gore's been listening to Texas. He thinks as we do. He thinks government should serve, not stand in the way. When Al Gore is president, we'll stop importing oil from countries that support terrorism. That's why I'm supporting Senator Al Gore of Tennessee for president." Although Gore ran a distant second to Massachusetts governor Michael Dukakis in Texas, he won several Southern states, including Tennessee, which convinced him to remain in the race at least through the New York primary in April. But when Dukakis beat Gore badly in that primary, Gore suspended his campaign. As a result, Hobby, who had already lost his enthusiasm for Gore because of his defeat in the Texas primary, switched his support to Dukakis, whom he had met in June 1987, when Hobby hosted a reception for the governor when he visited Austin.[9]

A few days after Dukakis defeated Gore in the Texas primary, Democratic National Committee chair Paul Kirk appointed Hobby chair of the committee's Victory Fund in Texas. The mission of the Texas fund was to raise money for all the state's Democratic candidates. Jim Calaway, a Houston oilman and Democratic Party fundraiser who was serving as national chairman of the Victory Fund, delivered Kirk's invitation to Hobby. Before his association with Calaway, Hobby had generally avoided official involvement in general political fundraising because of his need to raise money for his own campaigns. His leadership in Calaway's organization lured Hobby deeper into the Democratic presidential race. As one political commentator noted, Democratic Party leaders hoped Hobby's active involvement in the campaign would persuade moderate white businessmen whose support and money had been denied to Democratic presidential candidates in the recent past to return to the fold.[10]

Hobby was an active chairman of the Victory Fund. On May 5 he and Calaway spoke at a luncheon in Houston, and Hobby introduced the main speaker, Senator John D. "Jay" Rockefeller IV. Afterward, Hobby and Calaway flew to San Antonio, where they reunited with Rockefeller to speak at a Victory Fund reception and dinner at the Hyatt Regency Hotel. Before Hobby became immersed in the political campaign as the chair of the fund, he and Diana took time on May 6 and 7 to participate in the celebration of the centennial of the 1888 dedication of the Texas Capitol, including attending a gala grand ball, a parade on Congress Avenue in drizzling rain, and a ceremony in the House Chamber. In the latter ceremony, Hobby, Bill Clements, and Gib Lewis gave speeches lauding the foresight of the state's leaders in the 1880s who made construction of the massive building possible. The Capitol, Hobby declared, is "a monument to the strength and resourcefulness that have marked the history of Texas."[11]

A few days after the centennial celebration, Bill and Diana continued their almost frenetic lifestyle by flying to the United Kingdom with a group of friends that included Gib and Sandra Lewis. Joined by their daughter Kate, the Hobbys stayed at the Castle Hotel in Windsor, where they and the other members of their party spent three days attending various Royal Windsor Horse Show events as well as a performance of *The Phantom of the Opera* and a tour of the English countryside. On May 16, Diana returned to Houston, while Bill flew to Washington, DC, where he spent three days attending Hobby & Catto (H&C) business meetings with Jessica and Henry Catto, Jim Crowther, H&C Washington bureau personnel, and the general managers and news directors of the six H&C television stations. The entire group also met with legislators on May 19 to build relationships with members of Congress who represented the H&C television broadcast areas.[12]

On May 27, Hobby resumed his Victory Fund work, joining Gib Lewis, Ann Richards, and Garry Mauro as one of the featured speakers at a rally for Dukakis at Waterloo Park in Austin. Three weeks later, when the Texas Democratic Party held its state convention in Houston, Bill and Diana Hobby hosted a $1,000-per-person outdoor fundraising luncheon for Dukakis at their home in Houston. Speaking at the luncheon, Dukakis pointed at Lloyd Bentsen and praised him for recently helping Congress pass a welfare reform bill. "I know that you are proud of him, and I am, and I look forward to working with him next year in a Democratic Congress." The next day, Hobby further demonstrated his strong support for Dukakis's nomination by introducing the Massachusetts governor when he addressed the Democratic State Convention. Hobby was also elected a member of the Texas delegation to the Democratic National Convention, which was scheduled for Atlanta in July.[13]

The night before the Hobbys hosted the luncheon for Dukakis at their home, the Texas Democratic Party held a campaign kickoff dinner in honor of Bill Hobby at the downtown Houston Hyatt Regency Hotel. The dinner featured Bob Bullock and several of Hobby's allies in the Texas Senate, including Bob Glasgow, Hugh Parmer, Chet Brooks, and Chet Edwards. Each gave speeches praising the lieutenant governor. Before

Hobby made his remarks, Ann Richards delivered a humorous introduction with jokes about his lack of interest in how his clothes or hair looked.[14]

In Houston on the morning of July 12, a week before he and Diana were scheduled to fly to Atlanta to attend the Democratic National Convention, Bill heard the news that Dukakis had announced that if he won the party's nomination for president (which was practically assured), he would select Lloyd Bentsen to be his running mate. Bentsen was up for reelection to the US Senate in November, but a special Texas law passed in 1959 to allow LBJ to run simultaneously for the Senate and the presidency was still in force, which enabled Bentsen to run for reelection as well as for vice president. The unexpected possibility that Texas would have a vacant US Senate seat if Dukakis was elected president grabbed the keen attention of several Texas politicians who aspired to become a member of the upper chamber of Congress. Those aspirants included Bill Hobby, who immediately canceled the appointments he had scheduled in Houston for the day and arranged for Bob Cargill to fly him to Austin at noon to hold a news conference in the Senate Chamber that same afternoon.[15]

Hobby told reporters at the news conference that if the Dukakis-Bentsen ticket won the election in November, he would seriously consider running for the Senate seat Bentsen would be vacating. "I think the U.S. Senate is the greatest deliberative body in the world," Hobby stated. US senators had the opportunity "to have influence over national policy in many areas and to shape the future of the country." Hobby admitted that if Bentsen left the Senate, several political officeholders in Texas would also enter the contest to replace him, because it was an unusual opportunity for a free ride in a special election that would not require candidates to give up their current offices to run. When a reporter reminded Hobby that he had announced he would not be a candidate for any elected office in the near future, Hobby replied, "Circumstances have changed." Nevertheless, Hobby stressed, "First things first, we must elect Michael Dukakis president and Lloyd Bentsen vice president." That goal was achievable, he added, because the Dukakis-Bentsen ticket "is the best since the Kennedy-Johnson ticket in 1960."[16]

Four days after the press conference, Hobby was back in Austin, where he and Diana attended a benefit for the Texas Women's Political Caucus honoring Ann Richards. A highlight of the event was a program called "Capitol Comics" featuring Molly Ivins, Austin radio personality Cactus Pryor, comedian Jaston Williams, and Esther's Follies cofounder and comedian Shannon Sedwick. One of the program's comedy skits was a scripted newsroom interview, with Pryor and Ivins posing as news anchors interviewing Bill Hobby about Ann Richards. Ivins, who had long referred to Hobby in her newspaper column as "our Lite-Guv-for Life," had a field day with Hobby. She joked that he had decided not to run against Jim Mattox because "his advisors told him he couldn't even take a vacation—no fox-hunting in Ireland, which is what Hobby actually does for fun. Who the hell ever heard of a Governor of Texas who fox-hunts?" Hobby later admitted that he enjoyed the humorous skewering.[17]

On Monday, July 18, Bill and Diana flew to Atlanta to attend the Democratic National

Convention, where Dukakis easily defeated Reverend Jesse Jackson for the party's presidential nomination, and Lloyd Bentsen secured the convention's nomination for vice president. The night Dukakis won the nomination, Bill Hobby and Ann Richards, who had been attending receptions, were shocked when they arrived at the convention center and learned that the fire marshal had locked them out, along with all other late arrivers, because the convention center had reached its crowd capacity. As a result, both missed the roll call vote. When a reporter asked Bob Slagle, the chair of the Texas Democratic Party, if Hobby had reacted with bad temper to being denied entrance, Slagle laughed and said, "Bill Hobby doesn't get excited about anything." On July 18, the day after the convention adjourned, the Hobbys flew back to Houston early that morning in time for Bill to appear with Richards on a platform with Dukakis and Bentsen for a campaign rally at Tranquility Park in downtown Houston. Despite the late-afternoon, hot summer temperature, the rally attracted a large and enthusiastic crowd.[18]

Bentsen's nomination energized most of the Texans at the national convention, who believed it enhanced Dukakis's chance to carry their state in November despite his opponent, Vice President George H. W. Bush, being a Texas resident. Additionally, Bentsen's nomination furthered speculation about who, other than Hobby, was eager to fill Bentsen's seat in the Senate if the Democrats took the White House. Ann Richards, San Antonio mayor Henry Cisneros, Jim Hightower, and a few members of the Texas congressional delegation were among those believed to be interested, but most political observers doubted either Richards or Cisneros, who were close allies of Hobby, would oppose him. As for Hobby, once he had announced his intention to run if the opportunity arose, he ignored the issue and concentrated instead on campaigning for the Dukakis-Bentsen ticket in Texas, for incumbent state senator Richard Anderson's reelection, and for candidates he favored for the State Board of Education.

In the midst of the ongoing political campaigns during the summer of 1988, Hobby also took time in July to play an important role in making possible the state's purchase of oilman Robert O. Anderson's remote 215,000-acre Big Bend Ranch in West Texas as a state park. The ranch, which is located on the western edge of Big Bend National Park and the eastern bank of the Rio Grande in a Chihuahuan Desert environment, features deep canyons, waterfalls, grassy mesas, and high peaks. Texas Parks and Wildlife Commission member Bob Armstrong and other Texas land conservationists had long sought a way for the state to preserve the ranch as a natural area, but several obstacles, including legislative opposition, prevented an acquisition.

In July 1988 Texas parks officials finally negotiated an agreement acceptable to both sides of the deal, including an $8.8 million price tag. Buying the land was one of the rare public policy issues on which Bill Hobby and Bill Clements agreed. Comptroller Bob Bullock, however, claimed that the state lacked the funds to make the purchase. The deal could not be completed unless Bullock certified that the state had the money to buy the ranch. Hobby feared that if the state failed to take advantage of the opportunity, which would double the size of the Texas state park system, it would be lost to private developers. Hobby pleaded with Bullock to find money for the purchase. A Bullock aide later noted that Bullock always found it difficult to tell Hobby no. The sly Bullock responded that he might be able to find $10 million if he could give $1 million as a pay raise to the Texas Rangers. Bullock biographers Dave McNeely and Jim Henderson later wrote, "Hobby gulped and took the deal. Then Bullock immediately got the top Ranger on the phone. 'You've got a $1M pay raise,' Bullock told him. 'And don't think for a minute Hobby got it for you.'" The ranch deal closed in the fall of 1988, but it was eventually paid with funds from revenue bonds.[19]

On July 28, before Hobby returned to his campaign activities, his longtime advisor on mental health issues and social services for the poor, Helen Farabee, wife of his close friend Senator Ray Farabee, died in Austin at the age of fifty-three from lung cancer. Helen's death came at the same time Ray was leaving the state Senate to assume his duties as the new University of Texas System vice chancellor and legal counselor. Helen Farabee had been such an effective and tireless advocate for state support of services for mentally ill and impoverished Texans that members of the Capitol press corps often referred to her as Texas's thirty-second state senator. A few years before Hobby was elected to his first term as lieutenant governor, she had guided his committee in its work to modernize the state's health code, which led to the creation of the Texas Department of Mental Health and Mental Retardation. As lieutenant governor, Hobby appointed Helen chair of a task force that drafted successful legislation to reform the state's indigent healthcare system. When Hobby learned of her death, he issued a statement praising her record of public service. "Helen Farabee's contribution to the poor, the sick and the needy will live long after her. Helen Farabee enriched the lives of all who knew her." Respect for her accomplishments transcended partisanship. Bill Clements ordered flags at the Capitol lowered to half-mast in her honor. Hobby delayed a trip to the annual national lieutenant governors' conference in Minnesota so he could serve as a pallbearer at Helen's funeral in Wichita Falls on July 30.[20]

Except for a long vacation break from late August until mid-September, when he stayed at a hunting camp in Canada's Yukon Territory, Hobby campaigned across the state for Dukakis and Bentsen during the nearly three months remaining before the general election, often accompanied by Ann Richards. Before embarking on his Yukon hunting trip, Hobby hosted a reception for Lloyd Bentsen in Houston. Undoubtedly inspired by the memory of Helen Farabee's labor on behalf of the ill and the needy, Hobby's remarks at the reception included the charge that the "Reagan revolution is more accurately described as the Reagan retrenchment. The nation cannot afford to move from retrenchment to full-scale retreat. We cannot continue to turn our backs on the less fortunate, on those who do not yet share in the American dream. That is the danger of four more years of a Republican administration." Afterward, Hobby flew in his personal plane with Ann Richards to Dallas to attend Jess Hay's reception and gala dinner for Dukakis and Bentsen. The next day, Hobby and Richards flew to Johnson City, where they rejoined Dukakis and Bentsen for a rally in front of the Blanco County Courthouse.[21]

After Hobby returned to Houston in September, he immediately went on the campaign trail. The same day he arrived back from his vacation, he gave a speech in Houston in support of Bill Sarpalius, who was running for US Congress. That event was soon followed by campaign appearances on behalf of State Board of Education candidates in Lufkin and Lubbock and a trip to Sweetwater in support of Temple Dickson's bid for the Texas Senate. On September 21, he gave a speech to workers at an oil refinery in Big Spring in which he attacked George Bush's vice presidential running mate, Indiana senator Dan Quayle, as an enemy of the oil and gas industry. In October, he gave introductory remarks for Bentsen at a fundraising dinner in Houston—not for Bentsen's vice presidential campaign but for his separate Senate reelection bid. Hobby undoubtedly had in mind his own strong interest in replacing Bentsen in the US Senate. Hobby strengthened his ties to Bentsen's organization by loaning his press spokesman, Glenn Smith, to the Bentsen campaign.[22]

In October Hobby also continued his effort to get Richard Anderson reelected to the Texas Senate. Anderson faced a strong Republican opponent in Bill Ratliff, and polling indicated a close election. On October 10, Hobby, Ann Richards, Jim Mattox, Garry Mauro, and Jim Hightower went to Marshall to attend the opening of the Harrison County campaign headquarters and to boost Anderson's reelection bid. They also attended and spoke at a dinner "roast" of Anderson at the Marshall Civic Center. While in Marshall, Hobby removed any doubts about his interest in becoming a US senator. He told a reporter for the *Longview News-Journal*, "When Bentsen becomes vice president, I'm going to run for his Senate seat."[23]

As the general election day drew close, the Bush-Quayle campaign, led by Lee Atwater, increasingly used racist scare tactics to attack Dukakis. The chief example was the use of a sleazy television ad focused on the Willie Horton case in Massachusetts. Convicted murderer Horton, a Black man, was released from prison because of a controversial furlough program in Massachusetts that Governor Dukakis had supported. While on furlough, Horton raped a woman and stabbed her boyfriend. Republican television ads featured a scary-looking mug shot of Horton as a voice-over charged that Dukakis was easy on crime and criminals, despite his having no involvement in Horton's case. Hobby was outraged by the ads. He told reporters that he was "appalled and disgusted" by the Bush campaign's use of racist and false claims that Dukakis was weak on crime.[24]

On November 8, Hobby held an election watch party in the lieutenant governor's reception room at the Capitol. By this time, it had become clear to Hobby that he would not have an opportunity to take Bentsen's place in the US Senate. A major poll released a few days prior to the election had Bush leading Dukakis by seventeen points. There was little doubt, however, that Bentsen was going to win reelection to the US Senate. By eight seventeen that night, CBS declared Bush the winner. The final vote tally revealed that Bush won 426 electoral votes to Dukakis's 111. Shortly thereafter, Bentsen was at the Driskill Hotel ballroom celebrating his Senate victory. Hobby had an additional disappointment when Republican Bill Ratliff denied Richard Anderson a second term in the state Senate despite Hobby's efforts. In addition, the results for the seven candidates Hobby endorsed for the State Board of Education were mixed, with four wins and three losses. The day was not without clear successes, however. Temple Dickson, who had defeated Grant Jones in the primary, was able to keep his senatorial district in Democratic hands, while voters also approved a constitutional amendment that Hobby strongly favored that created a rainy day fund to allow the legislature to set aside state budget surpluses for use in years when revenues fell short.[25]

Hobby flew to Ireland two days after the election to join Diana at Beechwood House, where he could enjoy a three-week escape in isolation from the political wars, as well as get some badly needed rest before he presided over his last regular session of the Texas Senate in January 1989. Hobby was determined to make some lasting changes in Texas government during the session before finally giving up his lieutenant governor's gavel.[26]

CHAPTER 17

THE FINAL TERM

Bill and Diana Hobby ended their long stay at Beechwood House in Ireland on the first day of December, 1988. Diana returned to Houston, but Hobby went to Austin to meet with his Capitol office staff and to attend meetings of the Legislative Budget Board. During a session of the board, Bullock confirmed his earlier estimate that there would be a $300 to $400 million revenue surplus available to the Seventy-First Legislature in January 1989. Hobby was happy to have the surplus, but he knew it was likely to disappear quickly. He knew Texas's antiquated tax system was unlikely to provide sufficient funds to meet the state's many unaddressed needs, including the inequality in funding public schools. He was also aware that Bill Clements would argue that the revenue surplus was proof there was no need to reform the state's tax system.[1]

After his meetings, Hobby returned to Houston to speak at a $1,000-per-plate fundraiser at the Hyatt Regency Hotel for his good friend Ann Richards. It was obvious that Richards intended to run for governor in 1990, but she had not made an official announcement. Nonetheless, her fundraising efforts were now in full swing. She had recently raised money at a party in New York City attended by several native Texan expats, including CBS News anchor Dan Rather and celebrity columnist Liz Smith. After Hobby gave the introductory speech for Richards at the dinner in Houston, she thanked him profusely, declaring to loud applause, "Bill, you have convinced me we should start thinking seriously about the governor's race." On June 10, seven months after the Houston fundraiser, Richards officially entered the governor's race.[2]

At noon on Tuesday, January 10, Hobby formally convened the Senate's first official session of the Seventy-First Legislature. The news media made much of the fact that the day marked the beginning of Hobby's final regular session. When a reporter asked him how it felt, he replied in his typically laconic way, "Just another opening day."

The only business conducted on January 10 was a ceremony in which Texas Supreme Court justice Jack Hightower administered the oath of office to the five newly elected members. The Senate now had eight Republican members. The 1989 legislative session was Hobby's last chance to effect major changes on the course of state business. Accordingly, he was determined to bond with the new senators as soon as possible. On January 19, his fifty-seventh birthday, he hosted a skeet-shooting party for Democratic senators Temple Dickson and Steve Carriker and Republicans Bill Ratliff and Teel Bivens at the Cypress Valley Preserve, located in a rural area nearly forty miles northwest of Austin. Afterward, Hobby took the senators to dinner.[3]

Hobby also joined with Gib Lewis in an attempt to smooth over the hard feelings remaining from their budget battle with Clements in the previous legislative session. Not long after the Seventieth Legislature adjourned in 1987, Clements continued his criticism of the Democratic leadership, warning that in the Seventy-First Legislature, "Bill Hobby and other leaders want to keep the door open to a State Income Tax. I want to slam the door shut by passing a Constitutional Amendment to prohibit a State Income Tax." He urged his supporters to help him "restrain state spending and fight against the big spenders in the Senate and the House." Nevertheless, when the new legislative session began, Clements, who had not been well served by his staff and legislative advisors in 1987, lowered the heat by announcing that he would now rely on the same budget numbers as Hobby and Lewis. In response to Clements's peace offering, the two Democratic legislative leaders agreed to have a private breakfast with Clements at the Governor's Mansion every Tuesday morning to address issues during the session.[4]

The vastly improved state revenue situation helped efforts to make peace with Clements. It also resulted in a more upbeat atmosphere in the legislature as the new session began. On the opening day, Bullock informed lawmakers that the economy had improved to such an extent that he was now projecting a $1.6 billion surplus for the 1990–1991 fiscal year. Despite the optimistic atmosphere, Democratic representative Stan Schlueter of Killeen admitted to reporters that the newly found harmony might not survive the upcoming battles over the tax system, equitable public-school funding, and reform of the state's workers' compensation program. The legislative agenda also included addressing overcrowded prisons and an anti-crime initiative Hobby was known to be developing for the legislature.[5]

To members of the Capitol press corps, a key question was how much their lame-duck status would weaken the power and influence of Bill Hobby and Bill Clements. The issue was less significant in Clements's situation. As the first Republican governor elected in Texas since Reconstruction and one who had to maneuver through a Democratic-dominated legislature, Clements had never wielded as much legislative influence as Hobby, despite the governor's veto power. In addition, in Texas the governor's legislative powers are inferior to those of a skilled lieutenant governor. But this was obviously a new situation for Hobby, whose power and influence as the Senate's presiding officer had not been in doubt since 1975. In the past, Hobby would declare his candidacy for another term as lieutenant governor prior to each session before the next election, which put the senators on notice that it would be wise not to challenge him if they sought choice committee assignments or recognition when they wanted to speak on the floor. In 1989, however, legislative observers predicted that some senators would no longer be as easy to control as in the past. Three had already indicated a strong interest in succeeding Hobby as lieutenant governor, which meant potential grandstanding behavior was likely in their effort to gain attention and enhance their visibility. In addition, reporters predicted that the departure of two of Hobby's most important team leaders in the Senate, Ray Farabee and Grant Jones, would hurt his effectiveness. The accuracy of these assessments of Hobby's influence and power would soon be tested.[6]

Before Hobby turned his attention to the new session's business, he and Gib Lewis spoke at the swearing-in ceremony in the Capitol's old Texas Supreme Court Room for the fifteen newly elected members of the State Board of Education. He and Lewis both urged the board members to build on the Perot reforms and not reduce their efficacy. Hobby was particularly wary of the intentions of the new chairman, Monte Hasie of Lubbock. While campaigning for office, Hasie, a financial consultant, had criticized some of the reforms as well as disparaged Perot. After the ceremony, Hobby complained to reporters about the "unfortunate statements" the chairman had made during his campaign. He expected Hasie and his fellow board members to carry out their responsibility to work toward an improved school system. Hasie got at least part of the message. In his remarks after the swearing-in ceremony, he pledged as chairman to work closely with state leaders. "There are a lot of good things in House Bill 72," Hasie admitted, referring to Perot's educational reform act. But he also complained that the state had mandated but not funded programs that had forced many school districts to raise taxes to hire new teachers and to pay for building additional classrooms. He declared his hope that the legislature would act to fully fund these mandated education programs.[7]

Hobby rejected the argument that unfunded legislative mandates such as requiring students to pass their courses to be eligible for extracurricular activities needed additional state funding to be implemented. He was also concerned that funding state-mandated public-school programs would require either an increase in state revenue or deep cuts in existing state services and programs, which entangled the issue with the difficult overall problem of equitable public-school financing. An appellate court's decision to overturn Judge Harley Clark's ruling that Texas's system of public-school finance was unconstitutional had reduced pressure on the Seventy-First Legislature to overhaul school funding, but Hobby recognized the issue was far from dead, because the inequities remained. He also predicted the Texas Supreme Court would overrule the appellate court's decision and send the issue back to the legislature to resolve. No matter what the ultimate outcome in the courts might be, Hobby felt strongly that the legislature had to make funding equitable. A temporary state budget surplus was not going to solve the long-term problem. "In the 16 years I've been here," Hobby stated, "there's been a school finance bill every other session as regularly as clockwork. The nature of our school finance system is that it requires updating about every four years. There will be a school finance bill, but the court suit wasn't and isn't and won't be particularly the driving force." Hobby argued that resolution of the school-financing problem was inextricably tied to reform of the state's tax system.[8]

Representative Stan Schlueter, chair of the House Ways and Means Committee, agreed with Hobby, insisting that Texas simply had to have "a tax system that more clearly fits the state's economy and a better financial and more evenly funded public education system." Bill Clements had a different plan. He proposed a constitutional amendment to place school finance "under the sole purview of the Legislature and remove it from this constantly pressing situation in the courts." The amendment would essentially lock in place the current system of school finance. Hobby opposed the governor's proposed amendment, arguing that it "would be a constitutional amendment that says the constitution applies to everything except education. I don't think that would enjoy wide support."[9]

Hobby's effort to address the unequal funding of public schools was not only linked to his call for tax reform but also tied to his pet project for the session: a package of social justice and human services bills that he presented to the legislature as an anti-crime plan. Nationally, violent crime rates began to rise slowly at the end of the 1960s and continued to climb until they spiked in the 1980s and early 1990s. Few states were spared, including Texas. What caused the so-called crime epidemic of the 1980s was heavily debated at the time, and that argument has never been resolved. The main response to the crime wave in Texas, as in many other states, was to build more prisons and fill them with the convicted, largely men of color. The focus was on punishment, not prevention. Although Hobby made statements while campaigning for Senator Grant Jones in 1988 that boasted of Jones's support for new prisons, it's clear that Hobby's rhetoric in that case stemmed more from his desire to help the reelection of an important ally in the Senate than it was an accurate reflection of his views on how to solve the crime problem.[10]

As already discussed, Hobby and Clements had battled in 1987 over the appropriation for prisons. Hobby knew Texas prisons were vastly overcrowded, which had resulted in unacceptable living conditions. Ordered by a federal court to improve conditions, the state's answer was to build more prisons, which Hobby accepted as necessary to relieve overcrowding, but he wanted to build fewer prisons than did Clements. Hobby also believed there was a more effective way to reduce crime than building ever bigger and more penitentiaries. Influenced by social and economic justice advocates such as Helen Farabee and others, Hobby and two of his key staff members, Saralee Tiede and Glenn Smith, were convinced that a more rational approach to alleviating the crime problem was for state government to apply more resources to prevention than to punishment. Hobby had long criticized the state government's one-dimensional strategy for addressing crime. He and his staff were aware that public fears about the crime wave might be a way to get legislators to accept social and educational programs with the justification they were fighting crime. Accordingly, Glenn Smith persuaded Hobby to call the legislation the anti-crime plan. "People wanted all this anti-crime legislation," Smith remembered. "I said okay, here's your anti-crime plan. It wasn't a hard sell with Bill Hobby because it matched the things he wanted to do anyway." Hobby also hoped to take advantage of Bullock's forecast of a budget surplus for the upcoming biennial budget, as well as the existence of federal grants that could be tapped for funding.[11]

In preparation for the convening of the Seventy-First Legislature, Tiede and Smith spent several months in 1988 working on the legislative package, naming it the Hobby Anti-Crime Plan, possibly to avoid any "soft on crime" accusations due to the plan's emphasis on educational opportunity and social justice measures instead of jail time. "We wanted to attack crime by addressing some of its underlying causes," Tiede later recalled. After consulting with several prominent experts on criminal justice, Tiede and Smith produced a legislative package to deal more reasonably with low-level offenders and end the cycle of crime by targeting the school dropout problem, alcohol and drug abuse, child abuse, family violence, runaways, and teen pregnancies. "We knew the most significant way to deal with the root causes of crime was early intervention with kids," Smith later noted. "If you identify health needs or education needs early on, there was a good amount of research that you would save them from entering the criminal justice system."[12]

After accepting Tiede and Smith's basic twelve-point plan, Hobby circulated a draft to Kent Caperton, chair of the Senate Finance Committee, and to other likely allies in the Senate and the House, as well to Clements, who endorsed the plan. It won the governor's support mainly because of Hobby's agreement to support the construction of additional prisons, although not as many as Clements wanted. Because the cost of housing one prisoner for a year was $11,500, Hobby and his team projected that the eventual reduction in the size of the prison population would ultimately result in enough savings to pay a significant portion of the program's recurring expense. Fewer criminals meant less crime and fewer prisons. Those savings, however, would take a few years to kick in, but Hobby argued the delay was worth the wait. "When we project what the prison population will be in 10 years, we are assuming the unavoidable incarceration of children who are today 7, 8 and 9 years old. We are telling them that we do not have the resources to spend on them today, although we can commit millions of dollars to their future room and board in the Texas Department of Corrections."[13]

Hobby submitted his anti-crime legislation, now with the title "Unlocking the Future of Texas: The Anti-Crime Plan of 1989," to Caperton's Senate Finance Committee in early February 1989. The plan had a $164 million price tag spread over two years, but the state could count on $60 million in federal grants as well as approximately $38 million already budgeted for existing programs, leaving nearly $67 million left to be funded by the projected surplus. In Hobby's introduction to the official version of the plan, he argued that the state could "invest in quality education and preventive measures or continue to spend money on welfare and prisons. We pay a heavy cost in lost productivity, welfare payments, inequities in taxation, prison costs, and the loss of basic human potential."[14]

Mainly due to the availability of funding and the relatively small price tag in contrast with other programs, Hobby's anti-crime plan survived the legislative back-and-forth largely intact. The package was among the bills the Seventy-First Legislature passed before adjourning its regular session, making it one of the achievements of Hobby's last term in office.[15]

Passing Hobby's anti-crime package was relatively easy compared to the legislative struggle to reform the state's workers' compensation program. Ironically, the original law was written while Bill Hobby's father, Will, was governor. The issue had loomed as the main event of the Seventy-First Texas Legislature months before its first session convened. In 1987, amid growing employer complaints about the more than 100 percent rise in their insurance premiums in only four years, the legislature appointed a joint select committee to make recommendations for change. The committee found that the number of work-related fatalities and injuries was higher in Texas than the rest of the nation, that benefit rates were low compared to other states, and that medical costs were rising alarmingly. The committee also claimed that lawsuits driven by plaintiff's attorneys had resulted in excessive damage awards that were causing the spike in insurance rates. Business lobbyists charged that rising costs were forcing companies to close or leave the state, stifling economic development and job growth. Plaintiff's attorneys, however, accused the insurance industry of exaggerating its losses to boost premium rates and increase profits, while labor union leaders blamed the business community for unsafe working conditions and for viewing workers as disposable. The controversy not only pitted employers against workers but also involved the healthcare community and insurance companies. Each had a stake in the reform efforts.

Hobby's chief of staff, Saralee Tiede, sided with the plaintiff's attorneys. "I think the issue was exaggerated to destroy the trial lawyers," she said. "Workers' comp was the way a lot of trial lawyers made their living. It wasn't big money, but it was enough money to keep their practice going." Hobby, however, shared the business community's concerns. "Hobby's natural sympathies were with the business side because he was basically an employer," Hector Uribe later observed. "If it was going to be business versus labor, he'd be with business. But he could also see that the system wasn't compensating injured workers fairly." In preparation for what promised to be a difficult battle over workers' compensation insurance, Hobby held meetings in the summer and fall of 1988 with Governor Clements, Speaker Lewis, and business and labor leaders to discuss the issue. Seeking an outcome favorable to the business community, Clements and Lewis blamed the problem on plaintiff's attorneys who solicited injured workers as clients and sought what the business community claimed were excessive fees and settlements.[16]

To better understand the positions taken by all of the groups with an interest in the injured-workers issue, Hobby met with Kent Caperton, John Montford, and Bob Glasgow, who would represent Hobby's position in the Senate. He also sought the advice of former senators Grant Jones and Babe Schwartz, who were now working as lobbyists. Hobby knew he could get useful advice from Jones about the business community's interests, while Schwartz represented labor. That meeting was followed by one with Nick Kralj, a former aide to Ben Barnes, who represented the Texas Trial Lawyers Association.[17]

In March, the House passed a workers' compensation insurance reform bill with provisions that seemed to be acceptable, if grudgingly, to those on all sides of the issue. There was one exception, however, which proved to be extremely contentious in the Senate. The issue was over how to resolve the claims of injured workers who wanted to appeal the Texas Industrial Accident Board's decisions in their cases. That question generated heated debates that lasted from March through May. While the battle over the bill continued, Hobby hobbled around the Senate Chamber on crutches because of a fractured left ankle he suffered while skiing in Aspen, Colorado, on Easter Sunday, March 26. At the opening of the Senate session after the Easter recess, Hobby told the Senate, "Now I really know how it feels to be a lame duck." The lieutenant governor was forced to wear a cast until the end of April.[18]

On May 5, while the fight over the workers' compensation insurance reform bill continued, the members took a break from regular business to honor Bill Hobby with a surprise "roast" as he completed his last session as their presiding officer. During the ceremony, the members elected Hobby their president emeritus, a position that had no precedent in the Senate's history.[19]

Hobby's hope to pass the workers' comp bill before the end of the regular session was dashed when negotiations with the House broke down. Hobby called in all sides for two days of meetings, sitting in on many of them. Trial lawyers demanded that injured workers be allowed to go to court for a jury trial to resolve claim disputes. Employers wanted the state accident board's decisions to be final but were willing to allow a case to be heard by a judge. However, they adamantly opposed letting juries decide those cases. Clements's threat to veto any workers' compensation bill that retained the right to a jury trial complicated the negotiations. There also were arguments over whether injured workers' claims could be paid in a lump sum, as well as over how to calculate a worker's economic loss from suffering an injury on the job.[20]

Frustrated by the lack of progress, Hobby took the unusual move of placing his own name on a revised workers' compensation insurance bill. Hobby's bill called for two different classes of injury disputes. One would be eligible for a jury trial, the other for arbitration. Hobby persuaded labor and trial attorney lobbyists to support his bill. He gave Kent Caperton the job of leading the effort to pass it in the Senate. Hobby also decided to take the stalled bill out of the committee and submit it to a Senate "Committee of the Whole" that would bring the thirty-one members to the chamber to hear about, debate, and vote on his bill. That process would make it possible for every senator to hear the same information at the same time instead of having to rely on secondhand reports from their colleagues who were directly involved in writing the bill. It was also a strategic ploy that allowed suspension of the Senate's two-thirds rule, which prevented bills from proceeding to a vote if eleven members opposed the action. After a debate, a majority of the Committee of the Whole voted to send Hobby's version of the workers' compensation bill to a special subcommittee of seven senators. The subcommittee, which included Hobby's allies Kent Caperton, Carl Parker, and John Montford, was charged with the task of writing a version of the bill that retained an injured worker's right to a jury trial in disputed cases but could still pass the Senate and then be accepted by the joint House-Senate conference. As a result, Hobby told reporters he was "very optimistic" that a major overhaul of the workers' compensation law could be accomplished before the regular session ended.[21]

After revising Hobby's bill, the subcommittee sent it to a joint House-Senate conference committee. Because the House members of the conference committee refused to accept Hobby's compromise and the senators held their ground against the House version of reform, time ran out on the regular legislative session on May 29 without a bill. Governor Clements, angered by the failure to achieve his main legislative goal, quickly called the legislature to convene in a thirty-day special session on June 20 to focus exclusively on workers' compensation.[22]

Despite its failure to solve the workers' compensation problem, the Seventy-First Legislature did manage to pass a balanced budget without a tax increase, which was made possible by the surplus. It also passed Hobby's anti-crime package with some revisions, as well as a criminal justice system reform bill that expanded the state prison system. Other successful legislation increased funding for AIDS research, treatment, and education; boosted public-school funding; gave a higher minimum salary to beginning teachers; improved healthcare services in rural areas; increased Medicaid funding for maternal and child healthcare; and provided nursing home reform. With Hobby's active support and help, the legislature increased the budgets of the state's colleges and universities, which included a boost in faculty salaries. To improve access to higher education in the region south of San Antonio, the legislature also transferred the administration of Pan American University in Edinburg to the University of Texas System, and Corpus Christi State University, Laredo State University, and Texas A&I University in Kingsville to the Texas A&M University System. The Texas Legislature also provided more help to the poverty-stricken colonias scattered along the Rio Grande. Legislators passed bills to fund improvements in existing subdivisions, to build a new wastewater treatment facility, and to ban any new housing developments lacking water and sewer service. The lawmakers also passed bills to improve living conditions at migrant worker camps and to reduce pesticide exposure for farmworkers.[23]

Hobby told reporters that the colonia bills acknowledged lawmakers' "responsibility for allowing the existence of communities in our state that are really like Third World communities." Senator Hector Uribe, who was a leader in the effort to improve living and working conditions in South Texas, credited Hobby for supporting his efforts. "Hobby recognized the need to regulate the colonias and make sure that they had running water and sewers." Hobby had named Uribe chairman of the Natural Resources Committee's Subcommittee on Water, which positioned the senator to take a leadership role in the passage of the legislation to improve living conditions in the colonias. Ernesto Cortes, who was director of a progressive grassroots organization that advocated for low-cost housing and for clean water in the colonias, stated that "Hobby legitimized us. He was an incredible ally. He made it possible for us to be at the table. There are issues he and I would disagree on but those are issues of strategy."[24]

Despite the impressive list of legislative accomplishments, the legislature left the public-school funding issue unresolved while the Texas Supreme Court considered a request to reverse the appeals court's ruling that the system was constitutional. A decision from the Texas Supreme Court was expected during the coming fall. The legislature also failed to pass a bill banning assault rifles, although a bill allowing people to carry concealed handguns also failed. And bills to appoint state judges rather than elect them and to reform campaign financing both died during the session.

The legislature began its special session on June 20 to focus exclusively on workers' compensation. On the opening day, Hobby revealed his deep frustration over the failure to pass a bill during the regular session. Angered by the negative role the business lobby was playing in the negotiations, he complained to reporters, "We have idiots who represent the business community who say we don't want a trial by jury. You know this is really kind of silly." Senators Caperton and Parker, both trial lawyers, agreed to serve as Hobby's floor leaders for his version of the bill the Senate would send to the joint House-Senate conference committee.[25]

On July 5, as the Senate adjourned for a lunch break before continuing debate about the workers' compensation bill, Lonnie "Bo" Pilgrim, a wealthy Republican from northeast Texas who was one of the largest producers of chicken products in the United States, wandered around the Senate floor with his friend, Senator Ike Harris, handing out personal checks in the amount of $10,000 to the members who remained in the chamber. Nine senators accepted the checks, whose payees were left blank. "Pilgrim was just dumber than a box of rocks," Tiede recalled. "He walked around with these checks in his hand, totally oblivious that there might be anything wrong with doing that." Pilgrim was a Clements supporter who was well known to be an opponent of the Senate's version of the bill, which was scheduled for a vote in only two days. After Pilgrim offered a check to Senator Hugh Parmer, who declined it, Parmer went to the podium and told Hobby that Pilgrim had just tried to bribe him. Pilgrim, however, argued that the checks were political donations, not bribes, as some were charging. Pilgrim complained that he was concerned about the high cost of workers' compensation insurance and that his action was meant to bring attention to the issue. Pilgrim's explanation failed to persuade Hobby, who was infuriated by the incident. Hobby's anger deepened when he learned that nine senators had accepted the checks. "Hobby was incensed that these dumb Republicans thought they could buy integrity," Tiede said. "He was totally offended by the very thought of it."[26]

When Senator Caperton returned from lunch, Hobby called him to the podium and asked if he got his check. "I didn't know what he was talking about," Caperton recalled.

"Hobby kind of laughed and said, 'Obviously you're not one of the chosen ones, Caperton, because it seems like most everybody else got a check.'" Caperton joined Houston senator Craig Washington in urging Hobby to call Ronnie Earle, the Travis County district attorney, whose office had legal jurisdiction over corruption in government cases. "I was certain it was illegal to do what Pilgrim had done," Caperton observed, "but as it turned out, I was wrong." The DA's office informed Hobby that Pilgrim's action might have been unseemly but it was not criminal, because under then state law, it was not a bribe if it was officially reported. In addition, because the legislature was in a special session, the law prohibiting fundraising during the regular session did not apply. Nevertheless, aware the optics were bad, eight of the senators quickly returned their checks to Pilgrim, with the exception of Dallas senator Ike Harris, who had brought Pilgrim into the Senate Chamber. Harris, who had grown up with Pilgrim in Pittsburg, Texas, explained that because Pilgrim had done nothing illegal, he would keep his check.[27]

After a month of wrangling between the House and the Senate, the special session adjourned on July 21 without a workers' compensation bill. Caperton later recalled that Hobby submitted a bill to the Senate during the special session that "would have, I think, gone a long way towards reforming the comp system. But the House rejected it at Clements's urging."[28]

Clements soon announced his intention to call another special session late in the fall to get a workers' compensation bill passed. He said he would wait to call the session until after the insurance companies made their request in October to the state's insurance board for a 30 to 35 percent increase in premium charges. He predicted that voter outrage over the massive increase in premiums would force the legislators to act. The insurance board received the request for a hike in rates in October but deferred its decision for several weeks. While the board deliberated, Clements called the second special session to convene on November 13 with the charge to pass a workers' compensation bill. He warned he would keep calling the legislators back to Austin as many times as necessary until they resolved the issue.[29]

During the break between the first and second called sessions, Hobby met with his Senate team to discuss strategy. They agreed that Hobby would submit to the next session a heavily revised version of the bill he had pushed during the first session. The revision was a major compromise that still allowed workers to go to court, but it had provisions that would make it more difficult for injured workers to seek that option. According to Saralee Tiede, Hobby agreed to the compromise in the second special session because "he just wanted to move forward and get the workers' compensation fight over with. But ultimately, he was always in favor of compromising to get it done." Hobby's eagerness to move on was partially driven by the Texas Supreme Court's unanimous ruling on October 2 overturning the appeals court's decision that unequal funding for Texas public schools was constitutional. Because the state supreme court ordered the legislature to correct the problem by May 1, 1990, Hobby knew that at least one more special session would have to be called to meet that deadline.[30]

"My father was very patient, and process oriented during the regular and first sessions," Paul Hobby recalled. "But on workers' comp he finally had to wade in and just end it. That infuriated the trial lawyers and the left, who complained that he really is a rich white guy after all." Caperton, who had been the Senate leader for Hobby's proposed bill during the first special session, rejected Hobby's revised version. Another Hobby ally, Carl Parker, joined Caperton in opposition. They announced their plan to submit their own workers' compensation bill to the Senate, although it too was a weaker version than the trial lawyers and labor leaders had hoped for.[31]

Two weeks prior to the second special session, political reporter Sam Kinch noted that Hobby's new compromise plan had been characterized as a probusiness bill, despite Hobby's rejection of the business lobby's rigid demand that buying comprehensive workers' insurance coverage should not be mandatory. Nevertheless, Kinch continued, Hobby's plan would allow big business the option of self-insurance by setting aside funds to pay injury claims. The Hobby bill, however, would also establish a new state bureau that would compile data documenting worker safety violations, create a hotline for whistleblowers to report unsafe conditions at their jobsites, and impose a $5,000-a-day fine for violators.[32]

When Hobby gaveled open the Senate's second special session on November 14, the battle lines were clearly drawn, with Caperton and Parker on one side and Montford leading Hobby's supporters. Governor Clements and Speaker Lewis both accepted Hobby's compromise. Consumer groups, the Texas AFL-CIO, and the Trial Lawyers Association backed Hobby's opponents, although unenthusiastically. Caperton and Parker's rejection of his bill angered Hobby deeply. Both senators had normally been among his staunchest allies. "That's when the thing got unbelievably nasty," Saralee Tiede noted. "Hobby was the master of the Senate, so things normally went his way. But Caperton and Parker dug their heels in and fought him. Hobby wasn't used to having them cross him, especially not when he puts himself on the line with his own bill." Caperton recalled, "I had everybody mad at me. Governor Hobby was mad at me, and the trial lawyers didn't like my solution and neither did the labor unions, but Carl Parker and I and others were fighting to preserve the right of injured workers being able to have legal representation."[33]

Early in the session, Caperton and Parker won the first procedural vote on workers' compensation, causing Hobby, uncharacteristically, to lose his temper. Caperton recalled that after the vote, "Hobby pulled me aside in the hall and said, 'I think I'm just going to adjourn this session. Looks like we're not going to make any progress. I'm just going to send us all home.'" Caperton claimed that when he told Hobby he thought that was a bad idea, Hobby retorted, "Yeah, but I didn't ask your advice," and stormed away from the senator. "It just got rockier after that," Caperton remembered. "They were a tough thirty days, probably the hardest I had in my entire life." At one point, Montford called up Caperton and said he needed to make nice with the lieutenant governor. "It's eating [Hobby] alive and I know it's eating you," Montford told his colleague. Tiede later admitted the situation was "horrible. I mean, to be standing there watching those floor fights and the depths of the disagreement and the personal anger between old friends and allies. It was exhausting going to work in the morning and knowing you were going to have another big fight on the floor. It was just grueling."[34]

Largely because of Hobby's forceful backing and imaginative use of Senate rules, his version of the bill eventually passed the Senate during a late-night vote of eighteen to thirteen on December 12, the last day of the second special session. Hobby was able to coax Senators Judith Zaffirini, Chet Edwards, and Chet Brooks to provide the votes necessary for passage. With House approval already secured, the Texas Workers' Compensation Act was sent to Clements, who signed it into law the day after passage. At the ceremony, Gib Lewis and Bill Hobby stood behind the governor when he signed the bill. Clements praised Hobby for guiding the legislation through the Senate. Delighted by the major benefits the act would bestow on the business community, Clements engaged in a bit of hyperbole by declaring that the new law was the "most hard fought and the most significant piece of legislation to come out of the Texas Legislature in 20 years." That exaggerated view was not shared by the lieutenant governor. Clements also announced that the Texas Supreme Court's ruling that the state's public-school finance system was unconstitutional was forcing him to call the Seventy-First Legislature back to work in March 1990.[35]

The morning after the Senate passed the workers' compensation bill, Hobby sought out Caperton, who immediately congratulated the lieutenant governor on his victory. Hobby was determined to resolve the public-school financing problem once and for all in the upcoming year—his last as lieutenant governor—by passing a state income tax that would end dependence on the property tax. If successful, that effort would be a significant milestone capping Hobby's eighteen years in public office. "Kent, we've got to get through this school finance problem," he told Senator Caperton. "We have another special session coming up. Are you going to work with me on that and be part of the team and be part of the leadership? I need you." Caperton replied, "Of course I will." The bruised feelings on both sides of the issue lingered, but Caperton and Parker managed to patch up their differences with Hobby, and they would work with him on public-school funding during the next special session in the new year.[36]

CHAPTER 18

SINE DIE

As Bill Hobby entered what was to be his final full year as the longest-serving lieutenant governor in Texas history, resolving the intractable problem of providing equal funding for the education of all the state's public-school students ranked number one on his public policy agenda. That issue had once again become a crisis, with the Texas Supreme Court ordering the legislature to solve it by May 1, 1990. It was estimated that as much as $1 billion in new revenue would be needed to address the matter.

Characteristically, Hobby saw the crisis as an opportunity—not only to solve the school-funding problem once and for all but also to give serious consideration to a state income tax, another item on his agenda. School financing is largely based on local property taxes. The wide differences in property values throughout the state had resulted in inordinate disparities in funding between rich and poor school districts. Hobby, who had long been a critic of the state's reliance on property, sales, and business franchise taxes, believed education might be the one issue that would persuade Texans to drop their intense opposition to an income tax, especially if it lowered or even replaced the property and sales taxes.

Hobby was not naïve. He knew that passing an income tax was a long-shot proposition, especially with 1990 being an election year. It was also unlikely the Texas Legislature would consider such a politically radioactive proposal during the upcoming special session on school funding, even though an income tax would provide the solution they were seeking. The main problem was that for many years, conservative politicians in Texas had vigorously demagogued the income tax issue, driven largely by the self-interest of the upper economic class. After his years of experience as lieutenant governor, Hobby admitted he was frustrated that state government was so "handcuffed by political rhetoric that we can't consider realistic solutions." Hobby told reporters it was "time to put demagoguery aside. The landscape is littered with exclamations of 'No New Taxes.' This is an old promise that has been used, abused, and broken in the past few years. I suggest a new slogan for Texas: 'Pay Now or Pay Later.' It costs more to pay later. When we look at this state today, we find worse evils in the world than higher taxes."[1]

Despite his own considerable wealth, Hobby didn't see a state income tax as a threat to his economic self-interest. He believed his plan, which called for a 4 percent tax on a "broad measure of income," would allow for the lowering or even elimination of property taxes entirely, as well as for a reduction in the sales and business franchise taxes. He had often denounced the sales tax as regressive and argued that the property tax was an unreliable source because of fluctuating appraised values. Studies indicated that a state income tax would, at the least, keep taxation at the current rate or even reduce it for the wealthy, while lessening the overall tax burden on most Texans. It would also have the benefit of equalizing public-school financing and, more important to Hobby, provide the opportunity for all of the state's children to have a better education no matter where they happened to live.[2]

In the last months of 1989, Hobby took time away from the ongoing battle over workers' compensation insurance to make a public case for his tax plan. One of his most important audiences was the conservative Texas Association of Taxpayers, which he addressed in Austin on November 2. Aware of the business community's intense opposition to a state income tax, Hobby argued that the current property and franchise tax system was hostile to business because it required payments even in years when a business lost money, while an income tax would only be paid on profits. More important, Hobby claimed, the current system was incapable of providing the necessary revenue needed not only for a quality education system but also for badly needed improvements in the state's highways, healthcare, and criminal justice system. Those improvements, among others, were essential to the good health of the state's economy as well as the quality of life for the state's citizens. Hobby acknowledged the uphill nature of the fight he was waging, "but if the idea of an income tax is not put fairly and accurately into the debate about this state's future," he declared, "we are letting our children and grandchildren down."[3]

Because 1990 was an election year, Hobby assumed it was more than likely that the candidates would greet his call for an income tax with neutrality at best, or outright opposition at worst. That assumption proved to be accurate. The Associated Press noted that his proposal "brought widespread and bipartisan opposition." Quietly sympathetic to Hobby's proposal, House Speaker Gib Lewis was among the few officeholders who refrained from taking a rigidly negative position on the issue in public. Even though he faced a credible challenge from a Republican opponent in his district, Lewis told reporters that the tax proposal was "something that we need to examine." Lewis pointed out that Hobby's stand on an income tax was an easy target for political candidates running for statewide office.[4]

More typical was the reaction of Hobby's nemesis Jim Mattox, who was a candidate for the Democratic nomination for governor. Mattox promised that if elected governor, he would veto income tax legislation. Even Hobby's close political ally and friend Ann Richards announced her disapproval. "I oppose an income tax," Richards told the Capitol press, "but I respect Bill Hobby. I've disagreed with him before, and I disagree with him in this instance." Bill Clements, as well as the Republican candidates for office in 1990, uniformly opposed Hobby's proposal. When reporters asked Hobby for his reaction to the anti-income-tax stance that even his friends were taking, Hobby replied, "I think they are making a mistake. If I'm the father of the Texas income tax, can I also be the guy who abolished the franchise tax, lowered property taxes and lowered sales taxes?"[5]

Hobby, however, did have the support of the *Texas Observer*, the unofficial journal of the liberal wing of the state's Democratic Party. A week after Hobby called for a state income tax in his speech to the taxpayers' association, the *Observer* concluded that Hobby "might not have earned himself a chapter in *Profiles in Courage*, but the speech he made has to be considered an important event in the political history of the state." The *Observer* noted that Hobby's speech "was another one of several public stands that separates the Lieutenant Governor from the pack and that serves to define him as something more than a politician. Never before has someone of Hobby's stature publicly advocated an income tax. And then consider how unfortunate it is that this man's name will not appear on the ballot in 1990."[6]

A few days after Hobby called for a state income tax, he and Richards were back in sync on a different but even more controversial issue: abortion rights. On the afternoon of November 12, they appeared together at a pro-choice rally on the Capitol grounds that attracted several thousand participants. The event, one of several pro-choice rallies nationwide, was a reaction to President George H. W. Bush's veto of two major spending bills that would have expanded federal financing of abortions. Hobby was a featured speaker along with Richards, Mattox, and actors Cybill Shepherd and Morgan Fairchild. Bill and Diana Hobby had long supported the US Supreme Court's 1973 *Roe v. Wade* decision. They both were friends with former Texas state representative Sarah Weddington, lead plaintiff's counsel in the *Roe* case. Anti-abortion activists complained that Hobby was responsible for preventing the Texas Legislature from passing strong anti-abortion bills. When Hobby heard that charge, he told reporters, "I don't know if I deserve that honor, but I accept it gratefully. I do feel very strongly on the subject." When Hobby spoke at the pro-choice rally at the Capitol, he elicited a roar from the crowd when he declared, "Texas won't be the first state to roll back abortion rights."[7]

Governor Clements called for the third special session to convene on February 27, 1990, with only two items on the agenda: public-school funding and the method of selecting state judges. A month prior to the session, Bill Hobby busily took on new duties that he would continue after he left office in January 1991. One was membership on the board of the Dallas-headquartered Southwest Airlines, which included service on its audit committee, an assignment that took advantage of the math-loving Hobby's strong interest in budgeting. The other was a position on the Rice University faculty.

Back in 1989, Hobby had been appointed to a four-year term as a member of the Rice University Board of Governors, a position his mother once held. A year later, Rice appointed Hobby the Tsanoff Professor of Public Affairs. In January 1990, he began co-teaching an undergraduate political science class, Federalism and Intergovernmental Politics, with Robert Stein, who specialized in urban politics and public policy and would become the dean of the School of Social Sciences. The class met for two hours early every Monday morning during the spring semester, which included the third special legislative session. Hobby found his first experience teaching a regular class for an entire semester deeply satisfying, despite having to balance his time between the Rice campus in Houston and the Senate in Austin. He later recalled that he and Stein "enjoyed our co-teaching experiences, but even more than that we enjoyed our political discussions."[8]

Stein admitted in an interview with the *Houston Chronicle* that faculty "often look skeptically at politicians who become professors because they rely so much on war stories and so little on hard data. But in our team-taught classes, I found myself doing the anecdotal material because Bill has such a love for math and numbers. He could easily have had a career in academia." Stein recalled that one of his students asked him how to do a probability estimate on the computer. Before Stein could answer, Hobby asked the student to step over to his desk and gave him a quick lesson in statistics and research methods. Stein noted that in the classroom, Hobby was reflective. "He reads voraciously, works math puzzles he sometimes submits to journals, and invokes the Socratic method to challenge students in class." Hobby's experience at Rice convinced him that teaching would be in his future after he left public office.[9]

Two weeks before the third special session, Hobby took Gib Lewis on a two-day hunting trip near Albany, Georgia, to plot legislative strategy. When they returned to Austin, they agreed to renew their weekly Tuesday morning breakfasts with Bill Clements at the Governor's Mansion, with the hope that they might be able to coax Clements away from his threat to veto any new tax bill. When the legislature convened in late February, of the two issues Governor Clements placed on the agenda—school finance and state judge selection—school funding was by far the most difficult and controversial. Because of the high cost of equalized funding, most of the lawmakers arrived back in Austin deeply pessimistic about the chances for resolving the school financial problem to the satisfaction of the Texas Supreme Court. The legislature was once again in a too-familiar situation: either increase taxes, drastically reduce appropriations, or do both.[10]

All sixty of the Republican members of the House had pledged to vote against any tax bill, especially one that included an income tax. That was enough votes to kill legislation. In addition, Governor Clements had appointed a special task force on school financing weeks before the legislature convened. Hobby attended the task force meeting in early February. A majority of its members proposed a financing bill totaling $214 million that also included a plan to shift a significant amount of costs to local school districts. Those districts would be forced to raise school property taxes, thus protecting the legislators from the charge that they had raised the levies. Hobby and Lewis argued that the task force recommendations fell far short of actual needs. They also opposed shifting costs to local school boards.[11]

Bill Hobby gaveled open the third special session of the Senate on February 27, 1990, with the Senate meeting as a Committee of the Whole and Carl Parker serving as chair of the Education Committee. Despite the gloomy mood in the Senate, Hobby was delighted by his first task. He administered the oath of office to new senator Rodney Ellis, a former member of the Houston City Council who had won a special election earlier in February. Ellis filled the vacancy resulting from Craig Washington's election to US Congress to replace the late Mickey Leland, who died in August 1989 in a plane crash in Africa. Hobby had known Ellis since 1972 when Hobby recruited him to work on his campaign staff while he was still a high school student.[12]

When the legislature began work on the school funding issue, both houses ignored the governor's task force recommendations. Hobby guided the drafting of a bill, sponsored by Carl Parker, to increase school funding by $1.2 billion. Unable to gain support for his income tax proposal, Hobby and his Senate allies paid for the bill by tapping a surplus in the budget, hiking the cigarette tax, and increasing the state's property tax. In contrast, the Republican members of the House proposed a bill to increase school funding by only $450 million, but failed to identify how to pay for it. Clements announced he would veto those bills if passed. In response, Hobby called Clements "intransigent." He told reporters he could "only conclude that the governor's office doesn't want a bill to pass. I see no evidence, or any willingness, or, in fact, any desire on the governor's part to sign a bill."[13]

The party primary campaigns were a distraction during the third session for several members of the legislature who were seeking renomination or a new public office, including Senator Chet Edwards, who was a candidate for Congress. Hobby supported state treasurer Ann Richards for the Democratic gubernatorial nomination, but his leadership role in the battle over school financing limited his efforts to help her campaign. In addition, the fact that one of Richards's main opponents was former governor Mark White, who was also Hobby's friend, was a factor in Hobby's decision to take a lower profile in the primary campaign. Hobby attended a couple of Richards's campaign events in Houston prior to the primary election, including a major event for her at the Four Seasons Hotel, but he had no speaking role. However, Hobby did quietly make his personal plane available to Richards for a few campaign trips. On March 12, Hobby held an election watch party in the lieutenant governor's reception room, where he monitored the vote returns. In the race for the Democratic nomination for governor, Ann Richards edged out Jim Mattox by slightly less than thirty-four thousand votes but failed to win a majority, which forced her into a special runoff election in April.[14]

A few days after the primary election, the Senate passed Hobby's school finance bill by a vote of twenty-three to nine, with only two Democrats opposed, but it died in the

House on March 28, the last day of the session. Because of a federal appeals court ruling that allowed postponement of a decision, the legislature took no action on a new method of selecting state judges. As soon as the third session adjourned at midnight on March 28, Clements called a fourth session to convene five days later on April 2.[15]

At the end of the session, Hobby took a verbal shot at Republican Rob Mosbacher, chairman of the Texas Department of Human Services (DHS), who was opposing Bob Bullock in the race for lieutenant governor. Mosbacher revealed that the DHS faced an $851 million deficit that the legislature would have to address in the next regular session in January 1991. Hobby accused him of knowingly underestimating DHS budget figures for the legislature in 1989 in order to help Governor Clements fight off a tax increase, an allegation Mosbacher denied. Hobby also suspected that Mosbacher's request to shift revenue from the 1991 fiscal year to 1990 to cover DHS's deficit was "a Republican plot to somehow skate through another year without necessary taxes and leave the problem to blow up for whoever replaces Clements next year." Hobby told reporters the DHS was only weeks away "from going over a cliff." He charged that the department's estimate in 1989 of its needs for the 1990–1991 fiscal year had been "egregiously wrong. I think you can use the word low-balling or you can use the word falsification—either one." Hobby warned that there was "a very distinct possibility" of elderly nursing home patients being forced onto the streets. Although the DHS budget crisis was real, Hobby's attack on Mosbacher also benefitted Bullock's campaign, whether intended or not.[16]

On April 2, Bill Hobby called the Texas Senate to order for its fourth session in slightly less than one year. Eight days into the special session, he hosted a primary runoff watch party in the lieutenant governor's reception room. He was delighted when Richards easily vanquished the mudslinging attorney general whose demagoguery had played a role in Hobby's decision not to run for governor. Richards outpolled Mattox by a 57 to 43 percent margin, obviously benefitting from a decisive shift of Mark White's voters to her side.[17]

As soon as the fourth special session began, it was clear that a majority of members in the House were holding firm to their refusal to increase taxes to pay for the approximately $300 million that Clements said he would accept as an increase in public-school funding. To pay for a third of the $300 million, the House passed a $114 million cut in the higher education budget. It then considered Clements's demand to lay off enough state employees to pay for the remaining amount needed to reach $300 million. Despite a barrage of criticism, Clements held firm to his position. "We've had far too great a growth in our state employees," Clements explained. That proposal and the cut in the higher education budget were clearly unacceptable to Hobby and a majority of the Senate. "I know of no areas where significant reductions could take place without significant reduction of services," Hobby declared. He added that court decisions had already prohibited any cuts in the state's mental health, prison, and welfare departments. Bullock agreed with Hobby. "Texas has 124 state employees per 10,000 residents," Bullock explained, "and the national average is 147. I don't think we have any surplus as far as employees."[18]

The fourth special session ended in a stalemate on May 1. Clements immediately called a fifth session to convene the next day. The legislature passed a $555 million school finance bill after a majority of the House, tiring of the continuing grind of sessions and pressured by the teachers' lobby and hostile newspaper editorials, finally agreed to fund the finance bill with a relatively small increase in the sales tax. As he had promised, however, Clements vetoed the bill, claiming that it would eventually result in "massive budget deficits that could be paid for only through imposition of a state income tax." When the House failed to override the governor's veto, the session adjourned on May 31, once again with nothing accomplished. The back-and-forth between the legislature and Clements continued when he called yet another session, the sixth, to convene on June 4.[19]

At this point, Clements was wearing down, and he indicated his openness to a deal if he could get something in return to give him cover for going back on his word about vetoing any bill that raised taxes. As a result, on June 7, the legislature passed a school finance bill as well as a bill appropriating $100 million to cover the deficit facing the state's social service agencies in 1991. Clements signed the bills that same afternoon, finally ending the saga. The bill Clements signed included increases in the sales tax and the cigarette tax and a new tax on mixed drinks. The bill included relatively inconsequential reductions in the state budget, which allowed Clements to claim credit for a budget cut. Additionally, the legislature granted power to the governor to appoint the state education commissioner, to allow Clements to make the claim that he would be monitoring public-school spending through his commissioner, but in reality it was essentially a symbolic power. The total $633 million package more than doubled the amount the governor had previously said he would accept. When Clements signed the bill, he grumbled that it would eventually lead to Bill Hobby's state income tax.[20]

Confident the legislature would pass the new bill, Bill and Diana were in New York City the morning of June 7. The previous night Bill had attended the dedication of a new museum featuring the retired naval aircraft carrier USS *Intrepid*, which was docked at Pier 86 on the Hudson River. After the dedication ceremony, the attendees sat on the deck of the carrier for a black-tie dinner celebrating the forty-sixth anniversary of D-Day, which included a ceremony honoring Dwight Eisenhower. Bill was there to represent his eighty-five-year-old mother, Oveta, who was in poor health and unable to travel.[21]

The next morning, Bill and Diana flew to Texas in time for Bill to adjourn the Senate and attend Clements's bill signing. That day was Hobby's last as the presiding officer of the Texas Senate. Hobby told reporters the struggle to equalize public-school funding had been the "toughest" problem he had dealt with during his seventeen years as lieutenant governor. He warned that the recently passed bill fell far short of being a permanent solution to that problem. The plaintiffs in the court case, who were criticizing the legislation as inadequate, were already filing a new lawsuit to challenge it. Hobby complained that the appropriation for the Departments of Human Services, Health and Mental Health, and Mental Retardation was merely a Band-Aid that would only cover the year 1991. The legislature would have to face that problem as well as school funding again in January 1991. Hobby observed that when "you look around government—whether it's state government or federal government, or I guess international relations—there aren't ever any problems that are solved; there are situations that are managed."[22]

After Clements signed the bill, Hobby attended a party at Carl Parker's Austin residence celebrating the new legislation. The following week, he helped relieve some of the residual stress that had built up during the eighteen-month struggle to resolve the public-school funding crisis by playing racquetball nearly every afternoon with his favorite partners, Max Sherman, Ray Farabee, and Bill Cunningham. The next weekend Hobby was back in Houston catching up with the horseback riding he had not had time to enjoy during the almost continuous legislative sessions. Free of official duties until the next Legislative Budget Board meetings in the fall, Bill and Diana took a vacation the entire month of July, starting with a four-day visit to Beaver Creek, Colorado, where they stayed with Ray and Kay Bailey Hutchison at the Hutchisons' condominium. That was followed by a two-week visit to Ireland, where Bill and Diana attended a horse show, and London, where they were lodged at Winfield House as the guests of Bill's brother-in-law, Henry Catto, who was now the US ambassador to the United Kingdom. Max Sherman and his wife, Gene, and Bill Hobby's mentor from St. Albans, John Davis, joined them in London.[23]

On July 30, the Hobbys flew from London to Denver, where they boarded a flight to Aspen to attend the fortieth-anniversary conference of the Aspen Institute. On trips to Aspen, they would ordinarily reside at the Cattos' sprawling Woody Creek home, but on August 1, the Cattos would have a special houseguest, British prime minister Margaret Thatcher and her husband, Denis. The Thatchers had accepted Henry Catto's invitation to speak at the Aspen conference. President George H. W. Bush was also coming to Aspen to address the conference on August 2 and to visit with the prime minister at the Cattos' home, where he would also spend the night, surrounded by the White House press corps outside and Secret Service agents. As a result of the visit of these VIPs and their tight security arrangements, Bill and Diana stayed at Aspen's exclusive Snowmass Club.[24]

During the night of August 1, several hours prior to Bush's arrival at Aspen the next morning, Iraq invaded Kuwait, an action that would soon lead to US intervention and the Gulf War. General Brent Scowcroft called Henry Catto that morning and told him that Bush had decided to go forward with his speech in Aspen despite Iraq's invasion. Thatcher's coincidental presence in Aspen would give President Bush an opportunity to have a face-to-face discussion with the British prime minister about the crisis in the Middle East. However, the president would have to return to Washington that same night. The Hobbys were not at the Cattos' ranch during the meeting between Bush and Thatcher, but they did attend a small informal dinner the Cattos hosted at Woody

Creek for the president immediately following his address to the Aspen conference. The next day, Bill Hobby joined Albert Shanker, president of the American Federation of Teachers, to address a conference working group on education and economic competitiveness. On August 4, the Hobbys attended another private dinner at the Catto home in Woody Creek in honor of Margaret Thatcher. The following day, Bill and Diana departed from Aspen after attending Thatcher's speech to the conference.[25]

Hobby returned to Texas in time to take part in planning sessions for Ann Richards's campaign for governor and Bob Bullock's race for lieutenant governor in the general election in November. Polling indicated a probable victory for Bullock over Rob Mosbacher, his forty-year-old Republican opponent. However, Richards faced a much more difficult battle against her Republican opponent, fifty-seven-year-old Midland, Texas, rancher and banker Clayton "Claytie" Williams Jr., who enjoyed a twenty-point lead in the polls early in the campaign. Williams's nomination was a slightly awkward development for Hobby because of a minor and temporary connection he had with the West Texan's business enterprise, Claydesta Communications, a long-distance telephone service.

In 1988, before Williams became a candidate for governor, Hobby was an investor in his company, which was seeking to expand into Houston. In October of that year, Hobby had been a featured speaker at a dinner in Midland in honor of Williams. Later that same month, Hobby sent a letter to one hundred businessmen in Houston introducing Williams and announcing that he was bringing his fiber-optic long-distance telephone service to the Bayou City. Hobby invited the businessmen to attend a reception where they could meet Williams and hear his sales pitch for their businesses. Despite this relatively insignificant business connection with Williams, Hobby remained a stalwart supporter of his friend Ann Richards.[26]

In addition to serving with San Antonio mayor Henry Cisneros and former congresswoman Barbara Jordan as a Richards campaign cochair, Hobby once again aided Richards by giving her access to his airplane for campaign trips, attending occasional campaign strategy meetings in Houston, and appearing at a small number of special campaign events. The fact that Glenn Smith, Hobby's former chief of staff, served as Richards's campaign manager was further evidence of Hobby's close connection to Richards's gubernatorial crusade.[27]

Richards trailed Williams in the polls for most of the campaign, but a series of controversial comments proved to be the latter's undoing. He was quoted during the Republican primary campaign comparing rape to bad weather, stating, "If it's inevitable, just relax and enjoy it." As a result of that remark as well as other similar comments, significant numbers of outraged women voters, including Republicans, abandoned the Williams cause. On November 6, Richards narrowly defeated Williams by slightly more than ninety-nine thousand votes, while Bullock easily won his race for lieutenant governor. Hobby hosted another election night watch party in the lieutenant governor's reception room at the Capitol and was delighted by Richards's surprising victory.[28]

Bob Bullock was now lieutenant governor elect. Hobby formally remained in office until January 15, 1991, although his only remaining official duty was to attend his final Legislative Budget Board meeting in mid-December. Before Bill fulfilled that duty, he and Diana flew once again to their beloved Ireland for a retreat away from Texas. After spending a month at Beechwood House in County Tipperary, the Hobbys made an overnight stop in London on their return trip to Houston, where they once again stayed at Winfield House, the ambassador's residence, and attended Henry Catto's birthday party.[29]

When Hobby returned to Texas on December 7, Bullock announced the appointment of Bill and Diana's son Paul, a graduate of the University of Virginia and the University of Texas Law School, to be his executive assistant for the upcoming regular legislative session. Prior to his appointment, Paul had been on the US attorney's staff in Houston. His appointment immediately set off speculation about his political future. When a reporter asked Bill Hobby if his son was planning to continue the family tradition of seeking elected public office, Bill smiled and said, "Um, it's possible."[30]

On January 8, 1991, eleven days before his fifty-ninth birthday, Bill Hobby attended the opening ceremony of the new legislative session, where he formally handed his gavel over to Bob Bullock. John Montford unveiled a bronze bust of Hobby, which depicted him wearing his trademark bow tie. Montford declared that the bust, which was the work of Houston's Chinese American sculptor Wei Li "Willy" Wang, would be placed in a prominent place in the Senate Chamber to serve as "a lasting reminder of what public service should be all about." Bill and Diana had first seen and approved the finished sculpture in Wang's Houston studio the previous September. Ann Richards joined Hobby and Bullock on the rostrum. Addressing the Senate, Richards declared that Hobby had been "a mentor to me. I can think of no person in political life who has been more significant in my personal and political growth."[31]

During a meeting with reporters immediately after the ceremony, Hobby looked back on his eighteen years in office and observed that the "issues never change much," including problems with public-school finance, ethics scandals, and funding for highways, prisons, and human services. "Those were the basic problems 70 years ago when my father was here, and they will be the basic problems 20 years from now. People have been passing laws for about 5,000 years now. If it was possible to solve problems by passing laws, they would all be eliminated."[32]

Hobby told reporters he would not be hanging around the Capitol as a political advisor and certainly not as a lobbyist. "I'm not any senior statesman," he said. "I don't like to give gratuitous advice to people, and I've got other things to do." The things to do included chairing Hobby & Catto Communications and serving as a member of the board of rapidly growing Southwest Airlines. He also eagerly looked forward to continuing his teaching at the university level, not only at Rice but also at the University of Texas at Austin. In October 1990, as Bill Hobby's final term in office neared its end, his good friends UT Austin president Bill Cunningham and former state senator Max Sherman, who had become dean of the university's Lyndon B. Johnson School of Public

Affairs in 1983, arranged an appointment for Hobby to serve on the LBJ School's faculty as the Sid Richardson Chair in Public Affairs. Hobby's teaching duties would begin with the spring semester in 1991. When the news broke about Hobby's appointment, Lady Bird Johnson sent him a card expressing her delight. "I beam that you have become the Sid Richardson Professor! It makes me proud and satisfied that those students have you."[33]

CHAPTER 19

REQUIEM FOR THE POST

The Lyndon B. Johnson School of Public Affairs is housed in Sid Richardson Hall, a building on the east side of the University of Texas at Austin campus adjacent to the LBJ Library and Museum. Opened in 1970, the school's mission is to produce public policy specialists and analysts to fill positions at all levels of government. Beginning in late January 1991, teaching at the LBJ School became one of Bill Hobby's main professional interests as a former lieutenant governor of Texas. Those interests included chairing his family business, Hobby & Catto (H&C) Communications, serving on the Southwest Airlines board, and continuing to co-teach his course at Rice one day a week. But teaching at the LBJ School would take up most of his working time. Because H&C Communications no longer owned a newspaper, and Jack Harris, Jim Crowther, and their administrative teams managed the day-to-day affairs of the company's television and radio properties, Hobby had no full-time duties at the company; in addition, he and his sister, Jessica, were contemplating the sale of H&C's assets. As a Southwest Airlines director, Bill's responsibilities were largely restricted to quarterly meetings of the board.[1]

When the University of Texas announced the former lieutenant governor's appointment to the faculty, reporters asked UT System chancellor Hans Mark what Hobby would teach. "Whatever he wants," Mark answered. Hobby, however, was more specific. He told reporters he would teach practical courses about how state government "really" works. Hobby persuaded Saralee Tiede to serve as co-instructor in his Media and Public Policy seminar. Hobby would eventually teach courses on healthcare costs and access, public education, and the Texas budget process and statistics. He co-taught the latter class with Tom Keel, former director of the Legislative Budget Board staff and chief fiscal officer for the University of Texas System. Tiede later observed that because of

Hobby's deep interest in higher education, joining the faculty at the LBJ School was the logical next step for him. "I think he found university professors stimulating and he liked to be around them," she noted. "At the LBJ School he was trying to create for students a sense of the decision-making process in government. He had guest speakers, people like the publisher of the *Dallas Morning News* and key state senators. He didn't like to lecture. He would start the class with a good ten-minute introduction, but that would be about it, then it would go to discussion or to whoever was co-teaching with him at the time."[2]

Jack McGrew, who had been an executive at the Hobbys' radio and television stations in Houston before his retirement in 1981, audited one of Bill's first classes in the spring of 1991. He reported back to Oveta, who was now eighty-six years old and living in seclusion at her apartment in Houston, "Since you already know my affection for your son, you will not be surprised to learn that I expected to be impressed [with his teaching]. I was not disappointed. He is as much at home in the college classroom as he was in the Senate chamber, or in the board rooms. I was equally pleased to observe the attitude of the students toward him."[3]

To cap off the completion of Hobby's first semester as a professor at the university, as well as to honor him for his staunch support of higher education as lieutenant governor, UT Austin president Bill Cunningham invited Hobby to deliver the university's commencement address in May 1991. With slightly more than five thousand students in attendance at the ceremony held on the South Mall of the campus, Hobby urged the students, as the beneficiaries of a public-college degree, to do everything possible to support an investment in education at all levels in Texas and the nation. That investment, he pointed out, "doesn't have an immediate return. It takes a generation to see the results. But it is absolutely critical to our society." He called for a longer-than-nine-month public-school calendar, higher teacher salaries, improved working conditions, and smaller class sizes. He also stressed the need for supporting more research, "even if the immediate gain isn't clear." He continued to call for a major restructuring of the state's tax system "to fit our changed economy and retool our systems of education to face the future proudly." Afterward, Governor Ann Richards sent Hobby a handwritten note: "Your commencement address was (is) great. Who wrote it? Don't lie, I need good speech writers with a sense of humor. Love, as always, A."[4]

Although Hobby was now a professor, he was not entirely free of involvement in government. A few days after the end of UT Austin's spring semester, Hobby agreed to serve on Governor Richards's sixteen-member revenue task force, chaired by former Texas governor John Connally. Once again, Texas state government faced a budget shortfall. This time the Legislative Budget Board projected the amount to be approximately $4.7 billion for the 1992–1993 fiscal year if all current services were maintained at their present levels. In response to the board's estimate, Governor Richards called a special legislative session to convene on July 8. The governor asked her task force to recommend a plan for a more equitable state revenue system that would avoid or at least lessen the frequent budget shortfalls. That had long been one of Hobby's goals as lieutenant governor, which made him an obvious choice for the task force.

The task force soon produced two competing proposals—one by Connally and the other by Hobby—that reflected the conflicting views of two strong-minded former state officials. Connally's recommendations included doubling state college tuition fees, implementing a state lottery, and reducing the state's contribution to the Teacher Retirement System of Texas. Predictably, Hobby's plan called for a state income tax and an eventual reduction in sales and property taxes. He also recommended a 100 percent increase in tuition for four-year colleges and universities, explaining that Texas ranked last in the nation in tuition fees. Dallas businessman and Hobby ally Jess Hay, who also served on the task force, supported Hobby's plan. Senator John Montford, chair of the Senate Finance Committee, however, declared that Hobby's income tax proposal would be dead on arrival in the Texas Legislature. By the time the legislature adjourned its special session on August 13, Hobby's call for a state income tax had died a quiet death, although legislators did adopt part of Connally's and Hobby's plans and raised taxes by $2.1 billion, largely by broadening and raising the sales tax, increasing the fees for state services, and imposing a modest hike in college tuition. The legislature also passed a bill for a referendum on a constitutional amendment to permit a state lottery.[5]

In 1993 Texas voters passed a constitutional amendment banning a state income tax. When Bob Bullock distributed a newsletter boasting that the 1993 Senate sessions had been "the most productive" in many years, Bill sent him a handwritten note: "Bullock—Where did you get the stuff you smoke? The 1973–1991 sessions were pretty productive. At least we didn't ban an income tax!" Bullock replied, "Governor—You had 18 years to come out for an income tax. I always wondered why you didn't do it when you were elected instead of waiting until the last days in office. I appreciate you even reading my newsletter. Bullock."[6]

Hobby's concerns about the budgets of institutions of higher education included his alma mater, Rice University, although it was a private institution. In the spring of 1992, while serving on the Rice University Board of Directors, he caused a minor controversy when he complained publicly that Rice should stop spending $5.5 million a year on its football team. As Hobby's friend UT Austin president Bill Cunningham later observed, "Bill Hobby didn't care about football at all. I mean not at all." Hobby was quoted in Rice's student newspaper calling Rice's football program an "anachronistic albatross" with a budget that would be better spent on the library and on academics. His complaint was made after Rice president George Rupp issued a statement that athletics had lowered the university's academic standards and was a money loser. A cheating scandal in the athletics department a few months earlier had inspired these complaints. Several faculty members agreed with Hobby and called for athletics to be terminated. Board chairman and prominent Houston businessman Charles Duncan declared his strong disagreement with Hobby's and Rupp's comments. Led by Duncan, the Rice board voted to continue the football program.[7]

During this period, Hobby also publicly criticized Houston's historically Black Texas Southern University. Complaining that TSU seemed unable to resolve its serious, long-standing financial problems, he charged that the school was cheating its students out of a good education and that the school was an unnecessary duplication of educational offerings that were available at the nearby University of Houston. As was the case when he complained about Rice's football program, Hobby's comment about TSU stepped on many toes. One of the negative reactions came from the TSU faculty president. "We are completely and totally outraged at the lieutenant governor's position. He does make me wonder how much intellectual honesty he has." Other comments implied that Hobby's criticism had revealed his racism.[8]

Houston Post columnist Robert Newberry, a Black alumnus of the University of Houston, quickly came to Hobby's defense. Hobby had hired Newberry in the 1960s as a reporter for the *Post*. He was the only Black reporter on the *Post* when he was hired, at a time when the *Houston Chronicle* had no Black reporters. Newberry denied the charge that Hobby was a racist. He said Hobby was simply frustrated by TSU's poor management of its financial affairs. "And I can understand," he stated. "He has watched for years as TSU officials squandered money and failed to improve the school, while saying they were going to make improvements."[9]

Sometime during the final months that Hobby served as lieutenant governor in 1990, the Hobbys' legal and financial advisors persuaded Bill that it was time to reorganize or sell the family's media holdings. Those holdings not only included their radio and television properties in Houston but also five other television stations the Hobbys had purchased in the 1980s. The Hobbys' radio and television stations had been business subsidiaries of the Channel 2 Television Company, which had been a subsidiary of the Houston Post Company.

After the sale of the *Post* in 1983, which did not include the Channel 2 Television Company or their television stations in Nashville, Tennessee, and Tucson, Arizona, Oveta and her children, Bill and Jessica, had organized H&C Incorporated to serve as the corporate owner of the broadcast properties. The Hobbys appointed longtime family business executive and legal counsel Jim Crowther president of the new company. Two years after selling the *Post*, H&C purchased television stations in Des Moines, Iowa, and Daytona Beach–Orlando, Florida. A year later, the company added KSAT-TV in San Antonio to their holdings at a cost of $153 million in cash. The purchase of KSAT was apparently urged by Bill's brother-in-law, Henry Catto, who had become vice president of H&C and was still a partner in Catto & Catto, his family's insurance brokerage firm in San Antonio. At the time, Henry and Jessica Catto were living in McLean, Virginia, where Jessica published the *Washington Journalism Review*. The television stations were generating a combined total of more than $23 million in net income by the early 1990s.[10]

H&C was privately owned by Bill, Jessica, and Oveta. Paul Hobby was vice president, and Laura Hobby Beckworth was general counsel. Now in her late eighties, Oveta was experiencing a rapid decline in health. Her death would have serious inheritance tax complications that threatened a major loss of assets if the family failed to reorganize or sell off its holdings. Laura Hobby Beckworth later recalled that H&C also had "all the problems that go with running a business," including real estate, liability, personnel, and union issues that were becoming increasingly problematic. An additional reason for the decision to sell was Bill Hobby's lack of interest in running the company. Although his mother continued to participate in H&C management decisions, it was clear that Bill would have to perform most of the duties of chairmanship, for which he had little interest. Bill had always been more involved in the family's former newspaper property, the *Houston Post*, than the television stations.[11]

Two members of the family, Paul Hobby and Bill's brother-in-law, Henry Catto, opposed the sale. Paul wanted to run the company. "That was okay with my father because he didn't have any interest," Paul recalled. "And nobody else in my generation had the interest or the aptitude. My aunt [Jessica] initially thought it was a good idea. And then she thought it was a bad idea. There were times when I complained to my father that his sister was behaving inconsistently. And he would say, 'Welcome to my world. Are you sure you want to be part of that?' And I thought, 'Yeah, probably not.'" Henry Catto also opposed the plan to sell the media properties, but Bill and Jessica ultimately prevailed. Henry admitted in his memoir that the decision to liquidate was made only "after a great deal of debate. Jessica and Bill decided to sell the family television company, both having doubts about the industry's future and the best way of running things. I hated to see it happen. I loved the years spent working for H&C and I had thought I might return to it if my government career ended. That, however, was not to be."[12]

At the time, Paul explained to a reporter that the family wanted to diversify its holdings. "The media world is changing very quickly and, in that environment, our people want to broaden their base of investments." On May 19, 1992, H&C Communications announced that they had sold all five of their television stations to Young Broadcasting of New York City. The deal soon failed, however, when that company went into involuntary bankruptcy before the sale was completed. After the agreement collapsed, H&C sold the television stations in Florida and Iowa to the Pulitzer Company in February 1993 for $165 million in cash. Within a year they also sold their television properties in Tucson and San Antonio, as well as KPRC-TV, their pioneering station in Houston. After negotiations that began near the end of 1993, the *Washington Post* agreed to pay H&C $253 million for KPRC-TV. The cash deal was closed on January 31 and finalized on April 22, 1994. The *Washington Post*'s Katharine Graham and Oveta Culp Hobby were old friends who for years had talked about the Washington paper possibly buying the television station.[13]

The staff at KPRC-TV welcomed the sale of the station to the *Washington Post*. Former news anchor Ron Stone admitted that it had been "agonizing to watch the station just float along with no direction." According to a story in the *Houston Chronicle*, KPRC-TV had suffered during the two years it took for the Hobbys to sell the station. Media critic

Eric Gerber claimed that KPRC-TV had been "missing in action" the past few years. He predicted the *Washington Post*'s purchase "should mark the beginning of a new era, trying to revitalize a once-impressive news department that has been belt-tightened into mediocrity and mired in third place [in ratings]." Gerber explained that "when the Hobby family decided to sell the station, money for new purchases and maintenance was cut drastically to hold down expenses."[14]

In October 1993, the Hobbys sold their only remaining media property, KPRC-Radio, to Sunbelt Broadcasting (managed by future Texas lieutenant governor Dan Patrick, a right-wing talk-radio host). The sale of KPRC-Radio ended more than six decades of the Hobbys' association with the station, including five decades of ownership. The sale of these long-held Hobby broadcast venues occurred during the last two years of Oveta's life. No record can be found documenting any role she might have played in the decision to let the properties go, but Oveta was mentally alert and still actively engaged in family matters until only a few months before she died. It can be reasonably assumed that Bill and Jessica consulted with her in the matter and that she approved.[15]

While the Hobbys were trying to sell their television stations in 1992, the presidential campaign was dominating national attention. President George H. W. Bush was seeking a second term. A year earlier, because of the successful war to remove the Iraqi Army from Kuwait, his approval ratings had been so high that he seemed unbeatable. In 1992, however, the US economy took a serious downturn that was largely blamed on his administration, and his approval ratings plunged. Arkansas governor William J. "Bill" Clinton won the Democratic nomination for president in the summer of 1992, with Tennessee senator Al Gore as his vice presidential running mate.

Although Hobby normally favored Democratic candidates for public office and he abhorred the Republican right wing, his support for Democrats was never guaranteed. He had voted for George H. W. Bush when he ran unsuccessfully against Democrat Lloyd Bentsen in the 1970 Texas race for US Senate. He also supported the reelection of some Republican members of the Texas Senate, including moderates Cyndi Taylor Krier and Bill Ratliff, and on occasion, a Republican candidate for statewide office, especially Kay Bailey Hutchison. Hobby's support of Ratliff for an East Texas Senate seat angered Ed Martin, executive director of the state's Democratic Party. "Bill Hobby doesn't have a vote in that election," Martin peevishly told a reporter. "[Hobby] is from Houston, and I don't know if the people in northeast Texas are interested in having someone from Houston tell them how to vote." "Political parties don't interest Bill Hobby," Saralee Tiede has observed. "He thinks they're bad for public policy. He would help Republican senators to get reelected because he believes totally in merit."[16]

Hobby's basic disdain for political partisanship didn't prevent him from lashing out at what he considered to be Republican idiocy. For example, when angered, he wasn't shy about launching scorching verbal volleys at Republicans, calling Bill Clements a "fool," George Strake Jr. a "certifiable idiot," and US senator Phil Gramm "incredibly dumb." George Strake was a special Hobby target. "Most officeholders are affronted when anyone runs against them," Tiede noted. "But with Strake, he and Hobby shared the same social circles, and they had the same friends in Houston. I think it was a disappointment and surprise to [Hobby] that someone he thought he could get along with quite well should all of a sudden be running against him." Likewise, Hobby didn't exclude some Democrats from his pique. When he was lieutenant governor, Hobby frequently clashed with Democratic senator Carlos Truan, for whom Hobby had little respect. Hobby never appointed Truan to be chairman of a committee, despite his thirteen years in the Senate.[17]

Hobby didn't waver in his support for the Democrats' national ticket. Because he'd supported his friend Al Gore in his failed bid for the presidential nomination in 1988, it was no surprise when Hobby endorsed the Clinton-Gore ticket. On July 23, 1992, he made his support clear when he and Diana hosted a fundraiser for the Clinton-Gore campaign at their home on South Boulevard that Bill Clinton attended. Hobby actively worked for the Clinton campaign in Texas throughout the fall, but he was disappointed and frustrated that Clinton's team, assuming Bush was unbeatable in his home state, decided to send the candidates elsewhere and to not invest money in Texas. Hobby and Ann Richards sent several messages to Clinton headquarters in Little Rock insisting that Texas was winnable, but the Clinton team ignored their pleas. Hobby questioned his friends just before the election: "Do you know where Bill Clinton is today? He's in Colorado. Colorado has eight electoral votes. Hasn't anyone told him that Texas has thirty-two?" As it turned out, the Democrats didn't need Texas, as Bill Clinton defeated President Bush and Independent candidate Ross Perot for the presidency. It was the beginning of the national Democratic Party's long period of giving up on any prospects of carrying the Lone Star State.[18]

On December 10, 1992, President-elect Clinton appointed Lloyd Bentsen secretary of the treasury. Speculation about whom Governor Richards would choose to replace Bentsen in the US Senate began immediately. The three most likely candidates appeared to be Bill Hobby, former San Antonio mayor Henry Cisneros, and Comptroller John Sharp. The day after Clinton announced Bentsen's selection, Hobby's phone rang constantly with calls, and messages filled his mailbox urging him to lobby Richards for the Senate appointment. Kent Caperton and Grant Jones were among the strongest advocates for Hobby's candidacy. However, on January 5, 1993, Governor Richards appointed Texas Railroad Commissioner Robert Krueger to the US Senate seat vacated by Bentsen. Krueger, a moderate Democrat from New Braunfels, was a former member of the US Congress who had lost election campaigns for the US Senate in 1978 and 1984. Why did the governor appoint Krueger and not her friend and political mentor Bill Hobby? There are conflicting explanations. Paul Hobby stated that he didn't believe Richards ever officially offered the job to his father. "I don't know whether he would have accepted it or not. Probably he would have. It would have been an ending cap on his career. It would have been hard to turn that down. But I don't think she ever actually offered it to him." Saralee Tiede wasn't sure either. "I don't know what conversations

Bill had with Ann. But ultimately, I didn't feel like it was something that he wanted to campaign for in the special election or in the general election. He would have liked it if Ann had waved her wand and said you're going to be the senator. 'If I can have this job and just be a senator, that'll be fine. But if I have to campaign statewide again, no.'"[19]

In an oral history interview years later, however, Hobby said that Richards asked him if he would accept the Senate appointment, but he told her he was deeply conflicted about the job because of the lifestyle he would have to adopt as a senator. "I didn't like the idea of having to travel back and forth between Houston and Washington every weekend." Hobby also knew that Richards was under great pressure to appoint someone who would fight to hold the Senate seat for the Democrats in the coming elections. "I couldn't promise Ann that I would run for reelection in 1994, because I wasn't happy about campaigning, which was the main reason I decided against running for governor in 1990." Hobby's reluctance to take the job was probably a relief to Richards, who surely had doubts about how much effort Hobby would put into the special election campaign scheduled to be held in June. Hobby mailed a template letter to the individuals who had urged him to go after the Senate appointment: "Dear SUPPORTER: Many thanks for your interest in my potential involvement in the soon-to-be-vacated U.S. Senate seat in Texas. As you know, Governor Richards has appointed Railroad Commissioner Bob Krueger to that seat, and I shall support him in the forthcoming election."[20]

It's probable that Richards preferred the charismatic Henry Cisneros as Bentsen's replacement. But Clinton tapped Cisneros for his cabinet as secretary of housing and urban development. Some Democrats lobbied for Jim Mattox because he was progressive and a tough campaigner, but after all the mud he had tossed at her during the 1990 primary election campaign, Richards obviously was not going to appoint him and instead turned to Bob Krueger. Krueger's term as senator was brief, however. He lost a special election to Hobby's friend, Republican Kay Bailey Hutchison, in June 1993, six months after his appointment in January. Hobby was not brokenhearted by Krueger's defeat, because the victory went to his longtime friend. He sent his congratulations to Hutchison on the "termination of your opponent and your entry into the Rusk succession of the Texas seat in the U.S. Senate. Diana and I share your pride in your accomplishment and I wish you a long career of service to your state and nation."[21]

In March 1993, Richards found a position to which she could appoint Hobby: the nine-member board of the Texas Parks and Wildlife Commission. The appointment, which was for a six-year term, surprised Hobby. He told the *Austin American-Statesman*'s Dave McNeely that he hadn't sought the position, "but the governor asked me to do it and when governors ask me to do things I usually do it." In his newspaper column, McNeely noted that "Hobby is an avid bird hunter" and that he "[chases] foxes on horseback every November in Ireland and is mindful of the need to continue to expand the commission's role of reaching beyond the traditional hunting and fishing communities." McNeely also observed that Richards selected "her fishing and hunting buddy Hobby" because she trusted him implicitly.[22]

Membership on the commission was not an honorary, pro forma job. The commission is responsible for directing the overall management and protection of the state's wildlife habitats, parklands, and historic areas. McNeely wrote that "[Richards] owed [Hobby]; he probably could have prevailed on her to give him the U.S. Senate seat she gave to Bob Krueger—had he pushed it. But he didn't, and she respected that." Hobby served less than two years of his term on the Parks and Wildlife Commission. He resigned in early December 1994, explaining that his teaching duties demanded so much of his time that he couldn't contribute to the commission as much as he wanted.[23]

By January 1994, Bill Hobby was free from his governmental responsibilities, except for his duties as a member of the Parks and Wildlife Commission, which would end with his resignation by the end of the year. He did continue his involvement in the public policy arena with an op-ed column that was published on a semiregular basis in several newspapers in Texas, including the *Austin American-Statesman*, the *Dallas Morning News*, and the *San Antonio Express-News*. His topics ranged from healthcare reform to a new law to make it easier for veterans to be certified to teach in public schools.[24]

Hobby also remained on the board of Southwest Airlines, which had its own perks, including hunting trips to chairman Herb Kelleher's family ranch in West Texas with his friend and fellow board member Bill Cunningham and other directors. Those visits were elaborate affairs. "The first night at the ranch we would have a marvelous dinner with the best steaks and the finest wines," Cunningham later recalled. "The dinner would go on till eleven o'clock at night." At eight o'clock the next morning, the group would climb into the large SUVs Kelleher had on hand and go hunting. Hobby usually rode with Cunningham, John Montford, and Kelleher. "The bar in the back of the Suburban rivaled the bar at Austin's Four Seasons Hotel," Cunningham noted. "I'm not sure that combination of guns and alcohol makes a lot of sense, but we were out there five or six trips and never shot at an animal. No one wanted to kill anything. So, we spent the whole day driving around the ranch talking and bullshitting about world affairs." Cunningham observed that "it was clear Bill [Hobby] thoroughly enjoyed those escapades at Herb's ranch."[25]

According to Cunningham, Hobby was "a great board member. He was always very well prepared and highly regarded by management and his fellow board members." Cunningham also recalled that Hobby, who was a determined number cruncher, had a reputation on the board for being hard on Southwest's auditors, Ernst & Young. He was one of the only board members who paid detailed attention to the auditors' math, and he resisted paying the firm higher fees than he thought they deserved. "We always had to push him to vote to give any kind of increase in fees. We loved to kid him about it."[26]

Hobby also continued to teach at Rice and at the LBJ School. Because his teaching was a pleasure, not a burden, Hobby was spending much of his time on the two university campuses. During the spring semester of 1994, he co-taught an early-morning course on state legislative policy at Rice, and then he would fly to Austin to teach courses on the Texas state budget and state water policy at the University of Texas. He found his relationship with students and faculty intellectually stimulating.[27]

During an interview for a profile of Hobby in the *Houston Post* in 1994, longtime family employee Marguerite Johnston told a reporter that Hobby's retirement from politics and business had given him "a sense of freedom." A visible sign of that sense of liberty was the beard Hobby now sported, as well as even less concern about his clothing than when he'd been in public office. Journalist Robert Bryce described Hobby during the 1990s, writing that "whatever his clothing, [Hobby] always looked slightly rumpled, a look that is accentuated by his close-cropped beard. He hardly looks—or dresses—for the role of cultural and political heavyweight." When Bryce met Hobby at a meeting in Austin, he noted that the hem of the right sleeve of Hobby's blazer was ripped out and his black trousers had "a large, whitish stain on the right knee." To Bryce, the overall effect was "reminiscent of an absent-minded college professor. It's one of the traits that makes Hobby so intriguing. Here's a man with the kind of financial resources that most people can only dream about . . . yet he drives a . . . Chevrolet Caprice Classic station wagon with fake wood paneling on the sides. Political observers have never been sure what to make of him."[28]

Bill Hobby's newfound freedom also gave him and Diana the opportunity in 1994 to travel even more than they had in the past, which in 1994 included vacation trips to Mexico (February), Colorado (July), Montana (August), Spain (September), and Ireland (November), where they resided at Beechwood House for the entire month. Hobby also took advantage of his new independence to make two extended trips to Asia that resulted from his deepening relationship with the LBJ School of Public Affairs. On May 26, 1994, after the end of the spring semester, Hobby departed on a flight to Hong Kong, where he spent two days sightseeing before traveling to Mainland China for additional touring and then linking up with Max Sherman in Wuhan. Hobby and Sherman's mission was to establish formal ties between the LBJ School and Chinese universities in Wuhan, Beijing, and Shanghai. The expedition to Asia was followed with another in October. Hobby, who took a leave from teaching that fall semester, traveled to Bangladesh, where he lectured as part of a Ford Foundation–funded exchange program between the University of Texas at Austin and Bangladesh University. He also met with government officials in Bangladesh to discuss water regulatory policy. That trip, which included side visits to Thailand and Bhutan, lasted nearly three weeks.[29]

When Ann Richards faced reelection as governor in 1994, her opponent was George W. Bush, former president Bush's oldest son. Because of her high approval ratings in the polls early in the campaign and her national celebrity, most of the state's political prognosticators predicted her victory. Hobby shared those expectations, especially because her opponent was an inarticulate person whose only claim to fame was his last name. Never one to take election success for granted, Hobby helped his friend's campaign when he could, although his extensive travel plans kept him from much personal involvement. His main contribution was once again making his airplane and his longtime pilot, Bob Cargill, available to Richards. In a note thanking Hobby, Richards wrote, "Not only am I happy to have the plane ($10,000 worth) but I'm thrilled to spend more time with Cargill." Because he was out of the country for the last six weeks of the contest, Hobby found it difficult to keep up-to-date with developments. He did receive troubling reports before he went to Bangladesh, however, that Richards was waging a desultory campaign and that she and Bush were essentially tied in the polls. Bill and Diana were in Ireland when he received the news on November 9 that Bush had defeated Richards decisively.[30]

On January 19, 1995, Bill Hobby celebrated his sixty-third birthday and his mother's ninetieth at a dinner party in Austin at the Headliners Club. He assumed that the new year would not be much different from any of the years he had spent since leaving elected office. Oveta, whose health had continued its long decline, remained in seclusion at her home at the Huntingdon, a residential building in Houston. Bill would soon be on his way to attend another quarterly Southwest Airlines board meeting at the Biltmore Hotel in Phoenix. After being away from the classroom in the fall of 1994, he would renew his teaching at the LBJ School with a twice-weekly class on statistics and a weekly course on the news media and government. His involvement in the administrative workings of the LBJ School would deepen with faculty meetings, student counseling sessions, and budget planning with Max Sherman and his staff. In between those activities at the school, Bill kept busy playing racquetball with Bill Cunningham, Max Sherman, and Ray Farabee at UT Austin's Bellmont Hall; having meals with friends and colleagues at private clubs in Austin, including Tarry House and the Headliners; and giving an occasional guest lecture at Rice in Houston, where he spent most weekends at home. Hobby had left the Rice University Board of Directors, and in 1995 he was no longer teaching a regular class at the university. Traveling remained on his agenda, with trips scheduled to New Orleans, Colorado, Mexico, and Forest Home, Diana's family place in North Carolina, among other destinations.[31]

Two events in 1995, however, would mark the end of an era in the history of the Hobby family. The first occurred on April 18, 1995, when the front page of that day's *Houston Post* declared that it was the paper's last edition. The *Post* had sold its assets to the rival *Houston Chronicle*, including the flagship building on Southwest Freeway, and it ceased operations immediately. Although the Hobby family had not owned the newspaper since 1983, it was a sadly symbolic event for Bill Hobby, for whom it signified the end of the entity that had served as the foundation of the family's fortune and his parents' most important business legacy. The Toronto Sun Company, which had bought the *Houston Post* ten years earlier, had sold the paper only two years later to entrepreneurs Dean Singleton and Richard Scudder for $150 million. Singleton also owned the *Dallas Times Herald* at the time. Earlier, Singleton had tried to buy the *Houston Chronicle* from the Houston Endowment, but the Hearst Corporation outbid him. The *Post* had been a money loser for its Canadian owners, and it continued to be unprofitable for Singleton and Scudder, despite major staff layoffs and other cost reductions.[32]

Five days after the *Post* printed and distributed its last issue, the *Houston Chronicle* published Bill Hobby's op-ed piece "A Requiem for *The Houston Post*." "The *Houston*

Post is dead," Hobby lamented. It was "not just a business," he wrote, "but a voice, a personality, that was a vital part of Houston for more than a century. My family and I were involved with the *Post* for most of that century. My father went to work there on March 2, 1895, shortly before his 18th birthday." Hobby explained that Singleton and Scudder's decision to close the newspaper was understandable because of difficult economic conditions, including the rapid growth of competing news sources, the loss of advertising, and the ever-increasing cost of operations and printing equipment ("used only a few hours a day"). The price of newsprint had gone up 40 percent in the past year, yet the cost to readers of single copies as well as subscriptions was almost free. "When all the numbers are added up," Hobby explained, "a newspaper is dead."[33]

Hobby later observed in his memoir, "The death of a newspaper is not like the death of a grocery store or a bank or a movie theater. However noble grocery stores are, they do not entertain, enrage, or challenge people the way newspapers do. Grocery stores are not usually staffed with characters as colorful as those who populate newsrooms. But newspapers can fail just like grocery stores. When people don't shop at the grocery store, the store dies." The end of the *Houston Post* was a sad event for Bill, who ended his editorial with what was an unusually emotional public statement for him: "Please forgive the lump in my throat."[34]

The second event that marked the end of a Hobby era occurred on August 16. On that day, death came for Oveta Culp Hobby. Her passing was not unexpected. Oveta had suffered a severe, debilitating stroke four months earlier on April 17, the day after Easter and, by coincidence, the day before the *Houston Post* published its last issue. Oveta lingered, although conscious, for four months before she died. For several years before her stroke, she had rarely left her apartment. Nearly every Sunday, Bill and Diana went to her apartment to visit. "Mamaw was a very private person with a very public persona," her granddaughter Laura later reflected. "I think she got tired of being 'the public Oveta Culp Hobby,' and as a result, she never left her house without being immaculately turned out and prepared for whomever her company would be." Laura stressed that during the time Oveta withdrew from public life, before the stroke, her family life remained "incredibly rich." She was constantly in touch by telephone with her sister Lynn and her grandchildren. Laura felt that Diana was more attentive to Oveta during this time than anyone outside of her caregivers. "My mother was the best daughter-in-law, like ever," Laura said. "And Mamaw knew and appreciated it and trusted her completely."[35]

For a few years preceding Oveta's death, Bill had substituted for his mother at events of special importance to her. One such occasion was in mid-February 1993, when Bill and Diana flew in the Hobby airplane to Killeen, Texas, his mother's hometown, for the dedication of a children's swimming pool in honor of her parents, Ike and Emma Hoover Culp. The Hobby Family Foundation had donated funds for the swimming pool to Killeen's Peaceable Kingdom Retreat for Children.[36]

As Oveta requested, on August 18 she was given a "simple" funeral ceremony at Houston's Palmer Memorial Church, followed by burial at Glenwood Cemetery. Oveta had written precise instructions about how the church services should be performed, including delegating music selection to Diana Hobby. At the grave site, the flag she had used as commander of the Women's Army Corps was ceremoniously presented and placed in Bill's and Jessica's hands. Marguerite Johnston, longtime *Houston Post* columnist and Oveta's confidant, gave the funeral eulogy. "I remember Oveta's death well," Saralee Tiede recalled later. "Bill was very stoic, as he tends to be in those circumstances. He does not show a lot of emotion."[37]

CHAPTER 20

RESCUING THE UNIVERSITY OF HOUSTON

One evening in late May 1995, three months before Oveta Culp Hobby's death, Bill Hobby checked his telephone answering machine for messages before retiring for the night at the Austin duplex he owned and where he stayed when he was in town to teach classes at the LBJ School of Public Affairs. One of the messages was from Jim Crowther, who delivered surprising news. Crowther reported he had just learned that the University of Houston Board of Regents planned to offer Hobby the position of chancellor of the UH System. Hobby later recalled that his first reaction to the message was that there was something wrong with the answering machine. Hobby had served on the UH Board of Regents from 1965 until December 1969, but in the twenty-five years since he'd left the UH board he had not been much involved in the school's development. However, he knew the university was suffering from administrative turmoil. He had read in the *Houston Chronicle* that the faculty were in revolt and that four administrators, including the president, the chief financial officer, and the provost of the university's main campus, had recently resigned. With general, if not specific, knowledge of the school's troubles, he wondered why anyone would think he wanted that job.[1]

The last thing on Hobby's mind at the time was taking on the head leadership position at UH, although he had always thought well of the school. Not only had he served as a UH regent but his family had been involved in UH's development since the late 1930s, when it opened its new campus east of downtown in the city's Third Ward. In 1938 Bill's mother had cochaired a fundraising committee with oilman Hugh Roy Cullen that raised the school's first endowment. In the early 1950s, Bill's father had presided at the opening ceremonies for the Ezekiel Cullen Building—the university's landmark administrative headquarters—and he had helped UH organize the nation's first educational television station, KUHT. Bill's mother received an honorary degree from UH in what turned out to be her last major public appearance.[2]

The day after Hobby received Crowther's phone message, the chair of the UH System Board of Regents, Beth Robertson Morian, the granddaughter of H. R. Cullen, telephoned Hobby and asked for an appointment to discuss an important matter with him. Hobby, now aware of Morian's purpose and curious, agreed to meet with her in his office at the LBJ School on May 24.[3]

At her meeting with Hobby, Morian was candid and forthright, confirming that UH was in terrible shape. She revealed that the university would announce the resignation of Chancellor Alexander Schilt the next morning and that he was leaving under pressure from the board of regents. For several months, faculty dissidents had been charging that the UH System administration was too big, was too involved in the day-to-day workings of the main UH campus, and was wasting resources on the much smaller universities in the system. Enrollment at the main campus had been declining steadily, and the athletic program was in disarray and bleeding money. News reports about the problems within the UH System had greatly damaged its reputation. The Associated Press had recently distributed a story claiming UH had an "image of a system in crisis, with infighting between campuses, financial difficulties and a perceived lack of leadership." Morian explained that the UH System, which the Texas Legislature had formally established in 1977 with Hobby's support as lieutenant governor, desperately needed someone with political and administrative prestige to come in on a temporary basis to calm the waters. Morian and her colleagues were unanimous in agreeing that person was Bill Hobby. His reputation in Houston as an intellect, as a public servant who was above personal ambition, and as an expert on the public financing of higher education gave him the credibility UH badly needed. "Here's what we want to do," Morian told Hobby. "You'd be an interim chancellor. We need someone who knows the political ropes and is tightly bonded to higher education. Please don't say no right now," she pleaded. "Let's just talk about this."[4]

Hobby replied that he was traveling to Houston on a Southwest Airlines flight after their meeting. He invited her to go with him and they could continue to talk. During the flight, Hobby told Morian he was flattered by the regents' offer, and he promised to give it serious consideration. After they arrived in Houston, he asked Morian when she needed an answer. "Just as soon as you can," she responded. "Uncertainty of leadership is our most difficult problem now." Hobby explained that he needed to discuss the offer with Diana before he could give Morian an answer. He gave her hope when he stressed that "if" he took the job—the "if" being an encouraging sign—he wouldn't be able to start work immediately. For one thing, he and Diana were leaving on a trip to Paris, France, late the following morning. The other scheduling issue was his plan to attend a two-week statistical summer camp in late June and early July conducted by the Inter-University Consortium for Political and Social Research at the University of Michigan in Ann Arbor. Hobby had been attending the seminar (which his friends called

"Hobby's Math Camp") every summer beginning in 1991. Morian assured Hobby that the UH regents would not interfere with his travel plans if he accepted their offer.[5]

When Bill and Diana talked it over, Bill concluded that ending the turmoil at UH was a challenge he had to accept. In his memoir, Hobby wrote that "the dust kicked up by the comings and goings" of executive administrators had "obscured the greatness and vitality" of the university. He understood that UH's "greatest asset and virtue" was that it was in Houston, "a dynamic, growing city that I have called home all my life. Houston is the world center of the energy industry, a great international port, and a city with a powerful sense of entrepreneurship." Such a city needed a first-class public university. In addition, Hobby thought of the challenge as a way of capping his career with work that could make a real contribution to Houston and to Texas. "It would be a tremendous honor for people to say at the end of my term," Hobby said, "that I helped make the UH System better—or at least that I didn't make it any worse."[6]

Hobby called Beth Robertson Morian the next morning before he and Diana boarded their flight to Paris. He told her he was inclined to accept the regents' offer, but his acceptance was contingent on several conditions. He intended to continue his teaching relationship with the University of Texas LBJ School, although on a much-reduced schedule. He would serve for no more than two years, and he would not take a salary larger than one dollar a year. And finally, he would neither participate in fundraising nor move into the Wortham House, the official residence of the university's chancellor, located on South Boulevard. He also had no interest in hosting social events at the house. "I live just across the street," he pointed out. "I promise I will try and take good care of it; I just don't want to move." UH's regents quickly agreed to Hobby's conditions. While he and Diana were in France, Morian faxed him the news. Hobby later remembered that after his conditions were met, it was an easy decision for him to make. "It was a job that I could do in the city in which I lived, it was in academic administration, and I knew the landscape, having been a regent myself after [UH] became a state university. And, of course, my parents had both been active in the creation and building of the university."[7]

On June 6, the day after he and Diana returned from France, Bill had his first meeting with the departing UH executives, followed the next day by a meeting with the UH System Board of Regents to confirm arrangements. The following day Hobby was back in Austin to confer with Max Sherman, who assured him he would retain his professorship at the LBJ School. On June 13, Hobby attended a press conference on the UH main campus to announce he had accepted the offer to serve as chancellor of the four-university, 47,000-student UH System.[8]

The Houston news media reacted positively to the announcement that Hobby would take the reins at UH. In her column in the *Houston Chronicle*, veteran political reporter and columnist Jane Ely, who had once worked at the *Houston Post*, noted that Hobby's deep knowledge of Texas politics and his successful record as lieutenant governor made his appointment "especially fitting." Ely observed that "little of that success had to do with raw power. It was based in inherent political skills and a love for and understanding of complex budgets and numbers that are meaningless to the great majority of us. Be assured, Bill Hobby knows everything a university chancellor needs to know—and more."[9]

Leaders of other universities in Texas, including Bill Cunningham, who had become the University of Texas System chancellor, and former state senator John Montford, who had become chancellor of Texas Tech University, welcomed Hobby's appointment as a victory for the larger cause of higher education in Texas. "When Bill Hobby became interim chancellor of UH, the world changed for them," Cunningham later observed. "He was a player, no question about it. He was someone you had to respect. And we wanted to have a good strong University of Houston. That was not a problem for us [at the University of Texas]. In fact, we wished it had come quicker." Cunningham understood that Hobby would be an effective advocate for increased legislative funding for the state's universities. "If [UH] got more money for education, more money also went to UT, more money went to Texas Tech, and more money went to other UT System institutions."[10]

When Hobby agreed to become UH System chancellor, he was keenly aware that he had a limited amount of time to accomplish his goal of stabilizing and restructuring the system. He wasted no time and didn't wait until his formal appointment began on September 1. As soon as Hobby returned from his two weeks at the University of Michigan in late July, he spent the next four weeks focused on UH business—meeting with the regents both individually and as a board, the central campus's faculty council, the presidents of UH System universities, system management staff, and leaders of Houston's business community—while also finding time to do interviews at local television stations. That whirlwind of meetings was abruptly halted, however, when Bill's mother died on August 16.[11]

Hobby turned his attention back to his UH work a few days after Oveta's funeral on August 17. After Labor Day, Hobby moved into the chancellor's luxurious office on the thirty-fourth floor of a skyscraper at 1600 Smith Street in downtown Houston. His first appointment after officially assuming his duties as chancellor was with Beth Robertson Morian. She recalled, "The first thing he asked me was did his status as interim chancellor mean that he didn't have the authority to make real changes. I said, 'No, you are the chancellor with full authority.' That's when he really went to work." After his meeting with Morian, Hobby brought together administrators from all four UH System universities to identify and discuss the present challenges. He also held policy meetings with faculty representatives, despite being warned by UH administrators that it was a bad idea. "Well, faculty members typically don't respect any administrator," observed Saralee Tiede, whom Hobby brought in to serve as his deputy chancellor. "At first, there were a few unfriendly exchanges at meetings like, 'Why do you think you know what you're doing?' But the tone quickly changed, and it became, 'Help us out of this mess. We need leadership.' And by and large, everybody was on board with that. No question." For Hobby, the meetings confirmed his belief that although the system's problems had multiple causes, the most significant were the failed leadership in the office of the chancellor and at the main campus and the inherent flaws in the system's structure.[12]

After the UH regents forced Chancellor Schilt to resign, the board allowed his two vice chancellors, Dell Felder and Edward Whalen, to assume temporary leadership of the system. Critics of Schilt believed he had long allowed Felder and Whalen to make decisions and to manage the system while he dined with and entertained business executives and socialites at the Wortham House. Such criticism of a university chancellor or president was not unusual then nor later. It often stems from the faculty's misunderstanding of the role of a modern chief executive of a major university, whose main job is to raise money. Whether or not the criticism was justified, and in this case the evidence appears to have been supported by the facts, the result was that neither of the vice chancellors was a popular figure on the main UH campus.[13]

Whalen, an economist, managed the system's finances, and Felder, a professor of education, was the system's chief academic officer. At first, Hobby tried to work with both administrators, but he soon decided they had to go. Saralee Tiede, who characterized Schilt's, Felder's, and Whalen's administration as "imperial chancellorship," felt the vice chancellors seriously underestimated the degree to which Hobby was determined to make changes in the administrative structure of the UH System. "They thought he was going to be a nice quiet little figurehead that they could pat on the shoulder and have polite little briefing sessions while they continued to run things," she recalled. Hobby even had Felder go with him in mid-September to the McDonald Observatory in West Texas to show her the site where a new telescope named in his honor was being built. The trip didn't go well. Not long after Hobby and Felder returned to Houston after the visit to the observatory, Tiede came to work at the downtown office one morning around nine. "When I arrived, I learned that Hobby had asked Felder to meet with him an hour before I got to the office. It was unusual for Hobby to do anything before nine o'clock in the morning. But he called her in at eight o'clock and fired her."[14]

As he evaluated the problems at UH, Hobby drew on his experiences and the skills he'd honed as lieutenant governor presiding over the Texas Senate. As a result, he knew that UH had never had effective input or influence when decisions about higher education were made in the legislature. That was one problem he knew he could correct because of his still-considerable influence with many of his former colleagues in state government. During the legislative session that convened in January 1996, he went to Austin and lobbied Bob Bullock and other legislative leaders to secure funding for the university's Texas Center for Superconductivity, the brainchild of world-renowned UH professor of physics Paul Chu. Hobby's efforts were successful. In the years that followed, the center expanded its research efforts, and it continues today as UH's most prestigious program—one that led in 2016 to UH's designation as a tier-one research university.[15]

Hobby decided not to replace the vice chancellors or appoint a permanent president and provost at the main campus until he had the results of a study by the Vision

Commission, which he organized to examine the administrative structure of the UH System and all four campuses. Tiede stressed that Hobby "appointed people with really good minds to the commission. I think that was very important, because at that point, you just had one thousand wars going on at UH. He believes in expertise, and in letting experts work on the issues and come up with solutions. That approach suited him a great deal and he had the personal gravitas to attract top-notch people to the commission." Chaired by the soon-to-be-disgraced Enron CEO Kenneth Lay, a UH doctoral graduate, the commission consisted of nineteen national and local leaders in education, business, and the community who were asked to determine what UH should look like twenty years into the future. The main question for the Vision Commission was whether the UH System, with its four institutions, should retain the system form of governance it had had since 1977. Faculty at the UH main campus, by far the largest of the system's institutions, complained the system was taking resources away from the flagship university and was keeping it from fulfilling its mission to be a major research institution.[16]

In addition to the Vision Commission, Hobby persuaded the UH System Board of Regents to approve the creation of three organizational task forces consisting of regents, system officers, faculty, and administrators from all the system's universities. Those task forces conducted a review of UH System administrative functions to determine how the system could be made more efficient, responsive, and cost effective. The task forces were also asked to determine if the system should continue to be administrated by one chancellor, with a president at each university, or by one person in an executive position that combined the position of chancellor and president. Hobby, Morian, and the presidents and the chairs of faculty senates from each university directed the work of the task forces. It was the first comprehensive analysis of the UH System ever conducted. The task forces completed their work in March 1996.[17]

Using the information gathered by the Vision Commission and the task forces—a self-examination process that Hobby admitted had been "painstaking and sometimes painful"—Hobby closed units in the system administration that were ineffective or that duplicated services. He also returned the authority and responsibility for the internal operations of the main campus to its president. But his most far-reaching decision was to combine the position of system chancellor with that of the UH president, which included closing the system offices in downtown Houston and moving the staff to the UH main campus, resulting in considerable savings in salary as well as in rental costs. Bill's daughter, attorney Laura Hobby Beckworth, later noted that her father "immensely enjoyed his time at UH, especially when he combined the position of president and chancellor. He eliminated the fiefdoms that always exist in a dual system and it's always a fraught relationship. And he just eliminated it and I think UH has benefited hugely."[18]

Hobby also decided to move forward with a new UH campus in Sugar Land in rapidly growing Fort Bend County, only twenty-five miles south of the UH main campus. By the 1990s, the region's explosive growth had resulted in vast housing developments that covered much of the county and transformed Sugar Land into a suburb of Houston. The county's population had gone from approximately fifty thousand in 1970 to nearly three hundred thousand in 1995, and that growth was increasing at an exponential rate. Although the University of Houston–Victoria had provided some educational services to the area, Sugar Land is one hundred miles from Victoria, which greatly limited the services that could be provided from the Victoria campus.[19]

Local civic and business leaders in Fort Bend County were eager for its residents to have convenient access to the advanced learning opportunities a university can provide. Persuaded that the UH System could and should meet those needs, Hobby agreed to take the lead in the effort to establish a campus in the county. Initially, he directed the UH System universities in Harris County, including the UH main campus, to provide classroom instruction at Clements High School in Sugar Land and at a local junior college until the system could establish its own administration and classroom facilities. He also successfully lobbied the state legislature to transfer land from the state prison farm near Sugar Land to the UH System to serve as the site for a new UH campus. Because of the problems caused by having four separately administered universities in the UH System, Hobby worked with the board of regents to organize UH at Sugar Land as a branch of the main campus instead of as a separate university.[20]

Beth Morian later noted that because of the geographic proximity of most of the campuses in the system and the conflicts between the smaller universities and the flagship campus over resources, Hobby persuaded the regents that a system like the one operated by the University of Texas made little sense. Accordingly, the regents agreed to stop adding independent universities to the system. "It made more sense for us to make them branches of the main campus." Nevertheless, because the legislature had created the system's universities at Clear Lake, Downtown, and Victoria, they remained independent from the main campus, although they would soon be administered by the main campus's president in his or her dual capacity as chancellor.[21]

Several years after Hobby left the UH System chancellorship, he was asked what he thought his most important accomplishments had been. "One, I kept the place together because it was in a mess," he said. "The main thing I did was get them a new campus in Fort Bend County. It now has four thousand students or so. I also got the legislature to deed UH the land. So, when I say I got them a new campus, I got them the ground for it."[22]

In addition to his work at the UH System "to keep the place together," as he described it, Hobby also used his position as chancellor of one of the major state university systems in Texas as a "bully pulpit" to advocate more public support for higher education. For example, with the aid of Saralee Tiede, he authored op-ed essays making a case for the importance of education to the state's economy, which were published in several Texas newspapers, such as one in the *Houston Chronicle* on January 15, 1996, titled "Texas Future Requires a 'Can Do' on Education," which also appeared in the *Austin American-Statesman* on January 26, 1996. He also defended UH's affirmative action policies supporting race-based scholarships. When the US Court of Appeals for the Fifth

Circuit ruled against those policies in *Hopwood v. Texas*, he asked state attorney general Dan Morales for a clarification of the court's decision and how it would affect UH's financial aid policies, particularly at its law school. Morales issued an opinion that the court's decision applied to all institutional policies, not just admissions. Hobby believed that Morales's ruling, which was technically an opinion and not legally enforceable, was a misinterpretation of the court's decision, so he decided that UH would continue its affirmative action policy until the court clarified its ruling. In June 2003, the US Supreme Court overturned the Fifth Circuit's decision and upheld the use of race as a factor in admissions if quotas are not used.[23]

Seven months after Hobby's appointment as chancellor, Madeline Johnson, president of the University of Houston–Downtown Faculty Senate, pointed out the contrast between Hobby and his dismissed predecessor and the micromanaging former vice chancellors. She observed in an op-ed piece in the *Houston Chronicle* that Hobby understood the role of chancellor, which was "to see the big picture and to ascertain higher education needs throughout the community." Under Hobby's leadership, "UH officials and faculty have learned that a chancellor plus four presidents can work together effectively. Hobby recognized that authority over academic programs is best placed at the universities [not at the system]."[24]

Working closely with the UH System Board of Regents, Hobby moved quickly to find a suitable candidate to replace him as chancellor. The search found political scientist and US Naval Academy graduate Arthur K. Smith, the highly regarded president of the University of Utah. The UH regents had earlier accepted Hobby's recommendation to combine the positions of chancellor and president. In November 1996, when the board announced Smith's appointment, it made clear he was assuming the newly created dual position. Smith agreed to begin work on April 1, 1997. Accordingly, Hobby left his position as UH System chancellor on March 31, 1997, having placed the university back on the road to academic respectability. At the request of the regents, Hobby retained a formal relationship with the UH System until June 1997 to help with the university's legislative agenda.[25]

In an editorial published when Hobby gave up his temporary appointment as chancellor, the *Houston Chronicle* observed that UH "now seems poised to claim the long-sought mantle of a major urban research campus that offers excellent undergraduate education. Much of the credit for that development and promise goes to a single man, former Lt. Gov. Bill Hobby." Bill Fitzgibbon, a UH mathematics professor who had helped organize the faculty group that pressured the board of regents to replace Chancellor Schilt and to reform the system's administrative structure, told the *Dallas Morning News* that Hobby was the only person "who could have done it." State senator Rodney Ellis, who would later serve as a Harris County commissioner, believed it "was extremely helpful to have someone with Bill Hobby's stature willing to step into a leadership role at the University of Houston at a time when it gave them an opportunity to really harness their fair share of state resources. And that would not have happened but for him. He really put the University of Houston on track to become a tier-one university." Political reporter Paul Burka, who had covered Hobby's years as lieutenant governor for *Texas Monthly*, praised Hobby for pulling UH out of its mess. He observed that anyone who'd watched Hobby manage the Texas Senate for nearly two decades would not be surprised by his performance in Houston.[26]

With his mission accomplished at the University of Houston, Hobby turned his attention back to the LBJ School of Public Affairs, where Max Sherman was retiring as dean, effective at the end of August 1997. This was a job Hobby coveted. Eager to stay involved in teaching and academic administration, the deanship of the LBJ School was his dream job. He quickly informed the University of Texas administration that he was seeking the position. On May 25, the university announced that Hobby was one of five finalists for dean. Hobby had impeccable credentials for the job because of his decades of work on behalf of state support of higher education, his experience as a UH regent and as a member of the Rice University Board of Trustees, his teaching at Rice and at the LBJ School, and his work as UH System interim chancellor. Credentials he lacked, however, were graduate degrees—in particular a PhD—and peer-reviewed research published in scholarly journals, which was a serious problem for the faculty search committee.[27]

Departing dean Max Sherman lacked a PhD, but he had a law degree. In addition, Saralee Tiede believed some members of the faculty committee resented Hobby's lobbying for the appointment. "Hobby went around to talk to key people," Tiede recalled. "I don't know if they were in the decision-making process but at one point someone said to him, 'You're lobbying me,' and Hobby answered, 'Well, of course I am. I've got to tell you why I want it and what I can do. If you call that lobbying, that's it.' Well, that's not done in academia. At least not overtly. You find an eminent distinguished professor who will do the lobbying for you. Anyway, he apparently rubbed some of the academics at UT the wrong way because of that."[28]

According to some observers, the other roadblock to Hobby's candidacy might have been partisan politics. The chairman of the UT System Board of Regents was West Texas businessman and Republican Donald Evans, a close friend and supporter of Governor George W. Bush, who appointed Evans to the board. Paul Hobby, who was close to Lieutenant Governor Bob Bullock, stated that although Bullock supported Hobby's bid to be dean of the LBJ School, Bush "was not going to let that happen." Paul had reason to believe that Bush, who was keenly aware that Hobby was a close friend and supporter of Ann Richards, had Don Evans discourage the campus administration from giving the job to Hobby.[29]

At the end of May 1997, the university announced that the new dean of the LBJ School would be fifty-two-year-old UT graduate Edwin Dorn, an undersecretary in the Department of Defense who had earned a doctorate in political science from Yale. Dorn, who was highly qualified for the position because of his experience and education, was also a Black man, which undoubtedly played a key role in the decision because the university was eager to make the campus academic leadership more racially diverse.[30]

Losing his bid for the LBJ School deanship was a deeply disappointing event for Hobby. On July 1, he submitted his resignation as a member of the LBJ School faculty. He also released a four-sentence statement to the press on July 16 that he was ending his seven-year affiliation with the LBJ School, implying his departure was a result of not being selected to be dean. "The time has arrived to move on," he stated, "and I do so with considerable regret." At the time, Saralee Tiede told the *Austin American-Statesman* she doubted his resignation had any connection to his not being selected dean. Years later, however, Tiede admitted that Hobby's resignation was probably influenced by the university's decision but that she never discussed it with him. In an interview with Don Carleton, however, Hobby confirmed Tiede's assumption. In a personal note Lady Bird Johnson sent to Hobby a few months after his resignation, she wrote, "Dear Bill, this has been on my mind for some time. I do not want you and Diana to disappear from my life now that you have departed from the LBJ School of Public Affairs. I deeply valued your participation in the school. And how could I have not said so in the past? When I saw your name on the short list of candidates, I felt a sense of security in knowing the school would be in good hands. However, my opinion was never asked and therefore never given. I will always be grateful the faculty and students had the benefit of your ability, experience, caring and generosity."[31]

CHAPTER 21

A CHAMPION FOR HIGHER EDUCATION

Bill Hobby's departure from the LBJ School did not end his relationship with the University of Texas at Austin. On October 7, 1997, nearly three months after Hobby resigned from the school's faculty, he and Diana flew to Alpine and then were driven forty miles to the university's McDonald Observatory complex located 6,660 feet above sea level in the Davis Mountains. The Hobbys were there to attend the dedication program for the fourth-largest optical telescope in the world—the Hobby-Eberly Telescope—which Bill Hobby not only gave his name to but also played a crucial role in funding, along with natural gas company executive and Pennsylvania State University donor Robert E. Eberly.

On a sunny, clear, and pleasant day typical of the Davis Mountains in the fall, Bill Hobby joined Robert Eberly's wife, Carolyn Eberly, UT System chancellor Bill Cunningham, UT physicist and Nobel laureate Steven Weinberg, UT astronomer and McDonald Observatory director Frank Bash, Congressman Jake Pickle, Ludwig Maximilian University of Munich president Andreas Heldrich, and others on a temporary outdoor platform. They gathered in front of the golf-ball-shaped domed structure housing the telescope, located on Mount Fowlkes. Diana watched the proceedings from her front-row chair in the open area where she and approximately four hundred other guests were seated. After preliminary comments from Cunningham, Weinberg gave the dedication address. "The Hobby-Eberly Telescope will take the students and the faculty members who use it on quite a voyage," Weinberg said. "They will be traveling out thousands of light years, to visit stars and clusters of stars within our own galaxy, and millions of light years farther on to visit other galaxies, and billions of light years beyond that to see the most distant objects that can be seen, objects that were formed when the universe was about tenth its present age."[1]

After Weinberg's speech, master of ceremonies Frank Bash spoke, declaring his pride that the telescope project had been completed "on time and on budget." Whereupon Cunningham leaned over and whispered to Hobby, "Yes, but it was the ninth budget and the eighth timetable." Bash then asked Hobby to speak. Sporting dark sunglasses to protect his eyes from the glare of the bright day, Hobby spoke briefly and to the point. Referring to the telescope's engineer, Tom Sebring, Hobby declared, "It took a world-class project director to translate drawings and ideas into steel, glass, and concrete on time and on budget." He then paused, thought about what Cunningham had whispered to him, and commented, "Well, there were several times and several budgets—but never mind." The audience, which was filled with the planners and funders of the project, roared in knowing laughter.[2]

As Hobby later observed, the Hobby-Eberly Telescope began as a multimillion-dollar "pipe dream." The project's roots went back to the late 1970s, when Harlan Smith, the Harvard-trained director of UT Austin's McDonald Observatory, began to dream about constructing a giant telescope on Mount Locke with a mirror three hundred inches in diameter. At the time, the observatory had two major telescopes, but they were quickly being outpaced by newer instruments around the world. Smith's dream, however, had a price tag estimated to be $50 million.[3]

By 1980, Smith's proposal to build a much larger telescope had made its way to the UT System Board of Regents, who authorized a campaign to raise the money. At the time, the price of oil was continuing to soar, and the Texas economy was flush with petroleum-generated money. But oil prices soon crashed. When Bill Cunningham assumed the presidency of UT Austin in September 1985, only slightly more than $1.3 million had been raised for the project. It was obvious to Cunningham that with the Texas economy and the university's budget in bad shape, there was no way he could raise the remaining $49 million needed for a telescope. The project appeared to be dead at that point, but Harlan Smith was not one to give up easily.[4]

Smith soon found an alternative solution. In the spring of 1986, he learned from Frank Bash, one of his colleagues in the UT Austin Department of Astronomy, that Daniel Weedman, an expert on quasars at Penn State University, and his colleague, Lawrence W. Ramsey, had developed an innovative and economical design to replace the single large mirrors used on conventional telescopes with an array of many smaller, mass-produced mirrors in a honeycomb pattern. Weedman and Ramsey were convinced their telescope could be built for a cost of $6 million instead of the $50 million version that Smith was hoping to build. Their plan was to use spectroscopy, the study of the component wavelengths of light. The Penn State astronomers asked if UT Austin would partner with their university to finance and host their project at McDonald Observatory. Penn State president Bryce Jordan, who had held several important administrative positions in the UT System before going to Pennsylvania, was very familiar with the McDonald Observatory. He told his two faculty members that if UT Austin agreed to their proposal, Penn State would contribute $3 million toward the estimated $6 million total cost.

This was electrifying news to Smith, who presented the proposal to Cunningham, who agreed to take it to the UT System Board of Regents. In December 1986, no longer faced with a $50 million price tag, the regents told Cunningham that if he could raise $1.5 million, the UT System would match it. The regents gave Cunningham until January 1, 1989, to raise the money. At least sixteen potential donors rejected funding proposals. From the beginning, it had been obvious to Cunningham that a prospective donor might be enticed to give a major gift in return for having his or her name on a telescope that was certain to become widely known in international scientific circles. It was at this point in early 1987 that Bill Hobby became a target of the UT president's fundraising campaign.[5]

Hobby's friend George Christian was serving as chairman of the McDonald Observatory's board of visitors. He urged Smith and Cunningham to win Hobby over to the idea of naming the telescope after him, with the understanding that Hobby or his family would make a major financial donation as well as allow his name to be used in the fundraising campaign. Christian thought it would be an especially appropriate way to pay tribute to Hobby's many years of support for Texas higher education. Cunningham agreed that Hobby was an obvious choice. The Hobby Foundation had already committed $100,000 to support the telescope, and Cunningham and Christian were hopeful the foundation might contribute additional funds, especially if the telescope was named for Bill Hobby. In addition, it was likely there were several wealthy donor and foundation prospects eager to honor Hobby. Christian, who had extensive contacts with business lobbyists in Texas, agreed to lead the effort to raise money from that group.[6]

When Cunningham shared his new fundraising strategy with Harlan Smith, the astronomer replied that he had recently met Bill Hobby through Smith's wife, Joan Greene, who had been Diana Hobby's classmate at Radcliffe. Accordingly, Smith invited Bill and Diana and guests of their choice to the McDonald Observatory for a tour and a night of sky gazing. The Hobbys accepted the invitation and flew in the University of Texas airplane on March 12 with a small entourage that included Saralee Tiede, Ann Richards, Kay Bailey Hutchison, and Kay's husband, Ray Hutchison. After arriving in Alpine, they were driven to the Davis Mountains for an overnight visit to the observatory. The Hobbys enjoyed their visit so much that they made another overnight trip to the observatory six months later.[7]

Cunningham later noted that when Hobby was lieutenant governor, it was obvious he'd had a strong interest in the role the University of Texas played in research and economic development for the state. "He understood science and he was focused on technology," Cunningham said. "He was interested in McDonald and made trips there. So, telling him we'd like to name this telescope after him was easy. And it was something he was very excited about." Bill Hobby's son Paul felt that the telescope was "a really easy thing for my father, because of his intellectual curiosity, and it involved deep knowledge for its own sake and basic research and all these things that he was ultimately interested in. It also appealed to him as one of the ways to put Texas ahead of the scientific curve."[8]

In September 1988, Harlan Smith announced his retirement as observatory director, effective August 1989, because of ill health, but he would continue to help with fundraising. After Smith announced his retirement, Cunningham asked Smith's colleague, radio astronomer Frank Bash, to serve as acting director of the McDonald Observatory. Bash's familiarity with the telescope project from its inception was a strong point in his favor. By this time, Penn State had found its major donor in Robert Eberly, who donated almost $2 million to the project. Cunningham persuaded his friend Texas Commerce Bank chairman and Houston power broker Ben Love to take the job of chief fundraiser in Houston. Love and Hobby cohosted a luncheon at the Houston Club in September 1990 that raised more than $300,000.[9]

In August 1989 Penn State surprised the University of Texas with the news that it would limit its contribution to $2.25 million. Cunningham recalled that the "unsettling news arrived at about the same time that the astronomers were discussing among themselves the likelihood that several 'add-ons' would be necessary, increasing the original estimated cost by $2 million or more." Bash asked one of the McDonald Observatory engineers to do a detailed analysis to determine the project's cost. The answer was at least $10 million dollars, not $6 million. Shocked by the new estimate, Cunningham initiated a review to determine "with essential certainty that the telescope can be built and what it will actually cost." The reviewers confirmed that cost estimates had increased well beyond the original $6 million price tag, and they recommended that if project costs could not be "rigorously contained," the university should discontinue it.[10]

Armed with this candid assessment, Cunningham told Bash, "You and I are going to go down and tell Bill Hobby about this revised cost estimate." The new observatory director had the task of telling Hobby that the project was now going to cost $10 million, not $6 million. In his typically laconic manner, Hobby responded, "Well, Frank, that's your problem, you've got to raise that money." Hobby later explained, "As is always the case at a major research university, the competition for dollars was fierce. Raising money for a telescope, even an inexpensive telescope, is a more difficult proposition than raising money for, say, a football stadium."[11]

Cunningham and Bash weren't willing or able to pull the plug on the project at this late date in the process, and neither was Hobby, despite his obvious frustration at the constantly escalating cost estimates. The fundraising effort would continue. Bash had hoped Hobby would put more of his own family's money into the project. "I don't think he put in really anything much at all in terms of cash," Bash said years later, "although his foundation made a nice donation. But what he did do was put in a lot of shoe leather. Bill would gather people together, friends and associates of his, and I would speak to them about our telescope."[12]

At Bash's recommendation, Cunningham hired Tom Sebring, an engineer with broad experience in telescope building, to serve as the new project manager. Bash hosted a meeting of his board of visitors at the UT Austin Astronomy Department to introduce them to Sebring. Hobby attended the meeting. Sebring explained how he was going to manage the project and how he was going to be careful about the cost. He stressed that to save money, he could postpone the installation of certain items. If he found out at the end that he could afford those items, he would get those parts completed. Sebring cited the parking lot at the telescope site as an example. He would use gravel, and then if there was enough money left over, he would pave it. Bash later recalled that when Hobby heard that, he angrily complained, "I can't believe you wouldn't pave the parking lot!" Bash thought to himself, "I just hired this guy and he has just run into the namesake of the telescope, Bill Hobby, who's just blown up at him. It was really embarrassing. I was so proud of Tom Sebring for keeping his cool. He handled it beautifully. Hobby eventually calmed down and I was able to keep my project manager who didn't quit on the spot. And I was able to keep my namesake donor who didn't quit on the spot."[13]

As funding continued to be a problem, Bash persuaded Stanford University and two prestigious universities in Germany—Georg-August University in Göttingen and Ludwig Maximilian in Munich—to help fund the project. By the end of 1991, UT Austin had a 52 percent share, Penn State had 31 percent, Stanford had 7 percent, and each of the German universities had 5 percent. That same year, soon after Hobby left elected office, the project received an unexpected largesse from the Texas Legislature. "Hobby was determined to get more help from the state," Bash remembered. "He asked me to go to the Capitol with him during the legislative session to visit with some of the members. I reminded him that as a state employee I wasn't allowed to lobby. Hobby said, 'Now, Frank, you're not lobbying, your job is just to answer questions. I'm the guy who's lobbying.'" Bash and Hobby strolled through the marble-floored corridors of the vast building. "Walking through the Capitol with Hobby was like walking through Palestine with Jesus or something. He still had a lot of friends there, as well as influence."[14]

The Senate Finance Committee was meeting that day, and Hobby's old friend Rodney Ellis happened to be chairing it when its regular chairman, John Montford, was absent. "When Senator Ellis saw Hobby, he adjourned the meeting instantly and rushed over to greet us," Bash recalled. Hobby explained why he and Bash were there and what they needed. "It was obvious to me that Senator Ellis was going to help us get that special funding," Bash said. "We ended up not only getting one-time money from the legislature for construction, but even more importantly, also recurring funds to pay for operations."[15]

The legislature created the Center for Advanced Studies in Astronomy at the University of Texas as a special item appropriation in the state budget. Cunningham believes the appropriation saved the project. Hobby's close friend Senator John Montford played a key role in winning the legislative support. As Cunningham pointed out, "The fact that Montford was also chairman of the Senate Finance Committee increased our odds of success from negligible to virtually certain." Hobby later admitted, "I wasn't lieutenant governor any longer, but I still had some friends in high places who helped us secure the funding. I was, and I remain, grateful to them."[16]

By the end of 1991, Cunningham, Hobby, Bash, and their team had raised a little more than $2.4 million in cash gifts, including funds from several foundations. It was more than enough to qualify for the matching money from the UT System's permanent endowment. By March 1994, the Hobby-Eberly Telescope project was finally ready for the groundbreaking ceremony, which featured remarks by both Hobby and Eberly. Bash recalled that when Hobby learned that the telescope was going to include Eberly's name, "he wasn't completely happy with that." Eberly had assumed a relatively minor role in the overall effort to raise money for the telescope's construction, although his $2 million gift was clearly important. "That's one flash of Hobby's ego that I was a little amused by," Bash said. "But he appreciated Eberly's gift, and he was okay with it."[17]

Hobby was proud to have his name on the telescope. "When I left office, after serving longer than any other lieutenant governor of Texas, there were few monuments to Bill Hobby," he explained. "Only a state prison and a state office building in Austin acquired at the depths of the 1980s bust bore my name. But that telescope is a significant achievement that helps advance our attempt to understand the cosmos. I'm pleased to have helped make it a reality and I'm deeply honored by the naming."[18]

Hobby's disappointment about not being selected for the LBJ School's deanship failed to lessen his support for higher education. In 1997 he and Diana directed the Hobby Foundation to donate $22 million to Rice University for a major renovation and enlargement of its Fondren Library. It was one of the largest gifts to a university research library in US history. Diana was an active member of the Rice committee that studied and planned the library project. In May 2001, Rice recognized Bill and Diana's longtime involvement in and support of the university by awarding them its Gold Medal for "extraordinary service to the university." Rice also cited Diana's "distinguished" work in art and literature and mental health and children's issues.[19]

The gift to Rice signified there was new leadership at the Hobby Foundation, which Oveta had tightly controlled until her death. But after her passing, Bill assumed its direction, although Diana was behind the gift to Rice. "My grandmother, long after she was not active in running the family business, was very active in the foundation," Laura Hobby Beckworth later noted. "I was around then, so I was more in an administrative role, not decision-making. I know the Rice library gift was initiated by my mother. But the telescope was purely my father. That's his math-science person coming out." Bill Hobby eventually turned over leadership of the Hobby Foundation to Laura and Paul when he became deeply involved in the Hobby School of Public Affairs at the University of Houston. Paul Hobby stressed that before his father transferred leadership of the foundation to him and Laura, "there was no democracy, there was just him and he just did whatever. He might have consulted with my mother, but he wasn't big on democracy or process. He did whatever he wanted to do in allocating the gifts."[20]

Two years after the gift to Rice, Hobby personally gave $1 million to Texas State University to endow its Center for Public Service, which is a program in the Department of Political Science. Texas State named the center for Hobby. The endowment funds a professorship for public service, a distinguished lecture series, and scholarships, all in Hobby's name. The program trains Texas public employees and awards them a designation as Certified Public Managers.[21]

In a profile of Hobby published around the time these gifts were made, Robert Bryce noted that during his career,

> Hobby has done everything related to schooling but sweep the floors. He has been a teacher. He has been an administrator. He has given millions of dollars to schools. There really are no good explanations for what drives Bill Hobby. He has everything he needs and then some. He could retire and [spend] the rest of his days on his passions; hunting foxes in Ireland, riding horses in Montana and solving math problems. And yet, when it comes to educational issues, he can't sit in the hallway. He has to be at the chalkboard, drawing a graph, making a chart or figuring a plan of attack.[22]

Hobby's philanthropy in the late 1990s included a major gift in support of building a new performing arts facility in downtown Houston to replace the badly deteriorated music hall that had been built in the late 1930s as part of the Houston Coliseum complex. The site had once been the location of Sam Houston Hall, which had been hurriedly constructed entirely of wood in 1928 for that year's Democratic National Convention. Hobby's parents had been deeply involved in that convention. Houston's civic leaders had long seen the need to replace the aging music hall. In December 1995, a group of Houston's prominent business and cultural leaders organized the Houston Music Hall Foundation to raise funds to demolish the hall and replace it with a new state-of-the-art facility.[23]

On May 15, 1996, Marc Shapiro, the chairman of Texas Commerce Bank, met with Hobby when he was serving as University of Houston System chancellor and asked him to consider making the lead gift in the fundraising effort for a new performing arts hall. Shapiro said that the Music Hall Foundation was hoping Hobby would give $15 million to launch the campaign. Paul Hobby recalled that later that afternoon, Bill came to Paul's office and told him about Shapiro's request. Paul, who earlier had made an unsuccessful bid for the office of Texas comptroller, was now a private equity investor in Houston. "The fact that he was in my office asking what I thought about the idea made me realize that he was taking Shapiro's request seriously," Paul recalled. "I said, well, I think he'll take $10 million. But he eventually persuaded my father to donate a total of $15 million." Shapiro stressed to Bill Hobby that a new performing arts hall would take some pressure off the Alley Theatre, which was a venue for plays, and Jones Hall, which hosted the city's opera, ballet, and symphony. He also argued that the new hall would help local artists because it would increase the capacity of Houston to host live events. "That all made sense to my father," Paul noted. "And my mother liked the idea that there was going to be a black box theater there for local theatrical productions. She was not that interested in big touring shows." Bill, however, loved big musical productions, which played a role in his decision to support the performing arts hall. Whenever possible during trips to Manhattan, Hobby would take in a Broadway show such as *The Phantom of the Opera*. During his youth, he had worked as an usher at Houston's old music hall just to see the musical productions.[24]

Diana Hobby was soon actively involved in the planning for the center and the fundraising campaign. Three of the Hobbys' children, Paul, Laura, and Kate, also joined in the effort, hosting a series of luncheons and receptions to raise money. The fundraisers soon lined up other large donors. Investor Fayez Sarofim donated $5 million, Los Angeles oilman Selim Zilkha donated $4 million, and the El Paso Gas company donated $3.5 million. With pledges from the Houston Endowment and the Brown and Wortham Foundations, $29 million in private support was gathered within six months after the campaign's launch. In addition, the City of Houston agreed to join with the Houston Music Hall Foundation to make the project a joint public-private enterprise and pledged $13 million for future operational support.[25]

On May 10, 2002, after more than eight years of planning and fundraising, the Hobby Center for the Performing Arts opened with a morning ribbon-cutting ceremony, followed that evening by a two-hour grand-opening stage show featuring Shirley Jones and Tommy Tune in "A Centennial Salute to Richard Rodgers." The opening program attracted a full house of more than 1,200 guests, including former president George H. W. Bush and his wife, Barbara. The *Houston Chronicle* called the opening "a giddy celebration. Champagne flowed. Spirits ran high. And even more money was secured for the entertainment complex that has already garnered $92 million in commitments. The benefit evening brought in another $1.35 million." The Friends of the Hobby Center held another gala in the Sarofim Hall the next night, featuring musicians Lyle Lovett, John Hiatt, Guy Clark, and Joe Ely.[26]

The Hobby Center, designed by Robert A. M. Stern, dean of the Yale University School of Architecture, soon took its place as an architectural icon in Houston's Theater District. It has two theaters—the 2,650-seat Sarofim Hall and the 500-seat Zilkha Hall—as well as a restaurant. The center stands as a fitting honor to Bill Hobby's years of public service.[27]

After Bill Hobby left the lieutenant governorship in the early 1990s, he continued to pay close attention to public policy, especially at the state level. The Republican Party in Texas had begun its move to the extreme right, eventually taking control of state government by the beginning of the new century. The moderately liberal wing of the Republican Party with which Bill's mother had been associated for so long—the party of Eisenhower, Ford, and Rockefeller—was fast disappearing nationally. In Texas, even Republicans who had been relatively moderate earlier in their careers were undergoing a transformation to extremism—in some cases for opportunistic reasons.

Among those transformed was West Texan Rick Perry, who had entered electoral politics as a conservative Democrat. As a member of the Texas Legislature in the early 1980s, Perry, like Hobby, had supported Al Gore for the Democratic Party's presidential nomination. But in 1989, as partisan winds began to shift to the political right, he switched his loyalty to the Republican Party, eventually winning statewide races for the office of Texas agricultural commissioner and, later, lieutenant governor. After the US Supreme Court gave the presidency to Texas governor George W. Bush in 2000, Perry automatically succeeded Bush as governor. He subsequently won election on his own and then reelection to serve as the state's chief executive for fourteen years, longer than any other governor in Texas history.[28]

Hobby's disdain for Perry and the other right-wingers who had taken control of the Republican Party had been increasing for several years, but it grew more intense when Perry, a former Texas A&M Yell Leader, became a critic of higher education. He and many of his fellow Republicans believed that faculty members at the state's institutions of higher education, particularly the University of Texas at Austin, were politically indoctrinating their students to become liberals and even socialists. One of Perry's initial attempts to control the state's institutions of higher education was his attack on an important aspect of the budgets of some of the universities: an appropriation category known as special items.

On February 25, 2007, several Texas newspapers published Hobby's scathing op-ed criticizing what he considered to be Governor Perry's politically opportunistic attack on higher education. Hobby titled it "A History Lesson for Governor Perry's Benefit." The specific catalyst that inspired the op-ed piece was Perry's effort to veto special item appropriations for universities. Special items in the higher education budget provided funding for universities to conduct research and public service projects that reflected the special needs of the communities the universities served. They were called "special" because they weren't funded by the formulas that generated appropriations for teaching. A special item appropriation also applied to only a specific university. The op-ed was influenced by Hobby's deep knowledge of legislative issues related to higher education.[29]

"Governor Rick Perry doesn't like the way higher education is funded," Hobby complained in his column. "He wants to micromanage it. He doesn't care that higher education is poorly funded. (Texas ranks 50th in percentage of high school graduates, 27th in college graduates.) The issue is neither higher education nor funding, issues about which he knows little and cares less." Hobby claimed the real issue was the governor's line-item veto power versus the power of the legislature. "The Governor can veto certain 'items of appropriation' without vetoing the whole appropriations act," Hobby explained. "The line-item veto is almost meaningless because the Legislature can package items to keep a Governor from micromanaging." Hobby noted that Rick Perry wanted the power to veto "special items" even if they were protected in the total budget bill and not individually listed as line items. A provision in the Texas Education Code allows for special items to be in a lump sum. "In other words," Hobby pointed out, "the Governor would have to veto an entire university, not just a particular item."[30]

Hobby argued that special item funding provided support for research in subjects of importance to the public, especially in the natural, social, and political sciences. He cited three projects at the University of Houston as examples. One was in space exploration in partnership with NASA; another was in superconductivity to increase the efficiency of power transmission; and a third was for research by the Center for Public Policy on various government issues, with support from the City of Houston.

"Knowing that his plan [to eliminate special item funding] will be unpopular," Hobby wrote, "Governor Perry recently summoned the presidents of Texas public universities to his office and told them they would be in trouble if they criticized it. Governor Perry is pretty confused about the powers of the Governor and the powers of the Legislature. In power struggles between the Governor and the Legislature, the Legislature wins. Maybe the Governor should just issue another illegal executive order."[31]

Throughout Perry's years as governor, Hobby continued to use newspaper op-eds to criticize Perry and his fellow Republicans in state government. During Barack Obama's first term as president, Perry implied publicly that because of Obama's policies, Texas should secede from the United States. This was also when right-wing Republican ideologues on the Texas State Board of Education were waging war against sex education, the teaching of evolution, and textbooks that failed to glorify the history of Texas—a war that has continued to this day. Hobby, incensed at and embarrassed by the know-nothings in control of state government, published an op-ed critical of the Republican Party's political behavior and its role in Texas state government.[32]

"Texas, once the Lone Star State, first became the Let's Secede State (courtesy of Gov. Rick Perry) and is now the Laughingstock State (thanks to the State Board of Education)," Hobby lamented sarcastically. "Once a two-party state, Texas has become a tea party state," he added. He criticized the education board for wanting to "edit history books by expunging the names of Hispanics who helped Texas become free from Mexico," which would include such figures as Lorenzo de Zavala, interim vice president of the Republic of Texas. Years earlier, the legislature had named the Texas State Library and Archives building in the Capitol Complex for Zavala. "Have the folks who want to edit Texas history to suit their lily-white selves ever heard of him? Apparently not. Even before the Texas history fiasco, some board members had decided that they were better scientists than Charles Darwin. Seems they're not real happy about evolution." The outgoing State Board of Education chairman Don McLeroy had been quoted as believing dinosaurs and mankind lived at the same time. Hobby noted that McElroy was as ignorant as the "ill-informed" Tea Party demonstrators who held signs proclaiming, "Keep the government's hands off my Medicare!"[33]

Hobby, who was just getting started, added that "central to the theory of evolution is the mutant gene that causes the species to evolve, for better or worse. And the mutant gene that made the GOP evolve from the party of Eisenhower to the party of Rush Limbaugh and the wackos evolve from Birchers to Birthers is loose in Texas. Those of us who believe the Earth is round, that it goes around the sun and that President Barack Obama was born in Hawaii will try to avoid the conservative thought police."[34]

Hobby's criticism of how the Republicans were running the state had no discernable effect on their behavior or any impact on elections. But it was an outstanding example of his heeding the old warning that silence gives consent. Hobby wanted his disapproval to be on the record so that there would be no doubt about his stance.

The virulent anti-government and anti-intellectual ideology espoused by Republican Party leaders and the party's foot soldiers at the local level deeply troubled Bill Hobby, who believed fervently in the critical importance of public service and policy expertise. That concern drew him more and more toward the work of the University of Houston's Center for Public Policy.

In late summer 2006, Henry "Hank" Heitowit, head of the University of Michigan's Inter-University Consortium for Political and Social Research (ICPSR), called Hobby to encourage him to meet Jim Granato, who had recently accepted a job at the University of Houston. ICPSR is a research consortium that provides training on data access and analysis for social science research. Granato, who had taught at ICPSR, moved to Houston to serve as director of the UH Center for Public Policy after serving as a visiting professor at the University of Texas at Austin. Heitowit and Hobby had struck up a friendship when Hobby became a regular attendee of the ICPSR summer school program beginning in 1991. Heitowit also called Granato to suggest that he meet Hobby because of their strong mutual interests in data analysis for use in developing and shaping public policy. Heitowit was also aware that Granato's policy center at UH needed financial help and that Hobby might be useful in the effort to raise funds.[35]

Hobby and Granato eventually met at Hobby's office in October. Granato later recalled that during their initial visit, he and Hobby had an extended discussion about their shared interest in social science data. Hobby was curious about the UH policy center and Granato's plans for it. At the end of their visit, Hobby accepted Granato's invitation to serve on the policy center's new board of advisors beginning early in 2007. "My father was a data freak before that was cool," Paul later noted. "He believed strongly that data could provide the evidence needed to support policy decisions. There's no question that he can lay honest intellectual claim to being a pioneer in that. He was the first politician I ever saw using statistical charts."[36]

UH organized the Center for Public Policy in 1981 in its College of Social Sciences, with a Survey Research Institute, founded by political science professor Richard Murray, as its core unit. Murray, whose political polling results were frequently cited by Texas news media, became director of the policy center when it received special item funding from the Texas Legislature. In 2005 Murray gave up his position as director to devote full time to his polling work at the Survey Research Institute. With Murray leading the search, UH chose Granato as his replacement.[37]

By the end of the first meeting of the center's advisory board in January 2007, it was clear to Granato that Hobby wanted to be involved in developing the center. Hobby suggested to Granato that he consider establishing a Certified Public Manager (CPM) program such as the one Hobby had endowed at Texas State University. He recommended that Granato contact Texas State to see if they would agree to organize a branch campus of the CPM program at UH's public policy center. An agreement was reached, and the CPM branch at UH was soon a success. Soon thereafter, Kay Bailey Hutchison asked Hobby if he would conduct research on the factors that had made the University of California System successful. Hobby brought Hutchison's idea to Granato, who made it a formal research project of the center. Hobby and Granato worked on that project together and brought it to completion, helping to seal the bond between the two.[38]

In 2009 Hobby worked with Granato and Renee Cross, a researcher at the center who was also Granato's executive associate, on a qualitative research project to study issues related to the upcoming 2010 census and its potential impact on congressional redistricting. "Governor Hobby loves redistricting," Cross later noted, "because that's the ultimate math problem. So, we were spending a lot of time with him. And we saw him as a potential prospect for gifts." That potential soon became reality when Hobby made a major financial gift to the center. The UH administration decided to show its gratitude by renaming the program the Hobby Center for Public Policy. When Granato and Cross met with Hobby to discuss his gift pledge, he insisted that he did not want the research unit to be named for him. He wanted it named for the entire Hobby family. UH honored that request, although most observers assume that it is named for Bill Hobby, because the official title fails to indicate that family designation.[39]

The center had a new name, but it still lacked resources and remained a relatively unknown three-person operation. Progress was slow in coming. Turnover in the university's administration was a problem. "The institutional memory remained short," Granato recalled. "I had to educate new administrators every so often about who we were and why we existed. Even though I was brought in to build the center, the people who recruited me were no longer around." The financial situation improved in 2012 when Branch Banking and Trust granted $1 million to the Hobby Center. Nevertheless, Granato understood that if the center was ever going to become a serious player in the academic policy and public affairs sphere, it needed to become a school, with faculty and the authority to grant degrees. To accomplish that goal, Granato drafted a strategic plan based on the advice of his advisory board, including Bill Hobby, Beth Robertson (formerly Morian), UH System chancellor Renu Khator, and Paul Hobby. After Granato submitted the plan to the UH regents in 2013, they agreed to make the Hobby Center a school, contingent on final approval from the Texas Higher Education Coordinating Board.[40]

Once Granato and his allies jumped through the administrative hurdles at UH to establish the school and with Hobby's pledge, they sought special item funding from the state legislature. Early in 2016 Hobby, Robertson, Granato, Houston businessman Welcome Wilson Sr., and Chancellor Khator flew to Austin on Hobby's plane to lobby the legislature for funding. Hobby's task was to justify the appropriation in testimony to the Senate Higher Education Committee. Granato recalled that the members stopped what they were doing to let Hobby talk. "They were very respectful," he said. "Hobby took ten minutes to explain why the school was important."[41]

After Hobby's appearance before the Senate committee, he and his companions from Houston, with Rodney Ellis in tow, met with Lieutenant Governor Dan Patrick. "That was an amazing meeting," Granato noted. "We walked into his office and Dan Patrick stepped forward, shook Hobby's hand, and said, 'Governor, it's a pleasure to meet you.'" Patrick asked everyone to have a seat. Then he looked at Hobby and said, "I want you to know I'm in this chair because of you." Shocked, Hobby asked, "How?" Patrick replied, "When I wasn't doing well, I was able to purchase a radio station from your family and you gave me a really good price. That changed my life. Now, what can I do for you?" Hobby quickly answered, "We need $2 million." Patrick smiled and said, "Okay." Hobby later admitted that when he met Dan Patrick, an ultra-right-wing Republican whom Hobby had opposed in every race Patrick had run, he was less than pleased when Patrick told him that he had made it possible for his political success.[42]

As promised, Patrick supported special item funding for the Hobby School. In August 2016, the Texas Higher Education Coordinating Board gave official approval to UH to establish the Hobby School of Public Affairs, which included the Hobby Center for Public Policy and the newly created Elizabeth D. Rockwell Center on Ethics and Leadership as its component units. Former state senator Kirk Watson of Austin was appointed the founding dean of the school. When Watson resigned a year later, UH appointed Jim Granato dean, with Renee Cross serving as executive director of the school. Before age-related physical ailments put an end to Hobby's public activities by 2019, he enjoyed visiting classes at the school. "He lectured my classes on census and census data and voting participation," Granato noted. "He'd done a bunch of work on that as lieutenant governor." Hobby also participated in some of the school's programs and helped establish new projects. He also spoke at orientation sessions at the start of the school year to explain to the students what the program was all about. "We're training you to become good stewards of public policy," he would stress.[43]

"Hobby had great rapport with the students," Granato observed. "Hobby was not intimidating to the students, because he's such a nice guy. But he's also very introverted. My God, he's introverted. But he would talk when prompted and he'd answer questions and help the students with things." Granato also observed that Hobby was not afraid to tell students he had been wrong in some of his efforts as an elected official. "For example, his promotion of zero-based budgeting, which he thought was going to be a brilliant idea when he was lieutenant governor. He said, 'I was wrong. It didn't work.' He also admitted that his idea for the state legislature to set aside a rainy day fund was a mistake. 'The legislature just needs to spend the damn money,' Hobby said, 'when they have it. Just spend it.'"[44]

From the beginning of his involvement in the center, and later in the school, Hobby focused on the role it would play in the teaching of practical skills and applied, rather than theoretical, research. "Governor Hobby has no interest in academic research simply for the sake of ivory tower discussions," Renee Cross observed. "His interest is in research that can help people in government make better policy. I think what's different about the Hobby School is that it's blending the real-world side with this statistical skilled side." Laura Hobby Beckworth agreed with Cross's assessment. "My dad has very little patience with the theoretical, which is often never applied to real-life situations. He wants to actually solve problems that people have and that government is particularly well-suited to solve. He has no patience for ivory tower speculation; none."[45]

The Hobby School has flourished since its official establishment in 2016. It has an active research program that has included a major study of the impact of Hurricane Harvey on Houston in 2017. It continues to participate in the Certified Public Manager program, and it offers a master's degree in public policy. Bill Hobby donated money to fund student fellowships (Hobby fellows). In 2021, the Texas Legislature appropriated $40 million for UH to construct a building to house the school.

Those who knew Bill Hobby best felt that his support of and involvement in the Hobby School was the capstone to his long career in public service. "The Hobby School is definitely Dad's legacy piece," Laura Hobby Beckworth stated. Her brother, Paul, who was skeptical of the effectiveness of public policy schools on the actual workings of government, nevertheless agreed with Laura and added that his father was "as proud of the Hobby School at UH as anything he has ever done."[46]

At some point in the early 2000s, Bill Hobby began to drink in excess at home. It was rare that he was inebriated in public, such as when he was arrested in 1974 for DUI. After that incident, he never drove after he had a drink. Diana, staff members, or friends drove him home if he had drinks at dinner in the evening at a restaurant. When he was lieutenant governor, Hobby would have a glass or two of wine at lunch, but nothing else during the day, and he wasn't known to drink excessively at night. Glenn Smith, his press spokesman in the late 1980s, later noted that when Hobby's drinking "was measured against what others in the Capitol were doing when I got there, his drinking was very moderate. I mean, lord God, they had margarita machines in the hallway."[47]

Nevertheless, Hobby's drinking did become excessive, leading to some embarrassing incidents during social occasions. Paul Hobby believed his father's drinking problem was the result of boredom. "I think as he got older and he had less responsibility and more time on his hands, it did become a problem," Paul observed. The crisis point in Hobby's abuse of alcohol was reached when he tumbled down the stairs one night at his home in Houston and was injured, although not severely. Diana was away in North Carolina when it happened. This incident convinced Hobby that he had a problem. Two close friends, John Montford and Herb Kelleher, helped to persuade him to check into a Hazelden alcohol abuse treatment center in Minnesota during the spring of 2006. The treatment was successful and permanent. "There's a lot of things in [Bill Hobby's] life where he just decided he was going to change and he had the iron will to do it," Paul Hobby noted. "Whether it was alcohol later in life or stuttering in midlife. When he came home from Hazelden, he never drank again, despite never going to Alcoholics Anonymous or having a follow-up in rehab. I offered to go to AA meetings with him and he would just look at me and say, 'You don't understand. I just don't drink anymore, period.' And it wasn't a problem anymore."[48]

In March 2006, while Hobby was at Hazelden, Ann Richards—desperately fighting against the cancer that would soon kill her—handwrote Hobby a letter to boost his spirits. Richards, a recovered alcoholic, told her old political ally, "We are helpless when it comes to alcohol. It is a poison for us and despite our best intentions and strong will, we cannot drink alcohol—none—zip—zero. Much love to you Bill. I know this experience is sad and frightening but believe me—everyone will be filled with admiration and support when you choose to reveal this affirming step." Richards died six months later.[49]

In September 2009, when Bill Hobby was becoming involved in the University of Houston Center for Public Policy, his sister and only sibling, Jessica Catto, died at home on her ranch in Woody Creek, Colorado, after a struggle with colon cancer. She was seventy-two years old. Early in her life, Jessica made the decision to go on her own career path, with only a tenuous connection to the Hobby family enterprises until she became more involved in the last days of H&C Communications' ownership of its media properties. After she married Henry in 1958, she moved permanently to San Antonio, with other homes in Northern Virginia and Aspen, Colorado. Over the years, her many activities had included serving as a major fundraiser for the San Antonio PBS station KLRN, the publisher of the *Washington Journalism Review* (1980–1987), and a member of the National Parks System Advisory Board. Jessica was also deeply involved in the environmental movement, and despite her husband's activities in the Republican Party and service in Republican presidential administrations, she was a lifelong Democrat who often hosted fundraisers for Democrats at her home in Woody Creek. Jessica and Bill had a friendly but sometimes tense relationship, possibly rooted in sibling rivalry, age differences, a domineering mother, and dissimilarities in personality. Nevertheless, the Hobby and Catto families were close. Bill and Diana were frequent guests at the Catto ranch near Aspen, and the Cattos' four children and Bill and Diana's kids were good friends, with first cousins Laura Hobby and Heather Catto being especially close.[50]

Five years after Jessica's passing, Bill suffered the worst loss of his life. His beloved Diana died on July 4, 2014, from ovarian cancer after a thirteen-year gradual decline from Alzheimer's disease. After lunch on Christmas Day, 2001, when she was seventy, Diana fell while walking the family dogs and broke her hip. She underwent hip replacement surgery. Not long after, she began to show signs of possible dementia, eventually diagnosed as Alzheimer's. In August 2013, Diana became violently ill from eating wild mushrooms she had picked, and she was hospitalized. An MRI revealed terminal Stage IV ovarian cancer. She never had symptoms. Bill and the children decided against treatment because by this time, Diana was deep into her dementia. For the next eleven months, Bill focused on her care at home until her death on July 4, 2014.[51]

"Papa supervised Mom's care during those last months," Laura recalled. "I mean, if you had asked me whom I would have chosen to oversee my care at the late stage of life, he would have been the last person I would have chosen, and he turned out to be the best person. I mean, his devotion to her comfort was shocking just to watch him shift gears like that. Because her life in many ways had been focused on his career. All of a sudden, he was laser-focused on her comfort. And he was remarkable." Paul observed that his father was "very loving and considerate in her convalescence, maybe to a degree that surprised those of us that were watching. So, he finished well."[52]

Diana's services were held at 10:30 a.m. on July 8 at Houston's Palmer Memorial Episcopal Church, immediately followed by burial in the Hobby family plot at Houston's Glenwood Cemetery. Bill and Diana had been married for sixty years. "It was hard for my father to emote on her death," Paul Hobby later noted. "When we tried to do the graveside service, he just walked away from the gravesite and got in the car and closed the door and sat there alone. So, he just doesn't emote very well, even when he wants to. But he realized that she was the best thing that ever happened to him. No doubt about it. I don't know how you evaluate other people's marriages, much less your parents," Paul observed. "But [Dad] had certain weaknesses, and she didn't dwell on them. [Mom] would make the best of whatever situation, but there were times when she would get real mad at him, and you didn't know how it was going to end. But in general, they always sorted it out."[53]

After Diana's death, Bill Hobby was asked what he was happiest about in his life. He answered, "The greatest satisfaction of my life came from my wife, Diana, a scholar and editor. Diana was also that rarest of people—someone who enjoyed being married to a public official. Our four children, Laura, Paul, Andrew, and Kate, and their spouses are all wonderful people who have produced nine grandchildren who are fine, productive citizens. What more could one ask of life?"[54]

EPILOGUE

In the years after Diana's death, Bill increasingly withdrew from public life. The steady stream of essays and op-eds on the problematic state of Texas politics slowed, and public appearances became less frequent. He still held court at regular meals out with his friends and kept up on the ebb and flow of the state's affairs. But the loss of Diana, and of many of his friends, took its toll. As Jim Granato observed, "He's losing more and more people. He's tired of writing eulogies for people. He doesn't want to go to services anymore, I know that. He said, 'It's too hard.'"[1]

In January 2015, Hobby consented to a black-tie affair at Houston's River Oaks Country Club to celebrate his eighty-third birthday, a fundraiser that brought in more than $500,000 for Texas State University's Hobby Center for Public Policy and the University of Houston's Hobby School of Public Affairs. The event, cochaired by Beth Robertson and Lynne Bentsen, featured speeches from Hobby's close friends and "orner-ary chairmen and roasters" Rodney Ellis and Joe Jamail. Retired Southwest Airlines board chairman Herb Kelleher's impression of Marilyn Monroe singing "Happy Birthday" to President John F. Kennedy brought down the house. The guest list was, according to the *Houston Chronicle*, a "virtual who's-who of Texas politics," with many of Hobby's peers, friends, and family in attendance, including his children and Mark White, Ben Barnes, Don Adams, Jim Granato, and state representative Garnet Coleman. As Robertson noted, "We have a sea of senators, mayors, and governors tonight—it would take a lifetime to recognize each of you, so consider yourselves recognized."[2]

The event demonstrated that appreciation for Hobby's public service contributions persisted. Still, his record increasingly served as a reminder of a bygone era in politics. As Bob Moser noted in the *Texas Observer*, "If Bill Hobby was never a big-government liberal, at least he gave a damn about running government decently and fairly. In his heyday, that got him called a conservative Democrat. Today, it would qualify him as an outright socialist." Hobby himself leaned in to his role as political Jeremiah, reminding those who would listen that the state's trajectory needed to be corrected, particularly in funding for healthcare and education. "When I was lieutenant governor in the 1970s and '80s, health care wasn't a partisan issue. Nor were education or highways or corrections or regulatory policy. We made substantial progress in serving all of our citizens with the cooperation of Democrats and Republicans. Shocking though it sounds, Republicans joined Democrats in voting for the funding our public schools needed. . . . Should we marshal our resources and invest in the basic infrastructure of health care and education? We can. We must."[3]

In 2023, *Texas Monthly* included Hobby as one of the fifty "groundbreaking Texans who have shaped the Lone Star State—and the nation—over the past half-century." Hobby was joined by such luminaries as Lady Bird Johnson, President George H. W. Bush, Barbara Jordan, and Bob Bullock (not to mention Molly Ivins, Beyoncé, and Willie Nelson). Political reporter R. G. Ratcliffe's essay on Hobby captured his reputation as a powerful and effective leader of the Senate, best known for his budgetary acumen and his championship of state funding for education. But it crystallized Hobby's position as a touchstone of an earlier era when the state's politics could be characterized by compromise and cooperation. "The Senate Hobby took over in 1973 was very different from the one we have today," Ratcliffe wrote. "The business of the Legislature was business: the state budget and taxes, not culture war issues, were its raison d'etre." Ratcliffe continued, "For nearly two decades Hobby did an expert job of bridging those sorts of divides and delivering results to the people of the state. It was tempting to think that he represented the future of Texas politics: a centrist, consensus-driven, results-oriented process that would set an example for the rest of the nation. But if that is the future of Texas politics, from the vantage point of the early twenty-first century it looks like the very distant future indeed."[4]

Hobby agreed. As the state's politics increasingly shifted toward extremist right-wing conservatism, many of the causes he had championed were attacked, from funding for higher education and health and human services to abortion rights. Hobby decried the emphasis on public posturing on moral issues instead of policies that would benefit the people of Texas. As he stated in a televised interview in Houston in 2011, "These people are ideologues trying to run things. The only [bill] that matters is the general appropriations bill. The rest of it is poetry." Despite Hobby's frequent description of the workings of the legislature as poetry, any evaluation of his contributions reveals that he relished that poetry. The very process of governing offered him deep satisfaction. As he noted in an unpublished essay from the 1970s, "In the conduct of public affairs, process is often as important as content." That process—the intricacies and complexities of making government work for all its citizens—was a puzzle to which he devoted a lifetime. "The Texas system allows an official elected statewide to have significant input to the legislative process. In a state so large and diverse as Texas, this last consideration has particular meaning. Certainly there is no other state that offers its statewide elected officials so broad a challenge as balancing the interests and views of areas so diverse as the High Plains, the Piney Woods, the Gulf Coast, Central Texas, the Rio Grande Valley."[5]

In his later years, he also demonstrated his lifelong awareness of history—and his family's place in it. He assembled a chronicle of the Hobby family's role in Texas history, extending from the ancestors who fought in the Civil War to the many Hobbys who served in the state Capitol, from his great-uncle Alfred Hobby to his grandchildren, who were named "mascots" of the Senate. With coauthor Saralee Tiede, he wrote his memoir, *How Things Really Work: Lessons from a Life in Politics*. "Nostalgia is not my purpose," he explained. "But I do hope to convey . . . a sense of how things actually worked—at least in the legislative process." The memoir was consistent with Hobby's paradoxical ability to be a public figure from a prominent family and yet a deeply private man. As Bob Moser wrote in his review, "Hobby has no intention of giving readers a glimpse of his soul, or of anybody else's." Still, in his final years, Bill Hobby wanted to leave behind a record of the accomplishments of his family and himself.

Hobby's most lasting accomplishments may not be found in any specific policies or funding equations that have survived the shifts in the state's political landscape. Instead, his legacy is that he was a role model for public service and a reminder of the importance of the caliber of our elected officials. His manner might have made him an unlikely politician, but his brilliance and integrity made him an exemplary one. As a young man, Hobby was drawn to the priesthood. While he ultimately chose a different path, his lifelong devotion to the betterment of others became its own vocation. He dedicated himself to the advancement of our nation's ideals, as seen through his military service, his years as a journalist, his championship of higher education, and most importantly, his years in the Texas Legislature. Laura Hobby Beckworth noted, "Every role that life gave him to play—whether it was dutiful son, husband, newspaper editor, intelligence officer, public official, or academic leader—every one of those roles he took seriously, and he did a really good job. And I think he would want to be remembered for having taken each of those roles in life very seriously." For Hobby himself, the ultimate measure of his achievements came down to what he did on behalf of his fellow Texans: "If it is recorded that I cared about, that I preserved, that I protected, that I defended, and that I extended the fundamental liberties of every citizen, I shall leave a happy man."[6]

ACKNOWLEDGMENTS

BY DON CARLETON

The publication of *Bill Hobby: A Life in Journalism and Public Service* marks the completion of a research project that began in 2015, when former Texas lieutenant governor William P. Hobby Jr., better known as Bill, asked if I would research and write a book about his family reaching back to the eighteenth century but focusing mainly on his parents, William P. Hobby Sr. and Oveta Culp Hobby. Bill stressed that he did not want the book to be an exercise in hagiography. He wanted his family's story to be told objectively and based on original sources that would be identified in endnotes. He did not request preapproval of the final text. With that understanding, combined with my knowledge as a historian that the Hobby family's role in Texas and national history had failed to attract serious scholarly attention, I accepted Bill's invitation.

My initial goal was to tell the Hobby story in one volume. As I researched the lives of Bill and his parents, however, it became obvious that their historical significance, which spanned the twentieth century and part of the twenty-first, required two volumes, not one. Because Will's and Oveta's own histories were so closely linked and integrated, I decided to write the story of their partnership in a dual biography. That story was told in *The Governor and the Colonel: A Dual Biography of William P. Hobby and Oveta Culp Hobby*, which was published in 2021. It was clear to me that Bill's own accomplishments in the newspaper business and his impact on Texas politics and public policy as the longest-serving lieutenant governor in the state's history required their own detailed treatment.

After the publication of *The Governor and the Colonel*, and as I turned my attention to Bill, I invited my longtime Briscoe Center colleague Erin Purdy to serve as my coauthor. Erin is an outstanding researcher, a skilled and experienced oral historian, and a talented editor. She had worked closely with me as my chief editorial assistant for *The Governor and the Colonel*, and she helped edit Bill Hobby's 2010 memoir, *How Things Really Work*, which Bill wrote with journalist Saralee Tiede. Erin's extensive knowledge of Hobby family history and her research and editorial skills made her a natural choice. Along with her writing, Erin's interviews with several individuals with key knowledge of Bill Hobby's life and career have been a major contribution to this book. And now we have the second book in the Hobby family saga, *Bill Hobby: A Life in Journalism and Public Service*.

As with *The Governor and the Colonel*, the first person to thank is Bill Hobby, the best lieutenant governor who has ever served the citizens of Texas. Bill was unfailingly helpful throughout the research process for both books and provided essential insights through multiple interviews and conversations with me over many years. Thank you, Bill, for your forbearance and support.

The Briscoe Center is home to the papers of Bill Hobby and his father, Will, which were invaluable to this project. In addition to the Hobby papers, Erin and I were fortunate to have access to the center's other collections, notably the rich resources that document the news-media industry and twentieth-century Texas politics. Equally important to our effort were interviews with Bill's family, colleagues, and friends. Despite the challenges of conducting research and interviews during the COVID-19 pandemic, Erin and I had only to invoke Bill Hobby's name to be granted immediate and enthusiastic assistance. We are grateful to our interviewees for sharing their time and invaluable insights with us. Special thanks also go to the Hobby family, including Paul Hobby, Laura Hobby Beckworth, and Kate Hobby Gibson, all of whom were extremely forthcoming in their interviews. We also want to thank Saralee Tiede and Bill's longtime executive assistant, Delores Chambers. Along with the Hobbys, they provided candid observations, reviewed manuscript drafts, and made valuable suggestions that have greatly improved the final product.

Dr. Holly Taylor, the talented editor and historian who heads the Briscoe Center's publication program, helped make this book possible through her blend of expertise, encouragement, and gentle prodding. Thanks to Abby Webber for her meticulous copyediting and Derek George for his skillful design work. We also appreciate our partnership with the University of Texas Press and want to thank the staff, led by Robert Devens.

We would also like to thank our colleagues at the Briscoe Center for their patience as we devoted our time to this project. Special thanks are due to Alison Beck, the center's director of special projects, and Echo Uribe, director of finance and administration. It was also our good fortune to have the help of our Research and Collections staff, notably its director, Stephanie Malmros; Margaret Schlankey, head of reference services; Aryn Glazier, photography services coordinator; and Marisa Jefferson, off-site coordinator. Our team sets the standard for excellence, and this book is the better for it.

We have a deep appreciation for the invaluable services provided by reference staff of special collections at other institutions. Our thanks go to the staff members of the

Cushing Memorial Library and Archives, Texas A&M University; the Texas State Library and Archives; the Woodson Research Center, Fondren Library, Rice University (with special thanks to Amanda Focke, Rebecca Russell, Dara Flinn, and Melissa Kean); and the W. R. Poage Legislative Library, Baylor University (with special thanks to Amanda Fisher). We also are grateful for the oral histories found in collections across the state, notably those at the University of North Texas, the Center for Public History at the University of Houston, the LBJ Presidential Library, and the Austin History Center. We would also like to thank the St. Albans School archivist, Mark Wilkerson; Bob and Janis Daemmerich; and Bryan Luhn from the University of Houston for their assistance with photo research.

Bill Hobby: A Life in Journalism and Public Service was conducted as a formal research project of the Briscoe Center, and all sales income, including authors' royalties, will go directly into the center's publication support fund. Financial support has been provided by the center's Dolph Briscoe Endowment Fund and the J. R. Parten Chair in the Archives of American History. As a history research unit of the University of Texas at Austin, the Briscoe Center's mission includes the dissemination of historical knowledge resulting from its own research projects based on the center's vast holdings. Both volumes of the Hobby family history are examples of these projects. Accordingly, we want to thank former University of Texas president Greg Fenves, current president Jay Hartzell, and executive vice president and provost Sharon Wood for their support of this and all of the center's efforts.

Don would like to acknowledge the love, support, encouragement, and patience that his wife, Suzanne, has unselfishly given him for more than fifty years, without which this work would not have been possible. He also extends a very special thanks to his daughter, Aunna Fleur Carleton, whose research and editing were invaluable to her father's efforts on this book. And finally, he is grateful to his son, Ian Carleton, who continues to engage his father in discussions that keep him mentally sharp.

Erin would like to thank Don for his years of mentorship, wisdom, and camaraderie, all of which have enabled her to achieve more than she ever thought possible. Working with Don and the team he has assembled at the Briscoe Center is the singular honor of her professional life. Erin would also like to acknowledge her family and friends for their support and encouragement, especially her parents, Janis Purdy and Frederick Purdy, who gifted her with more than she can ever repay. She also wants to express her undying love and gratitude to her husband, Chris Miller, for the miracle that is their marriage.

NOTES

PROLOGUE

1. Hobby, *How Things Really Work*, 139.
2. Texas Senate Journal, 71st Leg., Reg. Sess., May 5, 1989; Saralee Tiede interview.
3. Letter to Delores Chambers, April 28, 1989, Bill Hobby Papers, Briscoe Center for American History (hereafter cited as BCAH); Burka et al., "1989"; Hector Uribe interview.
4. Saralee Tiede, introduction to Hobby, *How Things Really Work*, xxiii.
5. Jack Martin interview.
6. Laura Hobby Beckworth interview.
7. Paul Hobby interview; Saralee Tiede interview. Hobby's elder son, Paul, was unaware of his father's decision, as was Hobby's chief of staff, Saralee Tiede.
8. Texas Senate Journal, 71st Leg., Reg. Sess., May 5, 1989.
9. Texas Senate Journal, 71st Leg., Reg. Sess., May 5, 1989.
10. Texas Senate Journal, 71st Leg., Reg. Sess., May 5, 1989.
11. Carleton, *Governor and the Colonel*.
12. Hobby, *How Things Really Work*, xv; notes for oral history interview, 2002, Bill Hobby Papers, BCAH; Hobby, "Hobby Family in Texas"; Kent Caperton interview.
13. Texas Senate Journal, 71st Leg., Reg. Sess., May 5, 1989.
14. Texas Senate Journal, 71st Leg., Reg. Sess., May 5, 1989; Kent Caperton interview.
15. Texas Senate Journal, 71st Leg., Reg. Sess., May 5, 1989.
16. Texas Senate Journal, 71st Leg., Reg. Sess., May 5, 1989.
17. Texas Senate Journal, 71st Leg., Reg. Sess., May 5, 1989; Harrigan, *Big Wonderful Thing*, 775.
18. Texas Senate Journal, 71st Leg., Reg. Sess., May 5, 1989.
19. Texas Senate Journal, 71st Leg., Reg. Sess., May 5, 1989; Roberto Suro, "Texas Tory Democrats Go the Way of the Armadillo," *New York Times*, May 28, 1989. The bust is now located in the Capitol Extension, between busts of Ben Ramsey and Bob Bullock. The book of memories is in the collection of the Texas State Library and Archives.

CHAPTER 1: WILL AND OVETA

1. Newspaper clipping, Bill Hobby Papers, BCAH.
2. Hobby, *How Things Really Work*, 5.
3. Hobby, *How Things Really Work*, 7.
4. Carleton, *Governor and the Colonel*, 59–60, 68–69, 113, 119.
5. Carleton, *Governor and the Colonel*, 200, 204, 211, 220, 227.
6. Carleton, *Governor and the Colonel*, 230–233, 235.
7. Carleton, *Governor and the Colonel*, 236–240.
8. Carleton, *Governor and the Colonel*, 243–250.
9. Carleton, *Governor and the Colonel*, 265, 268.
10. *Dallas Morning News*, February 18, 1932; unidentified news clipping, March 4, 1932, Oveta Culp Hobby Papers, Rice University.

11. John Henry Kirby to Oveta Hobby, January 21, 1932, James V. Allred to Will Hobby, January 22, 1932, and Bob Poage to Will and Oveta Hobby, January 20, 1932, Bill Hobby Papers, BCAH.
12. Florence Sterling to Oveta and Will Hobby, January 27, 1932, Tom Connally to Bill Hobby, January 19, 1932, and Ross Sterling and Dan Moody to Will Hobby, January 20, 1932, Bill Hobby Papers, BCAH; Jessie Ziegler to Bill Hobby, January 19, 1932, Jessie D. Ziegler Papers, BCAH; Clark, *Tactful Texan*, 171; Johnston, *Houston*, 286.
13. Letter from Laura [possibly Will's sister], Bill Hobby Papers, BCAH; *New York Daily News*, March 21, 1953; Sutphen, "Conservative Warrior," 17, 21; Pando, "Oveta Culp Hobby," 54; Jessie Ziegler to her mother, August 18, 1932, Jessie D. Ziegler Papers, BCAH.
14. Carleton, *Governor and the Colonel*, 278.
15. *Houston Post*, May 14, 1933.
16. Carleton, *Governor and the Colonel*, 290.
17. *Houston Post*, undated clipping, Bill Hobby Papers, BCAH.
18. Carleton, *Governor and the Colonel*, 300.
19. *Houston Post*, undated clipping, Bill Hobby Papers, BCAH; Carleton, *Governor and the Colonel*, 302–303.
20. William P. Hobby Jr., "For the Young and Very Young: *Long Live the King!*," *Houston Post*, July 11, 1937, clipping from Bill Hobby Papers, BCAH. Restored in 1979, the Ideson Building now houses the Houston Metropolitan Research Center, an urban history archive and department of the Houston Public Library.
21. Bill Hobby interview. Unless otherwise indicated, "Bill Hobby interview" refers to his interview with the authors.
22. Bill Hobby interview, Houston Oral History Project.
23. Paul Hobby interview.
24. *Time*, May 4, 1953; Robert E. Connor, "Scout Haven," newspaper clipping in Bill Hobby Papers, BCAH.
25. Mrs. W. P. Hobby to Mrs. Laura L. Remer, the Oaks, 3204 Rosedale Avenue, Houston, April 15, 1938, Bill Hobby Papers, BCAH; *Daily News* interview, March 1953.
26. Bill Hobby, "An Account of National Affairs," October 1940, Bill Hobby Papers, BCAH.
27. Laura Hobby Beckworth interview.
28. Bill Hobby to Will Hobby, undated, Bill Hobby Papers, BCAH; Bill Hobby interview.
29. Bill Hobby interview; Jack McGrew to Bill Hobby, January 12, 1991, Bill Hobby Papers, BCAH.
30. Salazar, "Steiner, Thomas Casper"; Hobby, *How Things Really Work*, 12–13.
31. Laura Hobby Beckworth interview.
32. Carleton, *Governor and the Colonel*, 323.
33. Gary, *Green Fields Country Day*, 6, 10; Ralph Bowen to Oveta Culp Hobby, February 1, 1941, and Oveta to Bowen, February 7, 1941, Bill Hobby Papers, BCAH.
34. Ralph Bowen to Oveta Culp Hobby, February 1, 1941, Oveta to Mrs. G. A. Atchley, December 18, 1940, Oveta to Bowen, February 7, 1941, and Bill Hobby to Oveta, ca. February 1941, Bill Hobby Papers, BCAH; Bill Hobby interview.
35. Laura Hobby Beckworth interview; Paul Hobby interview.
36. Carleton, *Governor and the Colonel*, 325–326.
37. Carleton, *Governor and the Colonel*, 334.
38. For details about Oveta Culp Hobby's work as commander of the WAAC and the WAC, see Carleton, *Governor and the Colonel*.
39. Carleton, *Governor and the Colonel*, 356.
40. Carleton, *Governor and the Colonel*, 379, 409, 417.
41. Carleton, *Governor and the Colonel*, 395.
42. Carleton, *Governor and the Colonel*, 423.
43. Carleton, *Governor and the Colonel*, 424.

CHAPTER 2: ST. ALBANS AND THE RICE INSTITUTE

1. Brice McAdoo Clagett, "Our Founder: Harriet Lane Johnston," St Albans School, https://www.stalbansschool.org/about/history/our-founder-harriet-lane-johnston; Carleton, *Governor and the Colonel*, 265. Johnston married Henry Elliott Johnston, a Baltimore banker and railroad baron. The couple's two sons died in their early teens: fourteen-year-old James in March 1881 from fever, and twelve-year-old Henry the following year. Compounding Harriet's losses was the death of her husband in 1884. She died in 1903.
2. Hempstone, *Illustrated History of St. Albans*, 77.
3. Bill Hobby interview; Susan Barron, "Sons of St. Albans"; *Washington Post*, May 12, 1991.
4. Undated letter, Bill Hobby Papers, BCAH; *Albanian* yearbook, 1945; Bill Hobby interview; Laura Hobby Beckworth interview.
5. Hempstone, *Illustrated History of St. Albans*, 51; Hobby, *How Things Really Work*, 20. In his memoir, Bill Hobby recalled that "Mike [Collins] went on to West Point, joined the Air Force, became a test pilot and astronaut. During the flight of

Apollo 11 his wife Pat came and stayed with Diana and me because her front lawn was staked out by television news camera crews."
6. Hempstone, *Illustrated History of St. Albans*, 60; *Saint Albans News* 25, nos. 1 and 2.
7. "Memorial: John C. Davis *40," *Princeton Alumni Weekly*, https://paw.princeton.edu/memorial/john-c-davis-40; Hempstone, *Illustrated History of St. Albans*, 64, 86; Adam Berstein, "Outspoken Educator Enlarged St. Albans Curriculum," *Washington Post*, August 26, 2009; Hobby, *How Things Really Work*, 20.
8. Carleton, *Governor and the Colonel*, 428–429; Hobby, *How Things Really Work*, 13.
9. Carleton, *Governor and the Colonel*, 429–430. Jesse Jones despised the politically liberal Henry Wallace. When Jones met with the president in the Oval Office, FDR offered Jones an ambassadorship to the country of his choice, but Jones refused the offer.
10. Bill Hobby to Oveta and Will, November 6, 1945, Amy Sanders to Bill Hobby, September 4, 1946, "Dianne" to Bill Hobby, undated, and "Sam" to Bill Hobby, August 30 and September 2, 1946, Bill Hobby Papers, BCAH.
11. Bill Hobby to Oveta and Will, undated, and Bill Hobby to John Davis, undated, Bill Hobby Papers, BCAH.
12. Bill Hobby to John Davis, August 7, 1946, Bill Hobby Papers, BCAH.
13. Bill Hobby to John Davis, undated, and Hobby to Davis, June 26, 1946, Bill Hobby Papers, BCAH.
14. Bill Hobby to John Davis, June 26, 1946, and Davis to Hobby, July 7, 1946, Bill Hobby Papers, BCAH.
15. "The Vestry," *Albanian*, 1948; *Saint Albans News* 26, no. 11 (April 25, 1947); "The Cathedral Servers," *Albanian*, 1948.
16. *St. Albans News* 25, no. 3 (November 8, 1945); *St. Albans News* 28, no. 10 (April 14, 1949).
17. Bill Hobby interview; Hempstead, *Illustrated History of St. Albans*, 62; Jesse Jones to Henry Taylor, October 1947, Jesse Holman Jones Papers, BCAH. Hulen, who worked at the Associated Press and covered the US State Department for many years, had been a staff member at the *New York Times* Washington bureau since 1926. He died on July 12, 1949, in a plane crash in Bombay. *New York Times*, July 13, 1949.
18. "Men of Saint Albans: Bill Hobby," *St. Albans News* 28, no. 12 (May 20, 1949).
19. *St. Albans News* 28, no. 4 (November 24, 1948); Jesse Jones to Bill Hobby, May 26, 1949, Bill Hobby Papers, BCAH.
20. Bill Hobby to "Mother" (Oveta) and "Neeny" (Will), August 26, 1949, Bill Hobby Papers, BCAH.
21. Bill Hobby to John Davis, February 22, 1950, Bill Hobby Papers, BCAH.
22. Bill Hobby interview; Bill Hobby, "Dr. Houston's Speech Opens Orientation Day," *Rice Thresher*, September 23, 1949.
23. Bill Hobby, "Unfair?," *Rice Thresher*, January 20, 1950; *Houston Post*, January 3, 1940; transcript of column in Jesse Holman Jones Papers, BCAH.
24. Bill Hobby, "Casting Pearls," *Rice Thresher*, February 10, 1950, and March 17, 1950.
25. Bill Hobby to John Davis, March 25, 1950, Bill Hobby Papers, BCAH; Bill Hobby interview.
26. Bill Hobby to John Davis, May 13, 1950, Bill Hobby Papers, BCAH; Robertshaw, *Winant Volunteers*, 9–10; Winant Volunteers recruiting pamphlet, ca. 1952, Bill Hobby Papers, BCAH.
27. Robertshaw, *Winant Volunteers*, 3, 93–94. In 1959, the association helped to send British volunteers to America to do similar work, setting up a mutual-exchange scheme that has continued to this day. Later known as the Winant Clayton Volunteers, the organization ceased official operations in 2011.
28. Bill Hobby to Will and Oveta, July 18, 1950, and Bill Hobby to John Davis, July 6, 1950, Bill Hobby Papers, BCAH.
29. Bill Hobby to John Davis, July 6, 1950, Bill Hobby Papers, BCAH.
30. Bill Hobby to Will and Oveta, July 18, 1950, and Oveta to Bill, July 24, 1950, Bill Hobby Papers, BCAH.
31. Bill Hobby to John Davis, June 21, 1950, and Hobby to Davis, July 6, 1950, Bill Hobby Papers, BCAH.
32. Bill Hobby to Will and Oveta, undated, and Oveta to Bill, July 7, 1950, Bill Hobby Papers, BCAH.
33. William Hobby Jr., "British Coolness Must Be Accepted," *Houston Post*, August 13, 1950.
34. Oveta Hobby to Bill Hobby, July 7, 1950, and Bill Hobby to Oveta, Will, and Jessica Hobby, undated [June 1950], Bill Hobby Papers, BCAH. Laro was the managing editor of the *Post*.
35. Bill Hobby to John Davis, July 6, 1950, Bill Hobby Papers, BCAH; William Hobby Jr., "British Calloused by German Blitz," *Houston Post*, July 9, 1950. The mayor of Stepney, not named in the letter, was possibly Frederick George Spearing.
36. William Hobby Jr., "Irish Horseman Claim a Solution," *Houston Post*, August 20, 1950.

37. William Hobby Jr., "Suspicion Rampant," *Houston Post*, August 31, 1950.
38. Passion Play Oberammergau, https://www.passionsspiele-oberammergau.de/en/play/history; A. J. Goldmann, "New Kind of Passion in an 'Alpine Jerusalem,'" *Forward*, May 26, 2010, https://forward.com/news/128345/new-kind-of-passion-in-an-alpine-jerusalem/; William Hobby Jr., "Famed Oberammergau Play Is Worth Journey," *Houston Post*, September 3, 1950; Bill Hobby to John Davis, July 28, 1950, and telegram from W. P. H. to Oveta Hobby, Bill Hobby Papers, BCAH.
39. Bill Hobby, "KKK," *Rice Thresher*, October 27, 1950.
40. Bill Hobby, "Editor's Corner: Press Freedom Vital on Campus Too," *Rice Thresher*, February 15, 1952; "Allyce Tinsley Cole (Rice Institute, Class of 1953) Oral History Interview Audio and Transcript," 1996, Rice University Women's Studies Records, accessed via Rice Digital Scholarship Archive, https://scholarship.rice.edu/handle/1911/75872.
41. Abstract for photograph, "Dr. William Masterson at His Desk [ca. 1969]," Rice Digital Scholarship Archive, https://scholarship.rice.edu/handle/1911/63971; Bill Hobby, Rice University 40th Reunion survey, class of 1953, and Bill Hobby to John Davis, January 19 and November 7, 1952, Bill Hobby Papers, BCAH.
42. Bill Hobby to John Davis, August 7, 1952, Bill Hobby Papers, BCAH.
43. Bill Hobby to John Davis, November 7, 1952, Bill Hobby Papers, BCAH.
44. Carleton, *Governor and the Colonel*, 510–511.
45. Carleton, *Governor and the Colonel*, 511.
46. Carleton, *Governor and the Colonel*, 512.
47. Carleton, *Governor and the Colonel*, 501.
48. "Bill Hobby, "Politics: Is McCarthy's 'Subversion' Applicable to Education?," Rice *Thresher*, February 13, 1953; Bill Hobby, "Casting Pearls," *Rice Thresher*, February 10, 1950.
49. Carleton, *Governor and the Colonel*, 563–564.
50. Carleton, *Governor and the Colonel*, 566.
51. Hobby, *How Things Really Work*, 23.
52. Bill Hobby to John Davis, April 29, 1953, Bill Hobby Papers, BCAH.

CHAPTER 3: THE NAVY AND DIANA

1. Bill Hobby to John Davis, July 6, 1953, Bill Hobby Papers, BCAH.
2. Cheevers, "United States Naval Academy," 16; *Time*, "Change at Annapolis"; *Time*, "Books"; Bill Hobby to John Davis, November 11, 1953, Bill Hobby Papers, BCAH.
3. Bill Hobby to John Davis, December 14, 1953, Bill Hobby Papers, BCAH.
4. Bill Hobby, "Central Intelligence Agency" (1991), https://williamphobby.org/publications; *How Things Really Work*, 22. In 1965, Penguin Books published Morris's *The Washing of the Spears: The Rise and Fall of the Zulu Nation*.
5. National Register of Historic Places, nomination form, Poteat House/Forest Home.
6. Garrett, "His One and Only Novel," 244–258.
7. "Caswell County," *State: A Weekly Survey of North Carolina*, November 28, 1942; National Register of Historic Places, nomination form, Poteat House/Forest Home.
8. Laura Hobby Beckworth interview; Paul Hobby interview.
9. Diana Poteat Hobby to John Davis, March 11, 1968, Bill Hobby Papers, BCAH; National Register of Historic Places, nomination form, Poteat House/Forest Home.
10. Diana Hobby Papers, Rice University; Laura Hobby Beckworth interview.
11. Paul Hobby interview; Laura Hobby Beckworth interview.
12. Paul Hobby interview; "Ens. Will P. Hobby to Wed Diana Stallings of North Carolina," *Houston Post*, July 4, 1954.
13. Mary Blount, "News of Society," *Houston Post*, September 12, 1954; Diana Hobby to Helon Johnson, June 17, 1955, Bill Hobby Papers, BCAH.
14. Georgetown folder, Bill Hobby Papers, BCAH; *Dallas Morning News*, July 3, 1954, and February 29, 1972; *Austin American-Statesman*, undated news clipping, 1973; Hobby, *How Things Really Work*, 25; Bill Hobby, "Central Intelligence Agency" (1991), https://williamphobby.org/publications; Diana Hobby to Oveta Hobby, October 18, 1956, Oveta Culp Hobby Papers, Rice University.
15. Text of lecture presented by LCDH C. J. Lovell, USNH, to students of the Air Intelligence Division, Naval Intelligence School, September 13, 1957, declassified holdings of the National Archives; Paul Mullins, *A Brief History of the Naval Criminal Investigative Service* (1997), 5–6; Bill Hobby interview; Saralee Tiede interview. Saralee Tiede later noted how much the Naval Intelligence position meant to Bill, even later in life: "Bill loved Naval Intelligence. He told lots of stories about it."

16. Clark, *Tactful Texan*, 199; unidentified and undated clipping in Diana Hobby folder, Bill Hobby Papers, BCAH.
17. Bill Hobby, *How Things Really Work*, 28.
18. "Top Award Again Won by the Post," *Houston Post*, April 24, 1957; Hobby Foundation minutes, January 1954–March 1958, Hobby Foundation Papers, Rice University; Oveta Culp Hobby to Bill Hobby, September 28, 1956, Bill Hobby Papers, BCAH.
19. Laura Hobby Beckworth interview; news clippings, miscellaneous clippings file, Bill Hobby Papers, BCAH; Paul Hobby interview. The story appeared in newspapers throughout the country, including Bangor, Michigan; Shreveport, Louisiana; Norfolk, Nebraska; Evansville, Indiana; Piqua, Ohio; and Temple, Texas.
20. Carleton, *Governor and the* Colonel, 650.
21. *Houston Post*, October 17, 1957.
22. Bill Hobby, "Churchill Writes On," *Houston Post*, October 13, 1957.
23. Carleton, *Governor and the Colonel*, 666; *Houston Post*, April 27, 1958.
24. "Liberals Roll Up Big Harris Gains," *Houston Post*, July 28, 1958; "Widespread Support for Negro Leaves Puzzle for Vote Appraisers," *Houston Post*, November 5, 1958; "Sound-Off," *Houston Post*, September 2, 1958.
25. Laura Hobby Beckworth interview; Carleton, *Governor and the Colonel*, 669–670.
26. Hobby, *How Things Really Work*, 62; "Presiding Officers of the Texas Legislature, 1846–2016: 34th Lieutenant Governor Ben Ramsey," Legislative Reference Library, https://lrl.texas.gov/scanned/members/bios/PresidingOfficers2016/Ramsey.pdf; Morehead, "Ramsey, Ben"; Texas Senate Journal, 56th Leg., Reg. Sess., January 20, 1959, 25–26.
27. "Ben Ramsey," Legislative Reference Library; Morehead, "Ramsey, Ben."
28. Bowman, "Mister Ben."
29. "Citizen Handbook," Secretary of the Senate, Texas Senate, February 2015; Hobby, *How Things Really Work*, 62; Bill Hobby interview with Ariel Rogers, February 19, 2010, transcript in Bill Hobby Papers, BCAH.
30. Hobby, *How Things Really Work*, 62.
31. Hobby, *How Things Really Work*, 61–62. Ramsey would go on to win his sixth election as lieutenant governor in 1960, but he only served a short time before being appointed to the Texas Railroad Commission by Governor Price Daniel. He retired from that position in 1977 and died in 1985. A bronze bust was dedicated to his service in the Texas Capitol.
32. *Houston Post*, February 22, 1959.
33. *Houston Post*, August 10, 1959.
34. *Houston Post*, December 1, 1959.
35. *Houston Post*, December 7 and 9, 1959.
36. *Houston Post*, December 10 and 13, 1959.
37. "Athenians Stage Moving Welcome as Tribute to Ike," *Houston Post*, December 15, 1959.
38. *Houston Post*, December 27, 1959.
39. *Dallas Morning News*, December 3, 1958, and August 17, 1959.
40. Diana Poteat Hobby, "Books: Quarterlies," *Houston Post*, April 20, 1958; Hobby, "Journalism."
41. Hobby, "Journalism."

CHAPTER 4: THE JFK ASSASSINATION

1. *Dallas Morning News,* May 17, 1960; *Los Angeles Times*, August 3, 1991; *Time*, May 30, 1960; Hurt, "Last of the Great Ladies."
2. *Houston Post*, May 11, 1960. The report on the new printing plant is in the Oveta Culp Hobby Papers, Rice University.
3. *Houston Post*, April 28, 1962.
4. Anderson, "Eldrewey Stearns," 24–25; Cole, *No Color Is My Kind*, 43, 54–57.
5. Pando, "Oveta Culp Hobby," 184–185; Carleton, *Governor and the Colonel,* 672–673.
6. Bill Hobby interview; Cole, *No Color Is My Kind*, 43, 54–57; Pando, "Oveta Culp Hobby," 184–185.
7. *Texas Observer*, "Houston Changes"; *Time*, "Press."
8. Bill Hobby interview; *Time*, "Touchy Issue."
9. Bill Hobby interview; Laura Hobby Beckworth interview; Bill Hobby to John Davis, April 13, 1962, Bill Hobby Papers, BCAH.
10. Bill Hobby to John Davis, November 5, 1963, Bill Hobby Papers, BCAH; Laura Hobby Beckworth interview; Paul Hobby interview.
11. *Time*, "Three for the Post."
12. *Houston Post*, April 2, 1963; Bill Hobby interview.
13. Bill Hobby, typescript of formal statement to the Senate Committee on Constitutional Amendments, March 12, 1963, Bill Hobby Papers, BCAH.
14. Pierre Salinger to Oveta Hobby, October 23, 1961, and John F. Kennedy to Oveta, September 21, 1962, Oveta Culp Hobby Papers, Rice University; Bill Hobby interview. For Oveta's relationships with Presidents Roosevelt, Truman, and Eisenhower, as well as to former president Hoover, see Carleton, *Governor and the Colonel*.

15. Bill Hobby interview.
16. Hobby, *How Things Really Work*, 41–42.
17. Bill Hobby interview; Hobby, *How Things Really Work*, 41–44.
18. Bill Hobby interview; Hobby, *How Things Really Work*, 41–44 ; *Houston Post*, extra edition, November 22 and November 23–25, 1963.
19. Bill Hobby interview; *Houston Post*, November 25, 1963.
20. Oveta Culp Hobby interview; *Houston Post*, November 24, 1963; LBJ to Bill Hobby, December 9, 1963, Oveta Culp Hobby Papers, Rice University.
21. Paul Hobby interview.
22. *Houston Post*, February 7, 20, and 27, 1964.
23. *Houston Post*, June 7 and 8, 1964; Bill Hobby interview; Bill Hobby to John Davis, July 1, 1964, Bill Hobby Papers, BCAH. Don Carleton's *The Governor and the Colonel* incorrectly stated Will's death date as June 7.
24. *Austin American-Statesman*, June 8, 1964; *New York Times*, June 8, 1964; LBJ, "Statement on the Death of William P. Hobby, Sr.," June 8, 1964, copy in Oveta Culp Hobby Papers, Rice University.
25. *Houston Post*, June 8 and October 28, 1964, and January 22, 1965; *Houston Chronicle*, June 9, 1964; Carleton, *Governor and the Colonel*, 688; *Austin American-Statesman*, October 26, 1964.
26. LBJ, daily diary, August 28 and 29, 1964, and LBJ and Oveta Culp Hobby telephone conversation, August 28, 1964, LBJ Presidential Library (hereafter cited as LBJPL).
27. *Houston Post*, August 30, 1964; LBJ and Oveta Culp Hobby telephone conversation, August 30, 1964, LBJPL.

CHAPTER 5: THE HOUSTON POST

1. *Houston Post*, August 23, 1962; *Dallas Times Herald*, January 28, 1963; *Time*, "Three for the Post" 40; Hurt, "Last of the Great Ladies," 229; Bill Hobby interview; *Houston Chronicle*, July 7, 2005.
2. *Baytown Sun*, September 20, 1965; Bill Hobby interview; Hobby, *How Things Really Work*, 44–45; *Austin American-Statesman*, September 9, 1964; *Fort Worth Star-Telegram*, October 17, 1964; Goltz, *Pasadena Story*. A grand jury eventually indicted Mayor Brammer, his wife, Grace, and four others for theft of city funds in a payback scheme for bond fees from the city's financial advisors. It was later alleged that Brammer had hired a hit man from Chicago to kill Goltz, but the contract killer decided against killing the reporter after he saw him in person. The voters of Pasadena eventually adopted a new city charter and voted all incumbents out of office. However, prosecutors failed to convict anyone in the Pasadena scandals. Goltz moved to the *Detroit Press* in 1966.
3. Hurt, "Last of the Great Ladies," 229; Bill Hobby interview. Bill Hobby later denied Woestendiek's charge that he had censored stories to avoid angering advertisers.
4. Hurt, "Last of the Great Ladies," 229.
5. Bill Hobby interview.
6. Saralee Tiede interview; Laura Hobby Beckworth interview; Paul Hobby interview.
7. Keith, *Eckhardt*, 113, 198.
8. Paul Hobby interview; Bill Hobby interview.
9. *Dallas Morning News*, February 9, 1965.
10. Various clippings from unidentified newspapers, 1965, Bill Hobby Papers, BCAH; *Houston Post*, December 31, 1965, and January 16, 1966.
11. *Texas Press Messenger*, "Hobby Challenges a Closer Look."
12. *Houston Post*, November 17, 1965.
13. *Houston Post*, January 26, 1966; *Houston Chronicle*, January 9, 1966; *Dallas Morning News*, April 21, 1966.
14. Arthur B. Krim interview; Lady Bird Johnson, audio diary and transcript, September 6, 1965, LBJPL. For more about Oveta Culp Hobby's service in President Johnson's administration, see Carleton, *Governor and the Colonel*.
15. *Houston Post*, March 18, 1966; "Disability Legislation History," Student Disability Center, Colorado State University, https://disabilitycenter.colostate.edu/disability-awareness/disability-history. Coincidentally, the 1954 act was developed under Oveta Culp Hobby's general direction when she was US secretary of health, education, and welfare.
16. *Houston Post*, April 27, 1967; Bill Hobby to LBJ, April 26, 1967, Oveta Culp Hobby Papers, Rice University.
17. "NSA and the CIA," *Ramparts*, February 1967, 29–39; *New York Times*, February 16, 1967; Pando, "Oveta Culp Hobby," 143–146; Cummings, *Radio Free Europe's "Crusade."*
18. *Houston Post*, February 22, 1967; Pando, "Oveta Culp Hobby," 143–146. Many years later, Hobby wrote a column about his relationship with the CIA and noted, "I plead guilty to having helped

channel Agency funds to provide scholarships so that Third World . . . students could go to a journalism school in West Berlin in 1963. . . . What better way to show a student . . . the difference between Communism and Capitalism than to see first-hand the difference between East Berlin and West Berlin?" Hobby, "Central Intelligence Agency," 1991, https://williamphobby.org/publications.

19. *New York Times*, April 4, 1975; *Austin American-Statesman*, November 26, 1967; LBJ, daily diary, September 6, 1967, and Lady Bird Johnson, daily diary, September 6, 1967, LBJPL; Bill Hobby to LBJ, September 8, 1967, Oveta Culp Hobby Papers, Rice University; W. Marvin Watson to Bill Hobby, October 10, 1967, Bill Hobby Papers, BCAH. In November, Oveta, Bill and Diana, and Henry and Jessica Catto would host a private dinner-dance party at the exclusive Ramada Club in Houston in honor of Lynda Johnson and Chuck Robb's engagement. Bill and Diana Hobby would also attend the Robbs' marriage at the White House on December 9, 1967. Jake Jacobsen gained notoriety in the mid-1970s when he accused John B. Connally of accepting a bribe from him in return for Connally's assistance in raising federal milk price support when Connally was secretary of the treasury.

20. Bill Hobby interview. The Hobby Foundation had recently made a $500,000 donation to Rice to establish a chair in history named for Will Hobby. It was eventually filled by Dr. Harold Hyman, a specialist in American constitutional history. George R. Brown, who had long been on the board of trustees at Rice and one of its most generous financial backers, was one of Oveta's closest friends. Oveta was also a former trustee of the university. It can be assumed that the price Rice charged the Hobbys for the property was a fair one.

21. Papademetriou, *Houston*; Hurt, "Last of the Great Ladies," 144, 146; *Women's Wear Daily*, January 1971.

22. *Vogue*, "In Texas."

23. *Life*, July 26, 1968, 20–27; Bill Hobby's passport and file on the trip, Bill Hobby Papers, BCAH.

24. Catto, *Ambassadors at Sea*, 13; Richard Nixon to Oveta Culp Hobby, September 7, 1968, Oveta Culp Hobby Papers, Rice University.

25. *Women's Wear Daily*, January 1971; Marguerite Johnston in Shire, *Oveta Culp Hobby*, 20.

26. Middleton, *Double Vision*, 434.

27. Laura Hobby Beckworth interview; Paul Hobby interview; Diana Hobby to John Davis, March 11, 1968, Bill Hobby Papers, BCAH; Bill Hobby interview.

28. Laura Hobby Beckworth interview; Paul Hobby interview.

29. Laura Hobby Beckworth interview; Paul Hobby interview.

30. Laura Hobby Beckworth interview; Paul Hobby interview.

31. Laura Hobby Beckworth interview; Paul Hobby interview.

32. Laura Hobby Beckworth interview; Paul Hobby interview; Kate Hobby Gibson interview.

33. Laura Hobby Beckworth interview; Paul Hobby interview; Kate Hobby Gibson interview.

34. Laura Hobby Beckworth interview; Paul Hobby interview; Kate Hobby Gibson interview.

35. Kate Hobby Gibson interview; Laura Hobby Beckworth interview.

36. Paul Hobby interview.

37. Laura Hobby Beckworth interview; Paul Hobby interview.

38. Laura Hobby Beckworth interview; Paul Hobby interview; Kate Hobby Gibson interview.

39. Bill and Diana Hobby to John Davis, 1960–1968, and Bill Hobby's stamped passport, Bill Hobby Papers, BCAH.

40. Laura Hobby Beckworth interview; Paul Hobby interview; Kate Hobby Gibson interview.

41. Bill Hobby interview; Laura Hobby Beckworth interview; Paul Hobby interview.

42. Laura Hobby Beckworth interview; Paul Hobby interview; Kate Hobby Gibson interview.

43. Laura Hobby Beckworth interview; Paul Hobby interview.

44. Laura Hobby Beckworth interview; Paul Hobby interview; Kate Hobby Gibson interview.

45. Laura Hobby Beckworth interview; Paul Hobby interview; Kate Hobby Gibson interview.

46. Laura Hobby Beckworth interview; Paul Hobby interview.

47. Felton West to Bill Hobby, May 6, 2005, Bill Hobby Papers, BCAH.

48. *Round-Up* (Texas Daily Newspaper Association newsletter), March 1971, Bill Hobby Papers, BCAH.

CHAPTER 6: THE CAMPAIGN OF 1972

1. Bill Hobby interview.
2. *Dallas Morning News*, February 9, 1965; *Texas Press Messenger*, "Hobby Challenges a Closer

Look"; clipping from *Denton Record-Chronicle*, August 11, 1967, Bill Hobby Papers, BCAH; Hobby, *How Things Really Work*, 49; *Dallas Times Herald*, May 9, 1983; Bill Hobby interview.
3. Hobby, *How Things Really Work*, 49; Saralee Tiede interview.
4. Ron and Vicki Kessler interview; Maury Maverick to Ann Richards, April 1972, Ann Richards Papers, BCAH.
5. Saralee Tiede interview.
6. Bill Hobby interview.
7. Bill Hobby interview.
8. Bill Hobby interview; Ben Barnes interview.
9. *Corsicana (TX) Sun*, December 2, 1970; Bill Hobby interview; Hobby, *How Things Really Work*, 155.
10. Bill Hobby interview; Hobby, *How Things Really Work*, 155.
11. *Irving (TX) Daily News*, November 30, 1970; Bill Hobby interview; Hobby, *How Things Really Work*, 154–155.
12. Bill Hobby interview; Hobby, *How Things Really Work*, 49; J. Johnson, "Texas Air Control Board."
13. Hobby, *How Things Really Work*, 49; Bill Hobby interview; Max Sherman interview.
14. Bill Hobby interview; Babe Schwartz interview.
15. Hobby, *How Things Really Work*, 49–50; Bill Hobby interview; *Texas Observer*, "Christie for Lt. Governor."
16. *New York Times*, August 1, 1971; Kinch and Proctor, *Texas under a Cloud*; Kinch, "Sharpstown Stock-Fraud Scandal"; Campbell, *Gone to Texas*, 441–443.
17. Kinch, "Sharpstown Stock-Fraud Scandal"; Campbell, *Gone to Texas*, 441–443.
18. Kinch, "Sharpstown Stock-Fraud Scandal"; *New York Times*, March 8, 1973; Campbell, *Gone to Texas*, 441–443.
19. Kinch, "Sharpstown Stock-Fraud Scandal."
20. Bill Hobby interview; Hobby, *How Things Really Work*, 50.
21. *New York Times*, March 8, 1973; Ron and Vicki Kessler interview.
22. Hobby, *How Things Really Work*, 29–30; Bill Hobby interview; Oveta Culp Hobby to LBJ, April 20, 1971, and LBJ to Oveta, April 29, 1971, Oveta Culp Hobby Papers, Rice University.
23. *Dallas Morning News*, June 5, 1971.
24. Bill Hobby, typescript of speech announcing candidacy for lieutenant governor, July 6, 1971, Bill Hobby Papers, BCAH.
25. Bill Hobby interview; Saralee Tiede interview.
26. Ben Barnes interview; Hobby, *How Things Really Work*, 50.
27. Bill Hobby interview.
28. *Dallas Morning News*, July 7, 1971; *Austin American-Statesman*, July 7, 1971.
29. *Texas Observer*, April 14, 1972; *Austin American-Statesman*, July 6, 1971; *Houston Chronicle*, July 7, 1971; *Houston Post*, July 7, 1971.
30. Bill Hobby interview, Houston Public Library.
31. *Houston Post*, October 25, 1971, April 28, 1972, and May 21, 1972.
32. Bill Hobby interview; Bill Hobby interview with Ariel Rogers.
33. Laura Hobby Beckworth interview.
34. Hobby, *How Things Really Work*, 50; Bill Hobby interview; Ben Barnes interview; *Dallas Times Herald*, August 10, 1971.
35. Hobby, *How Things Really Work*, 50; Bill Hobby interview; Barnes, *Barn Burning Barn Building*; Ben Barnes interview.
36. *Dallas Morning News*, August 21 and September 7, 1971; *Texas Observer*, December 31, 1971, and March 17, 1972.
37. *New York Times*, September 24, 1971; *Dallas Morning News*, March 16, 1972; Kinch, "Sharpstown Stock-Fraud Scandal"; *Texas Observer*, March 31, 1972.
38. Hobby, *How Things Really Work*, 49; Bill Hobby interview.
39. *Dallas Times Herald*, January 14, 1972; *Houston Post*, October 25, 1971.
40. Bill Hobby interview; Hobby, *How Things Really Work*, 49–50; Ron and Vicki Kessler interview; Griffin Smith Jr., "Empires of Paper," *Texas Monthly*, November 1973.
41. Ron and Vicki Kessler interview.
42. Ron and Vicki Kessler interview.
43. *Dallas Times Herald*, January 20, 1972; *Houston Chronicle*, January 20, 1972.
44. Paul Hobby interview; O'Neil Ford to Oveta Culp Hobby, n.d., Oveta Culp Hobby Papers, Rice University.
45. Ron and Vicki Kessler interview; Reid, *Let the People In*, 73–75; *Texas Observer*, April 14, 1972.
46. *Houston Post*, February 5, 1972; *Texas Observer*, April 14, 1972.
47. Reid, *Let the People In*, 73–75; Maury Maverick to Ann Richards, April 1972, Ann Richards Papers, BCAH.
48. "Bill Hobby for Lieutenant Governor" press release, February 4, 1972, Ron Calhoun Papers,

BCAH; Ron and Vicki Kessler interview; *Texas Observer*, "Slow Start."
49. Ron and Vicki Kessler interview; Rodney Ellis interview; Saralee Tiede interview.
50. Rodney Ellis interview.
51. Ron and Vicki Kessler interview; Bryce, "Do Not Go Gentle."
52. Glenn Smith interview; Bill Hobby interview; *Dallas Times Herald*, May 9, 1983; *Dallas Morning News*, May 28, 1972; Kent Caperton interview; *Houston Post*, May 21, 1972; Rodney Ellis interview; *Houston Chronicle*, May 31, 1972. One of Hobby's staff members, Glenn Smith, recalled that Hobby smoked cigarettes "unless Diana [Hobby] was around. He kept a pack hidden in his desk." Smith claimed that whenever Diana caught her husband smoking, she would scold him in a playful manner: "'Bill, get off the cigarettes.'"
53. Laura Hobby Beckworth interview; Ron and Vicki Kessler interview; Hector Uribe interview.
54. Laura Hobby Beckworth interview; Ron and Vicki Kessler interview.
55. *Dallas Times Herald*, May 9, 1983; Ron and Vicki Kessler interview; Reid, *Let the People In*, 73; Saralee Tiede interview.
56. Ron and Vicki Kessler interview; Kent Caperton interview; Rodney Ellis interview.
57. Ron and Vicki Kessler interview; Bill Hobby interview.
58. Bill Hobby interview; *Dallas Times Herald*, August 10, 1971.
59. Catto, *Ambassadors at Sea*, 79.
60. Shire, *Oveta Culp Hobby*, 34–35; Laura Hobby Beckworth interview.
61. *Houston Post* editorials, 1972, Bill Hobby Papers, BCAH; *Time*, "Short Takes."
62. Clippings from various newspapers, 1972, and Jack McGrew to Bill Hobby, January 15, 1991, Bill Hobby Papers, BCAH.
63. Ron and Vicki Kessler interview; Oveta Culp Hobby to Billie Marcus, April 21, 1972, Bill Hobby Papers, BCAH.
64. *Dallas Times Herald*, April 12, 1972; *Houston Post*, April 12, 1972.
65. *Midland Reporter-Telegram*, April 13, 1972; Laura Hobby Beckworth interview.
66. *Dallas Times Herald*, April 13, 1972; Joe William Christie interview.
67. *Dallas Times Herald*, April 1974, clipping in Diana Hobby biography file, Bill Hobby Papers, BCAH; Max Sherman interview.
68. *Houston Post*, April 27 and May 21, 1972. Bill Hobby argued that current scientific studies "indicate that chronic marijuana use is no worse than that for long term use of other drugs that are legal. In the case of heroin, it's the drug that ruins a person's life. In the case of marijuana, it's the law—not the drug that does the ruining."
69. *Dallas Morning News*, May 28, 1972; *Houston Chronicle*, June 6, 1972; WBAP-TV (Fort Worth, TX) news script, August 22, 1972, University of North Texas Libraries Special Collections, Portal to Texas History, https://texashistory.unt.edu/ark:/67531/metadc1548926/.
70. *Dallas Morning News*, May 28, 1972.
71. *Texas Observer*, April 14, 1972; *Houston Post*, April 29, 1972.
72. Clippings from various newspapers, Bill Hobby Papers, BCAH; *Texas Observer*, "Christie for Lt. Governor."
73. *Houston Chronicle*, May 8, 1972; *New York Times*, May 9, 1972.
74. *Dallas Morning News*, May 28, 1972; Bill Hobby interview. The Hobby family's longtime connections with the top executives of the Harte-Hanks newspaper chain, specifically Houston Harte Jr., publisher of the *San Antonio Express-News*, and Ed Harte, publisher of the *Corpus Christi Caller-Times*, would result in strong editorials supporting Bill Hobby's campaign.
75. *Dallas Morning News*, May 28 and June 3, 1972.
76. Bill Hobby interview; *Houston Chronicle*, undated news clipping, Bill Hobby biography file, Bill Hobby Papers, BCAH.
77. *Houston Chronicle*, May 10, 1972; *Houston Post*, May 4, 1972; *Texas Observer*, "Oh Happy Day," May 26, 1972.
78. *Houston Post* and *Houston Chronicle*, undated news clippings, Bill Hobby biography file, Bill Hobby Papers, BCAH; *Texas Observer*, May 26, 1972.
79. *Dallas Morning News*, May 28, 1972; *Texas Observer*, "Oh Happy Day," May 26, 1972; *Dallas Times Herald*, May 18, 1972.
80. *Houston Post*, May 22, 1972; *Houston Chronicle*, May 21 and June 6, 1972; *Dallas Morning News*, May 28, 1972.
81. *Houston Chronicle*, May 21 and June 6, 1972.
82. *Dallas Morning News*, May 26, 1972; *Texas Observer*, "Oh Happy Day," May 26 and June 9, 1972.
83. *Texas Observer*, "Oh Happy Day," May 26 and June 9, 1972; *Dallas Morning News*, May 27, 1972;

Dallas Times Herald, May 31, 1972; *Houston Chronicle*, June 6, 1972; Bill Hobby interview; Hobby, *How Things Really Work*, 51.

84. *Houston Post*, May 21, 1972; Max Sherman interview; Bill Hobby campaign ads, Julian P. Kanter Political Commercial Collection, Carl Albert Congressional Research and Studies Center, University of Oklahoma.
85. Bill Hobby interview; Hobby, *How Things Really Work*, 52–53. Larry L. King included the Chicken Ranch story in his 1980 book, *Of Outlaws, Con Men, Whores, Politicians and Other Artists*.
86. Hobby, *How Things Really Work*, 52.
87. Hobby, *How Things Really Work*, 51; Max Sherman interview.
88. Bill Hobby interview; *Corpus Christi Caller-Times*, May 25, 1972.
89. *Dallas Morning News*, June 4, 1972; Harold S. Taxel to Oveta Culp Hobby, June 27, 1972, Bill Hobby Papers, BCAH.
90. *Houston Post*, June 5, 1972; Paul Hobby interview; Laura Hobby Beckworth interview.

CHAPTER 7: THE FIRST TERM

1. Caudill and Hancock, "Guild and the Post."
2. "Editorial," *Houston Journalism Review*, 1972.
3. *Dallas Morning News*, February 18, 1973.
4. *Dallas Morning News*, September 23, 1972; *Austin American-Statesman*, September 22, 1972.
5. *Dallas Times Herald*, June 16, 1972; *Houston Chronicle*, June 22 and July 7, 1972; *Houston Post*, December 10, 1972; Bill Hobby interview.
6. Bill Hobby interview; Hobby, *How Things Really Work*, 61–64; Don Adams interview.
7. *Austin American-Statesman*, August 26, 1972; *Texas Observer*, "Perils of the SA Expressway."
8. *Dallas Times Herald*, October 15, 1972; *Texas Observer*, October 6, 1972; Shire, *Oveta Culp Hobby*, 20–21; *Houston Post*, October 29, 1972; Richard Nixon to Oveta Culp Hobby, November 3, 1972, Oveta Culp Hobby Papers, Rice University.
9. *Houston Post*, December 10, 1972.
10. *Dallas Morning News*, December 30, 1972.
11. Oscar Mauzy interview; Don Adams interview.
12. Bill Hobby interview; Oscar Mauzy interview; Don Adams interview.
13. Oscar Mauzy interview; Don Adams interview; Bill Hobby interview.
14. Bill Hobby interview; Don Adams interview; Bill Hobby, "Days of Pomp and Ceremony," January 25, 1973, typescript in Bill Hobby Papers, BCAH.
15. Bill Hobby interview; Hobby, *How Things Really Work*, 67; Babe Schwartz interview.
16. Margaret Behrens obituary, *Austin American-Statesman*, March 8, 2005; *Austin American-Statesman*, August 13, 1973; Bill Hobby interview; *Houston Post*, November 26, 1972.
17. Bill Hobby, typescript journal, February 25, 1973, Bill Hobby Papers, BCAH; Babe Schwartz interview; Hobby, *How Things Really Work*, 66; Bill Hobby interview; O. H. "Ike" Harris interview.
18. Bill Hobby, typescript journal, February 25, 1973, Bill Hobby Papers, BCAH; *Dallas Morning News*, January 18, 1973; Hobby, *How Things Really Work*, 66; Bill Hobby interview; Tom Creighton interview.
19. Don Adams interview; Babe Schwartz interview.
20. Bill Hobby interview.
21. Hobby, *How Things Really Work*, 30.
22. Hobby, *How Things Really Work*, 30; Dolph Briscoe Jr. interview.
23. Briscoe, *Dolph Briscoe*, 200–201.
24. Briscoe, *Dolph Briscoe*, 200–201; Hobby, *How Things Really Work*, 30.
25. *Austin American-Statesman*, January 17, 1973; Briscoe, *Dolph Briscoe*, 200–201; Bill Hobby interview.
26. Briscoe, *Dolph Briscoe*, 200–201; Bill Hobby interview.
27. Briscoe, *Dolph Briscoe*, 203; *Austin American-Statesman*, January 17, 1973.
28. *Houston Post*, January 18, 1973; Bill Hobby interview. Will Hobby's other official portrait, as governor, was painted by Enrico Cerrachi and is displayed on the third floor of the Texas Capitol. A photographic portrait of Bill's grandfather, Edwin Hobby, is on the top row of a large, framed, posterlike composite of senatorial portraits taken in 1876. That composite hangs on a wall in the Senate Chamber.
29. *Houston Post*, January 18, 1973; Bill Hobby interview.
30. Hobby, *How Things Really Work*, 130; Bill Hobby interview; *Abilene Reporter-News*, April 9, 1978.
31. Hobby, *How Things Really Work*, 77–79.
32. Hobby, *How Things Really Work*, 64–66, 136; Bill Hobby interview.
33. Hobby, *How Things Really Work*, 64–67; Bill Hobby interview; *Houston Post*, December 10, 1972.
34. Bill Hobby interview; Hobby, *How Things Really Work*, 64–67; *Paris (TX) News*, October 4, 1987; Bill Hobby, typescript journal, February 25, 1973,

Bill Hobby Papers, BCAH; Northcott, "Needs Salt"; *Dallas Morning News*, January 18, 1973.

35. Oscar Mauzy interview; Bill Hobby interview; Hobby, *How Things Really Work*, 66; Bill Hobby, typescript journal, February 25, 1973, Bill Hobby Papers, BCAH; *Dallas Morning News*, January 18, 1973.
36. Bill Hobby interview; Hobby, *How Things Really Work*, 66; Bill Hobby, typescript journal, February 25, 1973, Bill Hobby Papers, BCAH; *Dallas Morning News*, January 18, 1973; Orozco, "Rodriguez v. San Antonio ISD."
37. *Austin American-Statesman*, February 6, 1973; Bill Hobby interview.
38. Hobby, "Days of Pomp and Ceremony."
39. Hobby, "Days of Pomp and Ceremony."
40. Hobby "Days of Pomp and Ceremony"; Bill Hobby interview.
41. Hobby "Days of Pomp and Ceremony"; Bill Hobby interview; Dolph Briscoe Jr. interview.
42. Hobby, *How Things Really Work*, 133–134.
43. Max Sherman interview.
44. Tom Creighton interview; *Austin American-Statesman*, February 6, 1973.
45. Bill Hobby interview; *Houston Chronicle*, December 9, 1990; *Austin American-Statesman*, February 6, 1973.
46. Bill Hobby interview; *Dallas Times Herald*, April 1, 1973.
47. Bill Hobby interview; Kent Caperton interview; Max Sherman interview; Babe Schwartz interview.
48. Hobby, *How Things Really Work*, 73–74. Price Daniel Jr.'s father was a former Speaker of the Texas House, state attorney general, US senator, governor, and justice of the Texas Supreme Court. His mother was a direct descendant of Sam Houston.
49. *Houston Post*, February 18 and 27, 1973; *Texas Observer*, March 2, 1973.
50. *Houston Post*, February 2, 1973; *Texas Observer*, March 2, 1973.
51. Oscar Mauzy interview; *Houston Post*, February 18 and 27, 1973; *Texas Observer*, March 2, 1973; *Houston Chronicle*, March 18, 1973; *Dallas Times Herald*, January 20, 1974.
52. *Texas Observer*, April 13, 1973; *Houston Post*, March 18, 1973.
53. *Houston Post*, March 21, 1973; Tom Creighton interview; Ferguson, Northcott, and Ivins, "Turn Out the Lights"; *Fort Worth Star Telegram*, October 30, 1973. Price Daniel tried to revive the ethics commission after the end of the regular legislative session. A special House Subcommittee on Ethics conducted hearings on the issue. Hobby testified at one of its hearings and repeated his opposition to a commission. He warned that it would create "a new bureaucracy that would open the door to political witch hunts. We certainly don't need to burden our taxpayers with a bureaucracy that would do less than our fine judicial system is doing now." Governor Briscoe and Secretary of State Mark White both agreed with Hobby.
54. *Texas Observer*, April 13, 1973.
55. Oscar Mauzy interview.
56. *Texas Observer*, April 13, 1973; Oscar Mauzy interview; Tom Creighton interview.
57. *Dallas Times Herald*, January 20, 1974; *Dallas Morning News*, April 14 and April 30, 1973.
58. Briscoe, *Dolph Briscoe*, 218.
59. Briscoe, *Dolph Briscoe*, 218; Mark White interview.
60. Briscoe, *Dolph Briscoe*, 213–214; Bill Hobby interview; Mark White interview.
61. Briscoe, *Dolph Briscoe*, 208, 210, 216; Max Sherman interview.
62. Briscoe, *Dolph Briscoe*, 13, 203; Hobby, *How Things Really Work*, 77–79; Bill Hobby interview. For more about Governor Ross Sterling and his relationship with the Briscoe and Hobby families, see Sterling and Kilman, *Ross Sterling, Texan*.
63. Briscoe, *Dolph Briscoe*, 210–211; Ferguson, Northcott, and Ivins, "Turn Out the Lights"; *Houston Post*, May 21, 1973.
64. Bill Hobby interview; Hill, *John Hill*, 31.
65. Bill Hobby interview; Hill, *John Hill*, 28–33.
66. Bill Hobby interview; Hill, *John Hill*, 28–33; *Texas Observer*, April 13, 1973.
67. Bill Hobby interview; Hill, *John Hill*, 28–33.
68. Max Sherman interview; Bill Hobby interview; *Dallas Times Herald*, June 3, 1973, and January 20, 1974; *Texas Observer*, April 13, 1973; *Houston Post*, June 3, 1974.
69. Don Adams interview.
70. *Dallas Morning News*, May 22, 1973; *Houston Chronicle*, May 27 and December 2, 1973; Bill Hobby interview; Kent Caperton interview.
71. Oscar Mauzy interview.
72. *Dallas Times Herald*, June 3, 1973; *Houston Post*, June 3, 1974; Bill Hobby interview; Dolph Briscoe Jr. interview.
73. *Texas Observer*, June 15, 1973.

74. Bill Hobby interview; Dolph Briscoe Jr. interview; *Houston Chronicle*, December 2, 1973; Ferguson, Northcott, and Ivins, "Turn Out the Lights."
75. *Dallas Times Herald*, January 20, 1974; Oscar Mauzy interview.

CHAPTER 8: ARTESIA HALL AND THE CONSTITUTIONAL CONVENTION

1. *Houston Post*, June 17, 1973; *Dallas Times Herald*, June 3, 1973. Texas and the other states, as well as the federal government, gave up on zero-based budgeting because it was such a costly process that rarely resulted in enough savings to be justified.
2. *Houston Post* and *Houston Chronicle*, June 16, 1973; Hobby, *How Things Really Work*, 90; Hill, *John Hill*, 96–97.
3. Chase Untermeyer, "A Life in Two Centuries," unpublished manuscript in Untermeyer's possession; *Houston Chronicle*, August 20, 1972; Hill, *John Hill*, 96–97; Hobby, *How Things Really Work*, 90. Chase Untermeyer was the *Chronicle* reporter who broke the news about problems at Artesia Hall. After that initial story, *Chronicle* editors rejected Untermeyer's pleas to continue coverage of Farrar and Artesia Hall, because they feared Farrar would file a lawsuit accusing the newspaper of libel.
4. Untermeyer, "A Life in Two Centuries"; *Houston Post*, June 16, 1973; Hobby, *How Things Really Work*, 90; Hill, *John Hill*, 96–97. Farrar claimed he earned his doctorate in psychology from the unaccredited Interamerican University in Saltillo, Mexico.
5. Hobby, *How Things Really Work*, 90; Hill, *John Hill*, 96–97.
6. Hobby, *How Things Really Work*, 90; Hill, *John Hill*, 90–92, 96–97.
7. Bill Hobby interview; Hill, *John Hill*, 97.
8. Hobby, *How Things Really Work*, 90–92; Hill, *John Hill*, 98.
9. Hobby, *How Things Really Work*, 91–92; Hill, *John Hill*, 99–100.
10. Dolph Briscoe Jr. interview; Hobby, *How Things Really Work*, 92; Hill, *John Hill*, 100.
11. Dolph Briscoe Jr. interview; Hill, *John Hill*, 103–104.
12. Hill, *John Hill*, 103–104; *Houston Chronicle*, February 7, 1987.
13. Hill, *John Hill*, 233f5; Farrar v. Hobby, 506 U.S. 103 (1992); Untermeyer, "A Life in Two Centuries." The Supreme Court's decision was largely based on the definition of "prevailing party." Per Seán Conley, the court ruled that "a plaintiff who wins nominal damages (Farrar) is a prevailing party, but nominal damages also may highlight the plaintiff's failure to prove actual, compensable injury. Furthermore, a test of reasonableness must be applied, based on the amount and nature of damages, so that the court may lawfully award low fees or no fees. When a plaintiff recovers only nominal damages because of his failure to prove an essential element of his claim for monetary relief . . . the only reasonable fee is usually no fee at all." For a legal analysis of *Farrar v. Hobby*, see Conley, "*Farrar v. Hobby*."
14. Hobby, *How Things Really Work*, 93; Dolph Briscoe Jr. interview; Mark White interview.
15. Bill Hobby interview; Dolph Briscoe Jr. interview.
16. Hobby, *How Things Really Work*, 96.
17. *Houston Post*, March 8, 1973.
18. *Houston Post*, October 2, 1973.
19. *Houston Post*, June 3, 1974.
20. Yergin, *Prize*, 602–632.
21. *Dallas Morning News*, October 11, 1973; *Houston Post*, October 24, 1973.
22. *Dallas Morning News*, October 11 and November 15, 1973; *Houston Post*, October 24, 1973.
23. *Dallas Times Herald*, April 1, 1973; Laura Hobby Beckworth interview.
24. *Houston Post*, December 5, 1973, and March 19, 1974; *Dallas Morning News*, December 6, 1973, and March 1, 1974; *New York Times*, January 3, 1974; *Dallas Times Herald*, March 1, 1974. In January 1974, Congress passed the Emergency Highway Energy Conservation Act, which included the national maximum speed limit. States had to agree to the limit if they wanted federal funding for highway repair.
25. *Dallas Morning News*, August 27, 1973.
26. Dolph Briscoe Jr. interview; Bill Hobby interview.
27. *Dallas Morning News*, October 17, 1973.
28. *Dallas Times Herald*, January 20, 1974; *Houston Post*, January 20, 1974.
29. *Houston Chronicle*, December 2, 1973, and January 20, 1974; *Dallas Times Herald*, January 20, 1974; *Dallas Morning News*, January 20, 1974.
30. *Dallas Times Herald*, January 20, 1974; *Austin American-Statesman*, February 6, 1973.
31. Barras and Daniel, "Constitutional Convention of 1974"; *Dallas Morning News*, October 2, 1973;

Houston Chronicle, June 30, 1973; *Houston Post*, January 9, 1974; Bill Hobby interview.

32. *Dallas Times Herald*, May 31, 1973; Hobby, *How Things Really Work*, 74; *Houston Post*, May 31, 1973, and January 24, 1974.
33. Carleton, *Governor and the Colonel*, 12–13; Campbell, *Gone to Texas*, 285.
34. *Houston Post*, January 9, 1974; Hobby, *How Things Really Work*.
35. *Fort Worth Star-Telegram*, April 27, 1974; *Dallas Times Herald*, March 7, 1974; Bill Hobby interview.
36. Bill Hobby interview; Hobby, *How Things Really Work*, 74.
37. Tom Creighton interview.
38. Dolph Briscoe Jr. interview; Briscoe, *Dolph Briscoe*, 233–234.
39. Briscoe, *Dolph Briscoe*, 235, 242–244; Untermeyer, "Give Me Liberty"; Max Sherman interview.
40. Hobby, *How Things Really Work*, 75.
41. *Dallas Times Herald*, March 7, 1974; *Daily Texan*, April 9 and 17, 1974; *Houston Chronicle*, April 16, 1974.
42. *Dallas Morning News*, June 21, 1974; *Austin American-Statesman*, June 21, 1974; *Daily Texan*, June 21, 1974; *Dallas Times Herald*, June 22, 1974; D. Richards, *Once upon a Time*, 226; Babe Schwartz interview. Anne Chisolm's biography of Nancy Cunard was eventually published in 1979. Dave Richards was future Texas governor Ann Richards's husband.
43. Paul Hobby interview; Hurt, "Last of the Great Ladies," 143, 237.
44. Babe Schwartz interview.
45. *Dallas Times Herald*, June 21 and 22, 1974; Paul Hobby interview. By coincidence, journalist Saralee Tiede, who would later become one of Bill Hobby's closest confidants and aides, broke the story in the *Dallas Times Herald* with the headline, "Hobby Sentenced for Drunk Driving."
46. D. Richards, *Once upon a Time*, 226.
47. *Austin American-Statesman*, November 6, 1974.
48. *Dallas Times Herald*, November 14, 1974; Saralee Tiede interview; *Texas Observer*, "Political Intelligence: Undoubtedly"; Hurt, "Last of the Great Ladies," 143, 237. In June 1975, one year after Hobby's DWI arrest, Senator Oscar Mauzy was also arrested for DWI, but it attracted little news media interest. Mauzy and Hobby joined a long list of other state officials who were arrested on the same charges.

CHAPTER 9: CONSTITUTIONAL REFORM REDUX

1. Murph, "Daniel, Marion Price, Jr."; *Dallas Times Herald*, February 2, 1975; O. H. "Ike" Harris interview; Briscoe, *Dolph Briscoe*, 241.
2. *Dallas Times Herald*, February 2, 1975; Bill Hobby interview. Hance defeated Doc Blanchard, Doggett filled Charles Herring's vacant seat, and Farabee replaced Jack Hightower, who was elected to US Congress.
3. Bill Hobby interview; Dolph Briscoe Jr. interview.
4. Bill Hobby interview; Dolph Briscoe Jr. interview.
5. Briscoe, *Dolph Briscoe*, 240; Ashworth, "Texas Higher Education Board."
6. Kent Caperton interview; Northcott, "Senate."
7. Tom Creighton interview; Ron and Vicki Kessler interview.
8. Hill, *John Hill*, 110; Dolph Briscoe Jr. interview; Bill Hobby interview.
9. *Washington Post*, October 13, 1978; Colloff, "Remember the Christian Alamo"; *New York Times*, November 4, 1982; Hill, *John Hill*, 110; Dolph Briscoe Jr. interview; *Texas Observer*, June 20, 1975; Bill Hobby interview; Hobby, *How Things Really Work*, 94–95; *Dallas Times Herald*, February 2, 1975. In November 1982, Roloff died when a small airplane he was piloting crashed near Normangee, Texas, during bad weather. Even after his death, the legal battles continued. Roloff's homes (he had opened more than one) were finally closed in 1985, but a ministry in his name continues.
10. Bill Hobby interview.
11. Oscar Mauzy interview; Ferguson, "School Financing," 12–13; Bill Hobby interview.
12. Bill Hobby interview; Oscar Mauzy interview.
13. Ferguson, "School Financing"; Dolph Briscoe interview.
14. Bill Hobby interview; Saralee Tiede interview.
15. Saralee Tiede interview; Bill Hobby interview; Hobby, *How Things Really Work*, 75–76.
16. Hobby, *How Things Really Work*, 75–76; Bill Hobby interview; Saralee Tiede interview; Tom Creighton interview.
17. Bill Hobby interview; Hobby, *How Things Really Work*.
18. Hopper, "Case for Regulation"; *Texas Observer*, June 20, 1975; Greenlee, "Public Utility Commission of Texas."
19. Hill, *John Hill*, 71, 82.
20. Hill, *John Hill*, 71, 82; Ivins and Northcott, "Utilities Regulation."

21. Ivins, "Utilities Regulation"; Bill Hobby interview; Greenlee, "Public Utility Commission of Texas." In the fall of 1977 the new Public Utility Commission of Texas held its first rate case. The commissioners granted Southwestern Bell Telephone Company a rate increase of $57.8 million instead of the $298.3 million the company had requested.
22. *Texas Monthly*, June 1975; *Dallas Times Herald*, June 8, 1975; *Texas Observer*, June 20, 1975; Bill Hobby interview.
23. Babe Schwartz interview; Oscar Mauzy interview; Tom Creighton interview.
24. Paul Hobby interview; Kate Hobby Gibson interview.
25. *Austin American-Statesman*, March 25, 1979.
26. Bill Hobby to Henry and Jessica Catto, November 21, 1975, Bill Hobby Papers, BCAH.
27. Bill Hobby to Henry and Jessica Catto, November 21, 1975, Bill Hobby Papers, BCAH.
28. *San Antonio Express*, October 7, 1975; *New York Times*, November 6, 1975; Ivins, "Vote Yes."
29. Bill Hobby interview; Hobby, *How Things Really Work*; Briscoe, *Dolph Briscoe*, 242–244.
30. *Texas Observer*, December 12 and 21, 1975; Hobby, *How Things Really Work*, 76. After the amendments were defeated, Molly Ivins noted there were "probably two main reasons." "First, the Legislature was once again asking for annual sessions for itself. Second, the people do not trust the Legislature."

CHAPTER 10: THE HOBBY-CLAYTON COMMISSION

1. *Fort Worth Star-Telegram*, January 7, 1976.
2. *Fort Worth Star-Telegram*, January 23, 1976.
3. "Documents Relating to the Impeachment of O. P. Carrillo," Legislative Reference Library of Texas, https://lrl.texas.gov/collections/impeachment.cfm; *Austin American-Statesman*, January 24, 1976.
4. *Fort Worth Star-Telegram*, January 1, 1976; *Abilene Reporter-News*, October 14, 1976; Bill Hobby interview; Hobby, *How Things Really Work*, 116.
5. *Fort Worth Star-Telegram*, January 1, 1976; *Abilene Reporter-News*, October 14, 1976; Bill Hobby interview; Hobby, *How Things Really Work*, 116.
6. Bill Hobby interview; *San Angelo (TX) Standard-Times*, January 23, 1977.
7. *Southlander*, Summer 1976, clipping in Bill Hobby Papers, BCAH.
8. Bill Hobby interview; Harris, Huhndorff, and McGrew, *Fault Does Not Lie*, 118–119.
9. Harris, Huhndorff, and McGrew, *Fault Does Not Lie*, 118–119; Bill Hobby interview.
10. *Nashville Banner*, June 24, 1976; *Tennessean*, June 25, 1976.
11. *Tennessean*, June 25, 1976; Shire, *Oveta Culp Hobby*, 26; Jack McGrew to Bill Hobby, January 15, 1991, Bill Hobby Papers, BCAH.
12. Carleton, *Governor and the Colonel*, 746.
13. Oveta Culp Hobby to Kaye McDermott, August 11, 1976, Oveta Culp Hobby Papers, Rice University; Harris, Huhndorff, and McGrew, *Fault Does Not Lie*, 118–122; Hurt, "Last of the Great Ladies," 233–234.
14. *San Antonio Express-News*, October 24, 1976; Dolph Briscoe Jr. interview; *Austin American-Statesman*, November 5, 1976; *Houston Chronicle*, November 30, 1976.
15. Dolph Briscoe Jr. interview; Bill Hobby interview; *Austin American-Statesman*, November 5, 1976; *Houston Chronicle*, November 30, 1976.
16. Briscoe, *Dolph Briscoe*; *San Antonio Express-News*, January 2, 1977.
17. *Waco Tribune-Herald*, September 3, 1976; *Times Record News* (Wichita Falls, TX), January 15, 1977. The Hobby-Clayton report also included drafts of seventy bills, five constitutional amendments, and sixteen resolutions it was proposing for the legislature's consideration.
18. *Fort Worth Star-Telegram*, January 2, 1977.
19. *San Antonio Express*, January 2, 1977; Bill Hobby interview.
20. *Austin American-Statesman*, November 14 and December 31, 1975; *Fort Worth Star-Telegram*, December 10, 1975.
21. *Austin American-Statesman*, January 6 and 7, 1976.
22. *Houston Chronicle*, October 30, 1975, and January 1 and February 11, 1976; *El Paso Times*, December 21, 1976.
23. *El Paso Times*, December 21, 1976; *Texas Observer*, "Political Intelligence: More against Schnabel"; Winston Bode column, *Bryan–College Station Eagle*, January 4, 1976; Bill Hobby interview.
24. *Austin American-Statesman*, undated [1976] news clipping in Bill Hobby Papers, BCAH.
25. *Houston Chronicle* and *Austin American-Statesman*, September 17, 1976. The charges against Schnabel included allowing Senate employees to perform work at a track-and-field event at the University of Texas while on the

Senate payroll, improperly placing persons on the Senate payroll for nonprofessional services, using improper procedures to pay for parking spaces for Senate employees, placing an ex-senator on the Senate payroll for a period of one month to make him eligible for retirement benefits under the Texas Employees Retirement System, and placing persons on the Senate payroll to reimburse them for travel expenses because they were not state employees and not otherwise eligible for state-paid travel. In two instances "persons were paid by the state to clear brush off Schnabel's ranch."

26. Lauren Caruba, "People We'll Miss," *Texas Monthly*, December 1, 2014; Ross Ramsey, "Betty King, Longtime Secretary of Texas Senate Dies," *Texas Tribune*, December 1, 2014; Bill Hobby interview. One month after Schnabel was dismissed from his job in the Senate, the Texas Rehabilitation Commission hired him. When Senator Charlie Wilson won election to US Congress, he hired Schnabel to be his executive assistant. Schnabel eventually spent the remainder of his career working as a lobbyist. Betty King remained in her position until she retired in 2001. She died on December 1, 2014, at the age of eighty-nine and was buried in the Texas State Cemetery.
27. *Austin American-Statesman*, January 19, 1977; *Fort Worth Star-Telegram*, January 20, 1977.
28. Burka and West, "1977"; Briscoe, *Dolph Briscoe*; Hobby, *How Things Really Work*; *Abilene Reporter-News*, April 9, 1978.
29. Bill Hobby interview; Hobby, *How Things Really Work*; *Texas Observer*, "Report of the Hobby Commission"; *Port Arthur (TX) News*, June 22, 1977; Billy Clayton interview; *Austin American-Statesman*, January 11, 1977; Smyrl, "Texas Sunset Advisory Commission"; Texas Sunset Advisory Commission homepage, https://www.sunset.texas.gov/.
30. Hobby, *How Things Really Work*, 85; Bill Hobby interview; *Austin American-Statesman*, June 1, 1977.
31. Tiede, "Drifting"; *Austin American-Statesman*, June 1, 1977.
32. Bill Hobby interview; *Austin American-Statesman*, June 1, 1977; Dolph Briscoe Jr. interview; Briscoe, *Dolph Briscoe*, 250; *Fort Worth Star-Telegram*, July 19, 1977.
33. *Fort Worth Star-Telegram*, July 16, 1977; *Houston Chronicle*, July 20, 1977.
34. Burka and West, "1977."
35. Bill Hobby, calendar, September 1977, Bill Hobby Papers, BCAH.
36. *Fort Worth Star-Telegram*, September 10, 1977.
37. Paul Hobby interview; Bill Hobby, calendar, December 26, 1977–January 7, 1978, Bill Hobby Papers, BCAH; Diana Poteat, "The Praise of Life: A Study of the Dramatic Work of William Butler Yeats as It Is Represented by Four Plays" (senior thesis, Radcliffe College, 1952); Diana Poteat Hobby, "William Butler Yeats and Edmund Dulac: A Correspondence, 1916–1938" (PhD diss., Rice University, 1981). Copies of the thesis and dissertation are in the William P. Hobby Jr. and Diana Poteat Hobby Family Collection, Rice University.
38. *Fort Worth Star-Telegram*, February 5, 1978; *San Angelo (TX) Times*, February 7, 1978.
39. Pennington, "John Hill Westbrook."
40. *Abilene Reporter-News*, February 14 and April 9, 1978; *Fort Worth Star-Telegram*, March 14 and April 1, 1978; *Bryan–College Station Eagle*, March 8, 1978. A few years after he ran against Hobby, Westbrook died suddenly of a pulmonary embolism at the age of thirty-six.
41. Murph, "Daniel, Marion Price, Jr." Daniel was shot by his second wife, Vickie, in January 1981 and died from the wound.
42. Slaughter, "Clements, William Perry, Jr."
43. Oscar Mauzy interview; Dolph Briscoe Jr. interview; Bill Hobby interview.
44. Bill Hobby interview; *Fort Worth Star-Telegram*, July 9, 1978.
45. Dolph Briscoe Jr. interview; Bill Hobby interview; *Houston Chronicle*, June 22, 1978; *Austin American-Statesman*, June 24 and 25, 1978; *Fort Worth Star-Telegram*, July 9, 1978.
46. *Fort Worth Star-Telegram*, July 9, 1978; *Victoria (TX) Advocate*, July 15, 1978.
47. *Austin American-Statesman*, July 17, 1978; *Fort Worth Star-Telegram*, August 6 and 8, 1978.
48. Burka, "Other Hobby"; Kent Caperton interview; *Austin American-Statesman*, August 10, 1978; *Fort Worth Star-Telegram*, August 10, 1978.
49. Laura Hobby Beckworth interview; Paul Hobby interview; Harte-Hankes newspapers, November 2, 1978.
50. *Galveston Daily News*, September 18, 1978; *Austin American-Statesman*, October 25, 1978.
51. *Abilene Reporter-New*s, September 13, 1978; Paul Hobby interview.
52. *Houston Post*, October 19, 1978; *Austin*

American-Statesman, October 19, 1978; Burka, "Other Hobby."

53. *Houston Chronicle*, November 8, 1978; Bridges, *Twilight of the Texas Democrats*, 117; Burka, "State Secrets" (January 1982), 180; *Abilene Reporter-News*, November 19, 1978.

CHAPTER 11: BILL CLEMENTS AND THE KILLER BEES

1. *Austin American-Statesman* and *Fort Worth Star-Telegram*, January 17, 1979; Hobby, *How Things Really Work*, 83.
2. *Texas Monthly*, July 1979; Barta, *Bill Clements*; Hobby, *How Things Really Work*, 82.
3. Hobby, *How Things Really Work*, 82–83.
4. Hobby, *How Things Really Work*, 116.
5. Hobby, *How Things Really Work*, 83–84; Bill Hobby interview.
6. Hobby, *How Things Really Work*, 83–84; Bill Hobby interview.
7. George Bristol to Bill and Diana Hobby, August 22, 1995, Bill Hobby Papers, BCAH; Bill Hobby interview.
8. Bill Hobby interview; *Houston Chronicle* and *Fort Worth Star-Telegram*, February 4, 1979; George Bristol to Bill and Diana Hobby, August 22, 1995, Bill Hobby Papers, BCAH; "Breakfast Honoring His Excellency Deng Xiaoping, February 3, 1979," program, Oveta Culp Hobby Papers, Rice University.
9. Saralee Tiede interview; Hobby, *How Things Really Work*, 80.
10. Saralee Tiede interview; Babe Schwartz interview.
11. Hobby, *How Things Really Work*, 81; Saralee Tiede interview; Babe Schwartz interview.
12. Saralee Tiede interview; Burka, "Bill Hobby."
13. Saralee Tiede interview; Bill Hobby interview; Hobby, *How Things Really Work*, 81; Babe Schwartz interview.
14. Ben Barnes interview. For Barnes's role in the lobbying effort for the split primary, see Jules Witcover's nationally syndicated column, multiple newspapers, April 23, 1979.
15. Bill Hobby interview; Oscar Mauzy interview; Knaggs, *Two Party Texas*, 179; Saralee Tiede interview.
16. *Fort Worth Star-Telegram*, March 11, 1979; Hobby, *How Things Really Work*, 134.
17. *Austin American-Statesman*, January 31, 1979.
18. Hobby, *How Things Really Work*, 135; Babe Schwartz interview; *Dallas Times Herald*, May 9, 1983; *Fort Worth Star-Telegram*, January 14 and February 7, 1979.
19. *Fort Worth Star-Telegram*, January 14 and February 7, 1979; *Washington Post*, May 22, 1979.
20. *Fort Worth Star-Telegram*, March 8, 1979.
21. *Fort Worth Star-Telegram*, March 11, 1979.
22. *Houston Chronicle*, April 20, 1979.
23. Hobby, *How Things Really Work*, 134–135.
24. *Austin American-Statesman*, May 2, 1979; Hobby, *How Things Really Work*; Bill Hobby interview.
25. Oscar Mauzy interview; Hobby, *How Things Really Work*, 134.
26. Babe Schwartz interview; Oscar Mauzy interview.
27. Babe Schwartz interview; Oscar Mauzy interview; *Dallas Times Herald*, May 18, 1979; Knaggs, *Two Party Texas*, 235–236.
28. *Dallas Times Herald*, May 18, 1979; *Fort Worth Star-Telegram*, May 18, 1979; *Washington Post*, May 22, 1979; *New York Times*, May 20 and 21, 1979; "Flight of the Killer Bees," *Time*, June 4, 1979.
29. Bill Hobby interview; Oscar Mauzy interview.
30. Oscar Mauzy interview.
31. Oscar Mauzy interview; Babe Schwartz interview.
32. Oscar Mauzy interview; Babe Schwartz interview.
33. *New York Times*, May 20, 1979; Rodney Ellis interview; Hobby, *How Things Really Work*, 135.
34. *New York Times*, May 21, 1979; Oscar Mauzy interview; Hobby, *How Things Really Work*, 135.
35. *Washington Post*, May 22, 1979; Knaggs, *Two Party Texas*, 235–236.
36. Hobby, *How Things Really Work*; Bill Hobby interview; Babe Schwartz interview.
37. Oscar Mauzy interview; *Time*, June 4, 1979; *New York Times*, May 23, 1979.
38. Oscar Mauzy interview; Rodney Ellis interview; Saralee Tiede interview; *Dallas Times Herald*, May 23, 1979; Hobby, *How Things Really Work*, 135.
39. *Dallas Times Herald*, May 23, 1979.
40. Gib Lewis interview.
41. "Ode to the Killer Bees," unattributed typescript, ca. 1979, Bill Hobby Papers, BCAH.
42. Burka, "1979."
43. *Texas Observer*, "Key Senate Votes."
44. Bill Hobby interview.
45. *Fort Worth Star-Tribune*, June 12, 1979.
46. *Houston Post*, August 25, 1979; *New York Times*, September 23, 1979.
47. *Corpus Christi Caller-Times*, August 8, 1979; *Austin American-Statesman*, August 8, 1979; *Dallas Times*, August 29, 1979; Allen Clark to William

P. Clements Jr., August 24, 1979, William P. Clements Jr. Papers, Texas A&M University.

48. Sarah Weddington to Bill Hobby, September 27, 1979, Bill Hobby Papers, BCAH; *Fort Worth Star-Telegram*, August 15, 1979; *Corpus Christi Caller-Times*, August 15, 1979.
49. *Dallas Times Herald*, October 10, 1979; Bill Hobby to John Davis, October 10, 1979, Bill Hobby Papers, BCAH.
50. *San Antonio Light*, November 28, 1979.

CHAPTER 12: THE CAMPAIGN OF 1982

1. Bill Hobby, calendar, 1980, Bill Hobby Papers, BCAH.
2. Bill Hobby interview; Bill Hobby, calendar, 1980, Bill Hobby Papers, BCAH.
3. Paul Hobby interview; Keith, *Eckhardt*, 113, 308.
4. Saralee Tiede interview.
5. Burka, "Other Hobby"; Bill Hobby interview; Glenn Smith interview.
6. Bill Hobby interview; *Houston Post*, November 21 and 25, 1980.
7. Diana Hobby to John Davis, December 30, 1980, Bill Hobby Papers, BCAH.
8. *Austin American-Statesman*, January 14, 1981. Clayton was indicted as part of the federal government's broad investigation of corruption known as BriLab (bribery-labor) that targeted public officials in Texas and several other states and in US Congress.
9. Bennett, "Senate Is Not the Same."
10. Sarpalius, *Grand Duke*, 160.
11. Sarpalius, *Grand Duke*, 173.
12. Sarpalius, *Grand Duke*, 176.
13. Sarpalius, *Grand Duke*, 176.
14. Sarpalius, *Grand Duke*, 176, 177; *Fort Worth Star-Telegram*, June 7, 1981.
15. Bennett, "Senate Is Not the Same"; Kent Caperton interview.
16. Bennett, "Senate Is Not the Same."
17. Burka, "Perot and Con"; *Washington Post*, June 10, 1992.
18. *Dallas Times Herald*, December 11, 1974; *Fort Worth Star-Telegram*, May 24, 1981.
19. Babe Schwartz interview; Bill Hobby interview; *Dallas Times Herald*, December 11, 1974; *Fort Worth Star-Telegram*, May 24, 1981.
20. *Fort Worth Star-Telegram*, May 24, 1981; Hobby, *How Things Really Work*; Saralee Tiede interview.
21. Bill Hobby interview; Dugger, "Break, Enter, Wiretap."
22. Bill Hobby interview; Hobby, *How Things Really Work*, 84–85; Dugger, "Break, Enter, Wiretap"; James Kaster interview; Saralee Tiede interview; Max Sherman interview.
23. *Fort Worth Star-Telegram*, June 7, 1981.
24. James Kaster interview.
25. *Fort Worth Star-Telegram*, June 3, 1979; *Houston Chronicle*, June 3, 1979.
26. Bill Hobby, calendar, June–July 1981, Bill Hobby Papers, BCAH; Bill Hobby interview; Laura Hobby Beckworth interview.
27. *Fort Worth Star-Telegram*, August 12, 1981; Knaggs, *Two Party Texas*, 256–263.
28. Associated Press news story clipping, August 31, 1981, Bill Hobby Papers, BCAH; *Fort Worth Star-Telegram*, October 22, 1981, and June 22, 1982. For a detailed discussion of the complicated story of the redistricting battle in the legislature during the 1981 special called session, see Knaggs, *Two Party Texas*, 256–263.
29. *Houston Chronicle*, October 7, 1981.
30. Oscar Mauzy interview.
31. Don Adams interview.
32. Bill Hobby, calendar, 1981, Bill Hobby Papers, BCAH; *New York Times*, November 11, 1981.
33. *Austin American-Statesman*, January 10 and 19, 1982.
34. *Paris (TX) News*, April 30, 1982.
35. *Victoria (TX) Advocate*, February 18, 1982; *Waco Tribune-Herald*, February 25, 1982.
36. Robert C. Christopher to Bill Hobby, March 10, 1982, and Bill Hobby, calendar, 1982, Bill Hobby Papers, BCAH; *Paris (TX) News*, April 30, 1982.
37. Bill Hobby, calendar, 1982, Bill Hobby Papers, BCAH; *Paris (TX) News*, April 30, 1982.
38. D. Richards, *Once upon a Time*, 224.
39. *Houston Chronicle*, May 2, 1982; D. Richards, *Once upon a Time*, 225.
40. *Houston Chronicle*, May 2, 1982; Knaggs, *Two Party Texas*, 265.
41. Bill Hobby interview.
42. McNeely and Henderson, *Bob Bullock*, 150.
43. Bill Hobby interview; Reid, *Let the People In*, 73, 78.
44. Reid, *Let the People In*, 92; Hobby, *How Things Really Work*, 71; Saralee Tiede interview.
45. Hobby, *How Things Really Work*, 71–72; *Austin American-Statesman*, February 3, 1985; Saralee Tiede interview.
46. Saralee Tiede interview; *Austin American-Statesman*, February 3, 1985; Paul Hobby interview.

47. Knaggs, *Two Party Texas*, 266, 272–274; Lloyd Grove, "Troublemaker," *New York Times*, December 24, 2009.
48. James Kaster interview.
49. Knaggs, *Two Party Texas*, 272; Hobby, *How Things Really Work*, 53.
50. Dave McNeely, *Austin American-Statesman*, undated news clipping, Bill Hobby biography file, Bill Hobby Papers, BCAH.
51. Don Adams interview.
52. *Texas Monthly*, "State Secrets," January 1982.
53. Knaggs, *Two Party Texas*, 272; *Fort Worth Star-Telegram*, October 19, 1982; Don Adams interview.
54. *Times Record News* (Wichita Falls, TX), June 20, 1982.
55. Laura Hobby Beckworth interview; Don Adams interview.
56. *Austin American-Statesman*, September 8–10, 1982.
57. Bill Hobby interview; Hobby, *How Things Really Work*, 54.
58. Bill Hobby, calendar, 1982, Bill Hobby Papers, BCAH; Hobby, *How Things Really Work*, 53.
59. Associated Press story in multiple newspapers, October 18, 1982; *Dallas Times Herald,* May 9, 1983; Saralee Tiede interview.
60. Bill Hobby, calendar, 1982, Bill Hobby Papers, BCAH; Bill Hobby interview; *Houston Post*, October 31, 1982.
61. Bill Hobby, calendar, 1982, Bill Hobby Papers, BCAH; *Houston Post*, October 31, 1982.
62. Lady Bird Johnson to Bill Hobby, November 1, 1982, Bill Hobby Papers, BCAH; *Austin American-Statesman*, November 3 and 4, 1982.
63. McNeely and Henderson, *Bob Bullock*, 154; Oscar Mauzy interview; Glenn Smith interview; D. Richards, *Once upon a Time*, 226.
64. Bill Hobby, calendar, 1982, Bill Hobby Papers, BCAH.

CHAPTER 13: HOBBY TAKES CONTROL

1. Bill Hobby, calendar, January 18, 1983, Bill Hobby Papers, BCAH; *Austin American-Statesman*, January 10 and 18, 1983.
2. *Austin American-Statesman*, January 19, 1983; Oveta Culp Hobby to Helen Gruber, February 11, 1983, Oveta Culp Hobby Papers, Rice University.
3. *Austin American-Statesman*, January 19, 1983; *Houston Post*, January 19, 1983; Saralee Tiede interview.
4. *Austin American-Statesman*, January 19, 1983; *Houston Post*, January 19, 1983. In his poetic celebration of the election of "Marco Blanco" (Mark White), Hobby's statement about "cleans[ing] the Temple" is a reference to Buddy Temple, who was one of White's primary opponents. "Show[ing] no Clemency" refers to White's defeat of Bill Clements.
5. Bill Hobby, calendar, January 18, 1983, Bill Hobby Papers, BCAH; Saralee Tiede interview; *Austin American-Statesman*, January 19, 1983; *Dallas Morning News*, January 19, 1983.
6. *Austin American-Statesman*, January 19, 1983; Burka, Cook, and Northcott, "1983."
7. *Houston Chronicle*, January 20, 1983.
8. Bill Hobby interview*; Austin American-Statesman*, January 20, 1983; *Dallas Times Herald*, May 9, 1983.
9. *Austin American-Statesman*, January 20, 1983.
10. *Dallas Times Herald*, May 9, 1983; *Austin American-Statesman*, January 21 and 25, 1983, April 6, 1983, and April 18, 2013; Bill Hobby interview; Hobby, *How Things Really Work*, 85. The Senate confirmed Jack Pope to serve as chief justice of the Texas Supreme Court by a vote of twenty-nine to two. Pope retired in 1985 and lived to the age of 103. Included on the list of nominees sent back to White were several former employees and political allies of Clements's administration and reelection committee.
11. Bill Hobby interview; Bill Hobby, calendar, January 21–February 5, 1983, Bill Hobby Papers, BCAH; *Austin American-Statesman*, January 27, 1983.
12. Bill Hobby, calendar, February 5, 1983, Bill Hobby Papers, BCAH; *Austin American-Statesman*, February 7, 1983.
13. Hobby, *How Things Really Work*, 108–109; *Austin American-Statesman*, February 7, 1983.
14. *Austin American-Statesman*, February 7, 1983.
15. Hobby, *How Things Really Work*, 109; Kate Hobby Gibson interview.
16. Hobby, *How Things Really Work*, 109.
17. Hobby, *How Things Really Work*; *Austin American-Statesman*, February 7, 1983. The Zenith Company, which manufactured the television, eventually lost a lawsuit that Attorney General Jim Mattox filed claiming negligence. Zenith settled the case for $1.3 million.
18. Hobby, *How Things Really Work*, 110; *Austin American-Statesman*, February 7–8 and March 30, 1983.
19. Saralee Tiede interview; Max Sherman interview; Hobby, *How Things Really Work*, 110.

20. Hobby, *How Things Really Work*, 110.
21. *Austin American-Statesman*, February 8, 1983; Hobby, *How Things Really Work*, 109.
22. Hobby, *How Things Really Work*, 110–111.
23. Paul Hobby interview; *Fort Worth Star-Telegram*, June 5, 1983. Roy Eugene Graham was hired as the architect of the Capitol. He had directed historic preservation at the University of Virginia and been resident architect at Colonial Williamsburg. The first curator was Bonnie Campbell, who had served as curator of the California State Capitol.
24. Hobby, *How Things Really Work*, 112–114; Green, "Capitol."
25. Hobby, *How Things Really Work*, 112–114; Green, "Capitol."
26. Bill Hobby interview; *Houston Post*, January 19, 1983.
27. Farabee, *Ray Farabee*, 187; Hobby, *How Things Really Work*, 149; Saralee Tiede interview.
28. Saralee Tiede interview; John Montford interview.
29. Burka, Cook, and Northcott, "1983"; Kent Caperton interview.
30. Saralee Tiede interview; Burka, Cook, and Northcott, "1983"; *Dallas Morning News*, June 6, 1983.
31. Rodney Ellis interview; *Dallas Times Herald*, May 9, 1983; Hector Uribe interview; Saralee Tiede interview.
32. Bill Hobby interview; Mark White interview; Oscar Mauzy interview.
33. Oscar Mauzy interview; *Dallas Morning News*, June 6, 1983.
34. *Fort Worth Star-Telegram*, December 4, 1982; *Dallas Morning News*, June 6, 1983.
35. Miller, "Good Ol' Gib"; McNeely and Henderson, *Bob Bullock*, 160; *Dallas Morning News*, June 6, 1983. Lewis survived the financial disclosure controversy. The House Ethics Committee voted in June 1983 not to investigate him after he pleaded no contest to misdemeanor charges and paid a fine.
36. *Dallas Morning News*, June 6, 1983; *Fort Worth Star-Telegram*, May 3, 1983; John Leedom interview.
37. *Dallas Morning News*, June 6, 1983; *Fort Worth Star-Telegram*, May 3, 1983; *Dallas Times Herald*, May 9, 1983; Bill Hobby interview.
38. Hector Uribe interview.
39. Hector Uribe interview; Holley, Rips, and Gunderson, "Manager of the Year."
40. Hector Uribe interview.
41. Hector Uribe interview; *Austin American-Statesman*, July 29, 1987.
42. Hector Uribe interview.
43. *Fort Worth Star-Telegram*, May 31, 1983; *Dallas Times Herald*, May 9, 1983.
44. *Fort Worth Star-Telegram*, May 31, June 5, and July 14, 1983; Oscar Mauzy interview; Holley, Rips, and Gunderson, "Manager of the Year."
45. *Fort Worth Star-Telegram*, May 27, 1983; United Press International story in *Lubbock Evening Journal*, May 31, 1983; Associated Press wire story, June 20, 1983; *San Antonio Express-News*, June 26, 1983.
46. Oveta Culp Hobby to Helen Gruber, February 11, 1983, Oveta Culp Hobby Papers, Rice University.
47. Paul Hobby interview.
48. *Fort Worth Star-Telegram*, July 24, 1983; Barna, "Oveta Posts Notice," 116; Bill Hobby, "A Requiem for *The Houston Post*," *Houston Chronicle*, April 23, 1995; *New York Times*, July 30, 1983; Saralee Tiede interview.
49. *Fort Worth Star-Telegram*, July 24, 1983; Saralee Tiede interview; Barna, "Oveta Posts Notice," 116; *New York Times*, July 30, 1983; Oveta Culp Hobby to Evetts Culp, October 13, 1983, Oveta Culp Hobby Papers, Rice University.
50. Saralee Tiede interview.
51. Paul Hobby interview.
52. Laura Hobby Beckworth interview; Shire, *Oveta Culp Hobby*, 21.
53. Barna, "Oveta Posts Notice," 116; Hobby, "Requiem for *The Houston Post*"; *Fort Worth Star-Telegram*, July 24, 1983.
54. Bill Hobby interview; undated and unidentified news clipping, Bill Hobby Papers, BCAH.
55. Barna, "Oveta Posts Notice," 116; *New York Times*, July 30, 1983; Oveta Culp Hobby to Henry Taub, January 13, 1984, Oveta Culp Hobby Papers, Rice University; *USA Today*, July 22, 1983; *Advertising Age*, October 24, 1983, 6.
56. Photograph of announcement meeting in Shire, *Oveta Culp Hobby*, 42; United Press International news story, October 20, 1983; *New York Times*, July 30, 1983; *Advertising Age*, October 24, 1983.
57. Paul Hobby interview.
58. Diana Hobby to John Davis, October 10, 1983, and John Davis to Diana Hobby, November 16, 1986, Bill Hobby Papers, BCAH.
59. Ray Brady, "After the Fox in Ireland," *New York Times*, October 19, 1986.
60. Terry Clavin, "Ryan, Thady (Thaddeus) Francis," *Dictionary of Irish Biography*, https://www.dib

.ie/index.php/biography/ryan-thady-thaddeus-francis-a9500.
61. Ray Brady, "Hibernians, Away! Riding with Ireland's Scarteen Hunt," unnamed publication, and Bill Hobby to Chris Ryan, 1987, Bill Hobby Papers, BCAH.
62. Brady, "After the Fox in Ireland"; Brady, "Hibernians, Away!"
63. Bill Hobby to Chris Ryan, May 28, 2002, Bill Hobby Papers, BCAH.

CHAPTER 14: "NO PASS, NO PLAY"

1. Hobby, *How Things Really Work*, 102; Bill Hobby interview; "Public Education, Select - 68th R.S. (1983)," Legislative Reference Library of Texas, https://lrl.texas.gov/committees/cmtesDisplay.cfm?cmteID=8530; McNeely and Henderson, *Bob Bullock*, 161–162.
2. Huntington, "Perot, Henry Ross"; "Public Education, Select," Legislative Reference Library of Texas; McNeely and Henderson, *Bob Bullock*, 161–162; Bill Hobby interview. Other members of the committee included Senators Carl Parker and Grant Jones; Representative Bill Haley, the House Education Committee chairman; trial lawyer and Corpus Christi civic leader Tony Bonilla; State Board of Education chairman Joe Kelly Butler of Houston; former Carter administration cabinet member and Houstonian Charles W. Duncan Jr.; and university administrator Jon H. Fleming.
3. Huntington, "Perot, Henry Ross"; *Fort Worth Star-Telegram*, March 9 and 13, 1984; Hobby, *How Things Really Work*, 104.
4. *New York Times*, April 28, 1985; Hobby, *How Things Really Work*, 104–105.
5. *Dallas Morning News*, July 9, 2019; *Austin American-Statesman*, April 11, 1984; *Fort Worth Star-Telegram*, June 8, 1984; Huntington, "Perot, Henry Ross"; *New York Times*, June 23, 1992.
6. *Dallas Morning News*, July 9, 2019; McNeely and Henderson, *Bob Bullock*, 167; Hobby, *How Things Really Work*, 104–105.
7. Hobby, *How Things Really Work*, 104–105; Bill Hobby interview; McNeely and Henderson, *Bob Bullock*, 167.
8. *New York Times*, April 28, 1985; Hobby, *How Things Really Work*, 104–105; Saralee Tiede interview.
9. Bill Hobby interview; Hobby, *How Things Really Work*, 105.
10. *Fort Worth Star-Telegram*, March 10, 1984; Bill Hobby interview; Hobby, *How Things Really Work*, 105.
11. Bill Hobby interview; Hobby, *How Things Really Work*, 105–106; McNeely and Henderson, *Bob Bullock*, 168; *Dallas Morning News*, July 9, 2019; *New York Times*, June 23, 1992.
12. *New York Times*, July 4, 1984; Hobby, *How Things Really Work*, 106.
13. *New York Times*, July 4, 1984; Bill Hobby interview; Hobby, *How Things Really Work*.
14. *New York Times*, July 4, 1984; Hobby, *How Things Really Work*, 106.
15. McNeely and Henderson, *Bob Bullock*, 170; *New York Times*, July 4, 1984, and June 23, 1992; Hobby, *How Things Really Work*, 106–107.
16. Hobby, *How Things Really Work*, 69; Farabee, *Ray Farabee*, 200.
17. *Victoria (TX) Advocate*, April 13, 1986; Hobby, *How Things Really Work*, 106–107; Bill Hobby interview.
18. Copy of Perot reform poem in Bill Hobby Papers, BCAH; Huntington, "Perot, Henry Ross." In 1992 Ross Perot ran for US president as an independent candidate against Republican incumbent president George H. W. Bush and Democrat Bill Clinton. He won 19 percent of the vote, the largest vote total of a third-party candidate since Theodore Roosevelt's Progressive Party bid in 1912. Perot died in 2019.
19. *Austin American-Statesman*, July 14, 1983, and January 27, 1984; *Cincinnati Enquirer*, April 21, 1983; Bill Hobby to J. R. Parten, April 1, 1983, J. R. Parten Papers, BCAH; *New York Times*, August 3, 1984.
20. *Austin American-Statesman*, August 1, 1984; A. Richards, *Straight from the Heart*, 241–242.
21. *Austin American-Statesman*, July 14, 1983; Bill Hobby, calendar, August 1, September 7, 8, and 24, and October 17, 1984, Bill Hobby Papers, BCAH; *Fort Worth Star-Telegram*, September 25, 1984; Bill Hobby interview; *New York Times*, June 9, 1985.
22. *Fort Worth Star-Telegram*, January 17, 1985; Bill Hobby interview; Bill Hobby, calendar, November 8–December 9 and December 26–December 31, 1984, and January 1–2, 1985, Bill Hobby Papers, BCAH.
23. *San Angelo (TX) Standard-Times*, January 6, 1985.
24. *San Angelo (TX) Standard-Times*, January 6, 1985.
25. *San Angelo (TX) Standard-Times*, January 6, 1985.
26. *San Angelo (TX) Standard-Times*, January 6, 1985; Kent Caperton interview; Bill Hobby interview.

27. *San Angelo (TX) Standard-Times*, January 10, 1985; *Fort Worth Star-Telegram*, March 27, 1985; Hector Uribe interview.
28. *Victoria (TX) Advocate*, April 18, 1985.
29. *Austin American-Statesman*, March 27, 1985. For a concise history of MCC, see Frontain, "Microelectronics and Computer Technology Corporation."
30. Hobby interview; *Austin American-Statesman*, March 27, 1985.
31. *Fort Worth Star-Telegram*, January 6, 1985; *Austin American-Statesman*, March 27, 28, 1985; Hobby, *How Things Really Work*, 128; Bill Hobby interview; McNeely and Henderson, *Bob Bullock*, 177; *Corpus Christi Caller-Times*, June 17, 1985. Hobby's plan also phased in annual tuition hikes for four years.
32. Mark White interview.
33. Cottrell, "Farabee, Helen Jane Rehbein"; Kelly, "Health and Human Services."
34. *Austin American-Statesman*, May 31, 1985.
35. Bill Hobby interview; *Austin American-Statesman*, May 31, 1985.
36. *Fort Worth Star-Telegram*, May 30, 1985; *Austin American-Statesman*, May 29 and 31, 1985.
37. *New York Times*, June 9, 1985; Judge Woodrow Seals to Bill Hobby, June 14, 1985, Oveta Culp Hobby Papers, Rice University.
38. *Austin American-Statesman*, May 29 and 31, 1985.
39. Associated Press, May 29, 1985; *Austin American-Statesman*, May 29, 1985; *New York Times*, June 9, 1985.
40. *Times Record News* (Wichita Falls, TX), September 19, 1985.
41. *On Campus* (University of Texas at Austin), November 4–10, 1985.
42. *San Angelo (TX) Standard-Times*, December 17, 1985.
43. Bill Hobby interview.
44. *Kilgore (TX) News Herald*, December 19, 1985.
45. *Austin American-Statesman*, January 9, 1986.
46. *Austin American-Statesman*, January 14, 1986.
47. *Austin American-Statesman*, January 14, 1986.
48. Bill Hobby interview; Saralee Tiede interview.
49. Kent Caperton interview; Saralee Tiede interview; *Fort Worth Star-Telegram*, June 5, 1983. Senator Kent Caperton was among those who also experienced Hobby's occasional odd behavior during meetings. "Bill was easily distracted," Caperton recalled. "I remember walking out and thinking, 'I guess we're finished, but I'm not sure.'" A newspaper profile of Hobby published in the early 1980s also noted that Hobby "remains an enigma to all but his closest friends. He undoubtedly is one of the most private people in public office. Senators and reporters complain that Hobby sometimes walks away in the middle of a conversation, leaving them stranded in mid-sentence."
50. Saralee Tiede interview; Bill Hobby interview.
51. *Austin American-Statesman*, February 7, 1986; Bob Bullock to Bill Hobby, February 13, 1986, Bob Bullock Papers, Baylor University; *Fort Worth Star-Telegram*, March 2, 1986; Hobby, *How Things Really Work*; Cunningham, *Texas Way*, 303–304.
52. *Austin American-Statesman*, March 22, 1986.
53. *El Paso Times*, April, 27, 1986; Bill Hobby to J. R. Parten, April 10, 1986, J. R. Parten Papers, BCAH.
54. *Victoria (TX) Advocate*, April 13, 1986.
55. *Kerrville (TX) Mountain Sun*, March 4, 1986.
56. García, "Colonia"; *Fort Worth Star-Telegram*, June 4, 1986; Salinas, *Colonias Factbook*.
57. Cunningham, *Texas Way*, 254.
58. *Austin American-Statesman*, July 27, 1986; *Fort Worth Star-Telegram*, July 25, 1986.
59. Cunningham, *Texas Way*, 309–311. For more information about the Permanent School Fund, see Smyrl, "Permanent University Fund."
60. Cunningham, *Texas Way*, 308.
61. *Austin American-Statesman*, August 19, 1986; Kent Caperton interview; Lady Bird Johnson to Bill and Diana Hobby, September 2, 1986, Bill Hobby Papers, BCAH.
62. Hobby, *How Things Really Work*, 129; Cunningham, *Texas Way*, 314–316; *Austin American-Statesman*, September 5, 1986.
63. Cunningham, *Texas Way*, 313–314; *Austin American-Statesman*, September 5, 1986, and July 30, 1987; *Corpus Christi Caller-Times*, September 9, 1986; *New York Times*, October 2, 1986.
64. Bill Hobby to J. R. Parten, September 26, 1986, J. R. Parten Papers, BCAH.
65. *Dallas Morning News*, November 5, 1986; *Fort Worth Star-Telegram*, November 5, 1986; Hobby, *How Things Really Work*, 107.
66. John Davis to Bill Hobby, November 16, 1986, Bill Hobby Papers, BCAH.

CHAPTER 15: HOBBY VERSUS CLEMENTS

1. Bill Hobby interview; *Austin American-Statesman*, January 2, 1987.
2. Bill Hobby interview; *Austin*

American-Statesman, January 2, 1987; McNeely and Henderson, *Bob Bullock*, 185–186.
3. George Shipley to Don Adams, January 27, 1987, George Christian Papers, BCAH.
4. George Shipley to Don Adams, January 27, 1987, George Christian Papers, BCAH.
5. George Shipley to Don Adams, January 27, 1987, George Christian Papers, BCAH.
6. Bill Hobby, calendar, January 19, 1987, Bill Hobby Papers, BCAH.
7. Jess Hay interview; William H. Cunningham interview; Bill Hobby interview.
8. Cissy Stewart, "Inauguration Guests Cross All Party Lines," *Fort Worth Star-Telegram*, January 28, 1987.
9. Bill Hobby, typescript of inaugural speech, January 20, 1987, Bill Hobby Papers, BCAH; *Austin American-Statesman*, January 9, 1987; McNeely and Henderson, *Bob Bullock*, 186.
10. Bill Hobby, typescript of inaugural speech, January 20, 1987, Bill Hobby Papers, BCAH; *Austin American-Statesman*, January 9, 1987; McNeely and Henderson, *Bob Bullock*, 186.
11. Bill Hobby interview; Bill Hobby, calendar, January 26, 1987, Bill Hobby Papers, BCAH; *Houston Chronicle*, December 9, 1990; Hobby, *How Things Really Work*, 81–82.
12. Bill Hobby interview; Saralee Tiede interview; Glenn Smith interview; *Austin American-Statesman*, August 14, 1987.
13. *Austin American-Statesman*, August 26, 2001; McNeely and Henderson, *Bob Bullock*, 188; Saralee Tiede interview; Burka and Cook, "Ten Best and (Groan)"; Bill Hobby interview; Jess Hay interview.
14. *Austin American-Statesman*, April 15, 1987; Hobby, *How Things Really Work*, 118; Bill Hobby, calendar, May 23 and 31, 1987, Bill Hobby Papers, BCAH.
15. Bill Hobby, calendar, various dates in 1987 (e.g., March 17, 18, and 25), Bill Hobby Papers, BCAH; Jess Hay interview; William H. Cunningham interview; Bill Hobby interview. Hobby's other racquetball partners included Senators Ray Farabee and Buster Brown.
16. Jess Hay interview; William H. Cunningham interview.
17. Bill Hobby, calendar, March 31, 1987, Bill Hobby Papers, BCAH; Jess Hay interview; William H. Cunningham interview.
18. Associated Press story in multiple newspapers, May 19, 1987; *Austin American-Statesman*, May 27, 1987; *Fort Worth Star-Telegram*, May 27 and May 31, 1987.
19. Kent Caperton interview; *Austin American-Statesman*, May 7, 1987, and August 26, 2001.
20. Bill Hobby interview; Bill Hobby to George Christian, February 11, 1987, George Christian Papers, BCAH.
21. *New York Times*, October 31, 1993; Steven Weinberg, "The Crisis of Big Science," *New York Review of Books*, May 10, 2012; *Austin American-Statesman*, June 2, October 2, and November 1, 1987; *Fort Worth Star-Telegram*, May 15 and November 4, 1987; Bill Hobby interview. For an explanation of the Higgs particle, see Riordan, *Tunnel Visions*. The Superconducting Super Collider was an enormously expensive particle accelerator project advocated by members of the US High Energy Physics Advisory Panel and other physicists as a method to discover the subatomic Higgs particle. With key support from the then Speaker of the US House, Texas congressman Jim Wright, and aided by the passage of the Texas constitutional amendment pledging financial support, Texas won its bid against twenty-four other states to serve as the site for the project. A location was chosen near Waxahachie, south of Dallas. Because of charges of mismanagement and financial waste and overruns, Congress canceled the project in October 1993 after seventeen miles of tunnels were bored beneath the blackland prairie at a cost of $2 billion, including a $400 million contribution by the state of Texas.
22. *Austin American-Statesman*, May 13, 1987; Glenn Smith interview.
23. *San Angelo (TX) Standard-Times*, May 30, 1987; *Austin American-Statesman*, May 29, 1987.
24. Bill Hobby, calendar, June 1 and 2, 1987, Bill Hobby Papers, BCAH; Hobby, *How Things Really Work*, 131–132; *El Paso Times*, June 2, 1987; *Corpus Christi Caller-Times*, June 6, 1987.
25. McNeely and Henderson, *Bob Bullock*, 188–189; Bill Hobby, calendar, June 22, 1987, Bill Hobby Papers, BCAH; Hobby, *How Things Really Work*, 132.
26. McNeely and Henderson, *Bob Bullock*, 189; *El Paso Times*, July 16, 1987; Bill Hobby interview; Hobby, *How Things Really Work*, 132; *New York Times*, July 22, 1987; Bill Hobby, calendar, July 11, 15, and 21, 1987, and speech transcript, reception for Representative Al Luna, Houston, Texas, July 23, 1987, Bill Hobby Papers, BCAH.

27. Hobby, *How Things Really Work*, 132; Bill Clements to [addressee redacted], September 2, 1987, George Christian Papers, BCAH.
28. *New York Times*, April 11, 1987; *Fort Worth Star-Telegram*, July 23, 1987; McNeely and Henderson, *Bob Bullock*, 188–189; Bill Hobby interview; Hobby, *How Things Really Work*, 132; *Washington Post*, February 26 and March 11, 1987. SMU eventually also canceled its 1988 football season and did not field another team until 1989.
29. Slaughter, "Clements, William Perry, Jr."; *Fort Worth Star-Telegram*, August 7, 1987; *Austin American-Statesman*, July 16 and August 14, 1987; Cunningham, *Texas Way*, 322–324; Burka, "Bill Hobby." Clements served as deputy secretary for defense in the Nixon and Ford administrations.
30. *Fort Worth Star-Telegram*, August 7, 1987, and March 21, 1988; Jess Hay interview. In March 1988, in recognition of Hobby's efforts to support higher education, the Association of Texas Colleges and Universities presented him its Mirabeau B. Lamar Medal "for distinguished service that extends beyond benefitting a single institution."
31. Kent Caperton interview; Bill Hobby interview; McNeely and Henderson, *Bob Bullock*, 186–190.
32. Jim Mattox to James Atchley, May 19, 1987, George Christian Papers, BCAH.
33. McNeely and Henderson, *Bob Bullock*, 186–190; Reid, *Let the People In*, 170; Saralee Tiede interview.
34. D. Richards, *Once upon a Time*, 240–241; *Austin American-Statesman*, July 1, 1987; Saralee Tiede interview; McNeely and Henderson, *Bob Bullock*, 190–191; Reid, *Let the People In*, 170–171. Dave Richards is the source who mentioned Mattox's leak to the press.
35. McNeely and Henderson, *Bob Bullock*, 191; Bill Hobby interview.
36. Bill Hobby, calendar, July 24–26, 1987, and press release, July 27, 1987, Bill Hobby Papers, BCAH; Saralee Tiede interview.
37. *Houston Post*, July 29, 1987; *Austin American-Statesman*, July 30, 1987.
38. *Houston Post*, July 20, 1987; *Austin American-Statesman*, July 30, 1987.
39. *Fort Worth Star-Telegram*, July 28 and August 7, 1987; *Austin American-Statesman*, July 16 and 30, and August 14, 1987; McNeely and Henderson, *Bob Bullock*, 185–186; Saralee Tiede interview.
40. McNeely and Henderson, *Bob Bullock*, 185–186; Saralee Tiede interview; Bill Hobby interview.
41. Draft of Hobby's speech, Bill Hobby file, George Christian Papers, BCAH; Winston Bode, *On the Avenue*, July 30 and August 6, 1987.
42. *Houston Post*, July 29, 1987; Jim Mattox, statement, July 27, 1987, Bill Hobby Papers, BCAH; *Austin American-Statesman*, July 28, 1987. The *Houston Post*, no longer owned by the Hobby family, printed an editorial with a headline declaring, "Hobby's Exit a Loss." The *Post* urged the lieutenant governor to reconsider.
43. Bill Hobby interview; Bill Hobby, calendar, July 31, and August 1 and 2, 1987, Bill Hobby Papers, BCAH; Kay Bailey Hutchison interview.
44. Bill Hobby interview; Bill Hobby to George Christian, February 11 and April 30, 1987, George Shipley to Christian, July 7, 1987, and Christian to Tom Scott, August 6, 1987, George Christian Papers, BCAH; *Austin American-Statesman*; October 2, 1987; *Fort Worth Star-Telegram*, December 1, 1987; Bill Hobby, calendar, July 31, month of August, and September 1–5, 1987, Bill Hobby Papers, BCAH.
45. *San Angelo (TX) Standard-Times*, October 29, 1987; Bill Hobby, calendar, July 31, month of August, and September 1–5, 1987, Bill Hobby Papers, BCAH.
46. Bill Hobby, calendar, May 15, 16, and 17, and October 24–November 3, 1987, Bill Hobby Papers, BCAH.
47. Bill Hobby interview; *Austin American-Statesman*, November 5, 1987; Bill Hobby, calendar, November 30 and December 1–31, 1987, and January 1–18, 1988, Bill Hobby Papers, BCAH.
48. *Austin American-Statesman*, July 30, 1987.

CHAPTER 16: THE PRESIDENTIAL ELECTION OF 1988

1. Memorandum, Saralee Tiede to Bill Hobby, December 1, 1987, George Christian Papers, BCAH.
2. Saralee Tiede interview; Bill Hobby interview; *Dallas Morning News*, February 25, 1988.
3. *Fort Worth Star-Telegram*, April 23, 1988; *Austin American-Statesman*, January 7 and 22, 1988; Bill Hobby, transcript of speech to National Association of Realtors luncheon, San Antonio, TX, February 5, 1988, Bill Hobby Papers, BCAH.
4. Bill Hobby interview; Saralee Tiede interview.
5. *Gatesville (TX) Messenger and Star Forum*, February 25, 1988; *Marshall (TX) News Messenger*, February 19 and March 6, 1988.
6. *Houston Chronicle*, March 9, 1988; Associated

Press story, numerous newspapers, March 9, 1988; *Fort Worth Star-Telegram,* March 10, 1988.

7. Bill Hobby, speech for Gary Hart fundraiser, and calendar, April 28, 1987, Bill Hobby Papers, BCAH.
8. Bill Hobby, calendar, August 13, 1987, and Bill Hobby to Al Gore Jr., February 5, 1988, Bill Hobby Papers, BCAH.
9. Bill Hobby, calendar, June 25, 1987, and transcript of radio ad, February 25, 1988, Bill Hobby Papers, BCAH; *Fort Worth Star-Telegram,* February 11, 1988; *Austin American-Statesman,* February 12, 1988; *Dallas Morning News,* March 9, 1988; *New York Times,* April 20, 1988.
10. Paul Kirk to Bill Hobby, March 13, 1988, Bill Hobby Papers, BCAH; Bill Hobby interview; *Austin American-Statesman,* June 19, 1988.
11. Bill Hobby, calendar, May 6 and 7, 1988, Bill Hobby Papers, BCAH; *Austin American-Statesman,* May 6–8, 1988.
12. Bill Hobby, calendar, May 10–19, 1988, Bill Hobby Papers, BCAH.
13. Bill Hobby, calendar, May 27 and June 16–19, 1988, Bill Hobby Papers, BCAH; *Austin American-Statesman,* May 28 and June 19, 1988; *Fort Worth Star-Telegram,* June 17, 1988; *Houston Chronicle,* June 19, 1988.
14. Bill Hobby, calendar, June 16, 1988, Bill Hobby Papers, BCAH; Bill Hobby interview; *Houston Post,* June 13, 1988.
15. *New York Times,* July 13, 1988; Bill Hobby, calendar, July 12 and 13, 1988, Bill Hobby Papers, BCAH.
16. *Austin American-Statesman* and *Fort Worth Star-Telegram,* July 13, 1988.
17. Bill Hobby, calendar, July 16, 1988, Bill Hobby Papers, BCAH; Bill Hobby interview; Ivins, *Molly Ivins,* 275.
18. Bill Hobby, calendar, July 18, 1988, Bill Hobby Papers, BCAH; *New York Times,* July 21 and 22, 1988; *El Paso Times,* July 22, 1988; *Fort Worth Star-Telegram,* July 23, 1988.
19. *Fort Worth Star-Telegram,* July 23, 1988; *Austin American-Statesman,* August 14, 1988; McNeely and Henderson, *Bob Bullock,* 110.
20. *Austin American-Statesman,* July 29 and 30, 1988; Bill Hobby, calendar, July 30, 1988, Bill Hobby Papers, BCAH.
21. Bill Hobby, calendar, August 13–27, 1988, Bill Hobby Papers, BCAH; *Kerrville (TX) Mountain Sun,* August 17, 1988; Bill Hobby, speech transcript, Houston, TX, August 14, 1988, Bill Hobby Papers, BCAH.
22. Bill Hobby, speech transcript, Houston, Texas, October 7, 1988, and calendar, September 14, 16, 18, and 21, 1988, Bill Hobby Papers, BCAH; Reid, *Let the People In,* 209; *Austin American-Statesman,* September 25, 1988. Republican congressman Beau Boulter was Bentsen's opponent in the Senate race.
23. Glenn Smith interview; Bill Hobby, calendar, October 10, 1988; *Marshall (TX) News Messenger* and *Longview (TX) News-Journal,* October 11, 1988. Glenn Smith later recalled that Hobby made it clear to him and to others on Hobby's staff that he would seek the Senate seat Bentsen would be vacating. He told Smith that if Bentsen became vice president, "he was going to run for the Senate and wanted me to be ready to work on it." According to Smith, when Hobby met with members of his staff, he "would hold forth on the Senate and what a great place the Senate was."
24. *New York Times,* December 3, 2018; *Fort Worth Star-Telegram,* October 21, 1988.
25. *Austin American-Statesman,* November 8, 9, and 10, 1988.
26. Bill Hobby, calendar, October 30 and November 10–December 1, 1988, Bill Hobby Papers, BCAH.

CHAPTER 17: THE FINAL TERM

1. Bill Hobby, calendar, December 1–6, 1988, Bill Hobby Papers, BCAH; *Fort Worth Star-Telegram,* April 23, 1988; *Austin American-Statesman,* April 19 and 20, 1988.
2. *New York Daily News,* December 13, 1988; *Austin American-Statesman,* June 11, 1989.
3. Bill Hobby, calendar, January 10 and 19, 1989, Bill Hobby Papers, BCAH; *Corpus Christi Caller-Times,* January 11, 1989; Paul Burka and Patricia Hart, "Best and Worst Legislators," *Texas Monthly,* July 1993. Carriker was elected to fill Ray Farabee's vacant Senate seat. *Texas Monthly* would later dub Carriker one of the worst members of the Senate.
4. Bill Clements to [addressee redacted], September 2, 1987, George Christian Papers, BCAH; *Austin American-Statesman,* January 11, 1989.
5. *Austin American-Statesman,* January 11, 1989.
6. *Austin American-Statesman,* December 4, 1988.
7. *Austin American-Statesman,* January 13, 1989.
8. *Fort Worth Star-Telegram,* December 15, 1988; Associated Press story, December 26, 1988, clipping in Bill Hobby Papers, BCAH; Bill Hobby interview.

9. Bill Hobby interview; *Austin American-Statesman*, May 8, 1988.
10. The literature on the causes of and cures for the US crime wave in the 1980s is vast. See, for example, Boggess and Bound, "Did Criminal Activity Increase"; Ford, "What Caused the Great Crime Decline"; Levitt and Dubner, *Freakonomics*.
11. Glenn Smith interview; *Austin American-Statesman*, February 9, 1989. "Everybody was for building prisons," Smith said, "so there was all this spending pressure to just throw prisons at the problem. We'll just lock them all away. I knew that wasn't the long-term solution."
12. Saralee Tiede interview; "Unlocking the Future of Texas: The Anti-Crime Plan of 1989," copy in Bill Hobby Papers, BCAH; Glenn Smith interview.
13. *Austin American-Statesman*, February 9, 1989; *Abilene Reporter-News*, February 13, 1989.
14. *Fort Worth Star-Telegram*, February 9, 1989; *Austin American-Statesman*, February 9, 1989; "Unlocking the Future of Texas: The Anti-Crime Plan of 1989," copy in Bill Hobby Papers, BCAH; Glenn Smith interview.
15. Office of the Lieutenant Governor, "Accomplishments of the 71st Legislature" [1989], Bill Hobby Papers, BCAH.
16. Hector Uribe interview; *Odessa American*, January 1, 1989; Saralee Tiede interview; Bill Hobby interview.
17. Bill Hobby, calendar, August 10, 1988, and January 13, 1989, Bill Hobby Papers, BCAH; *Austin American-Statesman*, December 12, 1988; *Odessa (TX) American*, January 1, 1989.
18. Bill Hobby, calendar, March 26, 1989, Bill Hobby Papers, BCAH; *Fort Worth Star-Telegram*, March 29, 1989.
19. *Austin American-Statesman*, May 6, 1989. For a discussion of Bill Hobby Day, see the prologue to this book.
20. *Kerrville (TX) Times*, May 10, 1989; *Austin American-Statesman*, April 19 and 22, and May 5, 1989.
21. *Austin American-Statesman*, April 5, 7, 19, and 22, and May 5, 1989.
22. *Austin American-Statesman*, April 7 and May 30, 1989; Bill Hobby, calendar, May 28–29, 1989, Bill Hobby Papers, BCAH.
23. Office of the Lieutenant Governor, "Accomplishments of the 71st Legislature" [1989], Bill Hobby Papers, BCAH; Hector Uribe interview.
24. Hector Uribe interview; *Fort Worth Star-Telegram*, April 6, 1989; *Houston Chronicle*, December 9, 1990.
25. *Austin American-Statesman*, June 20 and 21, 1989; Kent Caperton interview.
26. *New York Times*, July 9, 1989; Saralee Tiede interview.
27. Kent Caperton interview; Saralee Tiede interview; *Fort Worth Star-Telegram*, July 8, 1989; *New York Times*, July 9, 1989.
28. *Austin American-Statesman*, June 20 and July 21, 1989; Kent Caperton interview.
29. *Austin American-Statesman*, July 29, 1989.
30. *Austin American-Statesman*, October 3 and December 10, 1989; *Houston Chronicle*, December 9, 1990; Saralee Tiede interview. During the break between special sessions, Hobby attended the wedding of his youngest son, Andrew, to Marion Farrar in Palm Beach, Florida.
31. Paul Hobby interview; Saralee Tiede interview; Kent Caperton interview; Hector Uribe interview; *Austin American-Statesman*, December 10, 1989; *Houston Chronicle*, December 9, 1990.
32. *Dallas Morning News*, October 31, 1989.
33. *Austin American-Statesman*, November 14, 1989; *San Antonio Light*, November 28, 1989; Hector Uribe interview; Saralee Tiede interview; Kent Caperton interview.
34. Kent Caperton interview; Saralee Tiede interview.
35. *Austin American-Statesman*, December 14, 1989; Bill Hobby interview.
36. *Austin American-Statesman*, December 13 and 14, 1989; Bill Hobby interview; Kent Caperton interview. The Texas Supreme Court eventually upheld Hobby's workers' compensation legislation.

CHAPTER 18: SINE DIE

1. Bill Hobby interview; *Austin American-Statesman*, November 3, 1989.
2. Bill Hobby interview; *Austin American-Statesman*, November 3, 1989.
3. *Austin American-Statesman*, November 3, 1989.
4. *Austin American-Statesman*, November 3, 1989; *San Antonio Light*, November 3, 1989; *Fort Worth Star-Telegram*, October 3, 1989.
5. *Austin American-Statesman*, November 3, 1989; *Dallas Morning News*, November 3, 1989.
6. Dubose, "Politics of Conviction." The *Observer*'s editor, Louis Dubose, was so impressed with Hobby's call for a state income tax that he published it in its entirety in the journal.
7. *Fort Worth Star-Telegram*, November 13, 1989;

Freedman, "Pro-choice Posturing"; *Houston Chronicle*, December 9, 1990. More than thirty years later, Texas would become one of the leading states in the anti-abortion effort.
8. Carleton, *Governor and the Colonel*, 719; Bill Hobby, calendar, February–May 1990, Bill Hobby Papers, BCAH; Hobby, *How Things Really Work*, 172–173; *Austin American-Statesman*, April 30, 1990. Oveta Culp Hobby was named to the Rice University Board of Trustees on June 17, 1967. She was the first woman member to serve on the board.
9. *Houston Chronicle*, June 18, 1995; Bill Hobby interview.
10. Bill Hobby, calendar, February 15–16, 1990, Bill Hobby Papers, BCAH; *Austin American-Statesman*, February 28, 1990.
11. *Fort Worth Star-Telegram*, February 27, 1990; *Austin American-Statesman*, February 28, 1990.
12. Bill Hobby, calendar, February 27, 1990, Bill Hobby Papers, BCAH; *Austin American-Statesman*, February 28, 1990; Rodney Ellis interview.
13. *Fort Worth Star-Telegram*, March 9 and 28, 1990; *El Paso Times*, May 18, 1990.
14. Bill Hobby, calendar, February and March 1990, Bill Hobby Papers, BCAH; Mark White interview; *Austin American-Statesman*, March 13, 1990.
15. *Fort Worth Star-Telegram*, March 29, 1990.
16. *Fort Worth Star-Telegram*, March 29, 1990; *Austin American-Statesman*, April 1, 1990.
17. *Austin American-Statesman*, April 10–14, 1990. For details about Mattox and his mudslinging campaign against Richards, see Reid, *Let the People In*, 222–229.
18. *Austin American-Statesman*, April 19, 1990; *Fort Worth Star-Telegram*, April 19, 1990.
19. *Austin American-Statesman*, May 23 and June 1, 1990.
20. *Fort Worth Star-Telegram*, June 8, 1990; *Austin American-Statesman*, June 8, 1990.
21. Bill Hobby, calendar, June 6 and 7, 1990, Bill Hobby Papers, BCAH; Laura Hobby Beckworth interview.
22. *Fort Worth Star-Telegram*, June 8, 1990; *Austin American-Statesman*, June 8, 1990.
23. Bill Hobby, calendar, June 11–17 and month of July, 1990, Bill Hobby Papers, BCAH.
24. Bill Hobby interview; Bill Hobby, calendar, July 30, 1990, Bill Hobby Papers, BCAH.
25. Catto, *Ambassadors at Sea*, 1–5; Bill Hobby, calendar, August 2–5, 1990, Bill Hobby Papers, BCAH.
26. Bill Hobby, calendar, October 27, 1988, Bill Hobby Papers, BCAH; Cochran, *Claytie*.
27. Bill Hobby, calendar, May 4, July 11, August 22, 24, and 25, September 24, and October 9, 1990, Bill Hobby Papers, BCAH; *Austin American-Statesman*, July 12, 1990; Reid, *Let the People In*, 209–211; Glenn Smith interview. One strategy meeting, for example, was with two of Richards's most influential advisors, Mary Beth Rogers and Jane Hickie, at Hobby's business office in Houston early in October.
28. Reid, *Let the People In*, 240–241; *New York Times*, March 26, 1990; Harrigan, *Big Wonderful Thing*, 792–793. Adding to Clayton Williams's problems during the campaign was his politically unwise admission that as an undergraduate at Texas A&M University, he had been a customer at the Chicken Ranch brothel in La Grange and that he had been "serviced" by prostitutes at "Boy's Towns" in Mexican red-light districts near the Texas border.
29. *Corpus Christi Caller-Times*, December 15, 1990; Bill Hobby, calendar, November 9–December 7, 1990, Bill Hobby Papers, BCAH. In his last Legislative Budget Board meeting, on December 14, 1990, Hobby went out swinging by strongly registering his opposition to a proposal made by the members representing the Texas House that the next legislature pass a "bare-bones, no new taxes" budget that would require a reduction in support for state services, including education.
30. *Austin American-Statesman*, December 8, 1990; *San Angelo (TX) Standard-Times*, December 23, 1990.
31. Bill Hobby, calendar, September 27, 1990, Bill Hobby Papers, BCAH; *Austin American-Statesman*, January 9, 1991.
32. *Austin American-Statesman*, January 9, 1991.
33. *Austin American-Statesman*, January 9, 1991; *Victoria (TX) Advocate*, December 23, 1990; Lady Bird Johnson to Bill Hobby, [January 1991], Bill Hobby Papers, BCAH.

CHAPTER 19: REQUIEM FOR THE POST

1. *Austin American-Statesman*, October 4, 1990, and January 9, 1991; "The LBJ Legacy," Texas LBJ School, lbj.utexas.edu/lbj-legacy. Sid Richardson Hall is divided into three units: the Nettie Lee Benson Latin American Collection in the south wing, the Dolph Briscoe Center for American

2. Hobby, *How Things Really Work*, 164–165; *Daily Texan*, January 30, 1995; Saralee Tiede interview.
3. Jack McGrew to Oveta Culp Hobby, March 4, 1991, Bill Hobby Papers, BCAH.
4. *Austin American-Statesman*, May 19, 1991; *On Campus* (University of Texas at Austin), June 3, 1991; Ann Richards to Bill Hobby, June 11, 1991, and Bill Cunningham to Bill Hobby, August 5, 1991, Bill Hobby Papers, BCAH. The day after his University of Texas commencement speech, Hobby addressed graduates of Huston-Tillotson, a historically Black private university in Austin. On May 20, 1991, Bill and Diana also attended the dinner hosted by Governor Richards at the LBJ Library for Queen Elizabeth and Prince Philip.
5. Bob Bullock to Bill Hobby, March 6, 1991, Bob Bullock Papers, Baylor University; *Houston Chronicle*, June 13, 1991; *Houston Post*, June 9, 1991; *Austin American-Statesman*, August 14, 1991. Officially, Bob Bullock, the new lieutenant governor, appointed Hobby to the task force.
6. Bill Hobby to Bob Bullock, August 13, 1993, and Bullock to Hobby, Bill Hobby Papers, BCAH.
7. *Austin American-Statesman*, March 30, 1992; *Houston Chronicle*, March 14 and April 12, 1992.
8. *Houston Post*, August 29, 1990.
9. *Houston Post*, August 29, 1990.
10. *Arizona Daily Star*, March 16, 1982; Harris, Huhndorff, and McGrew, *Fault Does Not Lie*, 120–122.
11. Laura Hobby Beckworth interview; Saralee Tiede interview.
12. Paul Hobby interview; Catto, *Ambassadors at Sea*, 357.
13. *Fort Worth Star-Telegram*, May 20, 1992; *Orlando Sentinel*, February 19 and September 2, 1993; Bill Hobby to Jessica Catto, October 25, 1993, Bill Hobby Papers, BCAH; *Austin American-Statesman*, December 2, 1993; Paul Hobby interview.
14. *Houston Chronicle*, December 2, 1993, and April 14, 1994.
15. Bill Hobby interview.
16. "Hobby Helping Incumbent Republican in State Senate Race," *Dallas Morning News*, July 25, 1992; Saralee Tiede interview; Bill Hobby interview.
17. Saralee Tiede interview; *Victoria (TX) Advocate*, December 23, 1990.
18. Bill Hobby to Albert Gore Jr., February 5, 1988, and Bill Hobby, calendar, July 23, 1992, Bill Hobby Papers, BCAH; Burka, "Bill's Bungle."
19. *Washington Post*, December 11, 1992; Bill Hobby interview; *New York Times*, January 3, 1993; miscellaneous telephone call notes and letters, Bill Hobby Papers, BCAH; *Fort Worth Star-Telegram*, January 5, 1993; Paul Hobby interview; Saralee Tiede interview.
20. A copy of the template letter, dated January 5, 1993, is in the Bill Hobby Papers, BCAH.
21. Bill Hobby, calendar, April 15 and May 28, 1993, Bill Hobby to Kay Bailey Hutchison, June 21, 1993, and Hutchison to Hobby, July 26, 1993, Bill Hobby Papers, BCAH; *Austin American-Statesman*, June 6, 1993; *Wall Street Journal*, December 11, 1992; Bill Hobby interview; Saralee Tiede interview. Hobby's involvement in Krueger's election campaign in 1993 was restricted to Houston. He and Diana hosted a reception at their home in April, and he attended a Krueger fundraiser at Houston attorney Mike Perrin's home in late May. Hutchison went on to win reelection to the US Senate in November 1994 and would remain in Congress until 2013.
22. Bill Hobby to Bob Bullock, March 18, 1993, Bob Bullock Papers, Baylor University; *Austin American-Statesman*, March 21, 1993.
23. *Austin American-Statesman*, March 21 and April 4, 1993, and December 3, 1994.
24. Clippings of Hobby's columns are in the Bill Hobby Papers, BCAH.
25. William H. Cunningham interview.
26. William H. Cunningham interview.
27. *Houston Post*, June 5, 1994.
28. Bryce, "Do Not Go Gentle."
29. *Austin American-Statesman*, February 24, 1994; *Houston Post*, June 5, 1994; Bill Hobby, calendar, February 9–12, May 26–June 12, July 3–4, August 10–15, September 2–10, October 1–30, 1994, and November 1–28, 1994, Bill Hobby Papers, BCAH.
30. Bill Hobby interview; Ann Richards to Bill Hobby, November 5, 1993, Bill Hobby Papers, BCAH.
31. Bill Hobby interview; Bill Hobby, calendar, January–December 1995, Bill Hobby Papers, BCAH.
32. *New York Times*, September 11, 1987.
33. Bill Hobby, "A Requiem for *The Houston Post*," *Houston Chronicle*, April 23, 1995; Hobby, *How Things Really Work*, 47–48.
34. Hobby, "Requiem for *The Houston Post*"; Hobby, *How Things Really Work*, 48.

35. Carleton, *Governor and the Colonel*, 758–761; Laura Hobby Beckworth interview.
36. Printed program, Culp Pool dedication, Killeen, TX, February 13, 1993, Bill Hobby Papers, BCAH.
37. For more about Oveta Culp Hobby's final days, see Carleton, *Governor and the Colonel*, 758–761; *Austin American-Statesman*, August 17, 1995. At the time of her death, *Forbes* magazine listed Oveta as the country's 287th-wealthiest person, estimating the worth of her family's assets at $400 million, which would be approximately $790 million in 2022.

CHAPTER 20: RESCUING THE UNIVERSITY OF HOUSTON

1. Bill Hobby interview; Burka, "Bill Hobby."
2. Burka, "Bill Hobby"; Carleton, *Governor and the Colonel*, 292, 466, 754; Hawes, *Public Television*, 20.
3. Mangan, "University of Houston System"; Fleck, "Insider"; Hobby, *How Things Really Work*, 166; Beth Robertson interview.
4. Beth Robertson interview; Bill Hobby interview.
5. Bill Hobby interview; Beth Robertson interview. Hobby eventually became an instructor in the summer program at the University of Michigan, teaching students how to work with datasets and software. He later noted that he had worked his "way up to become a teaching assistant when I was seventy-six, proving that it's never too late to find a new job."
6. Hobby, *How Things Really Work*, 167; Bill Hobby interview; Bill Hobby, calendar, May 24, 1995, Bill Hobby Papers, BCAH.
7. Bill Hobby interview; Beth Robertson interview; *Austin American-Statesman*, June 19, 1995; *Dallas Times Herald*, June 19, 1995. The foundation established by multimillionaire insurance tycoon Gus Wortham and his wife, Lyndall, donated the Worthams' former mansion to the University of Houston in 1986. Gus Wortham's father, John, had been a close friend of Will Hobby, and Gus had been a member of Houston's power-elite group known as the "8F crowd," which included Will and Oveta Culp Hobby. Lyndall Wortham was a member of the UH System Board of Regents for sixteen years, including the four years Bill Hobby was a regent. The Wortham Foundation's gift required that the UH chancellor live in the mansion.
8. Undated news clipping, and Bill Hobby, calendar, June 6–23, 1995, Bill Hobby Papers, BCAH; Bill Hobby interview; news clipping [ca. 1996], *Daily Texan*, Bill Hobby Papers, BCAH; *Austin American-Statesman*, June 14, 1995.
9. *Houston Chronicle*, June 25, 1995.
10. William H. Cunningham interview; Peter Flawn to Bill Hobby, June 20, 1995, Bill Hobby Papers, BCAH.
11. Bill Hobby interview; Bill Hobby, calendar, July 21–August 15, 1995, Bill Hobby Papers, BCAH.
12. Beth Robertson interview; Bill Hobby interview; Bill Hobby, calendar, August 15–September 8, 1995, Bill Hobby Papers, BCAH; Burka, "Bill Hobby"; Saralee Tiede interview.
13. Beth Robertson interview.
14. Frank Bash interview; Saralee Tiede interview.
15. William H. Cunningham interview; Bill Hobby interview; Burka, "Bill Hobby."
16. Hobby and Tiede, "Urban System," 173–174; *Houston Chronicle*, June 10, 1996; Saralee Tiede interview; Bill Hobby interview; Beth Robertson interview. Sociologist and future studies scholar Peter C. Bishop served as the commission's facilitator, and its members included Trinity University humanities professor Arturo Madrid; C. Peter Magrath, president of the National Association of State Universities and Land Grant Colleges; Frank Newman, president of the Education Commission of the States; Chester E. Finn Jr., fellow at the Hudson Institute; UH-Downtown professor Angela Patton; and Linda Gratch, former president of UH-Downtown. Ken Lay would be convicted of fraud in the Enron scandal in 2006, but he died before his appeal could be heard by the courts. The Vision Commission relied heavily on Texas A&M University professor Steve Murdock's report "Texas Challenged."
17. Bill Hobby to Bob Bullock, March 11, 1996, Bob Bullock Papers, Baylor University.
18. Bill Hobby to the secretary to the UH System Board of Regents, November 6, 1995, Bob Bullock Papers, Baylor University; *Houston Chronicle*, June 10, 1996; Bill Hobby interview; Laura Hobby Beckworth interview.
19. Ott, "Fort Bend County."
20. Bill Hobby interview.
21. Beth Robertson interview.
22. Bill Hobby interview.
23. *Houston Chronicle*, January 15, 1996; *Austin American-Statesman*, January 26, 1996; Bill Hobby interview; undated clipping from the *Daily Cougar* (UH), Bill Hobby Papers, BCAH.

24. *Houston Chronicle*, March 11, 1996.
25. *Houston Chronicle*, November 21, 1996; *Austin American-Statesman*, July 17, 1997.
26. Undated clippings from *Houston Chronicle* and *Dallas Morning News*, Bill Hobby Papers, BCAH; Rodney Ellis interview; Burka, "Bill Hobby."
27. *Austin American-Statesman*, May 26, 1997.
28. Saralee Tiede interview; Larry Temple interview.
29. Paul Hobby interview; James K. Galbraith interview.
30. *Austin American-Statesman*, May 31, 1997.
31. *Austin American-Statesman*, July 17, 1997; Saralee Tiede interview; Bill Hobby interview; Lady Bird Johnson to Bill Hobby, November 18, 1997, Bill Hobby Papers, BCAH.

CHAPTER 21: A CHAMPION FOR HIGHER EDUCATION

1. Cunningham, *Texas Way*; Hobby, *How Things Really Work*, 188; Bill Hobby interview.
2. William H. Cunningham interview; Bill Hobby interview. To view part of the dedication ceremony, including Hobby's speech, see "Telescope Dedication - The Film & Video Archive of the McDonald Observatory (1997)," Texas Archive of the Moving Image, https://texasarchive.org/2019_02350.
3. *New York Times*, October 20, 1991; Frank Bash interview; William H. Cunningham interview.
4. William H. Cunningham interview.
5. William H. Cunningham interview; Frank Bash interview.
6. William H. Cunningham interview.
7. Bill Hobby, speech transcript, September 30, 1987, and calendar, March 12–14, 1987, Bill Hobby Papers, BCAH; William H. Cunningham interview; Bill Hobby interview; Kay Bailey Hutchison interview.
8. William H. Cunningham interview; Paul Hobby interview.
9. *Austin American-Statesman*, September 18, 1988; Bill Hobby, calendar, September 20, 1990, Bill Hobby Papers, BCAH; *New York Times*, October 20, 1991. Harlan Smith died in 1991, eight years before the Hobby-Eberly Telescope was operational.
10. Frank Bash interview; William H. Cunningham interview.
11. Frank Bash interview; Hobby, *How Things Really Work*, 190.
12. Frank Bash interview.
13. Frank Bash interview.
14. Frank Bash interview.
15. Frank Bash interview; Bill Hobby interview.
16. William H. Cunningham interview; Cunningham, *Texas Way*; Bill Hobby interview; Hobby, *How Things Really Work*, 190.
17. Bill Hobby, calendar, March 25, 1994, Bill Hobby Papers, BCAH; Frank Bash interview. Foundations contributing to the telescope project included Houston's MD Anderson Foundation, the Brown Foundation, the Cullen Foundation, and the Houston Endowment. Each of those foundations had strong connections to Bill Hobby and the Hobby family. Hobby's Dallas friend Peter O'Donnell also directed his foundation to make a contribution.
18. Hobby, *How Things Really Work*, 186.
19. Bill Hobby interview; *Austin American-Statesman*, December 22, 1997.
20. Laura Hobby Beckworth interview; Paul Hobby interview.
21. Bill Hobby to Bob Bullock, February 11, 1998, Bob Bullock Papers, Baylor University; Texas State University, press release, 1999, Bill Hobby Papers, BCAH. Hobby's involvement in higher education after he left the LBJ School also included serving as chairman of the Texas Commission on a Representative Student Body in 1998. The commission was created by public and private institutions of higher education to address issues raised in the *Hopwood* decision.
22. Bryce, "Do Not Go Gentle."
23. Carleton, *Governor and the Colonel*, 251–252; Bill Hobby interview.
24. Paul Hobby interview; Delores Chambers to Bill Hobby, undated copy of email, Bill Hobby Papers, BCAH; *Fort Worth Star-Telegram*, July 28, 1997; Bill Hobby interview. Recalling his run for political office, Paul Hobby said in an interview, "I offered myself in public service. And [my father] was very supportive of that. I flew around the state every day on his airplane for sixteen months. But obviously, after twenty years, you realize, there just isn't any market for radically moderate white males in the state of Texas, not then, not now. But I tried."
25. *Houston Chronicle*, April 8, 1997, and October 18, 1998. By this time, Laura Hobby Beckworth was an equity investor who volunteered at the Pin Oak Charity Horse Show and was active with her alma maters, the University of North Carolina at Chapel Hill and the University of Texas at Austin. Kate Hobby Gibson was in the horse-raising

business, breeding, training, showing, and selling hunters and jumpers. Her husband, Steve Gibson, was a real estate developer. Andrew was a rancher who was active with the LBJ Museum of San Marcos.

26. *Houston Chronicle*, May 13, 2002.
27. Valdes, "Now Showing," 2–9.
28. Rick Perry would lose two attempts to become the GOP's nominee for president. In 2016, Donald Trump appointed Perry to his cabinet as secretary of energy. He resigned from the position in 2019.
29. Bill Hobby, "A History Lesson for Governor Perry's Benefit," clipping of newspaper column, *Austin American-Statesman*, February 25, 2007, Bill Hobby Papers, BCAH.
30. Hobby, "History Lesson for Governor Perry's Benefit."
31. Hobby, "History Lesson for Governor Perry's Benefit."
32. Bill Hobby interview.
33. *Austin American-Statesman*, February 25, 2007.
34. *Austin American-Statesman*, April 10, 2010.
35. Jim Granato interview; Renee Cross interview.
36. Jim Granato interview; Renee Cross interview; Paul Hobby interview.
37. Jim Granato interview.
38. Jim Granato interview; Bill Hobby interview.
39. Jim Granato interview; Renee Cross interview.
40. Jim Granato interview; Renee Cross interview.
41. Jim Granato interview.
42. Jim Granato interview; Dan Patrick's Facebook page, 2016; Bill Hobby interview.
43. Jim Granato interview; Renee Cross interview.
44. Jim Granato interview.
45. Renee Cross interview; Laura Hobby Beckworth interview.
46. Laura Hobby Beckworth interview; Paul Hobby interview. When asked if the school has had a significant effect on public policy in the short period of time it has existed, Paul Hobby said he couldn't say yes. "Let's be honest. I've been around the LBJ School and the Batten School at the University of Virginia. They have been in existence long enough for us to know whether they've affected public policy. And the answer is no. I've been in a lot of hot fights around public policy, and not once has the LBJ School ridden over the hill with the answer, because the decisions get made around political considerations, and academics tend to be scared of all that. Maybe for good reason."
47. Saralee Tiede interview; Glenn Smith interview.
48. Paul Hobby interview.
49. Ann Richards to Bill Hobby, March 23, 2006, Bill Hobby Papers, BCAH.
50. *Austin American-Statesman*, October 6, 2009; Laura Hobby Beckworth interview. Jessica Hobby Catto died on September 30, 2009. Henry Catto would die at the age of eighty-one, two years after his wife. Heather Catto died in 2014.
51. Laura Hobby Beckworth interview; *Houston Chronicle* and *Austin American-Statesman*, July 5, 2014.
52. Laura Hobby Beckworth interview; Kate Hobby Gibson interview; Paul Hobby interview.
53. Paul Hobby interview.
54. Bill Hobby interview.

EPILOGUE

1. Jim Granato interview.
2. Amber Elliott, "Bill Hobby's Birthday Roast and Toast," January 26, 2015, *Houston Chronicle*; Clifford Pugh, "Texas Legend Celebrates His 83rd Birthday with A-listers in River Oaks," *CultureMap Houston*, January 27, 2015.
3. Bob Moser, "Unchained," *Texas Observer*, September 20, 2010; Bill Hobby, "The Real Crisis in Texas Isn't Ebola," *Texas Tribune*, October 7, 2014.
4. R. G. Ratcliffe, "Bill Hobby," in *Lone Stars Rising: The Fifty People Who Turned Texas into the Fastest-Growing, Most Exciting, and, Sometimes, Most Exasperating State in the Country*, by the editors of *Texas Monthly* (New York: HarperCollins, 2023).
5. Bill Hobby, interview with Gabe Gutierrez, January 9, 2011, KHOU-TV; unpublished essay, Bill Hobby Papers, BCAH.
6. Hobby, *How Things Really Work*, xvi; Moser, "Unchained"; Laura Hobby Beckworth interview; Hobby, *How Things Really Work*, xxiv.

BIBLIOGRAPHY

ARCHIVAL SOURCES

Briscoe Center for American History, University of Texas at Austin (BCAH)
- Don Adams Papers
- Lloyd M. Bentsen Jr. Papers
- Dolph Briscoe Jr. Papers
- Ron Calhoun Papers
- George Christian Papers
- Robert C. Eckhardt Papers
- Jess Hay Papers
- Jim Hightower Papers
- Bill Hobby Papers
- William P. Hobby Sr. Papers
- Houston Post, Washington DC Bureau, Collection
- Molly Ivins Papers
- Jesse Holman Jones Papers
- Bob Krueger Papers
- Maury Maverick Jr. Papers
- New York Times Morgue
- Office of the Provost Records, University of Texas at Austin
- J. R. Parten Papers
- Ann Richards Papers
- Texas Observer Archive
- Jessie D. Ziegler Papers

Cushing Memorial Library and Archives, Texas A&M University
- William P. Clements Jr. Papers

LBJ Presidential Library, Austin, TX (LBJPL)
- Lady Bird Johnson Papers
- Lyndon B. Johnson Papers

Texas State Library and Archives
- William P. Hobby Jr. Papers

Woodson Research Center, Fondren Library, Rice University, Houston, TX
- Oveta Culp Hobby Papers
- Diana Hobby Papers
- Hobby Foundation Papers
- William P. Hobby Jr. and Diana Poteat Hobby Family Collection

Baylor Collections of Political Materials, W. R. Poage Legislative Library, Baylor University, Waco, TX
- Bob Bullock Papers

INTERVIEWS

By Don Carleton
- Dolph Briscoe Jr.
- James K. Galbraith
- Bill Hobby
- Howard Richards
- Babe Schwartz
- Larry Temple
- Mark White

By Erin Purdy
- Mike Andrews
- Ben Barnes
- Frank Bash
- Laura Hobby Beckworth
- Kent Caperton
- Delores Chambers
- Renee Cross

William H. Cunningham
Rodney Ellis
Kate Hobby Gibson
Jim Granato
Paul Hobby
Kay Bailey Hutchison
Ron and Vicki Kessler
Jack Martin
John Montford
Beth Robertson
Bill Sarpalius
Max Sherman
Glenn Smith
Saralee Tiede
Hector Uribe
By Patricia Kilday Hart
    Don Adams
    Babe Schwartz
    Max Sherman

ORAL HISTORY COLLECTIONS

Austin History Center, Austin, TX
    Bill Hobby, Texas Oral History Makers Oral History Project
Briscoe Center for American History, University of Texas at Austin
    Jane Hickie, Ann Richards Oral History Project
    Bill Hobby, interview conducted by Ariel Rogers, Bill Hobby Papers
    Peter Flawn, Shirley Bird Perry UT Oral History Project
    Jess Hay, Shirley Bird Perry UT Oral History Project
LBJ Presidential Library, Austin, TX
    Oveta Culp Hobby
    Arthur B. Krim
Rice University, Fondren Library, Woodson Research Center, Houston, TX
    Allyce Tinsley Cole, Rice University Women's Studies Records
    Bill Hobby, Jesse Jones Project
    Bill Hobby, Rice University Historical Commission Papers
Stephen F. Austin State University, East Texas Research Center, Nacogdoches, TX
    Joe William Christie
University of Houston, Center for Public History, Houston Oral History Project, University of Houston Libraries, Houston, TX
    Alison Cook
    Bill Hobby

Mark White
University of North Texas, Oral History Collection, Denton, TX
    Bill Clayton
    Tom Creighton
    O. H. "Ike" Harris
    James Kaster
    John Leedom
    Gib Lewis
    Oscar Mauzy

NEWSPAPERS

Abilene Reporter-News
Arizona Daily Star
Austin American-Statesman
Bryan–College Station Eagle
Cincinnati Enquirer
Corpus Christi Caller-Times
Corsicana (TX) Sun
Daily Texan (University of Texas at Austin)
Dallas Morning News
Dallas Times Herald
Denton (TX) Record-Chronicle
El Paso Herald Post
El Paso Times
Fort Worth Star-Telegram
Galveston Daily News
Gatesville (TX) Messenger and Star Forum
Houston Chronicle
Houston Post
Houston Press
Irving (TX) Daily News
Kerrville (TX) Mountain Sun
Kerrville (TX) Times
Kilgore (TX) News Herald
Longview (TX) News-Journal
Lubbock Evening Journal
Marshall (TX) News Messenger
Midland (TX) Reporter-Telegram
Nashville Banner
New York Times
New York Daily News
Odessa (TX) American
Orlando Sentinel
Paris (TX) News
Port Arthur (TX) News
Rice Thresher (Rice University)
Saint Albans News
San Angelo (TX) Standard-Times
San Antonio Express-News
San Antonio Light
Tennessean (Nashville, TN)

Texas Press Messenger

Texas Tribune

Times Record News (Wichita Falls, TX)

USA Today

Victoria (TX) Advocate

Waco Tribune-Herald

Wall Street Journal

Washington Post

Women's Wear Daily

PUBLISHED SOURCES

Adair, Wendy, and Oscar Gutiérrez. *The University of Houston: Our Time; Celebrating 75 Years of Learning and Leading*. Virginia Beach, VA: Donning, 2001.

Anders, Evan. "Parr, George Berham [1901–1975]." *Handbook of Texas Online*. Updated August 4, 2020. https://www.tshaonline.org/handbook/entries/parr-george-berham-1901-1975.

Anderson, Michael. "Eldrewey Stearns and Houston's Student Civil Rights Movement." *Houston History* 14, no. 2 (Spring 2017): 23–27.

Ashworth, Kenneth. "Texas Higher Education Coordinating Board." *Handbook of Texas Online*. Updated January 1, 1996. https://www.tshaonline.org/handbook/entries/texas-higher-education-coordinating-board.

Bagdikian, Ben H. "Houston's Shackled Press." *Atlantic*, August 1966.

Barna, Joel. "Oveta Posts Notice." *Houston City Magazine*, November 1983.

Barnes, Ben, with Lisa Dickey. *Barn Burning Barn Building: Tales of a Political Life, from LBJ to George W. Bush and Beyond*. Albany, TX: Bright Sky Press, 2006.

Barras, Mary Lucia, and Houston Daniel. "Constitutional Convention of 1974." *Handbook of Texas Online*. Updated September 11, 2019. https://www.tshaonline.org/handbook/entries/constitutional-convention-of-1974.

Barta, Carolyn. *Bill Clements: Texian to His Toenails*. Austin: Eakin Press, 1996.

Bennett, Scott. "The Senate Is Not the Same." *Texas Business*, February 1981. Clipping in Bill Hobby Papers, BCAH.

"Bill Hobby [Democratic] 1972 Campaign Ad 'Drugs.'" Julian P. Kanter Political Commercial Collection, Carl Albert Congressional Research and Studies Center, University of Oklahoma. YouTube, uploaded August 5, 2020, https://www.youtube.com/watch?v=jcyYv6Fv20A.

"Bill Hobby [Democratic] 1972 Campaign Ad 'Economy.'" Julian P. Kanter Political Commercial Collection, Carl Albert Congressional Research and Studies Center, University of Oklahoma. YouTube, uploaded August 5, 2020, https://www.youtube.com/watch?v=bd1uG5T_78M.

"Bill Hobby [Democratic] 1972 Campaign Ad 'Education.'" Julian P. Kanter Political Commercial Collection, Carl Albert Congressional Research and Studies Center, University of Oklahoma. YouTube, August 5, 2020, https://www.youtube.com/watch?v=SIiq2CW0Nfw.

"Bill Hobby [Democratic] 1972 Campaign Ad 'Insurance.'" Julian P. Kanter Political Commercial Collection, Carl Albert Congressional Research and Studies Center, University of Oklahoma. Uploaded August 5, 2020, https://www.youtube.com/watch?v=ecx-Yy-PUHY.

"Bill Hobby [Democratic] 1972 Campaign Ad 'Welfare.'" Julian P. Kanter Political Commercial Collection, Carl Albert Congressional Research and Studies Center, University of Oklahoma. YouTube, August 5, 2020, https://www.youtube.com/watch?v=7YVlJEbETlY.

Bloom, John. "The Ten Best and the Ten Worst Legislators." *Texas Monthly*, July 1979.

Boggess, Scott, and John Bound. "Did Criminal Activity Increase during the 1980s? Comparisons across Data Sources." *Social Science Quarterly* 78, no. 3 (September 1997): 725–739.

Bowman, Bob. "Mister Ben." *All Things Historical*, September 17–23, 2000. http://www.texasescapes.com/DEPARTMENTS/Guest_Columnists/East_Texas_all_things_historical/Bowman_Mister_Ben_91700.htm.

Bridges, Kenneth. *Twilight of the Texas Democrats: The 1978 Governor's Race*. College Station: Texas A&M University Press, 2008.

Briscoe, Dolph, with Don Carleton. *Dolph Briscoe: My Life in Texas Ranching and Politics*. Austin: Center for American History, 2008.

Brittain, Joan T. *Laurence Stallings*. Boston: Twayne, 1975.

Bryce, Robert. "Do Not Go Gentle: Former Lieutenant Governor Bill Hobby Fights on for Better, More Diverse Education in Texas." *Houston Press*, September 1998.

Burka, Paul. "Bill Hobby: A Lesson in Public Service." *Texas Monthly*, September 1997.

———. "Bill's Bungle: Why Clinton Lost Texas—And What It Means." *Texas Monthly*, December 1992.

———. "The Man in the Black Hat: Part One and Part Two." *Texas Monthly*, June–July 1984.

———. "1975: The Ten Best and (Sigh) . . . the Ten Worst Legislators." *Texas Monthly*, July 1975.

———. "1979: The Ten Best and the Ten Worst Legislators." *Texas Monthly*, July 1979.

———. "The Other Hobby." *Texas Monthly*, October 1978.

———. "Perot and Con." *Texas Monthly*, August 1996.

———. "State Secrets." *Texas Monthly*, January 1982.

———. "State Secrets." *Texas Monthly*, May 1987.

Burka, Paul, and Alison Cook. "The Ten Best and (Groan) the Ten Worst Legislators." *Texas Monthly*, July 1985.

Burka, Paul, Alison Cook, and Kaye Northcott. "1983: The Ten Best and the Ten Worst Legislators." *Texas Monthly*, July 1983.

Burka, Paul, Patricia Hart, Ellen Williams, and Jennifer Bradley. "1989: The Best and the Worst Legislators." *Texas Monthly*, July 1989.

Burka, Paul, and Richard West. "1977: The Ten Best and the Ten Worst Legislators." *Texas Monthly*, July 1977.

Campbell, Randolph B. *Gone to Texas: A History of the Lone Star State*. New York: Oxford University Press, 2003.

Carleton, Don. *A Breed So Rare: The Life of J. R. Parten, Liberal Texas Oil Man, 1896–1992*. Austin: Texas State Historical Association, 1998.

———. *The Governor and the Colonel: A Dual Biography of William P. Hobby and Oveta Culp Hobby*. Austin: Dolph Briscoe Center for American History, 2021.

———. *Red Scare: Right-Wing Hysteria, Fifties Fanaticism, and Their Legacy in Texas*. Austin: University of Texas Press, 2014.

Caro, Robert A. *The Path to Power*. Vol. 1 of *The Years of Lyndon Johnson*. New York: Knopf, 1982.

Carroll, Jeff. "Provident City, TX." *Handbook of Texas Online*. Updated March 1, 1995. https://www.tshaonline.org/handbook/entries/provident-city-tx.

Catto, Henry E., Jr. *Ambassadors at Sea: The High and Low Adventures of a Diplomat*. Austin: University of Texas Press, 1998.

Caudill, Susan, and Darrell Hancock. "The Guild and the Post." *Houston Journalism Review*, June 1972.

Cheevers, Jim. "The United States Naval Academy, 1845–2020." Annapolis, MD: US Naval Academy, 2020.

Clark, James A., with Weldon Hart. *The Tactful Texan: A Biography of Governor Will Hobby*. New York: Random House, 1958.

Cochran, Mike. *Claytie: The Roller-Coaster Life of a Texas Wildcatter*. College Station: Texas A&M University Press, 2007.

Cole, Thomas R. *No Color Is My Kind: The Life of Eldrewey Stearns and the Integration of Houston*. Austin: University of Texas Press, 1997.

Colloff, Pamela. "Remember the Christian Alamo." *Texas Monthly*, December 2001.

Conley, Seán W. "*Farrar v. Hobby*: When Moral Victories Will Not Feed the Attorney." *Mercer Law Review* 44, no. 4, article 20 (1993). https://digitalcommons.law.mercer.edu/jour_mlr/vol44/iss4/20.

Cottrell, Debbie Maudlin. "Farabee, Helen Jane Rehbein." *Handbook of Texas Online*. Updated September 21, 2019. https://www.tshaonline.org/handbook/entries/farabee-helen-jane-rehbein.

Cummings, Richard H. *Radio Free Europe's "Crusade for Freedom": Rallying Americans behind Cold War Broadcasting, 1950–1960*. Jefferson, NC: McFarland, 2010.

Cunningham, William H., with Monty Jones. *The Texas Way: Money, Power, Politics, and Ambition at the University*. Austin: Dolph Briscoe Center for American History, 2013.

Deaton, Charles. *The Year They Threw the Rascals Out*. Austin: Shoal Creek, 1973.

Dethloff, Henry C. *Suddenly, Tomorrow Came: The NASA History of the Johnson Space Center*. Mineola, NY: Dover Books, 1993.

Dubose, Louis. "Editorials: Politics of Conviction." *Texas Observer*, November 10, 1989.

Dugger, Ronnie. "Break, Enter, Wiretap: Clements Gets His Way." *Texas Observer*, May 29, 1981.

Farabee, Ray. *Ray Farabee: Making It Through the Night and Beyond*. Austin: self-published, 2008.

Ferguson, John. "School Financing." *Texas Observer*, June 20, 1975.

Ferguson, John, Kaye Northcott, and Molly Ivins. "Turn Out the Lights the Party's Over." *Texas Observer*, June 15, 1973.

Fleck, Tim. "Crisis on Cullen Blvd." *Houston Press*, September 1, 1994.

———. "The Insider." *Houston Press*, June 1, 1995.

———. "Station Break." *Houston Press*, [month unknown] 1996. Clipping in Bill Hobby Papers, BCAH.

Ford, Matt. "What Caused the Great Crime Decline in the U. S.?" *Atlantic*, April 15, 2016.

Freedman, Allan. "Pro-choice Posturing." *Texas Observer*, November 24, 1989.

Frontain, Michael. "Microelectronics and Computer Technology Corporation [MCC]." *Handbook of

Texas Online. Updated August 2, 2020. https://www.tshaonline.org/handbook/entries/microelectronics-and-computer-technology-corporation-mcc.

García, María-Cristina. "Colonia." *Handbook of Texas Online*. August 1, 1995. https://www.tshaonline.org/handbook/entries/colonia.

Garrett, George. "His One and Only Novel: Laurence Stallings's 'Plumes.'" *Sewanee Review* 114, no. 2 (Spring 2006).

Gary, Suzanne Tumblin. *Green Fields Country Day School: The First Fifty Years*. Tucson, AZ: Green Fields Country Day School, 1983.

Goltz, Gene. *The Pasadena Story*. Durham, NC: Lulu Press, 2014.

Green, William Elton. "Capitol." *Handbook of Texas Online*. Updated February 7, 2019. https://www.tshaonline.org/handbook/entries/capitol.

Greenlee, Tracy Anders. "Public Utility Commission of Texas." *Handbook of Texas Online*. November 1, 1995. https://www.tshaonline.org/handbook/entries/public-utility-commission-of-texas.

Harrigan, Stephen. *Big Wonderful Thing: A History of Texas*. Austin: University of Texas Press, 2019.

Harris, Jack, Paul Huhndorff, and Jack McGrew. *The Fault Does Not Lie with Your Set: The First Forty Years of Houston Television*. Austin: Eakin Press, 1989.

Hawes, William. *Public Television: America's First Station; An Intimate Account*. Santa Fe, NM: Sunstone Press, 1996.

Heard, Robert. *The Miracle of the Killer Bees: 12 Senators Who Changed Texas Politics*. Austin: Honey Hill, 1981.

Hempstone, Smith, editor. *An Illustrated History of St. Albans*. Washington, DC: Glastonbury Press, 1981.

Hightower, Jim. "Peering into the Worst Session in Memory." *Texas Observer*, June 8, 1979.

Hill, John L., Jr., with Ernie Stromberger. *John Hill for the State of Texas: My Years as Attorney General*. College Station: Texas A&M University Press, 2008.

Hobby, Bill. Essays published on Hobby's personal website. "Publications," William P. Hobby Jr., 1991–2014, https://williamphobby.org/publications/.

———. "The Hobby Family in Texas." December 2013. https://uh.edu/hobby/_docs/THE%20HOBBY%20FAMILY%20IN%20TEXAS%20HISTORY.PDF.

———. "Hobby on Taxes: A Speech by Lieutenant Governor Bill Hobby." *Texas Observer*, November 10, 1989.

———. "Journalism: Literature's Fourth Dimension." *Texas Quarterly* 2, no. 4 (Winter 1959).

———. "A Lesson from the Sports Page." *Reporter*, September 18, 1958.

———, with Saralee Tiede. *How Things Really Work: Lessons from a Life in Politics*. Austin: Dolph Briscoe Center for American History, 2010.

———, and Saralee Tiede. "The Urban System: The University of Houston." In *The Multicampus System: Perspectives on Practice and Prospects*, edited by Gerald Gaither. Sterling, VA: Stylus, 1999.

Holley, Joe, Geoff Rips, and Kay Gunderson. "COPS Meeting Educational." *Texas Observer*, June 24, 1983.

———. "Manager of the Year." *Texas Observer*, June 24, 1983.

Hopper, Jack, "A Case for Regulation." *Texas Observer*, February 14, 1975.

———. "The Urban System: The University of Houston." in *The Multicampus System: Perspectives on Practice and Prospects*, edited by Gerald Gaither. Sterling, VA: Stylus, 1999.

Huntington, John. "Perot, Henry Ross." *Handbook of Texas Online*. June 17, 2020. https://www.tshaonline.org/handbook/entries/perot-henry-ross.

Hurt, Harry, III. "The Last of the Great Ladies." *Texas Monthly*, October 1978.

Ivins, Molly. "Child Care Progress," *Texas Observer*, June 20, 1975.

———. *Molly Ivins Can't Say That, Can She?* New York: Random House, 1991.

———. "Oh, Happy Day." *Texas Observer*, May 26 and June 9, 1972.

———. "Utilities Regulation: Ball in Briscoe's Court," *Texas Observer*, June 20, 1975.

———. "Vote Yes." *Texas Observer*, October 31, 1975.

———, and Kaye Northcott. "Utilities Regulation." *Texas Observer*, January 17, 1975.

Johnson, John G. "Texas Air Control Board." *Handbook of Texas Online*. Updated October 1, 1995, https://www.tshaonline.org/handbook/entries/texas-air-control-board.

Johnson, Madeline. "Cooperation Is Solving UH System's Problems." *Houston Chronicle*, March 11, 1996.

Johnston, Marguerite. *Houston: The Unknown City; 1836–1946*. College Station: Texas A&M University Press, 1991.

Keith, Gary A. *Eckhardt: There Once Was a*

Congressman from Texas. Austin: University of Texas Press, 2007.

Kelly, Rita, "Health and Human Services Issues." *Texas Association of Counties*, January 14, 2015.

Kinch, Sam, Jr. "Sharpstown Stock-Fraud Scandal." *Handbook of Texas Online*. Updated November 1, 1995. https://www.tshaonline.org/handbook/entries/sharpstown-stock-fraud-scandal.

———, and Ben Procter. *Texas under a Cloud: Story of the Texas Stock Fraud Scandal*. Austin: Jenkins, 1972.

Knaggs, John R. *Two Party Texas: The John Tower Era, 1961–1984*. Austin: Eakin Press, 1986.

Levitt, Steven D., and Stephen J. Dubner. *Freakonomics: A Rogue Economist Explores the Hidden Side of Everything*. New York: William Morrow, 2005.

Mahler, Daniel. "Zero-Based Budgeting Is Not a Wonder Diet for Companies." *Harvard Business Review*, June 2016.

Mangan, Katherine. "University of Houston System Recovers from Major Shakeup." *Chronicle of Higher Education*, June 16, 1995.

McNeely, Dave, and Jim Henderson. *Bob Bullock: God Bless Texas*. Austin: University of Texas Press, 2008.

Meiners, Fredericka. *A History of Rice University: The Institute Years, 1907–1963*. Houston, TX: Rice University, 1982.

Middleton, William. *Double Vision: The Unerring Eye of Art World Avatars Dominique and John de Menil*. New York: Knopf, 2018.

Miller, Eric. "Good Ol' Gib." *D Magazine*, September 1983.

Montford, John T., and Will G. Barber. "1987 Texas Tort Reform: The Quest for a Fairer and More Predictable Texas Civil Justice System." *Houston Law Review* 25, no. 1 (January 1988).

Montford, John T., et al. "1989 Texas DTPA Reform: Closing the DTPA Loophole in the 1987 Tort Reform Laws and the Ongoing Quest for Fairer DTPA Laws." *St. Mary's Law Journal* 21, no. 3 (1990).

Morehead, Richard M. "Ramsey, Ben." *Handbook of Texas Online*. Updated April 30, 2019. https://www.tshaonline.org/handbook/entries/ramsey-ben.

Mosher, Bob. "Purple State Unchained." *Texas Observer*, September 17, 2010.

Mullis, H. Paul, editor. "A Brief History of the Naval Criminal Investigative Service." NCISA History Project, 1997. https://ncisahistory.org/wp-content/uploads/2017/07/A-Brief-History-of-the-Naval-Criminal-Investigative-Service-Editor-H.-Paul-Mullis-1997.pdf.

Murph, Daniel. "Daniel, Marion Price, Jr." *Handbook of Texas Online*. Updated July 5, 2017. https://www.tshaonline.org/handbook/entries/daniel-marion-price-jr.

National Register of Historic Places. Nomination form, Poteat House/Forest Home, Yanceyville, Caswell County, North Carolina.

Nicholson, Patrick J. *In Time: An Anecdotal History of the First Fifty Years of the University of Houston*. Houston, TX: Pacesetter Press, 1977.

Northcott, Kaye. "Needs Salt." *Texas Observer*, February 2, 1973.

———. "The Senate: No Style, Little Action." *Texas Observer*, June 20, 1975.

Orozco, Cynthia E. "Rodriguez v. San Antonio ISD." *Handbook of Texas Online*. Updated August 4, 2020, https://www.tshaonline.org/handbook/entries/rodriguez-v-san-antonio-isd

Ott, Virginia. "Fort Bend County." *Handbook of Texas Online*. Updated October 22, 2020. https://www.tshaonline.org/handbook/entries/fort-bend-county.

Pando, Robert T. "Oveta Culp Hobby: A Study of Power and Control." Ph.D. diss., Florida State University, 2008.

Papademetriou, Peter. *Houston: An Architectural Guide*. Houston, TX: American Institute of Architects, 1972.

Pennington, Richard. "John Hill Westbrook." *Handbook of Texas Online*. Updated September 9, 2021. https://www.tshaonline.org/handbook/entries/westbrook-john-hill.

Reid, Jan. *Let the People In: The Life and Times of Ann Richards*. Austin: University of Texas Press, 2012.

Richards, Ann, with Peter Knobler. *Straight from the Heart: My Life in Politics and Other Places*. New York: Simon and Schuster, 1989.

Richards, David. *Once upon a Time in Texas: A Liberal in the Lone Star State*. Austin: University of Texas Press, 2002.

Riordan, Michael. *Tunnel Visions: The Rise and Fall of the Superconducting Super Collider*. Chicago: University of Chicago Press, 2015.

Robertshaw, Nicholas. *The Winant Volunteers: A History*. Winant Clayton Volunteers, 2020.

Salazar, Stephanie M. "Steiner, Thomas Casper [Buck]." *Handbook of Texas Online*. Updated April 6, 2019. https://www.tshaonline.org/handbook/entries/steiner-thomas-casper-buck.

Salinas, Exiquio. *The Colonias Factbook: A Survey of*

Living Conditions in Rural Areas of South Texas and West Texas Border Counties. Austin: Texas Department of Human Services, 1988.

Sarpalius, Bill. *The Grand Duke from Boys Ranch*. College Station: Texas A&M University Press, 2018.

——. "The Grand Duke from Boys Ranch." Unpublished manuscript version of memoir. Copy in Don Carleton's possession.

Shire, Al, ed. *Oveta Culp Hobby*. Houston, TX: W. P. Hobby, 1997.

Slaughter, George. "Clements, William Perry, Jr. [Bill]." *Handbook of Texas Online*. Updated October 20, 2016. https://www.tshaonline.org/handbook/entries/clements-william-perry-jr-bill.

Smyrl, Vivian Elizabeth. "Permanent University Fund." *Handbook of Texas Online*. Updated June 9, 2020. https://www.tshaonline.org/handbook/entries/permanent-university-fund.

——. "Texas Sunset Advisory Commission," *Handbook of Texas Online*. September 1, 1995. https://www.tshaonline.org/handbook/entries/texas-sunset-advisory-commission.

The State (North Carolina). "Caswell County." November 28, 1942.

Sterling, Ross S., and Ed Kilman. *Ross Sterling, Texan: A Memoir by the Founder of Humble Oil and Refining Company*. Austin: University of Texas Press, 2007.

Sutphen, Debra Lynn. "Conservative Warrior: Oveta Culp Hobby and the Administration of America's Health, Education, and Welfare, 1953–1955." PhD diss., Washington State University, 1997.

Texas Legislative Council, Research Division. *Presiding Officers of the Texas Legislature, 1846–2016*. Texas Legislative Council, 2016.

Texas Monthly. "State Secrets." January 1982.

Texas Observer. "Christie for Lt. Governor." April 28, 1972.

——. "Houston Changes." September 2, 1960.

——. "Key Senate Votes." June 8, 1979.

——. "The Perils of the SA Expressway." September 8, 1972.

——. "Political Intelligence: More against Schnabel." February 27, 1976.

——. "Political Intelligence: Undoubtedly." July 4, 1975.

——. "Report of the Hobby Commission." February 11, 1977.

——. "Slow Start in Senate Race." March 3, 1972.

Texas Senate Journal. 56th Texas Legislature. Regular Session, January 13, 1959–May 12, 1959.

——. 71st Texas Legislature. Regular Session, January 10, 1989–May 29, 1989.

Tiede, Saralee. "Drifting." *Texas Observer*, June 17, 1977.

Time. "Books: Realism without Obscenity." April 9, 1951.

——. "Change at Annapolis." January 20, 1947.

——. "The Heir Apparent." May 30, 1960.

——. "The Press: Blackout in Houston." September 12, 1960.

——. "Short Takes." *Time*, June 19, 1972.

——. "Three for the Post." March 1, 1963.

——. "The Touchy Issue." September 19, 1960.

Untermeyer, Chase. "Give Me Liberty." *Texas Monthly*, February 1975.

Valdes, Ernesto. "Now Showing: One Singular Sensation . . ." *Houston History Magazine*, December 18, 2010.

Vogue. "In Texas: Ten Personalities." April 1, 1968.

Waite, Charles. "Price Daniel, Texas Democrats, and School Segregation, 1956–1957." *East Texas Historical Journal* 48, no. 2 (2010).

Walsh, Kelly Cardenas. "Oveta Culp Hobby: Ability, Perseverance, and Cultural Capital in the Twentieth-Century Success Story." In *Texas Women: Their Histories, Their Lives*, edited by Elizabeth Hayes Turner, Stephanie Cole, and Rebecca Sharpless, 318–337. Athens: University of Georgia Press, 2015.

——. "Oveta Culp Hobby: A Transformational Leader from the Texas Legislature to Washington, D.C." PhD diss., University of South Carolina, 2006.

Weinberg, Steven. "The Crisis of Big Science." *New York Review of Books*, May 10, 2012.

Yergin, Daniel. *The Prize: The Epic Quest for Oil, Money and Power*. New York: Simon and Schuster, 1990.

INDEX

Note: "Hobby" in index refers to Bill Hobby

A

abortion and abortion rights, 109, 128, 258, 273, 275, 310, 390. *see also* women's rights.
abuse, child, 160
academics, 26, 47, 321
Adams, Don: at Bill Hobby Day, x; and committee assignments, 123; and ethics reform, 133; filibuster, 138; and Hobby, 121, 123, 213–214, 219–221, 260, 267, 281, 359; and Hobby *vs.* Clements, 275; and Provident City retreat, 120, 121; and Schnabel investigation, 175; on Strake, 213
Adenauer, Konrad, 57
Administration Committee, 122, 175, 176
adoption, consideration of, 53
ad valorem tax, 97
advertising: billboards, 102–103; for Build Texas plan, 282; and campaigns, 100, 110, 114, 219, 220–221; and *Houston Post*, 166, 239, 370; and Kennedy, 63; and news blackout, 62
affirmative action, 338–339
African Americans. *see* Black Texans.
Agnew, Spiro, 79–80, 129
agriculture, 46, 260, 268
AIDS research, 303
Aid to Families with Dependent Children (AFDC), 214, 255
Aiken, A. M. Jr., 122, 125, 127–128, 131, 151, 283
air-conditioning, 148, 177, 205
Air Control Board, 92, 97

airplane, 109, 272, 312, 316, 328–329
Alabama-Coushatta Tribe of Texas, 138
alcohol: ban on drinking while driving, 255–256, 275; and drinking age, 138, 207–208, 232, 238, 255; and Hobby, 156–157, 355–356, 377; and hunting, 327; postwar rationing, 32; prevention programs, 300; Prohibition, 128; and Provident City retreat, 120; and Senators, 120, 190; taxes on, 238, 247
Aldrin, Buzz, 21
Altgens, James W., 66
alumni and education funding, 178, 272
Alzheimer's disease, 356
amendments, constitutional: and bonds, 274; and Build Texas plan, 274, 282–283, 284; and constitutional reform, 118, 162–163, 165, 166–167, 174–175; and Hobby-Clayton report, 378; income tax, 297; and lottery, 321; and Permanent School Fund, 178; and prisons, 274, 288; and public-school finance, 299; and rainy day fund, 295; and State Board of Education, 274, 283, 286; statewide water plan, 255; and Super Collider, 386; and taxes, 177, 183, 297; and term lengths, 150; and welfare ceiling, 222. *see also* Constitution, Texas.
American Cancer Society, 61
American Civil Liberties Union (ACLU), 221–222
American Federation of Labor (AFL-CIO), 28, 112, 306. *see also* unions.
American Federation of Teachers, 316
American General Corporation, 171
Americanism Committee, American Legion, 39–40
American Society of Newspaper Editors, 61

amphibious car, 76
Anderson, Maxwell, 44
Anderson, Richard, 286, 287–288, 292, 294–295
Anderson, Robert O., 292
Annenberg, Walter, 79
annex, underground, 231
annual sessions, legislative, 118
anti-Communism, 38–40, 57, 71–72
anti-crime plan, Hobby, 299–301
anti-intellectualism, 188, 277–278, 352
antisemitism, 34
antiwar movement, 76–77
apartments: garage, 47; and Killer Bees, 196–197; in Lamar Hotel, 6–7, 9; lieutenant governor's, 116, 130, 228–230, 231, 280; Oveta's, 17, 320, 329, 330; in Washington, DC, 17, 49. *see also* homes.
Apollo 11, 20–21
appeals claims and workers' compensation, 302
appendicitis, 18
appropriations: ceiling for, 92; and Clements, 209; emergency, xii; and ethics reform, 134; and governor's veto, 350; and Hobby, 174, 206, 209; and Hobby-Clayton commission, 178; and Legislative Budget Board, viii; and legislature, 126, 159, 360; and New Federalism, 234; and permanent funds, 150; and school finance, 311; and women's shelter, 217. *see also* budget, state.
Armstrong, Bob, 119, 201–202, 212, 215, 292
Armstrong, Neil, 21
Army, US, 14–15
Arnold, Kelly, 197–198
Artesia Hall, 142–147, 159, 376
Ashby, Lynn, 168
Asia, 58, 328
Aspen Institute, 315–316
Associated Press Managing Editors, 61
asthma, 13–14
Atchley, George, 14
athletics, 20, 26, 271, 321. *see also* football.
Attlee, Clement, 33
attorney general's office, 137, 144, 145, 149
Atwater, Lee, 294
Audubon Society, x
Austin, TX: *Capital Eye,* 100; childhood visits to, 13; commuting from, 55, 166, 170, 327; and Diana, 165–166; DUI charge, 155–157; duplex, 166, 228, 229, 332; and Hobby family, 115, 116, 217; and *Post* Capitol news team, 50; as small town, 217; and technology sector, 252, 287; and Texas constitution, 152
Austin American-Statesman, 166, 327
automation, 166

automobile dealers, 255
aviation, advisory committee on, 61

B
Baby Blue sports, 20
bail bonds, 156–157
Balcones Research Campus, 253
ballet, 84
Bangladesh University, 328
Banking Commission, 3
Bank of Texas, 61
Baptists, 3, 19, 27, 44, 221
Barken, Eddie, 95
Barna, Joel, 239
Barnes, Ben: and Bill Hobby Day, x; and dual primaries, 191–192; and ethics reform, 134; governor's campaign, 90–91, 98–99, 110–111; and Hobby, 90–91, 96, 121, 359; as lieutenant governor, 89, 90, 130–131; and Senate rules, 118, 120, 127; and Sharpstown Bank Scandal, 94–95, 97, 98–99, 147
Barrientos, Gonzalo, 252
Barton Springs Pool, 13
baseball, 20
Bash, Frank, 342–343, 345
basketball, 20
Battise, Robert Fulton, 138
Battle of Belleau Wood, 44
Battle of Galveston, 64
Baum, Elmer, 93
Baylor Academy (Baylor Female College), 3
Bayoud, George, 276
beaches, 84, 211
Beaumont, TX, 1–2
Beaumont Enterprise, 1–2
Beckworth, Carter, x
Beckworth, John, 238
Beckworth, Laura Poteat Hobby: and Bill Hobby Day, ix; birth of, 53; career of, 393; childhood of, 81–82, 116; and cousins, 356; education of, 184, 205; on father, 14, 73, 98; and grandfather, 12, 68; and grandmother, 85–86, 98, 240, 330; and H&C, 322–323; and Hobby Family Foundation, 347; on Hobby School, 355; and *Houston Post,* 240; marriage of, 238, 241; on parents, 356–357; and performing arts center, 349; and Zimmermans, 84
Beckworth, Lindley, 238
Beckworth, Will, x
Bedell, W. D., 52
Beechwood House, 284, 295, 296, 317, 328
bees, africanized honey, 196
behavior and laws, 132, 210, 273
Behrens, Margaret, 122, x

Bennett, Constance, 37
Bentsen, Beryl Ann "B. A.," 214, 288
Bentsen, Lloyd Jr.: campaigns and elections, 214, 216–218, 223, 290, 291–292, 293–294, 324; and Carter inauguration, 177; and dual primaries, 129, 191, 204; and election watch party, 288; and fundraising, 119, 294; and *Houston Post* endorsement, 97; as secretary of the treasury, 325; as senator, 129, 145, 204, 224, 288, 294; and welfare reform, 290
Bentsen, Lloyd Sr., 150
Bentsen, Lynne, 359
Bernstein, Leonard, 34
Bertner, Ernst William, 16
Bertner, Julia, 16
The Best Little Whorehouse in Texas, 103, 114
Beyers, Bo, 110
Big Bend Ranch, 292–293
Big Four meeting, 57
billboards, 102–103
Bill Hobby Day, 302, vii–xiii
Biltmore Hotel, 23
Binion, Jack, 72
birthdays: and campaign opening, 101; eighty-third, 359–360; fifty-fifth, 268; at Headliners Club, 329; shared, 4, 5, 8–9; skeet-shooting party, 297; thirty-third, 73; in Washington DC, 37
Bivens, Teel, 297
Black Arts Festival, 80–81
Blackham, Sam, 103
Black-majority congressional district, 212
Black Texans: color barrier, 181–182; and congressional districts, 212; and fundraisers, 155; and Hobby campaigns, 103, 112, 151, 222, 267, 283; and *Houston Post*, 322; Hunter and Hobby, 122; in legislature, 254; and school board elections, 53; and Texas Constitution, 152; and Texas Southern University, 322. see also desegregation; segregation.
Blake, Roy, 231
Blanchard, H. J. "Doc," 120, 122, 140, 153, 377
Blanton, Ray, 172
blue laws, 232, 238, 251, 255
Board of Education, State: appointed *vs.* elected, 248, 274, 283; and Build Texas plan, 284; candidates for, 286–287, 292; criticism of, 259; elections, 294, 295; and Hobby campaigns, 260; and Perot reforms, 257; and Republican ideology, 351; swearing in of, 298
book and theater reviews: and Diana, 51–52, 58, 80, 83, 165; and Hobby, 9, 34, 51–52; passion play, 34; and Will's biography, 52
boots, riding, 32

Bowen, Ralph, 13, 14
bow ties, 237, ix, vii, xi
boxing gear, 191, 268
Boy Scouts, 11, 17
Bradbury, Ray, 43
Braeswood Addition, 4, 7, 9, 10
Brammer, James, 72, 370
breakfasts: with children, 83; and Killer Bees, 196; with legislative leaders, 130, 160, 297; with Lewis and Clements, 297, 311
"Breaking the Poverty Cycle" report, 91–92. see also Interim Committee on Welfare Reform.
Brezinski, Zbigniew, 202
bribery, 207, 304–305, 371, 381
Bridger Wilderness, 84
Briscoe, Dolph Jr.: and Artesia Hall, 145–146; and campaigns, 99, 111, 115, 149–150, 173, 182; and Carter, 177; and constitutional reform, 151, 154, 163, 167, 183; and consumer protection bill, 137; and Daniel, 136; and Energy Advisory Council, 148; and ethics commission, 375; fundraising dinner, 119; and Hobby, 135, 136, 149–150, 151, 167, 266; and Hobby-Clayton Commission, 170, 174; and Hobby-Price dispute, 135–136; inaugurations, 123–125, 225; and LBJ's funeral, 129; and public-school finance, 162, 179; and special sessions, 135, 140–141, 179; and speed limit, 149; and taxes, 159, 177, 182–183; and Texas Energy Advisory Council, 180; and utility regulation, 164–165; youth-care facilities, 146; and zero-based budgeting, 142
Briscoe, Dolph Sr., 135
Briscoe, Janey, 119, 123–124, 125, 145, 177
Bristol, George, 189
broadcast properties: Hobby & Catto (H&C) Communications, 317, 319, 322–324, 356; KDFW-TV, 95; KLEE-TV, 29–30; KPRC-TV and Radio, 3, 7, 10, 12–13, 29–30, 31, 42, 58, 68–69, 107, 166, 180, 204, 323–324; KSAT-TV, 172, 322; KTRK-Radio, 7; WTLV-TV (WLAC) Nashville station, 171–172, 204
Brooke Field hospital, 18
Brooks, Chet: campaign dinner, 290; dual primaries and Killer Bees, 193, 196, 198; and Hobby, 131, ix, xii; and Human Resources Committee, 207; and workers' compensation, 307; and youth-care facility reform, 160
Brooks, Jack, 201
brothel, 114, 390
Brown, Alice, 69, 75–76
Brown, Buster, 264, 386
Brown, George R.: and constitutional reform, 167; as donor, 150; and Huntland Farm, 46; and labor

movement, 73; at LBJ Ranch, 69, 75–76; and Oveta, 205; and Rice University, 78, 371; and unions, 73
Brown, Herman, 46, 78
Brown, Reagan, 215
Brownell, Herbert, 38
Brown Foundation, 349
Brown & Root Company, 28, 46, 49, 73
Brown v. Board of Education of Topeka, 51, 61
Bruce, A. D., 17
Bryant, John, 183, 194, 207
Bryce, Robert, 348
Buchwald, Art, 79
Buckley, William F. Jr., 35–36
budget, state: alternate revenue sources, 251; and Bullock, 276; and Clements, 187–188, 270–271; and constitutional amendments, 295, 297; crisis in, 259–260; deficits and shortfalls, 226, 232, 237–238, 250, 253, 256–257, 261–262, 276, 320–321; and education spending, 244; Hobby's expertise with, 184, 360; as legislature's primary work, 54, 248; Mosbacher and DHS, 313; and New Federalism plan, 234; and oil prices, 158–159, 174, 256–257, 259–260, 268; prison appropriations, 299; process of, 138, 140; and rainy day emergency fund, 173, 179, 274, 295, 354; and Ramsey, 54; revenue task force, 320–321; and Seventieth Legislature, 269–273, 287; and Seventy-First Legislature, 303; and Sixty-Eighth Legislature, 232, 234–235; and Sixty-Seventh Legislature, 209; special item funding, 346, 350–351, 352, 354; surplus in, 158–159, 173, 174, 287, 296, 297; teaching on, 327; and Toomey, 270–271; tuition and user fees, 253. *see also* appropriations; employees, state; taxes.
Budget and Planning Office, 188
budget-making process, 138, 140
Build Texas plan, 274, 282–283, 284
Bullock, Bob: and Big Bend Ranch, 292–293; and blue laws, 251; and budget, 250, 268, 271, 276, 296, 297; campaigns and elections of, 216, 223, 265, 313, 316; and constitutional reform, 163; and Dukakis campaign, 290; and economic recovery, 287; and education reform, 243, 247, 248; and energy council, 180–181; and Hobby, 282, 340, x, xii; as lieutenant governor, 317, 391; and redistricting, 212; as state comptroller, 215; and state employees, 314; and Texas Center for Superconductivity, 336
Bush, Barbara, 349
Bush, George H. W.: and abortion, 310; and Aspen Institute, 315–316; and dual primaries, 191–192, 193; inaugurations, 187; and performing arts center, 349; and *Post* endorsement, 97; presidential campaigns, 191, 288, 292, 294, 324, 384; senate race, 110
Bush, George W., 328–329, 340, 350
business lobby: and higher education, 263; and Hobby, 151, 180, 266, 336, xi; and initiative and referendum proposal, 209; and prisons, 250; and workers' compensation, 237, 301, 302, 304, 306, 307
busing, 109, 112
bust, bronze, 317, 365, xiii
Butler, George, 49
Butler, Joe Kelly, 248
Butler & Binion, 72, 100
Butt, Charles, 150
Buttrell, Jean, 66

C

Cain, Clarence, 145–146
Calaway, Jim, 289, 290
California, 23, 45
Calvert, Robert, 124
cameraman, 42
campaign contributions, corporate, 111
campaign laws, 129, 304
campaigns, presidential: of 1988, 288–289, 293–294; Bush *vs.* Clinton, 324, 325; Carter, 172–173, 191–192, 202, 204–205; and dual primaries, 191–192; Eisenhower, 36; FDR *vs.* Willkie, 11–12; Jackson, 292; Kennedy, 65; Nixon *vs.* Humphrey, 79–80; Nixon *vs.* McGovern, 119; and Perot, 384
campaigns and elections: advertising, 100, 110, 114, 219, 220–221; awkward candidate, 103–104; and Black voters, 103, 222; and Build Texas plan, 282–283; and Bullock, 316; campaign for lieutenant governor, 89–116; campaign staff, 100, 259; campaign strategy, 91, 100–101, 112–114, 266–268; college campuses, 108–109, 110; coordinated campaign, 216–218; and corporate contributions, 111; crisis of confidence, 102; for dean, 340–341; debates, 112–113, 221–222; and debates, 112–113; decision and preparing to run for office, 74–75, 89–90, 92–93, 279–281; dislike of campaigning, 104, 281, 325–326; dual primaries, 191–200; and DUI, 157; election results analysis, 52–53; and foxhunting, 278–279; fundraising for, 114, 214, 219, 250, 260; hand-shaking tours, 54, 104; headquarters of, 117, 119, 123; Hobby's gubernatorial campaign, 149, 173, 240–241, 266–268, 278–280, 387; and local volunteers, 109; name recognition, 93, 105–106, 213, 219–220, 260; one-stop shopping counties, 114–115; postcards, 114; press conferences, 95, 97, 150, 206, 279–280; re-election

campaigns, 150–151, 155, 181–182, 185, 212–223, 260–261; "Rose Garden strategy," 267; runoff elections, 109, 110–115, 215; Sharpstown Bank Scandal and anti-corruption candidates, 94, 96, 99; themes and slogans, 99–100, 102–103, 214, 267–268; at universities, 112; US Senate ambitions, 291, 294. *see also* campaigns, presidential.
Campbell, George, 144
Camp Rio Vista, 13
Camp Spring, 11
Caperton, Kent: and anti-crime plan, 300; and blank checks, 304–305; and budget, 263; and Build Texas plan, 282; and Clements, 270; and committee assignments, 252; and education reform, 246; election to Senate, 207; and Hobby, 307, 325, viii; on Hobby, 105, 157, 208–209, 233, xi; and lame-duck nominations, 227; and public utilities, 238; on Strake, 213; and tort law reform, 273–274; and workers' compensation, 301, 302–303, 304, 306
Capitol building, 228–232, 290, 383
Cargill, Bob: as Hobby's pilot, 107–108, 109, 114, 182, 213, 220, 291; on Hobby's reelection plans, 256; press spokesman, 122, 259; and Richards, 328–329
Carpenter, Les, 48
Carpenter, Liz, 48, 258
Carr, Waggoner, 93–94, 146
Carriker, Steve, 297, 388
Carrillo, O. P., 169–170
cars, 76, 83, 149, 238, 328
Carter, Amon Jr., 79
Carter, Amon Sr., 71
Carter, Jimmy: and Briscoe, 173, 183; and Deng's visit, 189; and dual primaries, 191, 192; energy policies of, 180–181; and Hobby, 173, 205; inauguration of, 177; presidential elections, 172–173, 191, 192, 202, 204–205; visit to Houston, 183; and Weddington, 258; and zero-based budgeting, 142
"Casting Pearls" column, 28–29
Catholics and Catholic Church, 94, 221
Catto, Heather, 356, 394
Catto, Henry: career of, 315, 356; Colorado ranch, 84; death of, 394; and H&C, 290, 323; and Hobby, 106, 125; and KSAT-TV, 322; marriage of, 73; profile of, 79; and Republican Party, 80, 98; and Thatcher, 315–316
Catto, Jessica Oveta Hobby: birthdays, 37; career of, 73, 356; childhood of, 9, 10–11, 15, 16, 17; Colorado ranch, 84; death of, 356, 394; and Democratic Party, 80, 356; education of, 11; and Eisenhower, 36–38; and family businesses, 172, 240, 241, 290, 322–323; and father, 68, 69; and Hobby, 47, 106, 125, 356; and Hobby Foundation, 49; and horses,
84; marriage of, 73; and mother, 38, 331; and Nixon, 49; profile of, 79; and Thatcher, 315–316; and *Washington Journalism Review*, 322, 356
Catto & Catto, 322
censorship, 42, 72, 370
census, 353, 354
centennials, 8, 230, 290
Center for Advance Studies in Astronomy, 346
Center for Public Service, 347
Center on Ethics and Leadership, Elizabeth D. Rockwell, 354
Central Intelligence Agency (CIA), 44, 48, 77, 370–371
Certified Public Manager programs, 347, 352–353, 355
Chambers, Delores, x
Chambers, James, 77–78
chandelier, 229–230
Chandler, Norman, 38
Chandler, Otis, 79
change, fear of, 167–168
Channel 2 Television Company, 322
Chaplin, Charlie, 39–40
Chappell, David, 100
Chatham Hall, 44, 46
checks, 113, 304
chemistry set, 17
Cherry, Bill, 32
Chicken Ranch, 114, 390
child abuse, 113–114, 142–147, 277
childcare facilities, 142–147, 159, 178
child support, 92
China, People's Republic of, 58, 189, 202
Chisolm, Anne, 156
choirboys, 19
Christ Church Cathedral, 32, 68–69, 86
christening ceremony, 16
Christian, George: and Build Texas plan, 282; as campaign advisor, 220, 221, 267, 281; and DUI charge, 156; on fiscal issues, 285; and LBJ, 95; and McDonald Observatory, 344
Christian Moral Majority, 87
Christie, Joe: campaign of, 93, 101, 102, 110; on Oveta, 108; and Richards, 217; and unions, 99
Christmas, 16, 17, 86, 356
Chu, Paul, 336
Churchill, Winston, 52
cigarette tax, 245, 254, 312, 314
Cisneros, Henry, 278, 292, 316, 325, 326
Citizens Conference on Ethics in Government, 132–133
citizenship rights, 152

City Coliseum, 125
Civil Rights Act, 69
Civil War, 44, 45, 64
Clark, Allen, 221
Clark, Ed, 150
Clark, Guy, 349
Clark, Harley, 298
Clark, James A., 52
Clark, Roy, 172
class president, 26
Claydesta Communications, 316
Clayton, Bill W.: bribery indictment, 207, 381; and Carter inauguration, 177; and Clements, 188–189; and constitutional reform, 162–163, 167; and drinking-age bill, 208; and dual-primary bill, 191–192, 194; and education finance, 179; elected Speaker, 158, 187, 207; and gasoline tax, 183; and Hobby-Clayton Commission, 170, 180; and Jones, 198; and redistricting, 212; and tax reductions, 177, 182–183; and Texas A&M, 226, 227; and utility regulation, 164
Clayton, Phillip "Tubby," 30, 31
Clements, William P. "Bill": and abortion, 273; and Big Bend Ranch, 292–293; breakfast meetings, 269–270, 311; and budget, 188–189, 211, 272, 296, 314; and Build Texas plan, 274; campaigns and elections, 182, 216, 218, 223, 263–265, 270, 276–277; and Capitol centennial, 290; and Collins, 218; criticism of, 269; as deputy secretary for defense, 387; and drinking-age bill, 208; and dual primaries, 193; and government size, 211; and Helen Farabee's death, 293; and higher education, 277–278; and Hobby, 187–188, 194, 201, 210–211, 266, 268, 269–275, 276–277, 281, 282, 297, 324, x, xii; and Hobby Anti-Crime plan, 300; vs. Hutchison, 193; impeachment threat, 277; inaugurations, 187, 225; initiative and referendum law, 187, 194, 209; and judge selection, 310; and Killer Bees, 198, 200; lame-duck appointments, 226–227, 297, 382; and oil industry, 270; opposing income tax, 297, 310, 314; and Pemex oil-well blowout, 201–202, 223; and Pope, 224; and prairie chickens, 271; and prisons, 299–300; and public-school finance, 299, 310, 311–312, 313, 315; and redistricting plan, 212; SMU football scandal, 277; and Strake, 218; and Texas Energy Plan, 201; and unemployment insurance, 214; and veto power, 277; and war on drugs, 209, 244; wiretapping bill, 209–211; and women's shelter, 217; and workers' compensation, 301–303, 305–307
Clements High School, 338
climate change, 148

Clinton, William J. "Bill," 204, 324, 325, 384
Clower, Ron, 160, 164, 194, 195–196, 205, 207
Coast Guard, US, 201–202
Cohen, George, 12
coin flip, 208
Cold War, 42, 47, 48, 57–58
Cole, Allyce Tinsley, 35
Coleman, Garnet, 359
College and University Coordinating Board, 138, 159, 227, 353–354. *see also* education, higher.
College of William and Mary, 142
colleges and universities: campaigning at, 108–109, 110; historically Black, 322; and naval training, 42–43; and Texas Coordinating Board, 138. *see also* education, higher; Higher Education Coordinating Board, Texas; specific institutions.
Collins, James "Jim," 215–216, 218, 223
Collins, Michael, 20–21, 366–367
colonias, 261, 284, 303–304
color barrier, football, 181
Columbia University, 36, 74
commencement address, 320
commissions, state: appointments to, 153, 163, 314; Banking Commission, 3; ethics commission, 132; government by, 152; Hobby-Clayton Commission, 170, 174, 177–178; Public Utility Commission, 159, 164, 232, 238; Sunset Advisory Commission, 178, 238; Texas Employment Commission, 214, 238; Texas Highway Commission, 149; Texas Parks and Wildlife Commission, 292–293, 326–327; Texas Railroad Commission, 118. *see also* constitutional reform.
Committee for the Preservation of Methodism, 40
Committee of the Whole Senate, 161–162, 246, 302–303, 312
Committee on Administration, 231
Committee on Constitutional Amendments, 65. *see also* constitutional reform.
committees, Senate: Administration Committee, 122, 175, 176; Affairs Committee, 193; appointments to, 118, 122–123, 127, 159, 252, viii; authority of, 137–138; Committee on Constitutional Amendments, 65; Consumer Affairs Committee, 206–207; Criminal Jurisprudence Committee, 209; critique of, 139–140; Economic Development Committee, 122, 123, 232; Education Committee, 128, 161–162, 232, 247, 251–252, 257, 312, 353–354; and ethics reform, 132–133, 151; Finance Committee, 122, 236, 248, 252, 263, 287, 300–301, 321, 346; Higher Education Committee, 353–354; and Hobby, 122–123, 130–131, 159, 177, 206–207, 232–233, 251–252, 325; Human Resources Committee, 207;

Jurisprudence Committee, 122, 123, 134, 207; and lieutenant governor, 118, 122; meetings with chairs, 160, 228, 269; Natural Resources Committee, 122; Rules Committee, 123; Schnabel investigation, 175, 176; State Affairs Committee, 122, 131, 159–160, 193, 232; talent *vs.* party, 232–233; and Truan, 325; and Uribe, 252; Vocational Rehabilitation, 76; Ways and Means Committee, 188; welfare reform committee, 91; working of, 130
Communion service, 25
Communism, 49, 57, 77, 189
competency tests, teacher, 245, 248, 264
compromises, 131, 134, 227, 246–247
computer industry, 252–253, 272
concert, Royal Albert Hall, 31
concerts, open air, 24
Connally, John: and bribery, 371; campaigns of, 191–192, 199; and dual primaries, 191–192; and Hobby, 74; inaugurations, 187, 225; and IRS, 192; and Nixon, 105; and revenue task force, 320–321; and Texas Democratic Party, 65, 215; and University of Texas Board of Regents, 226, 227; *Vogue* profile, 79; and Will's death, 68
Connally, Nellie, 79
Connally, Tom, 5
Connally, Wayne: and campaign contributions, 111; campaign of, 93, 101, 102, 105, 108, 112–114; and Nixon, 109–110; and Sharpstown Bank Scandal, 113; and voting age, 112
consensus, importance of, 131
conservationists, 251. *see also* environmentalism.
Constitution, Texas: of 1876, 118, 152–153; and budget deficits, 257; and citizenship rights, 152; constitutional convention, 152–155; and legislative sessions, 130; reform of, 136; and structure of state government, 126, 152; and tax bills, 235; and term lengths, 150. *see also* amendments, constitutional; constitutional reform.
constitutional reform: amendments for, 162–163, 166–168, 378; Committee on Constitutional Amendments, 65; constitutional convention, 141, 151–155; and Hobby, 108, 118, 151, 174–175
consumer protection and Consumer Protection Act, 136–137, 139, 140, 200–201
contractors, 190
controversy, book, 36
Cooper, Samuel Bronson, 2
Cooper, Willie Chapman, 2
Corpus Christi Caller-Times, 114
Corpus Christi State University, 303
corruption: bribery indictment, 207, 381; and Pasadena city hall, 71–72, 370; and Pilgrim, 304–305;

Pilgrim and blank checks, 304–305; Sharpstown Bank Scandal, 93–100, 110, 131–132, 138; and sunshine laws, 132. *see also* ethics.
Cortes, Ernesto, 304
Cotton Bowl games, 27
counterintelligence, 48
County Galway, 85
County Indigent Health Care, 253–254
county ordinances, 163
Court of Criminal Appeals, 163
courts, federal: and affirmative action, 338–339; Ferrar's lawsuit, 145–146; prisons and mental health facilities, 235, 250, 269–270, 299; and public-school funding, 128, 298; and Sharpstown Bank Scandal, 93. *see also* lawsuits.
Cowles, Gardner, 79
crash, plane, 8
Crawford, Walter, 1–2
Creighton, Douglas, 241
Creighton, Tom: as ally, 121, 131, 140, 207; breakfasts with, 160; and constitutional reform, 154, 163; and Economic Development Committee, 123; on Hobby, 130–131, 134, 165; and Hobby's DUI charge, 156; and Senate rules, 127
crime and crime prevention, 178, 299–300, 389. *see also* prisons and prison reform.
Croix de Guerre, 44
crop, riding, 83
Cross, Renee, 353, 354
Crowther, Jim: and campaign funds, 219; and H&C, 290, 319, 322; and Hobby businesses, 204, 240; and *Houston Post,* 240; and University of Houston, 332
Crusade for Freedom, 77
Cullen, Hugh Roy, 332, 333
Cullinan, Joseph, 27
Culp, Emma Hoover, 3, 15, 16, 330
Culp, Isaac "Ike," 3, 83–84, 330
Culp, Lynn, 6, 180
Culp, Oveta. *see* Hobby, Oveta Culp.
culture warriors, 273, 360
cum laude society, 26
Cunningham, William H. "Bill": and higher education funding, 262, 272; and Hobby, 317–318, 335; on Hobby, 321, 327; and hunting trips, 327; as racquetball partner, 315, 329; and Southwest Airlines, 327; and telescope, 342, 343, 344–345, 346
Cutrer, Lewis, 61–62

D

Dalí, Salvador, 23
Dallas: and Build Texas Plan, 282–283; campaign

debates, 112, 221; and Clements, 259; and Electronic Data Systems, 91, 244; Kennedy assassination, 65–67, 68; and plane crash, 8; redistricting, 211–212; and Sharpstown Bank Scandal, 93

Dallas Morning News: and Dealy, 71; and Hobby, 4, 103–104, 111, 135, 269; and Hobby's political ambitions, 74, 89, 266; *vs. Houston Post,* 71; on journalists in office, 117–118; and op-ed column, 327; and Vietnam War coverage, 77–78

Daniel, J. Neil, 99

Daniel, Price Jr.: ancestors of, 375; and Artesia Hall, 143; campaigns of, 151, 158, 182; and constitutional reform, 151–155; death of, 379; elected Speaker of the House, 132; and ethics reform, 133, 375; and Hobby, 132, 134–136; and Oveta, 126; and utility regulation, 164

Daniel, Price Sr., 37, 51, 124, 369

Darcy, Thomas, 72

Davidson, David, 261, 264

Davis, Bob, 188, 270

Davis, John: at Bill Hobby Day, x; dinner party, 129; and Hobbys, 63–64, 241–242, 315; and *Houston Post,* 52; letters to, 23–24; as mentor, 21, 24–25, 265; Mexico trip, 27; and St. Albans, 20, 21

day-care centers, free, 92

Dealy, Joe, 77–78

Dealy, Ted, 71

DeBakey, Michael, 79, 214

debate: campaigns, 112–113, 221–222; in legislature, 127, 130, 162, vii; Tower Hill, 47

Deceptive Trade Practices Act, 136–137

de Gaulle, Charles, 57

demagoguery, 40, 221

de Menil, Dominique, 79

de Menil, John, 79, 80–81

Democratic National Committee, 289–290

Democratic National Conventions, 3, 49, 205, 249, 290, 291–292, 349

Democratic Party: and Carter, 172–173; and Christie, 102; and Connally, 226; conservative faction of, 54, 151, 154–155, 191–192, 193, 199, 250, xii; and coordinated campaign, 216–218, 223; criticism of Hobby, 151; and delegate selection, 192–193; and dual-primary plan, 191–192, 193; and Eisenhower, 36; fundraising for, 155, 224, 289–290; and Hobby, 80, 97–98, 99, 119, 289–292, 324–325; and Jessica, 356; and Jones, 27; liberal faction of, 52, 54, 94, 102, 151, 154–155, 193, 215; and Nixon, 226; and Oveta, 3, 11, 79–80; as prairie chickens, 271; and Ramsey, 54; and redistricting, 211–212; and Republican Party, 205, 215, 250, 267; and Sharpstown Bank Scandal, 94; and suburban voters, 56; and tax increases, 271; and Texas, 325, xii; and unions, 28; and Victory Fund, 224, 289–290; and Will Hobby, 3, 11. *see also* Democratic National Conventions; politics.

Deng Xiaoping, 189, 202

Department of Corrections, 247

Department of Health, Education and Welfare (HEW), 38–39, 48, 76

Department of Human Services (DHS), 313

Department of Justice, US, 212

Department of Mental Health and Mental Retardation, 145, 293

Department of Public Safety (DPS), 144, 197–198, 200, 209

Department of Public Welfare, 91, 143–147, 160–161

deposit insurance, 93–94

Depression, Great, 7

desegregation: and affirmative action, 338–339; and busing, 109, 112; color barrier, football, 181; and lunch counters, 61–63; and public schools, 51; and Rice, 35. *see also* racism; segregation.

Dewey, Thomas, 37

de Zavala, Lorenzo, 351

Dickens, Charles, 39

Dickson, Temple, 288, 294, 295, 297

dinner parties, 49, 129, 329

diplomacy, 56–58

Dirty Thirty, 94

disabled persons, 76, 91–92

disarmament, call for, 57

Distinguished Service Medal, 22

Doctors for Freedom, 40

Doggett, Lloyd: and Clements, 227; and Consumer Affairs Committee, 206–207; and disruption in Senate, 190; election of, 158, 377; and farmworkers compensation, 236; Killer Bees and dual-primary bill, 195–196; and public utility regulation, 164; and Schnabel indictments, 175; and tax reductions, 183

Dorn, Edwin, 341

draft law, 33

drinking age, legal, 138, 207–208, 232, 238, 255. *see also* alcohol.

drugs, war on, 209, 244. *see also* marijuana.

drugstores, breakfast at, 83

drunk driving (DUI/DWI), 155–157, 181, 232, 377

dual-primary bills, 191–200, 204, 291, 380

Dublin Horse Show, 33

Duckworth, Allen, 74

Dukakis, Michael, 289, 290, 292

Duncan, Charles, 321, 384

Dundas, Robert, 62

duplex, Austin, 166, 228, 229, 332

E

Earle, Ronnie, 305
Easter egg hunts, 86
Eberly, Carolyn, 342
Eberly, Robert E., 342, 345
Eckhardt, Bob, 73–74, 129, 204, 205
Eckhardt, Celia, 205
economic aid and Cold War, 58
Economic Development Committee, 122, 232
economy, national, 223, 324
economy, Texas: and bonds, 274; and Build Texas plan, 274; diversification of, 252, 260, 287; and education, 225, 245; and oil and gas, 75, 225, 245, 264; and prison reform, 235; recession and recovery, 223, 226, 264, 287; and technology sector, 75, 225, 240, 252–253, 270, 272, 287
Edge Park Stables, 84, 259
editorials: and AFL, 28; anti-union, 28; endorsing Hobby, 106–107, 373; and Hobby, 73, 80, 166; and *Houston Post*, 72, 73, 80, 106–107; and LBJ, 69–70; and Nixon, 97–98; op-ed column, 327, 338, 350–351
editors: Hobby and *Houston Post*, 51–52, 58, 80, 83, 165; and *Houston Post*, 55–56, 60; *Thresher*, 27–28, 34–35; and Woestendiek, 69, 72
education: and anti-crime program, 300; bilingual, 138, 139, 161; and campaigning, 215; importance of, 74–75, 124, 244, 270, 320, 338; as partisan issue, 360; sex, 351; vocational, 245. *see also* education, higher; public-school funding; schools, public; teaching.
education, higher: and Clements, 188, 277; criticism of TSU, 322; and economy, 225, 245; and governor's veto power, 277, 350; Higher Education Coordinating Board, 138, 159, 227, 353–354; and Hobby, 225, 335, 360, 387, 393; and Legislative Budget Board, 268; Permanent School Fund, 150, 178, 262; and Perry, 350–351; Rice football program, 321; and state budget, 206, 211, 253, 261, 263, 269, 270–272, 313, 321; and Texas Education Code, 350; tuition and fees, 253, 255, 321; as University of Houston chancellor, 332–340; university systems, 303. *see also* colleges and universities; education; specific institutions.
education commissioner, state, 314
Education Committee: and education reform, 247, 251–252, 257; and Hobby Center, 353–354; and Mauzy, 128, 161–162; and Parker, 232, 312
education reform. *see* public-school funding; Select Committee on Public Education (Perot reforms).

Edwards, Chet, 232, 273, 290, 307, 312
Eisenhower, Dwight D. "Ike": and desegregation, 51; endorsement of, 97; and "Flight to Peace" tour, 56–58; and HEW, 38; honoring of, 314; inauguration of, 36–38; and Oveta, 35, 36–38, 97, x; and Shivers, 54; and suburban voters, 56
elections. *see* campaigns and elections.
elections, school board, 52–53
Electronic Data Systems (EDS), 91, 243–244
Elkins, James A., 12, 167
Ellis, Rodney: election of, 312; on Hobby, 197, 233, 339–340; and Hobby campaigns, 103, 267, 312; and Hobby Center, 354, 359; and telescope funding, 346
El Paso Gas company, 349
Ely, Joe, 349
embargo, oil, 140–141, 148
emergency fund. *see* rainy day fund.
employees, state: and budget, 261, 263–264, 313; and Hobby-Clayton Commission, 174; layoffs and number of, 174, 263, 313; pay raises for, 159, 173, 261, 264; and workers' compensation fund, 261
Employment Commission, 214, 238
Energy Advisory Council, 147–149, 180–181
energy industry: and China, 202; coastal drilling, 148, 201–202; and conservation, 148–149; and Democratic Party, 192; and Energy Advisory Council, 147–149, 180–181; and energy crisis, 147–149, 180–181; and Hobby campaign, 108; national policies, 147–149, 180–181, 202; nuclear energy, 147, 148; oil embargo, 140–141, 148; oil-well blowout, 201–202; and pollution, 137; price controls, 173, 181; and Quayle, 294; and speed limit, 140–141; state budget and economy, 158–159, 174, 250, 256–257, 259–260, 268; and Strake, 213; and university financing, 159; utility regulation, 165
England, 30–33, 284, 315
entitlement, 82–83
environmentalism: and fossil fuels, 148; and Hobby campaigns, 92, 97, 112, 140; and pollution controls, 92, 151; and water supply, 251
Episcopalian Church: and Hobby family, 19, 32, 68–69, 86–87, 330–331, 357; St. Albans, 18, 19–20
equality. *see* desegregation and integration; women's rights.
Equal Rights Amendment, 258
ethics: as campaign issue, 110; enforcement of, 132–133, 375; and Hobby, 114, 375; honesty and honestly slogan, 99–100, 102–103, 107, 110; and journalists, 87–88, 117; and legislative process, 96; and Lewis, 235, 383; in politics, 128; reform bills, 132–134, 136, 140, 151; and Schnabel, 175–176;

sunshine laws, 132, 138. *see also* Sharpstown Bank Scandal.
evangelicals, 160–161, 221
Evans, Donald, 340
evolution, 44, 351
exchange program, 328
executive sessions, 65
exit exams, 248, 257
exposé and anti-Communism, 71–72
extra editions, 66–67

F
Fainter, John, 228
Farabee, Helen: death of, 293; and Hobby, 100, 101, 158, 299; and indigent healthcare, 254; in Ireland, 283
Farabee, Ray: and budget deficit, 263; and Build Texas plan, 282; and campaigns, 100, 213, 220; and Clements, 227, 270; and education reform, 246; and Hart, 288; and Hobby, 283, 288, 386, x; on Hobby, 237; and prison reform, 233; as racquetball partner, 315, 329; and Senate, 158, 288, 298; and State Affairs Committee, 232; and water plan, 256; and worker's compensation, xii
Farenthold, Frances "Sissy," 94, 99, 102, 111, 115
farm management, 46
farmworkers compensation, 200, 236–237, 252, 255. *see also* workers' compensation.
Farrar, Dale, 146
Farrar, Joseph Davis, 142–146, 376
Federal Bureau of Investigation (FBI), 48, 209
Federal Communications Commission (FCC), 171–172
Federal National Mortgage Association (Fannie Mae), 200
Federal Security Agency (FSA), 36–37, 38
Felder, Dell, 336
Ferguson, James "Pa," 2, 99–100, 111, 128, 170
Ferguson, Miriam A. "Ma," 224
Ferraro, Geraldine, 249
ferryboat, 68
Fifty-Sixth Calvary Brigade, 4
filibusters: blocking of, 138–139; Brown and tax increase, 264; and constitutional reforms, 162; longest, 178; and Mauzy, 179; Sarpalius and farmworkers compensation, 236; and tenure bill, 140; Washington and tort reform bill, 275
Finance Committee, Senate: and Aiken, 122; and budget deficit, 263; and Hobby Anti-Crime Plan, 300–301; and Jones, 287; and Leedom, 248; and revenue task force, 321; and telescope funding, 346; and Uribe, 236, 252
financial statements, 134

fire, Capitol, 228–230, 383
"Fiscal Implications of the Property Tax Constitution," 163
fishing industry and water crisis, 251
Fitzgibbon, Bill, 339
flags, 48, 68, 69, 293, 331
Flawn, Peter, 252
"Flight to Peace" tour, 56–58
flood control, 250–251, 274
Flournoy, Jim, 114
flu epidemic, 7
Foley's department store, 62
Fondren, Gene, 193–194
Fondren Library, 347
Food Stamp Program, 92, 214
football: Baby Blue, 20; and budgets, 321, 345; Cotton Bowl, 27; and "No Pass, No Play," 244–245; and Rice, 27, 28, 321; and Southern Methodist University scandal, 277, 387; varsity letter, 26; Westbrook and color barrier, 181. *see also* athletics.
Ford, O'Neil, 101–102
Ford, Powell & Carson, 231
Ford Foundation exchange program, 328
foreign relations, 56–58
Forest Home, 45–46, 47, 82, 84, 329
Fort Hobby, 78–79, 241
Fort Hood, 17
foxhunting: and courtship, 46; and gubernatorial campaign, 278–279, 291; in Ireland, 34, 85, 181, 241–242, 284; Ivins on, 291; passion for, 48, viii; and Scarteen Hunt, 242; and Texas Parks and Wildlife Commission, 326. *see also* horses.
franchise taxes, 276, 308–309, 310. *see also* taxes.
Franco, Francisco, 57
freedom, 35, 328
free enterprise system, 27
fuel shortages, 140–141, 148
Fuermann, George, 80
fundamentalists, 160–161, 178, 221
fundraisers and fundraising: ACLU, 221–222; for Bentsen, 294; and blank checks, 304–305; for Clinton-Gore campaign, 325; for Dukakis, 290; and Hay, 271; for Hobby campaigns, 119, 150, 155, 214, 250, 260, 264, 267; and Hobby Center for Public Policy, 353–354, 359; for Richards, 296; for telescope, 343–347; Texas Victory Fund, 224, 289–290; and University of Houston, 334

G
Galveston, 28, 64–65, 84, 185
Galveston News and Galveston Tribune, 64
Gammage, Bob, 136–137, 164

Gardner, William "Bill," 50, 72
gas, natural. *see* energy industry.
gasoline taxes, 234, 246–247
gavel, 95, 125, 317
Georg-August University, 346
Georgetown University, 44, 47
German Blitz, 33
Gibson, Kate Hobby: birth of, 63, 80; and Capitol fire, 228–229; career of, 393–394; childhood of, 82–83, 184; graduation of, 238; and horses, 211, 228; and London, 283; and performing arts center, 349
Glasgow, Bob, 290, 301, xii
Glen Haven house, 6, 9, 10
Glenn, John, 228, 241, 249
Glenwood Cemetery, 330–331, 357
gloves, boxing, 191
Godfrey, Lee, 100, 156
Goldenson, Leonard, 76
Goldwater, Barry, 69, 70
Goltz, Gene, 71–72, 370
goodwill tour, 172
Gordon, Boris B, 6
Gore, Al, 289, 325, 349–350
government: by commissions, 152; compromise *vs.* partisanship, 360; federal *vs.* state, 75; and problem solving, 97, 112, 315, 317, 355; reverence for, 233; transparency in, 132
Government Club, 25–26
governor, powers of, 126, 151–152, 153, 314, 350
governors, Texas. *see* Briscoe, Dolph Jr.; Clements, William P. "Bill"; Perry, Rick; Richards, Ann; Smith, Preston; White, Mark.
Graham, Katharine, 323
Gramm, Phil, 254, 280, 324
Granato, Jim, 352–355, 359
Granberry, Jim, 157
Grandcamp explosion, 66
Great Society, 77
Greene, Joan, 344
Green Fields Preparatory School for Boys, 13–14, 15
Greenhill, Joe, 151, 187
Greensboro protests, 61
Gridiron Show, 49
Gronchi, Giovani, 56
Gulf War, 315, 324
guns, 304

H
Hagan, Tom, 122
Hall, Anthony, 267
Hall, Ralph, 93, 100, 101, 102, 110
Hance, Kent, 100, 158, 377, x

Hancock, J. D., 66
Hannah, John, 215
Hansen, Matt, 228–230
Harding, Warren, 215
Harper, Dick, xi
Harrington, Jim, 252
Harris, Ike, 232, 264, 304, 305
Harris, Jack: broadcast of *William P. Hobby* launch, 68; and H&C, 319; and Houston Post Company, 71; meetings with, 204; and television stations, 29, 171–172, 240; and Will's funeral, 69
Harris County Commissioner, 68, 339
Hart, Gary, 249, 288–289
Hart, Weldon, 52
Harte, Ed, 84, 114
Harte, Houston, 71, 84, 150, 371
Hasie, Monte, 298
Hay, Betty Jo, 282
Hay, Jess: fundraising dinners, 289, 293; and higher education funding, 262–263, 271–272, 321; and Hobby, 105–106, 278, 282, xi; and Santa Rita Award, 256; and University of Texas Board of Regents, 227, 277
Hayden Planetarium, 23
Haynes, Richard, 170
hazing, campus, 270
H&C Incorporated. *see* Hobby & Catto (H&C) Communications.
healthcare: courses on policy, 319; indigent, 253–254, 255, 260, 293; and Medicaid, 91, 214, 303; mental health, 250, 274, 284; as partisan issue, 360; rural, 303; and workers' compensation, 301
Heatley, W. S., 99
Heitowit, Henry "Hank," 352
Heldrich, Andreas, 342
HemisFair '68, 79
Henry, O., 12
hepatitis, 29
Hermann, George, 9
Hermann Hospital, 53
Hermann Park, 9–10, 24, 283
Herring, Charles: and consumer protection bill, 137; and ethics reform, 133, 134; and Hobby, 131, 139, 140; and Jurisprudence Committee, 122
Hiatt, John, 349
Higher Education Coordinating Board, Texas, 138, 159, 227, 353–354. *see also* education, higher.
Hightower, George, 10
Hightower, Jack, 122, 151, 297, 377, x
Hightower, Jim: election of, 223, 265; and Hobby, 216; and Mauro, 294; politics of, 200, 215; and US Senate, 292

Highway Commission, 149
Highway Patrol, 195–196, 197–198, 200
highways, 109, 177, 234, 247
Hill, John: and constitutional reform, 151, 152, 163, 167; and consumer protection, 136, 137; and energy council, 180–181; governor campaign, 182, 185; inaugurations, 269; and lobby control bill, 134–135; on Schnabel case, 176; and telephone rates, 164; and youth-care facilities, 144, 145, 160
Hilton, Conrad, 38
history, 42, 47, 258, 351, 361
Hobby, Alfred, 361
Hobby, Andrew, 63, 80, 113, 185, 238, 389, 394
Hobby, Bill (William Pettus Hobby Jr.): birth of, 1, 4–5; career in journalism (*see* editorials; editors; *Houston Post*); career in legislature, xii (*see* campaigns and elections; legislative sessions); career in navy, 88; career in teaching (*see* teaching); campaigns for office (*see* campaigns and elections); alcohol abuse, 355–356; and Andrew, 113–114; and antiwar movement, 77; and Artesia Hall, 144–147; and Aspen Institute, 315–316; authority of, 208–209; and beaches, 211; and beard, 328; and Big Bend Ranch, 292–293; and Bill Hobby Day, 302, xi–xii; birthdays (*see* birthdays); book reviews, 52; on British people, 32, 33; and budget (*see* budget, state); and Capitol, 228–231, 290; cars and frugality of, 83, 149, 238, 328; as chancellor, 332–340; character of, 14, 20, 87–88, 103–104, 220, 233, 385, viii–xi; childhood of, 1–18, x; and children, 53, 80, 81–87; and CIA, 77; and Claydesta Communications, 316; and Clayton, 158; comedic writing, 23; and constitutional reform (*see* constitutional reform); courtship and wedding, 46–47; criticism of, 132, 140, 151; dating, 23; and demagoguery, 40, 221; and Democratic Party, 80, 97–98, 99, 119, 289–292, 324–325; and Deng, 189; and Diana, 44, 46–47, 159, 356–357; drinking and DUI charges, 155–157, 181, 355–356; education of, 11, 13–42, 47; and Energy Advisory Council, 147–149, 180–181; enjoyment of lieutenant governor's role, 131, 149, 150, 173; and family businesses (*see* Hobby & Catto (H&C) Communications; *Houston Post*); and father, 5, 10–11, 12–13, 15, 16, 47, 68–69; and filibusters, 138–139, 140, 178; on final legislative session, 296–297; gavel, 95, 125, 317; on government and solving problems, 97, 112, 233, 315, 317, 355; on graduation, 42; health of, 7, 13–14, 354; and Hobby Family Foundation, 49, 330, 344, 347–348; homesickness, 14; honesty and integrity, 96, 99–100, 133, 333, viii, xi; horses and foxhunting (*see* foxhunting); and horses and foxhunting (*see* horses); and Houston Public Library, 9; humor of, 104, 113, 125, 191, 222, 225, 241; as hunt master, 242; identity of, 74, 90, 106; and Ideson, 9; inaugurations, 123–125, 197, 224–226, 269; and interviews, 259, 385; and Ireland (*see* Ireland); and IRS, 97, 192; and Jordan royalty, 214; on journalism, 58–59, 72; Kennedy and Kennedy assassination, 63, 65–67, 90; and Killer Bees, 199–200, 205; and King, 176–177; on Korean War, 33; lame-duck term, 297–298; on laws and human behavior, 132, 210, 273; and LBJ School (*see* Lyndon B. Johnson School of Public Affairs (LBJ School)); as leader, 26, 61, 140, 233, 235; legacy of, 359–361; and legislative staff, 121–122; and mathematics (*see* mathematics); on Mattox, 279, 280; and media, 111, 259; mentors of, 21, 24–25, 53–54, 55, 118–119, 265; on mistakes, 195–196, 198, 199, 354; and mother, 11, 15, 16, 73, 85, 90, 106, 107–108, 314, 330, 331; and musicals, 84, 283, 345–349; on Naval Intelligence, 48; on newspapers' influence, 87–88; and Nixon, 119, 128–129; and oil-well blowout, 201–202; op-ed column, 327; as parliamentarian, 54–55, viii; and partisanship (*see* partisanship); and passion play, 34; on Perot reforms, 248; on Perry, 350–351; personal appearance of, 105, 114, 127–128, 140, 171, 220–221, 291, 329, xi; as political analyst, 58; political beliefs of, 11–12, 26, 28, 98, 112, 161, 199, 206, 213, 218–219, 254, 273, 310; popularity of, 237; president emeritus, 302, x, xi; and priesthood, 24–25, 26; public life, 61, 74, 79, 83, 91; and public-school funding (*see* public-school funding); as public speaker (*see* speaking, public); Pulitzer Prize jury, 74, 215; on racism and segregation, 35, 51, 294; and Reagan, 214; and Redistricting Board, 212; and Red Scare, 39–40; and Republicans, 324, 349, 351–352; requiem for *Houston Post,* 329–330; and revenue task force, 320–321; on rhetoric *vs.* solutions, 308–309; and Rice University, 27–41, 311, 347; rule for Senate, 190–191; salary, 334; and Santa Rita Award, 256; and Schnabel, 175–177; on secret executive sessions, 65; Senate allies, 121, 207, 232, 287, 288, 298, 306–307, 312, 377; smoking, 104, 373; and Southwest Airlines (*see* Southwest Airlines); spirituality and religion, 19, 24–25, 34, 86–87; and *St. Albans News,* 21; as strategist, 130–131, 138–139, 165, 207–208, 210, 232–234, vii (*see also* legislative sessions); and stutter, 13, 74–75, 104–105, viii; and taxes (*see* income tax, state); on taxes, 28–29; and telescope, 342–343, 344, 345; on television, 29, 104; testimony at Senate hearing, 65; and Texas Daily Newspaper Association, 87, 99; and *Thresher,* 27–28, 34–35,

39; travel (*see* travel and vacations); and unions, 99, 112, 151; and University of Houston, 332–340; as US Senate candidate, 325–326; and Valentis, 67; and Vietnam War, 77–78; on voting age, 112; on Waldock, 32; and welfare reform committee, 91–92; and Winant Volunteers, 30–31; and wiretapping, 159, 209–211; and World War II, 21–22; and zero-based budgeting, 142

Hobby, Diana Poteat Stallings: and abortion rights, 273, 310; and acting, 46; and Artesia Hall, 145; and Bill Hobby Day, ix, xii; and Capitol fire and restoration, 228, 229, 231; career of, 47–48, 51–52, 58, 80, 83, 87, 165; character of, 45, 46, 101; childhood of, 45–46; and children, 53, 80, 81–87; courtship and wedding, 46, 47; death of, 356–357; education of, 46, 47, 181; and father, 45, 81; health of, 69, 356; and Hobby campaigns, 106, 107, 108; horses and foxhunting, 46, 83–84, 94, 181; and Houston, 165–166; and husband, 44, 46, 47, 156–157, 356–357; inaugurations, 125, 129, 177, 187; and Johnsons, 76, 80; and Jordan royalty, 214; open-door policy of, 81–82; and Oveta, 85, 330, 331; as parent, 81, 82–83; and performing arts center, 348–349; public life of, 79, 83, 166; religion, 86; and Rice University, 181, 347; and Richards, 291; and telescope, 344; travel and vacations, 84, 184, 211, 241–242, 284, 286, 290, 315, 333; and Valentis, 67

Hobby, Dora Pettus, 1

Hobby, Edwin, 1, 64, 152, 374

Hobby, Janet, ix

Hobby, Jessica Oveta. *see* Catto, Jessica Oveta Hobby.

Hobby, Kate. *see* Gibson, Kate Hobby.

Hobby, Laura Poteat. *see* Beckworth, Laura Poteat Hobby.

Hobby, Marmaduke, 64

Hobby, Oveta Culp: birthdays, 9, 37; and Brown brothers, 46; career of, 3–4, 15–16, 36–37, 38, 48, x; on censorship, 40; character of, 4, 6, 85–86; childhood and education of, 3; and children's names, 9; and CIA, 77; and Communism, 49; death of, 330–331, 335; and Deng's visit, 189; and desegregation, 62–63; and Eckhardt, 205; and Eisenhower, 35, 36–38, 97, x; as grandmother, 83, 85–86; and H&C, 322–323; health of, 6, 17, 22–23, 239, 314; and Hobby campaigns, 106, 107–108, 114, 219; and Hobby Family Foundation, 347; honors and awards, 22, 125, 185; and horses, 84; and *Houston Post*, 3, 10, 49, 71, 73, 78, 80, 166, 240–241; and husband, 3, 4, 15, 16, 17, 68–69; inaugurations, 22, 36–38, 125, 187, 224; and Jones, 7; and LBJ, 37, 65, 67–68, 76, 95; as mother, 5–6, 9, 11, 16–17; and Murphy, 64; and Nixon, 49, 79–80, 119, 147; and PanAm flight, 79; and plane crash, 8; politics of, 3–4, 97–98; and Red Scare, 38–39; and religion, 19; and Rice University, 371, 390; riding accident, 6; and Robins, 81; and Roosevelts, 8; seclusion of, 329; and sister's funeral, 180; and son, 13, 32–33, 42, 43, 46–47, 49, 50, 156; and Special Studies Project, 51; and strapless dress, 38; and television stations, 166, 171–172; and unions, 28; and University of Houston, 332–333; and Vietnam, 77; wealth of, 392; and Will's biography, 52; and Woestendiek, 72

Hobby, Paul William: birth of, 63; and Bullock, 317; campaign for office, 393; childhood of, 68, 81–82, 85–86, 116; education of, 184, 238; on father, 14, 50, 157, 185, ix; and father's alcohol abuse, 355–356; and Hobby businesses and foundation, 241, 322, 323, 347; and Hobby Center for Public Policy, 353, 355; inaugurations, 225; and Krueger, 82; and lieutenant governor's apartment, 116; on parents, 47, 357; and performing arts center, 348–349

Hobby, William "Bill" Pettus Jr. *see* Hobby, Bill (William Pettus Hobby Jr.).

Hobby, William "Will" Pettus Sr.: auto tours, 53; and Briscoe, 135; and Brown brothers, 46; career of, 1–3, 10, x; character of, 2; death of, 68–69; and Democratic party, 3; and Diana, 46; education of, 1; and Eisenhower, 36–38; and eulogies, 69; as father, 5, 10–11, 12–13, 15, 16, 47, 68–69; and Ferguson, 111, 170; as grandfather, 68; health of, 17, 23, 52, 53, 58, 68; and horses, 84; and *Houston Post*, 10; and Jones, 7; and LBJ, 67–68; as lieutenant governor, 206; and mother, 6; and networking, 12; and Oveta, 3, 4, 15, 16, 17; and plane crash, 8; politics of, 28; portraits of, 125, 374; on public opinion, 262; and public-school funding, 128; and religion, 19; and Roosevelts, 8; and television, 29–30; and University of Houston, 332–333; and worker's compensation, 301

Hobby Anti-Crime Plan, 299–301, 303

Hobby & Catto (H&C) Communications, 290, 317, 319, 322–324, 356. *see also* broadcast properties.

Hobby Center for Public Policy, 351, 352–355, 359

Hobby Center for the Performing Arts, 348–349

Hobby-Clayton Commission, 170, 174, 177–178, 378

Hobby-Eberly Telescope, 342–347, 393

Hobby Family Foundation, 49, 77, 330, 344, 347–348, 371. *see also* philanthropy.

Hobby Redistricting Plan, 211–212

Hobby Rule, 157, 377

Hobby School of Public Affairs, 353–355, 359

Hobby's Math Camp, 333–334, 392

Hogg, James Stephen, 12, 118
Holcombe, Oscar, 12
holidays, 16, 17, 86, 356
Holloway Plan, 42–43
Holmegreen, Ginny. *See* Zimmerman, Ginny.
homes, family: Austin duplex, 166, 228, 229, 332; Braeswood Addition, 4, 9, 10; garage, 47; Huntingdon apartment, 320, 329, 330; Lamar Hotel, 6–7, 9; Remington Lane (Shadyside), 65, 85–86; South Boulevard home, 63–64, 79, 81–82, 205; Washington, DC, 17, 49
homestead protections, 152, 177
honestly slogan, 100, 102–103, 110. *see also* ethics.
Hong Kong, 256
honor council, 28
Hoover, Cordelia, 3
Hoover, Herbert, 38
Hopper, Hedda, 37
horse-race betting, 210, 238, 251, 255
horses: in childhood, 9–10, 14; and courtship, 46; and family, 83–84; horse shows, 33, 84, 211, 215, 290, 315; and Ireland's economy, 34; love of, 83–84, viii; and Oveta, 6; and political career, 215, 281; show jumping, 181; stables, 10, 84, 211, 259; Texas Hunter Jumper Association, 228; and Tiede, 259. *see also* foxhunting.
House Appropriations Committee, 176
House Bill 72. *see* Select Committee on Public Education (Perot reforms).
House of Representatives, Texas: and budget deficit, 263; Carrillo impeachment, 169–170; and consumer protection bills, 136–137; and dual-primary bill, 194–195; and education finance, 235; and ethics reform, 136; and indigent healthcare bill, 254; and Killer Bees, 198; and mortgage rate bill, 138–139; and Oveta, 125; passion driven, 131; and public-school funding, 161–162, 313, 314; and Ramsey, 53; and redistricting, 212; and Sharpstown Bank Scandal, 131–132; Speakers of the House (*see* Clayton, Bill W.; Daniel, Price Jr.; Lewis, Gib); tax bills, 232; and tax bills, 232, 235; and taxes, 183, 188, 264, 270; and utility regulation, 164; Ways and Means Committee, 188, 299; and workers' compensation, 302, 303, 305. *see also* legislature, Texas.
Houston, TX: childhood in, 4–13, 16; City Hall protests, 61; and Democratic National convention, 3; demographics and elections, 52; and desegregation, 61–63; economic boom of, 166; and Hobby family, 2–3, 6, 10, 12–13, 165–166; and *Houston Post*, 78–79, 329–330; and Hurricane Harvey, 355; and Kennedy, 65; library, 9; performing arts facility, 348–349; and Red Scare, 39–40; and Roosevelts, 8; school board elections, 52–53; Strake Jesuit High School, 94; and suburbs, 55–56; and Sugar Land, 337–338; and Texas Southern University, 312. *see also* Rice University; University of Houston.
Houston, William V., 28
Houston Chamber of Commerce, 61
Houston Chronicle: and Artesia Hall, 143; and Deng's visit, 189; on Hobby, 1, 4, 104; and *Houston Post,* 29, 60, 71, 73, 239, 329–330; and Jones, 7; op-ed column for, 283
Houston Dispatch, 3. *see also Houston Post.*
Houston Endowment, 329, 349
Houston Journalism Review, 117
Houston Junior Chamber of Commerce, 75
Houston League of Women Voters, 3
Houston Livestock Show and Rodeo, 215
Houston Musical Hall Foundation, 349
Houston Post: and antiwar movement, 77; automation of, 166; and Black Arts Festival, 80–81; and Carpenter News Bureau, 48; censorship at, 72, 370; circulation and market share, 60, 71, 166, 239; and Deng's visit, 189; and desegregation, 61–63; and Diana, 51–52, 58, 80–81, 83, 165; editorials and editorial board, 73, 147, 166, 204, 211; and equal opportunity, 69; extra editions, 55–56, 66; as family legacy, 58, 239–240, x; final edition of, 329–330; headquarters of, 42, 78–79, 241; Hobby as editor, 55–56, 60; Hobby as president of, 69, 71, 170–171; Hobby as reporter for, 21, 27, 34, 49, 50–53, 56–58; Hobby's summer work for, 24, 32–33, 39; Hobby *vs.* Oveta, 73, 90; and Kennedy assassination, 65–67; and LBJ, 67–70; leave of absence from, 117, 147; legislative coverage, 51; lunch counter news blackout, 62–63; and McCarthyism, 39–40; and Morris, 45; and naval career, 49; and Newberry, 322; *Now,* 51–52; and O. Henry, 12; and Oveta, 3, 6, 10, 23, 49, 71, 73, 78, 80, 166, 240–241; Pulitzer Prize, 71–72; purchase of, 10; reporting on Hobby, 47, 92, 106–107, 114, 117, 156, 387; sale of, 228, 238–241; and Will Hobby, 1, 68–69; and Woestendiek, 69, 72–73. *see also Houston Post-Dispatch.*
Houston Post Company, 71, 322. *see also* Hobby & Catto (H&C) Communications; *Houston Post.*
Houston Post-Dispatch, 3, 7, 8, 10
Houston Press, 71
Houston Ship Channel, 73–74
Houston Symphony, 24, 61
Howard, Ed, 190, 209
How Things Really Work, 361, x

Hubbard, Harry, 221
Hughes, Lynn, 146
Hughes, Sarah T., 67
Hulen, Bertram, 26, 367
Humble Oil Company, 2, 3
Humphrey, Hubert, 69, 70, 79–80, 98
Hunter, Delores, 122
Hunter, Ed, 87
hunting, 10, 206, 275, 311, 327, x. see also foxhunting.
Hurricane Harvey, 355
Hussein of Jordan, 214
Hutchison, Kay Bailey, 282, 315, 324, 326, 344, 353
Hutchison, Ray, 155, 182, 193, 282, 315, 344, 391
Hvalboll, Danna Annette, 143–144, 145–146
Hyer, June, 91, 121–122

I

ideology, anti-intellectual, 352
Ideson, Julia, 9
impeachments: and Carrillo, 169–170; and Clements, 277; Ferguson, 2, 99–100, 111, 128, 170
inaugurations: Carter, 177; Eisenhower, 36–38; FDR, 22; Hobby's, 123–125, 187, 224–226, 269; Nixon, 128–129
income tax, state: advocating for, 268, 276, 297, 307–310, 321; and campaigning, 280; and Clements, 187, 297, 314; and constitutional reforms, 167; opposition to, 97. see also taxes.
India, 56, 57, 286
indigent healthcare, 253–254, 255, 260, 293
indoctrination, 350–351
inflation, 158–159, 202
influenza epidemic, 7
initiative and referendum law, 187, 194, 209
Inman, Bobby Ray, 252–253, 272
Institute of International Education, 47–48
insurance industry: auto rates, 139; Catto & Catto, 322; and consumer fraud laws, 136–137; premiums of, 305; and tort laws, 273; and workers' compensation, 301, 305
integration. see also segregation.
integrity, 96, 99–100, 133, 304–305, viii, xi
intent calendar, 130, 195–200, 207–208
interest rates, mortgage, 138–139, 140, 200
Interim Committee on Welfare Reform, 91–92, 144, 244
Internal Revenue Service (IRS), 97, 192
Inter-University Consortium for Political and Social Research (ICPSR), 333–334, 352
Ireland: annual trips, 84–85, 181, 206, 250, 256, 284, 286, 295, 296, 315, 317; and Davis, 241–242; with Farabees, 283; and foxhunting, 85, 94, 348; and gubernatorial campaign, 278–279, 291; horse shows, 33, 184; post-war, 33–34
Ivins, Molly, 112–114, 132, 139, 291

J

Jackson, Andrew, 95
Jackson, Jesse, 249, 292
Jack Tar Hotel, 64
Jacobsen, Jake, 78, 371
Jamail, Joe, 359
Jaworski, Leon, 170
Jenkins, Bill, 120, 122, 123–124
Jenkins, Walter, 49
Jennings, Coleman, 33
Jesuit Fathers of Houston Incorporated, 94
Jewish Settlement House, 30–31
J. J. Pickle Research Campus, 253
Johnson, Eddie Bernice, 273, 282–283
Johnson, Harriet Lane, 19, 366
Johnson, Helon, 16–17, 47
Johnson, Lady Bird: and Carpenter, 258; and dinner party, 49; as donor, 222–223; and higher education funding, 263; and Hobby family, 65, 75–76, 123–124, 125; and LBJ School, 318, 341
Johnson, Lynda, 78, 371
Johnson, Lyndon B. (LBJ): and campaign laws, 129; campaigns and elections, 56, 69; and Darcy, 72; death of, 129; dinner party, 49; and Hobby, 95, 123–124, 125; and Hobby family, 37, 65, 67–70, 75–76, 95; and Kennedy assassination, 67; and KPRC studios, 107; and media, 76–77; and Oltorf, 49; war on poverty, 75; and Will's death, 68
Johnson, Madeline, 339
Johnson, Owen, 66
Johnson, Richard "Dick" J. V., 189
Johnson, Sam, 6
Johnston, Marguerite, 52, 331
Joint Advisory Commission on Government Operations, 170, 174, 177–178
Jones, Gene, 195–196, 197, 198, 205, 207
Jones, Grant: and education, 384; and Hobby, 286, 287–288, 298, 299, 325; on Hobby, 237; and Senate Finance Committee, 287; and workers' compensation, 301–302
Jones, Jesse H.: and FDR, 8, 22, 367; and Government Club, 26; graduation note, 26–27; and Hobby family, 6–7, 29; retirement of, 71; and Rice Hotel, 9
Jones, Jim, 78
Jones, John T., 62
Jones, LeRoi, 80–81
Jones, Shirley, 349
Jordan, Barbara, 91, 119, 129, 316

Jordan, Bryce, 343
Josey, Jack, 7, 10
journalism, 58–59, 61, 72, 107, 117. *see also Houston Post;* newspapers.
judges, state, 143, 304, 310–311, 313
Jurisprudence Committee, 122, 123, 134, 209
Justice, Blair, 62
Justice, William Wayne, 269, 270

K
Kaster, James, 210
KDFW-TV, 95
Keel, Tom, 319
Kellam, J. C., 75–76
Kelleher, Herb, 327, 355, 359
Kelsey, Mavis, 68
Kennard, Don, x
Kennedy, Edward, 192
Kennedy, Jacqueline, 66, 67
Kennedy, John F. (JFK), 56, 61, 63, 65–67, 90, 98
Kennedy, Robert, 67
Kennedy, Ted, 205
Kessler, Ron, 90, 100, 102, 103, 105, 160, 282
Kessler, Vicki, 101, 105, 108, 282
keys, house, 81–82
Khator, Renu, 353
Kilgallen, Dorothy, 50
Killeen, TX, 3, 258, 330
Killer Bees, 196–200, 205, ix
Kinch, Sam Jr., 103–104, 111, 266, 306
King, Betty, 176–177, 190, 230, 379
King, Frank H., 60, 62
King, Larry L., 103
King, Martin Luther Jr., 112
Kinkaid, Margaret, 11
Kinkaid School, 11, 15
Kirby, John Henry, 2, 5
Kirk, Paul, 289
Kissinger, Henry, 51
KLEE-TV, 29–30
Knowland, William, 38
Korean War, 33, 42, 44, 48
Kothmann, Glenn, 195–196
KPRC-Radio and KPRC-TV: and election nights, 31; and ferryboat launch, 68; growth of, 58; and Hobby, 12–13, 42, 166, 180, 204; and Jones, 7; purchase and sale of, 10, 29–30, 323–324; and Sterling, 3; studios, 107; and Will's funeral, 68–69. *see also* broadcast properties.
Kreisle, Matthew, x
Krier, Cynthia "Cyndi" Taylor, 324, xi
Krim, Arthur B., 75–76

Krueger, Robert "Bob," 82, 185, 325–326, 327, 391
KSAT-TV, 172, 322
KTRK-Radio, 7
Kubiak, Don, 215
Kuchel, Thomas, 38
Ku Klux Klan protests, 35
Kuwait, 315, 324

L
labor unions. *see* unions, labor.
Lacy, Margaret, 47
Lamar Hotel, 6–7, 9
lame-duck nominations, 226–227, 382
Landry, Tom, 124
Laredo State University, 303
Laro, Arthur, 32–33
Latinos, 236, 254, 261
laws: blue law, 232, 238, 251, 255–256; campaign finance reform, 304; draft, 33; drinking age, 138, 207–208, 232, 238, 255; and dual primaries, 129, 191–200, 204, 291; eighteen-year-old right to vote, 108–109, 110, 112, 138; and human behavior, 132, 210, 273
lawsuits: Artesia Hall, 145–146, 376; frivolous, 314–315; prisons and mental health facilities, 235, 250, 269–270, 299; and public-school financing, 128, 314–315; and workers' compensation, 301. *see also* courts.
Lay, Kenneth, 337
LBJ Ranch, 69–70, 75–76, 77–78
LBJ School. *see* Lyndon B. Johnson School of Public Affairs (LBJ School).
Lebermann, Lowell, 202
Ledbetter, Harry, 144
Lee, Albert, 29
Lee, Robert E, 4, 5
Leedom, John, 235, 247–248, 251–252
legislation. *see* laws; legislative sessions.
Legislative Budget Board: and constitutional amendments, 163; and Hobby, 126, 173, 296, 317, 390; and Keel, 319; and state budget, 253, 268, 320, viii; and Strake, 218; and zero-based budgeting, 142
Legislative Redistricting Board, 212
legislative sessions: Sixty-Second Legislature, 119–121; Sixty-Third Legislature, 121–141, 149; Sixty-Fourth Legislature, 158–168, 169–170; Sixty-Fifth Legislature, 173–180, 182–184; Sixty-Sixth Legislature, 190–200; Sixty-Seventh Legislature, 206–212, 221; Sixty-Eighth Legislature, 226–228, 230–238, 245–249; Sixty-Ninth Legislature, 250–257, 259–260, 262–265, 268; Seventieth Legislature, 269–278; Seventy-First Legislature,

296–307, 310–315; as parliamentarian, 54–55; reporting on, 51; special sessions, 140–141, 149, 169–170, 179, 182–184, 237, 259–260, 275–277, 303, 304–307, 311–315
legislature, Texas: anti-intellectualism in, 188, 352; and Center for Public Policy, 352; and committees, 137; conservatives *vs.* liberals, 132, 360; and desegregation, 51; Hobby on business of, 360; and Hobby School of Public Affairs, 355; integrity of, 96; membership of, 131–132; procedures and process, 8, 61, 126, 130, 153, 163; and telescope, 346. *see also* House of Representatives, Texas; legislative sessions; Senate, Texas.
Leland, Mickey, 204, 267, 312
Lewis, George Jr., 69
Lewis, Gib: and budget, 262–263, 271, 275; and Build Texas plan, 274; and Capitol centennial, 290; and Clements, 275, 297; and Dukakis, 290; and education, 243, 246, 247, 253, 272, 298; elected Speaker of the House, 226; failure to disclose, 235, 383; and Hobby, 275, x; on Hobby, 199–200; hunting trip, 311; and indigent healthcare bill, 254; and MCC, 252; and taxes, 246, 263–264, 276, 309; traveling with, 290; and water crisis, 251; and workers' compensation, 301, 306, 307
Lewis, Jerry, 172
Lewis, Judd Mortimer, 7, 8
Lewis, Sandra, 290
libraries, 9, 347
licenses, 29, 146–147, 160
lieutenant governors: Barnes as, 90; and Bullock, 317; enjoyment of position, 131, 149, 150, 173; Hobby as, 130–131, 138–139, 165, 207–208, 210, 232–234, vii–viii, xii; powers and role of, 118, 119–122, 125–128, 136, viii; president emeritus, 302, x, xi; Ramsey as, 53–55; tiebreaker, 127; Will Hobby as, 2. *see also* legislative sessions.
Life magazine, 79
Limelight, 39–40
liquor laws: blue law, 232, 238, 251, 255–256; drinking age, 138, 207–208, 232, 238, 255
Little Theater Group, 46
loans, 87, 93, 150
lobbyists and lobbying: and alcohol, 134–135, 208, 232, 251; business lobby (*see* business lobby); Clark, 150; and constitutional reform, 153, 154; and consumer protection laws, 136–137; control bill, 134–135; dual-primary bill, 193–194; and education reform, 245–247, 314; and ethics reform, 132, 133, 134; and higher education, 262; and Hobby, 151, 180, 266, 336, xi; initiative and referendum proposal, 209; oil companies *vs.* service stations, 234; and Perot, 246; registration of, 133, 134; and University of Houston, 336, 338; and wiretapping bill, 209; and workers' compensation, 237, 301, 302, 304, 306, 307
Locke, Eugene, 77–78
London, 30–33, 284, 315
Longoria, Raul, 196, 237
lottery, state, 251, 321
Love, Ben, 263, 345
Lucas, Albert Hawley, 19, 20, 47
Luce, Tom, 246
Ludwig Maximilian University, 342, 346
lunch counter protests, 61–63
Lyndon B. Johnson School of Public Affairs (LBJ School): about, 319, 390–391, 394; and Chinese universities, 328; dean of, 340–341; as instructor, 317–320, 327, 332; and University of Houston, 334
Lyon, Ted, 273

M

Macmillan, Harold, 57
Madden, Wales, 150
Madison Square Gardens, 84
Manager of the Year award, 237
Manned Spacecraft Center, NASA, 65, 189
Marcus, Billie, 107
Marcus, Stanley, 107
marijuana, 109, 112, 128, 138, 209, 210, 244
Marines, US, 44
Mark, Hans, 272, 319
Marshall, Gaylord, 157, 185, 213
Marshall, George C., 15, 16, 22, 38
Marshall, Gordon P., 45
Martin, Ed, 324
Martin, Jack, viii
Mary Hardin-Baylor College, 3, 17
Masterson, Bill, 35
mathematics: and budget, 126, 161–162; failed class, 35; love of, 20; and math camp, 333–334, 392; and politics, 52–53, 74; and redistricting, 353; and Southwest Airlines, 310–311, 327; teaching of, 311. *see also* statistics.
Mattox, Jim: and abortion, 310; and Anderson, 294; campaigns and elections, 223, 265, 267, 268, 278–282, 312; Hobby on, 280; and income tax, 310; mudslinging of, 278–279; politics of, 215; and right-to-work provision, 153; and US Senate seat, 326
Mauro, Garry, 215, 223, 265, 290, 294
Mauzy, Oscar: and Clements's nominations, 227; and consumer protection, 136, 137, 139; and drunk driving, 377; education expertise, 233; and ethics

reform, 132–133, 136; and farmworkers' compensation, 236–237; and financial statements, 134; and Hobby, 101, 213, 223, 232, x; on Hobby, 120, 165, 234; and Jurisprudence Committee, 207; and Killer Bees, 193, 195–196, 199; and public-school funding, 161–162, 178, 179; and Senate rules, 118, 120–121, 127, 128; and wiretapping bill, 209, 210
Maverick, Maury Jr., 90, 102
McBride, Cecil, 10, 13
McCarthy, Joseph, 38–39
McCarthyism, 38–40
McConn, Jim, 183
McCree, Allen, 231
McDonald, Dora, 196
McDonald Observatory, 336, 342–347
McFarland, Bob, xi
McGovern, George, 119, 221
McGrew, Jack, 12–13, 320
McKaskle, Larry, 73
McKinley, William, 2
McKnight, Peyton, 163, 167, 169, 180–181, 196, 197, 211
McLeroy, Don, 351
McNeely, Dave, 192, 266–267, 280
medals, 185, 347, 387
media: and CIA funding, 77; dual-primary bill and Killer Bees, 196, 199; and education finance, 179–180, 243; and Hobby businesses, 171–172, 323; and Houston news blackout, 62–63; objectivity and neutrality, 59, 61, 107, 117; and Oveta, 48; press conferences, 95, 97, 133, 150, 199, 206, 236, 279–280; and Schnabel, 176; and University of Houston, 333, 334–335; and Vietnam War, 76–78; and wedding, 47. *see also* broadcast properties; newspapers; radio and radio stations; television and television stations.
Media and Public Policy seminar, 319
Medicaid and Medicare, 91, 214, 303, 351. *see also* healthcare.
Meet the Press, 48
Meier, Bill, 178, 195–196
memories, book of, 365, xiii
Mengden, Walter "Mad Dog," 162–163, 175, 184, 207–208, 215
mental health facilities, 250, 274, 284
merit in political candidates, 324
Mewhinney, Hubert, 40–41
Mewhinney, Leonard Sparks, 40–41
Mexican Americans, 106, 236
Mexico, 8, 27, 196, 211, 230, 328, 329, 351
Microelectronics and Computer Technology Consortium (MCC), 252–253, 272
Middle East, 140–141, 148, 315, 324

migrant workers, 220, 244, 252, 303
Miller, Arthur, 34
Miller, William, 202
Millikin, Eugene, 37
Millsap, Mike, 273
minorities. *see* Black Texans; Latinos; Mexican Americans.
Minute Women, 40
mirrors, telescope, 343
Mischer, Walter, 263
Mitchell, James, 228–229
Mondale, Walter, 172–173, 249
Montford, John: and Build Texas plan, 282; campaigns and elections, 287, 288; finance expertise of, 233; and Hobby, 232, 335, 355, viii, xi; and Hobby bust, 317; and hunting trips, 327; and "No Pass, No Play" repeal, 251–252; and revenue task force, 321; and tort law reform, 273–274; and workers' compensation, 301, 303, 306
Moody, Dan Jr., 5, 53
Moody, Daniel, 5
Moody, Nancy, 53
Moody, William L. Jr., 64
Moore, Bill: filibuster of, 138; and Hobby, 50, 131, 132, 140, 207; and mortgage rates, 139; and Schwartz, 190–191; and State Affairs Committee, 122, 159–160; and Strake, 220; and youth-care facility reform, 160
Morales, Dan, 338–339
Morian, Beth Robertson, 333–334, 337, 353, 359
Morris, Donald, 43–44, 77
Morris, Sylvia Stallings, 44, 45, 47, 52
mortgage loans, 138–139, 140, 200
Mosbacher, Rob, 313, 316
Mothers against Drunk Driving, 232
mountains, 84
Mount Locke, 342, 343
Movietone Studios, 45
Mr. Chairman, 8
mudslinging, 221, 268, 278–279, 313
Muniz, Ramsey, 157
Murphy (dog), 64
Murray, Richard, 352
museums, 314
musicals, 84, 283, 284, 290, 348–349. *see also* plays.
music halls, 23, 348–349
Mutscher, Gus, 93–94, 96–97, 99

N

name recognition, 93, 105–106, 213, 219–220, 260
nannies, 9, 16, 17, 81–82, 85, 284
NASA Manned Spacecraft Center, 65, 189

Nashville television station (WLAC/WTLV-TV), 171–172, 204. *see also* television and television stations.
National Bankers Life Insurance Company, 93–94, 113
National Cathedral, 18, 19, 25, 33, 42
National Citizens Advisory Committee on Vocational Rehabilitation, 76
National Collegiate Athletic Association (NCAA), 277
National Guard, Texas, 4
National Horse Show, 84
National Lieutenant Governors' Conference, 149
National Presbyterian Church, 37–38
National Student Association, 77
natural gas. *see* energy industry.
Natural Resources Committee, 122
Naval Reserve Officers Training Corps, 40
navy, US, 42–43; enlistment in, 40–41; Office of Naval Intelligence, 41–43, 48, 49–50, 368
Neches River, 2
neutrality in journalism, 59, 61, 107, 117
Newberry, Robert, 322
New Deal, 274
New Federalism plan, 214, 234
news blackout, 62–63
newspapers: and Build Texas campaign, 283; decline of, 238–239, 240; in Galveston, 64; and Hobby campaigns, 102–103, 111, 114, 115, 373, 378; importance of, 87–88, 329–330; newsmen as dissenters, 58–59; political reporting, 55, 87; and public-school funding, 314; syndicated features, 71. *see also* media; specific newspapers.
News-Sun Today, 64–65
New York City, NY, 16, 23, 44, 84, 283, 314
New York Times, 77, 80
New York World, 44
Nixon, Richard: campaigns and elections, 56, 109–110; and Eisenhower's inauguration, 37; endorsement from *Houston Post*, 79–80, 97, 98; and Hobby, 119, 147; and Hobby family, 49; inauguration of, 128–129; and oil crisis, 140–141, 149
Nixon administration, 97, 147
nominations, lame-duck, 226–227
Noor of Jordan, 214
"No Pass, No Play" rule, 247, 248, 251–252. *see also* education reform.
North Atlantic Treaty Organization, 57
North Carolina State University, 46
Northcott, Kaye, 139
Northen, Mary Moody, 64
nostalgia, 239–240
nuclear energy, 147, 148. *see also* energy industry.

O

Oaks, Steve, 100, 103, 122, 129, 142–147, 197
Oaks kindergarten, 11
Obama, Barack, 351
objectivity in journalism, 59, 61, 107, 117
Obregón, Álvaro, 12
O'Connor, Sandra Day, 146
O'Conor, Robert Jr., 146
O'Donnell, Kenneth, 66
O'Donnell, Peter Jr., 262, 272, 393, xi
Office of Naval Intelligence (ONI), 41–43, 48, 49–50, 368
Officer Candidate School (OCS), 40–41, 42
Ogg, Jack, 138–139, 194
oil and gas industry. *see* energy industry.
oil-well blowout, 201–202
O'Leary, Ralph S., 40, 62
Oliver, Jim, 247
Olson, Lyndon, 164
Oltorf, Frank "Posh" Calvert, 48–49
one-party state, Texas as, 115–116, 215
one-stop shopping counties, 114–115
Onion, John, 151
op-ed column, 327, 338, 350–351
open-door policy, 81–82
Organization of Petroleum Exporting Countries (OPEC), 148
Osorio, John, 93–94
Oswald, Lee Harvey, 67
Outstanding Young Texans, 75
Oxford University, 31–32

P

Page, Bob, 5
paintings and portraits, 6, 126, 189, 230
Palmer Memorial Episcopal Church, 86, 330–331, 357
Pan American Airways, 79
Pan American University, 303
parades: and campaigning, 114, 215, 281; Capitol centennial, 290; inaugural, 38, 125, 225–226; in India, 57
parenthood, 82–83
Parker, Carl: and Bill Hobby Day, x; and Build Texas plan, 282; campaigns and elections, 287, 288; and Clements, 270; and Education Committee, 232; on Hobby, xi; Killer Bees and dual-primary bill, 195; and public-school finance, 246, 312, 315, 384; and tort law reform, 273; and workers' compensation, 303, 304, 306
Parks and Wildlife Commission, Texas, 292–293, 326–327
parliamentarian: Hobby as, 53–55, 89, 121–122, x; *Mr. Chairman*, 8; Oveta as, 3–4, x

parliamentary procedure, 8, 61, 126, 130, 153, 163
Parmer, Hugh, 290, 304
partisanship: and conservatives, 213, 215, 227; and dean of LBJ school, 340; and education, 360; and healthcare, 360; and Hobby, 97–98, 185, 191, 207, 301, 324; and Republican Party, 324–325; in Texas Democratic party, 54
Pasadena city hall, 71–72, 370
passion play, 34
Patman, Bill, 138–139, 140, 170, 195–196, x
Patrick, Dan, 324, 354
Peaceable Kingdom Retreat for Children, 330
Peach Tree, TX, 2
Peal and Co. boots, 32
Pearl Harbor, 15
Pemex (Petróleos Mexicanos), 201–202
Penn State University, 343, 345
Pentagon Papers, 80
Perlman, Jason, 122
Permanent School Fund, 150, 178, 262
Perot, H. Ross: and budget, 263; and education reform, 243–244, 245, 248, 384; and lobbyists, 246; and State Board of Education, 248, 283, 286–287; and war on drugs, 209, 244
Perot reforms, 243–249, 255, 257, 260, 287, 298, 384
Perry, Edgar "Commodore," 13
Perry, Rick, 349–351, 394
personal appearance, 220–221
Peterson, Arthur, 228
Petróleos Mexicanos (Pemex), 201–202
philanthropy, 347–349, 355. see also Hobby Family Foundation.
phone calls, 164, 272
Pickle, J. J. "Jake," 78, 342
Piedmont Airlines, 84
Pilgrim, Lonnie "Bo," 304
Pin Oak Stables, 211
plane crash, 8
Planned Parenthood, 108
plant, printing, 60–61
plays, 32, 34, 44–45, 48. see also musicals.
Plumes, 44–45
poems and poetry: constitutional reform, 168; and education reform, 246, 249; honoring Hobby, 7, 8, xi; and Killer Bees, 200; legislation as poetry, 174, 248, 360; and White, 225, 382
policy themes. see budget, state; education, higher; public-school funding; welfare and social services; workers' compensation.
political action committee, 287
political analysis, 35, 55, 56, 58
politics: Dallas and Hay, 105–106; ethics in (see ethics); Hobby's personal politics, 11–12, 26, 28, 98, 112, 161, 199, 206, 213, 218–219, 254, 273, 310; and LBJ School, 340; one-party state, 54, 115–116, 215; partisanship, 191, 207, 213, 215, 227, 301, 324–325, xii; party tickets, 98–99; shift to extreme right, 360; and St. Albans Government Club, 25–26. see also campaigns and elections; Democratic Party; House of Representatives, Texas; legislature, Texas; Republican Party; Senate, Texas.
polls and polling, 223, 284, 316, 352
pollution and pollution control: and Anderson, 294; in China, 202; legislation, 97, 137, 151, 274; and Pemex oil-well blowout, 201–202; Texas Air Control Board, 92
Pool, Brady, 229
Pope, Jack, 224, 226, 227, 382
Porter, William Sydney, 12
Port of Galveston strike, 28
portraits and paintings, 6, 126, 189, 230, 374
Poteat, Diana. see Hobby, Diana Poteat Stallings.
Poteat, Helen Purefoy. see Stallings, Helen Purefoy Poteat.
Poteat, Ida Isabella, 45
Poteat, James, 45
Poteat, William Louis, 44
Poteat House. see Forest Home.
poverty, 75, 108. see also welfare and social services.
prairie chickens, 271
Preservation Board, State, 230–231
president emeritus, 302, x, xi
press and press conferences. see media.
presses, high-speed color, 60
Pride, Charley, 224
priesthood, 24–25, 26
printers, Teletype, 65
printing plants, 60–61, 64, 202, 241
prisons and prison reform: and anti-crime plan, 299–300, 303, 389; bond financing, 278; and Build Texas plan, 274; and Clements, 299–300; cost of, 270, 300; and courts, 232, 269–270, 299; and economy, 235; and Farabee, 233; federal courts, 250; and higher education, 269, 300; and Jones, 288; and Justice, 270; and taxes, 234
privacy clause, 178
problem solving and government, 97, 112, 315, 317, 355
Prohibition, 2, 128
propeller, broken, 109
property taxes. see taxes, property.
Proposition 13, 182–183
protests, 39, 52–53, 61–63, 189, 253
Provident City retreat, 120–121

INDEX | 421

public-school funding: as chronic problem, 174; and federal courts, 128, 298; and House plan, 313; inequality of, 128, 137; and legislature, 161–162, 177, 179, 209, 237–238, 304, 308–315; Mauzy's filibuster, 178; and property taxes, 162, 174, 308, 312; Select Committee on Public Education (Perot reforms), 243–249, 255, 257, 260, 287, 298; and teachers (*see* teachers). *see also* education.
Public Utility Commission (PUC), 159, 164–165, 232, 238, 378
Public Utility Regulatory Act, 163–165
Pulitzer Company, 323
Pulitzer Prize, 71–72, 74, 215
Purefoy, Emma, 44

Q
Quayle, Dan, 294
Quintanilla, Joel, 228
quorum, breaking of, 195–196

R
racism, 35, 44, 61–63, 294. *see also* desegregation; segregation.
racquetball, 315, 329
Radcliffe College, 46, 181
radio and radio stations: and Build Texas plan, 282; and H&C, 322–323; and Hobby campaigns, 100, 105, 113; and Killer Bees, 198; Radio Free Europe, 77. *see also* broadcast properties; KPRC-Radio.
Radio City Music Hall, 23
Radio Free Europe, 77
Rainey, Homer, 36
rainy day fund, 173, 179, 274, 295, 354
Ramparts, 77
Ramsey, Ann, x
Ramsey, Ben, 53–54, 55, 118–119, 229, 231, 369
Ramsey, Lawrence W., 343
Ransom, Harry, 58
rates, interest, 138–139, 140, 200, 274
Rather, Dan, 296
Rather, Mary, 123
rationing, gas, 148–149
Ratliff, Bill, 294–295, 297, 324
Reagan, Ronald: and dual primaries, 191–192, 193; and Hobby campaign, 222; New Federalism plan, 214; and presidential elections, 191, 204–205; and Texas Republican Party, 213, 250
Reaganomics, 222
Rebekah Home, 160. *see also* youth-care facilities.
reception, public, 125
recession, economic, 223, 226, 264, 287. *see also* economy, Texas.

Reconstruction, 152
redistricting, 209, 211–212, 213, 353
Red Scare, 38–40
Reefer Madness commission, 209
referendum and initiative law, 187, 194, 209
rehabilitation programs, 142–147, 156–157
religion: Baptists, 3, 19, 27, 44, 221; Episcopal church, 18, 19–20, 86; evangelicals and fundamentalists, 160–161, 178, 221; football as, 244; hypocrisy in, 86–87; interest in priesthood, 24–25, 26; Methodism, 19; and passion play, 34
Reno, 45
reporting and reporters. *see Houston Post;* media; newspapers.
Republican Party: campaigns and elections, 182, 215–216, 223; and Catto, 80, 356; and Clements, 182, 187; and Collins, 215–216; and Connally, 226; criticism of, 351–352; and Davidson, 261; and dual primaries, 191–192, 193, 198; and higher education, 350–351, 352; and Hobby, 212–213, 261, 266, 267, 269, 278, 281, 324, xii; ideology of, 271, 349–350, 352; and partisanship, 324–325; power of, 200, 205, 207, 213, 265, 281, 349–352, xii; and public-school financing, 311–312; and redistricting, 211–212; and sex education, 351; and state board of education, 351; and Strake, 212–213; and suburban voters, 56; and tax bills, 311–312
residential childcare facilities, 142–147, 160–161
Retail Merchants' Association, 62–63
Rhodes Trust, 31
Rice, William Marsh, 27
Rice Hotel, 9
Rice University: and Oveta, 371, 390
Rice University (Rice Institute): and Board of Governors, 311; cheating scandal, 321; and Diana, 181, 347; Fondren Library project, 347; and Hobby Foundation, 371; and *Houston Post,* 78; and segregation, 35; as student, 27–41; teaching at, 311, 317, 319, 327, 329; and *Thresher,* 34–35. *see also* education, higher.
Richards, Ann: and abortion rights, 310; and Anderson, 294; and Bentsen's Senate seat, 325–326; and birthday lunch, 258–259; and boxing trunks, 268; and Build Texas plan, 283; campaigns and elections of, 215, 221, 222, 223, 265, 312, 313, 316, 328–329, 390; and Christie, 102; and Clinton-Gore ticket, 325; on commencement address, 320; death of, 356; and Democratic Convention, 292; and Dukakis, 290, 293; and Ferraro, 249; fundraiser for, 296; and Hobby, 216–218, 224, 249–250, 291, 317, 340, 356; on Hobby, 90; hosting royalty, 391; and income tax, 310; revenue task

force, 320–321; and telescope, 344; and Texas Parks and Wildlife Commission, 326–327; and Texas Women's Political Caucus, 291; and US Senate, 292
Richards, Dave, 156, 157, 223
rifles, assault, 304
right to scrutinize, 65
right-to-work provision, 153, 154–155, 162–163
ring, engagement, 46–47
Rives, Don, 100
Robb, Chuck, 78, 371
Robb, Lynda Johnson, 78
Robertson, Beth. *see* Morian, Beth Robertson.
Robins, Joan, 81–82, 85, 283
Rockefeller, Nelson, 50–51
Rockefeller IV, John D. "Jay," 290
Rodriguez v. San Antonio Independent School District, 128
Roe v. Wade, 109, 217, 258
Roloff, Lester, 160, 178, 377
Rome, 57
Roosevelt, Eleanor, 8
Roosevelt, Franklin Delano (FDR), 8, 11–12, 22, 367
Roosevelt, Teddy, 2
"Rose Garden strategy," 267
Rosenfeld, Arnold, 280
roses, 217
Ross Volunteers, 124
Rove, Karl, 218–219
Ruby, Jack, 67
Rules Committee, 123
Rupp, George, 321
Rusk, Howard A., 76
Rusk State Hospital, 145
Ryan, Chris, 242
Ryan, Thaddeus "Thady," 242

S

salary, chancellor's, 334
sales tax. *see* tax, sales.
San Antonio Express-News, 71, 327
Sanders, Amy, 23
Santa Rita Award, 256
Santiesteban, Tati, 237
Sarofim, Fayez, 349
Sarofim Hall, 349
Sarpalius, Bill, 207, 236, 294
Satterwhite, Lee, 4
Scarteen Hunt, 242. *see also* foxhunting.
Schacher, Eugene, 8
Schilt, Alexander, 333, 336, 339
Schlesinger, James, 181
Schlueter, Stan, 297, 299
Schnabel, Charles, 175–177, 378–379
scholarships, race-based, 338–339
schools, private: Artesia Hall, 142–147; Chatham Hall, 44, 46; Green Fields Preparatory School for Boys, 13–14, 15; and Hobby children, 87, 184; Kinkaid School, 11, 15; St. Albans, 19–27, 87; St. Johns School, 87; unlicensed, 146–147
schools, public, 51, 74–75, 152, 218–219, 220, 257–258. *see also* public-school funding.
Schwartz, A. R. "Babe": campaigns, 185; and constitutional reform, 151, 165; and Hobby, 92, 121, 131, 156, 205, 207, x; Killer Bees and dual-primary bill, 193, 195–196, 198; and Moore, 190–191; and mortgage rate bill, 139; and Senate rules, 118, 122, 127; and workers' compensation, 301–302
Scowcroft, Brent, 315
Scudder, Richard, 329, 330
sculpture dedication, 283
Seals, Woodrow, 255
Sebring, Tom, 345–346
secession, 351
secretary, Senate, 130, 175–177, 190, 230
secretary of state, Texas, 53, 146, 213, 216, 227–228
Securities and Exchange Commission (SEC), US, 93–94
Sedco of Dallas, 201–202
Sedwick, Shannon, 291
segregation: and football, 181; and lunch counters, 61–63; and public Schools, 51; and Rice, 27, 35; and St. Albans, 20; and Texas Constitution, 152; and University of Texas Law School, 35. *see also* desegregation; racism.
Select Committee on Public Education (Perot reforms), 243–249, 255, 257, 260, 287, 298, 384. *see also* public-school funding.
Sematech, 287
Senate, Texas: and Bill Hobby Day, xii–xiii; and Capitol fire, 230; and committee appointments, 118, 122–123, viii; Committee of the Whole Senate, 161–162, 246, 302–303, 312; composition of, 232; and dual primaries and Killer Bees, 191–200; and Hobby, 173, 190–191, 206; lieutenant governor's role in, 119–122, 125–128, 131, 136, viii; parliamentarian, 53–54, 121–122; procedures and process of, 55, 97, 118, 119–122, 126–128, 130, 177, 194–195; and Provident City retreat, 119–120; respect for Hobby, vii; and Schnabel trial, 175–176; secretary of, 130, 175–177, 190, 230; and Sharpstown Bank Scandal, 99–100, 131–132; testimony before, 65; two-thirds rule, 127, 130, 302–303. *see also* committees, Senate; legislative sessions; legislature, Texas.

Senate, US: and Bentsen, 145, 224, 288; and dual primaries, 291; Hobby's interest in, 267, 291, 294, 388; meeting with, 202; vacant seat, 325–326
Senate Ladies' Club, xii
service, public, 1, 74, 90, 206, x–xi
service fees, state, 321
sewage treatment plant, 217
Shakespeare, 10, xi–xii
Shamrock Hotel, 10
Shanker, Albert, 316
Shannon, Tommy, 93–94, 99
Shapiro, Marc, 348
Sharp, Frank, 93–94, 95, 99
Sharp, John, 232, 325, x
Sharpstown Bank Scandal, 93–100, 110, 131–132, 138. *see also* corruption.
Sherman, Gene, 286, 315
Sherman, Max: in China, 328; and constitutional reform, 151, 154, 155; on Diana, 108; and Hobby, 92, 286, 317–318, x; on Hobby, 114, 130; and LBJ School, 317–318, 329, 340; and Natural Resources Committee, 122; politics of, 215; as racquetball partner, 315, 329; travel with, 315, 334
Shipley, George, 220–221, 267, 282
Shivers, Allan, 54, 124
Shorb, Bob, 43, 129
Shorb, Katherine "Teeny," 43, 129
Shuptrine, Carl, 62
Sid Richardson Chair in Public Affairs, 317–318, 391–392. *see also* Lyndon B. Johnson School of Public Affairs (LBJ School).
signs, highway directional, 109
Silver Star, 44
Sims, Bill, 251–252
Singleton, Dean, 329, 330
sinusitis, chronic, 13
Slagle, Bob, 292
slavery, 44, 45, 152
slogan, campaign, 99–100
Smith, Arthur K., 339
Smith, Bob, 175, 176
Smith, Glenn, 270, 286, 299–300, 316, 388
Smith, Harlan, 343, 344–345, 393
Smith, Liz, 296
Smith, Preston: at Bill Hobby Day, x; campaigns of, 89, 110–111; inaugurations, 124, 225; and Sharpstown Bank Scandal, 93–94, 99; and Strake, 220; and Texas Air Control Board, 92
smoking, 104, 373
Snelson, Pete, 215
soccer, 20, 26
socialism, 27, 32

social services. *see* welfare and social services.
softball team, 271
Southeastern Drilling Company, 182
Southern Methodist University, 277, 387
South Texas Press Association, 61
Southwest Airlines, 310–311, 317, 319, 327, 329, 333
Southwestern Bell, 164, 210, 378
Southwest Texas State University, 238
Soviet Union, 148
Spanish language, 23, 27
Speakers of the House, Texas. *see* Clayton, Bill W.; Daniel, Price Jr.; Lewis, Gib.
speaking, public: campaign speeches, 95–96; commencement address, 320; and Hobby as, 103–104, viii, xi; and South Texas Press Association, 61; speech lessons, 13; and television, 114; in Tower Hill, 31
Special Committee on Delivery of Human Services: and Richards, 216–217
Special Studies Project, 50–51
speed limit, 140–141, 149, 376
Spinks, Wilfred, 228
split-primary bill. *see* dual-primary bill.
spokesperson, press, 286
sports. *see* athletics.
sprinkler system, capitol, 230
St. Albans News, 21, 25, 26
St. Albans School, 19–27, 87
Stallings, Diana Poteat. *see* Hobby, Diana Poteat Stallings.
Stallings, Helen Purefoy Poteat, 44, 45–46
Stallings, Laurence Tucker, 44–45, 81
Stallings, Sylvia. *see* Morris, Sylvia Stallings.
Stanford University, 346
Stansbury, Philip, 19, 21
State Affairs Committee, 122, 131, 159–160, 193, 232
state boards and commissions. *see* Board of Education, State; commissions, state; Preservation Board, State.
state budget. *see* budget, state.
state parks, 292–293, 326–327
statistics, 52–53, 74, 311, 319, 329, vii. *see also* mathematics.
Stearns, Eldrewey, 61
Stein, Robert, 311
Steiner, T. C. "Buck," 13
Stemmons, John, 150
Sterling, Florence, 3, 5
Sterling, Jim, 144–145
Sterling, Ross, 2, 3, 4, 5, 7, 135–136
Stern, Robert A. M., 349
Stevenson, Adlai, 36, 54

Stimson, Henry, 15, 22
St. Johns School, 87
stocks, 93–94
Stone, Harlan, 22
Stone, Ron, 323–324
Strake, George W. Sr., 213
Strake, George W. Jr., 212–214, 216, 218–222, 256, 324–325
Strake Jesuit High School, 94
Strategic Arms Limitation Talks (SALT), 202
Strauss, Robert, 189
students: and Artesia Hall, 142–145; and education reform, 247, 248, 249, 257, 260, 298; Hobby and, 311, 320, 327, 354; indoctrination of, 350; protests, 61–62, 253; and segregation, 20, 35; tuition fees, 253; as voters, 108–109, 112, 147
stutter, 13, 74–75, 104–105, viii
"Suburbia" special edition, 55–56
suburbs, 55–56, 166
suffrage movement, 2, 3
Sugar Land, 337–338
summer camps, 14, 17, 333–334
Sunbelt Broadcasting, 324
Sun Media, 241
Sunset Advisory Commission, 174, 178, 238
sunshine laws, 132, 138
Superconducting Super Collider project, 274, 386
Supreme Court, Texas: and Court of Criminal Appeals, 163; and Hill, 269; and Pope, 224, 226; and public-school finance, 298, 305, 308; and Rebekah Home, 160. *see also* courts, federal.
Supreme Court, US, 128, 146, 339, 350. *see also* courts, federal.
Survey Research Institute, 352
Sweatt, Heman, 35

T

The Tactful Texan: A Biography of Governor Will Hobby, 52
Taiwan, 256
task force to review New Federalism impact, 234
Taub, Ben, 12
taxes: ad valorem, 97; alternate revenue sources, 251; and Anderson, 288; and Briscoe, 136; and budget, 139, 226, 234, 243, 251, 257, 264, 268; business and franchise, 188, 276; cigarette, 245, 254, 312, 314; and Clements, 187–188, 211; and constitutional reform, 167; gasoline, 188, 234, 246–247; Hobby on, 28–29, 206, 272; and *Houston Post*, 239; inheritance, 183, 184, 228, 239, 323; and legislature, 177, 182–184, 238; and permanent funds, 150; and Proposition 13, 182–183; and public-school funding, 174, 245–247, 314; reform of, 136, 159, 182–183, 288, 299, 320; and utilities, 159, 183, 184. *see also* income tax, state; taxes, property; taxes, sales.
taxes, property: and public-school funding, 162, 174, 308–309, 312; reform of, 159, 182–183, 184. *see also* taxes.
taxes, sales: ceiling, 97, 280; denouncement of, 309; and education finance, 245, 314; and public-school financing, 314; and state budget, 174, 247, 262, 264, 276, 321; and utilities, 159, 183, 184. *see also* taxes.
Teacher Retirement System of Texas, 321
teachers: competency tests, 245, 248, 264; and education reform, 244, 245–246, 260; salary of, 159, 161, 187, 243, 248, 255, 275; unemployment insurance, 161–162
teaching: LBJ School, 317–320, 327, 332; practical skills *vs.* theory, 354; Rice University, 311, 317, 327, 329; University of Michigan summer program, 392
Tea Party demonstrators, 351
technology sector, 75, 225, 244, 252–253, 270, 272, 287
telephones, 82, 165, 316
telescope, 336, 342–347, 393
Teletype bulletin, 66, 67
Teletype printers, 65
television and television stations: debates, 112–113, 221–222; and H&C, 319; and Hobby campaigns, 100, 104, 107, 114, 220–221; Nashville station, 171–172, 204; paying the bills, 42; political interview program, 121; public affairs program, 149; purchase of, 29–30, 171–172; sale of, 322–323; and University of Houston, 335. *see also* broadcast properties; specific stations.
Temple, Arthur "Buddy" Jr., 132
Temple, TX, 3
term lengths, of state officials, 150
Terrace Square Ballroom, 125
Texans for Blue Law Repeal Incorporated, 251
Texas, 23, 24, 30, 31, 360–361, 390
Texas A&M University System: and Clayton, 226, 227; funding of, 150, 159, 262; and Ross Volunteers, 124; schools in system, 303
Texas Association of Taxpayers, 309
Texas Automobile Dealers Association, 251
Texas Bill of Rights Foundation, 74
Texas Center of Superconductivity, 336
Texas City Sun, 64
Texas College and University System Coordinating Board (Texas Higher Education Coordinating Board), 138, 159, 227, 353–354. *see also* education, higher.

Texas Daily Newspaper Association, 87, 99
Texas Education Agency (TEA), 257, 259
Texas Election Bureau, 74
Texas Energy Plan, 201
Texas Exes, 272
Texas Farm Bureau, 236
Texas Hunter Jumper Association, 228
Texas Instruments, 142
Texas Medical Center, 10
Texas Quarterly, 58
Texas Rangers, 195–196, 293
Texas Social Welfare Association, 74
Texas Southern University (TSU), 61, 322
Texas state budget. *see* budget, state.
Texas State Teachers Association (TSTA), 161–162, 244, 260, 264. *see also* teachers.
Texas State University, 347, 359
Texas Sunset Act, 178
Texas Tech University, 335
Texas Welfare Association, 75
Texas Women's Political Caucus, 291
Texas Workers' Compensation Act, 304–307. *see also* workers' compensation.
Thatcher, Denis, 315–316
Thatcher, Margaret, 315–316
"The Editor's Corner," 35
"The Praise of Life," 46
Thomas, Albert, 65, 73
Thoor Ballylee Castle, 85
Thornberry, Homer, 75–76
Thresher, 27–29, 34–35, 39
thyroid condition, 17, 18, 22–23
tiebreaker, 127
Tiede, John, 259
Tiede, Saralee: and campaign staff, 286; and Hobby, 259, 299; on Hobby, 90, 217–218, 279–281, 341; and Hobby's memoir, 361; on *Houston Post,* 73, 239; as instructor, 319; op-ed articles, 338; on Senate, 190, vii; and telescope, 344; and workers' compensation, 301
ties, bow, 237, ix, vii, xi
ties, neck, 105
Tipps, Kern, 12–13
Toomey, Mike, 270–271, 272
Toronto Sun Company, 329
tort law reform, 273–274, 275
tour, "nonpartisan," 180
Tower Hill, 31
transparency in government, 132
trapshooting, 275
travel and vacations: beaches, 84, 211; campaigning, 54, 104, 108–109, 172; childhood, 23; Europe, 31–34; "Flight to Peace" tour, 56–58; Hawaii, 256; for leisure, 329; London, 30–33, 284, 315; Mexico, 27, 211, 328, 329; Paris, 43, 47, 333, 334; skiing, 168, 182, 205, 215, 250; summer vacations, 11, 84, 205, 329; and University of Houston chancellorship, 333–334. *see also* Ireland
Travis County Commissioners Court, 215, 217
Travis County district attorney, 175, 305
Trial Lawyers Association, 306
trials, jury, 302, 303
Truan, Carlos, 160, 195–196, 325
trucking industry, 232, 238
Truman, Harry, 27
Tsanoff Professor of Public Affairs, 311
T-shirts, 197–198, 271
tuition and user fees, university, 253, 255, 321
Tully, Grace, 22
Tune, Tommy, 349
Tunisia, 57
tuxedo, 23
two-thirds rule, 127, 130, 302–303

U

unemployment, 260, 274
Unemployment Compensation Fund, 209, 214, 221, 232, 238. *see also* workers' compensation.
uniforms, 16, 17
unions, labor: and Brown, 73; and constitutional reform, 153–155; and Eckhardt, 73; and Hobby, 99, 112, 151; and Mattox, 278; and Will Hobby, 11; and workers' compensation, 301
United Fund, 61
United Kingdom, 290
University of Houston: and Board of Regents, 74, 92, 334; and Center for Public Policy, 351, 352–355, 359; as chancellor, 332–340; expansion of, 159; and Hobby School of Public Affairs, 354–355; leadership failure at, 332–337; and legislature, 339; reputation of, 333; as research campus, 336, 339; and Smith, 339; Sugar Land campus, 337–338; and TSU, 322; Vision Commission, 336–337, 392; and Wortham House, 334, 392
University of Mary Hardin-Baylor, 1
University of Michigan, 333–334, 352
University of North Carolina, 184, 205
University of Texas System: Board of Regents, 226, 227; and campaigning, 112; Center for Public Service, 347; commencement address, 320; and Erwin, 159; and ethics reform, 133; exchange program, 328; and expansion of system, 303; and Farabee, 288, 293; financing for telescope, 346–347; funding for, 150, 159, 262, 271–272; and Hay,

227, 277; and Hobby-Eberly telescope, 342–347; indoctrination of students, 350; Law School, 3, 35, 205; and MCC, 252–253; and Pan American University, 303; and Paul Hobby, 238; and Santa Rita Award, 256; teaching at, 317–319, 327; and Texas Constitution, 152; and University of Houston chancellor, 334. *see also* education, higher.

University of Virginia, 86, 184, 238, 283

Uribe, Hector: and Bill Hobby Day, ix; and colonias, 303–304; on Hobby, 104, viii; and Senate committees, 236, 252; and workers' compensation, 236–237, 301

user fees and tuition, 253, 255, 321

USS *Intrepid,* 314

utility regulation, 163–165, 378

V

vacations. *see* travel.

Vale, Bob, 195–196

Valenti, Jack, 65, 67, 75–76

Valenti, Mary Margaret, 67

vestry, student, 20, 25

veto power, governor's, 277, 350

Vickers, Tom, 267

Victory Fund, Democratic, 224, 289–290

Vietnam War, 76–78

Vinson, Fred, 38

Vision Commission, 336–337, 392

Vogue, 79

volunteers, local, 109

voters: Black voters, 103, 110, 222, 283; and Build Texas plan, 284; and constitutional reforms, 162–163, 167–168, 295; and coordinated campaign, 216, 223; desires of, 206; and highway bonds, 262; independent voters, 215; and lieutenant governor's duties, 267; minorities, 103, 106, 151; and off-year election voting, 282; and Proposition 13, 182; student, 108–109, 110, 112; suburban, 56; and taxes, 182, 184, 271; turnout of, 101, 111, 115, 180; and water plan, 255

voting age, 108–109, 110, 112, 138

voting sessions, secret, 61, 64

Vowell, Raymond, 144–145

W

wage garnishment, 92

Wakefield House, 30

Wake Forest University, 44

Waldock, Humphrey, 31–32

Wallace, George, 98

Wallace, Henry A., 22, 367

Wallace, Mack, 201–202

Wang, Wei Li "Willie," 317

war, declaration of, 33

War Department, 14–15

War on Drugs, Texan, 209, 244. *see also* marijuana.

Warren, Beth, 147

Warren, Earl, 37

Warwick Castle, 32

Washington, Craig, 151, 153–154, 232, 273, 275, 305, 312

Washington, DC: and Carter Administration, 202, 204; Democratic fundraiser, 181; and H&C business meetings, 290; National Lieutenant Governor's Conference, 149; and Oveta, 14–15, 16, 17, 185; social circle in, 48–49; and Texas congressional delegates, 129, 201, 204

Washington Journalism Review, 322, 356

Washington Post, 20, 323

wastewater treatment, 303

watch parties, 288, 294, 312, 313, 316. *see also* campaigns and elections.

Waterman, Jimmy, 228–230

Waterman, Joan, 228–230

water supply: and Build Texas plan, 274; colonias, 261, 284, 303–304; flood control, 250–251, 274; statewide plan, 255, 256; teaching on, 327

Watkins, Joe Bill, 100

Watson, John, 100

Watson, Kirk, 354

Wayman, Stan, 79

Ways and Means Committee, House, 188, 299

Weddington, Sarah, 202, 217, 258, 310

Weedman, Daniel, 343

Weinberg, Steven, 342

Weiss, Harry, 16

Weiss, Olga, 16

Welch, Louie, 61

welfare and social services: Aid to Families with Dependent Children (AFDC), 214, 255; Department of Human Services (DHS), 313; and disabled, 76, 91–92; Food Stamp Program, 92, 214; funding of, 314; and Hobby Anti-Crime plan, 300; importance of, 75; indigent healthcare, 253–254, 255, 260, 293; and McCarthyism, 38–39; payments and payment ceiling, 91, 178–179, 222; and Reagan, 214, 293; reform of, 91–92, 97, 144, 244; report on, 91–92; and Vocational Rehabilitation, 76; youth-care facilities, 142–147, 160–161

welfare queens, 91

West, Felton, 50, 87

Westbrook, John, 181–182, 379

Westmoreland, William, 76–77

WFAA-TV, 112

Whalen, Edward, 336

What Price Glory?, 44–45
White, Hattie Mae, 52–53
White, John, 119
White, Linda Gale, 225
White, Mark: campaigns and elections, 182, 185, 215, 216, 223, 264, 312; and Capitol fire and restoration, 229, 230; and Clements, 226, 276, 382; and colonias, 261; and education reform, 247, 248; and ethics commission, 375; and higher education funding, 253; and Hobby, 216, 225, 228, 266, 359; on Hobby, 253; and Hobby-Price dispute, 135; inauguration of, 224–226; and MCC, 252; and media, 259; and redistricting, 212; and Richards, 313; and special legislative sessions, 245, 261, 262; and taxes, 235, 253, 255; and teachers, 243; victory party, 224; and water crisis, 251; on youth-care facilities, 146
Whitmire, John, 144, 145, 232, 273
Wiggins, Patricia, 49–50
Wiley, Vernon, 10
William P. Hobby, 68
Williams, Clayton Jr., 316, 390
Williams, Mary Pearl, 156–157
Willkie, Wendell, 11–12
Wilson, Charles, 38, 91, 379
Wilson, John, 164
Wilson, Morris, Crain & Anderson, 78
Wilson, Welcome Sr., 353
Wilson, Woodrow, 12
Winant, John Gilbert, 30
Winant Volunteers, 30–33, 367
wind power, 147
Winfield House, 315, 317
wire copy, Associated Press, 65–66
wiretapping, 159, 209–211, 218
wiring, electrical, 229
WLAC-TV and Radio. *see* WTLV-TV (WLAC) and Radio.
Woestendiek, Bill, 69, 72–73
Wolters, Jacob, 4
Women's Army Corps (WAC) / Women's Auxiliary Army Corps (WAAC), 15–16, 17, 21–22, 23, x
women's rights: abortion, 109, 128, 258, 273, 275, 310, 390; and credit bill, 138; equality in employment, 155; Equal Rights Amendment, 258; as ongoing issue, 128; and Richards, 217, 310; suffrage movement, 2, 3
women's shelter, 217
Woodcock, Leonard, 189
workers, undocumented, 218–219, 220
workers' compensation insurance: and appeals process, 302; and business lobby, 301, 306; and employer self-insurance, 306; and Farabee, 288; for farmworkers, 200, 236–237, 252, 255; for injured workers, 301–306; overhaul of, 138; and Pilgrim, 304–305; and privacy clause, 178; and school employees, 161–162, xii
world's fair, 79
World War I, 2, 12, 44
World War II, 14–16, 21–23
Wortham, Gus, 69, 167, 171–172, 392
Wortham, Lyndall, 69, 392
Wortham Foundation, 349
Wortham House, 334, 392
Wouk, Herman, 43
Wrotenbery, Paul, 188
WTLV-TV (WLAC) and Radio, 171–172, 204. *see also* television and television stations.

Y

Yarborough, Ralph, 65, 215
Yeats, William Butler, 46, 85, 181
Yom Kippur War, 140, 148
York, Larry, 145
Young, David, 260
Young Broadcasting, 323
youth-care facilities, 142–147, 160–161

Z

Zaffirini, Judith, 267, 307
zero-based budgeting, 142, 149, 173, 354, 376
Ziegler, Jessie, 5
Zilkha, Selim, 349
Zilkha Hall, 349
Zimmerman, Charlie, 46, 84
Zimmerman, Ginny, 46, 84